Oxford
Children's
Dictionary

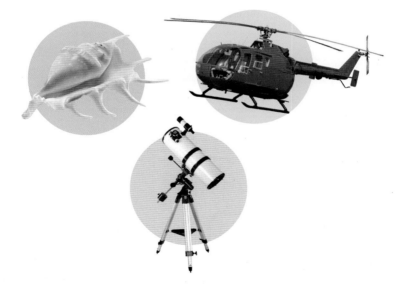

OXFORD
UNIVERSITY PRESS

OXFORD
UNIVERSITY PRESS

Oxford University Press is a department of the University of Oxford.
It furthers the University's objective of excellence in research, scholarship,
and education by publishing worldwide. Oxford is a registered trade mark of
Oxford University Press in the UK and in certain other countries

First published 1976
Second edition 1985
Third edition 1993
Redesigned impression 1994
Fourth edition 2000
Fifth edition 2013
This new edition 2015

British Library Cataloguing in Publication Data
Data available
ISBN: 9780 19 274401 2
5 7 9 10 8 6 4
Printed in China

Paper used in the production of this book is a natural,
recyclable product made from wood grown in sustainable forests.
The manufacturing process conforms to the environmental
regulations of the country of origin.

*The publishers would like to thank Shutterstock and Wikipedia for permission to use their material.
Every care has been taken to trace copyright holders. However, if there have been unintentional
omissions or failure to trace copyright holders, we apologize and if informed, endeavour to make
corrections in any future editions.*

Oxford
OWL

For school
Discover eBooks, inspirational
resources, advice and support

For home
Helping your child's learning
with free eBooks, essential
tips and fun activities

www.oxfordowl.co.uk

Contents

Introduction
and how to use this dictionary

The **Oxford Children's Dictionary** helps children aged 8+ discover the meaning of a wide range of words and how to spell them.

guide words
The first and last word on a page are given at the top of each page so that you can find your way when you are searching for a word.

headword
The words you look up are in blue and in alphabetical order.

pronunciation
This helps you to say the word but remember it is not how to spell it.

illustrations
Photographs and illustrations help to explain meaning.

label
If a word is usually used in a certain way, a label helps you understand this.

---

hyphen

hyphen *noun* a short dash used to join words or parts of words together, for example in *red-handed*

hypnosis *noun* (hip-**noh**-sis) to be under hypnosis is to be in a condition like a deep sleep in which a person follows the instructions of another person

hypnotism *noun* (**hip**-no-tizm) hypnotizing people hypnotist *noun* someone who hypnotizes people

hypnotize *verb* hypnotizes, hypnotizing, hypnotized to hypnotize someone is to put them to sleep by hypnosis This word can also be spelled **hypnotise**.

hypocrite *noun* (**hip**-o-krit) someone who pretends to be a better person than they really are hypocrisy *noun* being a hypocrite hypocritical *adjective* someone is being hypocritical when they are pretending to be a better person than they really are

hypodermic *adjective* (hy-po-**der**-mik) a hypodermic needle or syringe is one used to inject a drug under the skin

hypotenuse *noun* (hy-**pot**-i-newz) the side opposite the right angle in a right-angled triangle

hypothermia *noun* a person suffers from hypothermia when they become so cold that their body temperature falls well below normal

hysteria *noun* wild uncontrollable excitement or emotion

hysterical *adjective* 1. extremely excited or emotional 2. (*informal*) very funny hysterically *adverb*

hysterics *plural noun* a fit of hysteria to be in hysterics (*informal*) is to be laughing a lot

---

icing

Ii

I is always a capital letter when you are talking about yourself.

I *pronoun* a word used by someone to speak about himself or herself

ice *noun* ice is frozen water

ice *verb* 1. to ice or ice up is to become covered in ice 2. to ice a cake is to put icing on it

ice age *noun* a time in the past when ice covered large areas of the earth's surface

iceberg *noun* a large mass of ice floating in the sea, with most of it under water

ice cream *noun* 1. ice cream is a sweet creamy frozen food 2. an ice cream is a portion of this

ice hockey *noun* ice hockey is a game like hockey played on ice

ice lolly *noun* ice lollies a piece of flavoured ice on a stick

ice-skating *noun* moving on ice wearing special boots with blades on the bottom

icicle *noun* a thin pointed piece of hanging ice formed from dripping water

icing *noun* a sugary substance for decorating cakes

166

4

The text has been created using the *Oxford Children's Corpus*, a unique database of writing for and by children, to ensure the vocabulary is age-appropriate and carefully-levelled.

For help with spelling, punctuation and grammar there is a quick reference supplement at the back of the book.

---

icon — illuminate

icon *noun* **1.** a small picture or symbol standing for a program on a computer screen **2.** a painting of a holy person

ICT short for *information and communication technology*

icy *adjective* icier, iciest **1.** an icy road has ice on it **2.** an icy wind is very cold **3.** very unfriendly; hostile • *He gave them an icy stare.* icily *adverb* in an unfriendly way

idea *noun* something that you have thought of; a plan

ideal *adjective* exactly what you want; perfect • *If things were perfect • Ideally, I'd like to live by the sea.*
ideal *noun* something that is perfect or the best thing to have

identical *adjective* exactly the same • *identical twins* identically *adverb* in exactly the same way • *They were identically dressed.*

identification *noun* **1.** identification is any document, such as a passport, that proves who you are **2.** identification is the process of discovering who someone is or what something is

identify *verb* identifies, identifying, identified to identify someone or something is to discover who or what they are

identity *noun* identities who someone is or what something is • *Can you discover the identity of our mystery guest?*

idiom *noun* (id-i-om) a phrase or group of words that together have a special meaning that is not obvious from the words themselves, for example *to keep your head* means to stay calm

idiot *noun* (informal) a stupid or foolish person idiotic *adjective* stupid or foolish

idle *adjective* **1.** a person is idle when they are lazy or doing nothing **2.** a machine is idle when it is not being used **3.** idle talk or gossip is talk that is silly or pointless
idle *verb* a machine or engine idles when it is working slowly idly *adverb* in a lazy way

idol *noun* **1.** a famous person who is admired by a lot of people **2.** a statue or image that people worship as a god

idolize *verb* to idolize someone is to admire them very much This word can also be spelled **idolise**.

i.e. short for the Latin *id est*, which means 'that is', used to explain something • *The world's highest mountain (i.e. Mount Everest) is in the Himalayas.*

if *conjunction* **1.** on condition that • *I'll tell you what happened if you promise to keep it secret.* **2.** although; even though • *I'll finish this job if it kills me!* **3.** whether • *Do you know if lunch is ready?*

igloo *noun* a round house made of blocks of hard snow, built by the Inuit people of the Arctic

The word **igloo** comes from an Inuit word *iglu* meaning 'house'.

ignite *verb* **1.** to ignite something is to set fire to it **2.** to ignite is to catch fire

ignition *noun* **1.** igniting **2.** ignition is the system in a motor engine that starts the fuel burning

ignorant *adjective* not knowing about something; knowing very little ignorance *noun* someone shows ignorance when they don't know about something or know very little

ignore *verb* to ignore someone or something is to take no notice of them

ill *adjective* **1.** not well; in bad health **2.** bad or harmful • *There were no ill effects.*

illegal *adjective* something is illegal when it is against the law illegally *adverb*

illegible *adjective* (i-**lej**-i-bul) illegible writing is not clear enough to read illegibly *adverb*

illegitimate *adjective* (il-i-**jit**-i-mat) (old use) someone is illegitimate when they are born to parents who are not married

illiterate *adjective* (i-**lit**-er-at) unable to read or write

illness *noun* **1.** illness is being ill **2.** an illness is something that makes people ill; a disease

illogical *adjective* not logical or having any good reason

illuminate *verb* to illuminate a place or street is to light it up or decorate it with lights illuminations *plural noun* lights put up to decorate a place or street

a b c d e f g h i j k l m n o p q r s t u v w x y z

167

---

example sentence
Examples show how the word is used.

alphabet
The alphabet runs down the side of every page and the letter that you are in is highlighted so you can find your way around the dictionary quickly and easily.

word origin
These tell you the interesting origins of different words.

word forms
Tricky plurals and word forms are given in full.

word class
This tells you if the word is a noun, adjective, verb, adverb, pronoun or determiner; sometimes a word may have more than one word class.

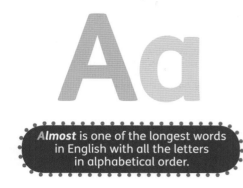

Almost is one of the longest words in English with all the letters in alphabetical order.

a *determiner* (called the indefinite article) **1.** one; any • *I would like a holiday.* **2.** each; every • *I go there twice a month.*

abacus *noun* a frame with rows of beads that slide on wires, used for counting and doing sums

abandon *verb* to abandon something or someone is to go away and leave them, without intending to go back for them • *Someone abandoned these poor kittens on the street.* abandon ship passengers abandon a sinking ship when they get into the lifeboats to save their lives

abbey *noun* a place where monks or nuns live and work

abbreviation *noun* a word or group of letters that is a shorter form of something longer • *BBC is an abbreviation of 'British Broadcasting Corporation'.*

abdomen *noun* **1.** the part of the human body where the stomach is **2.** the back part of the body of an insect

ability *noun* abilities **1.** ability is the skill or talent to do something • *They have a lot of ability at games.* **2.** an ability is a special skill or talent • *a person of many abilities*

able *adjective* **1.** having the power or skill or opportunity to do something • *They were not able to find our house.* **2.** having a special talent or skill • *John is a very able musician.* ably *adverb* to do something ably is to do it well and use skill or talent

abnormal *adjective* unusual or strange, not normal abnormality *noun* something abnormal • *a physical abnormality*

aboard *adverb, preposition* someone is aboard when they have got on on a train, ship or aircraft • *The passengers were now all aboard.* • *It's time to get aboard the train.*

abolish *verb* to get rid of a rule or custom • *Some people would like to abolish homework.*

abolition *noun* (ab-o-**lish**-on) getting rid of something

abominable *adjective* very shocking, dreadful • *an abominable crime*

aboriginal *noun* one of the original inhabitants of a country. When **Aboriginal** refers to Australia you spell it with a capital A.

Aborigines *plural noun* (ab-er-**ij**-in-eez) the people who lived in Australia before the European settlers arrived there

about *preposition* **1.** to do with, connected with • *The story is about animals.* **2.** approximately, roughly • *She's about five feet tall.*

about *adverb* **1.** in various directions or places • *They were running about.* **2.** somewhere near by • *There were wild animals about.* to be about to do something is to be just going to do it • *He was about to leave.*

above *preposition* **1.** higher than, over • *There was a window above the door.* **2.** more than • *The temperature was just above freezing.*

above *adverb* at a higher point or to a higher point • *Look at the stars above.*

abreast *adverb* side by side • *They walked three abreast.*

abroad *adverb* in a foreign country • *They live abroad now.*

abrupt *adjective* **1**. sudden and unexpected • *The van came to an abrupt halt.* **2**. rude and unfriendly • *He gave an abrupt reply.*

abscess *noun* a painful swelling on the body containing pus

abseil *verb* to abseil is to lower yourself down a steep cliff or rock by sliding down a rope

absence *noun* not being in a place where you are expected, for example school or work

absent *adjective* not present; away

absentee *noun* someone who is away, for example not at school or work

absent-minded *adjective* forgetting things easily

absolute *adjective* total, complete • *For a moment there was absolute silence.*

absolutely *adverb* **1**. completely **2**. *(informal)* definitely • *'Are you going to Beth's party?' 'Absolutely!'*

absorb *verb* **1**. to absorb something like liquid is to soak it up **2**. to be absorbed in something is to be interested in it and give it all your attention • *He was very absorbed in his book.*

absorbent *adjective* an absorbent material soaks up liquid easily

abstract *adjective* to do with ideas and not with physical things • *abstract ideas like love or beauty*

absurd *adjective* silly or ridiculous • *It was an absurd thing to say.* **absurdity** *noun* something that is silly or ridiculous

abundant *adjective* large in amount, plentiful **abundance** *noun* a large amount, plenty • *There was an abundance of good food.*

abuse *verb* (a-**bewz**) **1**. to abuse something is to treat it badly and harm it **2**. to abuse someone is to say unpleasant things about them **3**. to abuse someone also means to hurt them or treat them cruelly
abuse *noun* (a-**bewss**) **1**. treating something badly **2**. unpleasant words said about someone • *She got a lot of abuse from her so-called friends.* **3**. physical harm or cruelty done to someone

abusive *adjective* saying unpleasant things about someone

academic *adjective* to do with learning in a school or university • *an academic subject*

academy *noun* academies a college or school

accelerate *verb* to accelerate is to go faster **acceleration** *noun* an increase in speed, going faster

accelerator *noun* a pedal that you press down to make a motor vehicle go faster

accent *noun* **1**. your accent is the way you pronounce words, which shows where you are from • *a Yorkshire accent* **2**. a mark put over a letter, usually when it's a foreign word, to show its pronunciation • *The word 'resumé' has an accent on the second 'e'.*

accept *verb* **1**. to accept something is to take it when someone offers it to you **2**. to accept an invitation is to say 'yes' to it **3**. to accept an idea or suggestion is to agree that it is true or worth thinking about **acceptance** *noun* taking something that someone offers you

acceptable *adjective* good enough, satisfactory • *Their behaviour was not acceptable.*

access *noun* a way to reach or get into a place • *Does the building have disabled access?*
access *verb* (*in ICT*) to access data is to find and use it on a computer

accessible *adjective* easy to reach or approach

accident *noun* something unexpected that happens, especially when something is broken or someone is hurt or killed **by accident** by chance, not intentionally

accidental *adjective* something is accidental when it happens by accident, not because you want it to happen • *accidental damage* **accidentally** *adverb* to do something accidentally is to do it by mistake or without meaning to • *Anthony accidentally dropped a tin on his foot.*

accommodate *verb* to accommodate someone or something is to provide them with a place to stay or find space for them

accommodation *noun* accommodation is a place to live or stay • *They were looking for cheap accommodation.*

accompaniment *noun* the music played on an instrument while a singer sings

accompany *verb* accompanies, accompanying, accompanied **1**. to accompany someone is to go somewhere with them **2**. to accompany a singer is to play an instrument while they sing

accomplish *verb* to accomplish something is to do it successfully **accomplished** *adjective* good at doing something, skilful **accomplishment** *noun* something you do well

accordingly *adverb* **1**. consequently; therefore **2**. in a way that is suitable • *You are older now and must behave accordingly.*

according to *preposition* You say **according to someone** to show where a piece of information comes from • *According to Katie, there is a party tomorrow.*

accordion *noun* a portable musical instrument with sides that squeeze together and a set of keys like a piano's at one end

account *noun* **1**. a description or story about something that happened **2**. an amount of money someone has in a bank or building society **3**. a statement of the money someone owes or has received, a bill **on account of something** because of it **to take something into account** is to consider it along with other things

account *verb* to account for something is to be or give an explanation of it • *How do you account for these marks?*

accountant *noun* a person whose job is to write and organize the money accounts of a person or organization

accumulate *verb* **1**. to accumulate things is to collect them or pile them up **2**. things accumulate when they form a heap or pile **accumulation** *noun*

accuracy *noun* accuracy is being exactly right or correct

accurate *adjective* correct, done exactly and carefully • *The police keep accurate records.* **accurately** *adverb* carefully and exactly • *Measure the temperature accurately.*

accuse *verb* to accuse someone is to say that they did something wrong **accusation** *noun* a statement accusing someone of something

accustomed *adjective* **to be accustomed to something** is to be used to it • *She was not accustomed to being treated so rudely.*

ace *noun* **1**. the four aces in a pack of cards are the cards with an A in the corner and a large emblem of the suit in the centre **2**. someone or something very clever or skilful

ache *noun* a dull steady pain **ache** *verb* to ache is to feel a dull steady pain

achieve *verb* to achieve something is to succeed in doing it or getting it **achievement** *noun* something you succeed in doing • *Winning the prize was a fine achievement.*

acid *noun* a substance that contains hydrogen and causes chemical change. Acids are the opposite of alkalis. **acid** *adjective* sour or bitter to taste **acidic** *adjective* containing a lot of acid **acidity** *noun* the level of acid in a substance

acid rain *noun* rain that contains harmful acids from pollution in the air

acknowledge *verb* **1**. to acknowledge something is to admit that it is true **2**. to acknowledge a letter is to say that you have received it **acknowledgement** *noun*

acne *noun* (**ak**-ni) a skin disease with red pimples on the face

acorn *noun* the oval seed of an oak tree

acoustics *plural noun* (a-**koo**-stiks) **1**. the acoustics of a place are the qualities that make it good or bad for sound **2.** *(singular noun)* the science of sound

acquaint *verb* **1.** to acquaint someone with something is to tell them something about it, so they know what it is **2.** to be acquainted with someone is to know them slightly

acquaintance *noun* someone you know slightly to make someone's acquaintance is to get to know them

acquire *verb* to acquire something is to obtain it, usually with some effort or difficulty

acquit *verb* acquits, acquitting, acquitted to acquit someone is to decide in a court of law that they are not guilty of a crime

acre *noun* (**ay**-ker) an acre is the area of a piece of land containing 4,840 square yards or 0.4 hectares

acrobat *noun* (**ak**-ro-bat) an entertainer who gives displays of jumping and balancing **acrobatic** *adjective* to do with an acrobat; like what an acrobat does • *They were amazed at her acrobatic skills.*

acrobatics *plural noun* exercises such as jumping or balancing that an acrobat does

acronym *noun* (**ak**-ro-nim) a word or name that is formed from the first letters of other words, for example *UFO* is an acronym of *unidentified flying object*

across *adverb, preposition* **1.** from one side of something to the other • *The table measures 1.5 metres across.* **2.** to the other side of something • *How can we get across the busy road?*

act *noun* **1.** something that someone does **2.** an individual performance in a programme of entertainment, for example a juggling act or a comic act **3.** one of the main sections of a play or opera **4.** a new law that a government makes to put on an act is to show off or pretend to be something that you are not

act *verb* **1.** to do something useful or necessary • *We need to act straight away.* **2.** to behave in a certain way • *She's been acting very strangely recently.* **3.** to act in a play or film is to perform in it

action *noun* **1.** an action is something that you do **2.** action is fighting in a battle • *He was killed in action.* out of action not working

properly to take action is to do something decisive

activate *verb* to activate a machine or device is to start it working

active *adjective* **1.** busy, taking part in lots of activities **2.** doing things, working • *an active volcano*

activity *noun* activities **1.** activity is doing things **2.** an activity is something special that someone does • *They enjoy outdoor activities.*

actor *noun* someone who takes part in a play or film

actress *noun* a girl or woman who takes part in a play or film

actual *adjective* really there or really happening

actually *adverb* really, in fact • *Actually, I think you are wrong.*

acupuncture *noun* acupuncture is a way of curing disease or taking away pain by pricking parts of the body with needles

acute *adjective* **1.** sharp or intense • *She has an acute pain.* **2.** severe • *The explorers were suffering from an acute shortage of food.* **3.** an acute accent is the mark ´ put over a letter, as in *resumé* **4.** an acute angle is an angle of less than 90 degrees

AD short for *Anno Domini*, used with dates that come after the birth of Jesus Christ, for example AD 1492 is the year Columbus reached America

adapt *verb* **1.** to change something so you can use it in a different way **2.** to adapt to something is to make yourself cope with it • *They adapted to life in the country very quickly.* **adaptation** *noun* an adaptation is a book or play that someone has adapted into a film or television programme

adaptor *noun* a device for connecting different pieces of equipment

add *verb* **1.** to add one number to another is to put them together to get a bigger number **2.** to add one thing to another is to mix them together, for example the different things in a recipe to add up is what numbers do to make a bigger number, called a total to add numbers up is to make them into a bigger number

adder *noun* a small poisonous snake

addict *noun* someone with a habit they can't give up, for example taking drugs or drinking alcohol **addicted** *adjective* someone who is addicted to a habit can't give it up **addiction** *noun* a habit that someone can't give up

addition *noun* **1**. addition is the process of adding numbers together or adding other things **2**. an addition is something or someone that has been added • *James is an addition to the class.* **in addition** also, as well

additional *adjective* extra, added on

additive *noun* something that is added to food, for example as a flavouring

address *noun* **1**. the details of the place where someone lives • *My address is 29 High Street, Newtown.* **2**. *(in computing)* words and symbols you use to send an email or find a website • *What's your email address?* **3**. a speech

address *verb* **1**. to address a letter or parcel is to write the address on it before sending it **2**. to address a person or a group of people is to make an important remark or speech to them • *The judge addressed the prisoner.*

adenoids *plural noun* your adenoids are the spongy flesh at the back of your nose, which can become swollen making it difficult to breathe

adequate *adjective* enough, sufficient

adhesive *noun* something such as glue that you use to stick things together

adhesive *adjective* causing things to stick together

Adi Granth *noun* (ah-di **grunt**) the holy book of the Sikhs

adjacent *adjective* near or next to something • *Her house is adjacent to the shop.*

adjective *noun* a word that describes a noun or adds to its meaning, for example *big, honest, red*

adjust *verb* **1**. to adjust something is to change it slightly or change its position **2**. to adjust to something is to try to get used to it • *They found it hard to adjust to life in the city.* **adjustment** *noun* a small change you make to something

administration *noun* administration is running a business or governing a country **administrator** *noun* someone who helps to run a business or organization

admirable *adjective* worth admiring; excellent • *You have done an admirable piece of work.* **admirably** *adverb* in an admirable way • *The instructions are admirably simple and clear.*

admiral *noun* an officer of the highest rank in the navy

admiration *noun* admiration is a feeling you have for someone or something when you think they are very good or very beautiful • *He was filled with admiration for his sister.*

admire *verb* **1**. to admire someone or something is to think they are very good or very beautiful **2**. to admire something is also to look at it and enjoy it • *They went to the top of the hill to admire the view.* **admirer** *noun* • *Prince Charming has many admirers.*

admission *noun* **1**. admission is being allowed to go into a place • *Admission to the show is by ticket only.* **2**. an admission is something that someone admits or confesses • *He is guilty by his own admission.*

admit *verb* **admitting, admitted** **1**. to admit someone is to let them come into a place **2**. to admit something is to say that it has happened or that you have done it

admittance *noun* admittance is being allowed to go into a private place

admittedly *adverb* although it is true; without denying it • *Admittedly I was teasing the dog, but I didn't expect it to bite.*

adolescent *noun* a young person who is older than a child and not yet an adult, from about 15 to 18 **adolescence** *noun* the time between being a child and being an adult

adopt *verb* **1**. to adopt a child is to take them into your family and bring them

A
B
C
D
E
F
G
H
I
J
K
L
M
N
O
P
Q
R
S
T
U
V
W
X
Y
Z

up as your own **2.** to adopt a system or method is to start using it **adoption** *noun* adoption is adopting someone or something **adopted** *adjective* an adopted child is one that someone has adopted **adoptive** *adjective* adoptive parents are parents who have adopted a child

adorable *adjective* lovely, worth adoring

adore *verb* to adore someone or something is to love them or admire them very much **adoration** *noun* adoration is adoring someone or something

adorn *verb* to adorn something is to decorate it or make it pretty **adornment** *noun* adornment is making something pretty

adrenalin *noun* a hormone that stimulates your nervous system and makes you feel ready to do something

adrift *adverb, adjective* something such as a boat is adrift when it is loose and drifting about

adult *noun* a fully grown person or animal

advance *noun* **1.** an advance is a forward movement **2.** advance is improvement or progress **3.** an advance of money is a loan **advance warning** a warning given beforehand **in advance** beforehand **advance** *verb* **1.** to advance is to move forward **2.** to advance is also to make progress

advanced *adjective* **1.** a long way forward **2.** an advanced course or exam is one at a higher level

advantage *noun* something useful or helpful **to take advantage of someone** is to treat them unfairly when they are not likely to complain **to take advantage of something** is to make good use of it

Advent *noun* in the Christian Church, the period before Christmas

adventure *noun* an adventure is an exciting, dangerous or interesting event or journey **adventurous** *adjective* an adventurous person likes to do interesting or exciting things

adverb *noun* An adverb is a word that tells you how or when or where or why something happens. In these sentences, the words in italics are adverbs: They moved *slowly*. Come back *soon*. I *only* want a drink.

advert *noun (informal)* an advertisement

advertise *verb* to advertise a product or service is to tell people about it so that people will want it

advertisement *noun* a public notice or short film that tries to persuade people to buy something

advice *noun* advice is something you say to someone to help them decide what to do

advisable *adjective* sensible, worth doing

advise *verb* to advise someone is to tell them what you think they should do

aerial *noun* a wire or metal rod for receiving or sending radio or television signals **aerial** *adjective* from or in the air or from aircraft • *an aerial photograph of the city*

aerobatics *plural noun* an exciting display by flying aircraft **aerobatic** *adjective* to do with aerobatics • *They went to see an aerobatic display.*

aeroplane *noun* a flying machine with wings

aerosol *noun* a container that holds a liquid under pressure and lets it out in a fine spray

affair *noun* **1.** something interesting that happens, an event **2.** someone's affairs are their private business • *Keep out of my affairs.*

affect *verb* to affect someone or something is to cause them to change or to harm them • *The dampness might affect his health.*

affection *noun* love or fondness • *I have a great affection for my nephew.* **affectionate** *adjective* showing love or fondness

afflict *verb* to be afflicted by something unpleasant, like an illness, is to suffer from it **affliction** *noun* a great illness or problem that makes someone suffer

afford *verb* **1.** to be able to afford something is to have enough money to pay for it **2.** to be unable to afford the time to do something is not to have enough time for it

afforestation *noun* the process of covering an area of land with trees

afloat *adjective, adverb* floating; on a boat • *Somehow we kept the boat afloat.* • *We trod water to keep afloat.*

afraid *adjective* frightened **I'm afraid** I am sorry; I regret • *I'm afraid I've burnt the cakes.*

after *preposition, adverb* meaning 'later' or 'later than' • *Come after dinner.* • *I'll do it after.*

afternoon *noun* the time from midday or lunchtime until evening

afterwards *adverb* at a later time

again *adverb* **1.** once more; another time **2.** as before • *You will soon be well again.* **again and again** lots of times

against *preposition* **1.** touching or hitting • *He was leaning against the wall.* **2.** opposed to, not liking • *Are you against smoking?*

age *noun* **1.** your age is how old you are **2.** an age is a period of history • *the Elizabethan age* **ages** (*informal*) a long time • *We've been waiting ages.*
age *verb* to age is to become old

aged *adjective* **1.** (ayjd) having the age of • *The girl was aged 9.* **2.** (**ay**-jid) very old • *We saw an aged man.*

agent *noun* **1.** someone whose job is to organize things for other people • *We sold our flat through an estate agent.* **2.** a spy • *He is a secret agent.* **agency** *noun* an agent's office or business

aggravate *verb* to aggravate something is to make it worse **aggravation** *noun*

aggression *noun* starting a war or attack; being aggressive **aggressor** *noun* someone who starts an attack

aggressive *adjective* **1.** an aggressive person or group of people is one that is likely to attack or use violence **2.** an aggressive activity is one that people do with force or energy • *an aggressive sales campaign*

agile *adjective* able to move quickly and easily **agility** *noun* agility is being agile

agitated *adjective* worried and anxious • *Why are you getting so agitated?* **agitation** *noun* agitation is getting worried or anxious • *He could not hide his agitation.*

ago *adverb* in the past • *She died long ago.*

agonizing *adjective* **1.** an agonizing pain is one that hurts terribly **2.** an agonizing choice or decision is one that you find very difficult to make

agony *noun* **agonies** severe pain or suffering

agree *verb* **1.** to agree with someone is to think the same as them **2.** to agree to do something is to say that you are willing to • *She agreed to go with him.* **3.** something agrees with someone when it suits them or does them good • *Spicy food doesn't agree with her.*

agreeable *adjective* **1.** willing to do something that someone suggests • *We shall go if you are agreeable.* **2.** pleasant • *It was an agreeable journey.*

agreement *noun* **1.** agreement is thinking the same • *Are we in agreement?* **2.** an agreement is an arrangement that people have agreed on

agriculture *noun* agriculture is farming or growing food on the land **agricultural** *adjective* to do with agriculture

aground *adverb* stuck on the bottom of a river or the sea in shallow water • *The ship has run aground.*

ahead *adverb* forwards, in front • *Ali went ahead to show us the way.*

aid *noun* **1.** aid is help you give someone **2.** aid is also money or food or other help that a country sends to a poorer country **3.** an aid is something that helps you to do something better • *He was wearing a hearing aid.*
aid *verb* to aid someone is to help them

Aids *noun* a disease caused by a virus, which destroys the body's immunity to other diseases

ailment *noun* a minor illness

aim *verb* **1.** to aim a gun at someone or something is to point it at them **2.** to aim something like a ball is to throw it or kick it in a particular direction **3.** to aim to do something is to try to do it
aim *noun* **1.** a person's aim is what they intend to do **2.** aim is also pointing a weapon in a particular direction • *I took aim and fired.*

aimless *adjective* not having any definite aim or purpose • *He led an aimless life.* **aimlessly** *adverb*

air *noun* **1.** air is the mixture of gases which surrounds the earth and which everyone breathes **2.** an air of mystery or secrecy is a feeling that things are mysterious or secret **to**

go by air is to travel in an aeroplane **to be on the air** is to be on the radio or television

air verb **1.** to air clothes or washing is to put them in a warm place to finish drying **2.** to air a room is to let fresh air into it **3.** to air views or opinions is to say them so that people know them

airborne adjective **1.** flying in an aircraft **2.** carried by the air • an airborne virus

aircraft noun an aeroplane or a helicopter

air force noun the part of a country's fighting force that uses aircraft

airline noun a company that takes people to places by aircraft.

airliner noun a large aircraft for carrying passengers

airlock noun **1.** a bubble of air that forms in liquid and stops it flowing through a pipe **2.** a compartment with airtight doors at each end

airmail noun airmail is mail that is sent by air

airport noun a place where aircraft land and take off, with passenger terminals and other buildings

air raid noun an attack by bombs dropped from aircraft

airship noun a large balloon with engines, designed to carry passengers or cargo

airtight adjective not letting air get in or out

airy adjective airier, airiest with plenty of fresh air

aisle noun (rhymes with mile) a passage between or beside rows of seats in a church, theatre or cinema or on an aeroplane

alarm verb to alarm someone is to make them frightened or anxious

alarm noun **1.** an alarm is a warning sound or signal **2.** alarm is a feeling of fear or anxiety • He cried out in alarm.

alarm clock noun a clock with a loud ring or bleep, which can be set to wake you up

albatross noun a large seabird with long wings

album noun **1.** a book in which you keep things like photographs or stamps or autographs **2.** a collection of songs on a CD, record or digital download

alcohol noun **1.** a colourless liquid made by fermenting sugar or starch **2.** drinks containing this liquid (for example beer, wine, gin), which can make people drunk if they have too much

alcoholic adjective containing alcohol

alcoholic noun someone who drinks a lot of alcohol and cannot stop drinking

alcove noun a part of a room where the wall is set back from the main part

alert adjective watching for something; ready to act

alert verb to alert someone to a danger or problem is to warn them about it

A level noun a higher standard of examination that is taken after the GCSE, especially by pupils who want to go to university

algebra noun (**al**-ji-bra) mathematics in which letters and symbols are used to represent numbers

> The word **algebra** comes from an Arabic word **al-jabr** meaning 'putting broken parts together', which was the title of a book on mathematics by an Arab mathematician.

alias noun (**ay**-li-as) a false or different name that someone uses instead of their real name

alias adverb also named • Clark Kent, alias Superman

alibi noun (**al**-i-by) evidence showing that someone accused of a crime was not there when the crime was committed

alien noun (**ay**-li-en) **1.** someone who is not a citizen of the country where they are living **2.** in science fiction, a being from another world

alien adjective foreign

alight adjective on fire, burning

alike adjective similar, like each other

alike adverb in the same way • He treats everybody alike.

alive adjective living, existing • Is he alive?

alkali noun alkalis (**al**-ka-ly) a substance that neutralizes acids or that combines with acids to form salts **alkaline** *adjective* containing an alkali

all *determiner, adverb, noun* meaning 'everything' or 'everyone' • *That is all I know.* • *All my books are in the desk.* • *She was dressed all in white.*

Allah the Muslim name of God

allegation *noun* (a-li-**gay**-shun) you make an allegation when you accuse someone of doing something wrong

allege *verb* (a-**lej**) to allege that someone has done something is to accuse them of it, usually without proof • *He alleged that I stole his ring.*

allegiance *noun* (a-**lee**-jans) loyalty shown to a person or organization

allergy *noun* a medical condition that causes you to react badly or feel ill when you eat or drink some types of food or touch or breathe in something such as dust **allergic** *adjective* someone is allergic to something if they become ill or uncomfortable when they eat, touch or breathe it in • *She must be allergic to goat's milk.*

alley *noun* **1.** a narrow street or passage **2.** a place where you can play at skittles or tenpin bowling

alliance *noun* an agreement between countries to support each other, especially in a war

allied *adjective* on the same side • *Allied troops advanced across France.*

alligator *noun* a large reptile like a crocodile

allotment *noun* a small rented piece of ground used for growing vegetables

allow *verb* **1.** to allow someone to do something is to let them do it • *We will allow you to leave now.* • *Smoking is not allowed.* **2.** to allow an amount of money is to provide it for some reason • *She was allowed £10 for books.*

allowance *noun* a sum of money given regularly to someone

alloy *noun* a metal formed from a mixture of other metals

all right *adjective* satisfactory; in good condition • *She fixed my bike, so it's all right.*

ally *noun* **allies** (**al**-I) a person or country that helps and supports another

almighty *adjective* **1.** having a lot of power **2.** *(informal)* very great • *an almighty explosion*

almond *noun* (**ah**-mond) a flat oval nut that you can eat

almost *adverb* very close to but not quite • *I am almost ready.*

alone *adjective, adverb* without any other people or other things; on your own • *She was alone that evening.* • *She lives alone.*

along *preposition, adverb* **1.** from one end of something to the other **2.** on; onwards • *Move along, please!* **3.** accompanying someone • *I have brought my brother along.*

alongside *preposition, adverb* next to something

aloud *adverb* in a voice that can be heard

alphabet *noun* the letters used in a language, usually arranged in a set order **alphabetical** *adjective* to do with the alphabet **alphabetically** *adverb* something is arranged alphabetically when it is in the order of the alphabet

already *adverb* by or before now • *I've already told you once.*

also *adverb* as an extra, besides • *We also need some bread.*

altar *noun* a table or raised surface used in religious ceremonies

alter *verb* to alter something is to change it **alteration** *noun* a change you make to something

alternate *adjective* (ol-**ter**-nat) **1.** happening on every other one • *My sister and I take the dog for a walk on alternate days.* **2.** following one after the other • *alternate layers of fruit and cream* **alternately** *adverb* one after the other in turn • *The weather was alternately fine and wet.*

alternate *verb* (**ol**-ter-nayt) to alternate is to happen in turns

alternative *noun* (ol-**ter**-na-tiv) something you can choose instead of something else • *If you don't like this book there is an alternative.*

alternative *adjective* for you to choose instead of something else • *The cafe has an alternative menu for vegetarians.*

although *conjunction* in spite of the fact that • *Although the sun was shining, it was still cold.*

altitude *noun* the height of something, especially above sea level

alto *noun* **1.** a female singer with a low voice; also called a **contralto 2.** a male singer with a voice higher than a tenor's

altogether *adverb* **1.** completely • *He is altogether wrong.* **2.** on the whole • *Altogether, it wasn't a bad holiday.*

aluminium *noun* a silver-coloured metal that is light in weight

always *adverb* **1.** all the time, at all times **2.** often, constantly • *You are always crying.* **3.** whatever happens • *You can always sleep on the floor.*

a.m. short for Latin *ante meridiem* which means 'before midday'

amateur *noun* (**am**-a-ter) someone who does something because they like it, without being paid for it

amateur *adjective* done by amateurs

amaze *verb* to amaze someone is to surprise them greatly **amazement** *noun* amazement is a feeling of great surprise

ambassador *noun* someone sent to a foreign country to represent their own government

amber *noun* **1.** a hard, clear, yellowish substance used for making ornaments **2.** a yellowish colour, used as the signal for caution in traffic lights

ambiguous *adjective* having more than one possible meaning, uncertain • *His reply was ambiguous.*

ambition *noun* **1.** ambition is a strong desire to be successful **2.** an ambition is something you want to do very much • *His ambition is to run his own airline.* **ambitious** *adjective* an ambitious person wants very much to be successful

amble *verb* to amble along is to walk slowly

ambulance *noun* a vehicle for carrying sick or injured people

ambush *noun* a surprise attack from a hidden place

ambush *verb* to ambush someone is to attack them suddenly from a hidden place

amend *verb* to amend something like a piece of writing is to change or improve it **amendment** *noun* a change to a piece of writing or a law

amiable *adjective* friendly, good-tempered **amiability** *noun* friendliness **amiably** *adverb*

ammonia *noun* a gas or liquid with a strong smell, used to make cleaning liquids

ammunition *noun* bullets, bombs and other explosive objects used in fighting

amnesty *noun* amnesties a decision to pardon people who have broken the law

amoeba *noun* (a-**mee**-ba) An amoeba is a tiny creature made of one cell. It can change shape and split itself in two.

among or **amongst** *preposition* **1.** surrounded by, in the middle of • *She was hiding among the bushes.* **2.** between • *Let's divide the money amongst ourselves.*

amount *noun* a quantity or total

amount *verb* to amount to something is to reach it as a total • *The bill amounted to £55.*

amphibian *noun* an animal that can live on land and in water **amphibious** *adjective* an amphibious animal is able to live on land and in water

ample *adjective* more than enough; plenty • *We had an ample supply of food.* **amply** *adverb* generously • *They were amply rewarded.*

amplifier *noun* an electronic device for making music or other sounds louder

amplify *verb* amplifies, amplifying, amplified to amplify sounds is to make them louder or stronger **amplification** *noun* amplification is making voices or other sounds louder

amputate *verb* to amputate an arm or a leg is to cut it off when it is diseased or badly injured **amputation** *noun* amputation is cutting off a part of your body

amuse *verb* **1.** to amuse someone is to make them laugh or smile **2.** to amuse yourself is to find pleasant things to do

amusement *noun* **1.** an amusement is something pleasant that you enjoy doing **2.** amusement is being amused; laughing or smiling

amusing *adjective* making you laugh or smile • *It was an amusing story.*

an *determiner* (called the indefinite article) a word used instead of **a** when the next word begins with a vowel-sound or a silent **h** • *Take an apple.* • *You can hire boats for £5 an hour.*

anaemia *noun* (a-**nee**-mi-a) a poor condition of the blood that makes someone look pale **anaemic** *adjective* an anaemic person suffers from anaemia

anaesthetic *noun* (an-iss-**thet**-ik) a drug or gas that makes you unable to feel pain

anagram *noun* a word or phrase made by rearranging the letters of another word or phrase, for example *carthorse* is an anagram of *orchestra*

analyse *verb* **1.** to analyse something is to examine it carefully **2.** to analyse a substance is to divide it into its parts

analysis *noun* analyses a detailed study or examination of something

anarchy *noun* **1.** anarchy is having no government or effective controls, leading to a breakdown in law and order **2.** complete disorder and confusion **anarchist** *noun* someone who thinks that government and laws are bad and should be abolished

anatomy *noun* the study of the parts of the body **anatomical** *adjective* to do with anatomy

ancestor *noun* a person from your family who lived in the past **ancestry** *noun* a person's ancestors

anchor *noun* a heavy object joined to a ship by a chain or rope and dropped to the bottom of the sea to stop the ship from moving

ancient *adjective* belonging to times that were long ago

and *conjunction* linking words and phrases • *We had cakes and lemonade.* • *Touch that and you'll get burnt.* • *Go and buy a pen.*

anecdote *noun* a short amusing or interesting story about a real person or thing

anemone *noun* (a-**nem**-on-i) **1.** a small flower with the shape of a cup **2.** a sea anemone

angel *noun* a being that some people believe in, who is a messenger or attendant of God

anger *noun* a strong feeling of not liking what someone has said or done, making you want to quarrel or fight with them

angle *noun* the space between two lines or surfaces that meet

angle *verb* to angle something is to put it in a slanting position

angler *noun* someone who fishes with a fishing rod **angling** *noun* the sport of fishing with a fishing rod

angry *adjective* angrier, angriest feeling or showing anger **angrily** *adverb*

anguish *noun* great suffering or unhappiness **anguished** *adjective* suffering or unhappy

animal *noun* a living thing that can move and feel, such as a horse, snake, fish, bird or insect

animated *adjective* an animated film is one made by photographing a series of still pictures and showing them rapidly one after another, so they appear to move **animation** *noun* a way of making films from still pictures so they appear to move

aniseed *noun* a seed with a strong sweet taste like liquorice

ankle *noun* the part of your leg where it is joined to your foot

annihilate *verb* (a-**ny**-il-ayt) to annihilate something is to destroy it completely **annihilation** *noun* annihilation is destroying something completely

anniversary *noun* **anniversaries** a day when you remember something special that happened on the same date in an earlier year

announce *verb* to announce something is to say it publicly **announcer** *noun* someone who announces something, especially on radio or television

announcement *noun* something that is made known publicly, especially on the radio, on the Internet or in a newspaper

annoy *verb* to annoy someone is to make them feel slightly angry

annoyance *noun* **1.** annoyance is the feeling of being annoyed **2.** an annoyance is something that annoys you • *Wasps are a great annoyance at a picnic.*

annual *adjective* happening or coming every year **annually** *adverb* once every year • *The award is given annually.*
annual *noun* a children's book that comes out once a year

anonymous *adjective* an anonymous book or letter is one without the name of the writer being known **anonymously** *adverb* with the name unknown

anorak *noun* a thick warm jacket with a hood

anorexia *noun* (an-er-**eks**-ee-a) an illness that makes someone not want to eat **anorexic** *adjective* an anorexic person is suffering from anorexia

another *determiner, pronoun* a different person or thing • *Have another look.* • *May I have another?*

answer *noun* **1.** an answer is what you say when someone asks you a question **2.** the answer to a problem is something that solves it

answer *verb* **1.** to answer someone is to give them an answer **2.** to answer a phone is to pick it up when it rings

ant *noun* a tiny insect that lives in large groups

antelope *noun* an animal like a deer, that lives in Africa and parts of Asia

antenna *noun* **1.** **antennae** a long thin feeler on the head of an insect or shellfish **2.** **antennas** an aerial

anthem *noun* a religious or patriotic song, usually sung by a choir or group of people on special occasions

anthology *noun* **anthologies** a collection of poems, stories or songs in one book

antibiotic *noun* An antibiotic is a drug that kills bacteria. Penicillin is an antibiotic.

anticipate *verb* to anticipate something is to expect it and be ready for it • *The police were anticipating trouble.*

anticipation *noun* looking forward to doing something

anticlimax *noun* a disappointing ending or result after something exciting

anticlockwise *adverb, adjective* moving in the opposite direction to the hands of a clock • *Turn it anticlockwise.* • *Turn it in an anticlockwise direction.*

anticyclone *noun* an area where air pressure is high, usually causing fine weather

antidote *noun* something which takes away the bad effects of a poison or disease

antique *noun* (an-**teek**) a very old and valuable object

antiseptic *noun* a chemical that kills germs

antler *noun* the horn of a deer, which divides into several branches

antonym *noun* (**ant**-o-nim) a word that is opposite in meaning to another • *'Soft' is an antonym of 'hard'.*

anvil *noun* a large block of iron on which a blacksmith hammers metal into shape

anxiety *noun* anxieties **1.** anxiety is a feeling of being worried **2.** an anxiety is something that worries you

anxious *adjective* **1.** worried and nervous **2.** eager to do something • *They were anxious to help us.*

any *determiner* **1.** one or some • *Have you any wool?* **2.** no matter which • *Come any day you like.* **3.** every • *Any fool knows that!*

any *adverb* at all; in some degree • *Is it any good?*

anybody *noun, pronoun* anyone

anyhow *adverb* **1.** anyway **2.** (*informal*) carelessly, without much thought • *Books were placed anyhow on the shelves.*

anyone *noun, pronoun* any person

anything *noun, pronoun* any thing

anyway *adverb* whatever happens; whatever the situation may be • *If it rains, we'll go anyway.*

anywhere *adverb* in any place or to any place

apart *adverb* **1.** away from each other; separately • *Keep your desks apart.* **2.** into pieces • *It fell apart.*

apartment *noun* **1.** a set of rooms **2.** (*in America*) a flat

ape *noun* a monkey without a tail, such as a gorilla or a chimpanzee

aphid or **aphis** *noun* a tiny insect that sucks juices from plants

apologetic *adjective* saying you are sorry for something **apologetically** *adverb* in a way that shows you are sorry • *He replied apologetically.*

apologize *verb* to apologize to someone is to tell them you are sorry This word can also be spelled **apologise**.

apology *noun* apologies a statement that you are sorry for doing something wrong

apostle *noun* in Christianity, one of the twelve men sent out by Christ to tell people about God

apostrophe *noun* (a-**pos**-tro-fi) a punctuation mark (') used to show that letters have been left out, as in *can't* and *he'll*; it is also used with *s* to show who owns something, as in *the boy's books* (one boy), *the boys' books* (more than one boy)

appal *verb* appalling, appalled to appal someone is to shock them a lot • *The violence appalled everyone.*

appalling *adjective* dreadful, shocking • *The room was in an appalling mess.*

apparatus *noun* an apparatus is a set of equipment for a special use

apparent *adjective* **1.** clear, obvious • *He burst out laughing for no apparent reason.* **2.** appearing to be true • *Despite its apparent success, the film actually lost money.*

apparently *adverb* as it seems, so it appears • *The door had apparently been locked.*

appeal *verb* **1**. to appeal for something you need is to ask for it urgently • *They are appealing for money to rebuild the church roof.* **2**. to appeal to someone is to interest or attract them • *The film really appeals to me.* **3**. to appeal against a decision is to ask for it to be changed • *He appealed against his prison sentence.*

appeal *noun* **1**. an appeal is asking for something you need **2**. appeal is what makes something interesting • *Adventure stories have a lot of appeal for older children.* **3**. an appeal is asking for a decision to be changed

appear *verb* **1**. to appear is to become visible **2**. to appear is also to seem • *They appeared very anxious.* **3**. to appear in a film or play is to take part in it

appearance *noun* **1**. coming into sight **2**. taking part in a play, film, show, etc. **3**. what someone looks like

appendicitis *noun* an inflammation or disease of the appendix

appendix *noun* **1**. appendixes a small tube leading off from the intestines in the body **2**. appendices an extra section at the end of a book

appetite *noun* a desire for something, especially for food

appetizing *adjective* looking good to eat This word can also be spelled **appetising**.

applaud *verb* to applaud someone or something is to show that you like them, especially by clapping

applause *noun* clapping or cheering after someone has given a speech or given a performance

apple *noun* a round fruit with skin that is red, green or yellow

appliance *noun* a device or gadget

application *noun* **1**. an application is a letter or form you use to ask for something important, such as a job **2**. application is when you make a lot of effort to do something

applied *adjective* used for something practical • *Engineering is an applied science.*

apply *verb* applies, applying, applied **1**. to apply something is to put it on something else • *She applied some lipstick.* **2**. to apply

for a job is to write formally and ask for it **3**. to apply to someone is to concern them • *These rules apply to everybody.*

appoint *verb* to appoint someone is to choose them for a job

appointment *noun* **1**. an arrangement to meet or visit someone **2**. a job or position

appreciate *verb* **1**. to appreciate something is to enjoy or value it **2**. to appreciate a fact is to understand it • *You don't appreciate how lucky you are.* **3**. to appreciate is to increase in value

appreciation *noun* **1**. appreciation is showing that you enjoy or value something **2**. appreciation is also an increase in the money value of something, for example a house

appreciative *adjective* an appreciative person or group shows how much they enjoy or value something • *I enjoy playing to an appreciative audience.*

apprehension *noun* nervous fear or worry **apprehensive** *adjective* nervous and worried

apprentice *noun* someone who is learning a trade or craft **apprenticeship** *noun* the time when someone is an apprentice

approach *verb* **1**. to approach a place is to come near to it **2**. to approach someone is to go to them with a request or offer **approach** *noun* **1**. movement towards a place **2**. a way of tackling a problem **3**. a road, path, etc. leading up to a building • *The approach to the house had trees on each side.*

approachable *adjective* friendly and easy to talk to

appropriate *adjective* suitable

approval *noun* thinking well of someone or something

approve *verb* to approve of someone or something is to think they are good or suitable

approximate *adjective* roughly correct but not exact • *The dates in brackets are approximate only.* **approximately** *adverb* roughly but not exactly • *It will cost approximately twenty pounds.*

approximation *noun* something that is a rough estimate and not exact

apricot *noun* a juicy, orange-coloured fruit like a small peach, with a stone in it

April *noun* the fourth month of the year

apron *noun* a piece of clothing worn over the front of your body to protect your clothes

aptitude *noun* a natural ability to do something well

apt *adjective* 1. likely to do something • *He is apt to be careless.* 2. suitable • *I need to find an apt quotation.*

aquarium *noun* a tank or building for keeping live fish

aquatic *adjective* to do with water and swimming • *aquatic sports*

aqueduct *noun* a bridge that carries water across a valley

arabic figures or **arabic numerals** *plural noun* the figures 1, 2, 3, 4 and so on (compare *Roman numerals*)

arable *adjective* to do with the growing of crops

arbitrary *adjective* (**ar**-bi-trer-i) done or chosen without a proper reason and seeming unfair • *It was an arbitrary decision.*

arc *noun* part of the circumference of a circle, a curve

arcade *noun* a covered place to walk, with shops down each side

arch *noun* a curved structure that helps to support a bridge or building
arch *verb* to make a curved shape • *The cat arched its back.*

archaeology *noun* (ar-ki-**ol**-o-ji) the study of ancient people from the remains of their physical objects **archaeological** *adjective* an archaeological site or discovery is one to do with people from the ancient past

archaeologist *noun* someone who studies archaeology

archbishop *noun* the chief bishop of a region

archer *noun* someone who shoots with a bow and arrows

archery *noun* the sport of shooting with a bow and arrows

architect *noun* (**ar**-ki-tekt) someone whose work is to design buildings

architecture *noun* 1. the work of designing buildings 2. a style of building • *Victorian architecture*

area *noun* 1. part of a country, place, surface, etc. 2. the space occupied by something • *The area of this room is 20 square metres.*

arena *noun* (a-**ree**-na) a place where a sports event takes place

argue *verb* 1. to argue with someone is to quarrel with them 2. to argue is also to give reasons for something • *She argued that flying is safer than going by train.*

argument *noun* 1. a quarrel 2. a reason you give to show that something is right or wrong

arise *verb* arising, arose, arisen to arise is to appear or to come into existence • *If problems arise, we will deal with them.*

aristocracy *noun* aristocracies the aristocracy are the people of the highest social rank who often have titles like *Lord* and *Lady*

aristocrat *noun* (**a**-ris-to-krat) a nobleman or noblewoman **aristocratic** *adjective* to do with aristocrats

arithmetic *noun* the study of using numbers and working things out with them **arithmetical** *adjective* to do with arithmetic or using arithmetic

ark *noun* in the Bible, the ship in which Noah and his family escaped the Flood

arm *noun* 1. the part of your body between your shoulder and your hand 2. the sleeve of a coat or dress 3. the side part of a chair, on which you can rest your arm

arm *verb* 1. to arm people is to give them weapons 2. to arm is to prepare for war

armada *noun* (ar-**mah**-da) a fleet of warships, especially the Spanish Armada which attacked England in 1588

armadillo *noun* armadillos a South American animal whose body is covered with a shell of bony plates

armchair *noun* a chair with parts on either side to rest your arms on

armed forces *plural noun* the army, navy and air force of a country

armistice *noun* an agreement to stop fighting in a war or battle

armour *noun* armour is a metal suit or covering to protect people or equipment in battle **armoured** *adjective* having armour

armpit *noun* the hollow part under your arm at your shoulder

arms *plural noun* weapons • *Lay down your arms.*

army *noun* armies a large number of soldiers ready to fight

aroma *noun* (a-**roh**-ma) a pleasant smell, for example of food **aromatic** *adjective* having a pleasant smell

around *adverb, preposition* **1.** round • *They stood around the pond.* **2.** about • *Stop running around.*

arouse *verb* **1.** to arouse someone is to make them wake up **2.** to arouse feelings in someone is to cause them to have those feelings

arrange *verb* **1.** to arrange things is to put them all in the position you want **2.** to arrange a meeting or event is to organize it

arrangement *noun* **1.** arrangement is how you arrange or display something, for example flowers **2.** an arrangement is something you agree with someone else • *We made arrangements to meet in Paris.*

arrest *verb* to arrest someone is to take them to a police station because they may have committed a crime
arrest *noun* the act of arresting someone • *The police made several arrests.*

arrival *noun* **1.** an arrival is when someone or something arrives at a place **2.** an arrival is also someone who is new or has just arrived • *Have you met the new arrivals?*

arrive *verb* **1.** to arrive at a place is to get there at the end of a journey **2.** to arrive is also to happen • *The great day arrived.*

arrogant *adjective* an arrogant person is unpleasantly proud and thinks they are more important than anyone else **arrogance** *noun* arrogant behaviour

arrow *noun* **1.** a pointed stick shot from a bow **2.** a sign used to show direction or position

arsenal *noun* a place where bullets, shells and weapons are made or stored

arsenic *noun* a strong poison made from a metallic element and used in insecticides

arson *noun* the crime of deliberately setting fire to a building

art *noun* **1.** art is producing something by drawing or painting or sculpture **2.** the arts are subjects such as history and languages, as distinct from the sciences such as physics and chemistry **3.** an art is also a skill that can be developed with training and practice • *Public speaking is an art.*

artery *noun* arteries a tube carrying blood from the heart to parts of the body

arthritis *noun* (arth-**ry**-tiss) a disease that makes joints in the body painful and stiff **arthritic** *adjective* (arth-**rit**-ik) suffering from arthritis

article *noun* **1.** an object or thing that you can touch or pick up **2.** a piece of writing published in a newspaper, magazine or other publication **3.** *(in grammar)* the word 'a' or 'an' (called the *indefinite article*) or the word 'the' (called the *definite article*)

articulate *adjective* (ar-**tik**-yoo-lat) an articulate person is able to speak clearly and fluently

artificial *adjective* made by human beings and not by nature **artificially** *adverb*

artillery *noun* artilleries **1.** artillery is a collection of large guns **2.** the artillery is the part of the army that uses large guns

artist *noun* **1.** someone who produces art, especially a painter **2.** an entertainer **artistry** *noun* the skill of an artist • *The carving showed great artistry.*

artistic *adjective* **1**. to do with art and artists **2**. showing skill and beauty • *The food was presented in an artistic way.*

as *conjunction, adverb, preposition* linking words and phrases • *As you were late, you had better stay behind.* • *Leave it as it is.* • *She slipped as she got off the bus.* • *It is not as hard as you think.* • *He was dressed as a sailor.*

asbestos *noun* a fireproof material that is made up of fine soft fibres

ascend *verb* to ascend something like a hill or staircase is to go up it

ascent *noun* an ascent is a climb, usually a hard or long one

ash[1] *noun* ash is the powder that is left after something has been burned

ash[2] *noun* an ash or ash tree is a tree with silvery bark and winged seeds

ashamed *adjective* feeling guilty or upset about something you have done

ashore *adverb* on the shore

aside *adverb* to or at one side; away • *Step aside and let them pass.*

ask *verb* **1**. to ask someone something is to speak to them so as to find out or get something **2**. to ask someone to something like a party is to invite them

asleep *adverb, adjective* sleeping

aspect *noun* one way of looking at a problem or situation • *Perhaps the worst aspect of winter is the dark mornings.*

aspirin *noun* a drug used to relieve pain or reduce fever

ass *noun* a donkey

assassinate *verb* to assassinate someone such as a ruler or leader is to murder them to stop them having power **assassin** *noun* a person who assassinates someone **assassination** *noun* the murder of a ruler or leader

assault *noun* a violent attack on someone **assault** *verb* to assault someone is to attack them violently

assemble *verb* **1**. to assemble people or things is to bring them together in one place **2**. to assemble something is to make it by putting the parts together **3**. to assemble is to come together in one place • *Please assemble in the playground.*

assembly *noun* **1**. an assembly is when a lot of people come together and someone speaks to them, for example in a school **2**. an assembly is also a group of people who meet together, such as a parliament **3**. assembly of a machine or piece of furniture is putting the parts together to make it

> The words **assemble** and **assembly** come from Latin words *ad* meaning 'to' or 'towards' and *simul* meaning 'together'.

assert *verb* to assert something is to say it strongly and clearly **assertion** *noun* something you say clearly and strongly

assess *verb* to assess someone or something is to decide how good or useful they are **assessment** *noun* an opinion about something after thinking about it carefully

asset *noun* something useful or valuable to someone

assign *verb* to assign something to someone is to give it to them as their share or duty • *A different teacher is assigned to each subject.*

assignment *noun* a piece of work that someone is given to do

assist *verb* to assist someone is to help them, usually in a practical way

assistance *noun* help someone gets when they need information or support

assistant *noun* **1**. someone whose job is to help another person in their work **2**. someone who serves in a shop

associate *verb* (a-**soh**-shi-ayt) to associate one thing with another is to connect them in your mind • *I associate Christmas with ice and snow.*

association *noun* an association is an organization for people sharing an interest or doing the same work

assorted *adjective* of various kinds; mixed and different

assortment *noun* a mixture of different things or people

assume *verb* to assume something is to think it is true or likely without being sure of it • *I assume you will be coming tomorrow.* **assumed** *adjective* an assumed name is one that is not the person's real name

assumption *noun* something you assume or take for granted

assurance *noun* **1**. an assurance is a promise or guarantee **2**. assurance is confidence in yourself

assure *verb* to assure someone is to tell someone something definite • *I can assure you that we will make every effort to help.*

asterisk *noun* a star-shaped sign * used in printing and writing to draw attention to something

asteroid *noun* one of the small planets found mainly between the orbits of Mars and Jupiter

asthma *noun* (**ass**-ma) a disease which makes breathing difficult

asthmatic *adjective* suffering from asthma
asthmatic *noun* someone who is suffering from asthma

astonish *verb* to astonish someone is to surprise them very much **astonishment** *noun* a feeling of great surprise

astound *verb* to astound someone is to amaze or shock them very much

astrology *noun* astrology is studying how the planets and stars may affect people's lives **astrological** *adjective* to do with astrology **astrologer** *noun* someone who studies astrology

astronaut *noun* someone who travels in a spacecraft

astronomy *noun* astronomy is studying the sun, moon, planets and stars **astronomical** *adjective* to do with astronomy **astronomer** *noun* someone who studies astronomy

at *preposition* showing where someone or something is • *I was at the hospital.* • *They are looking at their new books.*

atheist *noun* someone who does not believe in a God **atheism** *noun* a belief that there is no God

athlete *noun* someone who is good at athletics or other sports

athletic *adjective* **1**. to do with athletics • *an athletic competition* **2**. good at sports; strong

athletics *plural noun* physical exercises and sports such as running and jumping

atlas *noun* a book of maps

Atlas was a Titan in Greek mythology who offended the gods and was punished by having to support the universe on his shoulders. A picture of him was often put at the beginning of old atlases and this is how they got their name.

atmosphere *noun* **1**. the earth's atmosphere is the air around it **2**. an atmosphere is a feeling you get in a room or at a place • *The atmosphere of the house was cheerful and friendly.*

atmospheric *adjective* **1**. to do with the earth's atmosphere **2**. having an exciting quality or creating an emotional mood

atom *noun* the smallest possible part of a chemical element

atom bomb or **atomic bomb** *noun* a bomb that uses atomic energy to make the explosion and has nuclear fallout

atomic *adjective* involving atoms; nuclear

attach *verb* to attach one thing to another is to fix or fasten it

attachment *noun* **1**. an extra part you fix to a device so that it can do a special kind of work • *The garden hose has an attachment for washing cars.* **2**. a fondness or friendship • *The boys felt a real attachment to their pet hamster.* **3**. *(in computing)* a document that you send to someone with an email message

attack *noun* **1**. an attempt to hurt or harm someone **2**. a sudden illness or pain
attack *verb* to attack someone is to try to hurt them with violence or to harm them with unfriendly words

attain *verb* to attain something is to reach or achieve it • *I have attained Grade 3 on the violin.* **attainment** *noun* something you have achieved

attempt *verb* to attempt to do something is to make an effort to do it

attempt *noun* an attempt at something is making an effort to do it

attend *verb* 1. to attend something like a meeting or a wedding is to be there 2. to attend school or college is to be a pupil or student there

attendance *noun* 1. attendance is being somewhere where you are supposed to be 2. the attendance at an event is the number of people who are there to see it

attendant *noun* someone who helps or goes with another person

attention *noun* giving care or thought to someone or something to stand to attention is to stand with your feet together and your arms straight down, like soldiers on parade

attic *noun* a room or space under the roof of a house

attitude *noun* your attitude is the way you think or feel about something and the way you behave

attract *verb* 1. to attract someone is to seem pleasant to them and get their attention or interest 2. to attract something unwelcome is to make it come • *Empty pop bottles attract wasps.* 3. to attract something is also to pull it by a physical force like magnetism • *Magnets attract metal pins.*

attraction *noun* 1. attraction is the power to attract someone 2. an attraction is something pleasant that visitors to a place like to see, such as a fair or a museum

attractive *adjective* 1. pleasant, good-looking 2. interesting or welcome • *They made us an attractive offer for the house.*

auburn *adjective* auburn hair is a reddish-brown colour

auction *noun* a sale at which things are sold to the person who offers the most money for them **auctioneer** *noun* an official in charge of an auction

audible *adjective* loud enough to be heard

audience *noun* the people who have come to see or hear an event like a concert or film

audition *noun* a test to see if a performer is suitable to act in a play or sing in a choir

auditorium *noun* (aw-dit-**or**-i-um) the part of a theatre or concert hall where the audience sits

August *noun* the eighth month of the year

aunt *noun* 1. the sister of your mother or father 2. your uncle's wife

auntie or **aunty** *noun* **aunties** (*informal*) an aunt

authentic *adjective* real, genuine **authenticity** *noun* being authentic

author *noun* the writer of a book or something like a poem or story

authority *noun* **authorities** 1. authority is the power to give orders to other people 2. the authorities are the people who have the power to make decisions 3. an authority on a subject is an expert on it

autistic *adjective* having a condition that makes someone unable to communicate with other people **autism** *noun*

autobiography *noun* **autobiographies** the story of someone's life that they have written themselves **autobiographical** *adjective* autobiographical writing is written by a person about their own life

autograph *noun* the signature of a famous person

automatic *adjective* 1. an automatic process is one that works on its own, without people operating it 2. an automatic action is one that you do without having to think **automatically** *adverb* by automatic means; without having to use controls all the time

automobile *noun* (*in America*) a motor car

autumn *noun* (**aw**-tum) the season when leaves fall off the trees, between summer and winter

available *adjective* able to be found or used • *The film is now available to rent.* **availability** *noun* availability is how easily you can find or get something

avalanche *noun* (**av**-a-lahnsh) a sudden heavy fall of snow and ice down the side of a mountain

avenue *noun* a wide street with trees along each side

average *noun* **1.** an average is the number you get by adding several amounts together and dividing the total by the number of amounts • *The average of 2, 4, 6 and 8 is 5.* **2.** the average is the usual or ordinary standard • *Their work is well above the average.*
average *adjective* of the usual or ordinary standard
average *verb* to average is to have as an average • *In the rainforest the rainfall can average more than 2500 mm a year.*

aviary *noun* aviaries a place where birds are kept

aviation *noun* aviation is flying in aircraft

avid *adjective* keen, eager • *She is an avid reader.*

avoid *verb* **1.** to avoid something or someone is to stay away from them • *She swerved in time to avoid a tree.* **2.** to avoid something is also to find a way of not doing it • *They wanted to avoid extra homework.*

awake *adjective* not sleeping
awake *verb* awakes, awaking, awoke, awoken to awake is to wake up

award *noun* something such as a prize given to a person who has done something successful
award *verb* to award something to someone is to give it to them as an award

aware *adjective* to be aware of something is to know about it or realize it is there • *They soon became aware of the danger.*
awareness *noun* awareness is knowing about something

away *adverb* at a distance or somewhere else • *I wish those people would go away.* • *The ice cream melted so I threw it away.*
away *adjective* an away match is one that is played at the opponent's ground

awe *noun* fear and wonder • *The mountains filled him with awe.* awed filled with fear and wonder

awful *adjective* **1.** (informal) very bad; very great • *I've been an awful fool.* **2.** causing fear or horror • *It was an awful sight.*

awfully *adverb* (informal) very, extremely • *It's awfully hot in June.*

awhile *adverb* for a short time

awkward *adjective* **1.** difficult to use or cope with • *The box was an awkward shape.* **2.** embarrassed and uncomfortable • *She felt awkward and shy in his presence.*

axe *noun* a tool for chopping

axis *noun* axes a line through the centre of a spinning object • *The earth rotates on its axis once every 24 hours.*

axle *noun* the rod through the centre of a wheel, on which it turns

Byte is a word that was invented in the 1960s to mean a unit that measures data or memory.

babble *verb* **1.** to babble is to talk quickly, without making much sense **2.** to babble is also to make a murmuring or bubbling sound • *They came across a babbling brook.*

baboon *noun* a large kind of monkey with a long muzzle

baby *noun* babies a very young child

babysit *verb* babysits, babysitting, babysat to babysit is to look after a child while its parents are out **babysitter** *noun* someone who babysits

bachelor *noun* a man who has not married

back *noun* **1**. the part of your body between your shoulders and your bottom **2**. the upper part of a four-legged animal's body **3**. the part of a thing that is furthest away from the front • *The back of the house faces a river.*
back *adjective* placed at or near the back • *Let's sit in the back row.*
back *adverb* **1**. backwards or towards the back • *Go back!* **2**. to where someone or something was before • *When will you be coming back?* **3**. to an earlier time • *Think back to when you were little.*
back *verb* **1**. to back a vehicle is to move it backwards **2**. to back someone is to support or help them

backbone *noun* your backbone is your spine

background *noun* **1**. the background of a picture or view is the part that is farthest away from you, behind the main subject **2**. the background to an event or situation is all the things that help to explain why it happened **3**. a person's background is their family, education and what they have done in their working life

backing *noun* **1**. backing is support or help • *Did you receive any financial backing from a bank?* **2**. the backing on a pop song is the music that is played or sung to support the main singer or tune

backstroke *noun* a stroke you use when swimming on your back

backward *adjective* facing or aimed towards the back • *She walked past him without a backward glance.*
backward *adverb* backwards

backwards *adverb* **1**. towards the back **2**. with the back end going first **3**. in the opposite order to the usual one • *Can you say the alphabet backwards?*

backyard *noun* an open area at the back of a building

bacon *noun* smoked or salted meat from the back or sides of a pig

bacteria *plural noun* tiny organisms that can cause diseases **bacterial** *adjective* to do with bacteria

bad *adjective* worse, worst **1**. not good or well done • *We were watching a very bad film on television.* **2**. someone who is bad is wicked

or naughty **3**. harmful to your health • *Eating fatty foods is bad for you.* **not bad** fairly good, all right

badge *noun* a small piece of metal, plastic or cloth that you pin or sew on your clothes to tell people something about you

badger *noun* a grey animal with a black and white head, which lives underground and comes out at night to feed
badger *verb* to badger someone is to keep asking them to do something • *He's been badgering his mum for weeks for a new bike.*

badly *adverb* **1**. not well • *They did the work badly.* **2**. seriously • *He was badly wounded.* **3**. very much • *I need a drink of water badly.* **badly off** poor or unfortunate

badminton *noun* a game in which players use rackets to hit a light object called a *shuttlecock* backwards and forwards across a high net

bad-tempered *adjective* a bad-tempered person is one who often becomes angry

baffle *verb* to baffle someone is to puzzle or confuse them completely

bag *noun* a container made of soft material, for holding or carrying things **bags of something** (informal) plenty • *There's bags of room.*

baggage *noun* baggage is the suitcases and bags you take on a journey

baggy *adjective* baggier, baggiest baggy clothes hang loosely from your body

bagpipes *plural noun* bagpipes are a musical instrument you play by squeezing air out of a bag into a set of pipes

bail[1] *noun* bail is money that has to be paid so that a person accused of a crime will not be kept in prison before their trial

bail[2] *noun* bails are the two small pieces of wood placed on top of the stumps in cricket

bail[3] *verb* to bail water out of a boat is to scoop it over the side

Bairam *noun* (by-**ram**) either of two Muslim festivals, one in the tenth month and one in the twelfth month of the Islamic year

Baisakhi *noun* a Sikh festival held in April

bait *noun* bait is a small amount of food put on a hook or in a trap to catch fish or animals

bait *verb* to bait a hook or trap is to put the bait on it or in it, to catch fish or animals

bake *verb* **1**. to bake food is to cook it in an oven, especially bread or cakes **2**. to bake something like clay is to make it hard by heating it in an oven

baker *noun* someone who makes or sells bread and cakes

bakery *noun* bakeries a place where bread is made or sold

balance *noun* **1**. a person's balance is their feeling of being steady • *He lost his balance and fell over.* **2**. a balance is a device for weighing things, with two trays hanging from the ends of a horizontal bar **3**. the balance of a bank account is the difference between the money paid into it and the money taken out of it **4**. a balance is also an amount of money that someone owes • *I will pay you the balance on Saturday.*

balance *verb* to balance something is to keep it steady • *He was balancing a tray on one hand.*

balcony *noun* balconies **1**. a platform built out from the wall of a building, with a railing round it **2**. the upstairs part of a cinema or theatre

bald *adjective* a bald person does not have much hair or any hair on their head

bale[1] *noun* a large bundle of hay or straw tied up tightly

bale[2] *verb* to bale out is to jump out of an aircraft with a parachute

ball *noun* **1**. a round object used in many games **2**. anything that is made into a round shape • *a ball of string* **3**. a grand or formal party where people dance

ballad *noun* a simple song or poem that tells a story

ballerina *noun* (bal-e-**ree**-na) a female ballet dancer

ballet *noun* (**bal**-ay) a form of dancing in which a group of dancers perform special steps and movements to tell a story to music

balloon *noun* **1**. a small rubber pouch that you fill up with air or gas and use as a toy or for decoration **2**. a large round or

pear-shaped bag filled with a light gas or hot air, so that it can carry people into the air

ballot *noun* (**bal**-ot) a method of voting in secret by making a mark on a piece of paper and putting it into a box

ballpoint *noun* a pen with a tiny ball at the tip, round which the ink flows

ballroom *noun* a large room where dances are held

balsa *noun* (**bol**-sa) a kind of lightweight wood used to make models

bamboo *noun* a tall tropical plant with hard hollow stems, used for making furniture

ban *verb* bans, banning, banned to ban something is to forbid people to do it

banana *noun* a long curved fruit with a yellow skin

band *noun* **1**. a group of people playing music together **2**. an organized group of people doing something together **3**. a circular strip of something

band *verb* to band together is to join together to form an organized group

bandage *noun* (**ban**-dij) a strip of material that you wrap round a wound to protect it

bandit *noun* a member of a gang of robbers who attack travellers

bandstand *noun* a platform for a band playing music outdoors, usually in a park

bandy *adjective* bandier, bandiest bandy legs curve outwards at the knees

bang *noun* **1**. a sudden loud noise **2**. a heavy blow or knock

bang *verb* **1**. to bang something is to hit or shut it noisily • *Don't bang the door when you go out.* **2**. to bang something is to knock it hard against something else • *She banged her knee on the desk.*

banish *verb* to banish someone is to punish them by sending them away and ordering them not to return • *The emperor banished him to a remote island.*

banisters *plural noun* banisters are a rail with upright supports at the side of a staircase

banjo *noun* **banjos** a musical instrument like a small guitar with a round body

bank *noun* **1**. a business which looks after people's money **2**. the ground beside a river or lake **3**. a piece of raised or sloping ground **4**. a place where something is stored and collected • *a blood bank*

bank *verb* **1**. to bank money is to put it in a bank **2**. to bank is to lean over while changing direction • *The plane banked as it turned to land.*

bank holiday *noun* a public holiday, when the banks are closed

bankrupt *adjective* not able to pay your debts

banner *noun* a large strip of cloth with writing on it, carried on a pole or between two poles in a procession or demonstration

banquet *noun* (**bank**-wit) a large formal dinner, often with speeches

baptism *noun* baptism is the ceremony of baptizing someone

baptize *verb* to baptize someone is to sprinkle them with water or dip them in water, in a ceremony welcoming them into the Christian Church This word can also be spelled **baptise**.

bar *noun* **1**. a long piece of something hard **2**. a counter or room where drinks and refreshments are served **3**. one of the small equal sections into which music is divided • *A waltz has three beats in a bar.*

bar *verb* **barring, barred 1**. to bar a widow or door is to fasten it with a bar **2**. to bar someone from something is to prevent them from taking part in it

barbarian *noun* an uncivilized or savage person

barbaric or **barbarous** *adjective* savage and cruel **barbarity** *noun* savage cruelty

barbecue *noun* **1**. a metal frame used for grilling food over a charcoal fire outdoors **2**. a party at which food is cooked outdoors on a barbecue

barbed wire *noun* wire with sharp twisted spikes on it, used to make fences

barber *noun* someone whose job is to cut men's hair

bar code *noun* a set of black lines that are printed on goods, library books, etc. so that they can be identified by a computer

bare *adjective* **1**. not covered with anything • *The trees were bare.* **2**. empty or almost empty • *The cupboard was bare.* **3**. only just enough • *They just had the bare necessities of life.*

barely *adverb* only just; with difficulty • *They were barely able to see in the fog.*

bargain *noun* **1**. something that you buy cheaply **2**. an agreement between two people to do something for each other • *I expect you to keep your side of the bargain.*

bargain *verb* to bargain over something is to argue over its price

barge *noun* a long flat-bottomed boat used especially on canals

barge *verb* to barge into someone is to bump clumsily into them or push them out of the way

bark *noun* **1**. a bark is the sound made by a dog or a fox **2**. bark is the outer covering of a tree's branches or trunk

bark *verb* a dog or fox barks when it makes its special sound

barley *noun* a kind of grain which is used for food and to make beer

bar mitzvah *noun* A bar mitzvah is a religious ceremony for Jewish boys who have reached the age of 13, when they accept some of the responsibilities of an adult. The ceremony for a girl is called a **bat mitzvah**.

barn *noun* a building on a farm used to store things such as grain or hay

barnacle *noun* a shellfish that attaches itself to rocks and the bottoms of ships

barometer *noun* (ba-**rom**-it-er) an instrument that measures air pressure, used in forecasting the weather

baron *noun* a member of the lowest rank of noblemen

baroness *noun* a female baron or a baron's wife

barracks *noun* the buildings where soldiers live

barrage *noun* (**ba**-rahzh) **1.** heavy gunfire **2.** a large amount of something • *We received a barrage of complaints.*

barrel *noun* **1.** a large container for liquids, with curved sides and flat ends **2.** the metal tube of a gun, through which the shot is fired

barren *adjective* barren land or plants cannot produce any crops or fruit

barricade *noun* a barrier, especially one put up quickly to block a street

barricade *verb* to barricade a place is to block or defend it with a barrier

barrier *noun* a fence or wall put up to stop people getting past

barrister *noun* a lawyer who argues legal cases in the higher courts

barrow *noun* a small cart

barter *verb* to barter is to exchange goods for other goods, without using money

base *noun* **1.** the lowest part of something or the part on which something stands **2.** a place from which an army or police operation is controlled

base *verb* to base one thing on another thing is to use the second thing as the starting point for the first • *She based the story on an event in her own childhood.*

baseball *noun* **1.** baseball is an American game in which the players hit a ball and run round a series of four 'bases' to score points **2.** a baseball is the ball used in this game

basement *noun* a room or part of a building below ground level

bash *verb* (*informal*) to bash someone or something is to hit them hard

bashful *adjective* shy

basic *adjective* forming the first or most important part • *He has a basic knowledge of French.* • *Food is a basic human need.*

basically *adverb* in the most important ways; essentially • *She is basically lazy.*

basin *noun* **1.** a deep bowl for mixing food in **2.** a large container to hold water for washing your face and hands in **3.** a river basin is the area of land where the river's water comes from

basis *noun* **bases** **1.** the basis of something is what you start from or add to • *These players will be the basis of a new team.* **2.** a basis is the way in which something is arranged or organized • *You will be paid on a monthly basis.*

bask *verb* to bask is to lie or sit comfortably warming yourself in the sun

basket *noun* a container made of strips of wood, cane or wire woven together

basketball *noun* **1.** basketball is a team game in which players try to throw a large ball through a high net hanging from a hoop **2.** a basketball is the ball used in this game

bass *adjective* (bayss) forming the lowest sounds in music

bass *noun* (bayss) a bass singer or instrument

bassoon *noun* a woodwind instrument that plays low notes

bat[1] *noun* a shaped piece of wood used to hit the ball in cricket, baseball and other games

bat[1] *verb* batting, batted to bat is to take a turn at using a bat in cricket, baseball and other games

bat[2] *noun* A bat is a flying mammal that looks like a mouse with wings. Bats come out at night to feed.

batch *noun* a set of things made at one time or dealt with together

bath *noun* **1.** a bath is a large container you fill with water and get into to wash yourself **2.** a bath sometimes means the water in a bath • *Your bath is getting cold.*

bath *verb* **1.** to bath someone is to give them a bath **2.** to bath is to have a bath

bathe *verb* **1.** to bathe is to go swimming in the sea or a river **2.** to bathe a sore part of your body is to wash it gently

bathe *noun* a bathe is a swim

bathroom *noun* a room for having a bath or wash in

bat mitzvah *noun* A bat mitzvah is a religious ceremony for Jewish girls who have reached the age of 12, when they accept some of the responsibilities of an adult. The ceremony for a boy is called a **bar mitzvah**.

baton *noun* a short stick, especially one you use to conduct an orchestra or in a relay race

batsman *noun* batsmen a player who uses a bat in cricket

battalion *noun* an army unit consisting of two or more companies

batter *verb* to batter someone or something is to hit them hard and often • *Huge waves battered the rocks.*

batter *noun* batter is a mixture of flour, eggs and milk beaten together and used to make pancakes or to coat food before you fry it

battery *noun* batteries **1.** a portable device for storing and supplying electricity **2.** a series of cages in which animals are kept close together on a farm • *battery farming* **3.** a set of devices that are used together, especially a group of large guns

battle *noun* **1.** a fight between two armies **2.** a struggle

battlefield *noun* a place where a battle is or was fought

battlements *plural noun* the top of a castle wall, usually with gaps for firing arrows

battleship *noun* a large warship armed with powerful guns

bawl *verb* to bawl is to shout or cry loudly

bay *noun* **1.** a place by the sea or a lake where the shore curves inwards **2.** an area for parking vehicles, storing things, etc.

bayonet *noun* a steel blade that can be fixed to the end of a rifle and used for stabbing

bazaar *noun* **1.** a sale held to raise money for charity **2.** a covered market in an Eastern country

BC short for *before Christ*, used with dates that come before the birth of Jesus Christ • *Julius Caesar came to Britain in 55 BC.*

be *verb* I am; you are; he, she or it is; they are; I, he, she or it was, you were, they were; I, you or they have been; he, she or it has been **1.** to be is to exist or happen • *There is a bus stop at the corner.* • *The final is on Saturday.* **2.** to be someone or something is to have that position or quality • *She is my teacher.* • *You are very tall.*

beach *noun* the strip of pebbles or sand close to the sea

beacon *noun* a light or fire used as a warning signal

bead *noun* **1.** a small piece of glass, wood or plastic with a hole through it, threaded on a string or wire to make a necklace or bracelet **2.** a small drop of liquid • *Beads of sweat ran down her face.*

beady *adjective* beadier, beadiest beady eyes are small and bright

beak *noun* the hard, horny part of a bird's mouth

beaker *noun* **1.** a tall drinking mug, usually without a handle **2.** a glass container used for pouring liquids in a science laboratory

beam *noun* **1.** a long, thick bar of wood or metal **2.** a ray of light or other radiation

beam *verb* **1.** to beam is to send out a beam of light or radio waves **2.** you can say a person beams when they smile very happily

bean *noun* **1.** a kind of plant with seeds growing in pods **2.** the seed or pod of this kind of plant, eaten as food

bear¹ *verb* bore, born or borne **1.** to bear something is to carry or support it **2.** to bear something is to put up with it or suffer it • *I can't bear all this noise.*

bear² *noun* a large heavy animal with thick fur and sharp hooked claws

bearable *adjective* something that is bearable is something you are able to put up with • *His toothache was hardly bearable.*

beard *noun* hair on the lower part of a man's face bearded *adjective* a bearded man is a man with a beard

bearing *noun* **1.** your bearing is the way you stand and walk **2.** the direction or position of something in relation to something else

beast *noun* any large four-footed animal

beat *verb* beating, beat, beaten **1.** to beat someone or something is to hit them repeatedly, especially with a stick **2.** to beat someone in a game or match is to do better than them and win it **3.** to beat a cooking mixture is to stir it quickly so that it becomes thicker **4.** to beat something is to shape or flatten it by hitting it many times **5.** to beat is also to make regular movements like your heart does to beat someone up is to attack them very violently

beat *noun* **1.** a regular rhythm or stroke, like your heart makes **2.** a strong rhythm in pop music **3.** the regular route of a police officer

beautiful *adjective* very pleasing to look at or listen to beautifully *adverb*

beauty *noun* beauties beauty is a quality that gives delight or pleasure, especially to your senses • *They enjoyed the beauty of the sunset.*

Beaver *noun* a member of the most junior section of the Scout Association

beaver *noun* a brown furry animal with strong teeth and a long flat tail, which builds dams in rivers

because *conjunction* for the reason that • *We were happy because it was a holiday.* because of someone or something for that reason; on account of them • *He limped because of his bad leg.*

become *verb* becoming, became, become to start being something described • *It gradually became darker.*

bed *noun* **1.** a bed is a piece of furniture for sleeping on **2.** bed is the place where you sleep • *I'm going to bed now.* **3.** a bed is also a part of a garden where plants are grown **4.** the bed of the sea or of a river is the bottom of it

bedclothes *plural noun* sheets, blankets, duvets, etc. for using on a bed

bedding *noun* things for making a bed, such as sheets, blankets, duvets, etc.

bedraggled *adjective* (bi-**drag**-uld) wet and dirty

bedroom *noun* a room where you sleep

bedside *noun* the space beside a bed, especially the bed of someone who is ill • *He sat by his son's bedside all night.*

bedspread *noun* a covering put over the top of a bed

bedtime *noun* the time when you usually go to bed

bee *noun* a stinging insect that makes honey

beech *noun* a tree with smooth bark and glossy leaves

beef *noun* the meat of an ox, bull or cow

beefburger *noun* a hamburger

beehive *noun* a container for bees to live in

beer *noun* beer is an alcoholic drink made from malt and hops

beet *noun* beet or beets beet is a plant used as a vegetable or for making sugar

beetle *noun* an insect with hard, shiny covers over its wings

beetroot *noun* beetroot the dark red root of beet used as a vegetable

before *adverb, preposition* 1. earlier or earlier than • *Have you been here before?* • *They came the day before yesterday.* 2. in front of • *He stood up before the whole school.*

beforehand *adverb* earlier or before something else happens • *She had tried to phone me beforehand.* • *Let me know beforehand if you want to come.*

beg *verb* begging, begged 1. to beg is to ask people to give you money or food 2. to beg someone is to ask them seriously or desperately • *He begged me not to tell the teacher.*

beggar *noun* someone who lives by begging in the street

begin *verb* beginning, began, begun to begin something is to start doing it **beginner** *noun* someone who is just starting to learn or is still learning a subject

beginning *noun* the start of something

behalf *noun* on behalf of something for a cause • *They were collecting money on behalf of cancer research.* on someone's behalf for them or in their name • *Will you accept the prize on my behalf?*

behave *verb* 1. to act in a certain way • *My sister has been behaving very strangely recently.* 2. to show good manners • *Why can't you behave?*

behaviour *noun* 1. your behaviour is the way you behave 2. animal behaviour is the way animals normally behave

behind *adverb, preposition* 1. at or to the back • *The others are a long way behind.* • *She hid behind a tree.* 2. not making good progress • *He's behind the rest of the class in French.* 3. supporting or encouraging • *We're all behind you.*

behind *noun* your behind is your bottom

beige *noun, adjective* (bayzh) a light yellowish-brown colour

being *noun* a being is a person or creature of any kind

belch *verb* 1. to belch is to make a noise by letting air come up from your stomach through your mouth 2. a chimney or factory belches smoke or fumes when it sends out thick smoke or fumes into the air

belch *noun* the act or sound of belching

belief *noun* a belief is something you believe

believe *verb* 1. to believe something is to think that it is true 2. to believe someone is to think that they are telling the truth 3. to believe in something is to think it exists • *Do you believe in ghosts?*

bell *noun* a hollow metal object that makes a ringing sound when it is struck

bellow *verb* to bellow is to shout loudly and deeply

bellows *plural noun* bellows are a device for blowing out air, especially into a fire to make it burn more strongly

belly *noun* **bellies** 1. the abdomen or the stomach of a human 2. the part underneath the body of a four-legged animal

belong *verb* 1. to belong to someone is to be their property • *The pencil belongs to me.* 2. to belong to a club or group is to be a member of it • *We both belong to the tennis club.* 3. to belong somewhere is to have a special place where it goes • *The butter belongs in the fridge.*

belongings *plural noun* your belongings are the things that you own

below *preposition* lower than, under • *We have nice neighbours in the flat below us.*
below *adverb* at a lower point or to a lower point • *I'll have the top bunk and you can sleep below.*

belt *noun* a strip of material, often leather or cloth, that you wear round your waist
belt *verb* (informal) to belt someone is to hit them hard

bench *noun* 1. a long seat 2. a long table for working at

bend *verb* **bending, bent** 1. to bend something is to make it curved or crooked 2. to bend is to become curved or crooked • *The trees were bending in the wind.* 3. to bend is also to move the top of your body downwards • *She bent down to pick up the cat.*

bend *noun* a part where something curves or turns

beneath *preposition, adverb* under • *Beneath the soil there is clay.*

benefit *noun* 1. a benefit is something that is useful or helpful • *Television is one of the benefits of modern science.* 2. benefit is money that the government pays to help people who are poor, sick or out of work
benefit *verb* you benefit from something or it benefits you, when it helps you

bent *adjective* curved or crooked

bequeath *verb* (rhymes with breathe) to bequeath something to someone is to leave it to them in a will

bereaved *adjective* a bereaved person is someone with a close relative who has recently died **bereavement** *noun* someone suffers bereavement when a close relative dies

beret *noun* (**bair**-ay) a soft, round, flat cap

berry *noun* **berries** a small, juicy fruit

berserk *adjective* to go berserk is to become extremely angry or lose control

berth *noun* 1. a sleeping place on a ship or train 2. a place where a ship is tied up

beside *preposition* next to; close to • *The little house stood beside a lake.*

besides *preposition* in addition to • *Who came besides you?*
besides *adverb* also; in addition to this • *The coat cost too much. Besides, it's the wrong colour.*

besiege *verb* (bi-**seej**) to besiege a place is to surround it until the people inside surrender

best *adjective* most excellent; most able to do something • *She's the best swimmer in the class.*
best *adverb* 1. in the best way; most • *We'll do what suits you best.* 2. most usefully; most wisely • *He is best ignored.*
best *noun* the best person or thing or the best people or things • *She was the best at tennis.* • *These apples are the best you can buy.* **to do your best** is to do as well as you can

best man *noun* someone who helps the bridegroom at his wedding

bestseller *noun* a book or other product that has sold in very large numbers

bet *noun* **1.** an agreement that you will risk money on the result of a race, game, etc. or on saying something will happen **2.** the money you risk losing in a bet
bet *verb* **betting, bet** or **betted 1.** to bet or to bet money, is to make a bet **2.** *(informal)* to bet something is to say you are sure about it • *I bet I'm right.*

betray *verb* to betray someone is to do them harm when they are expecting your support
betrayal *noun* betrayal is betraying someone

better *adjective* **1.** of a higher standard or quality • *I need a better bike.* **2.** to be better is to feel well again after an illness
better *noun* a better person or thing **to get the better of someone** is to defeat or outwit them
better *adverb* in a better way • *Try to do it better next time.* **to be better off** is to be more fortunate in some way, for example by having more money
better *verb* to better something is to improve on it • *She hopes to better her own record time.*

between *preposition, adverb* within two or more points; among • *Call me between Tuesday and Friday.* • *The train runs between London and Glasgow.* • *Divide the sweets between the children.* • *The two houses are side by side with a fence between.*

beware *verb* only as **beware** a warning to be careful • *Beware of pickpockets.*

bewilder *verb* to bewilder someone is to puzzle them completely

bewitch *verb* to bewitch someone is to put a spell on them

beyond *preposition, adverb* farther on • *Don't go beyond the end of the street.* • *You can see the next valley and the mountains beyond.*

bias *noun* **biases** bias is a strong feeling in favour of one person or side and against another • *The referee was accused of bias.*
biased *adjective* someone is biased when they show that they prefer one person or side over another

bib *noun* a piece of cloth or plastic you put under a baby's chin to protect its clothes when eating

Bible *noun* the holy book of Christianity and Judaism **biblical** *adjective* to do with the Bible

bicycle *noun* a two-wheeled vehicle that you ride by pushing down on pedals with your feet

bid *noun* **1.** an offer to pay a particular amount of money for something, especially at an auction **2.** an attempt • *He will make a bid for the world record tomorrow.*
bid *verb* **bidding, bid** to bid an amount of money is to offer it for something at an auction

bide *verb* **to bide your time** is to wait, expecting something to happen that will help you

big *adjective* **bigger, biggest 1.** more than the normal size; large **2.** important • *This is a big decision.* **3.** elder • *Have you met my big sister?*

bike *noun* *(informal)* a bicycle or motor cycle

bikini *noun* a woman's two-piece swimsuit

bilingual *adjective* speaking two languages well

bill *noun* **1.** a piece of paper that tells you how much money you owe for something **2.** a plan for a new law in parliament **3.** a poster **4.** a bird's beak

billiards *noun* a game played with long sticks (called *cues*) and three balls on a cloth-covered table

billion *noun* a thousand million (1,000,000,000) **billionth** *adjective, noun* a thousand-millionth

billow *verb* to billow is to rise up or move like waves on the sea • *Her cloak billowed out behind her.*

bin *noun* a large or deep container, especially one that you put rubbish or litter in

binary *adjective* having two parts • *a binary star*

binary system *noun* a system of expressing numbers by using the digits 0 and 1 only; for example, 21 is written 10101

bind *verb* binding, bound **1.** to bind things is to tie them up or tie them together **2.** to bind something is to wrap a piece of material round it **3.** to bind a book is to fasten the pages inside a cover **4.** to bind someone is to make them do something or promise something

bingo *noun* Bingo is a game played with cards with numbered squares. These are covered or crossed out as the numbers are called out and the first person to complete the card wins the game.

binoculars *plural noun* a device with lenses for both eyes, for making distant objects seem nearer

biodegradable *adjective* able to be broken down by bacteria in the environment • *All our packaging is biodegradable.*

biography *noun* biographies the story of a person's life **biographer** *noun* someone who writes a biography **biographical** *adjective* a biographical story or history is one that is about a person's life

biology *noun* the science or study of living things **biological** *adjective* to do with biology **biologist** *noun* a person who studies biology

birch *noun* a thin tree with shiny bark and slender branches

bird *noun* a feathered animal with two wings, two legs and a beak

bird of prey *noun* birds of prey a bird that feeds on animal flesh, such as an eagle or hawk

birth *noun* birth is the beginning of a person's or animal's life, when they come out of their mother's body

birthday *noun* the anniversary of the day on which you were born

birthmark *noun* a coloured mark which has been on someone's skin since they were born

birthplace *noun* the place where someone was born

biscuit *noun* a small flat kind of cake that has been baked until it is hard

bishop *noun* **1.** a senior priest in the Christian Church who is in charge of all the churches in a city or district **2.** a chess piece shaped like a bishop's hat

bison *noun* bison a wild ox with shaggy hair

bit *noun* **1.** a small piece or amount of something **2.** the part of a horse's bridle that is put into its mouth **3.** the part of a tool that cuts or grips **4.** *(in computing)* the smallest unit of data or memory **a bit** slightly • *I'm a bit worried.* **bit by bit** gradually • *The truth came out bit by bit.*

bitch *noun* bitches a female dog, fox or wolf

bite *verb* biting, bit, bitten **1.** to bite something is to cut it or hold it with your teeth **2.** to sting
bite *noun* **1.** to give a person or animal a bite is to bite them **2.** a mark or spot made by biting • *He was covered in insect bites.* **3.** a snack • *Would you like a bite?*

bitter *adjective* **1.** tasting sour and unpleasant **2.** feeling angry and resentful because you are disappointed about something • *She is very bitter about losing her place in the team.* **3.** extremely cold • *There was a bitter wind.*

black *adjective* **1.** of the darkest colour, like coal or soot **2.** having dark skin
black *noun* a black colour

blackberry *noun* blackberries a sweet black berry

blackbird *noun* a dark European songbird

blackboard *noun* a dark board for writing on with chalk

blacken *verb* **1.** to blacken something is to make it black **2.** to blacken someone's name is to say bad things about them

black eye *noun* an eye with heavy bruises round it

black hole *noun* a region in space with such strong gravity that no light escapes

blackmail *verb* to blackmail someone is to get money from them by threatening to tell people something that they want to keep secret

blackout *noun* **1.** a time when lights are turned off to keep them hidden **2.** when a person becomes unconscious for a short time

blacksmith *noun* someone who makes and repairs things made of iron and fits shoes on horses

bladder *noun* your bladder is the bag-like part of your body where urine collects

blade *noun* **1.** the sharp part of a knife, sword or cutting tool **2.** the flat, wide part of an oar or propeller **3.** a long narrow leaf of grass

blame *verb* to blame someone is to say that they have done something wrong • *My brother broke the window but they blamed me.*
blame *noun* to get the blame for something is to be blamed for it

blancmange *noun* (bla-**monj**) blancmange is a pudding like a jelly made with milk

blank *adjective* not written, drawn or printed on • *The piece of paper was blank.* **to go blank** is to suddenly forget everything • *When he asked me the way, my mind went blank.*
blank *noun* **1.** an empty space **2.** a cartridge for a gun which makes a noise but does not fire a bullet

blanket *noun* a large piece of thick cloth, used as a warm covering for a bed

blare *verb* to blare is to make a harsh, loud sound

blasphemous *adjective* (**blas**-fe-mus) disrespectful about God or a religion
blasphemy *noun* talking without respect about God or a religion

blast *noun* **1.** a strong rush of wind or air **2.** a sharp or loud noise • *The referee gave a long blast of his whistle.* **3.** an explosion
blast *verb* to blast something is to blow it up with explosives

blast-off *noun* the launch of a spacecraft

blaze *noun* a very bright fire or light
blaze *verb* to blaze is to burn or shine brightly

blazer *noun* a kind of jacket, often with a badge on the front

bleach *noun* a substance used to clean things or make clothes white
bleach *verb* to bleach something is to make it white

bleak *adjective* **1.** bare and cold • *No trees grew on this bleak hillside.* **2.** dreary and miserable • *The future looks bleak.*

bleary *adjective* blearier, bleariest bleary eyes are tired and do not see clearly

bleat *noun* the cry of a sheep or goat
bleat *verb* a sheep or goat bleats when it makes a bleat

bleed *verb* bleeding, bled to bleed is to lose blood from your body

bleep *noun* a small, high sound like the sound some digital watches make

blemish *noun* a mark or stain on something

blend *verb* to blend things is to mix them together smoothly or easily
blend *noun* a smooth mixture

bless *verb* **1.** to bless someone is to wish or bring them happiness **2.** to bless someone is also to ask God to look after them

blessing *noun* **1.** a prayer or act of blessing someone **2.** something you are glad of or happy about • *It's a blessing that they are safe.*

blight *noun* **1.** blight is a plant disease **2.** a blight is a thing that spoils or damages something • *Knee injury has blighted his career.*

blind *adjective* not able to see
blind *verb* **1.** to blind someone is to make them blind **2.** a bright light blinds you when it makes you unable to see for a time
blind *noun* a screen for a window

blindfold *noun* a piece of cloth used to cover someone's eyes so that they cannot see
blindfold *verb* to cover someone's eyes with a blindfold

blink *verb* to blink is to shut and open your eyes quickly

bliss *noun* bliss is great happiness
blissful *adjective* very happy **blissfully** *adverb* very happily

blister *noun* a swelling like a bubble on your skin

blitz *noun* a sudden violent attack, especially from aircraft

> The word **blitz** is a shortening of the German word *Blitzkrieg*, which means 'lightning war'.

blizzard *noun* a severe snowstorm with strong wind

bloated *adjective* swollen or puffed out

blob *noun* a small round lump of something like paint or ice cream

block *noun* **1.** a solid piece of something hard such as wood **2.** a large building or group of buildings with streets all around it **3.** something that stops people getting through • *They came to a road block and had to turn back.*
block *verb* **1.** to block something is to get in the way of it • *Tall buildings blocked our view.* **2.** to block something like a pipe or drain is to prevent water flowing through it

blockade *noun* when a city or port is surrounded to stop people or goods from getting in or out

blockage *noun* something that stops up a pipe or drain

block capitals or **block letters** *plural noun* large capital letters

blog *noun* a website on which someone writes regularly about their own life or opinions
blog *verb* to add material or update a blog

blond or **blonde** *adjective* fair-haired

blonde *noun* a fair-haired girl or woman

blood *noun* the red liquid that flows through your veins and arteries

bloodhound *noun* a large breed of dog which can track people over long distances by following their scent

bloodshed *noun* bloodshed is the killing and injuring of people

bloodshot *adjective* eyes are bloodshot when they are streaked with red from being strained or tired

bloodstream *noun* the bloodstream is the blood flowing round your body

bloodthirsty *adjective* **bloodthirstier**, **bloodthirstiest** enjoying killing and violence

bloody *adjective* **bloodier**, **bloodiest**
1. bleeding or covered in blood **2.** a bloody fight or battle is one in which a lot of people are killed or badly hurt

bloom *verb* to bloom is to produce flowers
bloom *noun* a bloom is a flower **in bloom** trees and plants are in bloom when they are producing flowers

blossom *noun* **1.** a blossom is a flower, especially on a fruit tree **2.** blossom is a mass of flowers on a tree
blossom *verb* **1.** a tree or bush blossoms when it produces flowers **2.** to blossom is also to develop into something very fine or good • *She has blossomed into a lovely singer.*

blot *noun* a spot or blob of ink
blot *verb* **blotting**, **blotted** to blot something is to make a blot on it **to blot something out** is to remove it or make it invisible

blouse *noun* a loose piece of clothing like a shirt that girls and women wear

blow *noun* **1.** a hard knock or hit **2.** a shock or disappointment • *The news came to her as a terrible blow.* **3.** the action of blowing
blow *verb* **blowing**, **blew**, **blown** **1.** to blow is to force out air from your mouth or nose • *He blew on his cold hands to warm them up.* **2.** to move in the wind • *Her hat blew off.* **3.** to blow something such as a whistle is to make a sound with it **to blow something up** is to destroy it with an explosion **to blow up** is to be destroyed in an explosion

blue *adjective* **1.** of the colour of a bright cloudless sky **2.** sad and miserable • *I'm feeling blue.*
blue *noun* a blue colour **out of the blue** with no warning • *My friend turned up out of the blue.*

bluebottle *noun* a large blue fly that makes a loud buzz

blues *plural noun* blues is a type of music that is often sad

bluff *verb* to bluff someone is to make them think that you will do something that you don't intend to do or that you know something that you don't really know

bluff *noun* a bluff is something that someone says or does to bluff someone else • *He said he'd report us, but that was just a bluff.*

blunder *noun* a careless mistake

blunt *adjective* **1.** having an edge that is smooth and not good for cutting **2.** saying what you mean without trying to be polite or tactful

blur *verb* blurring, blurred to blur something is to make it unclear or smeared

blur *noun* an unclear shape with no definite outline • *Without her glasses on, everything was a blur.*

blush *verb* to blush is to become slightly red in the face because you are embarrassed or ashamed

boa or **boa constrictor** *noun* a large South American snake that coils round its prey and crushes it

boar *noun* **1.** a wild pig **2.** a male pig

board *noun* **1.** a board is a flat piece of wood, used in building **2.** a board is also a flat piece of wood or cardboard used to play games with, for example a dartboard or a chess board **3.** a board is also a group of people who run a company or organization **4.** board is daily meals supplied in return for money or work • *The price of the holiday includes full board.* **on board** aboard a ship

board *verb* **1.** to board a ship or train or aircraft is to get on it for a journey **2.** to board is to get meals and accommodation **to board something up** is to cover it with boards

boarder *noun* **1.** a child who lives at a boarding school during the term **2.** a lodger

boarding school *noun* a school in which the pupils live during the term

boast *verb* to boast about something that you own or that you have done is to talk proudly about it, often in order to impress people

boastful *adjective* a boastful person likes to talk a lot about the things they own or the things they have done **boastfully** *adverb*

boat *noun* a vehicle designed to float and travel on water

bob *verb* bobbing, bobbed to bob is to move gently up and down, like something floating on water

bobble *noun* a small round ball of something soft such as wool, used as a decoration on a hat or clothing

bobsleigh or **bobsled** *noun* a large sledge with two sets of runners

bodice *noun* the upper part of a woman's dress

body *noun* bodies **1.** the body is the flesh and bones and other parts of a person or animal **2.** a body is a dead person or corpse **3.** the body of something is the main part of it **4.** a body is a distinct object or piece of matter • *Stars and planets are heavenly bodies.*

bodyguard *noun* a guard who protects someone from being attacked

bog *noun* bog or a bog is an area of wet, spongy ground **boggy** *adjective* boggy ground is wet and spongy

bogus *adjective* false; not real or genuine • *He gave a name that turned out to be bogus.*

boil[1] *verb* **1.** to boil a liquid is to heat it until it starts to bubble and give off vapour **2.** to boil is to start bubbling, like water **3.** to boil food is to cook it in boiling water **to be boiling** *(informal)* is to be very hot • *It's boiling outside.*

boil[2] *noun* a painful red swelling on the skin

boiler *noun* a container for heating water or making steam

boiling point *noun* the temperature at which a liquid boils

boisterous *adjective* noisy and lively

bold *adjective* **1.** brave and adventurous **2.** clear and easy to see

bollard *noun* a short thick post put up on a road, used to keep out traffic

bolt *noun* **1.** a sliding bar for fastening a door or window **2.** a thick metal pin for fastening things together **3.** a flash of lightning
bolt *verb* **1.** to bolt a door or window is to fasten it with a bolt **2.** to bolt is to run away in panic, as a horse does

bomb *noun* a container with explosives, which blows up when it is detonated
bomb *verb* to bomb a place is to attack it with bombs

bombard *verb* **1.** to bombard a place is to attack it with heavy gunfire **2.** to bombard someone with questions or complaints is to direct a large number of questions or complaints at them **bombardment** *noun* a heavy attack with guns

bomber *noun* **1.** an aircraft built to drop bombs **2.** a person who plants or sets off a bomb

bond *noun* **1.** a shared experience or feeling that brings people close together **2.** bonds are ropes or chains used to tie people up

bondage *noun* bondage is being a slave

bone *noun* a bone is one of the hard pieces of a skeleton

bonfire *noun* a large fire lit out of doors

bonnet *noun* **1.** the hinged cover over the front part of a car **2.** a baby's or woman's hat with strings that tie under the chin

bonus *noun* **1.** an extra payment that someone gets for their work **2.** an extra advantage or reward

bony *adjective* bonier, boniest **1.** bony people or animals have bones without much flesh on them **2.** full of bones **3.** thin and hard, like a bone

boo *verb* to boo is to shout out that you don't like what someone has said or done

book *noun* a set of sheets of paper, usually with printing or writing on, fastened together inside a cover

book *verb* to book something such as a seat in a theatre or on a train or a room in a hotel, is to arrange for it to be kept for you

bookcase *noun* a piece of furniture with shelves for holding books

booklet *noun* a small book with paper covers

bookmaker *noun* a person whose business is taking bets

bookmark *noun* something you use to mark a place in a book

boom *noun* **1.** a deep hollow sound **2.** a time when people are well off
boom *verb* **1.** to boom is to make a deep hollow sound, like a heavy gun **2.** to boom is also to speak in a loud deep voice **3.** to boom is also to grow quickly or be prosperous • *Business is booming.*

boomerang *noun* a curved stick which moves in a curve and comes back to you when you throw it

boost *verb* to boost something is to increase its size or value or power • *Being in the drama group has really boosted his confidence.* **booster** *noun*

boot *noun* **1.** a heavy shoe that covers the ankle and sometimes part of your leg **2.** the space for luggage at the back of a car

boot *verb* **1.** to boot someone is to kick them hard **2.** to boot up a computer is to switch it on and start it

booth *noun* a small compartment for a special purpose, such as making a telephone call or having your photo taken

border *noun* **1.** the border between two countries is the line where they meet • *We're about to cross the Scottish border.* **2.** an edge • *There is a black border around the poster.* **3.** a flower bed

bore *verb* **1.** to bore someone is to make them feel tired and uninterested **2.** to bore a hole is to drill it through something
bore *noun* a dull or uninteresting person or thing

boredom *noun* a feeling of tiredness and lack of interest

boring *adjective* dull and uninteresting • *The book was really boring.*

born *adjective* to be born is to start your life • *My little brother was born on the 17th of December.*

borough *noun* (**bu**-ro) an important town or district with its own local council

borrow *verb* to borrow something is to have it for a time and then return it to its owner

bosom *noun* a woman's breasts

boss *noun* (informal) a person who is in charge of a business or group of workers
boss *verb* (informal) to boss someone is to order them around

bossy *adjective* bossier, bossiest (informal) a bossy person is fond of ordering people about

botany *noun* botany is the study of plants
botanist *noun* someone who studies botany
botanical *adjective* to do with botany or plants

both *determiner, pronoun* the two of them, not just one • *I want them both in the team.* • *Both boys are taller than me.*

bother *verb* **1.** to bother someone is to cause them trouble or worry **2.** to be bothered to do something is to take trouble over it
bother *noun* bother is trouble or worry

bottle *noun* a glass or plastic container with a narrow neck for holding liquids

bottle *verb* to put or store something in bottles to bottle something up is to keep something you are worried about to yourself

bottle bank *noun* a large tank or drum for putting glass bottles and jars in for recycling

bottom *noun* **1.** the bottom of something is its lowest point **2.** the bottom of a garden is the farther end of it, away from the house **3.** your bottom is the part of you that you sit on, also called your buttocks

bough *noun* (rhymes with cow) a large branch of a tree that reaches out from the trunk

boulder *noun* a very large smooth stone

bounce *verb* **1.** to bounce is to spring back when thrown against something, like a rubber ball **2.** to bounce a ball is to throw it so that it bounces
bounce *noun* **1.** a bounce is the action of bouncing **2.** bounce is liveliness, such as a young child has bouncy *adjective* a bouncy person is lively and full of energy

bound[1] *adjective* to be bound for a place is to be travelling towards it • *This train is bound for London.* to be bound to do something is to have to do it or be likely to do it • *He is bound to come.*

bound[2] *verb* to bound is to leap or to run with leaping steps
bound[2] *noun* a leaping movement

boundary *noun* boundaries **1.** a line that marks a limit **2.** a hit to the outer edge of a cricket field

bounds *plural noun* a place that is out of bounds is somewhere you are not allowed to go

bouquet *noun* (boo-**kay** or boh-**kay**) an attractively arranged bunch of flowers

bout *noun* (bowt) **1.** a period of illness • *a bout of flu* **2.** a boxing or wrestling fight

bow[1] *noun* (rhymes with go) **1.** a knot made with loops **2.** the stick used for playing a stringed musical instrument such as a violin **3.** a long curved piece of wood with a tight string joining its ends, used for shooting arrows

bow[2] *noun* (rhymes with cow) the front part of a ship

41

bow³ *verb* (rhymes with cow) to bow is to bend your body forwards to show respect or as a greeting

bow³ *noun* (rhymes with cow) a movement of bowing your body • *The pianist stood up to take a bow.*

bowels *plural noun* your bowels are the long tubes in your body that carry waste food for passing out of the body

bowl¹ *noun* a deep round dish for eating from

bowl² *verb* (in cricket) **1.** to bowl is to send the ball towards the batsman **2.** to bowl someone is to get them out by hitting the wicket with the ball

bowler *noun* **1.** someone who bowls in cricket **2.** a hat with a rounded top and a narrow brim

bowling *noun* **1.** bowling is the game of bowls **2.** bowling is also another game, in which you have to knock down skittles with a ball you roll down an alley

bowls *plural noun* a game played on a smooth piece of grass, in which you roll heavy balls towards a small target ball called the 'jack'

bow tie *noun* a tie in the form of a bow, worn by men as part of formal dress

box *noun* **1.** a container made of wood or cardboard, often with a lid **2.** a small rectangle that you fill in on a form or computer screen **3.** a special compartment or booth, such as in a theatre, or a witness box in a lawcourt

box *verb* to box is to fight with the fists

boxer *noun* someone who boxes

Boxing Day *noun* the first weekday after Christmas Day

box office *noun* a place where you can buy seats for the theatre or cinema

boy *noun* a male child **boyhood** *noun* the time when a man was a boy **boyish** *adjective* looking or behaving like a boy

boycott *verb* to boycott something is to refuse to buy it or have anything to do with it

boyfriend *noun* someone's boyfriend is the male friend they have a romantic relationship with

bra *noun* a piece of underwear women wear to support their breasts

brace *noun* **1.** a device for holding something in place **2.** a wire device for straightening the teeth

bracelet *noun* a small band or chain you wear round your wrist

braces *plural noun* braces are a pair of stretching straps worn over the shoulders to hold trousers up

bracket *noun* **1.** A bracket is a kind of punctuation mark used in pairs round words or figures to separate them from what comes before and after. Brackets are round ( ) or square [ ]. **2.** a support attached to a wall to hold up a shelf or screen

brag *verb* bragging, bragged to brag is to boast

braid *noun* **1.** a plait **2.** a decorative ribbon or band

Braille *noun* Braille is a system of writing or printing using raised dots, which blind people can read by touch.

> **Braille** is named after a French teacher called Louis Braille, who was blind from the age of three and invented the system. He died in 1852.

brain *noun* **1.** your brain is the part inside the top of your head that controls your body **2.** brain also means a person's mind or intelligence • *He's got a good brain.*

brainy *adjective* brainier, brainiest (informal) clever, intelligent

brake *noun* a device for making a vehicle stop or slow down

bramble *noun* a bramble is a blackberry bush or a prickly bush like it

branch *noun* **1.** a part that sticks out from the trunk of a tree **2.** a part of a railway or river or road that leads off from the main part **3.** a part of a large organization

brand *noun* a particular make or kind of goods • *a brand of tea*

brand *verb* to brand sheep or cattle is to mark them with a hot iron

brand new *adjective* completely new

brandy *noun* brandy is a kind of strong alcoholic drink

brass *noun* **1.** brass is an alloy made from copper and zinc **2.** brass also means the wind instruments made of brass, such as trumpets and trombones

brave *adjective* ready to face danger or suffering

brave *noun* a Native American warrior
bravery *noun* bravery is being brave
bravely *adverb*

brawl *noun* a noisy fight or quarrel

brawn *noun* brawn is physical strength

bray *verb* to bray is to make a noise like a donkey

brazen *adjective* shameless or cheeky

breach *noun* **1.** the breaking of an agreement or rule **2.** a gap or broken place in something like a wall

bread *noun* bread is food made by baking flour and water, usually with yeast

breadth *noun* a thing's breadth is its width from side to side

break *verb* breaking, broke, broken **1.** to break something is to make it go into several pieces by hitting it or dropping it **2.** to break is to stop working properly • *I think my watch must have broken.* **3.** to break a law or rule or promise is to fail to keep it or observe it **4.** the weather breaks when it changes after being hot **5.** waves break over rocks when they hit them **6.** a boy's voice breaks when it starts to go deeper at about the age of 14 **7.** to break a record is to do better than the previous holder **to break down** a machine or vehicle breaks down when it stops working properly **to break out** is to start and spread rapidly, like a disease or fighting **to break up 1.** people break up when they leave one another after

a long time together **2.** to finish school at the end of term

break *noun* **1.** a broken place; a gap **2.** a sudden dash or attempt to escape **3.** a short rest from work

breakage *noun* something that is broken
• *All breakages must be paid for.*

breakdown *noun* **1.** a sudden failure to work, especially by a car • *We had a breakdown on the motorway.* **2.** a period of mental illness caused by anxiety or depression

breaker *noun* a wave breaking on the shore

breakfast *noun* breakfast is the first meal of the day

breakthrough *noun* an important discovery or step forward

breast *noun* **1.** one of the two parts of a woman's body where milk is produced after she has had a baby **2.** a person's chest **3.** a bird's chest

breaststroke *noun* a stroke you use when swimming on your front, by pushing your arms forward and bringing them round and back

breath *noun* (breth) the air that you take into your lungs and send out again **to be out of breath** is to gasp for air after exercise

breathe *verb* (breeth) to breathe is to take air into your lungs through your nose or mouth and send it out again

breathless *adjective* short of breath

breathtaking *adjective* extremely beautiful or exciting

breech *noun* the part of a gun barrel where the bullets are put in

breed *verb* breeding, bred **1.** to breed is to produce offspring **2.** to breed animals is to keep them in order to get young ones from them **breeder** *noun* someone who breeds animals

breed *noun* a variety of similar animals

breeze *noun* a gentle wind

breezy *adjective* breezier, breeziest slightly windy

brevity *noun* brevity is being brief or short
• *I was surprised by the brevity of her answer.*

brew *verb* **1.** to brew beer or tea is to make it **2.** to be brewing is to start or develop • *Trouble is brewing.*

brewery *noun* breweries a place where beer is made

bribe *noun* a bribe is money or a gift offered to someone to make them do something **bribe** *verb* to bribe someone is to give them a bribe bribery *noun* bribery is offering someone a bribe

brick *noun* a small hard block of baked clay used in building

bricklayer *noun* a worker who builds with bricks

bridal *adjective* to do with brides

bride *noun* a woman on her wedding day

bridegroom *noun* a man on his wedding day

bridesmaid *noun* a girl or woman who helps the bride at her wedding

bridge *noun* **1.** a bridge is a structure built over a river, railway or road, to allow people to cross it **2.** the bridge of a ship is the high platform above the deck, from where the ship is controlled **3.** the bridge of your nose is the bony upper part of your nose **4.** bridge is a card game

bridle *noun* the part of a horse's harness that fits over its head

bridle path *noun* a path for people on horseback

brief *adjective* lasting a short time or using only a few words

briefcase *noun* a flat case for keeping documents and papers in

briefs *plural noun* short underpants

brigade *noun* **1.** an army unit usually consisting of three battalions **2.** a group of people in uniform, for example the fire brigade

bright *adjective* **1.** giving out a strong light; shining **2.** a bright colour is strong and vivid **3.** clever • *He's a bright lad.*

brighten *verb* **1.** to brighten something is to make it brighter **2.** to brighten is to become brighter

brilliance *noun* **1.** brilliance is bright light • *the brilliance of the summer sky* **2.** brilliance is also being very intelligent or clever

brilliant *adjective* **1.** a brilliant person is very intelligent or clever **2.** *(informal)* really good or enjoyable • *That was a brilliant film!* **3.** very bright and sparkling

brim *noun* **1.** the edge round the top of a container **2.** the bottom edge of a hat that sticks out

brimming *adjective* completely full brimming over overflowing

brine *noun* brine is salty water

bring *verb* bringing, brought to bring someone or something is to make them come with you to a place to bring someone up is to look after them and educate them as a child to bring something up is to mention it in a conversation

brink *noun* the edge of a steep or dangerous place

brisk *adjective* quick and lively

bristle *noun* a short, stiff hair bristly *adjective* having lots of bristles

British *adjective* to do with Great Britain

Briton *noun* someone born in Great Britain

brittle *adjective* hard but likely to break or snap

broad *adjective* broader, broadest **1.** wide and open • *They walked down a broad avenue.* **2.** general, not detailed • *a broad outline*

broadband *noun* a system for connecting computers to the Internet and sending information very quickly

broad bean *noun* a large flat bean

broadcast *noun* a radio or television programme

broadcast *verb* to broadcast a radio or television programme is to transmit it or take part in it **broadcaster** *noun* a person who takes part in a radio or television programme

broaden *verb* to broaden something is to make it broader

broadly *adverb* in general terms • *They were broadly right.*

broccoli *noun* a vegetable with green or purple heads on green stalks

brochure *noun* (**broh**-sure) a booklet containing information

broke *adjective* (*informal*) not having any money

broken *adjective* a broken home is a home in which the parents have separated

bronchitis *noun* (brong-**ky**-tiss) bronchitis is a disease of the lungs

bronze *noun* bronze is an alloy of copper and tin

brooch *noun* (rhymes with coach) a piece of jewellery that can be pinned on to clothes

brood *noun* a brood is a number of young birds hatched together

brood *verb* **1.** birds brood when they sit on eggs to hatch them **2.** to brood over something is to keep worrying about it

brook *noun* a small stream

broom *noun* a broom is a brush with a long handle, for sweeping

broomstick *noun* the handle of a broom

broth *noun* broth is a thin kind of soup

brother *noun* your brother is a man or boy who has the same parents as you

brother-in-law *noun* brothers-in-law a person's brother-in-law is the brother of their husband or wife or the husband of their sister

brow *noun* **1.** your brow is your forehead **2.** your brows are your eyebrows **3.** the brow of a hill is the top of it

brown *adjective* of the colour of earth, wood or toast

brown *noun* a brown colour

Brownie *noun* a junior member of the Guides

brownie *noun* a small chocolate cake with nuts

browse *verb* **1.** to browse is to read or look at something casually **2.** animals browse when they feed on grass or leaves

bruise *noun* a dark mark that appears on your skin when it is hit or hurt

bruise *verb* to bruise your skin or a part of your body is to get a bruise on it

brunette *noun* a woman with dark brown or black hair

brush *noun* a tool with hairs or bristles for sweeping, painting or arranging the hair

brush *verb* **1.** to brush something is to use a brush on it • *Have you brushed your hair yet?* **2.** to brush against someone is to touch them gently as you pass them

Brussels sprout *noun* a green vegetable like a tiny cabbage

brutal *adjective* savage and cruel **brutality** *noun* brutality is savage cruelty **brutally** *adverb* with savage cruelty

brute *noun* a cruel person

bubble *noun* **1.** a thin transparent ball of liquid filled with air or gas **2.** a small ball of air in a liquid or a solid

bubble *verb* a liquid bubbles when it produces bubbles, as it does when it boils

bubbly *adjective* bubblier, bubbliest **1.** full of bubbles, like fizzy water **2.** a bubbly person is cheerful and lively

buck *noun* a male deer, rabbit or hare

buck *verb* a horse bucks when it jumps with its back arched

a
b
c
d
e
f
g
h
i
j
k
l
m
n
o
p
q
r
s
t
u
v
w
x
y
z

bucket *noun* a container with a handle, for carrying liquids or something such as sand

buckle *noun* a clip at the end of a belt or strap for fastening it

buckle *verb* **1.** to buckle something is to fasten it with a buckle **2.** to buckle is to bend or give way under a strain • *The arm of the crane was beginning to buckle.*

bud *noun* a flower or leaf before it has opened

Buddhism *noun* (**buud**-izm) Buddhism is a religion that started in Asia and follows the teachings of Buddha. **Buddhist** *noun* someone who practises Buddhism

budding *adjective* showing great promise • *The new class had several budding musicians.*

budge *verb* to budge is to move slightly • *The door was stuck and wouldn't budge.*

budgerigar *noun* (**bud**-jer-i-gar) an Australian bird often kept as a pet in a cage

budget *noun* **1.** the money someone plans to spend on something **2.** a plan for earning and spending money

budget *verb* to budget is to plan how much you are going to spend

budgie *noun* (*informal*) a budgerigar

buffalo *noun* buffalo or buffaloes a wild ox with long curved horns

buffer *noun* something that softens a blow or collision, especially a device on a railway engine or wagon or at the end of a railway line

buffet *noun* (**buu**-fay) **1.** a cafe or place for buying drinks and snacks **2.** a meal where guests serve themselves

bug *noun* **1.** a tiny insect **2.** (*informal*) a germ that causes illness • *a tummy bug* **3.** (*informal*) a hidden microphone **4.** a fault or problem in a computer program that stops it working properly

bugle *noun* (**byoo**-gul) a brass instrument like a small trumpet **bugler** *noun* someone who plays the bugle

build *verb* building, built to build something is to make it by putting the parts together **to build something up** is to make it larger or stronger • *Regular exercise will build up your strength.* **to build up** is to become larger or stronger • *The traffic was starting to build up.* **build** *noun* your build is the shape of your body

builder *noun* someone who puts up buildings

building *noun* a building is a structure that someone has built, such as a house

bulb *noun* **1.** the glass part of an electric light, with a wire or gas inside that glows when you switch it on **2.** an onion-shaped root which grows into a plant or flower when it is put in the ground

bulge *noun* a part that sticks out; a swelling **bulge** *verb* to bulge is to stick out or swell

bulk *noun* **1.** a thing's bulk is its size, especially when it is large **2.** the bulk of something is most of it • *He spends the bulk of his time on the computer.*

bulky *adjective* bulkier, bulkiest taking up a lot of space

bull *noun* **1.** the male of the cattle family **2.** a male seal, whale or elephant

bulldozer *noun* a heavy vehicle with a wide metal blade in front, used to clear or flatten land

bullet *noun* a piece of shaped metal shot from a rifle or pistol

bulletin *noun* a short announcement of news on radio or television

bullfight *noun* in Spain, a public entertainment in which people challenge bulls and sometimes kill them

bullfighter *noun* someone who takes part in a bullfight

bullion *noun* gold or silver in the form of bars

bullock *noun* a young bull

bull's-eye *noun* the centre of a target

bully *verb* bullies, bullying, bullied to bully someone is to hurt or frighten a person who is small or weak
bully *noun* bullies someone who bullies people

bumble-bee *noun* a large kind of bee with a loud buzz

bump *verb* to bump something is to knock against it accidentally to bump into someone (informal) is to meet them unexpectedly
bump *noun* 1. an accidental knock 2. a swelling or lump

bumper[1] *noun* a bar along the front or back of a motor vehicle to protect it from damage

bumper[2] *adjective* unusually large or fine • We had a bumper crop of apples this year.

bumpy *adjective* bumpier, bumpiest having lots of bumps

bun *noun* 1. a small round sweet cake 2. a round bunch of hair made at the back of the head

bunch *noun* a number of things joined or tied together, such as fruit or flowers or keys • a bunch of grapes

bundle *noun* a number of things tied or wrapped loosely together, such as clothes or papers
bundle *verb* to bundle things together is to tie or wrap them loosely

bung *noun* a stopper for a bottle or barrel

bungalow *noun* a house with all the rooms on one floor

bungle *verb* to bungle something is to do it badly and clumsily

bunk or **bunk bed** *noun* a single bed with another bed above it or below it

bunker *noun* 1. a container for storing fuel such as coal 2. a hollow filled with sand, made as an obstacle on a golf course 3. an underground shelter

bunny *noun* bunnies (informal) a rabbit

Bunsen burner *noun* a gas burner with a flame you can adjust, used in laboratories

buoy *noun* (boi) a floating object in the sea, used as a marker or warning sign

buoyant *adjective* able to float

burden *noun* 1. a heavy load 2. something troublesome that you have to put up with

bureau *noun* bureaux (**bewr**-oh) an office or department • They will tell you at the Information Bureau.

burger *noun* a hamburger

burglar *noun* someone who breaks into a building to steal things **burglary** *noun* burglary is the crime of stealing things from a building

burgle *verb* to burgle someone is to steal from their house

burial *noun* putting a dead body in a grave

burly *adjective* burlier, burliest a burly person is big and strong

burn *verb* burning, burnt or burned 1. to burn something is to damage or destroy it by fire or strong heat 2. to burn is to be damaged or destroyed by fire or heat 3. to be burning is to be on fire 4. to be burning is also to feel very hot
burn *noun* an injury or mark caused by fire or strong heat

burner *noun* the part of a lamp or cooker that forms the flame

burp *verb* to burp is to make a noise through your mouth by letting air come up from your stomach
burp *noun* the act or sound of burping

burrow *noun* a hole dug by an animal such as a rabbit or fox
burrow *verb* an animal burrows when it digs a burrow

burst *verb* bursting, burst 1. to burst is to break apart suddenly 2. to burst something is to make it break apart 3. to be bursting with energy or excitement is to have a lot of energy or to be very excited to burst in is to rush in noisily or clumsily to burst into tears is to suddenly start crying to burst out laughing is to start laughing noisily

burst *noun* something short and quick • *a burst of gunfire*

bury *verb* **buries, burying, buried 1.** to bury something is to put it under the ground **2.** to bury a dead person is to put them in a grave

bus *noun* a large road vehicle for carrying passengers

bush *noun* **1.** a bush is a plant like a small tree with a lot of stems or branches **2.** the bush is wild land, especially in Australia or Africa

bushy *adjective* **bushier, bushiest** thick and hairy • *bushy eyebrows*

busily *adverb* in a busy way

business *noun* (**biz**-niss) **1. 2.** business is what an organization does to make money • *She has made a career in business.* **3.** a person's business is what concerns them and no one else • *Mind your own business.* **4.** a business is also an affair or subject • *I am tired of the whole business.*

busker *noun* someone who plays music in the street, hoping for money from people passing by

bus stop *noun* a place where a bus regularly stops

bust[1] *noun* **1.** a sculpture of a person's head and shoulders **2.** a woman's breasts

bust[2] *adjective* (informal) broken • *My watch is bust.*

busy *adjective* **busier, busiest 1.** a busy person is one with a lot to do **2.** a busy place is one with a lot going on **3.** a busy telephone line is one that someone is already using

busybody *noun* **busybodies** someone who interferes in other people's affairs

but *conjunction* you use **but** to join two words or statements that say different or opposite things • *I wanted to go but I couldn't.* **but** *preposition* except • *There's no one here but me.*

butcher *noun* someone who runs a shop that cuts and sells meat

butler *noun* a male servant in charge of other servants in a large private house

butt[1] *noun* **1.** the thicker end of a weapon or tool **2.** a large barrel

butt[2] *verb* to butt someone is to hit them hard with your head **to butt in** is to interrupt suddenly or rudely

butter *noun* butter is a fatty yellow food made from cream

butterfly *noun* **butterflies 1.** an insect with a thin body and large white or brightly coloured wings **2.** a stroke you use when swimming on your front, by raising both arms together over your head

butterscotch *noun* butterscotch is a kind of hard toffee

buttocks *plural noun* your buttocks are the part of the body on which you sit, your bottom

button *noun* **1.** a flat plastic or metal disc sewn on clothes and passed through a buttonhole to fasten them **2.** a small knob you press to work an electric device

button *verb* to button clothes or to button up clothes is to fasten them with buttons

buttress *noun* **buttresses** a support built against a wall

buy *verb* **buying, bought** to buy something is to get it by paying for it **buyer** *noun* someone who buys something

buy *noun* something you buy • *That was a good buy.*

buzz *noun* a sharp humming sound, like bees make

buzz *verb* to buzz is to make a buzzing sound

buzzard *noun* a bird of prey like a large hawk

buzzer *noun* an alarm or signalling device that makes a buzzing noise

by *preposition, adverb* **1**. near, close • *Sit by me.* **2**. using; by means of • *I fixed the tyre by sticking on a patch.* **3**. before • *Do your homework by tomorrow.* **4**. past • *She went by the window.* • *I can't get by.*

bye-bye *interjection (informal)* goodbye

bypass *noun* a road that takes traffic round the edge of a town or city rather than going through the centre

bystander *noun* someone who sees something happening but takes no part in it

byte *noun (in computing)* a unit that measures data or memory

Only three words in English end with -*ceed*: exceed, proceed and succeed.

C 1. short for **Celsius** or **centigrade 2**. 100 in Roman numerals

cab *noun* **1**. a taxi **2**. the place in a train or lorry where the driver sits

cabbage *noun* a large round green vegetable with layers of closely packed leaves

cabin *noun* **1**. a hut or shelter **2**. one of the small rooms on a ship for sleeping in **3**. the part of an aircraft where the passengers sit

cabinet *noun* **1**. a cupboard with shelves and doors, used for storing things **2**. the group of chief ministers who run the government

cable *noun* **1**. a thick rope, wire or chain **2**. a telegram sent overseas

cable television *noun* a television system in which programmes are transmitted along underground cables into people's houses

cactus *noun* **cacti** a fleshy plant that is covered in prickles and grows in hot, dry places

caddie *noun* someone whose job is to help a golfer by carrying the clubs and giving advice

cadet *noun* a young person who is being trained for the armed forces or the police

cafe *noun* (**kaf**-ay) a place that sells drinks and small meals

cafeteria *noun* (kaf-e-**teer**-i-a) a cafe where customers serve themselves from a counter

caffeine *noun* caffeine is a substance in tea and coffee and some other drinks, which keeps you awake and makes you feel active

cage *noun* an enclosure made of bars or wires, for keeping birds or animals so that they can't get away

cagoule *noun* a lightweight waterproof jacket

cake *noun* **1.** a sweet food made from a baked mixture of flour, eggs, fat and sugar **2.** a small block of something, such as soap **a piece of cake** (*informal*) something very easy to do

caked *adjective* covered with something that has dried hard, like mud

calamity *noun* **calamities** a disaster **calamitous** *adjective* disastrous

calcium *noun* a greyish-white element contained in teeth, bones and lime

calculate *verb* to calculate something is to work it out by arithmetic or with a calculator **calculation** *noun* something you work out by using numbers or other information

calculator *noun* an electronic machine for doing sums

calendar *noun* a chart or display that shows the days of the year

calf[1] *noun* **calves** **1.** a young cow or ox **2.** a young seal, whale or elephant

calf[2] *noun* **calves** the back part of your leg below your knee

call *noun* **calls** **1.** a shout or cry • *They heard a call for help.* **2.** a short visit • *She decided to pay her father a call.* **3.** a telephone conversation with someone

call *verb* **1.** to call is to shout out **2.** to call someone is to telephone them • *I'll call you at the weekend.* **3.** to call someone is to ask them to come to you **4.** to call on someone is to visit them **5.** to be called something is to have it as your name • *His friend was called Damon.* **to call something off** is to cancel it

calling *noun* someone's calling is their profession or trade

callipers *plural noun* a device for measuring the width of tubes or of round objects

callous *adjective* a callous person is very unkind and doesn't care if other people are suffering

calm *adjective* **1.** quiet and still • *a calm sea* **2.** someone is calm when they are not excited or agitated **calmly** *adverb* **calmness** *noun*

calorie *noun* a unit for measuring the amount of heat or the energy produced by food

camcorder *noun* a video camera that can record pictures and sound

camel *noun* a large animal with a long neck and one or two humps on its back • *Arabian camels have one hump and Bactrian camels have two.*

camera *noun* a device for taking photographs, films or television pictures

camouflage *noun* (**kam**-o-flahzh) a way of hiding things by making them look like part of their surroundings
camouflage *verb* to camouflage something is to hide it by making it look like part of its surroundings

camp *noun* a place where people live in tents, huts or caravans for a short time
camp *verb* **1.** to camp or go camping is to have a holiday in a tent **2.** to camp is also to put up a tent • *Let's camp here for the night.*
camper *noun* a person who goes to a camp

campaign *noun* **1.** a planned series of actions, especially to get people to support you or become interested in something • *a campaign for human rights* **2.** a series of battles in one area or with one aim
campaign *verb* to campaign is to carry out a plan of action to raise people's interest in something such as a good cause • *They are campaigning to stop the destruction of the rainforests.*

campsite *noun* a place for camping

campus *noun* the buildings of a college or university and the land around them

can[1] *verb* present tense **can**; past tense **could** **1**. to be able to do something or to know how to do it • *Can you lift this stone?* • *They can speak French.* **2**. to be allowed to do something • *Can I go home?*

can[2] *noun* a sealed metal container holding food or drink
can[2] *verb* **canning**, **canned** to can food is to put it into cans and seal it

canal *noun* a long channel specially dug and filled with water for boats to travel along

canary *noun* **canaries** a small yellow bird that sings

cancel *verb* **cancelling**, **cancelled** **1**. to cancel something planned is to say that it will not be done or not take place after all **2**. to cancel an order or instruction is to stop it **cancellation** *noun* something that someone has cancelled

cancer *noun* a serious disease in which a harmful growth forms in the body

candidate *noun* **1**. someone who has applied for a job or position **2**. someone who is taking an exam

candle *noun* a stick of wax with a wick through it, giving light when it is burning

candlestick *noun* a holder for a candle or candles

candy *noun* **candies** **1**. candy is crystallized sugar **2**. a candy is a sweet

candyfloss *noun* candyfloss is a fluffy mass of sugar that has been spun into fine threads

cane *noun* a cane is the hollow stem of a reed or tall grass
cane *verb* to cane someone is to beat them with a cane

canine *adjective* to do with dogs

cannibal *noun* **1**. a person who eats human flesh **2**. an animal that eats animals of its own kind **cannibalism** *noun* cannibalism is eating other people or animals of the same kind

cannon *noun* a large gun that fires heavy balls made of metal or stone

cannonball *noun* a heavy metal or stone ball fired from a cannon

cannot can not • *I cannot believe it.*

canoe *noun* a light narrow boat driven with paddles **canoeist** *noun* someone who uses a canoe

canopy *noun* **canopies** a covering that hangs over something • *The larger trees form a canopy over the roof of the forest.*

can't short for **cannot** • *We can't see them.*

canteen *noun* a restaurant in a factory or office or school

canter *verb* a horse canters when it goes at a gentle gallop

canvas *noun* **1**. canvas is strong, coarse cloth **2**. a canvas is a piece of canvas used for painting on

canyon *noun* a deep valley with a river running through it

cap *noun* **1**. a soft hat without a brim but often with a peak **2**. a cover or top
cap *verb* **capping**, **capped** to cap something is to cover it

capable *adjective* able to do something **capability** *noun* being able to do something **capably** *adverb* to do something capably is to do it well

capacity *noun* **capacities** **1**. ability to do something • *He has a great capacity for work.* **2**. the amount that something can hold

cape[1] *noun* a piece of high land sticking out into the sea

cape[2] *noun* a cloak

capital *noun* **1.** the capital of a country is the most important city in it **2.** capital is money or property that can be used to make more wealth

capital letter *noun* a large letter of the kind used at the start of a name or a sentence, such as A, B, C

capital punishment *noun* capital punishment is when someone is killed as a punishment for a serious crime

capsize *verb* to capsize is to overturn in a boat in the water

capsule *noun* **1.** a hollow pill containing medicine **2.** a small spacecraft that separates from a larger rocket

captain *noun* **1.** an officer in charge of a ship or aircraft **2.** an officer in the army or navy **3.** the leader in a sports team

caption *noun* the words printed beside a picture to explain it

captivate *verb* to captivate someone is to charm them or make them interested **captivating** *adjective* charming and attractive

captive *noun* a prisoner
captive *adjective* imprisoned; unable to escape

captivity *noun* **1.** captivity is being held prisoner **2.** an animal in captivity is one kept in a zoo or wildlife park rather than living in the wild

capture *verb* to capture an animal or person is to catch or imprison them
capture *noun* catching or imprisoning an animal or person

car *noun* **1.** a motor vehicle for about four or five people **2.** a railway carriage • *Does the train have a buffet car?*

caramel *noun* **1.** caramel is burnt sugar used to give a sweet taste to food **2.** a caramel is a sweet made from butter, milk and sugar

carat *noun* a measure of the purity of gold

caravan *noun* **1.** a vehicle towed by a car and used for living in **2.** a large number of people travelling together across a desert

carbon *noun* carbon is an element found in charcoal, graphite, diamonds and other substances

carbon dioxide *noun* a colourless gas made by humans and animals breathing

carbon monoxide *noun* a colourless, poisonous gas found especially in the exhaust fumes of motor vehicles

carcass *noun* the dead body of an animal or bird

card *noun* **1.** card is thick stiff paper **2.** a card is a folded piece of thick paper that you use to send greetings to someone, for example a birthday card **3.** a card is also a playing card **4.** a card is also a small piece of plastic that a bank or shop gives to a customer, used to buy goods or obtain money **cards** is a game with playing cards

cardboard *noun* cardboard is thick stiff paper

cardigan *noun* a knitted jumper fastened with buttons down the front

cardinal number *noun* a number for counting things, for example 1, 2, 3

care *noun* **1.** care is worry or trouble • *She was free from care.* **2.** care is also serious thought or attention • *Take more care with your homework.* **3.** care is also protection or supervision • *You can leave your dog in my care.* **to take care** is to be especially careful **to take care of someone** or **something** is to look after them

care *verb* to care about something or someone is to feel interested or concerned about them **to care for someone** is to look after them • *He cared for his wife when she was ill.*

career *noun* a person's career is their job or profession, in which they make progress during their working life

career *verb* to career along or down somewhere is to rush along wildly

carefree *adjective* not having any worries or responsibilities

careful *adjective* making sure that you do something well without any mistakes and without causing any danger • *She is a careful driver.* • *He was careful to read the instructions first.* **carefully** *adverb* to do something carefully is to do it with a lot of care and attention

careless *adjective* not taking care; clumsy **carelessly** *adverb* to do something carelessly is to do it without much care **carelessness** *noun* carelessness is not taking care

caress *noun* (ka-**ress**) a gentle and loving touch

caress *verb* to caress someone is to touch them gently and fondly

caretaker *noun* someone who looks after a large building such as a school

cargo *noun* **cargoes** the goods carried in a ship or aircraft

caricature *noun* a drawing or description of someone that exaggerates their features and makes them look funny or ridiculous

carnation *noun* a garden flower with a sweet smell

carnival *noun* a festival or celebration with a procession of people in fancy dress

carnivore *noun* an animal that eats meat **carnivorous** *adjective* a carnivorous animal is one that eats meat

carol *noun* a hymn or song that you sing at Christmas time

carpenter *noun* someone who makes things out of wood **carpentry** making things from wood

carpet *noun* a thick soft covering for a floor

carriage *noun* 1. a carriage is one of the separate sections of a train where passengers sit 2. a carriage is also a passenger vehicle pulled by horses

carriageway *noun* the part of a road that vehicles travel on

carrier bag *noun* a large bag for holding shopping

carrot *noun* a long thin orange-coloured vegetable

carry *verb* **carries, carrying, carried** 1. to carry something is to lift it and take it somewhere 2. to carry something is also to have it with you • *He is carrying a weapon.* 3. a sound carries when it can be heard a long way away **to be carried away** is to become very excited **to carry on** is to continue doing something • *They carried on chatting.* **to carry something out** is to do it in the way you had planned

cart *noun* a small vehicle for carrying loads

cart *verb* (*informal*) to cart something somewhere is to carry it, especially when it is heavy or tiring • *I've been carting these books around the school all afternoon.*

carthorse *noun* a large heavy horse

cartilage *noun* (**kar**-ti-lij) cartilage is tough and flexible tissue attached to a bone such as in the nose or ear

carton *noun* a lightweight cardboard or plastic box

cartoon *noun* 1. a drawing that is funny or tells a joke 2. a series of drawings that tell a story 3. an animated film **cartoonist** *noun* someone who draws cartoons

cartridge *noun* 1. a container holding film to be put into a camera or ink to be put into a pen 2. the case containing the explosive for a bullet or shell

cartwheel *noun* a somersault done sideways, with your arms and legs spread wide

a
b
c
d
e
f
g
h
i
j
k
l
m
n
o
p
q
r
s
t
u
v
w
x
y
z

carve *verb* **1.** to carve wood or stone is to make something artistic by cutting it carefully **2.** to carve meat is to cut it into slices

case[1] *noun* **1.** a container **2.** a suitcase

case[2] *noun* **1.** an example of something existing or happening • *We've had four cases of chickenpox.* • *It's just a case of being patient.* **2.** a crime or incident that the police or a lawcourt are investigating **3.** the facts or arguments used to support something • *She made a good case for getting some extra money.* **in case** because something may happen • *Take an umbrella in case it rains.*

cash *noun* cash is coins and banknotes that you use to pay for something

cash *verb* to cash a cheque is to exchange it for coins and banknotes

cash dispenser *noun* a machine from which customers of a bank can get money

cashier *noun* someone in charge of the money in a bank, office or shop

casket *noun* a small box for jewellery or other small objects

casserole *noun* **1.** a covered dish in which food is cooked **2.** the food cooked in a dish of this kind

cassette *noun* a small sealed case containing recording tape or film

cast *verb* **1.** to cast something is to throw it **2.** to cast a vote is to make your vote in an election **3.** to cast something made of metal or plaster is to make it in a mould **to cast off** is to untie a boat and start sailing in it

cast *noun* **1.** a shape you make by pouring liquid metal or plaster into a mould **2.** the performers in a play or film

castanets *plural noun* two pieces of wood or ivory held in one hand and clapped together to make a clicking sound, as in Spanish dancing

castaway *noun* someone who has been left in a deserted place after a shipwreck

caster sugar *noun* finely ground white sugar

castle *noun* **1.** a large old building with heavy stone walls and battlements, made to protect people in it from attack **2.** a piece in chess, also called a *rook*

castor *noun* (**kah**-ster) a small wheel on the leg of a piece of furniture

casual *adjective* **1.** not deliberate or planned • *It was just a casual remark.* **2.** casual clothes are informal clothes that you wear for leisure time **3.** not regular or permanent • *His dad was doing casual work.* **casually** *adverb*

casualty *noun* **casualties** someone killed or injured in war or in an accident

cat *noun* **1.** a small furry animal, usually kept as a pet **2.** a larger member of the same family, for example a lion, tiger or leopard

catalogue *noun* a list of goods for sale or of books in a library

catamaran *noun* a sailing boat with two hulls fixed side by side

catapult *noun* a forked stick with elastic attached to each fork, used for shooting small stones

catastrophe *noun* (ka-**tas**-tro-fi) a great or sudden disaster **catastrophic** *adjective* absolutely disastrous or dreadful • *The tornado did catastrophic damage.*

catch *verb* **catching, caught 1.** to catch something is to get hold of it, for example a ball that is coming towards you **2.** to catch an animal is to capture it and not let it escape **3.** to catch someone is to discover them doing something wrong • *He was caught going home early.* **4.** to catch an illness is to get it from someone else **5.** to catch a bus or train is to get on it before it leaves **6.** to catch something someone says is to manage to hear it • *I'm afraid I didn't catch your question.* **7.** to catch your clothes is to get them entangled in something • *I've caught my sleeve on a bramble.* **to catch fire** is to start burning **to catch on** (*informal*) is to become popular **to catch up with someone** is to reach them when they have been ahead of you

catch *noun* **catches 1.** catching something • *Maya made a brilliant catch.* **2.** something you catch • *They had a large catch of fish.* **3.** a hidden difficulty or snag • *The car was so cheap there had to be a catch.* **4.** a device for keeping a door or window closed

catchment area *noun* the area where the pupils who go to a particular school live

catchphrase *noun* a phrase that someone famous has used and a lot of people now use

catchy *adjective* catchier, catchiest pleasant and easy to remember, like a tune

category *noun* categories a group or division of similar people or things • *She was a runner-up in the 8-10 age category.*

cater *verb* to cater for someone or something is to give them what they need • *The library caters for all ages.*

caterer *noun* someone whose job is to provide food for people, especially at an important party or occasion

caterpillar *noun* a long, creeping creature that turns into a butterfly or moth

cathedral *noun* a large and important church in a major city, with a bishop in charge of it

Catholic *adjective* belonging to the Roman Catholic Church
Catholic *noun* a member of the Roman Catholic Church

cattle *plural noun* cattle are cows and bulls

cauldron *noun* a large round iron cooking pot used especially by witches in stories

cauliflower *noun* a kind of cabbage with a large head of white flowers

cause *noun* **1.** what makes something happen, a reason • *The cause of the fire is still a mystery.* **2.** the aim or purpose that a group of people are working for • *They were raising money for a good cause.*
cause *verb* to cause something is to make it happen

caution *noun* **1.** caution is being careful to avoid danger or mistakes **2.** a caution is a warning

cautious *adjective* careful to avoid a risk or difficulty cautiously *adverb*

cavalry *noun* soldiers who fight on horseback

cave *noun* a large hole in the side of a hill or cliff or under the ground
cave *verb* to cave or go caving is to explore caves to cave in is to collapse

caveman or **cavewoman** *noun* cavemen or cavewomen a person who lived in a cave in prehistoric times

cavern *noun* a cave, especially a deep or dark cave

cavity *noun* cavities a hollow or hole

CD short for **compact disc**

CD-ROM short for *compact disc read-only memory*, a system for storing information that can be viewed on a computer screen

cease *verb* to cease doing something is to stop doing it

ceasefire *noun* an agreement to stop fighting, made by people who are fighting a war

cedar *noun* an evergreen tree with hard sweet-smelling wood

ceiling *noun* (**see**-ling) the flat surface along the top of a room

celebrate *verb* to celebrate a day or event is to do something special to show that it is important celebration *noun* a party or other special event to celebrate something

celebrity *noun* celebrities a famous living person, for example an actor

celery *noun* a vegetable with crisp white or green stems

cell *noun* **1.** a small room, especially in a prison **2.** a tiny part of a living creature or plant **3.** a device for producing electric current chemically

cellar *noun* an underground room for storing things

cello *noun* cellos (**chel**-oh) a large stringed musical instrument, held between the knees and played using a bow cellist someone who plays the cello

cellulose *noun* cellulose is a tissue that forms the main part of all plants and trees

Celsius *adjective* using a scale for measuring temperature in which water freezes at 0 degrees and boils at 100 degrees

cement *noun* cement is a mixture of lime and clay used in building to make floors and join bricks together

cemetery *noun* cemeteries (**sem**-e-tri) a place where dead people are buried

censor *verb* to censor films, plays or books is to take out any parts that do not seem suitable for people **censorship** *noun* the job or process of censoring films, plays or books

census *noun* an official count or survey of the number of people in a place

cent *noun* a coin and unit of money in America and some other countries

centenary *noun* **centenaries** the hundredth anniversary of something special or important

centigrade *adjective* another word for Celsius

centimetre *noun* one-hundredth of a metre

centipede *noun* a small, long creature with many pairs of legs

central *adjective* at or near the centre of something **centrally** *adverb* in a central position

central heating *noun* central heating is a system of heating a building by sending hot water round it in pipes and radiators

centre *noun* **1.** the middle of something **2.** an important place • *Vienna is one of the great music centres of Europe.* **3.** a building or place for a special purpose, such as a sports centre or a shopping centre

centurion *noun* an officer in the ancient Roman army, originally commanding a hundred men

century *noun* **centuries 1.** a period of a hundred years **2.** a hundred runs scored by one batsman in an innings at cricket

ceramics *plural noun* ceramics is the art of making pottery

cereal *noun* **1.** a grass that produces seeds which are used as food **2.** a breakfast food made from seeds of this kind

ceremony *noun* **ceremonies** (**se**-ri-mo-ni) a formal event such as a wedding or funeral **ceremonial** *adjective* a ceremonial event or duty is one to do with a ceremony

certain *adjective* **1.** something is certain when it is definitely true or is going to happen **2.** you are certain about something when you know it is definitely true **for certain** definitely, for sure **to make certain** is to make sure

certainly *adverb* as a fact, without any doubt • *They were certainly here last night.*

certainty *noun* **certainties 1.** a certainty is something that is sure to happen **2.** certainty is being sure

certificate *noun* an official document that records an important event or achievement, such as someone's birth or passing an exam

CFC short for *chlorofluorocarbon*, a chemical that can damage the earth's ozone layer and was once used in refrigerators and aerosols

chaffinch *noun* a small bird

chain *noun* **1.** a row of metal rings fastened together **2.** a connected series of things • *The story told of a strange chain of events.*

chair *noun* a seat with a back for one person

chalk *noun* **1.** a soft white rock **2.** a stick of a substance like chalk, used for writing on blackboards **chalky** *adjective* white or powdery like chalk

challenge *verb* to challenge someone is to demand that they perform some feat or take part in a fight **challenger** *noun* a person who makes a challenge, especially for a sports title

challenge *noun* something difficult that someone has to do

chamber *noun* (old use) a room

chameleon *noun* (ka-**mee**-li-on) a small lizard that can change the colour of its skin to match its surroundings

champagne *noun* (sham-**payn**) a bubbly white French wine

champion *noun* **1.** the person who has beaten all the others in a sport or competition **2.** someone who supports a cause by fighting or speaking for it • *He is a champion of human rights.*

championship *noun* a contest to decide who is the best player or competitor in a game or sport

chance *noun* **1.** a chance is a possibility or opportunity • *This is your only chance to see them.* **2.** chance is the way things happen accidentally • *It was pure chance that we met.* **by chance** accidentally, without any planning • *We found the place by chance.* **to take a chance** is to take a risk

chancellor *noun* **1.** an important government or legal official **2.** the chief minister of the government in some European countries

Chancellor of the Exchequer *noun* the minister of the British government in charge of finances and taxes

chandelier *noun* (shan-de-**leer**) a light fitting that hangs from the ceiling and has a lot of bright bulbs

change *verb* **1.** to change something or someone is to make them different **2.** to change is to become different • *My gran said I'd changed since she'd last seen me.* **3.** to change one thing for another is to exchange them • *I'm going to change my bike for a new one.* **4.** to change money is to give coins or notes of small values in exchange for higher value money **5.** to change trains or buses is to get off one and get on another

change *noun* **1.** change is the process of changing **2.** your change is the money you get back when you give more than the right money to pay for something **3.** a change of clothes is a set of fresh clothes **to do something for a change** is to do it because it is different or unusual • *Let's walk home for a change.*

channel *noun* **1.** a stretch of water joining two seas, like the English Channel between Britain and France **2.** a television or radio station **3.** a way for water to flow along

chant *noun* a group of words sung repeatedly

chant *verb* to chant words is to sing them out in a special rhythm

chaos *noun* (**kay**-oss) chaos is complete disorder or confusion • *The room was in chaos.*

chaotic *adjective* (kay-**ot**-ik) completely confused or in a mess

chap *noun* (informal) a man or boy

chapatti *noun* a flat thin cake of Indian bread made without yeast

chapel *noun* a small church or part of a large church

chapped *adjective* having rough, cracked skin

chapter *noun* a section of a book

char *verb* charring, charred to char something is to scorch it or blacken it with fire

character *noun* **1.** the special nature and qualities of a person or thing **2.** a person in a story or play

characteristic *noun* something that makes a person or thing noticeable or different from others

characteristic *adjective* typical of someone

charades *noun* (sha-**rahdz**) charades is a game in which you have to guess the title of a book or film when other people act it out

charcoal *noun* charcoal is a black substance made by burning wood slowly

charge *noun* **1.** the price asked for something **2.** an accusation that someone committed a crime • *He is facing three charges of burglary.* **3.** an attack in a battle **to be in charge of something** or **someone** is to be the one who decides what will happen to them

charge *verb* **1.** to charge a price for something is to ask people to pay it **2.** to charge someone is to accuse them of committing a crime **3.** to charge in a battle is to rush to attack the enemy

chariot *noun* a horse-drawn vehicle with two wheels, used in ancient times for fighting and racing **charioteer** *noun* someone who drove a chariot

charity *noun* **charities 1.** charity is giving money and help to other people **2.** a charity is an organization that helps those in need **charitable** *adjective* kind and generous

charm *noun* **1.** charm is being pleasant and attractive **2.** a charm is a magic spell **3.** a charm is also something small worn or carried to bring good luck

charm *verb* **1.** to charm someone is to give them pleasure or delight **2.** to charm someone is also to put a spell on them

charming *adjective* pleasant and attractive

chart *noun* **1.** a large plan or map **2.** a diagram or list with information set out in columns or rows **3.** a list of the most popular CDs, records and digital downloads sold

charter *noun* an official document explaining people's rights or privileges

charter *verb* to charter an aircraft or vehicle is to hire it for a special journey

chase *verb* to chase someone is to go quickly after them to try to catch them up

chase *noun* a chase is when you chase someone

chassis *noun* **chassis** (**shass**-i) the frame and wheels of a vehicle, which support the body

chat *noun* a friendly talk with someone

chat *verb* **chatting, chatted** to chat to someone is to talk to them in a friendly way **chatty** *adjective* liking to chat to people

château *noun* **châteaux** (**shat**-oh) a castle or large house in France

chatroom *noun* a place on the Internet where people can have a conversation by sending messages to each other

chatter *verb* **1.** to talk quickly too much **2.** to make a rattling noise • *She couldn't stop her teeth from chattering.*

chauffeur *noun* (**shoh**-fer) someone who is paid to drive a large smart car for someone important

cheap *adjective* **1.** low in price; not expensive **2.** not well made or of good quality

cheat *verb* **1.** to cheat someone is to trick them so they lose something **2.** to cheat is to behave dishonestly in an examination or game by breaking the rules

cheat *noun* someone who cheats

check *verb* to check something is to make sure that it is correct or all right **to check on something** or **check up on something** is to look at it carefully to see if it is correct or suitable

check *noun* **1.** a check is when you check something **2.** check is a position in chess where the king is threatened by another piece **3.** a check is a pattern of squares

checkmate *noun* checkmate in chess is when one player wins by trapping the other's king

checkout *noun* the place where you pay for your shopping in a supermarket or a large shop

check-up *noun* a careful check or examination by a doctor or dentist

cheek *noun* **1.** the side of your face below your eye **2.** being rude or impolite

cheeky *adjective* cheekier, cheekiest rude or impolite, without being unpleasant or nasty

cheer *noun* a shout praising or supporting someone

cheer *verb* **1.** to cheer someone is to support them by cheering **2.** to cheer someone is to comfort or encourage them to cheer someone up is to make them more cheerful to cheer up is to become more cheerful

cheerful *adjective* happy and bright

cheese *noun* a white or yellow food made from milk cheesy *adjective* tasting or smelling like cheese

cheetah *noun* a large spotted animal of the cat family, which can run very fast

chef *noun* (shef) the chief cook in a hotel or restaurant

chemical *noun* a substance used in or made by chemistry

chemical *adjective* to do with chemistry or made by chemistry

chemist *noun* **1.** someone who makes or sells medicines **2.** an expert in chemistry

chemistry *noun* the study of the way substances combine and react with one another

cheque *noun* a written form instructing a bank to pay money out of an account

cherish *verb* to cherish something is to look after it lovingly

cherry *noun* cherries a small bright red fruit with a large stone

chess *noun* a game for two players played with sixteen pieces each on a board of 64 squares

chest *noun* **1.** a chest is a large strong box **2.** your chest is the front part of your body between your neck and your waist

chestnut *noun* **1.** a hard brown nut **2.** the tree that produces this kind of nut

chest of drawers *noun* a piece of furniture with drawers for holding clothes

chew *verb* to chew food is to grind it into pieces between your teeth chewy *adjective* chewy food is tough and needs a lot of chewing

chewing gum *noun* a sticky flavoured gum for chewing

chick *noun* a young bird

chicken *noun* **1.** a chicken is a young hen **2.** chicken is the meat of a hen used as food
chicken *adjective (informal)* cowardly

chickenpox *noun* a disease that produces red itchy spots on your skin

chief *noun* a leader or ruler
chief *adjective* most important

a
b
c
d
e
f
g
h
i
j
k
l
m
n
o
p
q
r
s
t
u
v
w
x
y
z

chiefly *adverb* mainly, mostly • *Peter is the one who is chiefly to blame.*

chieftain *noun* the chief of a tribe or clan

child *noun* **children** 1. a young person, a boy or girl 2. someone's son or daughter • *Whose child is that?*

childhood *noun* the time when you are a child

childish *adjective* silly and immature • *Don't be so childish!*

childminder *noun* a person who is paid to look after children while their parents are out at work

childproof *adjective* not able to be opened or operated by small children • *The car has childproof door locks.*

chill *noun* 1. chill is an unpleasant feeling of being cold 2. a chill is a cold that makes you shiver

chill *verb* to make something cold

chilli *noun* **chillies** the hot-tasting pod of a red pepper

chilly *adjective* **chillier, chilliest** 1. slightly cold 2. unfriendly • *They went to see the head and got a chilly reception.*

chime *noun* a ringing sound made by a bell

chime *verb* to chime is to make a ringing sound • *The clock chimes every quarter-hour.*

chimney *noun* a tall pipe or passage that carries away smoke from a fire

chimpanzee *noun* an small African ape with black fur and large eyes

chin *noun* your chin is the part of your face under your mouth

china *noun* china is thin and delicate pottery

chink *noun* a narrow opening • *He looked through a chink in the curtains.*

chip *noun* 1. a small piece of something 2. a place where a small piece has been knocked off something 3. a small piece of fried potato 4. a small counter used in gambling games 5. a silicon chip

chip *verb* **chipping, chipped** to chip something is to knock a small piece off it by accident

chirp *verb* to chirp is to make short sharp sounds like a small bird

chisel *noun* a tool with a sharp end for shaping wood or stone

chisel *verb* **chiselling, chiselled** to chisel wood or stone is to shape or cut it with a chisel

chlorine *noun* a chemical used to disinfect water

chlorophyll *noun* the substance that makes plants green

chocolate *noun* 1. chocolate is a sweet brown food 2. a chocolate is a sweet made of or covered with chocolate

choice *noun* 1. choice is the process of choosing or the power to choose • *I'm afraid we have no choice.* 2. a choice is what someone chooses • *Let me know your choice of book.*

choir *noun* a group of singers, especially in a church

choke *verb* 1. to choke on something is to be unable to breathe properly because it is stuck in your throat 2. to choke someone is to stop them breathing properly

cholera *noun* (kol-er-a) cholera is a severe infectious disease that affects the intestines

cholesterol *noun* (ko-**less**-te-rol) cholesterol is a substance found in the cells of your body which helps to carry fat in the bloodstream

choose *verb* **choosing, chose, chosen** to choose something or someone is to decide that you want them rather than any of the others

choosy *adjective* **choosier, choosiest** (*informal*) a choosy person is fussy and difficult to please

chop *verb* chopping, chopped to chop something up is to cut it into small pieces
chop *noun* a small thick slice of meat

choppy *adjective* choppier, choppiest a choppy sea is fairly rough with lots of small waves

chopsticks *plural noun* a pair of thin sticks used for eating Chinese or Japanese food

choral *adjective* (**kor**-al) for a choir or chorus

chord *noun* (kord) a number of musical notes sounded together

chore *noun* (chor) a boring or difficult task

chorister *noun* (**kor**-is-ter) someone who sings in a choir

chorus *noun* (**kor**-us) **1.** a group of people singing or speaking together **2.** a piece of music sung by a group of people **3.** the words repeated after every verse of a song or poem

christen *verb* to christen a child is to baptize it and give it a name **christening** *noun* the ceremony at which a child is baptized

Christian *noun* someone who believes in Jesus Christ
Christian *adjective* to do with Christ or Christians

Christianity *noun* the religion of Christians

Christmas *noun* Christmases the time of celebrating the birth of Jesus Christ on 25 December

chrome or **chromium** *noun* a shiny silvery metal

chromosome *noun* in living things, the part of a cell that contains the genes

chronic *adjective* a chronic illness or problem is one that lasts for a long time **chronically** *adverb* to be chronically ill is to have an illness for a very long time

chronicle *noun* a list of events with their dates

chronological *adjective* a chronological list of events is arranged in the order in which the events happened **chronologically** *adverb*

chrysalis *noun* (**kris**-a-lis) the hard cover a caterpillar makes round itself before it turns into a butterfly or moth

chubby *adjective* chubbier, chubbiest plump and healthy

chuck *verb (informal)* to chuck something is to throw it roughly • *He chucked a brick through the window.*

chuckle *verb* to chuckle is to laugh quietly

chum *noun (informal)* a friend

chunk *noun* a thick lump of something **chunky** *adjective* big and thick

church *noun* **1.** a church is a building where Christians worship **2.** a church is also a particular Christian religion, for example the Church of England

churchyard *noun* the ground round a church, used as a graveyard

churn *noun* **1.** a large container for milk **2.** a machine for making butter
churn *verb* to churn butter is to make it in a churn

chute *noun* (shoot) a steep channel for people or things to slide down

chutney *noun* a spicy mixture of fruit and peppers in a sauce, eaten with meat or cheese

cigarette *noun* a small tube of paper containing tobacco, that some people smoke

cinder *noun* a small piece of coal or wood that is partly burned

cinema *noun* a place where people go to see films

circle *noun* **1.** a round flat shape, the shape of a coin or wheel **2.** a balcony in a cinema or theatre
circle *verb* **1.** to circle is to move in a circle • *Vultures circled overhead.* **2.** to circle a place is go round it • *The space probe circled Mars.*

circuit *noun* (**ser**-kit) **1.** a circular line or journey **2.** a racecourse **3.** the path of an electric current

circular *adjective* round like a circle

circulate *verb* to circulate is to move around and come back to the beginning • *Blood circulates in the body.*

circulation *noun* the movement of blood around your body

circumference *noun* the line or distance round a circle

circumstance *noun* a fact or event that affects something • *He won under difficult circumstances.*

circus *noun* an entertainment with clowns, acrobats and sometimes animals, usually performed in a large tent

cistern *noun* a water tank

citizen *noun* a citizen of a place is someone who was born there or who lives there

citizenship *noun* 1. the citizenship of a country is the right to live there and be a citizen of it • *She has applied for American citizenship.* 2. citizenship is also the duties a person has when they are the citizen of a country • *The school has lessons in citizenship.*

citrus fruit *noun* citrus fruits are juicy fruits with a tough skin, such as oranges, lemons, limes and grapefruit

city *noun* **cities** a large or important town

civic *adjective* to do with a city or its citizens

civil *adjective* 1. to do with the citizens of a place 2. to do with the ordinary people and not those who are in the armed forces 3. a civil person is polite to other people

civilian *noun* someone who is an ordinary citizen and not in the armed forces

civilization *noun* a civilization is a society or culture at a particular time in history • *We are learning about the ancient civilizations of Greece and Rome.* This word can also be spelled **civilisation**.

civilize *verb* to civilize someone is to improve their education and manners This word can also be spelled **civilise**.

civil rights *plural noun* people's civil rights are their rights as citizens to have freedom and fair treatment and to vote in elections

civil service *noun* the civil service is all the officials who do the work the government needs to do to run the country

civil war *noun* a war fought between people of the same country, such as the English Civil War (1642–51) or the American Civil War (1861–65)

clad *adjective* clothed or covered • *The story was about a knight clad in shining armour.*

claim *verb* 1. to claim something is to ask for it when you think it belongs to you • *You can claim the money for your train fare.* 2. to claim something is to state or assert it • *They claimed they had been at home all evening.*

claim *noun* 1. an act of claiming 2. something claimed

clam *noun* a large shellfish

clamber *verb* to clamber is to climb up or over something difficult using your hands and feet • *We clambered over the slippery rocks.*

clammy *adjective* **clammier, clammiest** damp and slimy

clamp *noun* a device for holding things together

clamp *verb* to clamp something is to fit a clamp on it

clan *noun* a number of families with the same ancestor • *The Scottish clans include the Campbells and the MacDonalds.*

clang *verb* to clang is to make a loud ringing sound

clap *verb* **clapping, clapped** to clap is to make a noise by hitting the palms of your hands together, especially to show you like something

clap *noun* 1. a round of clapping, especially to show you like something • *They gave the winners a loud clap.* 2. a clap of thunder is a sudden sound of loud thunder

clarify verb clarifies, clarifying, clarified to clarify something is to explain it and make it easier to understand **clarification** noun clarification is making something clear and easier to understand

clarinet noun a woodwind instrument with a low tone **clarinettist** noun someone who plays the clarinet

clarity noun clarity is clearness • *They spoke with clarity.*

clash verb **1.** to clash is to make a loud sound like cymbals banging together **2.** two events clash when they happen inconveniently at the same time • *My favourite TV programmes clash at 8 o'clock tonight.* **3.** two or more people clash when they have a fight or argument • *Gangs of rival supporters clashed outside the ground.* **4.** colours clash when they look bad together

clash noun **1.** a clashing sound **2.** a fight or argument

clasp verb to clasp someone or something is to hold them tightly

clasp noun a device for fastening things

class noun **1.** a class is a group of similar people, animals or things **2.** a class is also a division according to how good or important something is • *Send the letter by first class post.* **3.** a class is also a group of children or students who are taught together or a lesson **4.** class is a system of different ranks in society

class verb to class things is to put them in classes or groups

classic noun a book, film or story that is well known and thought to be very good and important

classic adjective **1.** a classic story is one that most people think is very good and important **2.** very typical or common • *They made the classic mistake of leaving things to the last moment.*

classical adjective **1.** to do with Greek and Latin literature **2.** classical music is serious music, often written in the past and still played

classify verb classifies, classifying, classified to classify things is to put them in classes or groups **classification** noun a system of classifying things

classmate noun your classmates are the people in the same class as you at school

classroom noun a room where lessons are given at a school

clatter noun a loud noise of things being rattled or banged

clatter verb to clatter is to make a clatter

clause noun **1.** *(in grammar)* a part of a sentence that has its own verb **2.** a part of a contract, treaty or law

claw noun one of the hard sharp nails that some birds and animals have on their feet

clay noun clay is a sticky kind of earth, used for making bricks and pottery

clean adjective **1.** something is clean when it does not have any dirt or stains on it **2.** fresh, not yet used • *Start on a clean page.*

clean verb to clean something is to make it clean

cleaner noun **1.** someone who cleans rooms or offices **2.** something used for cleaning

cleanliness noun (**klen**-li-nes) the practice of keeping things clean

cleanly adverb neatly, exactly • *He cut the brick cleanly in two.*

cleanse verb (klenz) to cleanse something is to clean it and make it pure **cleanser** noun something you use to make a thing clean

clear adjective **1.** easy to see or hear or understand • *He spoke with a clear voice.* **2.** easy to see through • *The window in the door has clear glass.* **3.** not covered or blocked by anything • *Make sure the table's clear for dinner.*

clear adverb **1.** clearly • *Speak loud and clear.* **2.** at a distance from something • *You'd better stand clear of the gates.*

clear verb **1.** to clear something is to make it free of unwanted things • *They cleared a space on the floor to sit on.* **2.** to clear is to become clearer • *After the storm, the sky slowly cleared.* **3.** to clear someone is to find out that they are not to blame for something people thought they had done **to clear up** is to make things tidy

clearing noun an open space in a wood or forest

clearly *adverb* **1**. in a clear way • *We could see the house clearly.* **2**. obviously • *They were clearly going to win.*

clef *noun* a sign that shows the pitch of a stave in music

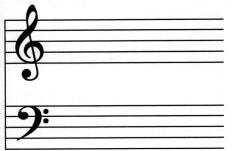

clench *verb* to clench your teeth or fingers is to close them tightly

clergy *plural noun* the clergy are the priests and other officials of a Christian Church **clergyman** *noun* **clergywoman** *noun*

clerk *noun* (klark) someone whose job is to keep records or deal with documents in an office

clever *adjective* quick to learn and understand things; skilful

cliché *noun* (**klee**-shay) a phrase that people use a lot, so that it doesn't mean very much

click *noun* a short sharp sound • *She heard a click as someone turned on the light.*

client *noun* someone who gets help or advice from a professional person such as a lawyer or architect; a customer

cliff *noun* a steep rock face, especially on the coast

climate *noun* the usual sort of weather in a particular area **climatic** *adjective* to do with the climate

climax *noun* the most important or exciting part of a story or series of events

climb *verb* **1**. to climb or climb up something is go up it **2**. to climb down something is to go down it **3**. to climb is to grow or rise upwards, like a tall plant or a building

climb *noun* an act of climbing • *It's a long climb to the top of the hill.*

climber *noun* someone who climbs mountains for sport

cling *verb* to cling to someone or something is to hold on tightly • *The child was clinging to its mother.*

clinic *noun* a place where people see doctors for treatment or advice

clink *verb* to clink is to make a short ringing sound, like a coin being dropped

clip *noun* a fastener for keeping things together
clip *verb* **clipping, clipped** **1**. to clip things together is to fasten them with a clip **2**. to clip something is to cut small pieces off it

cloak *noun* a piece of outdoor clothing, usually without sleeves, that hangs loosely from your shoulders

cloakroom *noun* **1**. a place where you can leave coats and bags while you are visiting a building **2**. a lavatory

clock *noun* an instrument that shows what the time is

clockwise *adverb, adjective* moving round a circle in the same direction as the hands of a clock

clockwork *adjective* worked by a spring which you wind up

clog *verb* **clogging, clogged** to clog something is to block it up accidentally
clog *noun* a shoe with a wooden sole

cloister *noun* a covered path that goes round the courtyard of a cathedral or monastery

clone *noun* an animal or plant made from the cells of another animal or plant
clone *verb* to clone something is to produce a clone of it

close[1] *adjective* (klohss) **1**. near, either in time or place • *They were close to finding the answer.* • *The shops were quite close to their new house.* **2**. careful and detailed • *Please pay close attention.* **3**. tight; with little empty space • *They got the wardrobe in but it was a close fit.* **4**. having a strong relationship • *The boys had been close friends for years.* **5**. a close race or finish is one in which competitors are nearly equal at the end **6.** stuffy; without fresh air • *It's very close in this room.*

close[1] *adverb* (klohss) at a close distance • *The children were following close behind.*

close[1] *noun* (klohss) **1.** a street that is closed at one end **2.** an enclosed area, especially round a cathedral

close[2] *verb* (klohz) **1.** to close something is to shut it **2.** to close an event or meeting is to finish it **to close down** is to stop doing business • *Several shops have closed down recently.*

closely *adverb* (**klohss**-li) **1.** carefully, with attention • *His friends were watching closely.* **2.** tightly • *The box was closely packed with toys.*

close-up *noun* (**klohss**-up) a photograph or film taken at short range

clot *noun* a mass of thick liquid like blood or cream that has become nearly solid
clot *verb* clotting, clotted to clot is to form into clots, like blood or cream

cloth *noun* **1.** cloth is material woven from wool, cotton or some other fabric **2.** a cloth is a piece of this material

clothe *verb* clothing, clothed to clothe someone is to put clothes on them

clothes *plural noun* clothes are the things you wear to cover your body

clothing *noun* clothing is the clothes you wear

cloud *noun* **1.** a mass of water vapour floating in the air **2.** a mass of smoke or dust in the air
cloud *verb* to cloud or cloud over is to become full of clouds • *In the afternoon the sky clouded over.* **cloudless** *adjective* a cloudless sky does not have any clouds

cloudy *adjective* cloudier, cloudiest **1.** full of clouds **2.** hard to see through • *The glass contained a cloudy liquid.*

clout *verb* to clout someone is to give them a hard blow

clove *noun* the dried bud of a tropical tree used as a spice

clover *noun* a small wild plant, usually with leaves in three parts

clown *noun* a circus performer who dresses up and wears bright face paint and does silly things to make people laugh
clown *verb* to clown is to behave in a silly way

club *noun* **1.** a heavy stick **2.** a stick for playing golf **3.** a group of people who meet together because they are interested in the same thing **4.** a playing card with a black clover-leaf printed on it
club *verb* clubbing, clubbed to club someone is to hit them hard with a heavy stick

cluck *verb* to cluck is to make a noise like a hen

clue *noun* something that helps you to solve a puzzle or a mystery

clump *noun* a cluster of trees or plants

clumsy *adjective* clumsier, clumsiest a clumsy person is careless and awkward and likely to knock things over or drop things clumsily *adverb* clumsiness *noun*

cluster *noun* a group of people or things close together

clutch[1] *verb* to clutch something or clutch at something is to grab hold of it
clutch[1] *noun* **1.** a tight grasp **2.** a device for disconnecting the engine of a motor vehicle from its gears and wheels

clutch[2] *noun* a set of eggs in a nest

clutter *verb* to clutter a place up is to make it untidy or messy
clutter *noun* clutter is a lot of things left around untidily

cm short for **centimetre** or **centimetres**

Co. short for **company**

coach *noun* **1.** a comfortable bus used for long journeys **2.** a carriage of a railway train **3.** a carriage pulled by horses **4.** a person who trains or instructs people in a sport or skill
coach *verb* to coach someone is to instruct or train them in a sport or skill

coal *noun* coal is a hard black mineral used as fuel

coarse *adjective* **1.** rough, not delicate or smooth • *coarse hands* **2.** rude or offensive • *a coarse sense of humour*

coast *noun* the seashore and the land close to it

coast *verb* to coast is to ride downhill without using power • *They stopped pedalling and coasted down the slope.*

coastal *adjective* by the coast or near the coast

coastguard *noun* someone whose job is to keep watch on coasts

coastline *noun* the edge of the land by the sea

coat *noun* **1.** a piece of clothing with sleeves that covers most of the body and is worn outdoors over other clothes **2.** a layer of paint

coat *verb* to coat something is to cover it with a coating

coating *noun* a covering or layer, especially of paint

coat of arms *noun* a design on a shield or building, representing a historic family or town

coax *verb* to coax someone is to persuade them gently or patiently

cobbler *noun* someone whose job is to mend shoes

cobbles *plural noun* cobbles are a surface of cobblestones on a road **cobbled** paved with cobbles

cobblestone *noun* a small smooth and rounded stone sometimes used in large numbers to pave roads in towns

cobra *noun* (**koh**-bra) a poisonous snake

cobweb *noun* a net of thin sticky threads that spiders spin to catch insects

cock *noun* a male bird, especially a male fowl

cockerel *noun* a young male fowl

cockle *noun* an edible shellfish

cockney *noun* **1.** a cockney is someone born in the East End of London **2.** cockney is a kind of English spoken by people from this part of London

cockpit *noun* the place in an aircraft where the pilot sits

cockroach *noun* a dark brown insect

cocky *adjective* **cockier, cockiest** *(informal)* conceited and cheeky

cocoa *noun* **1.** a hot drink that tastes of chocolate **2.** the powder from which you make this drink

coconut *noun* a large round nut containing a milky juice, that grows on palm trees

cocoon *noun* the covering round a chrysalis

cod *noun* **cod** a large edible sea fish

code *noun* **1.** a set of signs and letters for sending messages secretly **2.** a set of rules • *the Highway Code* • *a code of behaviour*
code *verb* to code a message is to use special signs and letters, so that other people cannot understand it

co-education *noun* the teaching of boys and girls together **co-educational** *adjective* a co-educational school or system is one that teaches boys and girls together

coffee *noun* **1.** a hot drink made from the roasted and crushed beans of a tropical plant **2.** the powder from which you make this drink

coffin *noun* a long box in which a dead body is buried or cremated

cog *noun* one of a number of pieces sticking out from the edge of a wheel and allowing it to drive another wheel

coil *noun* a circle or spiral of rope or wire
coil *verb* to coil something is to wind it into circles or spirals

coin *noun* a piece of metal money

coinage *noun* a country's coinage is the system of money that it uses

coincide *verb* to coincide is to happen at the same time as something else • *My birthday always seems to coincide with exams.*

coincidence *noun* coincidence or a coincidence, is when two things happen by chance at the same time

coke *noun* coke is a solid fuel made out of coal

cola *noun* cola is a sweet brown fizzy drink

cold *adjective* 1. low in temperature, not hot or warm 2. a cold person is unfriendly and distant

cold *noun* 1. cold weather or temperature 2. a cold is an illness that makes your nose run and gives you a sore throat **coldly** *adverb* to act coldly is to be very unfriendly **coldness** *noun* coldness is being unfriendly

cold-blooded *adjective* 1. having blood that changes temperature according to the surroundings 2. cruel, ruthless

coleslaw *noun* a salad made of chopped cabbage covered in mayonnaise

collaborate *verb* people collaborate when they work together or share their information **collaboration** *noun* working or sharing information with others

collage *noun* (**kol**-ahzh or kol-**ah**zh) a picture made by arranging many pieces of paper and other things on a card

collapse *verb* 1. to collapse is to fall or break into pieces because of too much weight 2. someone collapses when they fall from being very weak or ill

collapsible *adjective* a collapsible piece of furniture or equipment can be folded up

collar *noun* 1. the part of a piece of clothing that goes round your neck 2. a band that goes round an animal's neck

colleague *noun* someone's colleague is a person they work with

collect *verb* 1. to collect things is to get them together from various places, especially as a hobby • *She collects stamps.* 2. to collect someone or something is to go and get them **collector** *noun* someone who collects things for a hobby

collection *noun* 1. things you have collected as a hobby 2. money given by people at a meeting or concert or church service

college *noun* a place where people continue to study after they have left school

collide *verb* to collide with something is to hit it while moving

collision *noun* a crash between moving vehicles • *There has been a collision on the motorway.*

colon *noun* a punctuation mark (:) used to separate parts of a sentence or before items in a list

colonel *noun* (**ker**-nel) a senior army officer

colonial *adjective* from or to do with a country's colonies abroad

colony *noun* **colonies** 1. a country that another another country governs and sends people out to live there 2. a group of people or animals living together

colossal *adjective* huge, enormous

colour *noun* 1. the quality of being red, green, blue and so on, produced by rays of light of different wavelengths 2. the use of all colours, not just black and white • *Is this film in colour?* 3. the colour of someone's skin 4. a substance used to give colour to things

colour *verb* to colour something is to give it a colour or colours with paints or crayons

colour-blind *adjective* not able to see or distinguish between some colours, usually red and green

coloured *adjective* having a particular colour

colourful *adjective* having a lot of bright colours

colt *noun* a young male horse

column *noun* **1.** a pillar **2.** something long and narrow • *They could see a column of smoke in the distance.* **3.** a strip of printing in a book or newspaper **4.** a regular feature in a newspaper • *He always read the sports column.*

coma *noun* (**koh**-ma) someone is in a coma when they are unconscious for a long time

comb *noun* **1.** a tool with teeth for making the hair tidy **2.** the red, fleshy crest on a fowl's head
comb *verb* **1.** to comb your hair is to tidy it with a comb **2.** to comb an area is to search it carefully for something lost

combat *noun* a fight or contest
combat *verb* to combat something bad or unpleasant is to fight it and try to get rid of it • *The police force combats crime.*

combination *noun* **1.** combination is joining or mixing things **2.** a combination is a group of things that have been joined or mixed together

combine *verb* (kom-**byn**) to combine things is to join them or mix them together

combine harvester *noun* a machine that cuts and threshes the grain in the fields

combustion *noun* combustion is what happens when something burns

come *verb* coming, came, come **1.** to come is to move towards the person or place that is here and is the opposite of **go** • *Do you want to come to my house?* • *Has that letter come yet?* **2.** to come is also to occur or be present • *The pictures come at the end of the book.* to come to something is to add up to it • *The bill came to £50.* to come true is to actually happen • *Their holiday was a dream come true.*

comedian *noun* someone who entertains people with humour and jokes

comedy *noun* comedies **1.** a comedy is a play or film that makes people laugh **2.** comedy is using humour to make people laugh

comet *noun* an object moving across the sky with a bright tail of light

comfort *noun* **1.** comfort is a feeling of relief from worry or pain **2.** your comforts are the things you have around you that make your life comfortable and pleasant

comfort *verb* to comfort someone is to make them feel happier when they are feeling sad or worried

comfortable *adjective* **1.** pleasant to use or wear • *a comfortable chair* **2.** free from worry or pain • *The nurse made the patient comfortable.* comfortably *adverb*

comic *noun* **1.** a children's magazine that has stories with pictures **2.** a comedian
comical *adjective* funny, making people laugh
comically *adverb*

comic strip *noun* a series of drawings that tell a story

comma *noun* a punctuation mark (,) used to mark a pause in a sentence or between items in a list

command *noun* **1.** a command is an instruction telling someone to do something **2.** command is authority or control • *Who has command of these soldiers?*

command *verb* **1.** to command someone is to tell them to do something **2.** to command a group of people is to be in charge of them • *A centurion commanded a hundred soldiers.*

commander *noun* someone who commands, especially a senior naval officer

commandment *noun* a sacred command, especially one of the Ten Commandments in the Bible

commando *noun* commandos a soldier trained for making dangerous raids

commemorate *verb* to commemorate a past event is to do something special so that people remember it commemoration *noun*

commence *verb* to commence something is to begin it commencement *noun* the beginning of something

comment *noun* a remark or opinion

commentary *noun* commentaries a description of an event by someone who is watching it, especially for radio or television

commentator *noun* a person who gives a commentary, especially of a sports event

commerce *noun* commerce is trade or buying and selling goods

commercial *adjective* 1. connected with trade and making money 2. paid for by advertising • *a commercial radio station*

commercial *noun* an advertisement, especially on television or radio

commit *verb* committing, committed to commit a crime is to do something against the law

commitment *noun* 1. commitment is being determined to do something 2. a commitment is something you have promised to do

committee *noun* a group of people who meet to organize or discuss something

common *adjective* 1. ordinary or usual • *The dandelion is a common plant.* 2. happening or used often • *Traffic jams are common where we live.*

common *noun* a piece of open land that anyone can use

commonplace *adjective* ordinary, familiar

commonwealth *noun* a group of countries cooperating together the Commonwealth an association of Britain and various other countries, such as Canada, Australia and New Zealand

commotion *noun* an uproar • *Suddenly he could hear a commotion in the kitchen.*

commune *noun* a group of people who live in the same house and share the money and work

communicate *verb* to communicate information is to pass it on to other people communicative *adjective* a communicative person is willing to talk to people

communication *noun* 1. communication is giving people useful information 2. a communication is a message or piece of information that someone gives you 3. communication is also ways of sending information, for example television and text messaging and the Internet

Communion *noun* Communion is the Christian ceremony in which holy bread and wine are given to worshippers.

communism *noun* communism is a political belief that everyone should share the wealth of a country and the state should control its industry and resources communist *noun* someone who believes in communism

community *noun* communities the people living in one area

commuter *noun* someone who travels to work every day by train or bus commute *verb* to commute is to travel to work every day

compact *adjective* small and neat

compact disc *noun* A compact disc is a small plastic and metal disc on which music or information is stored as digital signals and is read by a laser beam. Usually called **CD**.

companion *noun* a companion is someone who spends a lot of time with you companionship *noun* companionship is being with someone and enjoying their friendship

company *noun* companies 1. a company is a group of people, especially a business firm 2. company is having people with you • *Jill was lonely and longed for some company.* 3. a company is an army unit consisting of two or more platoons

comparatively *adverb* in comparison, relatively • *They all went to bed comparatively late.*

compare *verb* 1. to compare things is to see how they are similar • *Compare your answers.* 2. to compare with something is to be as good as it • *Our football pitch cannot compare with Wembley Stadium.*

comparison *noun* comparison, or a comparison, is when you compare different things

compartment *noun* a special place or section where you can put something • *The coach had a luggage compartment under the floor.*

compass *noun* an instrument with a magnetized needle that shows which direction you are facing compasses or pair of compasses a device for drawing circles

compassion *noun* compassion is pity or mercy you show to people who are suffering **compassionate** *adjective* showing pity or mercy to people who are suffering

compatible *adjective* **1.** people are compatible when they are able to live or exist together without trouble **2.** machines and devices are compatible when they can be used together

compel *verb* compelling, compelled to compel someone to do something is to force them to do it

compensate *verb* to compensate someone is to give them something to make up for something they have lost or suffered **compensation** *noun* compensation is something given to someone to make up for a loss or injury

compete *verb* to compete in a competition is to take part in it and try to win it

competent *adjective* having the skill or knowledge to do something well • *He is not competent to teach French.* **competence** *noun* the ability to do something well

competition *noun* a game or race in which you try to do better than other people **competitive** *adjective* a competitive person enjoys competing with other people **competitor** *noun* someone who competes in a game or race or a rival in business

compile *verb* to compile information is to collect and arrange it, especially in a book • *She compiled a collection of children's poems.* **compilation** *noun* a collection of information, stories or poems that someone has compiled **compiler** *noun* someone who compiles something

complacent *adjective* smugly satisfied with the way things are, without wanting to improve them

complain *verb* to complain about something is to say that you are not pleased about it

complaint *noun* **1.** you make a complaint when you are not pleased about something **2.** you suffer from a complaint when you have a minor illness

complete *adjective* **1.** having all its parts, with nothing missing **2.** finished, achieved • *By evening the jigsaw puzzle was complete.* **3.** utter, total • *It came as a complete surprise.*

complete *verb* to complete something is to finish it or make it complete **completion** *noun* the completing of something, the finish

completely *adverb* totally, utterly • *You are completely wrong.*

complex *adjective* difficult and complicated **complexity** *noun* being difficult or complicated

complex *noun* a group of buildings, such as a sports centre

complexion *noun* the colour or appearance of your skin

complicate *verb* to complicate something is to make it difficult or awkward

complicated *adjective* difficult to understand or deal with because it has so many parts or details

complication *noun* a new problem that makes something else more difficult

compliment *noun* something you say to show that you admire someone or something

complimentary *adjective* praising someone or saying good things about them • *She liked Neil's work and was very complimentary about him.*

component *noun* one of the parts that a machine is made of

compose *verb* **1.** to compose music or poetry is to write it **2.** to be composed of several people or things is to be made up of them • *The class is composed of children up to the age of 8.* **composer** *noun* someone who writes music

composition *noun* **1**. composition is composing or writing something **2**. a composition is a piece of music or an essay

compost *noun* compost is a mixture of decayed leaves, grass and other natural refuse and is used as manure

compound[1] *noun* **1**. a substance that is made of two or more parts or ingredients **2**. *(grammar)* a word that is made from two or more other words, such as *bathroom* and *newspaper*

compound[2] *noun* a fenced area containing buildings

comprehend *verb* to comprehend something is to understand it

comprehension *noun* **1**. comprehension is understanding **2**. a comprehension is an exercise that tests or helps your understanding of a language

comprehensive school *noun* a secondary school for children of all abilities

compress *verb* **1**. to compress something is to press it or squeeze it together **2**. to be compressed is to be forced into a small space **compression** *noun* compression is pressing or squeezing something

comprise *verb* to comprise several people or things is to include them • *A football team comprises eleven players.*

compromise *verb* (**kom**-pro-myz) to compromise is to accept less than you really wanted, especially so as to settle a disagreement
compromise *noun* (**kom**-pro-myz) accepting less than you really wanted

compulsory *adjective* something is compulsory when you have to do it • *Wearing seat belts is compulsory.*

computer *noun* an electronic machine that does word processing and rapid calculations, sorts data and can control other machines

comrade *noun* a friend or companion

concave *adjective* A concave surface is curved like the inside of a circle or ball. The opposite of **convex**.

conceal *verb* to conceal something is to hide it carefully or cleverly **concealment** *noun* concealment is hiding something carefully

conceit *noun* conceit is thinking a lot about how clever or attractive you are **conceited** *adjective* a conceited person thinks a lot of themselves and is vain and proud

conceive *verb* **1**. to conceive an idea or plan is to form it in your mind **2**. a woman conceives when she becomes pregnant

concentrate *verb* **1**. to concentrate on something is to think hard about it **2**. to concentrate people or things is to bring them together in one place

concentrated *adjective* a liquid is concentrated when it is made stronger by having water removed from it

concentration *noun* concentration is thinking hard about something

concept *noun* a new idea about something

conception *noun* **1**. conception is forming an idea in your mind **2**. conception is also when a woman becomes pregnant

concern *verb* **1**. to concern someone is to be important or interesting to them **2**. to concern something is to be about a particular subject • *This story concerns a shipwreck.* **3**. to worry someone
concern *noun* something that matters to someone • *I think that is my concern.*

concerning *preposition* on the subject of; in connection with • *Do you have any information concerning his disappearance?*

concert *noun* a performance of music

concertina *noun* a portable musical instrument that you squeeze to push air past reeds

concerto *noun* concertos (kon-**cher**-toh) a piece of music for a solo instrument and an orchestra • *a violin concerto*

concise *adjective* giving a lot of information in a few words

conclude *verb* **1**. to conclude something is to end it **2**. to conclude something is also to decide about it • *The jury concluded that he was not guilty.*

conclusion *noun* **1**. the ending of something **2**. a decision that you reach after a lot of thought

concrete *noun* cement mixed with water and gravel or sand and used in building

concussion *noun* a temporary injury to the brain that is caused by a hard knock and leaves you feeling dizzy or unconscious

condemn *verb* **1**. to condemn someone or something is to say that you strongly disapprove of them **2**. to condemn criminals is to sentence them to a punishment • *He was condemned to death.* **3**. to condemn a building is to declare that it is not fit to be used

condensation *noun* drops of liquid formed from vapour that has condensed

condense *verb* **1**. to condense a piece of writing is to make it shorter **2**. to condense is to change from a gas or vapour into water or other liquid • *Steam condenses on cold windows.*

condition *noun* **1**. the state in which a person or thing is • *This bike is in good condition.* **2**. something that must happen if something else is to happen • *Learning to swim is a condition of going sailing.*

conduct *verb* (kon-**dukt**) **1**. to conduct something is to organize it or carry it out • *I decided to conduct a little experiment.* **2**. to conduct an orchestra or band is to direct it in a piece of music **3**. to conduct electricity or heat is to allow it to pass along • *Copper conducts electricity well.*

conduct *noun* (**kon**-dukt) a person's conduct is their behaviour

conduction *noun* the conducting of electricity or heat

conductor *noun* **1**. someone who conducts an orchestra or band **2**. something that conducts electricity or heat

cone *noun* **1**. an object which is circular at one end and pointed at the other end **2**. an ice cream cornet **3**. the fruit of a pine, fir or cedar

confectionery *noun* sweets that a shop sells

conference *noun* a meeting for discussion

confess *verb* to confess to something wrong or embarrassing is to admit that you have done it

confession *noun* an act of admitting that you have committed a crime or done wrong

confetti *plural noun* tiny bits of coloured paper thrown at the bride and bridegroom after a wedding

confide *verb* to confide in someone is to tell them a secret

confidence *noun* **1**. you have confidence when you are sure that you are right or can do something **2**. confidence in someone is trusting or believing them **in confidence** as a secret • *He told me all this in confidence.*

confident *adjective* **1**. being sure that you are right or can do something **2**. certain that something will happen • *We are confident it will be an enjoyable day.*

confidential *adjective* information is confidential when it has to be kept secret **confidentially** *adverb* in confidence, as a secret

confine *verb* **1**. to confine something is to restrict or limit it • *Please confine your comments to points of fact.* **2**. to confine someone is to lock them up or shut them in a place

confirm *verb* **1**. to confirm something is to say that it is true or to show that it is true **2**. to confirm an arrangement is to make it definite • *Please write to confirm your order.* **3**. to confirm someone is to make them a full member of a Christian Church

confirmation *noun* a fact or piece of information that shows something is true or has happened • *You will receive confirmation of your booking by email.*

confiscate *verb* to confiscate something is to take it away from someone as a punishment

conflict *noun* (**kon**-flikt) a fight or disagreement • *the conflict in the Middle East* • *a conflict between the unions and the bosses*

conflict *verb* (kon-**flikt**) two things conflict when they contradict or disagree with one another • *The two accounts of the incident conflict.*

conform *verb* to conform is to behave or think in the same way as most other people

confront *verb* **1.** to confront someone is to challenge them face to face for a fight or argument • *The police decided to confront the criminals there and then.* **2.** to confront a problem or difficulty is to deal with it firmly and positively **confrontation** *noun* meeting someone face to face for a fight or argument

confuse *verb* **1.** to confuse someone is to make them puzzled or muddled **2.** to confuse things is to mistake one thing for another **confusing** *adjective* difficult to understand, muddling **confusion** *noun* confusion is being confused or muddled

congratulate *verb* to congratulate someone is to tell them how pleased you are about something they have done **congratulations** *plural noun* congratulations are words that tell someone how well they have done

congregation *noun* the people who take part in a church service

congress *noun* a large meeting or conference **Congress** the parliament or government of the USA

conical *adjective* shaped like a cone

conifer *noun* (**kon**-i-fer) an evergreen tree with cones **coniferous** *adjective* a coniferous tree has cones

conjunction *noun* a word that joins other words and parts of a sentence, e.g. *and*, *but* and *whether*

conjure *verb* to conjure is to perform tricks that look like magic **conjurer** *noun* someone who performs magic tricks

conker *noun* a hard and shiny brown nut that grows on a horse chestnut tree **conkers** a game played with conkers

connect *verb* **connects**, **connecting**, **connected** to connect things is to join them together

connection *noun* **1.** a link between things **2.** joining together

conquer *verb* to conquer a people or country is to defeat them and take them over • *William I conquered England.* **conqueror** *noun* someone who conquers a country

conquest *noun* a victory over another country or people

conscience *noun* (**kon**-shens) a feeling people have about what is right or wrong

conscientious *adjective* (kon-shee-**en**-shus) careful and hard-working **conscientiously** *adverb*

conscious *adjective* (**kon**-shus) **1.** awake and knowing what is happening **2.** aware of something • *Are you conscious of the danger you are in?* **consciously** *adverb* **consciousness** *noun* being aware of what is happening

conscription *noun* conscription is a system of making people join the army for a time

consecutive *adjective* things are consecutive when they come one after another

consent *noun* consent is agreement or permission

consent *verb* to consent to something is to agree to it or permit it

consequence *noun* something which happens because of an event or action • *His injury was the consequence of an accident.* **consequently** *adverb* as a result

conservation *noun* conservation is keeping buildings and natural surroundings in a good state **conservationist** *noun* someone who takes an interest in conservation

Conservative *noun* someone who supports the Conservative Party, a British political party

conservative *adjective* **1.** a conservative person doesn't like change and wants things to stay the same **2.** a conservative estimate or guess is a careful or cautious one

conservatory *noun* conservatories a room built on to a house, with glass walls and a glass roof

conserve *verb* to conserve something is to keep it from being changed or spoilt

consider *verb* **1.** to consider something is to think carefully about it **2.** to consider something is also to believe it • *I consider myself to be a pretty good footballer.*

considerable *adjective* large or important • *The journey takes a considerable time.* **considerably** *adverb* very much • *Her new house is considerably larger.*

considerate *adjective* kind and thoughtful towards other people

consideration *noun* **1.** consideration is careful thought or attention **2.** a consideration is a serious thought or reason • *Money is a major consideration in this plan.*

considering *preposition* in view of • *The car goes well, considering its age.*

consist *verb* to consist of something is to be made from it • *The meal consisted of pasta and cheese.*

consistency *noun* consistencies **1.** consistency is being the same **2.** the consistency of a liquid is how thick it is

consistent *adjective* **1.** always the same, regular **2.** always acting in the same way **consistently** *adverb* in the same way, without changing • *He consistently misspells 'accommodation'.*

consolation *noun* consolation is comfort or sympathy given to someone

console *verb* to console someone is to give them comfort or sympathy

consonant *noun* A consonant is a letter that is not a vowel. The consonants in the English alphabet are b, c, d, f, g, h, j, k, l, m, n, p, q, r, s, t, v, w, x, y, z.

conspicuous *adjective* something conspicuous stands out and is easy to see or notice

conspiracy *noun* conspiracies a plot to do something bad or illegal **conspirator** *noun* someone who joins a conspiracy

constant *adjective* not changing; continual **constantly** *adverb* continually, all the time • *They are constantly complaining.*

constant *noun* (*in science and mathematics*) a number or quantity that does not change

constellation *noun* a group of stars that you can see in the sky at night

constipated *adjective* someone is constipated when they have difficulty getting rid of solid waste from their body **constipation** *noun* being constipated

constituency *noun* constituencies a district of the country that chooses its own Member of Parliament

constitute *verb* to constitute something is to form it or make it up • *50 states constitute the USA.*

constitution *noun* **1.** the set of principles or laws by which a country is governed **2.** a person's condition or state of health **constitutional** *adjective* to do with a constitution

construct *verb* to construct something is to build it

construction *noun* **1.** construction is the process of building **2.** a construction is something that someone has built

constructive *adjective* helpful and positive • *Their criticism was very constructive.*

consult *verb* to consult a person or book is to look for information or advice **consultation** *noun* a meeting with someone for information or advice

consultant *noun* **1.** a person who provides professional advice **2.** a senior hospital doctor

consume *verb* **1**. to consume food or drink is to eat or drink it **2**. to consume something is to use it up or destroy it • *The building was consumed by fire.*

consumer *noun* someone who buys goods or services

consumption *noun* the using up of food or fuel • *The consumption of oil has increased.*

contact *noun* **1**. contact is touching someone or something **2**. contact is also communication • *I've lost contact with my uncle.* **3**. a contact is a person to communicate with
contact *verb* to contact someone is to get in touch with them

contact lens *noun* a small plastic lens worn against the eyeball instead of glasses

contagious *adjective* (kon-**tay**-jus) you catch a contagious disease by having contact with people who are already infected with it

contain *verb* to contain something is to have it inside • *This book contains a great deal of information.*

container *noun* something that is designed to contain things

contaminate *verb* to contaminate something is to make it dirty or impure
contamination *noun* making something dirty or impure

contemplate *verb* **1**. to contemplate something is to look hard at it or think about it **2**. to contemplate doing something is to plan or intend to do it

contemporary *adjective* **1**. modern or up to date • *contemporary furniture* **2**. people or things are contemporary when they happen or exist during the same period of time • *Florence Nightingale was contemporary with Queen Victoria.*

contempt *noun* a feeling of strong disapproval when you despise someone or something **contemptible** *adjective* deserving contempt **contemptuous** *adjective* showing or feeling contempt

contend *verb* to contend is to struggle or compete **contender** *noun* someone who takes part in a competition

content[1] *noun* (**kon**-tent) **1**. the amount of a substance that there is in something • *Drink*

milk with a low fat content. **2**. the content of a book, magazine or piece of writing is what you read in it

content[2] *adjective* (kon-**tent**) happy and willing • *Are you content to stay behind?* **contentment** *noun* contentment is being happy

contented *adjective* (kon-**tent**-id) happy and satisfied • *After his big dinner he looked very contented.*

contents *plural noun* (**kon**-tents) **1**. the contents of a box or other container are what is inside it **2**. the contents of a book or magazine are the things you read in it

contest *noun* (**kon**-test) a competition

contest *verb* (kon-**test**) to contest something is to argue about it • *After her death, relatives contested her will.*

contestant *noun* (kon-**test**-ant) someone who takes part in a contest or competition

continent *noun* A continent is one of the main masses of land in the world. The continents are Africa, Antarctica, Asia, Australia, Europe, North America and South America **the Continent** the mainland of Europe from the pont of view of people living in Britain

continual *adjective* happening repeatedly • *I get fed up with his continual shouting.* **continually** *adverb* repeatedly, often

continue *verb* to continue something or to continue to do something, is to go on doing it **continuation** *noun* continuing something

continuous *adjective* going on all the time; without a break • *We could hear a continuous hum from the fridge.* **continuity** *noun* the process of going on without any breaks or changes **continuously** *adverb* all the time

contour *noun* **1**. the contour of something is its shape or outline **2**. a line on a map joining points that are the same height above sea level

contract *noun* (**kon**-trakt) a written legal agreement
contract *verb* (kon-**trakt**) **1**. to contract is to become smaller • *Heated metal contracts as it cools.* **2**. to contract an illness is to catch it • *She contracted pneumonia.*

contradict *verb* to contradict someone or something is to say they are wrong or untrue **contradiction** *noun* saying that someone or something is wrong or untrue **contradictory** *adjective* a contradictory statement says the opposite of what someone has just said

contrary *adjective* **1.** (kon-tra-ri) one thing is contrary to another when they are opposites or contradict one another • *Contrary to popular belief, Viking helmets didn't have horns* . **2.** (kon-**trair**-i) someone who is contrary is obstinate and difficult to deal with • *Mary, Mary, quite contrary.*

contrast *verb* (kon-**trahst**) **1.** to contrast two things is to show they are different **2.** one thing contrasts with another when it is clearly different
contrast *noun* (**kon**-trahst) a clear difference between things

contribute *verb* **1.** to contribute to something is to give money to help it **2.** to contribute to a result is to help cause it • *His tiredness contributed to the accident.* **contribution** *noun* money or help that someone gives towards something **contributor** *noun* someone who gives money or help

control *noun* **1.** control is the power to make someone or something do what you want **2.** the controls of a machine are the switches and levers that make it work **to be in control** is to have power or control over people or things
control *verb* **controlling, controlled** to control something or someone is to have power over what they do

controversial *adjective* a controversial action or statement is one that is likely to cause people to have strong opinions and disagree about it

controversy *noun* **controversies** (**kon**-tro-ver-si or kon-**trov**-er-si) a long argument or disagreement

conundrum *noun* a riddle

convalescent *adjective* recovering from an illness **convalescence** *noun* a period of recovery after an illness

convenience *noun* **1.** convenience is usefulness and comfort **2.** a convenience is something that is useful, such as central

heating **3.** a convenience is also a public lavatory

convenient *adjective* easy to use or reach

convent *noun* a group of buildings where nuns live and work

conventional *adjective* done in the accepted way; usual, traditional **conventionally** *adverb* in a conventional way, traditionally

converge *verb* to converge is to come together from different directions • *The two roads converge at the pub.* • *Thousands of fans converged on the football ground.*

conversation *noun* when you talk to someone for a while **conversational** *adjective* to do with conversation, like conversation • *Use a conversational style of writing.*

conversion *noun* changing or converting something

convert *verb* (kon-**vert**) **1.** to convert something is to change it so it is suitable for a new purpose **2.** to convert someone is to persuade them to change their religion or beliefs
convert *noun* (**kon**-vert) someone who has changed their beliefs

convex *adjective* A convex surface is curved like the outside of a circle or ball. The opposite of **concave**.

convey *verb* **1.** to convey someone or something is to take them somewhere **2.** to convey a message or idea is to get someone to understand it

convict *noun* (**kon**-vikt) a criminal in a prison
convict *verb* (kon-**vikt**) to convict someone of a crime is to decide at their trial that they are guilty of it and punish them

conviction *noun* **1.** being convicted of a crime **2.** being convinced of something; a strong opinion

convince *verb* to persuade someone that something is true or right

convoy *noun* a group of ships or vehicles travelling together

cook *verb* to cook food is to make it ready to eat by heating it
cook *noun* someone who cooks, especially as their job

cooker *noun* a device with an oven and hotplates for cooking food

cookery *noun* the art or skill of cooking food

cool *adjective* **1**. not very warm; fairly cold **2**. a cool person is calm and not easily excited **3**. *(informal)* good or fashionable • *He looks cool in those glasses.* **coolly** *adverb* calmly

cool *verb* **1**. to cool something is to make it cool **2**. to cool is to become cool

coop *noun* a cage for poultry

cooperate *verb* (koh-**op**-er-ayt) to cooperate with people is to work helpfully with them **cooperation** *noun* when people work together and help one another **cooperative** *adjective* someone who is cooperative is helpful and willing to do what people ask them

coordinate *verb* (koh-**or**-din-ayt) to coordinate people or things is to get them to work well together **coordination** *noun* coordination is your ability to control and use the different parts of your body well • *Tennis players have good hand to eye coordination.*

cope *verb* to cope with something awkward or difficult is to deal with it successfully

copper *noun* **1**. copper is a reddish-brown metal used for making wire and pipes **2**. a copper is a coin made of copper or bronze

copy *noun* **copies 1**. something made to look exactly like something else **2**. something written out a second time **3**. one example of a newspaper, magazine or book that is made in large numbers • *We each have a copy of 'Alice in Wonderland'.*

copy *verb* **copies**, **copying**, **copied 1**. to copy something is to make a copy of it • *Copy and save the document to the C drive.* **2**. to copy someone is to do the same as them **copier** *noun* a machine for copying pages

coral *noun* coral is a hard substance made of the skeletons of tiny sea creatures

cord *noun* a cord is a piece of thin rope

cordial *noun* a sweet drink

corduroy *noun* (**kor**-der-oi) thick cotton cloth with ridges along it

core *noun* the part in the middle of something

cork *noun* **1**. cork is the lightweight bark of a kind of oak tree **2**. a cork is a piece of this bark used to close a bottle

corkscrew *noun* **1**. a device for removing corks from bottles **2**. a spiral

cormorant *noun* a large black seabird

corn[1] *noun* grain • *a field of corn*

corn[2] *noun* a small, hard lump on your toe or foot

corner *noun* **1**. the point where two lines, roads or walls meet **2**. a kick from the corner of a football field; a hit from the corner of a hockey field

corner *verb* **1**. to corner someone is to trap them • *The police cornered the escaped prisoner.* **2**. to corner is to go round a corner • *The car cornered slowly and accelerated up the road.*

cornet *noun* **1**. a long cone-shaped biscuit open at the top for ice cream **2**. a musical instrument like a trumpet

cornflakes *plural noun* toasted maize flakes eaten for breakfast

cornflour *noun* fine flour used for making puddings

corny *adjective* **cornier**, **corniest** *(informal)* a corny joke is one that is silly and repeated too often to still be funny

coronation *noun* the ceremony of crowning a king or queen

coroner *noun* an official who holds an inquiry into the cause of an unnatural death

corporal *noun* a soldier just below sergeant in rank

corporation *noun* a large company or a group of companies acting together as one company

corps *noun* **corps** (kor) **1**. a large unit of soldiers **2**. a special army unit • *the Medical Corps*

corpse *noun* a dead body

correct *adjective* **1**. true or accurate; without any mistakes • *Your answers are all correct.* **2**. proper, suitable • *Is that the correct way to talk to your parents?* **correctly** *adverb* to do something correctly is to do it the right way and without any mistakes

correct *verb* to correct a piece of work is to mark the mistakes in it or to put them right

correction *noun* 1. correction is correcting something 2. a correction is a change made to something in order to make it right

correspond *verb* 1. to correspond with something is to agree with it or match it • *Your story corresponds with what I heard.* 2. to correspond with someone is to exchange letters with them

correspondence *noun* 1. similarity or agreement 2. letters or writing letters

correspondent *noun* 1. someone who writes letters 2. a journalist who sends reports to a newspaper or TV or radio station

corridor *noun* a long narrow passage from which doors open into rooms or compartments

corrode *verb* to corrode is to wear away by rust or chemical action **corrosion** *noun* corrosion is the process of corroding **corrosive** *adjective* a corrosive substance is likely to corrode

corrugated *adjective* shaped into folds or ridges • *The roof was made of corrugated iron.*

corrupt *adjective* a corrupt person is dishonest in carrying out their responsibilities or duties, for example by taking bribes

corrupt *verb* to corrupt someone is to make them dishonest, especially when they have important responsibilities

corruption *noun* corruption is dishonest behaviour by people who are in authority or have important responsibilities

cosmetics *plural noun* substances like lipstick and face powder, for making the skin or hair look attractive

cosmic *adjective* (**koz**-mik) to do with the universe

cost *verb* to cost a certain amount is to have that amount as its price • *The tickets cost £15.*

cost *noun* what you have to spend to do or get something

costly *adjective* **costlier, costliest** expensive

costume *noun* clothes, especially for a particular purpose or of a particular period

cosy *adjective* **cosier, cosiest** warm and comfortable

cot *noun* a baby's bed with high sides

cottage *noun* a small house in the country

cottage cheese *noun* soft white cheese made from skimmed milk

cotton *noun* 1. a soft white substance covering the seeds of a tropical plant 2. thread or cloth made from this substance

couch *noun* a long soft seat or sofa

cough *verb* (kof) to cough is to push air suddenly out of your lungs with a harsh noise **cough** *noun* 1. the action or sound of coughing 2. an illness which makes you cough a lot

could past tense of can[1]

council *noun* a group of people who run a city or town

councillor *noun* a member of a council

counsellor *noun* someone who gives advice, especially as their job

count[1] *verb* 1. to count is to use numbers to find out how many people or things there are in a place 2. to count or count out is to say numbers in their proper order 3. to count someone or something is to include them in a total • *There are 30 in the class, counting the teacher.* 4. to count is to have a particular value or importance • *Playing well counts a lot even if you lose.* **to count on someone** or **something** is to rely on them

count[1] *noun* the total reached by counting

count[2] *noun* a foreign nobleman

countdown *noun* a counting down to 0, especially before launching a rocket

counter *noun* 1. a long table where customers are served in a shop or cafe 2. a small plastic disc used in board games

counterfeit *adjective* (**kown**-ter-fit) made as a copy of something real, to deceive or swindle people • *counterfeit £20 notes*

countess *noun* the wife or widow of a count or earl; a female earl

countless *adjective* too many to count; very many

country *noun* countries **1.** a country is a part of the world where a particular nation of people lives **2.** the country is the countryside

countryside *noun* an area with fields, woods and villages, away from towns

county *noun* counties one of the areas that a country is divided into, for example Kent in England, Fife in Scotland and Powys in Wales

couple *noun* a couple is two people or things

coupling *noun* a link or fastening, especially for vehicles

coupon *noun* a piece of paper that gives you the right to receive or do something

courage *noun* the ability to be brave and overcome your fear

courageous *adjective* ready to face danger or pain

courgette *noun* a kind of vegetable like a small marrow

course *noun* **1.** the direction in which something moves along • *The ship's course was to the west.* **2.** a series of lessons or exercises in learning something • *My Mum's starting a cookery course at last.* **3.** a part of a meal, such as the meat course or the pudding course **4.** a racecourse or golf course of course naturally; certainly • *'Will you help us?' 'Of course!'*

court *noun* **1.** a place where legal trials take place; a lawcourt **2.** an area marked out for ball games like tennis or netball **3.** the place where a king or queen lives **4.** the people who are usually at a king's or queen's court
court *verb* to court someone is to try to win their love or support

courteous *adjective* (**ker**-ti-us) friendly and polite towards other people
courteously *adverb* courtesy *noun* courtesy is polite behaviour towards other people

court martial *noun* a trial of a soldier who is accused of breaking a military law

courtship *noun* courting someone

courtyard *noun* a paved area surrounded by walls or buildings

cousin *noun* a son or daughter of your uncle or aunt

cove *noun* a small bay

cover *verb* **1.** to cover something is to put something else over it to hide or protect it **2.** to cover a distance is to travel over it • *We managed to cover ten miles a day.* **3.** to cover a subject is to deal with it or include it • *This book covers everything you need to know about dinosaurs.* to cover something up is to make sure no one knows about something wrong or illegal
cover *noun* **1.** a cover is something used for covering something else; a lid or wrapper **2.** cover is a place where someone can hide or take shelter

coverage *noun* the amount of time or space given to reporting an event on radio, on television or in a newspaper or broadcast

cow *noun* a large female animal kept by farmers for its milk and beef

coward *noun* someone who has no courage and runs away from danger and difficulties cowardice *noun* being a coward cowardly *adjective* behaving like a coward

cowboy *noun* a man who looks after the cattle on a large farm in America, usually while riding a horse

coy *adjective* pretending to be shy or modest coyly *adverb*

crab *noun* a shellfish with a pair of pincers and four pairs of legs

crack *noun* **1.** a line on the surface of something where it has broken but not come completely apart; a narrow gap • *There's a crack in this cup.* **2.** a sudden sharp noise • *We heard a crack just before the branch fell down.*
crack *verb* **1.** to crack something is to make a crack in it **2.** something cracks when it splits without breaking • *The plate has cracked.* **3.** to crack is to make a sudden sharp noise

cracker *noun* **1.** a decorated paper tube with a small gift inside it, which bangs when two people pull it apart **2.** a thin crisp biscuit

cradle *noun* a cot for a baby

craft *noun* **1.** a craft is an activity which involves using your hands skilfully to make something **2.** a boat

craftsman or **craftswoman** *noun* craftsmen or craftswomen someone who is skilled at making things with their hands craftsmanship *noun* the skill of a craftsman or craftswoman

crafty *adjective* craftier, craftiest cunning and clever craftily *adverb* craftiness *noun*

crag *noun* a steep piece of rough rock craggy *adjective* steep and rocky

cram *verb* cramming, crammed **1.** to cram things is to force them into a small space **2.** to cram is to study very hard for an examination

cramp *noun* pain caused by a muscle tightening suddenly

cramped *adjective* in a space that is too small or tight • *We felt very cramped sleeping three in the same room.*

crane *noun* **1.** a machine for lifting and moving heavy objects **2.** a large bird with long legs and neck

crane *verb* to crane your neck is to stretch it so that you can see something

crane-fly *noun* crane-flies an insect with long thin legs

crank *noun* **1.** an L-shaped rod used to turn or control something **2.** a person with weird or unusual ideas

crank *verb* to crank an engine is to turn it by using a crank

cranny *noun* crannies a crevice; a narrow hole or space

crash *noun* **1.** the loud noise of something falling or breaking **2.** a collision between road vehicles

crash *verb* **1.** to crash is to collide or fall violently **2.** to crash a vehicle is to have a crash while driving it

crash helmet *noun* a padded helmet worn by racing drivers and motorcyclists

crate *noun* a container in which goods are transported

crater *noun* **1.** the mouth of a volcano **2.** a hole in the ground made by a bomb

crave *verb* to crave something is to want it very badly

crawl *verb* **1.** to crawl is to move along on your hands and knees **2.** to crawl is also to move slowly in a vehicle **3.** to be crawling with something unpleasant is to be full of it or covered in it • *This room's crawling with cockroaches.*

crawl *noun* **1.** a crawling movement **2.** a powerful swimming stroke in which you bring each arm over your head in turn

crayon *noun* a coloured pencil for drawing or writing

craze *noun* a brief enthusiasm or fashion for something

crazy *adjective* crazier, craziest mad or weird crazily *adverb* craziness *noun*

creak *noun* a sound like the noise made by a stiff door opening

creak *verb* to make a creak creaky *adjective* old and creaking

cream *noun* **1.** the rich fatty part of milk **2.** a yellowish-white colour **3.** something that looks like cream, for example face cream creamy *adjective* smooth and thick like cream

crease *noun* **1.** a line made in something by folding or pressing it **2.** a line on a cricket pitch where the batsman stands

crease *verb* to crease something is to make a crease in it

create *verb* to create something is to make it exist **creation** *noun* creating something **creator** *noun* someone who creates something

creative *adjective* showing imagination and thought as well as skill • *The older children have started some creative writing.* **creativity** *noun* the ability to use the imagination to create things

creature *noun* a living animal or person

crèche *noun* (kresh) a place where babies are looked after while their parents are at work

credible *adjective* able to be believed; trustworthy **credibility** *noun* being credible **credibly** *adverb*

credit *noun* **1.** praise or approval • *You have to give her credit for trying.* **2.** someone who brings honour or approval • *He is a credit to his family.* **3.** a system of allowing someone to pay for something later on • *Do you want cash now or can I have it on credit?* **4.** an amount of money in an account at a bank or building society **credits** the list of people who have produced a film, television programme, etc.

credit card *noun* a card allowing someone to buy goods and pay for them later

creep *verb* **creeping, crept** to creep is to move forward quietly or slowly **to creep up on someone** is to go up to them quietly from behind

creeper *noun* a plant that grows close to the ground or up walls

creepy *adjective* **creepier, creepiest** *(informal)* weird and slightly frightening

cremate *verb* to cremate a dead body is to burn it into fine ashes instead of burying it **cremation** *noun* the cremating of a dead body

crematorium *noun* **crematoria** (krem-a-**tor**-i-um) a place where dead bodies are cremated

crescent *noun* **1.** a narrow curved shape, pointed at both ends, like a new moon **2.** a curved street

cress *noun* a green plant used in salads and sandwiches

crest *noun* **1.** a tuft of hair, feathers or skin on an animal's head **2.** the top of a hill or wave **3.** a badge or emblem

crevasse *noun* a deep crack in a glacier

crevice *noun* a crack in rock or in a wall

crew *noun* the people who work on a ship or aircraft

crib *noun* a baby's cot
crib *verb* **cribbing, cribbed** to crib someone else's work is to copy it

cricket[1] *noun* a game played outdoors by two teams with a ball, two bats and two wickets **cricketer** *noun* someone who plays cricket

cricket[2] *noun* an insect like a grasshopper

crime *noun* an act that breaks the law

criminal *noun* someone who has committed one or more crimes
criminal *adjective* to do with crime or criminals

crimson *noun* and *adjective* a dark red colour

crinkle *verb* to crinkle something is to crease or wrinkle it **crinkly** *adjective* full of creases, wrinkled

cripple *verb* to cripple someone is to make them unable to walk properly

crisis *noun* **crises** (**kry**-sis) a difficult or dangerous time or situation

crisp *adjective* **1.** very dry so that it breaks easily **2.** firm and fresh • *I'd like a nice crisp apple.* **3.** cold and frosty • *crisp winter mornings*
crisp *noun* a thin fried slice of potato, sold in packets

criss-cross *adjective, adverb* with crossing lines

critic *noun* **1.** a person who criticizes someone or something **2.** someone who gives opinions on books, plays, films, music or other performances

a
b
c
d
e
f
g
h
i
j
k
l
m
n
o
p
q
r
s
t
u
v
w
x
y
z

critical *adjective* **1**. criticizing **2**. to do with critics or criticism **3**. serious, reaching a crisis
critically *adverb* in a critical way; seriously

criticism *noun* (**krit**-i-si-zum) an opinion or judgement about something, usually pointing out its faults

criticize *verb* (**krit**-i-syz) to criticize something or someone is to give an opinion pointing out their faults This word can also be spelled **criticise**.

croak *noun* a deep sound, like a frog makes
croak *verb* to make a croak

crochet *noun* (**kroh**-shay) a kind of needlework done with a hooked needle

crockery *noun* dishes, plates and cups and saucers used for eating

crocodile *noun* a large reptile living in hot countries, with a thick skin, long tail and huge jaws

croissant *noun* (**krwa**-sahn) a curved roll of rich pastry, usually eaten for breakfast

crook *noun* (*informal*) someone who cheats or robs people; a criminal

crooked *adjective* (**kruuk**-id) **1**. bent or twisted **2**. (*informal*) dishonest or criminal

crop *noun* **1**. something grown for food, especially in a field • *a crop of wheat* **2**. a riding whip with a loop instead of a lash
crop *verb* **cropping, cropped** to crop something is to cut or bite the top off it • *They could see sheep in a field, cropping the grass.* **to crop up** is to happen or appear unexpectedly

cross *noun* **1**. a mark or shape like + or x **2**. an upright post with another post across it, used in ancient times for crucifixions **3**. an animal produced by mixing one breed with another • *A mule is a cross between a donkey and a horse.* **the Cross** the cross on which Christ was crucified, used as a symbol of Christianity
cross *verb* **1**. to cross something is to go across it • *She crossed the road to meet him.* • *A bit further on the road crossed a river.* **2**. to cross your fingers or legs is to put one over the other **to cross something out** is to draw a line across something because it is unwanted or wrong
cross *adjective* angry or bad-tempered

crossbar *noun* a horizontal bar between two upright bars

crossbow *noun* a kind of bow used for shooting arrows, held like a gun and fired by pulling a trigger

cross-country *noun* a running race through fields and country

crossing *noun* a place where people can cross a road or railway

crossroads *noun* a place where two or more roads cross one another

cross-section *noun* a drawing of something as if it has been cut through

crossword *noun* a puzzle with blank squares in which you put the letters of words worked out from clues

crotchet *noun* (**kroch**-it) a musical note equal to half a minim, written ♩

crouch *verb* to crouch is to lower your body, with your arms and legs bent

crow *noun* a large black bird
crow *verb* **1**. to make a noise like a cock **2**. to boast; to be proudly triumphant

crowbar *noun* an iron bar used as a lever

crowd *noun* a large number of people in one place
crowd *verb* to crowd or crowd round is to form a crowd

crowded *adjective* having too many people or things

crown *noun* **1**. a crown is an ornamental headdress worn by a king or queen **2**. the crown is the king or queen of a country

• *This land belongs to the crown.* **3.** the top of something, such as a hill or a person's head

crown *verb* **1.** to crown someone is to make them king or queen **2.** to crown something is to form the top of it

crucial *adjective* (**kroo**-shal) extremely important

crucifix *noun* a model of Christ on the Cross

crucify *verb* crucifies, crucifying, crucified to crucify someone is to execute them by fixing their hands and feet to a cross and leaving them to die **crucifixion** *noun* the execution of someone by crucifying them

crude *adjective* **1.** natural; not purified • *crude oil* **2.** rough and simple • *They made crude stone tools.*

cruel *adjective* crueller, cruellest causing pain and suffering to others • *They were ruled by a cruel tyrant.* **cruelly** *adverb* **cruelty** *noun* cruel acts or treatment

cruise *noun* a holiday on a ship, usually visiting different places

cruise *verb* **1.** to cruise is to travel at a gentle speed **2.** to cruise is also to have a cruise on a ship

crumb *noun* a tiny piece of bread or cake

crumble *verb* **1.** to crumble something is to break it into small pieces **2.** to crumble is to be broken into small pieces • *The cliff was slowly crumbling into the sea.* **crumbly** *adjective* soft and likely to crumble

crumpet *noun* a soft flat cake that you toast

crumple *verb* **1.** to crumple something is to make it creased **2.** to crumple is to become creased

crunch *noun* the noise made by chewing hard food or walking on gravel

crunch *verb* to crunch something is to chew or crush it with a crunch **crunchy** *adjective* making a crunching sound

crusade *noun* **1.** a campaign against something that you think is bad **2.** a military expedition to Palestine made by Christians in the Middle Ages **crusader** *noun* someone who takes part in a crusade

crush *verb* **1.** to crush something is to press it so that it gets broken or damaged **2.** to crush an enemy is to defeat them completely

crush *noun* **1.** a crowd; a crowded place **2.** *(informal)* a sudden liking you have for someone

crust *noun* **1.** the hard outside part of something, especially of a loaf **2.** the rocky outer part of a planet

crustacean *noun* (krus-**tay**-shan) a shellfish

crutch *noun* a stick that fits under the arm, used as a support in walking

cry *verb* cries, crying, cried **1.** to cry is to shout **2.** to cry is also to let tears fall from your eyes

cry *noun* cries **1.** a loud shout **2.** a period of weeping

crypt *noun* a large room underneath a church

crystal *noun* **1.** a clear mineral rather like glass **2.** a small solid piece of a substance such as snow and ice

crystallize *verb* to crystallize is to form into crystals This word can also be spelled **crystallise**.

cub[1] *noun* a young animal, especially a lion, tiger, fox or bear

cub[2] *noun* a junior Scout

cube *noun* **1.** an object that has six square sides, like a box or dice **2.** the result of multiplying something by itself twice • *The cube of 3 is 3 x 3 x 3 = 27.*

cube verb **1.** to cube a number is to multiply it by itself twice • *4 cubed is 4 x 4 x 4 = 64.* **2.** to cube something is to cut it into small cubes

cube root noun a number that gives another number if it is multiplied by itself twice • *2 is the cube root of 8.*

cubic adjective a cubic metre or foot is the volume of a cube with sides that are one metre or foot long

cubicle noun a small division of a room

cuckoo noun a bird that makes a sound like 'cuck-oo' and lays its eggs in other birds' nests

cucumber noun a long green vegetable, eaten raw

cud noun half-digested food that a cow brings back from its first stomach to chew again

cuddle verb to cuddle someone is to put your arms closely round them and squeeze them in a loving way **cuddly** adjective a cuddly person is nice to cuddle

cue[1] noun a word or signal that tells an actor when to start speaking or come on the stage

cue[2] noun a long stick used to strike the ball in billiards or snooker

cuff noun the end of a sleeve that fits round your wrist
cuff verb to cuff someone is to hit them with the hand

cul-de-sac noun a street that is closed at one end

culprit noun someone who is to blame for something

cultivate verb to cultivate land is to grow crops on it **cultivation** noun

culture noun **1.** culture is the development of the mind by education and learning **2.** a culture is the customs and traditions of a people • *They were studying Greek culture.* **cultural** adjective to do with culture **cultured** adjective well educated and knowledgeable

cunning adjective clever at deceiving people

cup noun **1.** a small container with a handle, from which you drink liquid **2.** a prize in the form of a silver cup, usually with two handles
cup verb **cupping, cupped** to cup your hands is to form them into the shape of a cup

cupboard noun (**kub**-erd) a piece of furniture with a door, for storing things

curator noun (kewr-**ay**-ter) someone in charge of a museum or art gallery

curb verb to curb a feeling is to hold it back or hide it

curd noun a thick substance formed when milk turns sour

curdle verb to curdle is to turn sour and form into curds

cure verb **1.** to cure someone who is ill is to make them better **2.** to cure something bad is to stop it **3.** to cure food is to treat it so as to preserve it • *Fish can be cured in smoke.*
cure noun something that cures a person or thing • *They are still trying to find a cure for cancer.*

curfew noun a time or signal after which people must stay indoors until the next day

curiosity noun **curiosities** curiosity is being curious

curious adjective **1.** wanting to find out about things **2.** strange or unusual **curiously** adverb

curl noun a curve or coil, especially of hair

curl *verb* to curl is to form into curls **to curl up** is to sit or lie with your knees drawn up

curly *adjective* **curlier, curliest** full of curls

currant *noun* **1.** a small black fruit made from dried grapes **2.** a small juicy berry

currency *noun* **currencies** the money that is in use in a country • *The British currency is the pound.*

current *noun* **1.** a flow of water or air **2.** a flow of electricity through a wire

current *adjective* happening or used now **currently** *adverb* now, at the moment • *The admission charge is currently £10.*

curriculum *noun* the subjects that you study in a school

curry *noun* **curries** food cooked with spices that make it taste hot

curse *noun* **1.** a call or prayer for someone to be harmed or killed **2.** an angry word or words

curse *verb* to curse someone is to use a curse against them

cursor *noun* a flashing signal showing your position on a computer screen

curtain *noun* a piece of material hung at a window or door or at the front of a stage

curtsy *noun* **curtsies** a greeting made by bending the knees, done by women as a mark of respect

curtsy *verb* **curtsies, curtsying, curtsied** to curtsy is to make a curtsy

curve *noun* a line that bends smoothly

curve *verb* to curve is to bend smoothly

cushion *noun* a fabric cover filled with soft material so that it is comfortable to sit on or rest against

custard *noun* a sweet yellow sauce eaten with puddings

custom *noun* **1.** the usual way of doing things • *It is the custom to go on holiday in the summer.* **2.** regular business from customers • *That rude man at the corner shop won't get my custom any more.* **customs** are the group of officials at a port or airport whose job is to check what goods people are bringing into the country

customary *adjective* something that is customary is usual or normal

customer *noun* someone who uses a shop, bank or business

cut *verb* **cutting, cut** **1.** to cut something is to divide it using a knife or scissors **2.** to cut yourself is make a slit in a part of your body with a knife or something sharp **3.** to cut hair or grass is to make it shorter **4.** to cut something like prices or taxes is to reduce them **to cut someone off** is to interrupt them • *She cut me off before I could finish my sentence.* **to cut something out** (*informal*) is to stop doing it • *Cut out the talking!*

cut *noun* **1.** an act of cutting; the result of cutting • *Your hair could do with a cut.* **2.** a small wound caused by something sharp

cute *adjective* (*informal*) attractive in a quaint or simple way

cutlass *noun* a short sword with a wide curved blade

cutlery *noun* knives, forks and spoons used for eating

cut-out *noun* a design or shape cut out of paper or cardboard

cutting *noun* **1.** something cut from a newspaper or magazine **2.** a piece cut off a plant to grow as a new plant **3.** a deep passage cut through high ground for a railway or road

cycle *noun* **1.** a bicycle **2.** a series of events that are regularly repeated • *Rainfall is part of the water cycle.*

cycle *verb* to cycle is to ride a bicycle **cyclist** *noun* someone who rides a bicycle

cyclone *noun* a strong wind rotating round a calm central area

cygnet *noun* (**sig**-nit) a young swan

cylinder *noun* **1.** an object with straight sides and circular ends **2.** part of an engine in which a piston moves

cylindrical *adjective* shaped like a cylinder

cymbal *noun* a cymbal is a round, slightly hollowed metal plate that you hit to make a ringing sound in music

cynical *adjective* (**sin**-ik-al) thinking that nothing is good or worthwhile **cynic** *noun* someone who doubts that anything is good or worthwhile **cynicism** *noun* being cynical

Only four words in English end with -d**ous**: tremen**dous**, horren**dous**, stupen**dous** and hazar**dous**.

dab *noun* a gentle touch with something soft
dab *verb* dabbing, dabbed to dab something is to touch it gently with something soft
• *I dabbed my eyes with a handkerchief.*

dad or **daddy** *noun* daddies *(informal)* father

daddy-long-legs *noun* a crane-fly

daffodil *noun* a yellow flower that grows from a bulb

daft *adjective* silly or stupid

dagger *noun* a pointed knife with two sharp edges, used as a weapon

daily *adjective, adverb* happening every day

dainty *adjective* daintier, daintiest small and delicate

dairy *noun* dairies a place where milk, butter, cream and cheese are made or sold

daisy *noun* daisies a small flower with white petals and a yellow centre

dale *noun* a valley

Dalmatian *noun* a large dog that is white with black or brown spots

dam *noun* a wall built across a river to hold the water back
dam *verb* damming, dammed to dam a river is to build a dam across it

damage *verb* to damage something is to injure or harm it
damage *noun* damage is injury or harm

damn *verb* to damn something is to say it is bad or wrong

damp *adjective* slightly wet; not quite dry
damp *noun* wetness in the air or on something

dampen *verb* to dampen something is to make it damp

dance *verb* to dance is to move about in time to music
dance *noun* **1.** a piece of music or set of movements for dancing **2.** a party or gathering where people dance **dancer** *noun* someone who dances

dandelion *noun* a yellow wild flower with jagged leaves

The word **dandelion** comes from the French words *dent-de-lion* meaning 'lion's tooth', because of the leaves having a jagged shape.

dandruff *noun* dandruff is small white flakes of dead skin in a person's hair

danger *noun* something that is dangerous

dangerous *adjective* likely to harm you

dangle *verb* to dangle is to swing or hang down loosely

dappled *adjective* marked with patches of different colours

dare *verb* **1.** to dare to do something is to be brave or bold enough to do it **2.** to dare someone to do something is to challenge them to do it
dare *noun (informal)* a challenge to do something risky

daredevil *noun* a person who enjoys doing dangerous things

daring *adjective* bold or brave

dark *adjective* **1.** with little or no light **2.** deep and rich in colour • *a dark green coat*
dark *noun* **1.** dark or the dark is when there is no light • *Cats can see in the dark.* **2.** dark is also the time when it becomes dark just after sunset • *Be home before dark.* **darkness** *noun* darkness is when there is no light

darken *verb* **1.** to darken something is to make it dark **2.** to darken is to become dark • *The sky suddenly darkened.*

darling *noun* someone who is loved very much

darn *verb* to darn a hole is to mend it by sewing across it

dart *noun* an object with a sharp point that you throw at a target called a dartboard in the game of **darts**

dash *noun* **1.** a quick rush or a hurry • *They made a dash for the door.* **2.** a dash of something is a small amount of it **3.** a short line (–) used in writing or printing
dash *verb* to dash somewhere is to rush there

dashboard *noun* a panel with dials and controls in front of the driver of a car

data *noun* data is pieces of information

database *noun* a store of information held in a computer

date¹ *noun* **1.** the day of the month or the year, when something happens or happened **2.** an appointment to go out with someone
date¹ *verb* **1.** to date something that happened is to give it a date **2.** to date from a time is to have existed from then • *The church dates from the 15th century.* **3.** to date is also to seem old-fashioned • *Some fashions date very quickly.*

date² *noun* a sweet brown fruit that grows on a palm tree

daughter *noun* a girl or woman who is someone's child

dawdle *verb* to dawdle is to walk or do something too slowly

dawn *noun* the time of the day when the sun rises
dawn *verb* **1.** to dawn is to begin to become light in the morning **2.** something dawns on you when you begin to realize it

day *noun* **1.** the 24 hours between midnight and the next midnight **2.** the light part of the day **3.** a period in time • *Write about what it was like in Queen Victoria's day.*

daybreak *noun* the first light of day; dawn

daydream *verb* to daydream is to think about nice things that you would like to happen

daylight *noun* **1.** the light of day **2.** dawn • *They left before daylight.*

daze *noun* to be in a daze is to be unable to think or see clearly

dazed *adjective* someone is dazed when they can't think or see clearly

dazzle *verb* a light dazzles you when it shines so brightly in your eyes that you are blinded for a moment

dead *adjective* **1.** no longer alive **2.** no longer working or active • *The phone went dead.* **3.** a dead place is not at all lively • *This town is dead at the weekend.*

deaden *verb* to deaden pain or noise is to make it weaker

dead end *noun* a road or passage that is closed at one end

dead heat *noun* a race in which two or more winners finish exactly together

deadline *noun* the time by which you must finish doing something

deadly *adjective* **deadlier, deadliest** likely to kill • *a deadly poison*

deaf *adjective* unable to hear **deafness** *noun* being deaf

deafen *verb* to be deafening is to be very loud

deal *verb* **dealing, dealt 1.** to deal in something is to buy and sell it • *He deals in scrap metal.* **2.** to deal playing cards is to give them to players in a card game **to deal with someone** or **something** is to spend time doing what needs to be done • *I'll deal with you later.* **to deal with something** is to be about it • *This book deals with cacti.*

deal *noun* **1.** an agreement or bargain **2.** someone's turn to give out playing cards • *Whose deal is it?* **a good deal** or **a great deal** a large amount

dealer *noun* **1.** someone who buys and sells things **2.** the person dealing at cards

dear *adjective* **1.** loved very much **2.** you use dear as the usual way of beginning a letter • *Dear Mary* **3.** expensive

death *noun* dying; the end of life

debate *noun* a formal discussion about a subject

debate *verb* to debate is to discuss something

debris *noun* (**deb**-ree) debris is pieces of something that are left after it has been destroyed

debt *noun* (det) something that someone owes **to be in debt** is to owe money

début *noun* (**day**-bew or **day**-boo) someone's first public appearance as a performer

decade *noun* a period of ten years

decay *verb* to decay is to rot or go bad

decay *noun* decay is going bad or rotting

deceased *adjective* (di-**seest**) a formal word for dead

deceit *noun* (di-**seet**) deceit is telling lies or doing something dishonest **deceitful** *adjective* someone who is deceitful tells lies or does something dishonest

deceive *verb* (di-**seev**) to deceive someone is to make them believe something that is not true

December *noun* the last month of the year

The word **December** comes from the Latin word *decem* meaning 'ten', because it was the tenth month in the Roman calendar.

decent *adjective* **1.** respectable and honest **2.** of good enough quality • *Was it a decent film?* **decency** *noun* respectable and honest behaviour **decently** *adverb* in a respectable and honest way

deception *noun* deception is making someone believe something that is not true

deceptive *adjective* not what it seems to be • *The sunshine was deceptive and the wind made it very cold.*

decibel *noun* a unit for measuring how loud a sound is

decide *verb* **1.** to decide something is to make up your mind about it or make a choice **2.** to decide a contest or argument is to settle it

deciduous *adjective* a deciduous tree loses its leaves in autumn

decimal *adjective* a decimal system uses tens or tenths to count things

decimal *noun* a fraction with tenths shown as numbers after a dot (¼ is 0.25; 1½ is 1.5)

decimal point *noun* the dot in a decimal fraction

decipher *verb* (di-**sy**-fer) to decipher writing is to work out what it means when it is in code or difficult to read

decision *noun* a decision is what someone has decided

decisive *adjective* **1.** ending or deciding something important • *The decisive battle of the war was fought here.* **2.** a decisive person decides things quickly and firmly **decisively** *adverb*

deck *noun* a floor on a ship or bus

deckchair *noun* a folding chair with a seat of canvas or plastic material

declaration *noun* an official or public statement

declare *verb* to declare something is to say it clearly and openly **to declare war** is to announce a state of war with another country

decline *verb* **1.** to decline is to become weaker or smaller **2.** to decline an offer is to refuse it politely

decode *verb* to decode something written in code is to work out its meaning

decompose *verb* to decompose is to decay or rot **decomposition** *noun* when something decays or rots

decorate *verb* **1.** to decorate something is to make it look more beautiful or colourful **2.** to decorate a room or building is to put fresh paint or paper on the walls **decorative** *adjective* colourful and pretty

decoration *noun* **1.** decorations are the paint, wallpaper and ornaments that make a place look more attractive **2.** decoration is making something look more attractive or colourful

decorator *noun* a person whose job is to paint rooms and buildings and to put up wallpaper

decoy *noun* (**dee**-koi or di-**koi**) something used to tempt a person or animal into a trap

decrease *verb* (di-**kreess**) **1.** to decrease something is to make it smaller or less **2.** to decrease is to become smaller or less

decrease *noun* (**dee**-kreess) the amount by which something decreases

decree *noun* an official order or decision

decree *verb* to decree something is to give an official order that it must happen

decrepit *adjective* (dik-**rep**-it) old and weak

dedicate *verb* **1.** to dedicate yourself or your life to something is to spend all your time doing it • *She dedicated her life to nursing.* **2.** to dedicate a book to someone is to name them at the beginning, as a sign of friendship or thanks

dedication *noun* **1.** dedication is hard work and effort **2.** a dedication is a message at the beginning of a book in which you name someone as a sign of friendship or thanks

deduce *verb* to deduce a fact or answer is to work it out from what you already know is true • *She deduced from my smile that I had won the prize.*

deduct *verb* to deduct an amount is to subtract it from a total

deduction *noun* **1.** something that you work out by reasoning **2.** an amount taken away from a total

deed *noun* **1.** something that someone has done **2.** a legal document that shows who owns something

deep *adjective* **1.** going down or back a long way from the top or front **2.** measured from top to bottom or from front to back • *The hole was two metres deep.* **3.** intense or strong • *The room was painted a deep blue.* **4.** a deep voice is very low in pitch **deeply** *adverb* very, extremely • *She was deeply upset.*

deepen *verb* to deepen is to become deeper • *The pool deepened to 2 metres halfway along.*

deer *noun* deer A deer is a fast-running, graceful animal. The male has antlers.

defeat *verb* to defeat someone is to beat them in a game or battle

defeat *noun* **1.** defeat is losing a game or battle **2.** a defeat is a lost game or battle

defect *noun* (**dee**-fekt) a flaw or weakness

defect *verb* (di-**fekt**) to defect is to desert a country or cause and join the other side **defection** *noun* **defector** *noun* someone who defects

defective *adjective* something is defective when it has flaws or faults or doesn't work properly

defence *noun* **1.** something that protects you • *High walls were built around the city as a defence against enemy attacks.* **2.** protecting yourself or a place from an attack or from criticism • *In her defence, she thought she was acting for the best.* **3.** the players whose job is to stop the other team scoring in football and other games **defenceless** *adjective* someone who is defenceless can't protect themselves

defend *verb* **1.** to defend someone or something is to protect them from an attack **2.** to defend an idea, belief or person is to argue in support of them **3.** to defend an accused person is to try to prove that they are innocent **defender** *noun* someone who defends something

defendant *noun* a person accused of something in a lawcourt

defensive *adjective* **1.** used to defend something • *We need to take defensive measures.* **2.** a defensive person is anxious about being criticized

defiant *adjective* openly showing that you refuse to obey someone **defiance** *noun* being defiant **defiantly** *adverb*

deficiency *noun* **deficiencies** a lack or shortage **deficient** *adjective* to be deficient in something is not to have enough of it

define *verb* to define a word is to explain what it means

definite *adjective* fixed or certain • *Is it definite that we are going to move?*

definite article *noun* the word *the*

definitely *adverb, interjection* certainly, without doubt • *We are definitely going to the party.*

definition *noun* an explanation of what a word means

deflect *verb* to deflect something that is moving is to make it go in a different direction **deflection** *noun* a deflection is a sudden change in direction of something that is moving

deforestation *noun* the cutting down of a large number of trees in an area

deformed *adjective* not properly shaped **deformity** *noun* a deformity is a part of someone's body that is deformed

defrost *verb* to defrost frozen food is to thaw it out

deft *adjective* skilful and quick **deftly** *adverb* in a skilful and quick way

defuse *verb* **1.** to defuse a bomb is to remove its fuse so that it won't blow up **2.** to defuse a situation is to make it less dangerous or tense

defy *verb* **defies, defying, defied** **1.** to defy someone is to refuse to obey them **2.** to defy someone to do something is to challenge them • *I defy you to find anything cheaper.*

degree *noun* **1.** a unit for measuring temperature • *Water boils at 100 degrees centigrade or 100°C.* **2.** a unit for measuring angles • *There are 90 degrees (90°) in a right angle.* **3.** an award to someone at a university or college who has successfully finished a course • *She has a degree in English.*

dehydrated *adjective* dried up, with all the water removed **dehydration** *noun* dehydration is losing too much water from your body

deity *noun* **deities** (**dee**-i-ti or **day**-i-ti) a god or goddess

dejected *adjective* sad or depressed **dejection** *noun* dejection is being sad or depressed

delay *verb* **1.** to delay someone is to make them late **2.** to delay something is to put it off until later **3.** to delay is to wait before doing something

delay *noun* **1.** delaying or waiting • *Do it without delay.* **2.** the period you have to wait when something happens late • *There will be a delay of 20 minutes.*

delete *verb* to delete something is to cross it out or remove it

deliberate *adjective* (di-**lib**-er-at) **1**. done on purpose • *It was a deliberate lie.* **2**. slow and careful • *He has a deliberate way of talking.* deliberately *adverb* to do something deliberately is to do it on purpose

delicacy *noun* delicacies **1**. delicacy is being delicate **2**. a delicacy is something small and tasty to eat

delicate *adjective* **1**. fine and graceful • *The cloth had delicate embroidery.* **2**. fragile and easily damaged **3**. becoming ill easily **4**. a delicate situation needs great care delicately *adverb*

delicatessen *noun* a shop that sells cooked or prepared food such as meat and cheese

delicious *adjective* tasting or smelling very pleasant deliciously *adverb* in a delicious way • *a deliciously creamy sauce*

delight *verb* to delight someone is to please them a lot
delight *noun* great pleasure
delightful *adjective* giving great pleasure delightfully *adverb*

delinquent *noun* a young person who breaks the law delinquency *noun* delinquency is criminal behaviour by young people

delirious *adjective* in a confused state of mind because you are ill or have a high fever

deliver *verb* **1**. to deliver letters or packages is to take them to a house or office **2**. to deliver a speech or lecture is to give it to an audience **3**. to deliver a baby is to help with its birth

delivery *noun* deliveries **1**. delivery is when letters or goods are taken to a house or office **2**. a person's delivery is the way they give a speech or lecture **3**. giving birth to a baby

delta *noun* a triangular area at the mouth of a river where it spreads into branches

deluge *noun* **1**. a large flood **2**. a heavy fall of rain **3**. something coming in great numbers • *After the speech there was a deluge of questions.*
deluge *verb* to be deluged with something is to get a huge amount of it

de luxe *adjective* of very high quality

demand *verb* to demand something is to ask for it forcefully

demand *noun* **1**. a demand is a very firm request for something **2**. demand is a desire to have something • *There's not much demand for ice cream at this time of year.* to be in demand is to be wanted or popular

demanding *adjective* **1**. asking for many things • *Toddlers can be very demanding.* **2**. needing a lot of time or effort • *She has a demanding job.*

democracy *noun* democracies **1**. democracy is government by leaders elected by the people **2**. a democracy is a country governed in this way

democrat *noun* a person who believes in or supports democracy

democratic *adjective* a democratic idea or process is one that involves ordinary people and takes account of their views democratically *adverb* to do something democratically is to take account of ordinary people and their views

demolish *verb* to demolish a building is to knock it down and break it up demolition *noun* the demolition of a building is when it is knocked down

demon *noun* a devil or evil spirit

demonstrate *verb* **1**. to demonstrate something is to show or prove it **2**. to demonstrate is to take part in a demonstration demonstrator *noun*

demonstration *noun* **1**. showing how to do or work something **2**. a march or meeting to show everyone what you think about something

den *noun* **1**. the home of a wild animal • *a lion's den* **2**. a hiding place, especially for children

denial *noun* saying that something is not true

denim *noun* strong cotton cloth, used to make jeans

denominator *noun* the number below the line in a fraction • *In ¼ the 4 is the denominator.*

dense *adjective* **1**. thick • *The fog was getting very dense.* **2**. packed close together • *They walked through a dense forest.* **densely** *adverb* thickly, close together • *a densely populated area*

density *noun* **densities** **1**. how thick or tightly packed something is **2**. *(in science)* the proportion of mass to volume • *Water has greater density than air.*

dent *noun* a hollow made in a surface by hitting it or pressing it

dent *verb* to dent something is to make a dent in it

dental *adjective* to do with the teeth or dentistry

dentist *noun* a person who is trained to treat teeth, fill them or take them out, and fit false ones **dentistry** *noun* the work of a dentist

denture *noun* a set of false teeth

deny *verb* **denies**, **denying**, **denied** **1**. to deny something is to say that it is not true **2**. to deny a request is to refuse it

deodorant *noun* a powder or liquid that removes unpleasant smells

depart *verb* to depart is to go away or leave **departure** *noun* a departure is when someone or something leaves a place

department *noun* one part of a large organization or shop

department store *noun* a large shop that sells many different kinds of goods

depend *verb* to depend on someone or something is to rely on them • *We depend on you for help.* to depend on something is to be decided or controlled by it • *Whether we can have a picnic depends on the weather.*

dependable *adjective* that you can depend on; reliable

dependant *noun* a person who depends on someone else, especially for money • *She has two dependants, a son and a daughter.*

dependent *adjective* depending or relying on someone • *He was dependent on his father.* • *She has two dependent children.* **dependence** *noun* dependence is being dependent on someone

depict *verb* **1**. to depict something is to show it in a painting or drawing **2**. to depict a scene is to describe it • *The book depicts life in a small village.*

deport *verb* to deport someone is to send them out of a country **deportation** *noun* deportation is when someone is sent out of a country

deposit *noun* **1**. an amount of money you pay into a bank **2**. a sum of money paid as a first instalment **3**. a layer of solid matter in or on the earth

deposit *verb* **1**. to deposit something is to put it down somewhere **2**. to deposit money is to pay it into a bank

depot *noun* (**dep**-oh) **1**. a place where things are stored **2**. a place where buses or trains are kept and repaired

depress *verb* to depress someone is to make them very sad

depressed *adjective* someone who is depressed feels very sad and without hope

depression *noun* **1**. a feeling of great sadness and hopelessness **2**. a long period when there is less trade and business than usual and many people have no work **3**. a shallow hollow or dip in the ground **4**. an area of low air pressure which may bring rain

deprive *verb* to deprive someone of something is to take it away from them

deprived *adjective* without all the things you need to live a happy and comfortable life, like enough food and good housing

depth *noun* how deep something is • *What is the depth of the river here?* in depth thoroughly

deputy *noun* **deputies** a person who acts as a substitute or chief assistant for someone and does that person's job when they are away

derail *verb* a train is derailed when something causes it to leave the track

derby *noun* **derbies** a sports match between two teams from the same city or area

derelict *adjective* (**de**-re-likt) abandoned and left to fall into ruin • *The factory is now completely derelict.*

derivation *noun* where a word comes from

derive *verb* **1**. to get a good feeling from something • *She derived a lot of pleasure from* music. **2.** to develop or come from something • *Many English words are derived from Latin.*

descend *verb* to descend something like a hill or staircase is to go down it to be descended from someone is to be in the same family as them but living at a later time

descendant *noun* a person's descendants are the people who are descended from them

descent *noun* a descent is a climb down, usually a hard or long one

describe *verb* to describe something or someone is to say what they are like

description *noun* **1.** description is saying what someone or something is like • *She's a writer who's very good at description.* **2.** a description is something you write or say that describes what someone or something is like • *He gave the police a description of the robbers.* **descriptive** *adjective* a descriptive word or piece of writing describes someone or something • *a descriptive poem*

desert *noun* (**dez**-ert) a large area of very dry, often sandy, land

desert *verb* (di-**zert**) to desert someone or something is to leave them without intending to return **deserter** *noun* a soldier who runs away from the army **desertion** *noun* desertion is when a soldier runs away from the army

deserted *adjective* a place is deserted when there is nobody there

desert island *noun* a tropical island where nobody lives

deserve *verb* to deserve something is to be worthy of it or to have a right to it **deservedly** *adverb* rightly, because it is deserved • *This restaurant is deservedly popular.*

design *noun* **1.** the way that something is made or arranged **2.** a drawing that shows how something is to be made **3.** lines and shapes forming a pattern
design *verb* to design something is to make a design or plan for it **designer** *noun* someone who designs things, especially clothes

desirable *adjective* worth having or doing • *This is a desirable place to live.*

desire *verb* to desire something is to want it very much

desire *noun* a feeling of wanting something very much

desk *noun* **1.** a piece of furniture with a flat top and drawers, used for writing, reading or working at **2.** a counter at which a cashier or receptionist sits

desktop *adjective* small enough to use on a desk • *a desktop computer*

desolate *adjective* **1.** lonely and sad **2.** a desolate place is empty, with no people living there

despair *noun* despair is a complete loss of hope
despair *verb* to despair is to lose hope completely

despatch *noun* and *verb* a different spelling of *dispatch*

desperate *adjective* **1.** extremely serious or hopeless • *We were in a desperate situation.* **2.** ready to do anything to get out of a difficulty • *There are three desperate criminals at large.* **3.** needing or wanting something very much • *She was desperate to go home.* **desperately** *adverb* seriously; recklessly **desperation** *noun* desperation is being desperate

despicable *adjective* very unpleasant or evil

despise *verb* to despise someone is to hate them and have no respect at all for them

despite *preposition* in spite of • *They went out despite the rain.*

dessert *noun* (di-**zert**) fruit or a sweet food eaten at the end of a meal

destination *noun* the place you are travelling to

destined *adjective* intended by fate; meant to happen • *We were destined to meet.*

destiny *noun* **destinies** your destiny is what is intended for you in the future; your fate

destroy *verb* to destroy something is to ruin it or put an end to it **destruction** *noun* when something is destroyed **destructive** *adjective* causing a lot of damage

detach *verb* to detach something is to remove it or separate it

detached *adjective* a detached house is one that is not joined to another house

detail *noun* **1.** a small piece of information **2.** a small part of a design or picture or piece of decoration in detail describing or dealing with everything fully

detain *verb* **1.** to detain someone is to keep them in a place **2.** to detain someone is also to keep them waiting • *I'll try not to detain you for long.*

detect *verb* to detect something is to discover or notice it **detection** *noun* detection is detecting something **detector** *noun* a detector is a device that detects something

detective *noun* a police officer who investigates crimes

detention *noun* detention is when someone is made to stay in a place as a punishment

deter *verb* deterring, deterred to deter someone is to put them off doing something

detergent *noun* a kind of washing powder or liquid

deteriorate *verb* to deteriorate is to become worse • *The weather was starting to deteriorate.* **deterioration** *noun* deterioration is when something becomes worse

determination *noun* a strong intention to achieve something, even though it is difficult

determined *adjective* having your mind firmly made up

deterrent *noun* something that is meant to put people off doing something

detest *verb* to detest something is to dislike it very much **detestable** *adjective* horrid

detonate *verb* to detonate a bomb is to make it explode **detonation** *noun* detonation is making a bomb explode **detonator** *noun* a device that makes a bomb explode

detour *noun* a less direct route you use instead of the normal route

deuce *noun* a tennis score when each player has 40 points and needs two more points in a row to win the game

devastate *verb* to devastate a place is to ruin or destroy it, making it impossible to live in **devastation** *noun* devastation is destruction of a place

devastated *adjective* someone is devastated when they are extremely shocked and upset

develop *verb* **1.** to develop something is to make it bigger or better **2.** to develop is to become bigger or better **3.** to develop photographic film is to treat it with chemicals so that pictures appear on it

developing country *noun* developing countries a poor country that is building up its industry and trying to improve its living conditions

development *noun* a development is something interesting that has happened

device *noun* a piece of equipment used for a particular purpose

devil *noun* an evil spirit or person **devilish** *adjective* cruel or wicked, like a devil

devious *adjective* using unfair and dishonest methods • *He got rich by devious means.*

devise *verb* to devise a plan or idea is to think it up

devolution *noun* handing over power from a central government to a local or regional government

devote *verb* to devote yourself or your time to something is to spend all your time doing it • *They devote all their free time to sport.*

devoted *adjective* loving and loyal • *They are devoted parents.* **devotion** *noun* great love or loyalty

devour *verb* to devour something is to eat or swallow it greedily

devout *adjective* deeply religious

dew *noun* tiny drops of water that form during the night on the ground and other surfaces out of doors

diabetes *noun* (dy-a-**bee**-teez) a disease in which there is too much sugar in a person's blood **diabetic** *noun* a person suffering from diabetes **diabetic** *adjective* suffering from diabetes

diabolical *adjective* like a devil; very wicked

diagnose *verb* to diagnose a disease is to find out what it is and what treatment is needed

diagnosis *noun* **diagnoses** a doctor makes a diagnosis when they decide what disease someone has

diagonal *noun* a straight line joining opposite corners **diagonally** *adverb* across from one corner to another

diagram *noun* a drawing or picture that shows the parts of something or how it works

dial *noun* a circular piece of plastic or card with numbers or letters round it
dial *verb* **dialling**, **dialled** to dial a telephone number is to choose it by pressing numbered buttons

dialect *noun* the form of a language used by people in one area of the country but not in the rest of the country

dialogue *noun* conversation in a play, film or book

diameter *noun* **1.** a line drawn from one side of a circle to the other, passing through the centre **2.** the length of this line

diamond *noun* **1.** a very hard jewel that looks like clear glass **2.** a shape which has four equal sides but which is not a square **3.** a playing card with red diamond shapes on it

diarrhoea *noun* (dy-a-**ree**-a) an illness that makes you have to keep going to the toilet and the waste matter you empty from your bowels is very watery

diary *noun* **diaries** a book in which you write down what happens to you each day

dice *noun* **dice** a small cube marked with one to six dots on each side, thrown to give a number in some games

dictate *verb* **1.** to dictate something is to speak or read it aloud for someone else to write down **2.** to dictate to someone is to give them orders in a bossy way **dictation** *noun* an exercise in writing down what someone reads out

dictator *noun* a ruler who has complete power over the people of a country **dictatorship** *noun* a country ruled by a dictator

dictionary *noun* **dictionaries** a book with words listed in alphabetical order, telling you what a word means and how to spell it

die *verb* **dying**, **died** to die is to stop living **to die down** is to gradually become less strong • *The wind died down at last.* **to die out** is to gradually disappear • *The tiger is beginning to die out.*

diesel *noun* **1.** a diesel is an engine that works by burning oil in compressed air **2.** diesel is fuel for this kind of engine

diet *noun* **1.** a diet is a choice of food that someone eats to be healthy or to lose weight • *I am on a diet.* **2.** someone's diet is the food they normally eat
diet *verb* to diet is to keep to a special diet, especially in order to lose weight

differ *verb* **1.** to differ from something is to be not the same as it **2.** to differ is to disagree • *The two writers differ on this point.*

difference *noun* **1.** the way in which something is different from something else **2.** the amount between two numbers • *The difference between 8 and 3 is 5.*

different *adjective* one person or thing is different from another when they are not the same **differently** *adverb* in a different way

difficult *adjective* needing a lot of effort or skill; not easy

difficulty *noun* **difficulties** **1.** difficulty is not being easy, trouble • *I had difficulty answering most of the questions.* **2.** a difficulty is something that causes a problem • *She has learning difficulties.*

dig *verb* **digging**, **dug** **1.** to dig soil or the ground is to break it up and move it **2.** to dig a hole is to make it **digger** *noun* a machine for digging

digest *verb* to digest food is to soften and change it in the stomach and intestine so that the body can absorb it **digestible** *adjective* easy to digest **digestion** *noun* the way your body digests food

digestive *adjective* to do with digesting food

digit *noun* (**dij**-it) **1.** any of the numbers from 0 to 9 **2.** a finger or toe

digital *adjective* **1.** a digital clock or watch has a row of digits to show the time **2.** a digital computer or recording stores the data or sound as a series of binary digits

dignified *adjective* having dignity

dignity *noun* a calm and serious manner

dike *noun* **1.** a long wall or embankment to hold back water and prevent flooding **2.** a ditch for draining water from land

dilemma *noun* an awkward choice between two possible actions, either of which would cause difficulties

dilute *verb* to dilute a liquid is to make it weaker by mixing it with water **dilution** *noun* diluting a liquid

dim *adjective* **dimmer**, **dimmest** only faintly lit and difficult to see **dimly** *adverb* to see something dimly is to find it hard to see clearly
dim *verb* **dimming**, **dimmed** a light dims when it becomes less bright

dimension *noun* a measurement such as length, width, area or volume • *What are the dimensions of the box?*

diminish *verb* **1.** to diminish something is to make it smaller **2.** to diminish is to become smaller

dimple *noun* a small hollow on a person's cheek or chin

din *noun* a loud noise

dine *verb* to dine is to have dinner **diner** *noun* someone eating a meal in a restaurant or hotel

dinghy *noun* **dinghies** (**ding**-i) a kind of small boat

dingy *adjective* **dingier**, **dingiest** (**din**-ji) shabby and dirty-looking

dinner *noun* the main meal of the day, eaten either in the middle of the day or in the evening

dinosaur *noun* a prehistoric reptile, often of enormous size

dip *verb* **dipping**, **dipped** **1.** to dip something is to put it into a liquid and then take it out again **2.** to dip is to go or slope downwards • *The road dips steeply after the hill.* **3.** to dip a vehicle's headlights is to lower the beam so that they do not dazzle other drivers
dip *noun* **1.** a downward slope **2.** a quick swim **3.** a mixture into which things are dipped

diploma *noun* a certificate awarded for skill in a particular subject

diplomacy *noun* **1.** the business of keeping friendly with other nations **2.** dealing with other people without upsetting or offending them

diplomatic *adjective* **1.** to do with diplomacy **2.** tactful and courteous **diplomat** *noun* someone who works in diplomacy **diplomatically** *adverb* in a tactful and courteous way

dire *adjective* dreadful or serious • *The refugees are in dire need of food and shelter.*

direct *adjective* **1.** as straight or quick as possible **2.** frank and honest **directness** *noun* directness is being frank and honest
direct *verb* **1.** to direct someone is to show them the way **2.** to direct a film or play is to decide how it should be made or performed

direction *noun* **1.** a direction is the way you go to get somewhere **2.** direction is directing something **directions** information on how to use or do something or how to get somewhere

directly *adverb* **1.** by a direct route • *Go directly to the shop.* **2.** immediately • *I want you to come directly.*

director *noun* **1.** a person who is in charge of something, especially one of a group of people managing a company **2.** a person who decides how a film or play should be made or performed

directory *noun* **directories** a book containing a list of people with their telephone numbers and addresses

dirt *noun* earth or soil; anything that is not clean

dirty *adjective* **dirtier**, **dirtiest** **1.** covered with dirt; not clean **2.** unfair or mean • *That was a dirty trick.* **dirtily** *adverb* **dirtiness** *noun*

disability *noun* disabilities something that restricts someone's movements or senses

disabled *adjective* having a disease or injury that restricts someone's movements or senses

disadvantage *noun* something that hinders you or makes things difficult

disagree *verb* to disagree with someone is to have or express a different opinion from them disagreement *noun* when people don't agree about something or argue about it

disappear *verb* 1. to disappear is to become impossible to see; to vanish 2. to disappear is also to stop happening or existing • *Her nervousness soon disappeared.* disappearance *noun* a person's or thing's disappearance is when they disappear

disappoint *verb* to disappoint someone is to fail to do what they want disappointing *adjective* causing someone to be disappointed disappointment *noun* a feeling of being disappointed

disapprove *verb* to disapprove of someone or something is to have a bad opinion of them disapproval *noun* having a bad opinion

disaster *noun* 1. a very bad accident or misfortune, often one where many people are killed or injured 2. a complete failure • *The first night of the play was a disaster.* disastrous *adjective* causing great misfortune; going completely wrong disastrously *adverb*

disc *noun* 1. a round flat object 2. a round, flat piece of plastic on which sound or data is recorded; a CD

discard *verb* to discard something is to throw it away

disciple *noun* a follower of a political or religious leader

discipline *noun* 1. training people to obey rules and punishing them if they don't 2. the control you have over how you behave • *You need lots of discipline to learn the piano.*

disc jockey *noun* someone who introduces and plays records on the radio or at a club

disclose *verb* to disclose information or a secret is to tell someone about it

disco *noun* discos a place or party where people dance to pop music

discomfort *noun* being uncomfortable

disconnect *verb* to disconnect something is to break its connection or detach it

discontented *adjective* unhappy and not satisfied discontent *noun* discontent is a feeling of being unhappy or not satisfied

discount *noun* an amount by which a price is reduced

discourage *verb* 1. to discourage someone is to take away their enthusiasm or confidence 2. to discourage someone from doing something is to try to persuade them not to do it discouragement *noun* a feeling of being discouraged

discover *verb* to discover something is to find it or learn about it by chance or for the first time

discovery *noun* discoveries 1. finding or learning about something, especially by chance or for the first time • *Columbus is famous for the discovery of America.* 2. something that is found or learned about for the first time • *This drug was an important discovery in the history of medicine.*

discreet *adjective* being careful in what you say and do discreetly *adverb*

discriminate *verb* 1. to discriminate between things is to notice the differences between them or to prefer one thing to another 2. to discriminate between people is to treat them differently or unfairly because of their race, sex or religion

discrimination *noun* discrimination is treating people differently or unfairly because of their race, sex or religion

discus *noun* (**dis**-kuss) a thick heavy disc thrown in an athletic contest

discuss *verb* (dis-**kuss**) to discuss a subject is to talk with other people about it or to write about it in detail

discussion *noun* 1. a conversation about a subject 2. a piece of writing in which the writer examines a subject from different points of view

disease *noun* a disease is an illness or sickness **diseased** *adjective* someone or something is diseased when they have a disease

disgrace *noun* **1**. disgrace is shame • *You have brought disgrace to your family.* **2**. a disgrace is a person or thing that is so bad that people should feel ashamed • *This room is an absolute disgrace.* **disgraceful** *adjective* so bad that people should feel ashamed about it **disgracefully** *adverb*

disgrace *verb* to disgrace someone or something is to bring them shame

disguise *verb* to disguise someone or something is to make them look different so that other people won't recognize them

disguise *noun* clothes or make-up you put on to change the way you look so that people won't recognize you

disgust *noun* a strong feeling of dislike or contempt

disgust *verb* to disgust someone is to make them feel disgust **disgusted** *adjective* disliking someone or something very much **disgusting** *adjective* very unpleasant; making you feel disgust

dish *noun* **1**. a plate or bowl for food **2**. food that has been prepared for eating

dishonest *adjective* not honest or truthful **dishonesty** *noun* dishonesty is being dishonest

dishwasher *noun* a machine for washing dishes

disinfect *verb* to disinfect something is to treat it to kill all the germs in it

disinfectant *noun* a liquid used to disinfect things

disintegrate *verb* to disintegrate is to break up into small pieces **disintegration** *noun* the disintegration of something is when it disintegrates

disk *noun* a disc, especially one used to store computer data

dislike *verb* to dislike someone or something is not to like them
dislike *noun* a feeling of not liking someone or something

dislocate *verb* to dislocate a bone or joint in your body is to make it come out of its proper place by accident

dislodge *verb* to dislodge something is to move it from its place

disloyal *adjective* not loyal

dismal *adjective* gloomy and sad

dismantle *verb* to dismantle something is to take it to pieces

dismay *noun* a feeling of strong disappointment and surprise **dismayed** *adjective* disappointed and surprised

dismiss *verb* **1**. to dismiss someone is to tell them that they have to leave their job **2**. to dismiss an idea or suggestion is to reject it **dismissal** *noun* losing your job

dismount *verb* to dismount is to get off a horse or bicycle

disobey *verb* to disobey someone is to refuse to do what they tell you to do **disobedience** *noun* disobedience is refusing to obey someone **disobedient** *adjective* someone who is disobedient doesn't do what someone tells them to do

disorder *noun* **1**. disorder is confusion or disturbance **2**. a disorder is an illness **disorderly** *adjective* behaving in a wild and noisy way

dispatch *verb* to dispatch something or someone is to send them somewhere

dispense *verb* **1**. to dispense something is to give it out to people • *The machine dispenses drinks and snacks.* **2**. to dispense medicine is to prepare it for patients **to dispense with something** is to do without it

disperse *verb* **1.** to disperse people is to send them away in various directions • *The police dispersed the crowd.* **2.** to disperse is to go off in various directions

display *verb* to display something is to arrange it so that it can be clearly seen

display *noun* **1.** a show or exhibition **2.** the showing of information on a computer screen

disposable *adjective* something that is disposable is made to be thrown away after it has been used

disposal *noun* getting rid of something **at your disposal** ready for you to use

dispose *verb* **to dispose of something** is to get rid of it

disprove *verb* to disprove something is to prove that it is not true

dispute *noun* a quarrel or disagreement

disqualify *verb* disqualifies, disqualifying, disqualified to disqualify someone is to remove them from a race or competition because they have broken the rules **disqualification** *noun* when someone is disqualified

disregard *verb* to disregard someone or something is to take no notice of them

disrespect *noun* lack of respect; rudeness **disrespectful** *adjective* showing disrespect **disrespectfully** *adverb* in a disrespectful way

disrupt *verb* to disrupt something is to stop it running smoothly or throw it into confusion • *Floods have disrupted local traffic.* **disruption** *noun* when something stops running smoothly **disruptive** *adjective* causing so much disorder that a meeting or lesson can't continue

dissatisfied *adjective* not satisfied or pleased **dissatisfaction** *noun* dissatisfaction is being dissatisfied

dissect *verb* to dissect something is to cut it up so that you can examine it **dissection** *noun* dissecting something

dissolve *verb* **1.** to dissolve something is to mix it with a liquid so that it becomes part of the liquid **2.** to dissolve is to mix with a liquid so as to become part of it • *The tablet dissolved in the water.*

dissuade *verb* to dissuade someone is to persuade them not to do something

distance *noun* the amount of space between two places or things **in the distance** a long way off but able to be seen

distant *adjective* far away

distil *verb* distilling, distilled to distil a liquid is to purify it by boiling it until it becomes a steam or vapour and then letting it cool so that it becomes liquid again

distillery *noun* distilleries a place where whisky and other alcoholic drinks are produced

distinct *adjective* **1.** easily heard or seen; clear or definite • *You have made a distinct improvement.* **2.** clearly separate or different • *A rabbit is quite distinct from a hare.*

distinction *noun* **1.** a distinction is a clear difference between two things **2.** distinction is excellence or honour • *She is a writer of distinction.*

distinctive *adjective* clearly different from all the others and easy to recognize or notice

distinguish *verb* **1.** to distinguish things is to notice the differences between them **2.** to distinguish something is to see or hear it clearly

distinguished *adjective* famous, successful and much admired by other people • *a distinguished writer*

distort *verb* **1.** to distort something is to change it into a strange shape • *His face was distorted with anger.* **2.** to distort facts is to change them so that they are untrue or misleading **distortion** *noun* distortion is distorting something

distract *verb* to distract someone is to take their attention away from what they are doing • *Don't distract the bus driver.* distraction *noun* when you are distracted

distress *noun* great sorrow, suffering or trouble **in distress** a ship or plane is in distress when it is in difficulty and needs help

distress *verb* to distress someone is to make them feel very upset or worried

distribute *verb* 1. to distribute things is to give them out or deliver them • *The teacher distributed textbooks to the class.* 2. to distribute something is to share it among a number of people • *The money was distributed among all the local schools.* distribution *noun* distribution is distributing things

district *noun* part of a town or country

distrust *noun* lack of trust; suspicion distrustful *adjective* not trusting people

distrust *verb* to think that someone or something can't be trusted

disturb *verb* 1. to disturb someone is to interrupt them or spoil their peace 2. to disturb someone is also to worry or upset them disturbance *noun* a disturbance is something that disturbs someone

disused *adjective* no longer used • *a disused warehouse*

ditch *noun* a narrow trench to hold or carry away water

dither *verb* to dither is to hesitate nervously

ditto *noun* Ditto means the same again. Ditto marks (") are sometimes used in lists or bills to show where something is repeated.

dive *verb* 1. to dive is to go into water head first 2. to dive is also to move downwards quickly • *The aeroplane then dived.*

diver *noun* 1. a swimmer who dives 2. someone who works under water using special breathing equipment

diverse *adjective* very different from each other and of several different kinds • *He has a diverse collection of rocks.* diversity *noun* diversity is variety

diversion *noun* a different way for traffic to go when the usual road is closed

divert *verb* to divert something is to change the direction it is moving in

divide *verb* 1. to divide something is to separate it into smaller parts or shares 2. *(in mathematics)* to divide a number by another number is to find out how many times the second number is contained in the first • *Divide six by two and you get three ($6 \div 2 = 3$).*

divine *adjective* 1. belonging to God or coming from God 2. like a god 3. *(informal)* excellent; extremely beautiful divinity *noun* divinity is the fact of being a god or like God

division *noun* 1. the process of dividing numbers or things 2. one of the parts into which something is divided divisible *adjective* able to be divided exactly • *27 is divisible by 9.*

divorce *noun* the legal ending of a marriage

divorce *verb* a husband and wife divorce when they end their marriage by law

Diwali *noun* (di-**wah**-li) a Hindu festival held in October or November

DIY short for **do-it-yourself**

dizzy *adjective* dizzier, dizziest giddy and feeling confused dizzily *adverb* dizziness *noun*

DJ short for **disc jockey**

do *verb* does, doing, did, done 1. to do something is to perform it or deal with it • *Are you doing your work? • I can't do this sum.* 2. to do well is to manage; to do badly is not to manage very well 3. you say that something will do when it is all right or suitable • *I'd really like some football boots but trainers will do.* 4. you also use **do** with other verbs in special ways • *Do you want this? • He does not want it. • I do like crisps. • We work as hard as they do.* to do something up is to fasten it • *Do up your coat.* to do without something is to manage without having it

docile *adjective* gentle and obedient

dock[1] *noun* a part of a harbour where ships are loaded, unloaded or repaired

dock[1] *verb* a ship docks when it comes into a dock

dock[2] *noun* a place for the prisoner on trial in a lawcourt

docker *noun* a person whose job is loading and unloading ships

doctor *noun* a person trained to heal sick or injured people

document *noun* **1.** an important written or printed piece of paper **2.** something stored in a computer or on a disk, such as a piece of text or a picture

documentary *noun* documentaries a film or a television programme that tells you about real events or situations

dodge *verb* to dodge something is to move quickly to avoid it

doe *noun* a female deer, rabbit or hare

dog *noun* a four-legged animal that barks, often kept as a pet

do-it-yourself *adjective* suitable for anyone to make or use at home, rather than paying for someone else to do it

doldrums *plural noun* the ocean regions near the equator, where there is little or no wind **in the doldrums** bored and unhappy

dole *noun* (informal) the dole is money paid by the government to unemployed people

doll *noun* a toy model of a child or person

dollar *noun* a unit of money in the United States and some other countries

dolphin *noun* a sea mammal like a small whale with a snout like a beak

dome *noun* a roof shaped like the top half of a ball

domestic *adjective* **1.** to do with the home **2.** a domestic animal is tame and kept at home

dominant *adjective* most powerful or important **dominance** *noun* being dominant

dominate *verb* to dominate people is to control them by being the most powerful **domination** *noun* dominating people

domino *noun* dominoes a small flat oblong piece of wood or plastic with dots (1 to 6) or a blank space at each end, used in the game of **dominoes**

donate *verb* to donate money is to give it to a charity or organization **donation** *noun* a donation is money that is donated

donkey *noun* donkeys an animal that looks like a small horse with long ears

donor *noun* someone who gives something • *blood donors*

doodle *noun* a quick drawing or scribble

doodle *verb* to doodle is to draw a doodle

doom *noun* something bad that is certain to happen

door *noun* a movable panel that opens and closes the entrance to a room, building or cupboard

doorway *noun* the opening into which a door fits

dormitory *noun* dormitories a room for several people to sleep in, especially in school

dose *noun* the amount of a medicine that you are meant to take at one time • *You can take one dose in the morning and another at bedtime.*

dot *noun* a tiny spot

dot *verb* dotting, dotted to dot something is to mark it with dots **dotted** *adjective* made of dots • *Write on the dotted line.*

double *adjective* **1**. twice as much or twice as many **2**. having two of something • *Smith-Jones is a double-barrelled surname.* **3**. suitable for two people • *a double bed*

double *noun* **1**. double is twice the amount or cost **2**. a double is someone who looks exactly like someone else **3**. you play doubles in tennis when you play with someone else against another pair of players

double *verb* **1**. to double something is to make it twice as big **2**. to double is to become twice as big

double bass *noun* a musical instrument with strings, like a large cello

double-cross *verb* to double-cross someone is to cheat or betray them when you are supposed to be supporting them

doubly *adverb* twice as much • *It's doubly important that you should go.*

doubt *noun* not feeling sure about something

doubt *verb* to doubt something is to feel unsure about it • *I doubt whether he is telling the truth.*

doubtful *adjective* **1**. having doubts • *She looked doubtful.* **2**. making you feel doubt • *Their story was very doubtful.* **doubtfully** *adverb*

dough *noun* a thick mixture of flour and water used for making bread or pastry

doughnut *noun* a round or ring-shaped bun that has been fried and covered with sugar

dove *noun* a kind of pigeon, often used as a symbol of peace

down[1] *adverb, preposition* **1**. to or in a lower place • *It fell down.* • *Run down the hill.* **2**. along • *Go down to the shops.*

down[2] *noun* very soft feathers or hair • *Ducks are covered with down.*

downcast *adjective* sad or dejected

downfall *noun* **1**. a person's downfall is their ruin or fall from power **2**. a heavy fall of rain or snow

downhill *adverb* down a slope

download *verb* to transfer data or programs to a computer from the Internet

download *noun* a computer program or file that you have downloaded

downpour *noun* a heavy fall of rain

downright *adjective, adverb* very, completely • *I felt downright angry about it.*

downs *plural noun* grass-covered hills

downstairs *adverb, adjective* to or on a lower floor

downstream *adverb* in the direction that a river or stream flows

downward or **downwards** *adverb* towards a lower place

doze *verb* to doze is to sleep lightly

dozen *noun* a set of twelve

Dr short for **Doctor**

draft *noun* a rough plan for something you are going to write

draft *verb* to draft something you are going to write is to make a rough plan of it

drag *verb* dragging, dragged to drag something heavy is to pull it along

dragon *noun* a winged lizard-like monster that breathes fire in stories

dragonfly *noun* **dragonflies** an insect with a long body and two pairs of transparent wings

drain *noun* a pipe or ditch for taking away water or sewage

drain *verb* **1.** to drain water is to take it away with drains **2.** to drain is to flow or trickle away **drainage** *noun* a system of drains

drama *noun* **1.** drama is writing or performing plays **2.** a drama is a play

dramatic *adjective* **1.** to do with drama **2.** exciting and impressive • *A dramatic change has taken place.* **dramatically** *adverb*

dramatist *noun* someone who writes plays

dramatize *verb* **1.** to dramatize a story is to make it into a play **2.** to dramatize an event is to exaggerate it **dramatization** *noun* a dramatization is a play made from a story This word can also be spelled **dramatise**.

drape *verb* to drape a cloth is to hang it loosely over something

drastic *adjective* having a strong or violent effect **drastically** *adverb*

draught *noun* (rhymes with craft) a current of cold air indoors **draughty** *adjective* a draughty room has lots of draughts

draughts *noun* a game played with 24 round pieces on a chessboard

draw *verb* **drawing, drew, drawn 1.** to draw a picture is to make it with a pencil or pen **2.** to draw people is to attract them • *The fair drew large crowds.* **3.** to draw is to end a game or contest with the same score on both sides • *They drew 2-2 last Saturday.*

draw *noun* **1.** a raffle or similar competition in which the winner is chosen by picking tickets or numbers at random **2.** a game that ends with the same score on both sides

drawback *noun* a disadvantage

drawbridge *noun* a bridge over a moat, hinged at one end so that it can be raised or lowered

drawer *noun* a sliding box-like container in a piece of furniture

drawing *noun* something you draw with a pencil or pen

drawing pin *noun* a short pin with a large flat top that you use for fixing paper to a surface

dread *verb* to dread something is to fear it very much

dread *noun* great fear

dreadful *adjective* very bad • *We've had dreadful weather.* **dreadfully** *adverb* very badly

dream *noun* **1.** things you picture happening while you are sleeping **2.** something you would like to do or have very much • *His dream is to be famous.* **dreamy** *adjective* like a dream; not real

dream *verb* **dreaming, dreamt** or **dreamed 1.** to dream is to have a dream **2.** to dream is also to want something badly

dreary *adjective* **drearier, dreariest 1.** dull or boring **2.** gloomy

dredge *verb* to dredge something is to drag it up, especially mud from the bottom of water **dredger** *noun* a machine for clearing mud from the bottom of a river

drench *verb* to drench someone or something is to soak them • *They got drenched in the rain.*

dress *noun* **1.** a dress is a woman's or girl's piece of clothing, having a top and skirt in one **2.** dress is clothes or costume • *a fancy dress party*

dress *verb* **1.** to dress is to put clothes on **2.** to dress a wound is to put a bandage or plaster on it

dresser *noun* a sideboard with shelves at the top

dressing *noun* **1.** a sauce for a salad **2.** a bandage or plaster

dressing gown *noun* a loose light indoor coat you wear over pyjamas or a nightdress

dribble *verb* **1.** to dribble is to let saliva trickle out of your mouth **2.** to dribble with a ball is to kick it gently as you run along, so that it stays close to your feet

drier *noun* a device for drying hair or washing

drift *verb* to drift is to be carried gently along by water or air

drift *noun* a mass of snow or sand piled up by the wind

drill *noun* **1.** a tool for making holes **2.** repeated exercises in military training, gymnastics or sport

drill *verb* to drill a hole is to make a hole with a drill

drink *verb* drinking, drank, drunk **1.** to drink is to swallow liquid **2.** to drink can also mean to drink a lot of alcohol • *Don't drink and drive.* **drinker** *noun* someone who drinks alcohol

drink *noun* **1.** a liquid for drinking **2.** an alcoholic drink

drip *verb* dripping, dripped **1.** to drip is to fall in drops **2.** to drip is also to let liquid fall in drops

drip *noun* a falling drop of liquid

drive *verb* driving, drove, driven **1.** to drive a vehicle is to operate it **2.** to drive someone or something is to make them move • *The farmer was driving his herd across the road.* **3.** to drive someone into a state or feeling is to force them into it • *That music is driving me mad!* **driver** *noun* someone who drives a vehicle

drive *noun* **1.** a drive is a journey in a vehicle **2.** drive is energy and enthusiasm **3.** a drive is a road leading to a house

drizzle *noun* gentle rain

drizzle *verb* to rain gently

droop *verb* to droop is to hang down weakly

drop *noun* **1.** a tiny amount of liquid **2.** a fall or decrease • *There has been a sharp drop in prices.* **droplet** *noun* a small drop

drop *verb* dropping, dropped **1.** to drop is to fall **2.** to drop something is to let it fall **3.** to drop is also to become less or lower • *The temperature suddenly dropped.* to drop in is to visit someone casually to drop out is to stop taking part in something

drought *noun* (rhymes with out) a long period of dry weather

drown *verb* **1.** to drown is to die from being under water and unable to breathe **2.** to drown a person or animal is to kill them by forcing them to stay under water **3.** to drown sounds is to make so much noise that they cannot be heard

drowsy *adjective* drowsier, drowsiest sleepy **drowsiness** *noun*

drug *noun* **1.** a substance that kills pain or cures a disease **2.** A drug is also a substance that people take because it affects their senses or their mind. Some drugs cause addiction or are illegal.

drug *verb* drugging, drugged to drug someone is to make them unconscious with drugs

drum *noun* **1.** a musical instrument made of a cylinder with a thin skin stretched over one end or both ends **2.** a cylindrical container • *an oil drum*

drum *verb* drumming, drummed **1.** to drum is to play a drum or drums **2.** to drum on something is to tap it repeatedly • *He drummed his fingers on the table.* **drummer** *noun* someone who plays the drums

drumstick *noun* **1.** a stick used for hitting a drum **2.** the lower part of a cooked bird's leg

drunk *adjective* not able to control your behaviour through drinking too much alcohol

dry *adjective* drier, driest not wet or damp

dry *verb* dries, drying, dried **1.** to dry is to become dry **2.** to dry something is to make it dry

dry-cleaning *noun* a method of cleaning clothes using chemicals rather than water

dual *adjective* having two parts or aspects; double • *This building has a dual purpose.*

dual carriageway *noun* a road with several lanes in each direction

dub *verb* dubbing, dubbed to change or add new sound to the sound on a film • *It's a Japanese film but has been dubbed into English.*

dubious *adjective* **1.** feeling doubtful or uncertain • *I'm dubious about our chances of winning.* **2.** probably not honest or not good

duchess *noun* a duke's wife or widow

duck *noun* **1.** a web-footed water bird with a flat beak **2.** a batsman's score of nought at cricket
duck *verb* **1.** to duck is to bend down quickly to avoid something **2.** to duck someone is to push them under water quickly

duckling *noun* a young duck

due *adjective* **1.** expected to arrive • *The train is due in five minutes.* **2.** needing to be paid • *Payment for the trip is due next week.*
due to something or someone because of something or someone • *The traffic jam was due to an accident.*
due *adverb* directly • *The camp is due north.*

duel *noun* a fight between two people with pistols or swords

duet *noun* a piece of music for two players or two singers

duke *noun* a member of the highest rank of noblemen

dull *adjective* **1.** not bright or clear; gloomy • *It was a dull day.* **2.** boring • *What a dull programme.* **3.** not sharp • *I had a dull pain.*

duly *adverb* rightly; as expected • *They promised to come and later they duly arrived.*

dumb *adjective* **1.** unable to speak; silent **2.** *(informal)* stupid

dumbfounded *adjective* unable to say anything because you are so astonished

dummy *noun* dummies **1.** a large doll or model made to look like a human being **2.** an imitation teat for a baby to suck

dump *noun* **1.** a place where something, especially rubbish, is left or stored **2.** *(informal)* a place you don't like

dump *verb* **1.** to dump something is to get rid of it when you don't want it **2.** to dump something somewhere is to put it down carelessly

dumpling *noun* a lump of boiled or baked dough, usually eaten with a stew

dune *noun* a hill of loose sand formed by the wind

dung *noun* solid waste matter from an animal

dungarees *plural noun* trousers with a piece in front covering your chest, held up by straps over your shoulders

dungeon *noun* (**dun**-jon) an underground prison cell

dunk *verb* to dunk something is to dip it into a liquid

duo *noun* duos a pair of people, especially playing music

duplicate *noun* (**dew**-pli-kat) something that is exactly the same as something else
duplicate *verb* (**dew**-pli-kayt) to duplicate something is to make an exact copy of it
duplication *noun* making an exact copy of something

durable *adjective* lasting and strong

duration *noun* the time something lasts

during *preposition* while something else is going on • *Let's meet in the cafe during the interval.*

dusk *noun* the time of the day just after sunset when it is starting to get dark

dust *noun* a fine powder made up of tiny pieces of dry earth or other material
dust *verb* **1.** to dust things is to clear the dust off them **2.** to dust something is to sprinkle it with powder • *You can dust the cake with sugar.*

dustbin *noun* a bin kept outside a house for rubbish

duster *noun* a cloth for dusting things

dustman *noun* dustmen a person whose job is to empty dustbins

dustpan *noun* a pan into which you brush dust

dusty *adjective* **dustier, dustiest** covered with or full of dust

dutiful *adjective* doing your duty; obedient

duty *noun* **duties** **1.** your duty is what you have to do, because it is right or part of your job **2.** a duty is a kind of tax

duvet *noun* (**doo**-vay) a kind of quilt used instead of other bedclothes

DVD *noun* **DVDs** short for *digital video disc* or *digital versatile disc*, a disc on which large amounts of sound and pictures can be stored, especially films

dwarf *noun* **dwarfs** or **dwarves** a very small person or thing
dwarf *verb* to dwarf something is to make it seem very small • *The skyscraper dwarfs all the buildings round it.*

dwell *verb* **dwelling, dwelt** to dwell in a place is to live there

dwelling *noun* a house or other place to live in

dwindle *verb* to dwindle is to get smaller gradually • *Their food supplies were starting to dwindle.*

dye *verb* to dye something is to change its colour by putting it in a special liquid
dye *noun* a liquid used to dye things

dyke *noun* another spelling of **dike**

dynamic *adjective* energetic and active

dynamite *noun* a powerful explosive

dynamo *noun* **dynamos** a machine that makes electricity

dynasty *noun* **dynasties** (**din**-a-sti) a series of kings and queens from the same family

dyslexia *noun* (dis-**lek**-si-a) special difficulty in being able to read and spell words
dyslexic *adjective* someone is dyslexic when they have dyslexia

Education has all the vowels – **a, e, i, o, u** – in it.

each *determiner, pronoun* each person or thing in a group is every one of them when you think of them separately • *Each film lasts an hour.* • *You get ten marks for each of these questions.* • *We all knew each other.*

eager *adjective* wanting to do something very much; enthusiastic **eagerly** *adverb* **eagerness** *noun*

eagle *noun* a large bird of prey

ear[1] *noun* the part of your body that you hear with

ear[2] *noun* the spike of seeds at the top of a stalk of corn

earache *noun* a pain inside your ear

earl *noun* a British nobleman

earlobe *noun* the rounded part that hangs down at the bottom of your ear

early *adverb, adjective* **earlier, earliest** **1.** arriving or happening before the usual or expected time • *Jane caught a bus and got home early.* **2.** happening near the beginning • *The flowers bloom in early spring.* • *The equalizer came early in the second half.*

earn *verb* **1.** to earn money is to get it by working for it **2.** to earn a reward or praise is to do something good so that you deserve it

earnest *adjective* serious about something you want to do or about something important

earnings *plural noun* earnings are money that someone earns

earphones *plural noun* earphones are a device for listening to music that fit in your ears

earring *noun* a piece of jewellery worn on the ear

earshot *noun* a sound is in earshot when it is close enough for you to hear it

earth *noun* **1.** the earth is the planet that we live on **2.** earth is soil or the ground **3.** an earth is a hole where a fox or badger lives

earthly *adjective* to do with life on earth

earthquake *noun* a violent movement of part of the earth's surface caused by pressure that has built up under the earth's crust

earthworm *noun* a common worm that is found in the soil

earwig *noun* a crawling garden insect with pincers at the end of its body

ease *noun* to do something with ease is to do it without any difficulty or trouble **to be at ease** is to be comfortable and relaxed • *She liked Sarah and felt at ease with her.*
ease *verb* **1.** to ease something unpleasant is to make it easier or less troublesome **2.** a pain or problem eases when it becomes less severe

easel *noun* a stand or frame for holding a blackboard or a painting

easily *adverb* **1.** without difficulty; with ease • *Pencil marks can be easily rubbed out afterwards.* **2.** by far • *This was easily the best victory of his career.* **3.** very likely • *They could easily be wrong.*

east *noun* **1.** the direction in which the sun rises • *A gale was blowing from the east.* **2.** the part of a country or city that is in this direction
east *adjective, adverb* **1.** towards the east or in the east • *An east wind made the day very cold.* **2.** coming from the east • *Travelling east, they walked for two days.*

Easter *noun* a Christian festival in spring, commemorating Christ's rising from the dead

eastern *adjective* coming from or to do with the east

eastward or **eastwards** *adjective, adverb* towards the east

easy *adjective* **easier, easiest** something easy can be done or understood without trouble • *He started with easy questions.* • *The machine is easy to use.*

eat *verb* **eating, ate, eaten** to eat food is to chew it and swallow it **to eat something up** or **eat something away** is to use it up or destroy it • *Acid rain has eaten away the forests.* • *Housekeeping eats up most of my free time.*

eatable *adjective* food is eatable when it is good and pleasant to eat

eaves *plural noun* eaves are the overhanging edges of a roof

ebb *noun* the movement of the tide when it is going out **to be at a low ebb** is to be in a poor or weak condition
ebb *verb* **1.** the tide ebbs when it goes away from the land **2.** something ebbs or ebbs away when it gradually becomes weaker • *After a while, his enthusiasm ebbed away.*

ebony *noun* ebony is a hard black wood

eccentric *adjective* (ik-**sen**-trik) behaving strangely **eccentricity** *noun* strange or unusual behaviour

echo *noun* **echoes** a second sound that you hear when the original sound bounces back off something solid such as walls or high rocks
echo *verb* **echoes, echoing, echoed** **1.** to echo is to make an echo **2.** to echo something said is to repeat it

éclair *noun* (ay-**klair**) a finger-shaped cake of pastry with a cream filling

eclipse *noun* An eclipse is the blocking of light from the sun or moon, causing a short period of darkness. An eclipse of the sun happens when the moon comes between the sun and the earth and blocks out the light from the sun; and an eclipse of the moon happens when the earth comes between the moon and the sun and casts a dark shadow on the surface of the moon.

ecology *noun* (ee-**kol**-o-ji) ecology is the study of living creatures and plants in their surroundings **ecological** *adjective* to do with ecology

economic *adjective* (eek-o-**nom**-ik or ek-o-**nom**-ik) to do with economics or the economy • *Coal no longer dominates the country's economic scene.*

economical *adjective* (eek-o-**nom**-ik-al) using money and resources carefully **economically** *adverb* to do something economically is to use money and resources carefully when you do it

economics *noun* (eek-o-**nom**-iks or ek-o-**nom**-iks) economics is the study of how money is used and how goods and services are provided and used

economist *noun* (i-**kon**-o-mist) someone who studies economics

economize *verb* (i-**kon**-o-myz) to economize is to use money more carefully This word can also be spelled **economise**.

economy *noun* economies (i-**kon**-o-mi) **1**. an economy is a country's or family's income and the way it is spent **2**. economy is being careful with money

ecstasy *noun* ecstasies a feeling of great happiness or delight **ecstatic** *adjective* delighted about something

eczema *noun* (**ek**-si-ma) eczema is a skin disease that causes rough itching patches

edge *noun* **1**. the part along the side or end of something **2**. the sharp part of a knife or other cutting device

edge *verb* to edge is to move gradually and carefully • *He edged a little closer to the door.*

edgy *adjective* **edgier**, **edgiest** nervous and irritable

edible *adjective* an edible substance is one that you can eat and is not poisonous

edit *verb* **1**. to edit a book, newspaper or magazine is to get it ready for publishing **2**. to edit a film or tape recording is to choose parts of it and put them in the right order **editorial** *adjective* to do with editing or editors

edition *noun* **1**. the form in which something is published • *There is a special illustrated edition of the book.* **2**. all the copies of a newspaper, magazine or book issued at the same time

editor *noun* **1**. someone who prepares a book, newspaper or magazine for publishing **2**. the person who manages a newspaper and is in charge of everything that is published in it

educate *verb* to educate someone is to teach them and give them knowledge and skills

education *noun* the process of teaching people and giving them knowledge and skills **educational** *adjective* to do with learning or teaching

eel *noun* a long thin fish that looks like a snake

eerie *adjective* weird and frightening • *It was dark outside and there was an eerie silence.* **eerily** *adverb* in an eerie way • *Her voice echoed eerily in the cold air.*

effect *noun* something that happens because of something else • *the harmful effect of smoking*

effective *adjective* producing what you want; successful • *Dieting is much more effective when you combine it with exercise.* **effectively** *adverb* **effectiveness** *noun*

effervescent *adjective* (ef-er-**vess**-ent) an effervescent liquid is fizzy and gives off bubbles **effervescence** *noun* effervescence is being effervescent

efficient *adjective* doing work well; effective **efficiency** *noun* efficiency is being efficient and doing work well **efficiently** *adverb*

effort *noun* **1**. effort is using energy or hard work **2**. an effort is an attempt
effortless *adjective* not needing much work or effort

e.g. for example • *There are lots of ways of finding out, e.g. ask a teacher.*

egg[1] *noun* **1**. an oval or round object with a thin shell that birds, fish, reptiles and insects lay and in which their young develop **2**. a hen's or duck's egg used as food

egg[2] *verb* **to egg someone on** is to encourage them with taunts or dares • *He didn't want to dance but his friends egged him on.*

Eid *noun* (eed) a Muslim festival that marks the end of the fast of Ramadan

eiderdown *noun* (I-der-down) a quilt stuffed with soft material

eight *noun* the number 8

eighteen *noun* the number 18
eighteenth *adjective, noun* 18th

eighth *adjective, noun* the next after the seventh

eighty *noun* **eighties** the number 80
eightieth *adjective, noun* 80th

either *determiner, pronoun* **1**. one or the other of two people or things • *Either road will take us there.* • *Either of them might have seen the killer.* **2**. both of two things • *The houses on either side were all boarded up.*

either *adverb* also; similarly • *I don't like cabbage and my brother doesn't either.*

either *conjunction* **either ... or ...** one thing or another, but not both • *You can choose either a CD or a DVD.*

eject *verb* **1**. to eject something is to send it out with force **2**. to eject someone is to make them leave

elaborate *adjective* (i-**lab**-er-at) complicated or detailed

elastic *noun* cord or material with strands of rubber in it so that it can stretch
elastic *adjective* able to stretch and then return to its original shape or length

elated *adjective* very pleased and excited

elbow *noun* the joint in the middle of your arm, where it bends

elbow *verb* to elbow someone is to push or prod them with your elbow

elder *adjective* older • *Josh is my elder brother.*

elderly *adjective* rather old

eldest *adjective* oldest • *Their eldest son George was born in 1660.*

elect *verb* to elect someone is to choose them by voting

election *noun* the process of voting for people to be the government or to run an organization

electric or **electrical** *adjective* to do with electricity or worked by electricity
electrically *adverb* by using electricity

electrician *noun* someone whose job is to fit and repair electrical equipment

electricity *noun* electricity is a kind of energy used to produce light and heat and to make machines work

electrocute *verb* to electrocute someone is to kill them when a large charge of electricity passes through them **electrocution** *noun* electrocution is electrocuting someone

electron *noun* a particle of matter that is smaller than an atom and has a negative electric charge

electronic *adjective* electronic equipment uses transistors and silicon chips which control electric currents **electronically** *adverb* by means of electronic devices

electronics *plural noun* the use or study of electronic devices

elegant *adjective* graceful and smart
elegance *noun* elegance is being graceful and smart **elegantly** *adverb*

element *noun* **1**. a substance that cannot be split up into simpler substances, for example copper and oxygen **2**. one part of something **3**. the elements are forces that make the weather, such as rain and wind **4**. a wire or coil that gives out heat in an electric heater or cooker

elementary *adjective* dealing with the simplest stages of something; easy

a
b
c
d
e
f
g
h
i
j
k
l
m
n
o
p
q
r
s
t
u
v
w
x
y
z

elephant *noun* a very large animal found in Africa and India, with a thick grey skin, large ears, a trunk and tusks

elevate *verb* to elevate something is to lift it or raise it to a higher position

eleven *noun* elevens **1**. the number 11 **2**. a team of eleven people in cricket, football and other sports **eleventh** *adjective, noun* 11th

elf *noun* elves a tiny mischievous fairy in stories

eligible *adjective* a person is eligible for something when they are qualified or suitable for it **eligibility** *noun* eligibility is being eligible for something

eliminate *verb* to eliminate someone or something is to get rid of them **elimination** *noun* elimination is getting rid of someone or something

elk *noun* elk or elks a large kind of deer

ellipse *noun* an oval shape

elliptical *adjective* oval-shaped

elm *noun* a tall tree with large rough leaves

eloquent *adjective* speaking well and expressing ideas clearly

else *adverb* besides; instead • *Nobody else knows.* **or else** otherwise • *Run or else you'll be late.*

elsewhere *adverb* somewhere else

elusive *adjective* difficult to find or catch • *Deer are elusive animals.*

email *noun* **1**. email is a system of sending messages from one person to another, using computers. **Email** is short for *electronic mail*. **2**. an email is a message sent this way

email *verb* to email someone is to send them an email

embankment *noun* a long wall or bank of earth that holds back water or supports a road or railway

embark *verb* to embark is to go on board a ship **to embark on something** is to begin something important **embarkation** *noun* embarkation is going on board a ship

embarrass *verb* to embarrass someone is to make them feel shy or awkward **embarrassment** *noun* embarrassment is feeling embarrassed

embassy *noun* embassies a building where an ambassador from another country lives and has an office

embers *plural noun* the embers of a fire are small pieces of coal or wood that keep glowing when the fire is going out

emblem *noun* a symbol that stands for something • *The dove is an emblem of peace.*

embrace *verb* to embrace someone is to hold them closely in your arms

embroider *verb* embroiders, embroidering, embroidered to embroider cloth is to decorate it by stitching in designs or pictures **embroidery** *noun* embroidery is the art of embroidering

embryo *noun* embryos a baby or young animal that is growing in the womb

emerald *noun* **1**. a green jewel **2**. a bright green colour

emerge *verb* to emerge is to come out or appear

emergency *noun* emergencies a sudden dangerous or serious situation that needs to be dealt with very quickly

emigrant *noun* someone who leaves their own country and goes to live in another country

emigrate *verb* to emigrate is to leave your own country and go and live in another country emigration *noun*

eminent *adjective* famous and respected • *He is Britain's most eminent scientist.*

emission *noun* 1. the action of sending something out 2. something that is emitted, for example smoke or fumes

emit *verb* emitting, emitted to emit something such as smoke or fumes is to send it out

emotion *noun* 1. an emotion is a strong feeling in your mind, such as love or fear 2. emotion is being excited or upset • *Tears of emotion flooded his eyes.* emotional *adjective* showing emotion; to do with emotion emotionally *adverb*

emperor *noun* the ruler of an empire

emphasis *noun* emphases special importance given to something

emphasize *verb* to emphasize something is to give it special importance, for example by saying it more loudly or by explaining it more fully This word can also be spelled **emphasise**.

emphatic *adjective* an emphatic statement or expression is one that you make very firmly or strongly emphatically *adverb* you say something emphatically when you are very firm and definite about it

empire *noun* a group of countries ruled by one person or group of people

employ *verb* 1. to employ someone is to pay them to work for you 2. to employ something is to use it

employee *noun* (im-**ploi**-ee) someone who works for another person or group of people

employer *noun* a person or organization that has people working for them

employment *noun* work for which you are paid

empress *noun* a female emperor or the wife of an emperor

empty *adjective* emptier, emptiest an empty place or container has nothing or no one in it emptiness *noun* emptiness is being empty

empty *verb* empties, emptying, emptied 1. to empty something is to make it empty 2. to empty is to become empty • *After the show the hall quickly emptied.*

emu *noun* (**ee**-mew) a large Australian bird that cannot fly, like an ostrich but smaller

emulsion *noun* 1. emulsion is a creamy or slightly oily liquid 2. emulsion or emulsion paint, a kind of water paint used for decorating buildings

enable *verb* to enable someone to do something is to make it possible for them • *A calculator will enable you to multiply and divide quickly.*

enamel *noun* 1. enamel is a shiny glassy substance that is baked on to metal or pottery to form a hard bright surface 2. enamel is also the hard shiny surface of teeth

enchant *verb* 1. to enchant someone is to delight or please them 2. to enchant someone is also to put a magic spell on them in stories enchanted *adjective* under a magic spell enchanting *adjective* beautiful or delightful enchantment *noun* a feeling of wonder or delight

enclose *verb* 1. to enclose an area is to put a fence or wall round it 2. to enclose something is to put it in an envelope with a letter

enclosure *noun* a piece of ground with a fence or wall round it

encore *noun* (**on**-kor) an extra item performed at a concert or show

encounter *verb* **1.** to encounter someone is to meet them unexpectedly **2.** to encounter something is to experience it • *We have encountered a few problems.*

encourage *verb* **1.** to encourage someone is to give them confidence or hope • *We were encouraged by your support.* **2.** to encourage someone to do something is to urge and help them to do it • *They try to encourage schools to take part in these road safety schemes.* **encouragement** *noun* encouragement is supporting someone or something in what they do • *The crowd shouted their encouragement.*

encyclopedia *noun* a book or set of books containing a lot of information on a particular subject or on many different subjects

> The word **encyclopedia** comes from the Greek words *enkuklios* meaning 'complete' and *paideia* meaning 'education'.

end *noun* **1.** the end of something is the last part of it or the point where it stops • *Holly stood at the end of the pier.* • *This is the end of our journey.* **2.** an end is an aim or purpose • *They used the money for their own ends.* **on end 1.** upright • *His hair stood on end.* **2.** continuously • *She spoke for two hours on end.*

end *verb* **1.** to end something is to finish it **2.** to end is to finish

endanger *verb* to endanger someone or something is to put them in a situation where they could be harmed

endangered species *noun* a type of animal or plant that has become so rare that it is in danger of becoming extinct

endeavour *verb* to endeavour to do something is to try hard to do it

ending *noun* the last part of something • *They all wanted a story with a happy ending.*

endless *adjective* never stopping • *At work, he drank endless cups of tea.* **endlessly** *adverb* without ending

endure *verb* **1.** to endure pain or suffering is to put up with it **2.** to endure is to continue or last **endurance** *noun* endurance is suffering or putting up with something unpleasant

enemy *noun* **enemies 1.** someone who is opposed to someone else and wants to harm them **2.** a nation or army that is at war with another country

energetic *adjective* **1.** an energetic person has a lot of energy **2.** an energetic activity needs a lot of energy • *They then performed an energetic dance.* **energetically** *adverb* with a lot of energy

energy *noun* **energies 1.** energy is the ability to do work or provide power, for example electrical energy **2.** a person's energy is the strength they have to do things

enforce *verb* to enforce a law or order is to make people obey it **enforcement** *noun* enforcement is making people obey laws

engage *verb* to engage someone in conversation is to talk to them

engaged *adjective* **1.** someone is engaged when they have promised to marry someone **2.** a telephone line or lavatory is engaged when someone is already using it

engagement *noun* a promise to marry someone

engine *noun* **1.** a machine that turns energy into motion **2.** a vehicle that pulls a railway train

engineer *noun* a person who designs and builds machines, roads and bridges

engineering *noun* engineering is the designing and building of machines, roads, bridges and other large buildings

engrave *verb* to engrave a surface is to carve figures or words on it **engraving** *noun* a print made by engraving a design

engrossed *adjective* to be engrossed in something is to concentrate on it and ignore other things around you

engulf *verb* to engulf something is to flow over it and swamp it • *The house was quickly engulfed in flames.*

enjoy *verb* **1.** to enjoy something is to get pleasure from it **2.** to enjoy yourself is to have a good time **enjoyable** *adjective* able to be enjoyed; pleasant **enjoyment** *noun* enjoyment is a feeling of great pleasure

enlarge *verb* to enlarge something is to make it larger

enormous *adjective* very large; huge **enormously** *adverb* hugely; a lot • *I enjoyed the party enormously.*

enough *determiner, noun, adverb* as much or as many as you need or can cope with • *I've saved enough money for a new bike.* • *I have had enough.* • *Are you warm enough?*

enquire *verb* to enquire about something is to ask for information about it • *He enquired if I was well.* **enquiry** *noun* a question that asks for information

enrage *verb* to enrage a person or animal is to make them very angry

enrol *verb* **enrolling, enrolled** to enrol in a society or class is to become a member of it **enrolment** *noun* enrolment is becoming a member or making someone a member

ensure *verb* to ensure that something happens or has happened is to make sure of it • *Please ensure that you leave the room tidy when you go.*

entangle *verb* to entangle something is to get it tangled or caught up

enter *verb* **1.** to enter a place is to come into it or go into it **2.** to enter something in a list or book is to write or record it there **3.** to enter data in a computer is to key it in **4.** to enter for a competition or examination is to take part in it

enterprise *noun* **1.** enterprise is being bold and adventurous **2.** an enterprise is a difficult or important task or project

enterprising *adjective* an enterprising person or activity is one that is exciting or adventurous

entertain *verb* **1.** to entertain someone is to amuse them or give them pleasure, as a singer or comedian does **2.** to entertain people is to have them as guests and give them food and drink **entertainer** *noun* someone such as a singer or comedian who entertains people **entertainment** *noun* entertainment is something that entertains or amuses people

enthusiasm *noun* enthusiasm is a feeling of excitement and interest you show for something

enthusiastic *adjective* full of enthusiasm **enthusiastically** *adverb*

entire *adjective* whole or complete • *The entire school gathered in the field for a photograph.* **entirely** *adverb* completely; in every way • *The brothers look entirely different.*

entitle *verb* to entitle someone to something is to give them a right to it • *The voucher entitles you to a free drink with your pizza.*

entrance[1] *noun* (**en**-transs) **1.** the way into a place **2.** coming into a room or on to a stage or arena • *Everyone clapped when the clowns made their entrance.*

entrance[2] *verb* (in-**trahnss**) to entrance someone is to delight or enchant them

entrant *noun* someone who goes in for a competition or examination

entreat *verb* to entreat someone is to ask them seriously or earnestly

entrust *verb* to entrust someone with something or to entrust something to someone, is to give it to them to look after

entry *noun* **entries 1.** an entrance **2.** something written in a list or diary

envelop *verb* (in-**vel**-op) to envelop something is to cover or wrap it completely • *The mountain was enveloped in mist.*

envelope *noun* (**en**-ve-lohp or **on**-ve-lohp) a paper wrapper for a letter

envious *adjective* you are envious of someone when they have something you would like to have too **enviously** *adverb*

environment *noun* **1.** surroundings, especially as they affect people and other living things • *Plants can die out if their environment is damaged.* **2.** the environment is the natural world of the land and sea and air **environmental** *adjective* to do with the environment

envy *noun* the feeling of wanting something that someone else has got
envy *verb* **envies, envying, envied** to envy someone is to be envious of them

epic *noun* a story or poem about heroes

epidemic *noun* a disease that spreads quickly among the people of an area

epilepsy *noun* epilepsy is a disease of the nervous system, which causes fits

epileptic *adjective* to do with epilepsy • *an epileptic fit*
epileptic *noun* someone who suffers from epilepsy

epilogue *noun* (**ep**-i-log) words written or spoken at the end of a story or a play

episode *noun* **1.** one event that is part of a series of happenings or forms part of a story **2.** one programme in a radio or television serial

epitaph *noun* words written on a tomb or describing a person who has died

equal *adjective* things are equal when they are the same in amount, size or value
equal *noun* a person or thing that is equal to another
equal *verb* **equalling, equalled** to equal something is to be the same in amount, size or value

equality *noun* equality is being equal

equalize *verb* to equalize is to even the score in a game of football, hockey, etc. **equalizer** *noun* a goal that makes a score equal This word can also be spelled **equalise**.

equally *adverb* in the same way or to the same extent • *You are all equally to blame.*

equation *noun* (i-**kway**-zhon) *(in mathematics)* a statement that two amounts are equal, for example 3 + 4 = 2 + 5

equator *noun* (i-**kway**-ter) an imaginary line round the earth at an equal distance from the

North and South Poles **equatorial** *adjective* to do with the equator or near the equator

equestrian *adjective* to do with horse-riding

equilateral *adjective* (ee-kwi-**lat**-er-al) an equilateral triangle has all its sides equal

equilibrium *noun* **equilibria** (ee-kwi-**lib**-ri-um) equilibrium is a state of even balance

equinox *noun* the time of year when day and night are equal in length (about 20 March in spring and about 22 September in autumn)

equip *verb* **equipping, equipped** to equip someone or something is to supply them with what is needed

equipment *noun* equipment is a set of things needed for a special purpose

equivalent *adjective* things are equivalent when they are equal in value, importance or meaning

era *noun* (**eer**-a) a long period of history

erase *verb* **1.** to erase something written is to rub it out **2.** to erase a recording on magnetic tape is to remove it **eraser** *noun* a piece of rubber for rubbing out writing

erect *adjective* standing straight up
erect *verb* to erect something is to set it up or build it

erode *verb* **erodes, eroding, eroded** to erode something is to wear it away • *Water has eroded the rocks.*

erosion *noun* erosion is the wearing away of the earth's surface by the action of water and wind

errand *noun* a short journey to take a message or fetch something

erratic *adjective* (i-**rat**-ik) not reliable or regular **erratically** *adverb*

error *noun* a mistake **in error** by mistake

erupt *verb* **1.** a volcano erupts when it sends out lava **2.** something powerful or violent erupts when it suddenly happens **eruption** *noun* when a volcano erupts

escalate *verb* to escalate is to become gradually greater or more serious • *The riots escalated into a war.* **escalation** *noun* when something becomes greater or more serious

escalator *noun* a moving staircase that takes you from one floor to another in a building

escape *verb* **1.** to escape is to get free or get away **2.** to escape something is to avoid it • *He escaped the washing-up.*

escape *noun* an act or way of escaping • *What a lucky escape!* • *There was no escape.*

escort *noun* (**ess**-kort) a person or group who accompanies someone, especially to give protection

escort *verb* (i-**skort**) to escort someone is to act as an escort to them

especially *adverb* chiefly; more than anything else • *I like cheese, especially strong cheese.*

espionage *noun* (**ess**-pi-on-ahzh) espionage is spying on other countries or people

essay *noun* a short piece of writing on one subject

essence *noun* the most important quality or ingredient of something

essential *adjective* something is essential when it is very important and you must have it or do it • *A warm coat is essential in winter.* **essentially** *adverb* basically; in many ways • *The two stories are essentially the same.*

essential *noun* something you must have or do • *I've made a list of some essentials to pack.*

establish *verb* to establish a business, government or relationship is to start it on a firm basis

establishment *noun* **1.** a place where people do business **2.** establishing something

estate *noun* **1.** an area of land with a set of houses or factories on it **2.** a large area of land belonging to one person

estate agent *noun* someone whose business is selling or letting buildings and land

estimate *noun* (**ess**-ti-mat) a rough calculation or guess about an amount or value

estimate *verb* (**ess**-ti-mayt) to estimate is to make an estimate

estimation *noun* estimation is making a rough estimate

estuary *noun* estuaries (**ess**-tew-er-i) the mouth of a large river where it flows into the sea

etc. short for **et cetera**

et cetera and other similar things; and so on

etch *verb* to etch a picture is to make it by engraving on a metal plate with an acid **etching** *noun* a picture made by engraving

eternal *adjective* lasting for ever; not ending or changing **eternally** *adverb* for ever **eternity** *noun* eternity is time that goes on for ever

ethnic *adjective* belonging to a particular national or racial group

eucalyptus *noun* (yoo-ka-**lip**-tus) an evergreen tree from which an oil is obtained

euphemism *noun* A euphemism is a word or phrase which is used instead of an impolite or less tactful one. To 'pass away' is a euphemism for 'die'. • *She passed away in her sleep.*

euro *noun* **euros** or **euro** the single currency introduced in the European Union in 1999

euthanasia *noun* (yooth-an-**ay**-zi-a) euthanasia is causing someone to die gently and without pain when they are suffering from an incurable disease

evacuate *verb* to evacuate people is to move them away from a dangerous place **evacuation** *noun* evacuation is moving people away from a dangerous place **evacuee** *noun* someone who is evacuated during a war

evade *verb* to evade someone or something is to make an effort to avoid them

evaporate *verb* to evaporate is to change from liquid into steam or vapour **evaporation** *noun* when a liquid changes into steam or vapour

evasive *adjective* trying to avoid answering something; not honest or straightforward

eve *noun* the day or evening before an important day, for example New Year's Eve

even *adjective* 1. level and smooth 2. calm and stable • *He has a very even temper.* 3. equal • *The scores were even.* 4. able to be divided exactly by two • *6 and 14 are even numbers.* **evenly** *adverb* in an even way • *The money will be shared out evenly.* **evenness** *noun*
even *verb* 1. to even something is to make it even 2. to even or even out is to become even
even *adverb* used to emphasize another word • *You haven't even started your work!* • *I ran fast, but she ran even faster.*

evening *noun* the time at the end of the day before night time

event *noun* 1. something that happens, especially something important 2. an item in an athletics contest

eventful *adjective* full of happenings, especially remarkable or exciting ones

eventual *adjective* happening at last or as a result

eventually *adverb* finally, in the end • *We eventually managed to get the door open.*

ever *adverb* 1. at any time • *It's the best present I've ever had.* 2. always • *ever hopeful* 3. (*informal*) used for emphasis • *Why ever didn't you tell me?*

evergreen *adjective* having green leaves all through the year

evergreen *noun* an evergreen tree

everlasting *adjective* lasting for ever or for a long time

every *determiner* all the people or things of a particular kind; each • *Every child should learn to swim.* **every other** each alternate one; every second one • *Every other house had a garage.*

everybody *pronoun* everyone

everyday *adjective* happening or used every day; ordinary • *everyday life*

everyone *pronoun* every person; all people • *Everyone likes her.*

everything *pronoun* all things; all

everywhere *adverb* in all places

evict *verb* to evict someone is to make them move out of their house **eviction** *noun* making someone move out of their house

evidence *noun* evidence is facts and information that give people reason to believe something

evident *adjective* obvious; clearly seen • *It is evident that he is lying.* **evidently** *adverb* clearly; obviously

evil *adjective* an evil person or action is one that is wicked and harmful
evil *noun* something wicked or harmful

evolution *noun* (ee-vo-**loo**-shon) the development of animals and plants over millions of years from earlier or simpler forms of life

evolve *verb* to develop gradually or naturally

ewe *noun* (yoo) a female sheep

exact *adjective* completely correct or accurate **exactly** *adverb* in an exact way; correctly **exactness** *noun* being correct

exaggerate *verb* to exaggerate something is to make it seem bigger or better or worse than it really is **exaggeration** *noun* making something seem more than it really is

exam *noun (informal)* an examination

examination *noun* **1.** a test of someone's knowledge or skill **2.** a close inspection of something

examine *verb* to examine something is to look at it closely or in detail

examiner *noun* a person who sets and marks an examination to test students' knowledge

example *noun* **1.** a single thing or event that shows what others of the same kind are like **2.** a person or thing that you should copy or learn from **for example** as an example

exasperate *verb* to exasperate someone is to make them very annoyed **exasperation** *noun* a feeling of being very annoyed

excavate *verb* to excavate a piece of land is to dig in it, especially in building or archaeology **excavation** *noun* digging in land

exceed *verb* **1.** to exceed an amount or achievement is to be more than it or do better than it **2.** to exceed a rule or limit is to go beyond it when you are not supposed to • *The driver was exceeding the speed limit.*

excel *verb* **excelling, excelled** to excel at something is to be very good at it and better than everyone else

excellent *adjective* extremely good; of the best kind **excellence** *noun* excellence is being extremely good

except *preposition* not including; apart from • *Everyone got a prize except me.*

exception *noun* something or someone that does not follow the normal rule

exceptional *adjective* very good in a way that is unusual • *Her eyesight is exceptional.* **exceptionally** *adverb* to an unusual degree

excerpt *noun* a piece taken from a book or story or film

excess *noun* too much of something • *We have an excess of food.*

excessive *adjective* too much or too great **excessively** *adverb* too; by too much • *They are excessively greedy.*

exchange *verb* to exchange something is to give it and receive something else for it
exchange *noun* changing one thing for another

excite *verb* **exciting, excited** to excite someone is to make them eager and enthusiastic about something **excitable** *adjective* easily excited

excitement *noun* excitement is being excited

exclaim *verb* to exclaim is to shout or cry out

exclamation *noun* an exclamation is a word or phrase you say out loud that expresses a strong feeling such as surprise or pain

exclamation mark *noun* the punctuation mark (!) placed after an exclamation

exclude *verb* to exclude someone or something is to stop them taking part in something **exclusion** *noun* exclusion is stopping someone or something from taking part

exclusive *adjective* **1.** not shared with others • *Today's newspaper has an exclusive report about the match.* **2.** allowing only a few people to be involved • *They joined an exclusive club.* **exclusively** *adverb*

excrete *verb* to excrete is to pass waste matter out of your body

excuse *noun* (iks-**kewss**) a reason you give to explain why you have done something wrong
excuse *verb* (iks-**kewz**) **1.** to excuse someone is to forgive them **2.** to excuse someone something is to allow them not to do it • *Please may I be excused swimming?* **excuse me** a polite apology for interrupting or disagreeing

execute *verb* to execute someone is to put them to death as a punishment **execution** *noun* putting someone to death **executioner** *noun* someone who executes people

executive *noun* a senior person in a business or government organization

exercise *noun* exercise is using your body to make it strong and healthy
exercise *verb* **1.** to exercise is to do exercises **2.** to exercise an animal is to give it exercise

exercise book *noun* a book for writing in

exert *verb* to exert oneself or one's ability is to make an effort to get something done • *He exerted all his strength to bend the bar.*
exertion *noun* exertion is making a big effort

exhale *verb* to exhale is to breathe out

exhaust *noun* **1.** the waste gases from an engine **2.** the pipe these gases are sent out through
exhaust *verb* **1.** to exhaust someone is to make them very tired **2.** to exhaust something is to use it up completely
exhaustion *noun* great tiredness

exhibit *verb* to exhibit something is to show it in a gallery or museum
exhibit *noun* something displayed in a gallery or museum

exhibition *noun* a collection of things put on display for people to look at

exile *verb* to exile someone is to send them away from their country
exile *noun* **1.** exile is having to live away from your own country **2.** an exile is a person who is exiled

exist *verb* **1.** to exist is to have life or be real • *Do ghosts exist?* **2.** to exist is also to stay alive • *They existed on biscuits and water.*

existence *noun* existing or being

exit *noun* the way out of a place
exit *verb* to exit is to leave a place

exotic *adjective* unusual and colourful because of coming from another part of the world

expand *verb* **1.** to expand something is to make it larger **2.** to expand is to become larger expansion *noun* expansion is becoming larger or making something larger

expanse *noun* a wide area

expect *verb* **1.** to expect something is to think that it will probably happen • *I expect it will rain.* **2.** to be expecting someone is to be waiting for them to arrive **3.** to expect something is to think that it ought to happen • *She expects us to be quiet.*

expecting *adjective* a woman is expecting when she is pregnant

expectant *adjective* full of expectation or hope

expectation *noun* **1.** expecting something or being hopeful **2.** something you hope to get

expedition *noun* a journey made in order to do something

expel *verb* expelling, expelled **1.** to expel something is to send or force it out • *The fan expels stale air and fumes.* **2.** to expel someone is to make them leave a school or country

expenditure *noun* expenditure is when you spend money or use effort • *We must reduce our expenditure.*

expense *noun* the cost of doing something

expensive *adjective* costing a lot of money

experience *noun* **1.** experience is what you learn from doing and seeing things **2.** an experience is something that has happened to you
experience *verb* to experience something is to have it happen to you

experienced *adjective* having skill or knowledge from much experience

experiment *noun* a test made in order to study what happens experimental *adjective* something is experimental when it is being tried out to see how good or successful it is experimentally *adverb* as an experiment
experiment *verb* to experiment is to carry out experiments experimentation *noun* doing experiments

expert *noun* someone who has skill or special knowledge in something
expert *adjective* having great knowledge or skill

expertise *noun* expert ability or knowledge

expire *verb* to expire is to come to an end or to stop being usable • *My bus pass has expired.* expiry *noun* the time when something expires

explain *verb* **1.** to explain something is to make it clear to someone else **2.** to explain a fact or event is to show why it happens • *That explains his absence.*

explanation *noun* something you say that explains something or gives reasons for it

explode *verb* **1.** to explode is to burst or suddenly release energy with a loud bang **2.** to explode a bomb is to set it off **3.** to explode is to increase suddenly or quickly

exploit *noun* (**eks**-ploit) a brave or exciting deed

exploit *verb* (iks-**ploit**) **1.** to exploit resources is to use or develop them **2.** to exploit someone is to use them selfishly or unfairly **exploitation** *noun* exploitation is exploiting something or someone

explore *verb* to explore a place is to travel through it to find out more about it **exploration** *noun* exploring a place **explorer** *noun* someone who explores a remote country to find out more about it

explosion *noun* **1.** the exploding of a bomb or other weapon **2.** a sudden or quick increase • *There was a population explosion after the war.*

explosive *noun* a substance that can explode

explosive *adjective* likely to explode; able to cause an explosion

export *verb* (iks-**port**) to export goods is to send them abroad to be sold **exporter** *noun* someone who exports goods

export *noun* (**eks**-port) something that is sent abroad to be sold

expose *verb* **1.** to expose something is to reveal or uncover it **2.** to expose film is to let light reach it in a camera when taking a picture

exposure *noun* **1.** exposure is being harmed by the weather when in the open without enough protection **2.** an exposure is a single photograph or frame on a film

express *adjective* going or sent quickly

express *noun* a fast train stopping at only a few stations

express *verb* to express an idea or feeling is to put it into words

expression *noun* **1.** the look on a person's face that shows what they are thinking or feeling **2.** a word or phrase **expressive** *adjective* an expressive look is one that clearly shows your feelings

expulsion *noun* when someone is forced to leave a place

exquisite *adjective* very delicate or beautiful **exquisitely** *adverb*

extend *verb* **1.** to extend is to stretch out **2.** to extend something is to make it longer or larger

extension *noun* **1.** an extension is something added on, especially to a building **2.** an extension is also an extra telephone in an office or house

extensive *adjective* covering a large area • *The bomb caused extensive damage.* **extensively** *adverb* over a large area • *She travelled extensively.*

extent *noun* **1.** the area or length of something **2.** an amount or level • *The extent of the damage was enormous.*

exterior *noun* the outside of something

exterminate *verb* to exterminate a people or breed of animal is to kill all the members of it **extermination** *noun* extermination is killing all the people or animals in a place

external *adjective* outside **externally** *adverb* on the outside

extinct *adjective* **1.** an animal or bird is extinct when there are no more examples of it alive **2.** a volcano is extinct when it is not burning or active any more **extinction** *noun* when something no longer exists

extinguish *verb* to extinguish a fire or light is to put it out **extinguisher** *noun* a device for putting out a fire

extra *adjective* more than usual; added • *There is no extra charge for taking a bicycle on the train.*

extra *noun* **1.** an extra person or thing **2.** someone acting as part of the crowd in a film or play

extract *noun* (**eks**-trakt) **1.** a short piece taken from a book, play or film **2.** something obtained from something else • *a plant extract*

extract *verb* (iks-**trakt**) to extract something is to remove it or take it out of something else

extraction *noun* **1.** a person's extraction is the place or people they come from • *She is of Indian extraction.* **2.** extraction is taking something out

extraordinary *adjective* unusual or very strange **extraordinarily** *adverb* in an extraordinary way

extraterrestrial *adjective* existing in or coming from another planet

extravagant *adjective* spending or using too much of something **extravagance** *noun* extravagance is being extravagant **extravagantly** *adverb*

extreme *adjective* 1. very great or strong • *They were suffering from extreme cold.* 2. farthest away • *She lives in the extreme north of the country.*
extreme *noun* **extremes** 1. something very great, strong or far away 2. either end of something

extremely *adverb* as much or as far as possible; very much • *They are extremely pleased.*

exuberant *adjective* very cheerful or lively **exuberance** *noun* exuberance is being exuberant

eye *noun* 1. the organ of your body used for seeing 2. the small hole in a needle 3. the centre of a storm
eye *verb* **eyeing**, **eyed** to eye someone or something is to look at them closely

eyeball *noun* the ball-shaped part of your eye, inside your eyelids

eyebrow *noun* the curved line of hair growing above each eye

eyelash *noun* one of the short hairs that grow on your eyelids

eyelid *noun* the upper or lower fold of skin that can close over your eyeball

eyesight *noun* a person's eyesight is their ability to see

eyesore *noun* something that is ugly to look at

eyewitness *noun* someone who actually saw something happen, especially an accident or crime

Fuselage comes from French and means 'something shaped like a spindle'.

F short for **Fahrenheit**

fable *noun* a short story about animals, which teaches a lesson about how people should behave

fabric *noun* cloth

fabulous *adjective* 1. very great • *The prince enjoyed fabulous wealth.* 2. *(informal)* wonderful; marvellous

face *noun* 1. the front part of your head 2. the look on your face • *She had a friendly face.* 3. the front or upper side of something • *Put the cards face down.* 4. a surface • *A cube has six faces.* **facial** *adjective* on or to do with your face • *He had some facial injuries.*
face *verb* 1. to face in a certain direction is to look there or be pointing in that direction • *Please face the front.* • *The church faces the school.* 2. to face a problem or danger is to accept that you have to deal with it

facility *noun* **facilities** (fa-**sil**-i-ti) something that helps you to do things • *The sports facilities at the youth club are very good.*

fact *noun* something that is true or certain **in fact** used to say that something is rather surprising • *He sounds like a local, but in fact he is French.*

factor *noun* 1. something that helps to bring about a result or situation • *Hard work has been a factor in her success.* 2. a number by which a larger number can be divided exactly • *4 and 5 are factors of 20.*

factory *noun* **factories** a large building where machines are used to make things

factual *adjective* based on or containing facts

fade *verb* **1.** to fade is to lose colour, freshness or strength **2.** to fade or fade away is to disappear gradually

Fahrenheit *adjective* (**fa**-ren-hyt) using a scale for measuring temperature that gives 32 degrees for freezing water and 212 degrees for boiling water

fail *verb* **1.** to fail is to try to do something but not be able to do it **2.** to fail an exam or test is not to pass it **3.** to fail is also to stop working • *The batteries are failing.* **4.** to fail to do something is not to do it when you should • *He failed to warn me of the danger.*

fail *noun* not being successful in an examination • *She has five passes and one fail.* without fail definitely or always • *I'll be there without fail.*

failing *noun* a fault or weakness

failure *noun* **1.** failure is not being successful **2.** a failure is someone or something that has failed

faint *adjective* **1.** weak; not clear or distinct **2.** nearly unconscious, often because you are exhausted or very hungry faintly *adverb* weakly or not clearly faintness *noun*

faint *verb* to faint is to become unconscious for a short time

fair[1] *adjective* **1.** right or just; honest • *It was a fair fight.* **2.** light in colour • *The sisters both had fair hair.* **3.** quite good • *We've got a fair chance of winning.* **4.** weather is fair when it is fine and not raining fairness *noun* fairness is being fair

fair[2] *noun* **1.** an outdoor entertainment with rides, amusements and stalls **2.** an exhibition or market • *a craft fair*

fairground *noun* a place where a fair is held

fairly *adverb* **1.** quite or rather • *It is fairly hard.* **2.** honestly; justly • *He promised to treat everyone fairly.*

fairy *noun* fairies an imaginary small creature with wings and magic powers

fairy story or **fairy tale** *noun* fairy stories or fairy tales a story about fairies or magic

faith *noun* **1.** faith is strong belief or trust • *We have great faith in her.* **2.** a faith is a religion

faithful *adjective* loyal and trustworthy faithfully *adverb*

fake *noun* a copy of something made to deceive people into thinking it is real

fake *adjective* not real or genuine • *fake diamonds*

fake *verb* **1.** to fake something is to make it look real in order to deceive people **2.** to fake something is also to pretend to have it

falcon *noun* a small kind of hawk

fall *verb* falling, fell, fallen **1.** to fall is to come down quickly towards the ground **2.** numbers or prices fall when they get lower or smaller **3.** a city or stronghold falls when it is captured **4.** to fall sick or ill is to become ill to fall for someone is to start loving them to fall for something is to be tricked into believing it to fall out is to quarrel and stop being friends

fall *noun* **1.** a time when a person or thing falls • *My grandma had a bad fall.* **2.** (in America) autumn

fallout *noun* fallout is radioactive dust that is carried in the air after a nuclear explosion

fallow *adjective* land that is fallow has been ploughed but not sown with crops

falls *plural noun* a waterfall

false *adjective* **1.** untrue or incorrect **2.** faked; not genuine falsely *adverb*

falsehood *noun* **1.** falsehood is telling lies **2.** a falsehood is a lie

falter *verb* **1.** to falter is to hesitate when you move or speak **2.** to falter is also to become weaker • *His courage began to falter.*

fame *noun* fame is being famous

familiar *adjective* **1.** well-known; often seen or experienced • *It was a familiar sight.* **2.** knowing something well • *Are you familiar with this story?* familiarity *noun* familiarity with something is being familiar with it

family *noun* families **1.** parents and their children, sometimes including grandchildren and other relations **2.** a group of animals, plants or things that are alike in some way • *The tiger is a member of the cat family.*

family tree *noun* a diagram showing how people in a family are related

famine *noun* a severe shortage of food that causes many people to die

famished *adjective* extremely hungry

famous *adjective* known to a lot of people

fan¹ *noun* a device for making the air move about, in order to cool people or things

fan¹ *verb* **fanning, fanned** to fan something is to send a draught of air at it • *She fanned her face with her hand.* **to fan out** is to spread out in the shape of a fan

fan² *noun* an enthusiastic follower or supporter of someone or something

fanatic *noun* **fanatics** (fa-**nat**-ik) someone who is too enthusiastic about something **fanatical** *adjective* too enthusiastic about something **fanatically** *adverb*

fanciful *adjective* imagined rather than based on facts or reason

fancy *adjective* **fancier, fanciest** decorated; not plain

fancy *verb* **fancies, fancying, fancied** to fancy something is to want or like it • *Does anyone fancy an ice cream?*

fancy dress *noun* unusual costume that you wear to a party or dance, often to make you look like someone else

fanfare *noun* a short burst of music, often with trumpets and to announce something

fang *noun* a long, sharp tooth

fantastic *adjective* **1.** strange or unusual • *The blocks of ice had been carved into the most fantastic shapes.* **2.** *(informal)* excellent **fantastically** *adverb* strangely or unusually

fantasy *noun* **fantasies 1.** something pleasant that you imagine but isn't likely to happen **2.** a very imaginative story

far *adverb* **farther, farthest 1.** a long way • *We didn't go far.* **2.** much; by a great amount • *She's a far better singer than I am.* **so far** up to now

far *adjective* **farther, farthest** distant; opposite • *She swam to the far side of the river.*

farce *noun* a far-fetched or absurd kind of comedy **farcical** *adjective* absurd and ridiculous

fare *noun* the money you pay to travel on a bus, train, ship or aircraft

fare *verb* the way that someone fares is how well they get on or progress • *How did you fare in your exam?*

farewell *interjection* goodbye

far-fetched *adjective* unlikely to be true; difficult to believe

farm *noun* **1.** an area of land where someone grows crops and keeps animals for food **2.** the buildings on land of this kind

farm *verb* to farm is to grow crops and raise animals for food

farmer *noun* someone who owns or looks after a farm

farmyard *noun* the open area surrounded by farm buildings

farther *adverb, adjective* at or to a greater distance; more distant • *She lives farther from the school than I do.*

farthest *adverb, adjective* at or to the greatest distance; most distant

fascinate *verb* to fascinate someone is to attract or interest them very much **fascinating** *adjective* very interesting **fascination** *noun* a feeling of being fascinated; a great interest in something

fashion *noun* the style of clothes or other things that most people like at a particular time

fashion *verb* to fashion something is to make it in a particular shape or style • *The ring had been fashioned from the finest gold.*

fashionable *adjective* something is fashionable when it follows a style that is popular at a particular time

fast¹ *adjective* **1.** moving or done quickly • *He's a fast runner.* **2.** a watch or clock is fast when it shows a time later than the correct time **3.** a fast colour is one that is not likely to fade

fast¹ *adverb* **1.** quickly **2.** firmly **fast asleep** deeply asleep

fast² *verb* to fast is to go without food

fasten *verb* **1.** to fasten something is to join it firmly to something else **2.** to fasten is to close or do up securely. • *Fasten your seatbelts.* **fastener** or **fastening** *noun* a device used to fasten something

fat *noun* **1.** the white greasy part of meat **2.** an oily or greasy substance used in cooking
fat *adjective* **fatter, fattest 1.** having a very thick round body **2.** thick • *What a fat book!* **3.** fat meat is meat with a lot of fat

fatal *adjective* **1.** causing someone's death • *There has been a fatal accident on the motorway.* **2.** likely to have bad results • *He then made a fatal mistake.* **fatally** *adverb* someone is fatally injured or wounded when they die as a result of their injuries

fate *noun* **1.** a power that is thought to make things happen **2.** someone's fate is what has happened or will happen to them

father *noun* your male parent

father-in-law *noun* **fathers-in-law** the father of your husband or wife

fatigue *noun* (fa-**teeg**) **1.** extreme tiredness **2.** weakness in metals, caused by stress

fatten *verb* **1.** to fatten something is to make it fat **2.** to fatten is to become fat

fatty *adjective* **fattier, fattiest** containing a lot of fat

fault *noun* **1.** something wrong that spoils a person or thing; a flaw or mistake **2.** the responsibility or blame for something • *It's my fault we are late.* **faultless** *adjective* something is faultless when it is perfect and has nothing wrong with it
fault *verb* to fault something is to find faults in it

faulty *adjective* **faultier, faultiest** having a fault or faults; not working properly

fauna *noun* (**faw**-na) the animals of an area or of a period of time

favour *noun* **favours** a favour is something kind that you do for someone • *Will you do me a favour?* **to be in favour of someone** or **something** is to like or support them
favour *verb* to favour someone or something is to like or support them or prefer them to others

favourable *adjective* **1.** helpful or advantageous **2.** showing approval
favourably *adverb*

favourite *adjective* that you like best • *What is your favourite book?*
favourite *noun* the person or thing that you like best • *This book is my favourite.*

favouritism *noun* favouritism is when someone is unfairly kinder to one person than to others

fawn *noun* a young deer

fax *noun* **1.** a machine that sends copies of documents through a telephone line **2.** a copy made by this process
fax *verb* to fax a document is to send a copy of it using a fax machine

fear *noun* fear or a fear, is a feeling that something unpleasant may happen
fear *verb* to fear someone or something is to be afraid of them

fearful *adjective* **1.** frightened **2.** *(informal)* awful or horrid • *They had a fearful quarrel.*

fearless *adjective* having no fear
fearlessly *adverb*

fearsome *adjective* frightening

feasible *adjective* able to be done; possible or likely

feast *noun* a large and splendid meal for a lot of people
feast *verb* to feast is to have a feast

feat *noun* something brave or difficult that you do

feather *noun* a bird's feathers are the very light coverings that grow from its skin **feathery** *adjective* soft or light like feathers

feature *noun* **1.** your features are the different parts of your face • *He has rugged features.* **2.** an important or noticeable part of something; a characteristic **3.** a newspaper article or television programme on a particular subject

feature *verb* **1.** to feature something is to make it an important part of something **2.** to feature in something is to be an important part of it • *Sport features a lot in the Sunday papers.*

February *noun* the second month of the year

fed up *adjective (informal)* depressed or unhappy

fee *noun* a payment or charge

feeble *adjective* weak; not having much strength or force **feebly** *adverb*

feed *verb* **feeding, fed** **1.** to feed a person or animal is to give them food **2.** to feed on something is to eat it • *Sheep feed on grass.*
feed *noun* **1.** a feed is a meal **2.** feed is food for animals

feel *verb* **feeling, felt** **1.** to feel something is to touch it to find out what it is like **2.** to feel a feeling or emotion is to experience it **to feel like something** is to want it
feel *noun* what something is like when you touch it • *I like the feel of this material.*

feeler *noun* an insect's feelers are the two long thin parts that extend from the front of its body and are used for feeling

feeling *noun* **1.** feeling is the ability to feel or touch things • *She lost the feeling in her right hand.* **2.** feeling is also what a person feels in the mind, such as love or fear • *I have hurt her feelings.*

feline *adjective* to do with cats; like a cat

fell[1] past tense of **fall** verb

fell[2] *verb* to fell a tree is to cut it down

fell[3] *noun* a hill or area of wild hilly country in the north of England

fellow *noun* **1.** a friend or companion; someone who belongs to the same group **2.** a man or boy

fellow *adjective* of the same group or kind • *She arranged a meeting with her fellow teachers.*

fellowship *noun* **1.** fellowship is friendship **2.** a fellowship is a group of friends; a society

felt[1] past tense of **feel**

felt[2] *noun* thick woollen material

felt-tip pen or **felt-tipped pen** *noun* a pen with a tip made of felt or fibre

female *adjective* of the sex that can produce offspring
female *noun* a female person or animal

feminine *adjective* **1.** to do with women or like women; suitable for women **2.** in some languages, belonging to the class of words that includes words referring to women **femininity** *noun* being feminine

feminist *noun* someone who believes that women should have the same rights and opportunities as men **feminism** *noun* the belief that women should have the same rights and opportunities as men

fen *noun* an area of low-lying marshy or flooded land

fence *noun* a wooden or metal barrier round an area of land
fence *verb* **1.** to fence something or to fence it in is to put a fence round it **2.** to fence is to fight with long narrow swords called *foils*, as a sport **fencer** *noun* someone who fences **fencing** *noun* the sport of fighting with swords

fend *verb* **to fend for yourself** is to take care of yourself

fender *noun* a low guard placed round a fireplace to stop coal from falling into the room

ferment *verb* Beer or wine ferments when it bubbles and changes chemically by the action of yeast or bacteria. This makes the sugar turn into alcohol. **fermentation** *noun* the process of fermenting

fern *noun* a plant with feathery leaves and no flowers

ferocious *adjective* fierce or savage **ferociously** *adverb* **ferocity** *noun* fierceness

ferret *noun* a small fierce animal with a long thin body, used for catching rabbits and rats

ferry *noun* **ferries** a boat that takes people or things across a river or other stretch of water

ferry *verb* **ferries, ferrying, ferried** to ferry people or things is to take them from one place to another in a boat or car

fertile *adjective* **1.** land that is fertile is good for growing crops and plants **2.** people or animals that are fertile can produce babies or young animals **fertility** *noun* being fertile

fertilize *verb* **1.** to fertilize the soil is to add chemicals or manure to it so that crops and plants grow better **2.** to fertilize an egg or plant is to put sperm or pollen into it so that it develops its young or seeds **fertilization** *noun* fertilizing the soil or an egg or plant This word can also be spelled **fertilise**.

fertilizer *noun* chemicals or manure added to the soil to make crops and plants grow better This word can also be spelled **fertiliser**.

festival *noun* **1.** a time of celebration, especially for religious reasons **2.** an organized set of concerts, shows or other events

festive *adjective* to do with joyful celebrating **festivities** *noun* events held to celebrate something

fetch *verb* **1.** to fetch something or someone is to go and get them **2.** something fetches a particular price when it is sold for that price • *My old bike fetched £10.*

fete *noun* (fayt) an outdoor event with stalls, games and things for sale

feud *noun* (fewd) a bitter quarrel between two people or families that lasts a long time

feud *verb* people feud when they keep up a quarrel for a long time

feudal *adjective* (**few**-dal) in the Middle Ages, the feudal system was a system in which people could farm land in exchange for working or fighting for the owner **feudalism** *noun* the feudal system

fever *noun* a person has a fever when their body temperature is higher than usual because they are ill

feverish *adjective* someone is feverish when they have a slight fever

few *determiner* not many

few *noun* a small number of people or things **a good few** or **quite a few** a fairly large number

fiancé *noun* (fee-**ahn**-say) a woman's fiancé is the man who she is engaged to be married to

fiancée *noun* (fee-**ahn**-say) a man's fiancée is the woman who he is engaged to be married to

fiasco *noun* **fiascos** (fi-**ass**-koh) a complete failure

fib *noun* a lie about something unimportant

fib *verb* to fib is to tell a lie about something unimportant **fibber** *noun* someone who tells fibs

fibre *noun* (**fy**-ber) **1.** a fibre is a very thin thread **2.** fibre is a substance made up of thin threads **3.** fibre is also a substance in food that helps you to digest it **fibrous** *adjective* made up of lots of fibres

fibreglass *noun* a kind of lightweight plastic containing glass fibres

fickle *adjective* someone is fickle when they often change their mind or do not stay loyal to one person or group

fiction *noun* fiction is writings about events that have not really happened; stories and novels **fictional** *adjective* existing only in a story, not in real life

fictitious *adjective* made up; not true

fiddle *noun* a violin

fiddle *verb* **1.** to fiddle is to play the violin **2.** to fiddle with something is to keep touching or playing with it with your fingers

fiddler *noun* someone who plays the violin

fiddly *adjective (informal)* awkward to use or do because it involves handling small objects • *Making the model of the ship was quite a fiddly job.*

fidget *verb* to fidget is to make small restless movements because you are bored or nervous **fidgety** *adjective* someone is fidgety when they fidget a lot

field *noun* **1.** a piece of land with crops or grass growing on it, often surrounded by a hedge or fence **2.** an area of grass where people play a sport **3.** a subject that someone is studying or interested in • *new developments in the field of science*

field *verb* **1.** to field a ball in cricket or other games is to stop it or catch it **2.** to be fielding in cricket is to be on the side that is not batting **fielder** *noun* a player who is fielding

fiend *noun* (feend) **1.** a devil or evil spirit **2.** a wicked or cruel person

fiendish *adjective* wicked or cruel

fierce *adjective* **1.** angry and violent and likely to attack you **2.** strong or intense • *The heat from the fire was fierce.* **fiercely** *adverb* **fierceness** *noun*

fiery *adjective* **fierier, fieriest** **1.** full of flames or heat **2.** easily made angry • *He had a fiery temper.*

fifteen *noun* the number 15 **fifteenth** *adjective, noun* 15th

fifth *adjective, noun* the next after the fourth

fifty *noun* **fifties** the number 50 **fiftieth** *adjective, noun* 50th

fifty-fifty *adjective, adverb* to share something fifty-fifty is to share it equally between two people or groups

fig *noun* a soft fruit full of small seeds

fight *noun* **1.** a struggle against someone, using hands or weapons **2.** an attempt to achieve or overcome something • *We can all help in the fight against crime.*

fight *verb* **fighting, fought** **1.** to fight someone is to have a fight with them **2.** to fight something is to try to stop it • *They fought the fire all night.*

fighter *noun* **1.** someone who fights **2.** a fast military plane that attacks other aircraft

figure *noun* **1.** one of the symbols that stand for numbers, such as 1, 2 and 3 **2.** the shape of someone's body **3.** a diagram or illustration in a book or magazine **4.** a pattern or shape • *He drew a figure of eight.*

figure *verb* **1.** to appear or take part in something • *His name does not figure in the list of entrants.* **2.** to think that something is probably true • *I figure the best thing to do is to wait.* **to figure something out** is to work it out • *Can you figure out the answer?*

file[1] *noun* a metal tool with a rough surface that you rub on things to make them smooth or shape them

file[1] *verb* to file something is to make it smooth or shape it with a file

file[2] *noun* **1.** a box or folder for keeping papers in **2.** *(in computing)* a document stored on a computer **to walk in single file** is to walk one behind the other

file[2] *verb* **1.** to file a paper or document is to put it in a box or folder **2.** to file is to walk one behind the other

fill *verb* **1.** to fill something is to make it full **2.** to fill is to become full • *The room was filling quickly.* **3.** to fill a tooth is to put a filling in it **to fill in a form** is to write answers to all the questions on it **to fill something up** is to fill it completely

fill *noun* enough to make you full • *Eat your fill.*

fillet *noun* a piece of fish or meat without bones

filling *noun* **1.** a piece of metal put in a tooth to replace a decayed part **2.** food you put inside a pie, sandwich or cake

filling station *noun* a place where petrol is sold

filly *noun* **fillies** a young female horse

film *noun* **1.** a story that you see in a cinema or on television **2.** a roll of thin plastic that you put in some cameras to take photographs **3.** a very thin layer of something • *The table was covered in a film of grease.*

film *verb* to film a book or story is to make a film of it

filter *noun* a device for removing dirt or other unwanted things from a liquid or gas that passes through it

filter *verb* to filter something is to pass it through a filter

filth *noun* disgusting dirt **filthy** *adjective* extremely dirty

fin *noun* **1.** a thin flat part that sticks out from a fish's body and helps it to swim **2.** a small part that sticks out from an aircraft or rocket and helps it to move smoothly

final *adjective* **1.** coming at the end; last **2.** a decision is final when it puts an end to argument or doubt • *You must not go and that's final!*

final *noun* the last of a series of contests, that decides the overall winner

finale *noun* (fin-**ah**-li) the last part of a show or piece of music

finalist *noun* a person or team taking part in a final

finally *adverb* **1.** after a long time, at last • *We finally got there around midnight.* **2.** as the last thing • *Finally, I would like to thank my parents.*

finance *noun* **1.** finance is the business of using and looking after money **2.** someone's finances are the amount of money or funds they have

finance *verb* to finance something is to provide money for it

financial *adjective* to do with money

finch *noun* a small bird with a short thick beak

find *verb* **finding, found 1.** to find something is to see or get it by chance or by looking for it **2.** to find something is also to learn it by experience • *He found that digging is hard work.* **to find something out** is to get information about it

findings *plural noun* things someone has found out

fine¹ *adjective* **1.** of high quality; excellent **2.** the weather is fine when it is sunny and not raining **3.** very thin or delicate • *The curtains were made of a fine material.* **4.** made of small particles • *The sand on the beach was very fine.* **finely** *adverb* into fine or small parts • *Slice the tomato finely.*

fine² *noun* money that someone must pay as a punishment

fine² *verb* to fine someone is to make them pay money as a punishment

finger *noun* one of the long thin parts that stick out on your hand

finger *verb* to finger something is to touch it with your fingers

fingernail *noun* the hard covering at the end of your finger

fingerprint *noun* a mark made by the pattern of curved lines on the tip of your finger

finish *verb* **1.** to finish something is to bring it to an end **2.** to finish is to come to an end

finish *noun* the end of something

fir *noun* an evergreen tree with leaves like needles

fire *noun* **1.** the flames, heat and light that come from burning things **2.** coal or wood burning in a grate or furnace to give heat **3.** a device using electricity or gas to heat a room **4.** the shooting of guns • *Hold your fire!* **to be on fire** is to be burning **to set fire to something** is to start it burning

fire *verb* **1.** to fire a gun is to shoot it **2.** (*informal*) to fire someone is to dismiss them from their job **3.** to fire pottery or bricks is to bake them in an oven to make them hard

fire brigade *noun* a team of people whose job is to put out fires and rescue people from fires

a b c d e f g h i j k l m n o p q r s t u v w x y z

fire engine *noun* a large vehicle that carries firefighters and equipment to fight fires

fire extinguisher *noun* a metal cylinder containing chemicals for putting out a fire

firefighter *noun* someone whose job is to put out fires

fireplace *noun* an open space for a fire in the wall of a room

fireproof *adjective* something is fireproof when it can stand great heat without burning

fire station *noun* the headquarters of a fire brigade

firework *noun* a cardboard tube containing chemicals that give off coloured sparks and make loud noises

firm *noun* a business organization • *a clothing firm*

firm *adjective* 1. fixed or solid so that it will not move 2. definite and not likely to change • *She has made a firm decision to go.* **firmly** *adverb* in a strong or definite way **firmness** *noun*

first *adjective* 1. coming before all others 2. the most important • *My first priority is to get a job.*

first *adverb* before everything else • *Finish your work first.*

first *noun* a person or thing that is first **at first** at the beginning; to start with

first aid *noun* simple medical treatment that is given to an injured person before a doctor comes

first-class *adjective* 1. belonging to the best part of a service • *Send the letter by first-class post.* 2. excellent

first-hand *adjective, adverb* you get first-hand information directly, rather than from other people or from books

firstly *adverb* as the first thing • *Firstly, let me tell you about our holiday.*

fish *noun* an animal that lives and breathes in water

fish *verb* fishes, fishing, fished to fish is to try to catch fish

fisherman *noun* fishermen someone who tries to catch fish

fishy *adjective* fishier, fishiest 1. smelling or tasting of fish 2. *(informal)* suspicious or doubtful

fist *noun* a tightly closed hand with the fingers bent into the palm

fit[1] *adjective* fitter, fittest 1. healthy and strong because you get a lot of exercise 2. suitable or good enough • *It was a meal fit for a king.*

fit[1] *verb* fitting, fitted 1. to fit someone or something is to be the right size and shape for them 2. to fit something is to put it into place • *We need to fit a new lock on the door.* 3. to fit something is to be suitable for it • *Her speech fitted the occasion perfectly.* **to fit in** is to be suitable for something • *Does this fit in with your plans?*

fit[1] *noun* the way something fits • *The coat is a good fit.*

fit[2] *noun* a sudden illness that makes you move violently or become unconscious

fitness *noun* being healthy and strong because of doing a lot of exercise

fitting *adjective* suitable or proper

fitting *noun* fittings are pieces of furniture or equipment in a room or building

five *noun* the number 5

fix *verb* 1. to fix something is to join it firmly to something else or to put it where it will not move 2. to fix something is also to decide or settle it • *We have fixed a date for the party.* 3. to fix something that is broken is to mend it • *He's fixing my bike.*

fix *noun* *(informal)* an awkward situation • *I'm in a fix.*

fixture *noun* 1. a sports event planned for a particular day 2. something fixed in its place, like a cupboard or a washbasin

fizz *verb* liquid fizzes when it produces a lot of small bubbles **fizzy** *adjective* a fizzy drink has a lot of bubbles

fizzle *verb* to fizzle out is to end in a disappointing or unsuccessful way

flabby *adjective* flabbier, flabbiest fat and soft; not firm

flag *noun* a piece of material with a coloured pattern or shape on it, often used as the symbol of a country or organization

flag *verb* flagging, flagged to flag is to become weak or tired

flagship *noun* the main ship in a navy's fleet, which has the commander of the fleet on board

flagstone *noun* a flat slab of paving stone

flake *noun* 1. a very light thin piece of something 2. a piece of falling snow
flaky *adjective* like flakes or likely to break into flakes
flake *verb* to flake is to come off in light thin pieces

flame *noun* a bright strip of fire that flickers and leaps
flame *verb* to flame is to produce flames or become bright red

flamingo *noun* flamingos a large wading bird with long legs, a long neck and pale pink feathers

flammable *adjective* that burns easily

flan *noun* a pie without any pastry on top

flank *noun* the side of something, especially an animal's body or an army

flannel *noun* 1. a flannel is a piece of soft cloth you use to wash yourself 2. flannel is a soft woollen material

flap *noun* a part that hangs down from one edge of something, usually to cover an opening
flap *verb* flapping, flapped 1. to flap something is to move it up and down or from side to side • *The bird flapped its wings.* 2. to flap is to wave about • *The sails were flapping in the breeze.*

flapjack *noun* a cake made from oats and syrup

flare *verb* 1. to flare is to burn with a sudden bright flame 2. to flare up is to become suddenly angry 3. things flare when they get gradually wider
flare *noun* 1. a bright light fired into the sky as a signal 2. a gradual widening, especially in skirts or trousers

flash *noun* 1. a sudden bright burst of light 2. a device for making a brief bright light when you take a photograph in a flash immediately or very quickly

flash *verb* 1. to flash is to make a sudden bright burst of light 2. to flash past or across is to approach and go past very quickly • *The bus flashed past without stopping.*

flashy *adjective* flashier, flashiest showy and expensive

flask *noun* 1. a bottle with a narrow neck 2. a vacuum flask

flat *adjective* flatter, flattest 1. having no curves or bumps; smooth and level 2. spread out; lying at full length • *Lie flat on the ground.* 3. dull or uninteresting • *He spoke in a flat voice.* 4. a liquid is flat when it is no longer fizzy 5. a tyre is flat when it is punctured and has lost its air 6. below the proper musical pitch • *The clarinet was flat.* **flatness** *noun*

flat *adverb* exactly and no more • *He won the race in ten seconds flat.* **flat out** as fast as possible • *They all worked flat out to get everything ready in time.*

flat *noun* 1. a set of rooms for living in, usually on one floor of a building 2. *(in music)* the note that is a semitone lower than the natural note; the sign (♭) that indicates this

flatly *adverb* in a definite way, leaving no room for doubt • *He flatly refused to go out.*

flatten *verb* 1. to flatten something is to make it flat 2. to flatten is to become flat

flatter *verb* to flatter someone is to praise them more than they deserve, often because you want to please them **flattery** *noun* too much praise

flavour *noun* the taste and smell of something

flavour *verb* to flavour something is to give it a particular taste and smell **flavouring** *noun* something added to food or drink to give it a particular flavour

flaw *noun* a fault that stops a person or thing from being perfect • *The diamond had a flaw.* **flawed** *adjective* having a fault **flawless** *adjective* perfect, with no faults

flax *noun* a plant that produces fibres from which cloth is made and seeds from which oil is obtained

flea *noun* a small jumping insect that sucks blood

fled past tense of **flee**

flee *verb* **flees**, **fleeing**, **fled** to flee is to run away from something

fleece *noun* **1.** a sheep's fleece is the wool that covers its body **2.** a piece of clothing made from a soft warm material **fleecy** *adjective* soft and warm like a fleece

fleet *noun* a number of ships, aircraft or vehicles owned by one country or company

fleeting *adjective* very brief; passing quickly • *I caught a fleeting glimpse of him.*

flesh *noun* the soft substance of the bodies of people and animals, made of muscle and fat

flex *noun* flexible insulated wire for carrying an electric current

flex *verb* to flex something is to move or bend it • *Try flexing your muscles.*

flexible *adjective* **1.** easy to bend or stretch **2.** able to be changed • *Our plans are flexible.* **flexibility** *noun* something that has flexibility can bend or stretch easily • *I'm gaining flexibility in gymnastics.*

flick *noun* a quick light hit or movement

flick *verb* to flick something is to hit or move it with a flick

flicker *verb* to flicker is to burn or shine unsteadily

flight[1] *noun* **1.** flight is the action of flying • *a flock of birds in flight* **2.** a flight is a journey in an aircraft or rocket **3.** a flight of stairs is one set of stairs

flight[2] *noun* running away; escape

flimsy *adjective* **flimsier**, **flimsiest** light and thin; fragile

flinch *verb* to flinch is to make a sudden movement because you are frightened or in pain

fling *verb* **flinging**, **flung** to fling something is to throw it violently or carelessly

flint *noun* **1.** flint is a very hard kind of stone **2.** a flint is a piece of this stone or hard metal used to produce sparks

flip *verb* **flipping**, **flipped** to flip something is to turn it over quickly

flipper *noun* **1.** a limb that water animals use for swimming **2.** a large flat rubber shoe you wear to help you swim faster

flit *verb* **flitting**, **flitted** to flit is to fly or move lightly and quickly

float *verb* **1.** to float is to stay or move on the surface of a liquid or in the air **2.** to float something is to make it stay on the surface of a liquid

float *noun* **1.** a light object that is designed to float • *She learned to swim with the help of floats.* **2.** a vehicle used for carrying a display in a parade

flock *noun* a group of sheep, goats or birds

flock *verb* to flock is to gather or move in a crowd

flog *verb* **flogging**, **flogged** **1.** to flog someone is to beat them severely with a whip or stick **2.** *(slang)* to flog something is to sell it

flood *noun* **1.** a large amount of water spreading over a place that is usually dry **2.** a great amount of something • *They received a flood of complaints.*

flood *verb* **1.** to flood something is to cover it with a large amount of water **2.** a river floods when it flows over its banks **3.** to arrive in large amounts • *Offers of help came flooding in from all over the country.*

floodlight *noun* a lamp that gives a broad bright beam, used to light up a public building or a sports ground at night **floodlit** *adjective* lit up by floodlights

floor *noun* **1.** the part of a room that people walk on **2.** all the rooms on the same level in a building • *The sports department is on the top floor.*

floorboard *noun* one of the long flat boards in a wooden floor

flop *verb* flopping, flopped **1.** to flop or flop down, is to fall or sit down heavily **2.** to flop is also to hang loosely • *Her hair flopped over her eyes.* **3.** (informal) to flop is to be a failure

flop *noun* (informal) a failure or disappointment • *The play was a complete flop.*

floppy *adjective* floppier, floppiest hanging loosely or heavily • *Our dog has huge floppy ears.*

flora *noun* (**flor**-a) the plants of an area or of a period of time

floral *adjective* made of flowers or to do with flowers

florist *noun* a shopkeeper who sells flowers

flounder *verb* to flounder is to move clumsily through water, mud, etc.

flour *noun* a fine powder made from corn or wheat and used for making bread, cakes and pastry **floury** *adjective* powdery like flour

flourish *verb* to flourish is to grow or develop strongly; to be successful

flow *verb* **1.** to flow is to move along smoothly, like a river does **2.** to flow is also to hang loosely • *She had long flowing hair.*

flow *noun* a continuous steady movement of something

flower *noun* **1.** the part of a plant from which the seed or fruit develops **2.** a plant with a flower

flower *verb* a plant flowers when it produces flowers

flowerpot *noun* a pot in which plants are grown

flu *noun* influenza

fluent *adjective* skilful at speaking, especially a foreign language **fluency** *noun* skill at speaking a language **fluently** *adverb*

fluff *noun* fluff is the small soft bits that come off wool and cloth **fluffy** *adjective* soft like fluff

fluid *noun* a substance that flows easily, like liquids and gases

fluke *noun* a success that you achieve by unexpected good luck

fluorescent *adjective* a fluorescent light or lamp is one that produces a bright light by means of radiation

fluoride *noun* a chemical that is added to water and toothpaste to help prevent tooth decay

flush¹ *verb* **1.** to flush is to go slightly red in the face **2.** to flush something is to clean or remove it with a fast flow of liquid

flush¹ *noun* **1.** a slight blush **2.** a fast flow of water

flush² *adjective* level; without any part sticking out • *The doors are flush with the walls.*

flustered *adjective* nervous and confused

flute *noun* a musical instrument which you hold sideways across your mouth and play by blowing across a hole in it at one end

flutter *verb* **1.** to flutter is to move with a quick flapping of wings **2.** to flutter is to move or flap quickly and lightly • *The flags fluttered in the breeze.*

fly *verb* **flies, flying, flew, flown** **1.** to fly is to move through the air with wings or in an aircraft **2.** to fly something is to make it move through the air **3.** to fly is to wave in the air • *Flags were flying.* **4.** to fly is to move or pass quickly • *The door flew open.* • *The weeks just flew by.*

fly *noun* **flies** **1.** a small flying insect with two wings **2.** the front opening of a pair of trousers

flying saucer *noun* a saucer-shaped flying object believed to come from outer space, especially in science fiction stories

flyover *noun* a bridge that carries one road over another

foal *noun* a young horse

foam *noun* **1.** a mass of tiny bubbles on a liquid **2.** a spongy kind of rubber or plastic
foam *verb* to foam is to form a mass of tiny bubbles

focus *noun* **focuses** or **foci** **1.** the distance at which something appears most clearly to your eye or in a lens **2.** the part of something that people pay most attention to **to be in focus** is to appear clearly and not blurred **to be out of focus** is to appear blurred
focus *verb* **1.** to focus your eye or a camera lens is to adjust it so that objects appear clearly **2.** to focus your attention on something is to concentrate on it

fodder *noun* fodder is food for horses and farm animals

foe *noun* (*old use*) an enemy

foetus *noun* (**fee**-tus) a developing embryo, especially an unborn human baby

fog *noun* thick mist which makes it difficult to see **foggy** *adjective* it is foggy when there is a lot of fog

foil[1] *noun* a very thin sheet of metal

foil[2] *noun* a long narrow sword you use in fencing

foil[3] *verb* to foil someone or something is to prevent them from succeeding

fold[1] *verb* **1.** to fold something is to bend it so that one part lies over another part **2.** to fold is to bend or move in this way • *The table folds up when we are not using it.*
fold[1] *noun* a line where something has been folded

fold[2] *noun* an enclosure for sheep

folder *noun* **1.** a folding cardboard or plastic cover you use to keep loose papers in **2.** (*in computing*) a place where a set of files are grouped together in a computer

foliage *noun* the leaves of a tree or plant

folk *plural noun* people

folklore *noun* old beliefs and legends

folk song *noun* a song in the traditional style of a country

follow *verb* **1.** to follow someone or something is to go or come after them or to do something after they have **2.** to follow someone's instructions is to obey them **3.** to follow a road or path is to go along it **4.** to follow a sport or team is to take an interest in them or support them **5.** to follow someone is to understand them • *Do you follow me?* **6.** to follow is to happen as a result • *Who knows what trouble may follow?* **follower** *noun* a person who follows or supports someone or something

following *preposition* after or as a result of • *Following the break-in we had new locks fitted.*

fond *adjective* kind and loving • *She wished me a fond farewell.* **to be fond of someone** or **something** is to like them very much **fondly** *adverb* **fondness** *noun*

font *noun* a stone or wooden basin in a church, to hold water for baptism

food *noun* anything that a plant or animal can take into its body to make it grow or give it energy

food chain *noun* a series of plants and animals, each of which is eaten as food by the one above in the series

fool *noun* **1.** a silly or stupid person **2.** a jester or clown • *Stop playing the fool.*
fool *verb* to fool someone is to trick or deceive them **to fool about** or **fool around** is to behave in a silly or stupid way

foolhardy *adjective* **foolhardier, foolhardiest** bold but foolish; reckless **foolhardiness** *noun* being foolhardy

foolish *adjective* stupid or unwise **foolishly** *adverb* **foolishness** *noun*

foolproof *adjective* a plan or method is foolproof when it is easy to follow and certain to be successful

foot *noun* feet **1.** the lower part of your leg below your ankle **2.** the lowest part of something • *They met up at the foot of the hill.* **3.** a measure of length, 12 inches or about 30 centimetres on foot walking

football *noun* footballs **1.** a game played by two teams which try to kick an inflated ball into their opponents' goal **2.** the ball used in this game footballer *noun* someone who plays football

footing *noun* your footing is the position of your feet when you are standing firmly on something • *He slipped and lost his footing.*

footnote *noun* a note printed at the bottom of the page

footpath *noun* a path for people to walk along

footprint *noun* a mark made by a foot or shoe

footstep *noun* the sound made each time your foot touches the ground when you are walking or running

for *preposition* used to show **1.** purpose or direction • *This letter is for you.* • *We set out for home.* • *Let's go for a walk.* **2.** length of time or distance • *We've been waiting for hours.* • *They walked for three miles.* **3.** price or cost • *She bought it for £2.* **4.** an alternative • *New lamps for old!* **5.** cause or reason • *He was rewarded for bravery.* • *I only did it for the money.* **6.** support • *Are you for us or against us?* for ever always

for *conjunction* because • *They paused, for they heard a noise.*

forbid *verb* forbidding, forbade, forbidden **1.** to forbid someone to do something is to tell them that they must not do it **2.** to forbid something is not to allow it • *Smoking is forbidden in this station.*

force *noun* **1.** strength or power **2.** *(in science)* an influence that pushes or pulls objects **3.** an organized team of soldiers or police

force *verb* **1.** to force someone to do something is to use your power or strength to make them do it **2.** to force something is to break it open using your strength

forceful *adjective* strong and effective forcefully *adverb*

forceps *plural noun* (**for**-seps) a pair of pincers or tongs that a dentist or surgeon uses

ford *noun* a shallow place where you can wade or drive across a river

forecast *noun* a statement about what the weather is likely to be
forecast *verb* forecasting, forecast or forecasted to forecast something is to say what is likely to happen • *Snow is forecast for tomorrow.*

forefinger *noun* the finger next to your thumb

foregone conclusion *noun* a result that is certain to happen

foreground *noun* the part of a picture or view that is nearest to you

forehead *noun* (**for**-hed or **fo**-rid) the part of your face above your eyes

foreign *adjective* belonging to or coming from another country

foreigner *noun* a person from another country

foremost *adjective* most important

forename *noun* a person's first name

foresee *verb* foreseeing, foresaw, foreseen to foresee something is to realize that it is likely to happen

foresight *noun* the ability to realize that something is likely to happen in the future and prepare for it

forest *noun* a large area of trees growing close together

forestry *noun* the science of planting forests and looking after them

foretell *verb* foretelling, foretold to foretell something is to say it will happen

forever *adverb* continually or always • *He is forever complaining.*

forfeit *noun* something that you lose or have to pay as a penalty
forfeit *verb* to forfeit something is to lose it as a penalty

A
B
C
D
E
F
G
H
I
J
K
L
M
N
O
P
Q
R
S
T
U
V
W
X
Y
Z

forge *noun* a place where metal is heated and shaped; a blacksmith's workshop
forge *verb* **1.** to forge metal is to shape it by heating and hammering **2.** to forge money or a signature is to copy it in order to deceive people

forgery *noun* forgeries **1.** forgery is copying something in order to deceive people **2.** a forgery is a copy of something made to deceive people

forget *verb* forgetting, forgot, forgotten **1.** to forget something is to fail to remember it **2.** to forget something is also to stop thinking about it • *Try to forget your worries.*

forgetful *adjective* often forgetting things forgetfulness *noun*

forgive *verb* forgiving, forgave, forgiven to forgive someone is to stop being angry with them for something they have done forgiveness *noun*

fork *noun* **1.** a small tool with prongs for lifting food to your mouth **2.** a large tool with prongs used for digging or lifting things **3.** a place where a road or river divides into two or more parts
fork *verb* to fork is to divide into two or more parts • *Further downstream, the river forks in two.*

fork-lift truck *noun* a truck with two metal bars at the front for lifting and moving heavy loads

forlorn *adjective* looking sad and lonely

form *noun* **1.** a form is a kind or type of thing • *What is your favourite form of transport?* **2.** the form of something is its shape and general appearance • *They could see a shadowy form in front of them.* **3.** a form is also a class in a school **4.** a form is also a piece of paper with printed questions and spaces for the answers
form *verb* **1.** to form something is to shape or make it **2.** to form is to come into existence or develop • *Icicles formed on the window sill.*

formal *adjective* **1.** strictly following the accepted rules or customs; not casual • *She has a formal manner and never calls me by my first name.* **2.** official or ceremonial • *The formal opening of the bridge takes place tomorrow.* formally *adverb*

formality *noun* formalities **1.** formality is formal behaviour **2.** a formality is something you do to obey a rule or custom

formation *noun* **1.** the process of forming something • *This chapter is about the formation of ice crystals.* **2.** something that is formed • *rock formations* **3.** a special pattern or arrangement • *The aircraft were flying in formation.*

former *adjective* earlier; in the past • *He is a former President of the US.*

formerly *adverb* once; previously

formidable *adjective* (**for**-mid-a-bul) **1.** deserving respect because of being so powerful or impressive **2.** very difficult to deal with or do • *This is a formidable task.* formidably *adverb* something is formidably difficult when it is very difficult indeed

formula *noun* formulas or formulae **1.** a set of chemical symbols showing what a substance consists of • H_2O is the formula for water. **2.** a rule or statement expressed in symbols or numbers

forsake *verb* forsaking, forsook, forsaken to forsake someone is to abandon them

fort *noun* a building that has been strongly built against attack

forth *adverb* forwards or onwards • *From that day forth they never fought again.*

fortification *noun* a tower or wall that is built to help defend a place against attack

fortify *verb* fortifies, fortifying, fortified **1.** to fortify a place is to make it strong against attack **2.** to fortify someone is to make them stronger • *A bowl of hot soup will fortify you.*

fortnight *noun* a period of two weeks
fortnightly *adverb* every two weeks

fortress *noun* a castle or town that has been strongly built against attack

fortunate *adjective* lucky **fortunately** *adverb* luckily

fortune *noun* **1.** fortune is luck or chance **2.** a fortune is a large amount of money

fortune-teller *noun* someone who tells you what will happen to you in the future

forty *noun* **forties** the number 40
fortieth *adjective, noun* 40th

forward *adjective* **1.** going towards the front **2.** placed in the front **3.** too eager or bold
forward *adverb* forwards
forward *noun* a player in an attacking position in a football, hockey, etc. team

forwards *adverb* to or towards the front; in the direction you are facing

fossil *noun* the remains of a prehistoric animal or plant that has been in the ground for a very long time and become hardened in rock **fossilized** *adjective* a fossilized animal or plant has been formed into a fossil

foster *verb* to foster someone is to look after someone else's child as if they were your own, but without adopting them

foster child *noun* **foster children** a child brought up by foster parents

foster parent *noun* a parent who is fostering a child

foul *adjective* disgusting; tasting or smelling unpleasant **foulness** *noun*

foul *noun* an action that breaks the rules of a game

foul *verb* to foul a player in a game is to commit a foul against them

found *verb* to found an organization or society is to start it or set it up

foundation *noun* **1.** a building's foundations are the solid base under the ground on which it is built **2.** the basis for something **3.** the founding of something

founder[1] *noun* someone who founds something • *Guru Nanak was the founder of the Sikh religion.*

founder[2] *verb* to founder is to fill with water and sink • *The ship foundered on the rocks.*

foundry *noun* **foundries** a factory or workshop where metal or glass is made

fountain *noun* an outdoor structure in which jets of water shoot up into the air

fountain pen *noun* a pen that has a nib and can be filled with a cartridge or a supply of ink

four *noun* the number 4 **to be on all fours** is to be on your hands and knees

fourteen *noun* the number 14
fourteenth *adjective, noun* 14th

fourth *adjective, noun* the next after the third

fowl *noun* **fowl** or **fowls** a bird, such as a chicken or duck, that is kept for its eggs or meat

fox *noun* a wild animal that looks like a dog with a long furry tail
fox *verb* to fox someone is to puzzle them

foxglove *noun* a tall plant with flowers like the fingers of gloves

foyer *noun* **foyers** (**foi**-ay) the entrance hall of a cinema, theatre or hotel

fraction *noun* **1.** a number that is not a whole number, for example ½ and 0.5 **2.** a tiny part or amount of something

fracture *verb* to fracture something, especially a bone, is to break it
fracture *noun* the breaking of something, especially a bone

fragile *adjective* (**fra**-jyl) easy to break or damage **fragility** *noun* being easy to break or damage

fragment *noun* a small piece broken off something

fragrant *adjective* (**fray**-grant) having a sweet or pleasant smell **fragrance** *noun* a sweet or pleasant smell

frail *adjective* weak or fragile **frailty** *noun* being weak or fragile

frame *noun* **1.** a set of wooden or metal strips that fit round the outside of a picture or mirror to hold it **2.** a rigid structure that supports something • *I've broken the frame of my glasses.* **3.** a human body • *He has a small frame.* **your frame of mind** is the way you think or feel for a while • *Wait till he's in a better frame of mind.*

frame *verb* **1.** to frame a picture is to put a frame round it **2.** *(informal)* to frame someone is to make them seem guilty of a crime by giving false evidence against them

framework *noun* **1.** a structure that supports something **2.** a basic plan or system

frank *adjective* honest and saying exactly what you think • *I'll be frank with you.* **frankly** *adverb* **frankness** *noun*

frank *verb* to frank a letter or parcel is to mark it with a postmark

frantic *adjective* wildly anxious or excited **frantically** *adverb*

fraud *noun* **1.** fraud is the crime of getting money by tricking people; a fraud is a swindle **2.** a fraud is also someone who is not what they pretend to be **fraudulent** *adjective* dishonest

fraught *adjective* someone is fraught when they are tense and upset

frayed *adjective* **1.** frayed material is worn and ragged at the edge • *Your shirt collar is frayed.* **2.** tempers or nerves are frayed when people feel strained or upset • *Tempers were becoming frayed.*

freak *noun* a very strange or unusual person, animal or thing

freckle *noun* a small brown spot on someone's skin **freckled** *adjective* covered in freckles

free *adjective* **1.** able to do what you want to do or go where you want to go **2.** not costing any money • *Entrance to the museum is free.* **3.** available; not being used or occupied • *Is this seat free?* **4.** not busy doing something • *Are you free tomorrow morning?* **5.** generous • *She is very free with her money.* **to be free of something** is not to have it or be affected by it • *The roads are free of ice.* **freely** *adverb* to do something freely is to do it as you want, without anyone or anything stopping you

free *verb* to free someone or something is to make them free

freedom *noun* the right to go where you like or do what you like

freehand *adjective, adverb* to draw something freehand is to do it without using a ruler or compasses

free-range *adjective* **1.** free-range hens are allowed to move about freely in the open instead of being caged **2.** free-range eggs are those laid by free-range hens

freewheel *verb* to freewheel is to ride a bicycle without pedalling

freeze *verb* freezing, froze, frozen **1.** to freeze is to turn into ice or another solid or to become covered with ice • *The pond froze last night.* **2.** to be freezing or to be frozen is to be very cold • *My hands are frozen.* **3.** to freeze food is to store it at a low temperature to preserve it **4.** a person or animal freezes when they suddenly stand still with fright

freezer *noun* a large refrigerator for keeping food frozen

freezing point *noun* the temperature at which a liquid freezes

freight *noun* (frayt) goods carried by road or in a ship or aircraft

frenzy *noun* **frenzies to be in a frenzy** is to be wildly excited or angry about something **frenzied** *adjective* wildly excited or angry about something

frequency *noun* **frequencies 1.** how often something happens **2.** the number of vibrations made each second by a wave of sound or light

frequent *adjective* happening often **frequently** *adverb* often

fresh *adjective* **1.** newly made or produced; not old or used • *fresh bread* **2.** not tinned or preserved • *fresh fruit* **3.** cool and clean • *It's nice to be out in the fresh air.* **4.** fresh water is water that is not salty **freshly** *adverb* newly or recently • *freshly made biscuits* **freshness** *noun*

freshen *verb* **1.** to freshen something is to make it fresh **2.** to freshen is to become fresh

freshwater *adjective* freshwater fish live in rivers or lakes and not the sea

fret *verb* **fretting, fretted** to fret is to worry or be upset about something

friar *noun* a man belonging to a religious group that has vowed to live a life of poverty **friary** *noun* a place where friars live

friction *noun* **1.** when one thing rubs against another **2.** disagreement and quarrelling

Friday *noun* the sixth day of the week

fridge *noun* *(informal)* a refrigerator

friend *noun* someone you like and who likes you

friendly *adjective* **friendlier, friendliest** kind and pleasant **friendliness** *noun*

friendship *noun* friendship or a friendship, is being friends with someone

frieze *noun* (freez) a decorative strip along the top of a wall

fright *noun* a sudden feeling of fear

frighten *verb* to frighten someone is to make them afraid

frightful *adjective* awful; very great or bad • *It's a frightful shame.* **frightfully** *adverb* awfully or very • *I'm frightfully sorry.*

frill *noun* a decorative strip on the edge of a dress or curtain **frilly** *adjective* decorated with frills

fringe *noun* **1.** a straight line of short hair that hangs down over your forehead **2.** a decorative edge of hanging threads on clothing or a curtain **fringed** *adjective* having a fringe

frisk *verb* *(informal)* to frisk someone is to search them by moving your hands over their body

frisky *adjective* **friskier, friskiest** playful or lively

fritter[1] *noun* a slice of meat, potato or fruit that is covered in batter and fried

fritter[2] *verb* to fritter something or fritter it away is to waste it gradually • *He frittered all his money on comics.*

frivolous *adjective* light-hearted and playful; not serious

frizzy *adjective* **frizzier, frizziest** frizzy hair has tight short curls

fro *adverb* **to and fro** backwards and forwards

frog *noun* a small jumping animal that can live both in water and on land

frolic *verb* **frolicking, frolicked** to frolic is to play in a lively and cheerful way

from *preposition* used to show **1.** a beginning or starting point • *She comes from London.* • *Buses run from 8 o'clock.* **2.** distance • *We are a mile from home.* **3.** separation • *She was freed from prison.* **4.** origin or source • *Get water from the tap.* **5.** cause • *I suffer from headaches.* **6.** difference • *Can you tell margarine from butter?*

front *noun* **1.** the part of a person or thing that faces forwards • *He walked up to the* front of the house. **2**. the part of a thing or place that is furthest forward • *Go to the front of the class.* **3**. a wide road or path that runs alongside the seashore **4**. the place where fighting is happening in a war • *More troops were moved to the front.* **in front** at or near the front

front *adjective* placed at or near the front • *We sat in the front row.*

frontier *noun* the boundary between two countries or regions

frost *noun* **1**. powdery ice that forms on things in freezing weather **2**. weather with a temperature below freezing point

frostbite *noun* harm done to a person's body by very cold weather **frostbitten** *adjective* suffering from frostbite

frosty *adjective* so cold that there is frost • *It was a frosty morning.*

froth *noun* a white mass of tiny bubbles on or in a liquid **frothy** *adjective* a frothy liquid has froth on top

froth *verb* to froth is to form a froth

frown *verb* to frown is to wrinkle your forehead because you are angry or worried

frown *noun* the wrinkling of your forehead when you frown

fruit *noun* **fruit** or **fruits 1**. the part of a tree or plant that contains the seeds and is often used as food, such as apples, oranges and bananas **2**. the good result of doing something • *He lived to see the fruits of his efforts.*

fruitful *adjective* something is fruitful when it is successful or has good results • *Their talks were fruitful.*

fruitless *adjective* something is fruitless when it is unsuccessful or has no results • *It was a fruitless search.* **fruitlessly** *adverb* without success

fruity *adjective* **fruitier, fruitiest** tasting like fruit

frustrate *verb* to frustrate someone is to prevent them from doing something or from succeeding in something, in a way that annoys them **frustration** *noun* the feeling of annoyance you have when you can't do what you want to do

fry *verb* **fries, frying, fried** to fry food is to cook it in hot fat

frying pan *noun* a shallow pan in which things are fried

fudge *noun* a soft sweet made with milk, sugar and butter

fuel *noun* something that is burnt to make heat or power, such as coal and oil

fugitive *noun* (**few**-ji-tiv) a person who is running away from something, especially from the police

fulfil *verb* **fulfilling, fulfilled** to fulfil something is to achieve it or carry it out • *She fulfilled her promise to come.* **fulfilment** *noun* the feeling that you have achieved something

full *adjective* **1**. containing as much or as many as possible • *The cinema was full.* **2**. having many people or things • *You are full of ideas.* **3**. complete • *Tell me the full story.* **4**. the greatest possible • *They drove at full speed.* **in full** not leaving anything out **fully** *adverb* completely

full moon *noun* the moon when you can see the whole of it as a bright disc

full stop *noun* the dot used as a punctuation mark at the end of a sentence or an abbreviation

full-time *adjective, adverb* you do something full-time when you do it for all the normal working hours of the day • *She has a full-time job.* • *She works full-time.*

fumble *verb* to fumble is to handle or feel for something clumsily • *He fumbled in the dark for the light switch.*

fume *verb* **1**. to be fuming is to be very angry **2**. to fume is to give off smoke or gas

fumes *plural noun* strong-smelling smoke or gas

fun *noun* amusement or enjoyment **to make fun of someone** or **something** is to make unkind jokes about them

function *noun* **1**. what someone or something does or ought to do • *The function of a doctor is to cure sick people.* **2**. an important event or party **3**. a basic operation of a computer or calculator

function *verb* to function is to work properly or perform a function • *The phone functions as a camera.*

fund *noun* a fund is an amount of money collected or kept for a special purpose

fundamental *adjective* basic and necessary • *Let me explain the fundamental rules of the game.* **fundamentally** *adverb* basically

funeral *noun* the ceremony where a person who has died is buried or cremated

fungus *noun* **fungi** a plant without leaves or flowers that grows on other plants or on decayed material, such as mushrooms and toadstools

funnel *noun* **1.** a tube that is wide at the top and narrow at the bottom, to help you pour things into bottles or other containers **2.** a chimney on a ship or steam engine

funny *adjective* **funnier, funniest 1.** that makes you laugh or smile • *a funny joke* **2.** strange or odd • *There's a funny smell in here.* **funnily** *adverb*

funny bone *noun* part of your elbow which gives you a strange tingling feeling if you knock it

fur *noun* **1.** the soft hair that covers some animals **2.** animal skin with the hair on it, used for clothing • *a fur hat*

furious *adjective* very angry **furiously** *adverb*

furnace *noun* an oven in which great heat can be produced for making glass or heating metals

furnish *verb* to furnish a room or building is to put furniture in it

furniture *noun* tables, chairs, beds, cupboards and other things inside a building

furrow *noun* **1.** a long cut in the ground made by a plough **2.** a deep wrinkle on the skin

furry *adjective* **furrier, furriest 1.** soft and hairy like fur **2.** covered with fur

further *adverb* & *adjective* **1.** at or to a greater distance; more distant • *I can't walk any further.* **2.** more • *We need further information.*

furthermore *adverb* also; moreover

furthest *adverb* & *adjective* at or to the greatest distance; most distant

furtive *adjective* cautious, trying not to be seen • *He gave a furtive glance and helped himself to the biscuits.*

fury *noun* **furies** violent or extreme anger

fuse[1] *noun* a safety device containing a short piece of wire that melts if too much electricity passes through it

fuse[1] *verb* a piece of electrical equipment fuses when it stops working because a fuse has melted • *The lights have fused.*

fuse[2] *noun* a device for setting off an explosive

fuselage *noun* (**few**-ze-lahzh) the main body of an aircraft

fuss *noun* fuss or a fuss, is unnecessary excitement or worry about something that is not important **to make a fuss of someone** is to pay a lot of attention to them in a kind way

fuss *verb* to fuss is to be excited or worried about something that is not important

fussy *adjective* **fussier, fussiest** worrying too much about something that is not important

futile *adjective* (**few**-tyl) useless or having no purpose **futility** *noun* being useless or having no purpose

futon *noun* (**foo**-ton) a seat with a mattress that you can roll out to form a bed

future *noun* **1**. the time that will come **2**. what is going to happen in the time that will come **in future** from now onwards

fuzzy *adjective* **fuzzier**, **fuzziest** **1**. blurred or not clear **2**. covered in something soft and hairy

Gg

There is a silent *g* in **g**nash, **g**nat, **g**naw and **g**nome.

g short for **gram** or **grams**

gable *noun* the three-sided part of a wall between two sloping roofs

gadget *noun* (**gaj**-it) a useful device or tool

gag *noun* **1**. something put over someone's mouth to stop them from speaking **2**. *(informal)* a joke

gag *verb* **gagging**, **gagged** to gag someone is to put a gag over their mouth

gain *verb* **1**. to gain something is to get it when you did not have it before **2**. a clock or watch gains when it goes ahead of the correct time **to gain on someone** is to come closer to them when you are following them

gala *noun* (**gah**-la) **1**. a festival **2**. a series of sports contests, especially in swimming

galaxy *noun* **galaxies** (**gal**-ak-si) a very large group of stars **galactic** *adjective* to do with a galaxy

gale *noun* a very strong wind

gallant *adjective* brave or courteous **gallantly** *adverb* **gallantry** *noun* gallantry is being gallant

galleon *noun* a large Spanish sailing ship used in the 16th and 17th centuries

gallery *noun* **galleries** **1**. a building or room for showing works of art **2**. a long room or passage

galley *noun* **1**. an ancient type of long ship driven by oars **2**. the kitchen in a ship

gallon *noun* a measure of liquid, 8 pints or about 4.5 litres

gallop *noun* **1**. the fastest pace that a horse can go **2**. a fast ride on a horse

gallop *verb* to gallop is to ride fast on a horse

gallows *plural noun* gallows are a framework with a noose for hanging criminals

galore *adjective* in large amounts • *There are bargains galore in the sale.*

gamble *verb* to gamble is to play a betting game for money **gambler** *noun* someone who gambles

gamble *noun* a risk • *We were taking a bit of a gamble on the weather being good.*

game *noun* **1**. something that you can play, usually with rules **2**. a section of a long game like tennis or whist **3**. wild animals or birds hunted for sport or food

gammon *noun* gammon is a kind of ham or thick bacon

gander *noun* a male goose

gang *noun* **1.** a group of criminals **2.** a group of people who do things together
gang *verb* to gang up on someone is to form a group to bully them

gangplank *noun* a plank for walking on to or off a ship

gangster *noun* a member of a gang of violent criminals

gangway *noun* **1.** a gap between rows of seats **2.** a bridge for getting on or off a ship

gaol *noun* and *verb* a different spelling of **jail**

gaoler *noun* a different spelling of **jailer**

gap *noun* **1.** an opening or break in something **2.** an interval

gape *verb* to gape is also to stare at something, especially with your mouth open, because you are surprised or shocked
gaping *adjective* wide open • *There was a gaping hole in the ice.*

garage *noun* (**ga**-rahzh or **ga**-rij) **1.** a building for keeping motor vehicles in **2.** a place where motor vehicles are serviced and repaired and where petrol is sold

garbage *noun* garbage is household rubbish

garden *noun* a piece of ground where flowers, fruit or vegetables are grown

gardener *noun* someone who looks after gardens, especially as a job

gardening *noun* gardening is looking after a garden

gargle *verb* to gargle is to wash your throat by holding liquid at the back of your mouth and breathing air through it

gargoyle *noun* an ugly or comical carving of a face near the roof of a building, used as a spout for rainwater

garland *noun* a wreath of flowers worn as a decoration

garlic *noun* a plant with a bulb divided into sections (called cloves), which have a strong smell and taste and are used in cooking

garment *noun* a piece of clothing

garnish *verb* to garnish food is to decorate it with extra items such as salad

gas *noun* **1.** a substance, such as oxygen, that can move freely and is not liquid or solid at normal temperatures **2.** a gas that burns and is used for heating or cooking
gaseous *adjective* in the form of a gas
gas *verb* gassing, gassed to gas a person or animal is to kill them with a poisonous gas

gash *noun* a long deep cut or wound

gasp *verb* **1.** to gasp is to breathe in suddenly when you are shocked or surprised **2.** to gasp is also to struggle to breathe when you are ill or tired

gate *noun* **1.** a movable barrier on hinges, used as a door in a wall or fence **2.** a place where you wait before you board an aircraft

gateau *noun* gateaux (**gat**-oh) a rich cream cake

gateway *noun* an opening containing a gate

gather *verb* **1.** to gather is to come together **2.** to gather people or things is to collect them and bring them together **3.** to gather something is to think it from what you have heard or read • *I gather you went to the same school as me?* to gather speed is to move gradually faster

gathering *noun* an assembly or meeting of people; a party

gaudy *adjective* gaudier, gaudiest very showy and bright

gauge *noun* (gayj) **1.** a measuring instrument, such as a fuel gauge **2.** the distance between a pair of railway lines
gauge *verb* to gauge something is to measure it or estimate it • *He looked down into the canyon, trying to gauge how deep it was.*

gaunt *adjective* a gaunt person is thin and tired-looking

gauntlet *noun* a glove with a wide covering for the wrist

gauze *noun* gauze is thin transparent material

gaze *verb* to gaze at something or someone is to look at them hard for a long time
gaze *noun* a long steady look

GCSE short for **General Certificate of Secondary Education**

gear *noun* **1.** a gear is a set of wheels with teeth, which work together to connect the engine to the wheels of a vehicle **2.** gear is equipment or clothes • *climbing gear*

Geiger counter *noun* a device that detects and measures radioactivity

gel *noun* gel is a substance used to give a style to hair

gelatine *noun* gelatine is a clear tasteless substance used to make jellies

gem *noun* a precious stone or jewel

gender *noun* (**jen**-der) the group to which a noun or pronoun belongs in some languages (masculine, feminine and neuter)

gene *noun* (jeen) the part of a living cell that controls which characteristics (such as the colour of your hair or eyes) you inherit from your parents

general *adjective* **1.** to do with most people or things • *The general feeling is that we should go to the beach.* **2.** not detailed or special • *The website has lots of general information on marine life.* **in general** usually; to do with most people

general *noun* an army officer of high rank

general election *noun* an election of Members of Parliament for the whole country

generally *adverb* usually; by most people

generate *verb* to generate something is to produce or create it

generation *noun* **1.** a single stage in a family • *Three generations were included: children, parents and grandparents.* **2.** all the people born about the same time • *He was one of the most famous film stars of his generation.*

generator *noun* a machine for producing electricity

generous *adjective* ready to give or share what you have **generosity** *noun* being generous and ready to give a lot **generously** *adverb*

genetic *adjective* (ji-**net**-ik) to do with genes and with characteristics inherited from parents **genetically** *adverb* by means of genes

genetics *plural noun* genetics is the study of genes

genie *noun* a magical being in stories who can grant wishes

genius *noun* **1.** an unusually clever person **2.** an unusually great ability or talent

gentle *adjective* kind and quiet; not rough or severe **gentleness** *noun* **gently** *adverb*

gentleman *noun* **gentlemen** **1.** a man **2.** a well-mannered or honest man • *He's a real gentleman.*

genuine *adjective* **1.** something is genuine when it is real and not fake **2.** a person is genuine when they are honest and sincere **genuinely** *adverb* really; in a genuine way

genus *noun* **genera** (**jee**-nus) a group of similar animals or plants

geography *noun* geography is the science or study of the world and its climate, peoples and products **geographer** *noun* someone who studies geography **geographical** *adjective* a geographical area is a region of the earth that you can see on a map

geology *noun* (ji-**ol**-o-ji) geology is the study of the earth's crust and its layers **geologist** *noun* someone who studies geology **geological** *adjective* a geological era or period is a time in the past that you can see in the layers of the earth

geometry *noun* geometry is the study of lines, angles, surfaces and solids in mathematics **geometric** *adjective* a geometric shape or pattern has regular lines and angles **geometrical** *adjective*

gerbil *noun* (**jer**-bil) a small brown animal with long back legs

germ *noun* a tiny living thing, especially one that causes a disease

germinate *verb* a seed germinates when it starts growing and developing **germination** *noun* germination is the process of germinating

gesture *noun* (**jes**-cher) a movement or action which expresses what you feel

get *verb* **getting, got** This word has many meanings, depending on the words that go with it **1.** to get something is to obtain or receive it • *I got a new bike yesterday.* **2.** to get (for example) angry or upset is to become angry or upset **3.** to get to a place is to reach

it • *We had to borrow money to get home.*
4. to get something (for example) on or off is take it on or off • *I can't get my shoe on.* **5.** to get (for example) a meal is to prepare it **6.** to get an illness is to catch it **7.** to get someone to do something is to persuade or order them to do it • *Lara might get him to say yes.* **8.** (informal) to get something is to understand it • *Do you get what I mean?* to get by is to manage to get on is to make progress or to be friendly with someone to get out of something is to avoid having to do it to get over something is to recover from an illness or shock

getaway *noun* an escape

geyser *noun* (**gee**-zer or **gy**-zer) a natural spring that shoots up columns of hot water

ghastly *adjective* ghastlier, ghastliest horrible; awful

ghetto *noun* ghettos (**get**-oh) an area of a city where poor people or people from another country live

ghost *noun* the spirit of a dead person seen by a living person ghostly *adjective* reminding you of a ghost • *The moon gave a ghostly light to the scene.*

giant *noun* **1.** a creature in stories, like a huge man **2.** something that is much larger than the usual size
giant *adjective* huge

giddy *adjective* giddier, giddiest feeling unsteady or dizzy giddily *adverb* giddiness *noun*

gift *noun* **1.** a present **2.** a talent • *She has a special gift for drawing.*

gifted *adjective* a gifted person has a special talent or ability

gigantic *adjective* huge; enormous

giggle *verb* to giggle is to laugh in a silly way
giggle *noun* a silly laugh the giggles (informal) are a fit of giggling

gild *verb* to gild something is to cover it with a thin layer of gold paint or gold

gills *plural noun* the gills are the part of a fish's body that it breathes through

gimmick *noun* something unusual done or used to attract people's attention

ginger *noun* **1.** a hot-tasting tropical root, used as a flavouring for food **2.** a reddish-yellow colour

gingerbread *noun* a cake or biscuit flavoured with ginger

gingerly *adverb* you do something gingerly when you do it carefully and cautiously because you are not sure about it • *She stepped gingerly onto the ice.*

gipsy *noun* gipsies a different spelling of **gypsy**

giraffe *noun* a tall African animal with a very long neck

girder *noun* a metal beam supporting part of a building or bridge

girl *noun* **1.** a female child **2.** a young woman girlhood *noun* the time when a woman was a girl girlish *adjective* looking or behaving like a girl

girlfriend *noun* a person's female friend with whom they have a romantic relationship

girth *noun* the measurement round something

gist *noun* (jist) the main points or general meaning of a speech or conversation

give *verb* giving, gave, given **1.** to give someone something is to let them have it • *She gave me a sweet.* **2.** to give (for example) a laugh or shout is to laugh or shout out **3.** to give a performance is to present or perform something **4.** something gives if it bends or goes down under a strain • *Will this branch give if I sit on it?* to give in is to surrender to give up is to stop doing or trying something giver *noun* a person who gives something

glacial *adjective* (**glay**-shal) made of ice or formed by glaciers

glacier *noun* (**glas**-i-er) a mass of ice moving slowly along a valley

glad *adjective* gladder, gladdest happy and pleased gladly *adverb* you do something gladly when you are pleased to do it gladness *noun*

gladden *verb* to gladden someone is to make them glad

gladiator *noun* a man who fought with a sword or other weapons at public shows in ancient Rome

glamorous *adjective* attractive and exciting

glamour *noun* a person's glamour is their beauty or attractiveness

glance *verb* **1**. to glance at something is to look at it quickly **2**. to glance off something is to hit it and slide off • *The ball glanced off his bat.*

glance *noun* a quick look

gland *noun* an organ of the body that separates substances from the blood, so that they can be used by the body or secreted out of it

glare *verb* **1**. to glare is to shine with a bright or dazzling light **2**. to glare at someone is to look angrily at them

glare *noun* **1**. a strong light **2**. an angry stare

glaring *adjective* **1**. very bright **2**. very obvious and embarrassing • *The report is full of glaring errors.*

glass *noun* **1**. glass is a hard brittle substance that lets light through **2**. a glass is a container made of glass, for drinking out of glassy *adjective* glassier, glassiest like glass • *He gave a glassy stare.*

glasses *plural noun* a frame holding two lenses that you wear over your eyes to improve your sight; spectacles

glaze *verb* **1**. to glaze something is to cover or fit it with glass **2**. to glaze pottery is to give it a shiny surface

glaze *noun* a shiny surface

gleam *noun* a beam of soft light

gleam *verb* to gleam is to shine with beams of soft light

glee *noun* glee is when you feel happy and excited about something gleeful *adjective* happy and excited gleefully *adverb*

glen *noun* a narrow valley in Scotland

glide *verb* **1**. to glide is to fly or move smoothly **2**. to glide is also to fly without using an engine

glider *noun* an aircraft that does not use an engine and floats on air currents

glimmer *noun* a faint light

glimmer *verb* to glimmer is to shine with a faint light

glimpse *verb* to glimpse something is to see it briefly

glimpse *noun* a brief view of something

glint *verb* to glint is to shine with a flash of light

glint *noun* a brief flash of light

glisten *verb* to glisten is to shine like something wet or oily

glitter *verb* to glitter is to shine with tiny flashes of light

gloat *verb* to gloat is to be pleased in an unkind way that you have succeeded or that someone else has failed

global *adjective* to do with the whole world globally *adverb* all over the world

global warming *noun* the gradual increase in the average temperature of the earth's climate, caused by the greenhouse effect

globe *noun* **1**. a globe is something shaped like a ball, especially one with a map of the world on it **2**. the globe is the world • *These stories come from all over the globe.*

gloom *noun* gloom is a depressed condition or feeling

gloomy *adjective* **gloomier, gloomiest**
1. almost dark; not well lit **2.** sad or depressed **gloomily** *adverb* **gloominess** *noun*

glorious *adjective* splendid or magnificent

glory *noun* **glories 1.** glory is fame and honour **2.** the glory of something is its splendour or beauty

gloss *noun* the shine on a smooth surface

glossary *noun* **glossaries** a list of words with their meanings explained

glossy *adjective* **glossier, glossiest** smooth and shiny

glove *noun* a covering for the hand, with a separate division for each finger

glow *noun* **1.** a brightness and warmth without flames • *the red glow of the fire* **2.** a warm or cheerful feeling • *Sarah felt a deep glow of satisfaction at her win.*
glow *verb* to glow is to shine with a soft light

glower *verb* (rhymes with flower) to glower is to stare with an angry look

glucose *noun* glucose is a type of sugar found in fruits and honey

glue *noun* glue is a thick liquid for sticking things together
glue *verb* to glue something is to stick it with glue

glum *adjective* **glummer, glummest** sad or depressed **glumly** *adverb*

glutton *noun* someone who is greedy and enjoys eating **gluttonous** *adjective* greedy; eating too much **gluttony** *noun* when someone eats too much

gnarled *adjective* (narld) twisted and knobbly, like an old tree

gnash *verb* (nash) to gnash your teeth is to grind them together

gnat *noun* (nat) a tiny fly that bites

gnaw *verb* (naw) to gnaw something hard is to keep biting it

gnome *noun* (nohm) a kind of dwarf in fairy tales that usually lives underground

go *verb* **going, went, gone 1.** to go is to move or lead from one place to another • *Let's go in and see Mrs Cooper.* • *We'll have to go soon.*
• *This road goes to Bristol.* **2.** a machine or device goes when it is working • *My watch isn't going.* • *A car that doesn't go is not much use.* **3.** you say that someone or something has gone when they are no longer there and you can't find them • *All her money had gone.* **4. Go** also has many special uses shown in these examples • *The milk went sour.* • *The plates go on that shelf.* • *The party went well.* • *The firework went bang.* **to be going to do something** is to be ready to do it **to go in for something** is to take part in it **to go off** is to explode **to go off someone or something** is to stop liking them **to go on** is to happen or continue • *What's going on?*

go *noun* **goes 1.** a go is a turn or try • *May I have a go?* **2.** *(informal)* go is energy or liveliness • *She's full of go.* **on the go** always working or moving

goal *noun* **1.** the two posts that the ball must go between to score a point in football, hockey and other games **2.** a point scored in football, hockey, netball and other games **3.** something that you try to do or to achieve • *Her goal is to become a pilot.*

goalkeeper *noun* the player who guards the goal in football and hockey

goalpost *noun* each of the upright posts of a goal in sports

goat *noun* an animal with horns, belonging to the same family as sheep

gobble *verb* to gobble something is to eat it quickly and greedily

goblin *noun* an evil or mischievous fairy in stories

The word **goblin** comes from an Old French word *gobelin*, which may be related to a Greek word *kobalos* meaning 'a mischievous goblin'.

God *noun* the creator of the universe in Christian, Jewish and Muslim belief

goddess *noun* a female being that is worshipped

goggles *plural noun* goggles are large glasses that you wear to protect your eyes, for example when you are swimming

gold *noun* **1**. gold is a precious yellow metal **2**. gold is also a bright yellow colour

golden *adjective* **1**. made of gold **2**. coloured like gold

goldfinch *noun* a small, brightly-coloured bird with yellow feathers in its wings

goldfish *noun* goldfish a small red or orange fish kept as a pet

golf *noun* golf is an outdoor game played on a prepared course by hitting a small ball into a series of small holes, using a club **golfer** *noun*

gondola *noun* (**gon**-do-la) a boat with high pointed ends, used on the canals in Venice **gondolier** *noun* a person who moves a gondola along with a pole

gong *noun* a large metal disc that makes a deep hollow sound when it is hit

good *adjective* better, best **1**. of the kind that people like, want or praise • *They wanted to have a good time.* **2**. kind • *It was good of you to come.* **3**. well-behaved • *Be a good boy.* **4**. healthy; giving benefit • *Exercise is good for you.* **5**. thorough; large enough • *Let's give it a good clean.*

good *noun* **1**. something good or right • *Do good to others.* **2**. benefit or advantage • *I'm telling you for your own good.* for good for ever no good useless

goodbye *interjection* a word you use when you leave someone or at the end of a telephone call

Good Friday *noun* the Friday before Easter, when Christians remember Christ's death on the Cross

good-looking *adjective* attractive or handsome

good-natured *adjective* kind

goodness *noun* goodness is being good

goods *plural noun* goods are things that people buy and sell

goodwill *noun* goodwill is a kindly and helpful feeling towards people

gooey *adjective* sticky or slimy

goose *noun* geese a water bird with webbed feet

gooseberry *noun* gooseberries a small green fruit that grows on a prickly bush

goose pimples *plural noun* goose pimples are lots of tiny bumps you get on the skin when you are cold or afraid

gore *verb* to gore a person or animal is to wound them badly with a horn or tusk

gorge *noun* a narrow valley with steep sides

gorgeous *adjective* magnificent; beautiful

gorilla *noun* a large strong African ape

gorse *noun* gorse is a prickly bush with small yellow flowers

gory *adjective* gorier, goriest having a lot of blood and violence

gosling *noun* a young goose

gospel *noun* the gospel is the teachings of Jesus Christ the Gospels the first four books of the New Testament

gossip *verb* to gossip is to talk a lot about other people

gossip *noun* **1**. gossip is talk or rumours about other people **2**. a gossip is someone who likes talking about other people

gouge *verb* (gowj) to gouge something is to press or scoop it out

govern *verb* to govern a country or organization is to be in charge of it

government *noun* the group of people who are in charge of a country

governor *noun* someone who governs or runs a place

gown *noun* a loose flowing piece of clothing

GP short for **general practitioner** a GP is a doctor who treats all kinds of illnesses

grab *verb* grabbing, grabbed to grab something is to take hold of it firmly or suddenly

grace *noun* grace is beauty, especially in movement

graceful *adjective* beautiful and elegant in movement or shape gracefully *adverb*

gracious *adjective* kind and pleasant to other people

grade *noun* a step in a scale of quality, value or rank

grade *verb* to grade things is to sort or divide them into grades

gradient *noun* (**gray**-di-ent) **1.** a slope **2.** the amount that a road or railway slopes

gradual *adjective* happening slowly but steadily gradually *adverb* slowly or in stages

graduate *noun* (**grad**-yoo-at) someone who has a degree from a university or college

graffiti *plural noun* (gra-**fee**-tee) graffiti is words or drawings scribbled on a wall

> **Graffiti** is an Italian word meaning 'scratches'.

grain *noun* **1.** grain is cereals when they are growing or after they have been harvested **2.** a grain is the hard seed of a cereal **3.** a grain of something is a small amount of it • *The story had a grain of truth in it.* **4.** the grain on a piece of wood is the pattern of lines going through it

gram *noun* a unit of weight in the metric system, a thousandth of a kilogram

grammar *noun* **1.** grammar is the rules for using words **2.** a grammar is a book that gives the rules for using words grammatical *adjective* following the rules of grammar

grammar school *noun* a kind of secondary school

grand *adjective* **1.** great or splendid **2.** a grand total is one that includes everything

grandchild *noun* grandchildren A grandchild is a child of a person's son or daughter. A girl is a **granddaughter** and a boy is a **grandson**.

grandfather *noun* the father of a person's mother or father

grandfather clock *noun* a clock in a tall wooden case

grandmother *noun* the mother of a person's mother or father

grandparent *noun* a grandmother or grandfather

grandstand *noun* a building at a racecourse or sports ground, that is open at the front with rows of seats for spectators

granite *noun* granite is a very hard kind of rock

grant *verb* to grant someone something is to give or allow them what they have asked for
grant *noun* a sum of money given for a special purpose

grape *noun* a small green or purple fruit that grows in bunches on a vine

grapefruit *noun* grapefruit a large round yellow citrus fruit with a soft juicy pulp

graph *noun* a diagram that shows how two amounts are related

graphic *adjective* **1.** short and lively • *He gave a graphic account of the journey.* **2.** to do with drawing or painting • *She wants to be a graphic artist.* graphically *adverb* in a graphic way

graphics *plural noun* graphics are diagrams, lettering and drawings, especially pictures that are produced by a computer

graphite *noun* graphite is a soft kind of carbon used for the lead in pencils

grapple *verb* 1. to grapple someone or grapple with someone is to fight them 2. to grapple with a problem is to try to deal with it

grasp *verb* 1. to grasp someone or something is to hold them tightly 2. to grasp something is to understand it
grasp *noun* 1. a firm hold 2. a person's grasp of a subject is how well they understand it

grass *noun* 1. grass is a green plant with thin stalks 2. the grass is an area of ground covered with grass **grassy** *adjective* covered in grass

grasshopper *noun* a jumping insect that makes a shrill noise

grate¹ *noun* 1. a metal framework that keeps fuel in the fireplace 2. a fireplace

grate² *verb* to grate something is to shred it into small pieces

grateful *adjective* feeling glad that someone has done something for you **gratefully** *adverb*

grating *noun* a framework of metal bars placed across an opening

gratitude *noun* you show gratitude when you are grateful or thankful for something

grave¹ *noun* the place where a dead body is buried

grave² *adjective* serious or solemn • *We've had grave news.* **gravely** *adverb* • *The man nodded gravely.*

gravel *noun* gravel is small stones mixed with coarse sand, used to make paths

gravestone *noun* a stone monument over a grave

graveyard *noun* a place where dead bodies are buried

gravity *noun* 1. gravity is the force that pulls all objects in the universe towards each other 2. the earth's gravity is the force that pulls everything towards itself

gravy *noun* a hot brown sauce made from meat juices

graze *verb* 1. to graze is to feed on growing grass 2. to graze your skin is to scrape it slightly against something rough
graze *noun* a sore place where skin has been scraped

grease *noun* grease is thick fat or oil
greasy *adjective* oily like grease

great *adjective* 1. very large 2. very important or distinguished • *She was a great writer.* 3. (informal) very good or enjoyable • *It's great to see you again.* 4. older or younger by one generation, as in *great-grandmother* and *great-grandson*
greatly *adverb* **greatness** *noun*

greed *noun* greed is being greedy and wanting too much

greedy *adjective* **greedier**, **greediest** wanting more food or money than you need
greedily *adverb*

green *adjective* 1. of the colour of grass and leaves 2. concerned with protecting the natural environment
green *noun* 1. green is a green colour 2. a green is an area of grass

greenery *noun* green leaves or plants

greenhouse *noun* a glass building that is kept warm inside for growing plants

greenhouse effect *noun* the warming of the earth's surface by gases (called **greenhouse gases**) such as methane and carbon dioxide, which trap heat in the earth's atmosphere

greet *verb* to greet someone is to welcome them when they arrive

greeting *noun* a greeting is the words or actions used to greet someone **greetings** are good wishes when you meet someone or talk to them

grenade *noun* a small bomb, usually thrown by hand

grey *adjective* of the colour between black and white, like ashes or dark clouds
grey *noun* a grey colour

grid *noun* a framework or pattern of bars or lines crossing each other

grief *noun* grief is deep sadness or sorrow people feel when someone has died

grievance *noun* something that people are unhappy or angry about

grieve *verb* to grieve is to feel sad or sorrowful when someone has died

grill *noun* **1.** a part of a cooker that sends heat downwards **2.** grilled food **3.** a grating
grill *verb* to grill food is to cook it under a grill

grim *adjective* grimmer, grimmest **1.** stern or severe **2.** frightening or unpleasant • *They had a grim experience.* grimly *adverb*

grimace *noun* a strange or twisted expression on your face

grime *noun* grime is a layer of dirt on a surface grimy *adjective* very dirty

grin *noun* a smile showing your teeth
grin *verb* grinning, grinned to grin is to smile showing your teeth

grind *verb* grinding, ground **1.** to grind something is to crush it into a powder **2.** to grind something hard is to sharpen or polish it by rubbing it on a rough surface grinder *noun* a machine that grinds things

grip *verb* gripping, gripped **1.** to grip something is to hold it tightly **2.** a story, film, game or other activity grips you when you find it very interesting or exciting
grip *noun* **1.** a firm hold on something **2.** a handle

grisly *adjective* grislier, grisliest disgusting or horrible • *the scene of a grisly murder*

gristle *noun* gristle is the tough rubbery part of meat gristly *adjective* gristly meat is tough and full of gristle

grit *noun* **1.** grit is tiny pieces of stone or sand **2.** a person's grit is their courage and determination to do something difficult gritty *adjective* rough like grit
grit *verb* gritting, gritted **1.** to grit your teeth is to clench them tightly when in pain or trouble **2.** to grit a road or path is to put grit on it

grizzly bear *noun* a large bear of North America

groan *verb* to groan is to make a long deep sound when in pain or distress
groan *noun* a long deep sound of pain or distress

grocer *noun* someone who keeps a shop that sells food, drink and other goods for the house

grocery *noun* groceries a grocer's shop groceries goods sold by a grocer

groin *noun* the flat part where your thighs join the rest of your body

groom *noun* **1.** someone whose job is to look after horses **2.** a bridegroom
groom *verb* to groom a horse or other animal is to clean and brush it

groove *noun* a long narrow channel cut in the surface of something

grope *verb* to grope for something is to feel about for it when you cannot see it

gross *adjective* **1.** having bad manners; crude or vulgar **2.** very bad or shocking • *They showed gross stupidity.* **3.** total, without anything taken off grossly *adverb* extremely or too much • *That's grossly unfair!*
gross *noun* a gross is twelve dozen or 144

grotesque *adjective* (groh-**tesk**) strange and ugly grotesquely *adverb*

ground *noun* grounds **1.** the ground is the surface of the earth **2.** a ground is a sports field

grounded *adjective* **1.** aircraft are grounded when they are prevented from flying, for example because of the weather **2.** *(informal)* someone is grounded when they are not allowed to go out

ground floor *noun* in a building, the floor that is level with the ground

grounds *plural noun* **1.** the reasons for doing something • *There are grounds for suspecting that a crime has been committed.* **2.** the gardens of a large house

group *noun* a number of people, animals or things that belong together in some way
group *verb* to group people or things is to make them into a group

grouse *noun* a large bird with feathered feet, that some people like to hunt as a sport

grove *noun* a group of trees; a small wood

grovel *verb* grovelling, grovelled **1.** to grovel is to crawl on the ground **2.** to grovel is to be extremely humble and obedient towards someone, usually because you want something from them

grow *verb* growing, grew, grown **1.** a person grows when they become bigger with age **2.** a plant or seed grows when it develops in the ground **3.** to grow something is to plant it in the ground and look after it **4.** to grow is also to become • *It was growing dark.* • *He grew richer and richer.* to grow out of something is to become too big or too old for it to grow up is to become an adult grower *noun* someone who grows things

growl *verb* to growl is to make a deep rough sound, like an angry dog

growl *noun* a deep rough sound

grown-up *noun* an adult

growth *noun* **1.** growth is growing or development **2.** a growth is something that has grown, especially something unwanted in the body such as a tumour

grub *noun* **1.** a grub is a tiny creature that will become an insect; a larva **2.** *(slang)* grub is food

grubby *adjective* grubbier, grubbiest rather dirty

grudge *noun* a dislike of someone who has hurt or annoyed you in the past

grudge *verb* to grudge someone something is to feel unwilling to let them have it grudgingly *adverb* you do something grudgingly when you don't really want to do it and only do it because you have to

gruelling *adjective* a gruelling journey or experience is one that is very hard and tiring

gruesome *adjective* horrible or disgusting to look at

gruff *adjective* having a rough unfriendly voice or manner gruffly *adverb*

grumble *verb* to grumble is to complain in a bad-tempered way

grumpy *adjective* grumpier, grumpiest bad-tempered grumpily *adverb* grumpiness *noun*

grunt *verb* grunts, grunting, grunted to grunt is to make a snorting sound like a pig

grunt *noun* grunts a snort like that of a pig

guarantee *noun* a formal promise to do something, especially to repair something you have sold someone if it goes wrong

guarantee *verb* to guarantee something is to make a promise to do it

guard *verb* **1.** to guard something or someone is to keep them safe **2.** to guard a prisoner is to prevent them from escaping to guard against something is to be careful to prevent it happening

guard *noun* **1.** guard is protecting or guarding people or things • *Keep the prisoners under close guard.* **2.** a guard is someone who protects or watches a person or place **3.** a guard is also an official in charge of a railway train **4.** a guard is a shield or device protecting people from danger on guard protecting; acting as a guard

guardian *noun* **1.** someone who protects something **2.** someone who is legally in charge of a child instead of the child's parents

guerrilla *noun* (ge-**ril**-a) a member of a small army or band that fights by means of surprise attacks

guess *noun* an opinion or answer that you give without working it out in detail or being sure of it

guess *verb* to guess is to make a guess

guest *noun* (gest) a person who is invited to a party or is staying at another person's house or at a hotel

guidance *noun* guidance is giving help or information to someone or telling them how to do something

guide *noun* **1.** someone who shows people the way, helps them or points out interesting sights **2.** a book that tells you about a place Guide a member of the Girl Guides Association, an organization for girls

guide *verb* to guide someone is to show them the way or help them do something

guide dog *noun* a dog specially trained to lead a blind person

guidelines *plural noun* guidelines are rules and information about how to do something

guillotine *noun* (**gil**-o-teen) **1.** a machine once used in France for beheading people **2.** a device with a sharp blade for cutting paper

guilt *noun* **1**. guilt is an unpleasant feeling you have when you have done something wrong **2**. a person's guilt is the fact that they have done something wrong • *Everyone was convinced of his guilt.*

guilty *adjective* guiltier, guiltiest **1**. someone is guilty when they have done wrong **2**. someone feels guilty when they know they have done wrong

guinea pig *noun* **1**. a small furry animal without a tail, kept as a pet **2**. a person who is used in an experiment

guitar *noun* a musical instrument played by plucking its strings **guitarist** *noun* someone who plays the guitar

gulf *noun* a large area of sea partly surrounded by land

gull *noun* a seagull

gullet *noun* the tube from the throat to the stomach

gullible *adjective* someone is gullible when they can be easily fooled about something

gully *noun* gullies a narrow channel that carries water

gulp *verb* to gulp something is to swallow it quickly or greedily
gulp *noun* a loud swallowing noise

gum[1] *noun* the firm fleshy part of the mouth that holds your teeth

gum[2] *noun* **1**. a sticky substance used as glue **2**. chewing gum

gun *noun* a weapon that fires shells or bullets from a metal tube

gun *verb* gunning, gunned
to gun someone down is to shoot them with a gun

gunfire *noun* gunfire is the firing of guns or the noise they make

gunman *noun* gunmen a man armed with a gun

gunpowder *noun* gunpowder is a type of explosive

gurdwara *noun* a building where Sikhs worship

gurgle *verb* to gurgle is to make a bubbling sound • *Water gurgled down the pipe.*

guru *noun* **1**. a Hindu religious teacher **2**. a wise and respected teacher

Guru Granth Sahib *noun* the holy book of the Sikh religion

gush *verb* to gush is to flow quickly

gust *noun* a sudden rush of wind or rain gusty *adjective*

gut *noun* the lower part of the digestive system; the intestine
gut *verb* gutting, gutted **1**. to gut a dead fish or animal is to remove its insides before cooking it **2**. to gut a place is to remove or destroy the inside of it • *The fire left the house a gutted ruin.*

guts *plural noun* **1**. the insides of a person or animal, especially the stomach and intestines **2**. *(informal)* courage and determination

gutter *noun* a long narrow channel at the side of a street or along the edge of a roof, to carry away rainwater

guy *noun* **1**. *(informal)* a man **2**. a figure in the form of Guy Fawkes, burnt on or near 5 November in memory of the Gunpowder Plot to blow up Parliament in 1605

guzzle *verb* to guzzle food or drink is to eat or drink it greedily

gym *noun* (jim) *(informal)* **1**. a gym is a gymnasium **2**. gym is gymnastics

gymkhana *noun* (jim-**kah**-na) a show of horse-riding contests and other events

gymnasium *noun* a place equipped for gymnastics

gymnast *noun* a person who does gymnastics

gymnastics *plural noun* gymnastics are exercises and movements that show the body's agility and strength

gypsy *noun* gypsies a member of a community of people, also called **travellers**, who live in caravans and travel from place to place

gyroscope *noun* a device used in navigation, that keeps steady because of a heavy wheel spinning inside it

> The word **gyroscope** comes from a Greek word *gyros* meaning 'a ring or circle'.

A *hyphen* can make a big difference in meaning, for example, in **a little used car** or **a little-used car**.

habit *noun* something that you do often and almost without thinking **habitual** *adjective* something is habitual when you do it regularly, as a habit **habitually** *adverb*

habitat *noun* an animal's or plant's habitat is the place where it naturally lives or grows

hack *verb* to hack something is to chop or cut it roughly

hacker *noun* someone who uses a computer to get access to a computer system without permission

hacksaw *noun* a saw with a thin blade for cutting metal

haddock *noun* haddock a sea fish used for food

hag *noun* an ugly old woman

haggard *adjective* looking ill or very tired

haggis *noun* a Scottish food made from some of the inner parts of a sheep mixed with oatmeal

haggle *verb* to haggle is to argue about a price or agreement

haiku *noun* haiku (**hy**-koo) a Japanese short poem, with three lines and 17 syllables in the pattern 5,7,5

hail[1] *noun* frozen drops of rain
hail[1] *verb* it hails or it is hailing when hail falls

hail[2] *verb* to hail a taxi is to wave in order to make it stop

hailstone *noun* a piece of hail

hair *noun* **1.** hair is the soft covering that grows on the heads and bodies of people and animals **2.** a hair is one of the fine threads that makes up this soft covering

hairbrush *noun* a brush for tidying your hair

haircut *noun* cutting a person's hair when it gets too long; the style into which it is cut

hairdresser *noun* someone whose job is to cut and arrange people's hair

hair-raising *adjective* terrifying or dangerous

hairstyle *noun* a way or style of arranging your hair

hairy *adjective* hairier, hairiest having a lot of hair

Hajj *noun* the Hajj is the journey to Mecca that all Muslims try to make at least once in their lives

hake *noun* hake a sea fish used for food

halal *adjective* halal meat is prepared according to Muslim law

half *noun* halves each of the two equal parts that something is or can be divided into
half *adverb* partly; not completely • *This meat is only half cooked.*

half-hearted *adjective* not very enthusiastic **half-heartedly** *adverb* not very enthusiastically

half-mast *noun* a flag is at half-mast when it is lowered to halfway down its flagpole, as a sign that someone important has died

half-term *noun* a short holiday from school in the middle of a school term

half-time *noun* a short break in the middle of a game

halfway *adverb, adjective* at a point half the distance between between two places in the middle of a period of time or an event

hall *noun* **1.** a space or passage inside the front door of a house **2.** a very large room for meetings, concerts or other large gatherings of people **3.** a large important building or house

hallo *interjection* a word used to greet someone or to attract their attention

Hallowe'en *noun* the night of 31 October, when people used to think that ghosts and witches might appear

hallucination *noun* something you think you can see or hear when it isn't really there

halo *noun* haloes a circle of light shown round the head of a saint or angel in a painting

halt *verb* to halt is to stop

halt *noun* to call a halt is to stop something to come to a halt is to stop

halter *noun* a rope or strap put round a horse's head so that it can be controlled

halve *verb* **1.** to halve something is to divide it into halves **2.** to halve something is to reduce it to half its size or amount • *If the shop had another checkout it would halve the queues.*

ham *noun* ham is meat from a pig's leg

hamburger *noun* a round flat cake of minced beef that is fried and usually eaten in a bread roll

hammer *noun* a tool with a heavy metal head at the end of a handle, used for hitting nails

hammer *verb* **1.** to hammer something is to hit it with a hammer **2.** to hammer is to knock loudly • *We heard someone hammering on the door.*

hammock *noun* a bed made of a strong net or piece of cloth hung up above the ground or floor

hamper[1] *noun* a large box-shaped basket with a lid

hamper[2] *verb* to hamper someone or something is to get in their way or make it difficult for them to work

hamster *noun* a small furry animal with cheek pouches, often kept as a pet

hand *noun* **1.** the part of your body at the end of your arm **2.** a pointer on a clock or watch **3.** the cards held by one player in a card game **4.** a worker, especially a member of a ship's crew to give someone a hand is to help them on hand ready and available to get out of hand is to get out of control

hand *verb* to hand something to someone is to give or pass it to them something is handed down when it is passed on from one generation to the next

handbag *noun* a small bag for holding money, keys and other personal items

handcuffs *plural noun* a pair of metal rings joined by a chain, used for locking a person's wrists together

handful *noun* **1.** as much as you can carry in one hand **2.** a small number of people or things

handicap *noun* a disadvantage

handicraft *noun* artistic work done with your hands, such as woodwork and pottery

handiwork *noun* something you have done or made with your hands

handkerchief *noun* (**hang**-ker-cheef) a square piece of material for wiping your nose

handle *noun* the part of a thing by which you can hold or control it or pick it up

handle *verb* **1.** to handle something is to touch or feel it with your hands **2.** to handle a task or problem is to deal with it

handlebars *plural noun* a bar with a handle at each end, used to steer a bicycle or motor cycle

handsome *adjective* attractive or good-looking

handstand *noun* an exercise in which you balance on your hands with your feet in the air

handwriting noun writing done by hand; a person's style of writing **handwritten** adjective written by hand, not typed or printed

handy adjective handier, handiest useful or convenient

hang verb hangs, hanging, hung or hanged **1**. to hang something is to fix the top part of it to a hook or nail • *Hang your coat on one of the pegs.* **2**. something hangs when it is supported from the top and does not touch the ground • *The bat was hanging by its feet.* **3**. to hang wallpaper is to paste it in strips on to a wall **4**. (in this meaning, the past tense and past participle are **hanged**) to hang someone is to execute them by hanging them from a rope that tightens around their neck **to hang about** or **hang around** is to wait around doing nothing **to hang on** (informal) is to wait • *Hang on! I'm not ready yet.* **to hang on to something** is to hold it tightly **to hang up** is to end a telephone conversation

hangar noun a large shed where aircraft are kept

hanger noun a curved piece of wood, plastic or wire with a hook at the top, that you use to hang clothes up on

hang-glider noun a frame like a large kite on which a person can glide through the air **hang-gliding** noun the sport of using a hang-glider

hanker verb to hanker after something is to want it badly

hanky noun hankies (informal) a handkerchief

Hanukkah noun a Jewish festival held in December

haphazard adjective (hap-**haz**-erd) done or chosen in no particular order or without any plan • *The books were arranged on the shelf in a haphazard way.* **haphazardly** adverb

happen verb to happen is to take place or occur **to happen to do something** is to do it by chance without planning it • *I happened to see him in the street.*

happening noun something that happens; an unusual event

happy adjective happier, happiest **1**. pleased or contented **2**. satisfied that something is

good • *My teacher is happy with my work this term.* **happily** adverb **happiness** noun

harass verb (**ha**-ras) to harass someone is to annoy or trouble them a lot **harassment** noun

harbour noun a place where ships can shelter or unload

hard adjective **1**. firm or solid; not soft • *The ground was hard.* **2**. difficult • *These sums are quite hard.* **3**. severe or harsh • *There has been a hard frost.* **4**. energetic; using great effort • *She is a hard worker.* **hard up** short of money **hardness** noun being hard

hard adverb **1**. with great effort • *We must work hard.* **2**. with a lot of force • *It was raining hard.*

hardboard noun stiff board made of compressed wood pulp

hard disk noun a disk fitted inside a computer, able to store large amounts of data

harden verb **1**. to harden is to become hard • *Wait for the glue to harden.* **2**. to harden something is to make it hard • *What's the best way to harden a conker?*

hardly adverb only just; only with difficulty • *She was hardly able to walk.*

hardship noun **1**. hardship is suffering or difficulty **2**. a hardship is something that causes suffering

hardware noun **1**. tools and other pieces of equipment you use in the house and garden **2**. the machinery and electronic parts of a computer, not the software

hard-wearing adjective able to stand a lot of wear

hardy adjective hardier, hardiest able to endure cold or difficult conditions

hare noun a fast-running animal like a large rabbit

harm verb to harm someone or something is to hurt or damage them
harm noun injury or damage
harmful adjective causing injury or damage
harmless adjective safe; not at all dangerous

harmonica noun a mouth organ

harmonious adjective **1**. music is harmonious when it is pleasant to listen to

2. peaceful and friendly **harmoniously** *adverb* when people live or work harmoniously they do it in a friendly way without disagreeing

harmonize *verb* to harmonize is to combine together in an effective or pleasant way This word can also be spelled **harmonise**.

harmony *noun* **harmonies 1**. a pleasant combination of musical notes played or sung at the same time **2**. agreement or friendship • *They live in perfect harmony.*

harness *noun* the straps put over a horse's head and round its neck to control it
harness *verb* **1**. to harness a horse is to put a harness on it **2**. to harness something is to control it and make use of it • *We can harness the power of the wind to make electricity.*

harp *noun* a musical instrument made of a frame with strings stretched across it that you pluck with your fingers **harpist** *noun* someone who plays the harp

harpoon *noun* a spear attached to a rope, fired from a gun to catch whales and large fish

harpsichord *noun* a musical instrument like a piano but with the strings plucked and not struck

harsh *adjective* **1**. rough and unpleasant **2**. cruel or severe **harshly** *adverb* **harshness** *noun*

harvest *noun* **1**. the time when farmers gather in the corn, fruit or vegetables they have grown **2**. the crop that is gathered in
harvest *verb* to harvest crops is to gather them in

hassle *noun* (*informal*) something that is difficult or causes problems

haste *noun* hurry or speed

hasten *verb* **1**. to hasten is to hurry **2**. to hasten something is to speed it up

hasty *adjective* **hastier, hastiest** hurried; done too quickly • *a hasty decision* **hastily** *adverb* in a hurried way **hastiness** *noun*

hat *noun* a covering for the head

hatch[1] *noun* an opening in a floor, wall or door, usually with a covering

hatch[2] *verb* **1**. to hatch is to break out of an egg • *The chicks hatched this morning.* **2**. to hatch an egg is to keep it warm until a young bird hatches from it **3**. to hatch a plan is to form it

hatchet *noun* a small axe

hate *verb* to hate someone or something is to dislike them very much
hate *noun* **1**. hate is a feeling of great dislike **2**. (*informal*) a hate is someone or something that you dislike very much

hateful *adjective* hated; very nasty **hatefully** *adverb*

hatred *noun* (**hay**-trid) a strong feeling of great dislike

hat trick *noun* getting three goals, wickets or victories one after another

haughty *adjective* **haughtier, haughtiest** (**haw**-ti) proud of yourself and looking down on other people **haughtily** *adverb* **haughtiness** *noun*

haul *verb* to haul something is to pull it using a lot of power or strength
haul *noun* an amount that someone has won or gained • *The trawler brought home a large haul of fish.*

haunt *verb* a ghost haunts a place or person when it appears often **haunted** *adjective* a haunted place is one that people think is visited by ghosts

have *verb* **has, having, had** This word has many meanings, depending on the words that go with it **1**. to have something is to own or possess it • *We haven't any money.* **2**. to have something in it is to contain it • *I thought this tin had biscuits in it.* **3**. to have (for example) a party is to organize it **4**. to have (for example) a shock or accident is to experience it • *I'm afraid she has had an accident.* **5**. to have to do something is to be obliged or forced to do it • *We really have to go now.* **6.** to have something (for example) mended or built is to get someone to mend or build it • *I'm having my watch mended.* **7.** to have (for example) a letter is to receive it • *I had a letter from my cousin.* **8.** The verb **have** can also be used to help make other verbs • *They have gone.* • *Has he seen my book?* • *We had eaten them.*

haven *noun* (**hay**-ven) **1.** a safe place **2.** a harbour

hawk *noun* a bird of prey with very strong eyesight

hawthorn *noun* a thorny tree with small red berries

hay *noun* cut grass that is dried and used to feed to animals

hay fever *noun* an allergy to pollen that makes you sneeze and makes your eyes water or itch

haystack *noun* a large neat pile of stored hay

hazard *noun* a risk or danger
hazardous *adjective* dangerous or risky

haze *noun* thin mist

hazel *noun* **1.** a type of small nut tree **2.** a nut from this tree

hazy *adjective* **hazier, haziest 1.** misty • *hazy sunshine* **2.** vague and unclear • *He has only a hazy memory of what happened.* **hazily** *adverb* **haziness** *noun*

he *pronoun* a male person or animal

head *noun* **1.** the part of your body containing your brain, eyes and mouth **2.** brains or intelligence • *Use your head!* **3.** the side of a coin on which someone's head is shown **4.** a person • *It costs £10 per head.* **5.** the top or front of something, such as a pin or nail **6.** the person in charge • *She's the head of this school.* **to keep your head** is to stay calm

head *verb* **1.** to head a group or organization is to be the person in charge **2.** to head a ball is to hit it with your head **3.** to head in a particular direction is to start going there • *They headed for home.*

headache *noun* a pain in your head that goes on hurting

headdress *noun* a decorative covering for the head

header *noun* the act of hitting the ball with your head in football

heading *noun* a word or words at the top of a piece of printing or writing

headlight *noun* a strong light at the front of a vehicle

headline *noun* a heading in a newspaper, printed in large type

headlong *adverb, adjective* **1.** falling with your head forward **2.** in a hasty or thoughtless way • *He's always rushing headlong into trouble.*

head-on *adverb, adjective* with the front parts hitting each other • *He hit the post head-on.* • *a head-on collision*

headphones *plural noun* a device for listening to music that fits over the top of your head

headquarters *noun* **headquarters** the place from which an organization is controlled

headteacher *noun* the person in charge of a school

heal *verb* **1.** to heal someone is to make them healthy **2.** a wound or injury heals when it gets better

health *noun* how well or ill a person is • *His health is good for his age.*

health food *noun* food that contains only natural substances and is thought to be good for your health

healthy *adjective* **healthier, healthiest 1.** free from illness; having good health **2.** good for you • *Eat a healthy diet.* **healthily** *adverb* **healthiness** *noun*

heap *noun* an untidy pile

heap *verb* **1.** to heap things is to pile them up **2.** to heap something is to put large amounts on it • *She heaped his plate with food.*

hear *verb* **hearing, heard 1.** to hear is to take in sounds through your ears **2.** to hear news or information is to receive it **3.** you hear from someone when they write to you or phone you

hearing *noun* **1.** the ability to hear **2.** a chance to be heard • *Please give me a fair hearing.* **3.** a trial in court

hearing aid *noun* a device to help a partially deaf person to hear

hearse *noun* a vehicle for taking a coffin to a funeral

heart *noun* **1.** the part of the body inside your chest that pumps blood around your body **2.** a person's feelings or emotions • *She has a kind heart.* **3.** courage or enthusiasm • *We must take heart.* **4.** the middle or most important part of something **5.** a curved shape representing a heart or a playing card with this shape on it **to break someone's heart** is to make them very unhappy **by heart** by using your memory

heart attack *noun* a sudden failure of the heart to work properly, causing pain and sometimes death

hearth *noun* (harth) the floor of a fireplace or the area near it

heartless *adjective* cruel or without pity

hearty *adjective* heartier, heartiest **1.** strong and healthy **2.** enthusiastic or sincere • *Hearty congratulations!*

heat *noun* **1.** being hot; great warmth **2.** a race or contest to decide who will take part in the final
heat *verb* **1.** to heat something or heat something up, is to make it hot **2.** to heat or heat up, is to become hot

heater *noun* a device for heating a room or a car

heath *noun* wild flat land often covered with heather or bushes

heather *noun* a low bush with small purple, pink or white flowers

heatwave *noun* a long period of hot weather

heave *verb* to heave something is to lift or move it with great effort

heaven *noun* **1.** the place where, in some religions, good people are thought to go when they die and where God and the angels are thought to live **2.** a very pleasant place or condition **the heavens** the sky

heavenly *adjective* **1.** to do with the sky or in the sky **2.** *(informal)* pleasing or delicious • *The cake is heavenly.*

heavy *adjective* heavier, heaviest **1.** weighing a lot; hard to lift or carry **2.** you talk about how heavy something is when you are talking about how much it weighs **3.** strong or severe • *Heavy rain was falling.* **4.** hard or difficult • *The climb up the hill was heavy going.* heavily *adverb* heaviness *noun*

Hebrew *noun* the language of the ancient Jews, with a modern form used in Israel

hectare *noun* (**hek**-tar) a unit of area equal to 10,000 square metres or nearly 2½ acres

hectic *adjective* very active or busy

hedge *noun* a row of bushes forming a barrier or boundary

hedgehog *noun* a small animal covered with prickles

hedgerow *noun* a row of bushes forming a hedge

heed *verb* to heed something is to pay attention to it
heed *noun* attention given to something heedless *adjective* taking no notice of something

heel *noun* **1.** the back part of your foot **2.** the part of a sock or shoe round or under the back part of your foot

heifer *noun* (**hef**-er) a young cow

height *noun* **1.** how high someone or something is **2.** a high place • *She's afraid of heights.* **3.** the highest or most important part of something • *We shall be going at the height of the holiday season.*

heighten *verb* **1.** to heighten something is to make it higher or more intense **2.** to heighten is to become higher or more intense • *Their excitement heightened as the kick-off approached.*

heir *noun* (air) someone who inherits money or a title heiress *noun* a girl or woman who inherits money or a title

helicopter *noun* a kind of aircraft without wings, lifted by a large horizontal propeller on top

helium *noun* (**hee**-li-um) a colourless gas that is lighter than air, often used in balloons

hell *noun* **1.** a place where, in some religions, wicked people are thought to be punished after they die and where the Devil is thought to live **2.** a very unpleasant place or situation

hello *interjection* a word used to greet someone or to attract their attention

helm *noun* the handle or wheel used to steer a ship

helmet *noun* a strong hard hat or covering that you wear to protect your head

help *verb* **1.** to help someone is to do something useful for them or make things easier for them **2.** when you cannot help doing something, you cannot avoid doing it • *I couldn't help sneezing.* **helper** *noun* someone who helps another person

help *noun* **1.** doing something useful for someone • *Do you need any help?* **2.** someone who does something for someone • *Thank you, you've been a great help.*

helpful *adjective* giving help; useful **helpfully** *adverb*

helping *noun* a portion of food at a meal

helpless *adjective* not able to do things or look after yourself **helplessly** *adverb*

hem *noun* the edge of a piece of cloth that has been folded over and sewn down

hem *verb* **hemming, hemmed** to hem material is to fold it over and sew down its edge

hemisphere *noun* each half of the earth, above or below the equator • *Australia is in the southern hemisphere.*

hen *noun* a female bird, especially a chicken

hence *adverb* **1.** from this time on **2.** therefore

her *pronoun* a word used for *she* when it is the object of a verb or when it comes after a preposition • *I can see her.* • *He took the books from her.*

her *determiner* belonging to her • *That is her book.*

herald *noun* an official who in the past used to make announcements or carry messages for a king or queen

heraldry *noun* the study of coats of arms **heraldic** *adjective* to do with heraldry

herb *noun* a plant used for flavouring or for making medicines **herbal** *adjective* made from herbs or using herbs

herbivore *noun* an animal that only eats plants

herd *noun* a large group of animals, especially cattle
herd *verb* to herd a group of animals or people is to move them in a large group

here *adverb* in or to this place **here and there** in various places or directions

hereditary *adjective* passed down to a child from a parent

heredity *noun* (hi-**red**-i-ti) the passing down of characteristics from parents to children through their genes

heritage *noun* things that have been passed from one generation to another; a country's history and traditions

hermit *noun* someone who lives alone and keeps away from people

hero *noun* **heroes 1.** a man or boy who has done something very brave **2.** the most important man or boy in a story, film or play **heroic** *adjective* very brave, like a hero **heroically** *adverb* bravely **heroism** *noun* being a hero; great bravery

heroine *noun* **1.** a woman or girl who has done something very brave **2.** the most important woman or girl in a story, film or play

heron *noun* a wading bird with long legs and a long neck

herring *noun* **herring** or **herrings** a sea fish that swims in large groups and is used for food

hers *pronoun* belonging to her • *Those books are hers.*

herself *pronoun* she or her and nobody else, used to refer back to the subject of a verb • *She has hurt herself.* **by herself** on her own; alone • *She did the work all by herself.*

hesitant *adjective* being slow or uncertain when you speak or move **hesitantly** *adverb*

hesitate *verb* to hesitate is to be slow or uncertain when you speak or move **hesitation** *noun* when you hesitate; a pause

hexagon *noun* a flat shape with six sides
hexagonal *adjective* having six sides

hibernate *verb* (**hy**-ber-nayt) animals hibernate when they sleep for a long time during cold weather **hibernation** *noun* hibernating

hiccup *noun* a high gulping sound made when your breath is briefly interrupted
hiccup *verb* **hiccupping, hiccupped** to make this high gulping sound

hide *verb* **hiding, hidden, hid, hidden** 1. to hide is to get into a place where you cannot be seen or found 2. to hide someone or something is to keep them from being seen • *The gold was hidden in a cave.* 3. to hide information is to keep it secret • *Are you hiding the truth from me?*

hide-and-seek *noun* a game in which one person looks for others who are hiding

hideous *adjective* very ugly or unpleasant
hideously *adverb*

hideout *noun* a place where someone hides

hiding[1] *noun* **to go into hiding** is to hide yourself so that people can't find you

hiding[2] *noun* a thrashing or beating

hieroglyphics *plural noun* (hyr-o-**glif**-iks) pictures or symbols used in ancient Egypt to represent words

high *adjective* 1. reaching a long way up • *high mountains* 2. far above the ground or above sea level • *The clouds were high in the sky.* 3. measuring from top to bottom • *The post is two metres high.* 4. above average in amount or importance • *They are people of a high rank.* • *Prices are high.* 5. lively; happy • *They are in high spirits.* 6. a high note is one at the top end of a musical scale
high *adverb* **higher, highest** 1. far above the ground or a long way up • *She jumped high into the air.* 2. at a high level • *The temperature is going to rise even higher this week.*

high jump *noun* an athletic contest in which competitors jump over a high bar

highland *adjective* in the highlands; to do with the highlands

highlands *plural noun* mountainous country, especially in Scotland **highlander** *noun* someone who lives in the highlands

highlight *noun* the most interesting part of something • *We watched the highlights of the match on the TV.*
highlight *verb* to highlight something is to draw attention to it

highly *adverb* extremely • *He is highly amusing.* **to think highly of someone** is to admire them very much

Highness *noun* **Highnesses** a title of a prince or princess • *His Royal Highness, the Prince of Wales.*

high-pitched *adjective* high in sound

highway *noun* an important road or route

highwayman *noun* **highwaymen** a man who in earlier times robbed travellers on highways

hijack *verb* to hijack an aircraft or vehicle is to take control of it by force during a journey **hijacker** *noun* someone who hijacks an aircraft or vehicle

hike *noun* a long walk in the countryside
hike *verb* to hike is to go for a long walk in the countryside **hiker** *noun* someone who goes for long walks in the countryside

hilarious *adjective* very funny
hilariously *adverb* if something is hilariously funny it is extremely funny **hilarity** *noun* loud laughter

hill *noun* a piece of ground that is higher than the ground around it **hillside** *noun* the side of a hill **hilly** *adjective* a hilly area has lots of hills

hilt *noun* the handle of a sword or dagger

him *pronoun* a word used for *he* when it is the object of a verb or when it comes after a preposition • *I like him.* • *I gave it to him.*

himself *pronoun* he or him and nobody else, used to refer back to the subject of a verb • *He has hurt himself.* **by himself** on his own; alone • *He did the work all by himself.*

hind[1] *adjective* (hynd) at the back • *The donkey had hurt one of its hind legs.*

hind[2] *noun* (hynd) a female deer

hinder *verb* (**hin**-der) to hinder someone is to get in their way or to make it difficult for them to do something **hindrance** *noun* something that gets in your way or makes it difficult for you to do something

Hindi *noun* a language spoken in northern India

Hindu *noun* someone who believes in **Hinduism**, one of the religions of India

hinge *noun* a joining device on which a door, gate or lid swings when it opens

hinged *adjective* a hinged door, window or lid is fixed on a hinge

hint *noun* a slight indication or suggestion • *Give me a hint of what you want for your birthday.*

hint *verb* to hint is to suggest something without actually saying it • *She hinted that she'd like to have a puppy.*

hip *noun* your hips are the bony parts at the side of your body between your waist and your thighs

hippo *noun* hippos *(informal)* a hippopotamus

hippopotamus *noun* a very large African animal that lives near water

hire *verb* to hire something is to pay to use it for a time

hire *noun* something is for hire when you can hire it

his *determiner* belonging to him • *That is his book.*

hiss *verb* to hiss is to make a sound like a continuous s, as some snakes do

historian *noun* someone who writes or studies history

historic *adjective* famous or important in history

historical *adjective* to do with history

history *noun* histories **1**. what happened in the past **2**. the study of past events

hit *verb* hitting, hit **1**. to hit someone or something is to come up against them with force or to give them a blow **2**. something hits you when you suddenly realize or feel it **3**. to hit a place or people is to have a bad effect on them • *The tax will hit poorest families hardest.* **4**. to hit a note is to reach it when you are singing to hit on something is to think of an idea suddenly

hit *noun* **1**. a knock or stroke **2**. a shot that hits the target **3**. a successful song or show

hitch *verb* **1**. to hitch something is to tie it up with a loop **2**. *(informal)* to hitch a lift is to hitch-hike

hitch *noun* a slight difficulty or delay

hitch-hike *verb* to hitch-hike is to travel by getting lifts in other people's vehicles hitch-hiker *noun* someone who hitch-hikes

hitherto *adverb* up to now

HIV short for *human immunodeficiency virus*, the virus that causes the disease Aids

hive *noun* **1**. a beehive **2**. a very busy place • *The office was a hive of activity.*

hoard *noun* a hidden store of something valuable

hoard *verb* to hoard things is to collect them and store them away for the future hoarder *noun* someone who likes keeping things rather than throwing them out

hoarding *noun* a tall fence covered with advertisements

hoarse *adjective* having a rough or croaking voice • *He was hoarse from shouting.*

hoax *noun* a trick played on someone in which they are told about something but it isn't true • *The bomb scare was a hoax.*

hoax *verb* to hoax someone is to trick them by telling them about something that isn't true

hobble *verb* to hobble is to walk with unsteady steps because your feet are sore

hobby *noun* hobbies something that you enjoy doing in your spare time

hockey *noun* an outdoor game played by two teams with long curved sticks and a small hard ball

hoe *noun* a gardening tool with a long handle and a metal blade, used for scraping up weeds and making soil loose

hog *noun* a male pig

Hogmanay *noun* New Year's Eve in Scotland

hoist *verb* to hoist something is to lift it up using ropes or pulleys

hold *verb* holding, held **1.** to hold something is to have it in your hands **2.** to hold something is also to possess it or be the owner of it • *She holds the world high jump record.* **3.** to hold a party, meeting or event is to organize it • *The 2012 Olympic Games were held in London.* **4.** a container holds an amount when that is what you can put in it • *This jug holds a litre.* **5.** to hold someone or something is to support them • *This plank won't hold my weight.* **6.** to hold someone is to keep them and stop them getting away • *They held the thief until help arrived.* **7.** to hold an opinion is to believe it to hold on (informal) is to wait • *Hold on! I'm not ready yet.* to hold out is to last or continue to hold someone up is to rob them with threats of force to hold someone or something up is to hinder or delay them • *We were held up by the traffic.*

hold *noun* **1.** holding something • *Don't lose hold of the rope.* **2.** the part of a ship where cargo is stored to get hold of someone is to make contact with them

hold-up *noun* **1.** a delay **2.** a robbery with threats or force

hole *noun* **1.** a gap or opening made in something **2.** an animal's burrow • *a rabbit hole*

Holi *noun* a Hindu festival held in the spring

holiday *noun* a day or time when you do not go to work or school; a time when you go away to enjoy yourself to be on holiday is to be away from work or school enjoying yourself

hollow *adjective* having an empty space inside; not solid

hollow *verb* to hollow something is to make it hollow

hollow *noun* **1.** a hollow or sunken place **2.** a small valley

holly *noun* an evergreen bush with shiny prickly leaves and red berries

holster *noun* a leather case for a pistol, usually attached to a belt

holy *adjective* holier, holiest **1.** to do with God and treated with religious respect **2.** a holy person is devoted to God or a religion holiness *noun*

home *noun* **1.** the place where you live **2.** the place where you were born or where you feel you belong **3.** a place where people are looked after • *a home for the elderly* to feel at home is to feel comfortable and happy

home *adverb* **1.** to or at the place where you live • *Is she home yet?* **2.** to the place aimed at • *Push the bolt home.* to bring something home to someone is to make them realize it

home *verb* homes, homing, homed to home in on something is to aim for it

homeless *adjective* not having a place to live

homely *adjective* simple or ordinary

home-made *adjective* made at home and not bought from a shop

homesick *adjective* sad or upset because you are away from home homesickness *noun*

homeward or **homewards** *adverb* towards home

homework *noun* school work that you have to do at home

honest *adjective* truthful and able to be trusted; not stealing, cheating or telling lies honesty *noun* being honest and truthful

honestly *adverb* **1.** to say something honestly is to say it truthfully **2.** to do something honestly is to do it without stealing or cheating

honey *noun* a sweet sticky food made by bees

honeycomb *noun* a wax framework made by bees to hold their honey and eggs

honeymoon *noun* a holiday that a newly-married couple spend together

honour *noun* **1.** honour is great respect or reputation **2.** an honour is something given to a person who deserves it because of the good work they have done **3.** an honour is also something a person is proud to do • *It is an honour to meet you.*

honour *verb* **1.** to honour someone is to show you respect them or to give them an honour **2.** to honour a promise or agreement is to keep it

honourable *adjective* someone is honourable when they can be trusted and always try to do the right thing **honourably** *adverb*

hood *noun* **1.** a part of a coat or sweatshirt that covers your head and neck **2.** a folding roof or cover **hooded** *adjective* having or wearing a hood

hoof *noun* **hoofs** or **hooves** the hard part of the foot of horses, cattle or deer

hook *noun* a piece of bent or curved metal or plastic for hanging things on or catching hold of something **hooked** *adjective* having a curved shape like a hook

hook *verb* **1.** to hook something is to fasten it with or on a hook **2.** to hook a fish is to catch it with a hook

hooligan *noun* a rough or noisy person

hoop *noun* a large ring made of metal, wood or plastic

hooray *interjection* a shout of joy or approval; a cheer

hoot *noun* **1.** a sound like the one made by an owl **2.** a jeer

hoot *verb* to hoot is to make a sound like an owl

hop[1] *verb* **hopping, hopped** **1.** to hop is to jump on one foot **2.** animals hop when they move in jumps

hop[1] *noun* a jump you make on one foot

hop[2] *noun* a climbing plant used to give beer its flavour

hope *noun* **1.** the feeling of wanting something to happen and thinking that it will happen **2.** a person or thing that makes you feel like this • *She is our big hope for a gold medal.*

hope *verb* to hope for something is to want it and expect it to happen

hopeful *adjective* **1.** having hope **2.** likely to be good or successful • *The future did not seem very hopeful.*

hopefully *adverb* **1.** in a hopeful way **2.** I hope that ... • *Hopefully we can all go to the sea tomorrow.*

hopeless *adjective* **1.** without hope **2.** very bad at something • *I'm hopeless at cricket.* **hopelessly** *adverb*

hopscotch *noun* a game in which you hop into squares drawn on the ground

horde *noun* a large group or crowd

horizon *noun* (ho-**ry**-zon) the line where the sky appears to meet the land or sea

horizontal *adjective* (ho-ri-**zon**-tal) level or flat; going across from left to right **horizontally** *adverb* in a horizontal direction

hormone *noun* a substance made in glands in the body and sent directly into the blood to make other organs work in special ways

horn *noun* **1.** a kind of pointed bone that grows on the head of a bull, cow, ram and other animals **2.** a brass musical instrument that you blow **3.** a device for making a warning sound

hornet *noun* a large kind of wasp

horoscope *noun* an astrologer's forecast of future events

horrendous *adjective* extremely unpleasant

horrible *adjective* very unpleasant or nasty **horribly** *adverb*

horrid *adjective* nasty or unkind

horrific *adjective* shocking or terrifying **horrifically** *adverb*

horrify *verb* horrifies, horrifying, horrified to horrify someone is to make them feel shocked and disgusted

horror *noun* horror is great fear or disgust

horse *noun* **1.** a four-legged animal used for riding on or pulling carts **2.** a tall box that you jump over when you are doing gymnastics

horseback *noun* to be on horseback is to be riding a horse

horse chestnut *noun* a large tree that produces dark brown nuts called conkers

horsepower *noun* horsepower a unit for measuring the power of an engine, equal to 746 watts

horseshoe *noun* a U-shaped piece of metal nailed as a shoe to a horse's hoof

hose *noun* a long flexible tube through which liquids or gases can travel

hospitable *adjective* welcoming and friendly to visitors and guests

hospital *noun* a place where sick or injured people are given medical treatment

hospitality *noun* welcoming people and giving them food and entertainment

host[1] *noun* someone who has guests and looks after them

host[2] *noun* a large number of people or things

hostage *noun* someone who is held prisoner until the people who are holding them get what they want

hostel *noun* a building with rooms where people can stay cheaply

hostess *noun* a woman who has guests and looks after them

hostile *adjective* **1.** unfriendly and angry • The crowd outside was hostile. **2.** opposed to someone or something **hostility** *noun* unfriendliness and strong dislike

hot *adjective* hotter, hottest **1.** having a high temperature; very warm **2.** having a burning taste like pepper or mustard

hot dog *noun* a hot sausage in a bread roll

hotel *noun* a building where people pay to stay for the night

hotly *adverb* strongly or forcefully • He hotly denied that he'd done it.

hot-water bottle *noun* a container that you fill with hot water to make a bed warm

hound *noun* a dog used for hunting or racing

hound *verb* to hound someone is to keep on chasing and bothering them • The family was hounded by newspaper reporters.

hour *noun* **1.** one of the twenty-four parts into which a day is divided **2.** a particular time • Why are you up at this hour?

hourglass *noun* an old-fashioned device for telling the time, with sand running from one half of a glass container into the other through a narrow middle part

hourly *adjective, adverb* every hour; done once an hour

house *noun* (howss) **1.** a building where people live **2.** a building used for a special purpose • Sydney's famous opera house **3.** one of the divisions in some schools for sports competitions and other events

house *verb* (howz) to house someone or something is to provide a house or room for them

household *noun* all the people who live together in the same house

housewife *noun* housewives a woman who stays at home to look after her children and do the housework rather than doing a paid job

housework *noun* the work like cooking and cleaning that has to be done in a house

hover *verb* to hover is to stay in one place in the air

hovercraft *noun* hovercraft a vehicle that travels just above the surface of water or land, supported by a strong current of air sent downwards by its engines

how *adverb* **1**. in what way • *How did you do it?* **2**. to what extent • *How much do you want?* **3**. in what condition • *How are you?*

however *adverb* **1**. no matter how; in whatever way • *You will never catch him, however hard you try.* **2**. nevertheless • *It was snowing; however, he went out.*

however *conjunction* in any way • *You can do it however you like.*

howl *noun* a long loud cry like an animal in pain

howl *verb* to howl is to make a long loud cry like an animal in pain or to weep loudly

HQ short for **headquarters**

hub *noun* the centre of a wheel

huddle *verb* to huddle is to crowd together with other people for warmth or comfort

hue *noun* a colour or tint

hug *verb* **hugging, hugged 1**. to hug someone is to clasp them tightly in your arms **2**. to hug something is to keep close to it • *The ship hugged the shore.*

hug *noun* clasping someone tightly in your arms

huge *adjective* extremely large
hugely *adverb* greatly; very

hulk *noun* the remains of an old decaying ship

hull *noun* the main part or framework of a ship

hum *verb* **humming, hummed 1**. to hum is to sing a tune with your lips closed **2**. to hum is also to make a low continuous sound like a bee

hum *noun* a humming sound

human *noun* a man, woman or child; a human being
human *adjective* to do with humans

human being *noun* a man, woman or child; a human

humane *adjective* (hew-**mayn**) showing kindness and a wish to cause as little suffering or pain as possible **humanely** *adverb*

humanity *noun* **1**. all the people in the world **2**. kindness and sympathy to other people

humble *adjective* modest and not proud
humbly *adverb*

humid *adjective* (**hew**-mid) damp and warm in the air **humidity** *noun* how damp it is in the air

humiliate *verb* to humiliate someone is to make them feel ashamed or foolish in front of other people **humiliation** *noun* a feeling of shame because you have been made to look foolish in front of other people

humility *noun* being humble

hummingbird *noun* a small tropical bird that makes a humming sound by beating its wings rapidly

humorous *adjective* amusing or funny

humour *noun* **1**. being amusing; what makes people laugh **2**. being able to enjoy things that are funny • *He has a good sense of humour.* **3**. a person's mood • *Keep him in a good humour.*

humour *verb* to humour someone is to keep them happy by doing what they want

hump *noun* a rounded lump or mound
hump *verb* to hump something heavy is to carry it with difficulty on your back

hunch[1] *noun* a feeling that you can guess what will happen • *I have a hunch that she won't come.*

hunch[2] *verb* to hunch your shoulders is to bring them up and forward so that your back is rounded

hunchback *noun* someone with a hump on their back

hundred *noun* the number 100
hundredth *adjective, noun* 100th

hundredweight *noun* a unit of weight equal to 112 pounds or 50.8 kilograms

hunger *noun* the feeling you get when you want or need to eat

hungry *adjective* hungrier, hungriest you are hungry when you want or need to eat **hungrily** *adverb*

hunk *noun* a thick piece of something

hunt *verb* 1. to hunt animals is to chase and kill them for food or sport 2. to hunt for something is to look hard for it
hunt *noun* 1. a time when a group of people chase and kill animals for food or sport 2. a group of people who go hunting 3. a search

hunter or **huntsman** *noun* huntsmen someone who hunts for sport

hurdle *noun* 1. an upright frame that runners jump over in an athletics race 2. a problem or difficulty

hurl *verb* to hurl something is to throw it as far as you can

hurrah or **hurray** *interjection* a shout of joy or approval; a cheer

hurricane *noun* a severe storm with a strong wind

hurry *verb* hurries, hurrying, hurried 1. to hurry is to move or act quickly 2. to hurry someone is to try to make them be quick **hurriedly** *adverb* in a hurry • *We hurriedly got dressed.*
hurry *noun* moving quickly; doing something quickly in a hurry hurrying or impatient

hurt *verb* 1. to hurt a person or animal is to harm them or cause them pain 2. part of your body hurts when you feel pain there 3. to hurt someone is also to upset them by being unkind
hurt *noun* pain or injury **hurtful** *adjective* a hurtful remark upsets someone because it is unkind

hurtle *verb* to hurtle is to move quickly or dangerously • *A mass of snow and rocks hurtled down the mountain.*

husband *noun* the man that a woman is married to

husk *noun* the dry outer covering of a seed

husky[1] *adjective* huskier, huskiest a voice is husky when it is deep and rough

husky[2] *noun* huskies a large strong dog used in the Arctic for pulling sledges

hut *noun* a small roughly made house or shelter

hutch *noun* a box or cage for a rabbit or other pet animal

hybrid *noun* an animal or plant that combines two different species

hydrant *noun* an outdoor water-tap connected to the main water supply, for fixing a hose to

hydraulic *adjective* worked by the movement of liquid

hydroelectric *adjective* using water-power to make electricity

hydrofoil *noun* a boat designed to skim over the surface of the water

hydrogen *noun* a very light gas which with oxygen makes water

hyena *noun* (hy-ee-na) a wild animal that looks like a wolf and makes a shrieking howl

hygiene *noun* (**hy**-jeen) keeping clean and healthy and free of germs

hygienic *adjective* clean and healthy and free of germs **hygienically** *adverb*

hymn *noun* a Christian religious song, especially one that praises God

hypermarket *noun* a very large supermarket, usually outside a town

hyphen *noun* a short dash used to join words or parts of words together, for example in *red-handed*

hypnosis *noun* (hip-**noh**-sis) to be under hypnosis is to be in a condition like a deep sleep in which a person follows the instructions of another person

hypnotism *noun* (**hip**-no-tizm) hypnotizing people **hypnotist** *noun* someone who hypnotizes people

hypnotize *verb* hypnotizes, hypnotizing, hypnotized to hypnotize someone is to put them to sleep by hypnosis This word can also be spelled **hypnotise**.

hypocrite *noun* (**hip**-o-krit) someone who pretends to be a better person than they really are **hypocrisy** *noun* being a hypocrite **hypocritical** *adjective* someone is being hypocritical when they are pretending to be a better person than they really are

hypodermic *adjective* (hy-po-**der**-mik) a hypodermic needle or syringe is one used to inject a drug under the skin

hypotenuse *noun* (hy-**pot**-i-newz) the side opposite the right angle in a right-angled triangle

hypothermia *noun* a person suffers from hypothermia when they become so cold that their body temperature falls well below normal

hysteria *noun* wild uncontrollable excitement or emotion

hysterical *adjective* **1.** extremely excited or emotional **2.** (*informal*) very funny **hysterically** *adverb*

hysterics *plural noun* a fit of hysteria to be in hysterics (*informal*) is to be laughing a lot

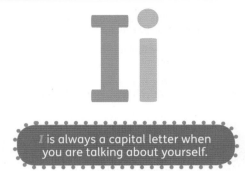

I is always a capital letter when you are talking about yourself.

I *pronoun* a word used by someone to speak about himself or herself

ice *noun* ice is frozen water

ice *verb* **1.** to ice or ice up is to become covered in ice **2.** to ice a cake is to put icing on it

ice age *noun* a time in the past when ice covered large areas of the earth's surface

iceberg *noun* a large mass of ice floating in the sea, with most of it under water

ice cream *noun* **1.** ice cream is a sweet creamy frozen food **2.** an ice cream is a portion of this

ice hockey *noun* ice hockey is a game like hockey played on ice

ice lolly *noun* ice lollies a piece of flavoured ice on a stick

ice-skating *noun* moving on ice wearing special boots with blades on the bottom

icicle *noun* a thin pointed piece of hanging ice formed from dripping water

icing *noun* a sugary substance for decorating cakes

icon *noun* **1.** a small picture or symbol standing for a program on a computer screen **2.** a painting of a holy person

ICT short for *information and communication technology*

icy *adjective* **icier**, **iciest** **1.** an icy road has ice on it **2.** an icy wind is very cold **3.** very unfriendly; hostile • *He gave them an icy stare.* **icily** *adverb* in an unfriendly way

idea *noun* something that you have thought of; a plan

ideal *adjective* exactly what you want; perfect **ideally** *adverb* if things were perfect • *Ideally, I'd like to live by the sea.*
ideal *noun* something that is perfect or the best thing to have; a very high standard

identical *adjective* exactly the same • *identical twins* **identically** *adverb* in exactly the same way • *They were identically dressed.*

identification *noun* **1.** identification is any document, such as a passport, that proves who you are **2.** identification is the process of discovering who someone is or what something is

identify *verb* **identifies**, **identifying**, **identified** to identify someone or something is to discover who or what they are

identity *noun* **identities** who someone is or what something is • *Can you discover the identity of our mystery guest?*

idiom *noun* (**id**-i-om) a phrase or group of words that together have a special meaning that is not obvious from the words themselves, for example *to keep your head* means to stay calm

idiot *noun* (*informal*) a stupid or foolish person **idiotic** *adjective* stupid or foolish

idle *adjective* **1.** a person is idle when they are lazy or doing nothing **2.** a machine is idle when it is not being used **3.** idle talk or gossip is talk that is silly or pointless
idle *verb* a machine or engine idles when it is working slowly **idly** *adverb* in a lazy way

idol *noun* **1.** a famous person who is admired by a lot of people **2.** a statue or image that people worship as a god

idolize *verb* to idolize someone is to admire them very much This word can also be spelled **idolise**.

i.e. short for the Latin *id est*, which means 'that is', used to explain something • *The world's highest mountain (i.e. Mount Everest) is in the Himalayas.*

if *conjunction* **1.** on condition that • *I'll tell you what happened if you promise to keep it secret.* **2.** although; even though • *I'll finish this job if it kills me!* **3.** whether • *Do you know if lunch is ready?*

igloo *noun* a round house made of blocks of hard snow, built by the Inuit people of the Arctic

> The word **igloo** comes from an Inuit word *iglu* meaning 'house'.

ignite *verb* **1.** to ignite something is to set fire to it **2.** to ignite is to catch fire

ignition *noun* **1.** igniting **2.** ignition is the system in a motor engine that starts the fuel burning

ignorant *adjective* not knowing about something; knowing very little **ignorance** *noun* someone shows ignorance when they don't know about something or know very little

ignore *verb* to ignore someone or something is to take no notice of them

ill *adjective* **1.** not well; in bad health **2.** bad or harmful • *There were no ill effects.*

illegal *adjective* something is illegal when it is against the law **illegally** *adverb*

illegible *adjective* (i-**lej**-i-bul) illegible writing is not clear enough to read **illegibly** *adverb*

illegitimate *adjective* (il-i-**jit**-i-mat) (*old use*) someone is illegitimate when they are born to parents who are not married

illiterate *adjective* (i-**lit**-er-at) unable to read or write

illness *noun* **1.** illness is being ill **2.** an illness is something that makes people ill; a disease

illogical *adjective* not logical or having any good reason

illuminate *verb* to illuminate a place or street is to light it up or decorate it with lights **illuminations** *plural noun* lights put up to decorate a place or street

illusion *noun* something that you think is real or happening but is not

illustrate *verb* 1. to illustrate something is to show it with pictures or examples 2. to illustrate a book is to put pictures in it

illustration *noun* a picture in a book

image *noun* 1. a picture or statue of a person or thing 2. what you see in a mirror or through a lens 3. a picture you have in your mind 4. the way someone seems to other people

imaginary *adjective* not real; existing only in your mind

imagination *noun* your ability to form pictures and ideas in your mind

imaginative *adjective* showing that you are good at thinking of new and exciting ideas

imagine *verb* to imagine something or someone is to form a picture of them in your mind **imaginable** *adjective* that you can imagine

imam *noun* a Muslim religious leader

imitate *verb* to imitate someone or something is to do the same as them **imitation** *noun* copying someone or something **imitator** *noun* someone who copies someone or something else

immature *adjective* 1. not fully grown or developed 2. behaving in a silly or childish way **immaturity** *noun* being immature

immediate *adjective* 1. happening or done without any delay 2. nearest; with nothing or no one between • *The Smiths are our immediate neighbours.*

immediately *adverb* without any delay; at once

immense *adjective* huge **immensely** *adverb* extremely

immerse *verb* 1. to immerse something is to put it completely into a liquid 2. to be immersed in something is to be very interested or involved in it **immersion** *noun* the immersion of something is when you put it into a liquid

immigrant *noun* someone who has come into a country to live there

immigrate *verb* to immigrate is to come into a country to live there **immigration** *noun* people coming into a country to live there

immobile *adjective* not moving

immoral *adjective* not following the usual standards of right and wrong **immorality** *noun* immoral behaviour

immortal *adjective* someone who is immortal lives for ever **immortality** *noun* living for ever

immune *adjective* someone is immune to a disease if they cannot catch it **immunity** *noun* protection against a disease

immunize *verb* to immunize someone is to make them safe from a disease, usually by giving them an injection **immunization** *noun* immunization is immunizing someone This word can also be spelled **immunise**.

imp *noun* a small devil

impact *noun* 1. the force of one thing hitting another 2. a strong influence or effect • *The Internet has a big impact on our lives.*

impair *verb* to impair something is to harm or weaken it • *The accident has impaired his health.*

impartial *adjective* fair and not supporting one side more than the other **impartiality** *noun* someone shows impartiality when they are fair and do not support one side more than the other **impartially** *adverb*

impatient *adjective* annoyed because you can't wait for something to happen **impatience** *noun* annoyance because you can't wait for something to happen **impatiently** *adverb*

imperative *adjective* essential • *Speed is imperative.*

imperceptible *adjective* too small or gradual to be noticed • *The difference is imperceptible to the naked eye.* **imperceptibly** *adverb*

imperfect *adjective* not perfect or complete **imperfection** *noun* being imperfect

imperial *adjective* belonging to an empire or its rulers

impersonal *adjective* not showing friendly human feelings

impersonate *verb* to impersonate someone is to pretend to be them **impersonation** *noun* an act in which you impersonate someone **impersonator** *noun* a person who impersonates someone else

impertinent *adjective* rude to someone and not showing them respect **impertinence** *noun* being impertinent

implement *noun* a tool or device you use to do something

implication *noun* 1. an implication is something that someone suggests without actually saying it 2. an implication is also a possible effect or result

implore *verb* to implore someone to do something is to beg them to do it

imply *verb* implies, implying, implied to imply something is to suggest it without actually saying it • *Are you implying that I'm lazy?*

impolite *adjective* not having good manners; not respectful and thoughtful towards other people

import *verb* (im-**port**) to import goods is to bring them in from another country to sell them **importer** *noun* someone who imports goods
import *noun* (**im**-port) something brought in from another country to be sold

important *adjective* 1. needing to be taken seriously; having a great effect 2. an important person is powerful or influential **importance** *noun* being important **importantly** *adverb* seriously • *Try to win the match but, more importantly, don't lose.*

impossible *adjective* not possible **impossibility** *noun* something that is not possible

impostor *noun* someone who is not what he or she pretends to be

impractical *adjective* 1. impractical people are not good at making or doing things 2. not likely to work or be useful

impress *verb* 1. to impress someone is to make them admire you 2. to impress something on someone is to make them realize or remember it

impression *noun* 1. a vague idea that you have about something • *I had the impression*

that he was waiting for me to speak. 2. the effect that something has on your mind or feelings • *The book left a strong impression on me.* 3. an imitation of a person or a sound

impressive *adjective* something is impressive when it makes you admire it

imprison *verb* to imprison someone is to put them in prison **imprisonment** *noun* being put in prison

improbable *adjective* unlikely **improbability** *noun* being improbable

improper *adjective* 1. not proper; wrong 2. rude or indecent

improve *verb* 1. to improve something is to make it better 2. to improve is to become better **improvement** *noun* something that is better or makes a thing better

improvise *verb* to improvise is to do something without any rehearsal or preparation, especially to play music without rehearsing **improvisation** *noun* improvisation is improvising something

impudent *adjective* not respectful; rude **impudence** *noun* being impudent

impulse *noun* a sudden desire to do something

impulsive *adjective* doing things suddenly without much thought **impulsively** *adverb*

impure *adjective* not pure **impurity** *noun* something in a substance that makes it not pure

in *preposition, adverb* 1. showing position at or inside something • *They live in London.* • *Please come in.* • *She fell in the water.* 2. **In** also has some special uses, shown by the following examples • *We came in April.* • *I paid in cash.* • *The serial was in four parts.* • *He is in the army.* • *We knocked on the door but no one was in.* **in all** including everything • *The bill comes to £120 in all.*

inability *noun* inability is being unable to do something

inaccessible *adjective* an inaccessible place is impossible to reach

inaccurate *adjective* not accurate **inaccuracy** *noun* inaccuracy is being inaccurate **inaccurately** *adverb*

inactive *adjective* not working or doing anything **inactivity** *noun* inactivity is being inactive

inadequate *adjective* not enough **inadequacy** *noun* inadequacy is being inadequate **inadequately** *adverb*

inanimate *adjective* (in-**an**-im-at) not living or moving

inappropriate *adjective* not appropriate or suitable **inappropriately** *adverb*

inaudible *adjective* not able to be heard

incapable *adjective* not able to do something

incapacity *noun* incapacity is inability or disability

incense *noun* (**in**-senss) incense is a substance that makes a spicy smell when it is burnt

incense *verb* (in-**senss**) to incense someone is to make them very angry

incentive *noun* something that encourages a person to do something or to work harder

incessant *adjective* going on in an annoying way without stopping • *They were bothered by the incessant noise.* **incessantly** *adverb*

inch *noun* a measure of length, one twelfth of a foot or about 2½ centimetres

incident *noun* a strange, serious or violent event

incidental *adjective* happening along with something else; not so important **incidentally** *adverb* by the way

incinerator *noun* a container for burning rubbish

inclination *noun* a feeling that makes you want to do something • *He showed no inclination to move house.*

incline *verb* (in-**klyn**) to incline is to lean or bend **to be inclined to do something** is to feel like doing it

incline *noun* (**in**-klyn) a slope

include *verb* to include something or someone is to make or consider them as part of a group of things • *Did you include Peter in the party?* **inclusion** *noun* being included

inclusive *adjective* including everything; including all the things mentioned • *We want to stay from Monday to Thursday inclusive.*

income *noun* the money that a person earns regularly for their work

incompatible *adjective* **1.** not able to live or exist together without trouble **2.** machines and devices are incompatible when they cannot be used together

incompetent *adjective* unable to do something properly **incompetence** *noun* the inability to do something properly **incompetently** *adverb*

incomplete *adjective* not complete

incomprehensible *adjective* not able to be understood

inconsiderate *adjective* not thinking of other people

inconsistent *adjective* not consistent **inconsistency** *noun* being inconsistent **inconsistently** *adverb*

inconspicuous *adjective* not easy to see or notice

inconvenient *adjective* not convenient; awkward **inconvenience** *noun* when something is inconvenient • *Sorry for the inconvenience.*

incorporate *verb* to incorporate something is to include it as a part of something else

incorrect *adjective* not correct; wrong **incorrectly** *adverb* wrongly

increase *verb* (in-**kreess**) **1.** to increase something is to make it bigger **2.** to increase is to become bigger **increasingly** *adverb* more and more • *They were becoming increasingly angry.*

increase *noun* (**in**-kreess) **1**. increasing **2**. the amount by which something increases

incredible *adjective* hard to believe; unbelievable **incredibly** *adverb*

incredulous *adjective* finding it difficult to believe someone

incubate *verb* to incubate eggs is to hatch them by keeping them warm **incubation** *noun* incubation is the hatching of eggs

incubator *noun* a specially heated container for keeping newly born babies warm and well supplied with oxygen

indecent *adjective* not decent; improper **indecency** *noun* indecency is being indecent **indecently** *adverb*

indeed *adverb* used for emphasis • *He was very wet indeed.*

indefinite *adjective* not definite; vague and unclear

indefinite article *noun* the word *a* or *an*

indefinitely *adverb* for an indefinite or unlimited time

independent *adjective* **1**. free from the control of another person or country **2**. not needing help from other people **independence** *noun* being independent **independently** *adverb* without help from other people

index *noun* **indices** or **indexes** a list of names or topics in alphabetical order at the end of a book

index finger *noun* the finger next to the thumb

indicate *verb* to indicate something is to point it out or show that it is there **indication** *noun* a sign of something

indicator *noun* **1**. something that tells you what is happening **2**. a flashing light on a vehicle, to show that it is turning left or right

indifferent *adjective* you are indifferent to something when you have no interest in it at all **indifference** *noun* you show indifference when you have no interest at all in something

indigestible *adjective* not easy to digest

indigestion *noun* indigestion is pain that you get when food is hard to digest

indignant *adjective* angry at something that seems wrong or unjust **indignantly** *adverb* **indignation** *noun* indignation is a feeling of being indignant

indirect *adjective* not direct or straight **indirectly** *adverb*

indispensable *adjective* essential; that you have to have

indistinct *adjective* not clear **indistinctly** *adverb*

individual *adjective* **1**. of or for one person **2**. single or separate **individually** *adverb* separately; one by one
individual *noun* an individual is one person

indoctrinate *verb* to indoctrinate someone is to fill their mind with particular ideas or beliefs, so that they accept them without thinking **indoctrination** *noun* indoctrination is indoctrinating someone

indoor *adjective* placed or done inside a building • *indoor cricket*

indoors *adverb* inside a building • *We'd better go indoors.*

induce *verb* to induce someone to do something is to persuade them to do it **inducement** *noun* something given or done to persuade someone to do something

indulge *verb* to indulge someone is to let them have or do what they want

indulgent *adjective* kind and allowing people to do what they want **indulgence** *noun* indulgence is being indulgent

industrial *adjective* to do with industry

industrious *adjective* hard-working **industriously** *adverb*

industry *noun* **industries** **1**. industry is making or producing goods to sell, especially in factories **2**. an industry is a branch of this, such as the motor industry **3**. industry is also working hard

ineffective *adjective* not effective; not working well **ineffectively** *adverb*

inefficient *adjective* not working well and wasting time or energy **inefficiency** *noun* being inefficient **inefficiently** *adverb*

inequality *noun* **inequalities** inequality is not being equal

inevitable *adjective* something is inevitable when it cannot be avoided **inevitability** *noun* being inevitable **inevitably** *adverb*

inexhaustible *adjective* that you cannot use up completely; never-ending

inexpensive *adjective* not expensive; cheap

inexperience *noun* inexperience is lack of experience **inexperienced** *adjective* someone is inexperienced when they don't have much experience

inexplicable *adjective* impossible to explain **inexplicably** *adverb* in a way that is impossible to explain

infallible *adjective* never wrong **infallibility** *noun* infallibility is being infallible **infallibly** *adverb*

infamous *adjective* (**in**-fa-mus) well-known for being bad or wicked **infamy** *noun* being infamous

infant *noun* a baby or very young child **infancy** *noun* the time when someone is an infant

infantile *adjective* childish and silly

infantry *noun* infantry are soldiers who fight on foot

infect *verb* to infect someone is to pass on a disease to them

infection *noun* **1.** infection is infecting someone **2.** an infection is an infectious disease

infectious *adjective* an infectious disease is one that can spread from one person to another

infer *verb* **inferring, inferred** to infer something is to work it out from what someone says or does • *I inferred from his words that he did not really want to come.* **inference** *noun* something that you infer

inferior *adjective* not as good or important as something else; lower in position or quality **inferiority** *noun* being inferior

inferior *noun* a person who is lower in position or rank than someone else

inferno *noun* **infernos** (in-**fer**-noh) a fierce fire

infested *adjective* a place is infested with (for example) insects or rats when it is full of them

infinite *adjective* (**in**-fi-nit) endless; too large to be measured or imagined **infinitely** *adverb* to an infinite extent

infinitive *noun* (in-**fin**-i-tiv) The infinitive is the basic form of a verb. In English it often comes after *to*, as in *to go* and *to hit.*

infinity *noun* (in-**fin**-i-ti) infinity is an infinite number or distance

infirm *adjective* someone is infirm when they are weak because they are ill or old **infirmity** *noun* being infirm

infirmary *noun* **infirmaries** a place for sick people; a hospital

inflame *verb* **1.** a part of the body is inflamed when it has become red and sore **2.** to inflame someone is to make them angry

inflammable *adjective* an inflammable material can be set alight

inflammation *noun* a painful swelling on the body

inflate *verb* to inflate something is to fill it with air or gas so that it swells up **inflatable** *adjective* something is inflatable when it can be inflated

inflation *noun* inflation is a general rise in prices

inflexible *adjective* that you cannot bend or change • *There are a lot of inflexible rules.* **inflexibility** *noun* being inflexible

inflict *verb* to inflict something on someone is to make them suffer it • *The dog inflicted serious injuries on the boy.*

influence *noun* the power to affect someone or something

influence *verb* to influence someone or something is to have an effect on what they are or do • *The tides are influenced by the moon.*

influential *adjective* having a big influence; important

influenza *noun* (in-floo-**en**-za) Influenza is an infectious disease that causes fever, catarrh and pain. It is more usually called **flu.**

inform *verb* to inform someone of something is to tell them about it **to inform against** or **on someone** is to give information about them to the police

informal *adjective* not formal; casual and relaxed **informality** *noun* informality is being informal **informally** *adverb*

information *noun* information is facts or what someone tells you

information technology *noun* information technology is ways of storing, arranging and giving out information, especially the use of computers and telecommunications

informative *adjective* (in-**form**-a-tiv) containing a lot of helpful information

informed *adjective* you are informed about something when you know about it

informer *noun* a person who tells the police about a criminal activity

infrequent *adjective* not frequent **infrequently** *adverb* only now and then

infuriate *verb* to infuriate someone is to make them very angry

ingenious *adjective* **1.** clever at doing things **2.** cleverly made or done **ingeniously** *adverb* **ingenuity** *noun* cleverness or skill in doing things

ingot *noun* a lump of gold or silver that has been cast in the form of a brick

ingratitude *noun* ingratitude is not showing that you are grateful for something that someone has done for you

ingredient *noun* (in-**greed**-i-ent) **1.** one of the parts of a mixture **2.** one of the things used in a recipe

inhabit *verb* to inhabit a place is to live in it **inhabitant** *noun* one of the people who live in a place

inhale *verb* **1.** to inhale is to breathe in **2.** to inhale something is to breathe it in

inherit *verb* **1.** to inherit money, property or a title is to receive it when its previous owner dies **2.** to inherit qualities or characteristics is to get them from your parents **inheritance** *noun* something you inherit **inheritor** *noun* a person who inherits something

inhospitable *adjective* (in-hos-**pit**-a-bul or in-**hos**-pit-a-bul) **1.** unfriendly to visitors **2.** an inhospitable place is difficult to live in because it gives no shelter • *an inhospitable barren island*

inhuman *adjective* cruel; without pity or kindness **inhumanity** *noun* cruel behaviour

initial *noun* the first letter of someone's name

initial *adjective* first; of the beginning • *the initial stages of the work* **initially** *adverb* at the beginning

initiate *verb* (in-**ish**-i-ayt) to initiate something is to start it

initiative *noun* (in-**ish**-a-tiv) **1.** the action that starts something • *She took the initiative in planning the party.* **2.** initiative is the ability to start things or to get them done on your own

inject *verb* to inject someone is to put a medicine or drug through their skin using a hollow needle **injection** *noun* injecting someone with medicine

injure *verb* to injure someone is to harm or hurt them

injury *noun* injuries harm or damage done to someone

injustice *noun* unfairness in the way someone is treated

ink *noun* ink is a black or coloured liquid used for writing and printing

inkling *noun* a slight idea or suspicion • *I had an inkling that we'd find them in here.*

inland *adverb* away from the coast

inn *noun* a hotel or public house **innkeeper** *noun* someone who runs an inn

inner *adjective* inside; nearer the centre
innermost *adjective* furthest inside

innings *noun* the time when a cricket team or player is batting

innocence *noun* **1**. when someone is not guilty of doing something wrong **2**. lack of experience of the world and the evil things in it

innocent *adjective* **1**. not guilty of doing something wrong **2**. not knowing much about the world and the evil things in it
innocently *adverb*

innovation *noun* **1**. innovation is inventing or using new things **2**. an innovation is something new that you have just invented or started using **innovative** *adjective* new or original

innumerable *adjective* too many to be counted

inoculate *verb* to inoculate someone is to inject them with a vaccine to protect them against a disease **inoculation** *noun* inoculation is being inoculated

input *noun* what you put into something, especially data put into a computer
input *verb* **inputting, input** *(in computing)* to input data or programs is to put them into a computer

inquest *noun* an official investigation to decide why someone died

inquire *verb* **1**. to inquire about something is to ask about it **2**. to inquire into something is to make an official investigation of it

inquiry *noun* **inquiries** an official investigation

inquisitive *adjective* always trying to find out things, especially about other people
inquisitively *adverb*

insane *adjective* not sane; mad
insanely *adverb* **insanity** *noun* insanity is being insane

insanitary *adjective* dirty and unhealthy

inscribe *verb* to inscribe something is to write or carve it on a surface

inscription *noun* words written or carved on a monument, stone or coin or written in the front of a book

insect *noun* a small animal with six legs and a body divided into three parts

The word **insect** comes from a Latin word *insectum* meaning 'cut up'.

insecticide *noun* a chemical used for killing insects

insecure *adjective* **1**. not safe or protected properly **2**. not feeling safe or confident
insecurely *adverb* not firmly or safely
insecurity *noun* insecurity is not feeling safe or confident

insensitive *adjective* not sensitive or thinking about the feelings of other people
insensitively *adverb* **insensitivity** *noun* being insensitive

inseparable *adjective* **1**. unable to be separated **2**. people are inseparable when they are very good friends and always together

insert *verb* to insert something is to put it into something else

inside *noun* **1**. the middle or centre of something; the part nearest to the middle **2**. *(informal)* your insides are your stomach or abdomen
inside *adjective* placed on the inside of something • *Stick the picture on an inside page.*
inside *adverb, preposition* in or to the inside of something • *Come inside.* • *It's inside that box.*

insignificant *adjective* not important or influential **insignificance** *noun* being insignificant

insincere *adjective* not sincere
insincerely *adverb* **insincerity** *noun* not being sincere

insist *verb* to insist something is to be very firm in saying it • *He insisted that he was innocent.* **to insist on something** is to demand it

insistent *adjective* insisting on doing or having something **insistence** *noun* being insistent

insolent *adjective* very rude and insulting
insolence *noun* speaking to someone rudely and without respect

insomnia *noun* (in-**som**-ni-a) insomnia is being unable to sleep

inspect *verb* to inspect something or someone is to look carefully at them, especially to check them **inspection** *noun* a close or careful look at something to check it

inspector *noun* **1.** someone whose job is to inspect things or people **2.** a police officer next in rank above a sergeant

inspire *verb* to inspire someone is to fill them with ideas or enthusiasm **inspiration** *noun* a person or thing that encourages you and fills you with ideas

install *verb* to install something is to put it in position ready for use **installation** *noun* being installed

instalment *noun* one of the parts into which something is divided so that it is spread over a period of time • *He is paying for his bike in monthly instalments.*

instance *noun* an example **for instance** for example

instant *adjective* **1.** happening immediately • *It has been an instant success.* **2.** that can be made very quickly • *Do you like instant coffee?*
instant *noun* a moment • *I don't believe it for an instant.*

instantaneous *adjective* happening or done in an instant or without any delay **instantaneously** *adverb* in an instant; immediately

instantly *adverb* to do something instantly is to do it without any delay

instead *adverb* in place of something else; as a substitute • *There were no potatoes, so we had rice instead.*

instep *noun* the top of your foot between the toes and the ankle

instinct *noun* a natural tendency to do or feel something without being taught • *Spiders spin webs by instinct.* **instinctive** *adjective* done by instinct **instinctively** *adverb* in an instinctive way • *He knew instinctively that something was wrong.*

institute *noun* an organization set up for a special purpose

institution *noun* a large organization

instruct *verb* **1.** to instruct someone is to teach them a subject or skill **2.** to instruct someone is also to give them information or orders

instruction *noun* **1.** instruction is teaching a subject or skill **2.** an instruction is an order or piece of information • *Follow the instructions carefully.*

instrument *noun* **1.** a device for making musical sounds **2.** a device for delicate or scientific work

instrumental *adjective* instrumental music uses musical instruments without any singing

insufficient *adjective* not enough

insulate *verb* to insulate something is to cover it to stop heat, cold or electricity from passing in or out **insulation** *noun* insulation is insulating something

insult *verb* (in-**sult**) to insult someone is to speak or behave in a rude way that offends them
insult *noun* (**in**-sult) a rude remark or action that offends someone

insurance *noun* a business agreement to receive money if you suffer a loss or injury, in return for a regular payment called a premium

insure *verb* **insures**, **insuring**, **insured** to insure yourself or your goods is to protect them with insurance

intact *adjective* complete and undamaged

intake *noun* the number of people or things taken in • *The school had a high intake of pupils this year.*

integer *noun* (**in**-ti-jer) a whole number, such as 0, 1, 24 and not a fraction

integrate *verb* (**in**-ti-grayt) **1.** to integrate different things or parts is to make them into a whole **2.** to integrate people, especially of different origins, is to bring them together into a single community **integration** *noun* integration is being integrated

integrity *noun* (in-**teg**-ri-ti) integrity is being honest and behaving well

intellect *noun* the ability to think and work things out with your mind

intellectual *adjective* **1**. involving the mind and thinking **2**. able to think effectively; keen to study and learn

intellectual *noun* an intellectual person

intelligence *noun* your intelligence is your ability to think and learn

intelligent *adjective* good at thinking and learning **intelligently** *adverb*

intelligible *adjective* able to be understood • *The message was barely intelligible.*

intend *verb* to intend to do something is to plan to do it

intense *adjective* **1**. very strong or great • *The heat was intense.* **2**. having or showing strong feelings **intensely** *adverb* very strongly **intensity** *noun* how strong or great something is

intensive *adjective* using a lot of effort; thorough • *We have made an intensive search.*

intent *adjective* showing a lot of attention and interest **to be intent on something** is to be eager or determined to do it **intently** *adverb* with a lot of attention

intent *noun* your intent is what you intend to do

intention *noun* what you intend to do

intentional *adjective* done on purpose; deliberate **intentionally** *adverb* deliberately

interactive *adjective* allowing information to be sent in either direction, especially between a computer system and its user

intercept *verb* to intercept someone or something is to stop them going from one place to another **interception** *noun* interception is intercepting someone or something

interchange *noun* a place where traffic moves from one main road or motorway to another

interchangeable *adjective* things are interchangeable when they can be changed or swapped round

intercom *noun* a device by which people in different rooms or places can communicate with one another

interest *verb* to interest someone is to make them want to look or listen or take part in something

interest *noun* **1**. interest is being interested **2**. an interest is a thing that interests you • *Jane's main interest is music.* **3**. interest is also money a borrower has to pay regularly for a loan

interface *noun* a connection between two parts of a computer system

interfere *verb* **1**. to interfere in something is to become involved in it when it has nothing to do with you **2**. to interfere is to get in the way • *I hope the weather won't interfere with our picnic.*

interference *noun* **1**. interfering in something **2**. a crackling or distorting of a radio or television signal

interior *noun* the inside of something

interjection *noun* an exclamation, such as oh!

interlude *noun* an interval

intermediate *adjective* coming between two things in place, order or time

interminable *adjective* seeming to go on for ever

internal *adjective* of or in the inside of something **internally** *adverb* on the inside

international *adjective* to do with more than one country • *an international chess tournament* **internationally** *adverb* for or in more than one country

Internet *noun* the Internet is a computer network that allows people all over the world to share information and send messages

interpret *verb* **1**. to interpret something is to explain what it means **2**. to interpret a foreign language is to translate it into another language **interpretation** *noun* an explanation or translation of something **interpreter** *noun* a person who translates what someone says into another language

interrogate *verb* to interrogate someone is to question them closely in order to get information **interrogation** *noun* when someone is interrogated

interrupt *verb* **1**. to interrupt someone is to stop them talking **2**. to interrupt something is to stop it continuing **interruption** *noun* when someone or something is interrupted

intersect *verb* to intersect something is to cross or divide it • *The cloth had a design of intersecting lines.*

intersection *noun* a place where lines or roads cross each other

interval *noun* a time between two events or between two parts of a play or film a space between two things

intervene *verb* 1. to intervene is to come between two events • *During the intervening years they went abroad.* 2. to intervene in an argument or fight is to interrupt it in order to stop it or affect the result **intervention** *noun* an intervention is when someone intervenes in something

interview *noun* a meeting with someone to ask them questions or discuss something

interview *verb* to interview someone is to have an interview with them **interviewer** *noun* a person who interviews someone

intestine *noun* the long tube along which food passes after leaving your stomach

intimate *adjective* (**in**-ti-mat) 1. very friendly with someone 2. intimate thoughts are thoughts that are private or personal **intimacy** *noun* closeness **intimately** *adverb*

intimidate *verb* to frighten a person with threats into doing something **intimidation** *noun* intimidation is intimidating someone

into *preposition* 1. to the inside of something • *Go into the house.* 2. **Into** also has some special uses, shown by the following examples • *He got into trouble.* • *She went into acting.* • *3 into 12 goes 4 times.*

intolerable *adjective* unbearable • *The noise outside was intolerable.*

intolerant *adjective* not willing to accept people or ideas that are different in some way **intolerance** *noun* intolerance is being intolerant **intolerantly** *adverb*

intonation *noun* the way your voice gets higher or lower when speaking

intoxicate *verb* a person is intoxicated when they are drunk **intoxication** *noun* being drunk

intrepid *adjective* brave or fearless

intricate *adjective* an intricate pattern or design is detailed and complicated **intricacy** *noun* intricacy is being intricate **intricately** *adverb*

intrigue *verb* (in-**treeg**) to intrigue someone is to interest them very much and make them curious **intriguing** *adjective* very interesting because it is unusual

introduce *verb* 1. to introduce someone is to make them known to other people 2. to introduce something is to get it into general use

introduction *noun* 1. introducing someone or something 2. a piece at the beginning of a book, explaining what it is about **introductory** *adjective* coming at the beginning of something

intrude *verb* to intrude is to come in or join in without being wanted **intrusion** *noun* coming in where you are not wanted

intruder *noun* someone who forces their way into a place where they are not supposed to be

intuition *noun* (in-tew-**ish**-on) the ability to know or understand things without having to think hard **intuitive** *adjective* using intuition

invade *verb* to invade a country or place is to attack and enter it **invaders** *plural noun* people who invade a place

invalid[1] *noun* (**in**-va-leed or **in**-va-lid) someone who is ill or weakened by a long illness

invalid[2] *adjective* (in-**val**-id) not valid • *This passport is invalid.*

invaluable *adjective* very valuable

invariable *adjective* never changing; always the same **invariably** *adverb* always

invasion *noun* when an army or a large number of people attack and enter a place

invent *verb* to invent something is to be the first person to make it or think of it **invention** *noun* something invented **inventor** *noun* a person who invents things

invertebrate *noun* (in-**vert**-i-brat) an animal without a backbone, such as a worm or an amoeba

inverted commas *plural noun* punctuation marks (' ') or (" ") that you put round spoken words and quotations

invest *verb* to invest money is to use it to earn interest or make a profit **investor** *noun* someone who invests money

investigate *verb* to investigate something or someone is to find out as much as you can about them **investigation** *noun* a careful search for information **investigator** *noun* a person who investigates someone or something

investment *noun* **1.** money someone invests **2.** something someone invests money in • *Houses are a safe investment.*

invincible *adjective* not able to be defeated

invisible *adjective* not visible; not able to be seen **invisibility** *noun* being invisible **invisibly** *adverb*

invitation *noun* a request for someone to do something, such as come to a party

invite *verb* to invite someone is to ask them to come to a party or do something special

inviting *adjective* attractive or tempting **invitingly** *adverb*

invoice *noun* a bill that you get when someone has sold you something or done a job for you

involve *verb* **1.** to involve something is to need it or result in it • *The job involved a lot of effort.* **2.** to be involved in something is to take part in it • *The police think he may have been involved in the robbery.* **involvement** *noun* being involved in something

involved *adjective* long and complicated

inward *adjective* on the inside or facing the inside

inward *adverb* inwards

inwardly *adverb* in your thoughts; privately • *He kept his face severe but inwardly he was smiling.*

inwards *adverb* towards the inside

iodine *noun* iodine is a chemical used to kill germs

IQ *noun* short for *intelligence quotient*, **IQ** is a measure of someone's intelligence, calculated from the results of a test

iris *noun* the coloured part of your eyeball

iron *noun* **1.** iron is a strong heavy metal **2.** an iron is a device heats up and is used for smoothing clothes
iron *verb* to iron clothes is to smooth them with an iron

ironic or **ironical** *adjective* **1.** an ironic situation is strange because the opposite happens to what you might expect **2.** you are being ironic when you say the opposite of what you mean **ironically** *adverb*

irony *noun* **ironies** **1.** irony is saying the opposite of what you mean in order to emphasize it or to be funny, for example *What a lovely day* when it is pouring with rain **2.** an irony is an unexpected or strange event or situation • *The irony is that she had sold all her jewels the day before the burglars broke in.*

irregular *adjective* not regular or usual **irregularity** *noun* being irregular or unusual

irrelevant *adjective* (i-**rel**-i-vant) not having anything to do with what is being discussed **irrelevance** *noun* something irrelevant

irresistible *adjective* too strong or attractive or tempting to resist

irresponsible *adjective* not thinking enough about the effects of your actions **irresponsibility** *noun* irresponsible behaviour **irresponsibly** *adverb*

irreverent *adjective* not respectful **irreverence** *noun* lack of respect

irrigate *verb* to irrigate land is to supply it with water so that crops can grow **irrigation** *noun* irrigating land

irritable *adjective* easily annoyed; bad-tempered **irritability** *noun* crossness; bad temper **irritably** *adverb*

irritate *verb* **1.** to irritate someone is to annoy them **2.** to irritate a part of your body is to make it itch or feel sore

irritation *noun* **1.** irritation is being annoyed **2.** an irritation is something that annoys you

Islam *noun* (**iz**-lahm) Islam is the religion of Muslims **Islamic** *adjective* to do with Islam

island *noun* a piece of land surrounded by water **islander** *noun* someone who lives on an island

isle *noun* an island

isolate *verb* to isolate someone or something is to keep them apart from others **isolation** *noun* being isolated or alone

issue *verb* **1.** to issue something is to send it or give it out to people • *They issued blankets to the refugees.* **2.** to issue a book or piece of information is to publish it

issue *noun* **1.** an issue is a subject that people are discussing • *Global warming is an important issue.* **2.** an issue of a magazine or newspaper is the edition sold on a particular day

it *pronoun* **1.** the thing being talked about, used as the subject or object of a verb • *When the tree fell it hit the greenhouse.* **2.** used to say things about the weather or the time • *It is raining.* • *Is it lunch time yet?*

italics *plural noun* letters printed with a slant, *like this*

itch *noun* a tickling feeling in your skin that makes you want to scratch it **itchy** *adjective* a part of your body is itchy when you want to scratch it

itch *verb* a part of your body itches when you want to scratch it

item *noun* one thing in a list or group of things

itinerary *noun* **itineraries** (I-**tin**-er-er-i) a list of places to be visited on a journey

its *determiner* of it; belonging to it • *The cat hurt its paw.*

it's short for *it is* and (before a verb in the past tense) *it has* • *It's raining.* • *It's been raining.*

itself *pronoun* it and nothing else, used to refer back to the subject of a verb • *I think the cat has hurt itself.* **by itself** on its own, alone • *The house stands by itself in a wood.*

ivory *noun* the hard creamy-white substance that forms elephants' tusks

ivy *noun* a climbing evergreen plant with shiny leaves

A *jeep* is a sturdy four wheel-drive vehicle whose name comes from the sound of the letters **GP** (which stand for **General Purpose**).

jab *verb* **jabbing, jabbed** to jab someone or something is to poke them roughly
jab *noun* **1.** a quick hit with something pointed or a fist **2.** *(informal)* an injection

jabber *verb* to jabber is to chatter a lot or to speak quickly and not clearly

jack *noun* **1.** a piece of equipment for lifting something heavy off the ground, especially a car **2.** a playing card with a picture of a young man
jack *verb* to jack something is to lift it with a jack

jackal *noun* a wild animal rather like a dog

jacket *noun* a short coat covering the top half of the body

jackpot *noun* the biggest prize in a game or lottery

a b c d e f g h i j k l m n o p q r s t u v w x y z

jade *noun* jade is a hard green stone which is carved to make ornaments

jagged *adjective* (**jag**-id) having an uneven edge with sharp points

jaguar *noun* a large fierce South American cat like a leopard

jail *noun* a prison
jail *verb* to jail someone is to put them in prison

jailer *noun* a person in charge of a jail

jam *noun* **1.** a sweet food made of fruit boiled with sugar until it is thick **2.** a lot of people or cars or other things crowded together so that it is difficult to move
jam *verb* jamming, jammed **1.** to jam something is to make it stuck and difficult to move **2.** to jam is to become stuck • *The door has jammed.*

jamboree *noun* **1.** a large party or celebration **2.** a rally of Scouts

jangle *verb* to jangle is to make a harsh ringing sound

January *noun* the first month of the year

jar[1] *noun* a container made of glass or pottery

jar[2] *verb* jarring, jarred to jar is to give you an unpleasant shock or jolt • *I jarred every bone in my body.*

jaundice *noun* jaundice is a disease that makes your skin turn yellow

jaunt *noun* a short trip for fun

jaunty *adjective* jauntier, jauntiest lively and cheerful

javelin *noun* a light spear used for throwing in athletics competitions

jaw *noun* **1.** one of the two bones that hold the teeth **2.** the lower part of the face; the mouth and teeth of a person or animal

jay *noun* a noisy brightly-coloured bird

jazz *noun* jazz is a kind of music with strong rhythm

jealous *adjective* **1.** unhappy or resentful because you feel that someone is better or luckier than you **2.** upset because you think that someone you love is interested in someone else **jealously** *adverb* **jealousy** *noun* the feeling of being jealous

jeans *plural noun* casual trousers made of denim

Jeep *noun* (trademark) a small strong vehicle that can be driven over rough ground

jeer *verb* to jeer is to laugh rudely at someone and shout insults at them

jelly *noun* jellies **1.** a soft sweet food with a fruit flavour **2.** any soft slippery substance

jellyfish *noun* jellyfish a sea animal with a body like jelly and tentacles that can sting

jerk *verb* **1.** to jerk is to make a sudden sharp movement **2.** to jerk something is to pull it suddenly
jerk *noun* a sudden sharp movement

jerky *adjective* jerkier, jerkiest moving with sudden sharp movements **jerkily** *adverb*

jersey *noun* a pullover with sleeves

jest *noun* a joke
jest *verb* to jest is to make jokes

jester *noun* an entertainer at a royal court in the Middle Ages

jet[1] *noun* **1.** a stream of liquid, gas or flame forced out of a narrow opening **2.** a narrow opening from which a jet comes out **3.** an aircraft driven by jet engines

jet[2] *noun* a hard black mineral

jet engine *noun* an engine that drives an aircraft forward by sending out a powerful jet of hot gas at the back

jetty *noun* jetties a small pier or landing stage for boats

jewel *noun* a precious stone such as a diamond

jeweller *noun* someone who sells or makes jewellery

jewellery *noun* jewels or ornaments that people wear, such as rings and necklaces

jig *noun* a lively jumping dance

jigsaw *noun* jigsaws **1.** a jigsaw puzzle **2.** a saw that can cut curved shapes

jigsaw puzzle *noun* a puzzle made of differently shaped pieces that you fit together to make a picture

jingle *verb* to jingle is to make a tinkling or clinking sound

jingle *noun* **1.** a tinkling or clinking sound **2.** a simple tune or song that is used in an advertisement

job *noun* **1.** work that someone does regularly to earn a living **2.** a piece of work that needs to be done

jockey *noun* jockeys someone who rides horses in races

jodhpurs *plural noun* (**jod**-perz) jodhpurs are trousers for riding a horse, fitting closely from the knee to the ankle

jog *verb* jogging, jogged to jog is to run slowly, especially for exercise to jog someone's memory is to help them remember something jogger *noun* someone who goes jogging

join *verb* **1.** to join things together is to put or fix them together **2.** two or more things join when they come together **3.** to join a society or group is to become a member of it to join in is to take part in something

join *noun* a place where things join

joiner *noun* someone whose job is to make furniture and other things out of wood joinery *noun* the work a joiner does

joint *noun* **1.** a place where things are fixed together **2.** the place where two bones fit together **3.** a large piece of meat

joint *adjective* shared or done by two or more people or groups • *The song was a joint effort.* jointly *adverb*

joist *noun* a long beam supporting a floor or ceiling

joke *noun* something that you say or do to make people laugh

joke *verb* to joke is to make jokes or to talk in a way that is not serious

joker *noun* **1.** someone who makes jokes **2.** an extra playing card with a picture of a jester on it

jolly *adjective* jollier, jolliest happy and cheerful

jolly *adverb* (informal) very • *It's jolly cold!*

jolt *verb* **1.** to jolt something or someone is to hit them or move them suddenly and sharply **2.** to jolt is to make a sudden sharp movement • *The bus jolted to a halt.*

jolt *noun* **1.** a sudden sharp movement • *The plane landed with a jolt.* **2.** a surprise or shock

jostle *verb* to jostle someone is to push them roughly

jot *verb* jotting, jotted to jot something down is to write it quickly

journal *noun* **1.** a newspaper or magazine **2.** a diary

journalist *noun* someone whose job is to write news stories for a newspaper or magazine or on television or radio journalism *noun* the job of writing news stories for a newspaper or magazine or on television or radio

journey *noun* going from one place to another

journey *verb* to journey is to go from one place to another

joust *verb* to joust is to fight on horseback with lances, as knights did in medieval times

jovial *adjective* cheerful and jolly

joy *noun* **1.** joy is great happiness or pleasure **2.** a joy is something that gives happiness

joyful *adjective* very happy joyfully *adverb*

joystick *noun* **1.** (informal) the lever that controls the movement of an aircraft **2.** a lever for controlling movement in a computer game

jubilant *adjective* (**joo**-bi-lant) very happy because you have won or succeeded jubilantly *adverb* jubilation *noun* rejoicing because you have won or succeeded

jubilee *noun* A jubilee is a special anniversary of an important event. A **silver jubilee** is the 25th anniversary, a **golden jubilee** is the 50th anniversary and a **diamond jubilee** is the 60th anniversary.

Judaism *noun* (**joo**-day-izm) Judaism is the religion of the Jewish people

judge *noun* **1.** someone who hears cases in a lawcourt and decides what should be done **2.** someone who decides who has won a contest or competition **3.** someone who knows enough to form an opinion or make a decision about something • *I'm a good judge of character.*

judge *verb* **1.** to judge something is to act as judge in a law case or a competition **2.** to judge an amount is to estimate or guess what it is

judgement *noun* **1.** a judgement is the decision made by a lawcourt **2.** judgement is also the ability to make decisions wisely • *Not arguing with him showed good judgement.*

judo *noun* (**joo**-doh) judo is a Japanese form of unarmed combat for sport

jug *noun* a container for pouring liquids, with a handle and lip

juggernaut *noun* a very large articulated lorry

juggle *verb* to juggle objects is to keep tossing and catching them so that you keep them moving in the air without dropping any **juggler** *noun* someone who juggles

juice *noun* the liquid from fruit, vegetables or other food **juicy** *adjective* juicy fruit or meat is full of juice

jukebox *noun* a machine that plays a record of your choice when you put a coin in

July *noun* the seventh month of the year

jumble *verb* to jumble things is to mix them up in a confused way

jumble *noun* a confused mixture of things

jumble sale *noun* a sale of second-hand clothes and other goods to raise money

jump *verb* **1.** to jump is to move suddenly from the ground into the air **2.** to jump a fence or other obstacle is to go over it by jumping **3.** to jump up or out is to move quickly or suddenly • *He jumped out of his*

seat. **to jump at something** (*informal*) is to accept it eagerly

jump *noun* a sudden movement into the air

jumper *noun* a pullover with sleeves

junction *noun* a place where roads or railway lines join

June *noun* the sixth month of the year

jungle *noun* a thick tangled forest in tropical countries

junior *adjective* **1.** younger **2.** for young children • *She goes to a junior school.* **3.** lower in rank or importance

junior *noun* **1.** a younger person • *Peter is my junior.* **2.** a person of lower rank or importance

junk[1] *noun* useless or worthless things that should be thrown away

junk[2] *noun* a Chinese sailing boat

junk food food that contains a lot of sugar and starch and is not good for you

jury *noun* juries a group of twelve people chosen to listen to evidence in a lawcourt and decide if an accused person is guilty or not guilty **juror** *noun* a member of a jury

just *adjective* **1.** fair and right; giving proper thought to everybody **2.** deserved • *He got his just reward.* **justly** *adverb* in a just or fair way

just *adverb* **1.** exactly • *It's just what I wanted.* **2.** only; simply • *I just wanted another cake.* **3.** barely; by only a short amount • *The ball hit her just below the knee.* **4.** a short time ago • *They had just gone.* **5.** now; immediately • *I'm just leaving.*

justice *noun* **1.** justice is being just or having fair treatment **2.** justice is also the actions of the law • *They were tried in a court of justice.*

justify *verb* justifies, justifying, justified to justify something is to show that it is reasonable or necessary • *Do you think that you were justified in taking such a risk?* **justifiable** *adjective* easy to justify **justification** *noun* a good reason for doing something

jut *verb* jutting, jutted to jut or to jut out, is to stick out

juvenile *adjective* (**joo**-vi-nyl) to do with young people

juvenile *noun* a young person who is not yet an adult

The letter *k* is silent at the beginning of the word **know**; **now** is a different word altogether.

kaleidoscope *noun* (kal-**I**-dos-kohp) a tube that you look through and turn to see brightly-coloured changing patterns

kangaroo *noun* an Australian animal that moves by jumping on its strong back legs

karaoke *noun* (ka-ri-**oh**-ki) a party entertainment in which people sing songs with a recorded background

karate *noun* (ka-**rah**-ti) karate is a Japanese method of self-defence using your hands, arms and feet

kayak *noun* (**ky**-ak) a small canoe with a covering that fits round the canoeist's waist

kebab *noun* small pieces of meat or vegetables grilled on a skewer

keel *noun* the long piece of wood or metal along the bottom of a boat
keel *verb* to keel over is to fall sideways or overturn

keen *adjective* **1**. enthusiastic or eager • *She is keen on swimming.* • *We are keen to go.* **2**. strong or sharp • *The knife had a keen edge.*

• *There was a keen wind.* **keenly** *adverb* a keenly fought contest is one in which people are competing very hard **keenness** *noun* being keen

keep *verb* **keeping, kept 1**. to keep something is to have it and not get rid of it **2**. to keep something in a place is to put it there when you aren't using it **3**. to keep (for example) well or still is to continue to be well or still **4**. something keeps when it lasts without going bad • *Will the milk keep until tomorrow?* **5**. to keep doing something is to continue to do it • *They kept laughing at her.* **6**. to keep your word or promise is to do what you have promised **7**. to keep animals or pets is to have them and look after them **to keep something up** is to continue doing it • *Keep up the good work!* **to keep up with someone** is to go as fast as them

keep *noun* **1**. someone's keep is the food or money they need to live • *They have to earn their keep.* **2**. a keep is a strong tower in a castle

keeper *noun* **1**. someone who looks after the animals in a zoo **2**. a goalkeeper

keeping *noun* something is in your keeping when you are looking after it • *The diaries are in safe keeping.*

keg *noun* a small barrel

kennel *noun* a shelter for a dog

kerb *noun* the edge of a pavement

kernel *noun* the part inside the shell of a nut

ketchup *noun* ketchup is a thick sauce made from tomatoes

kettle *noun* a container with a spout and handle, used for boiling water in

key *noun* **1**. a piece of metal shaped so that it opens a lock **2**. a small lever that you press with your finger, on a piano or keyboard **3**. a device for winding up a clock or clockwork toy **4**. a scale of musical notes • *It is played in the key of C major.*

keyboard *noun* a set of keys on a piano, typewriter or computer

keyhole *noun* the hole through which you put a key into a lock

kg short for **kilogram** or **kilograms**

khaki *noun* (**kah**-ki) a dull yellowish-brown colour

kick *verb* **1.** to kick someone or something is to hit them with your foot **2.** to kick is to move your legs about vigorously to kick off is to start a football match to kick someone out is to get rid of them
kick *noun* a kicking movement

kick-off *noun* the start of a football match

kid *noun* **1.** a young goat **2.** (*informal*) a child
kid *verb* kidding, kidded (*informal*) to kid someone is to deceive or tease them

kidnap *verb* kidnapping, kidnapped to kidnap someone is to capture them by force, usually to get a ransom kidnapper *noun* a person who kidnaps someone

kidney *noun* kidneys each of two organs in your body that remove waste products from your blood and send them as urine to your bladder

kill *verb* to kill a person or animal is to make them die killer *noun* a person who kills someone

kiln *noun* an oven for hardening or drying pottery or bricks

kilo *noun* kilos a kilogram

kilobyte *noun* (*in computing*) a unit that measures data or memory, equal to 1,024 bytes

kilogram *noun* a unit of weight equal to 1,000 grams or about 2.2 pounds

kilometre *noun* (**kil**-o-mee-ter or kil-**om**-i-ter) a unit of length equal to 1,000 metres or about ⅔ of a mile

kilowatt *noun* a unit of electrical power equal to 1,000 watts

kilt *noun* a kind of pleated skirt worn by men as part of traditional Scottish dress

kin *noun* a person's family or relatives your next of kin is your closest relative

kind[1] *noun* a type or sort of something • *What kind of food do you like?*

kind[2] *adjective* helpful and friendly kindness *noun*

kindergarten *noun* (**kin**-der-gar-ten) a school for very young children

kind-hearted *adjective* kind and generous

kindle *verb* **1.** to kindle something is to get it to burn **2.** to kindle is to start burning

kindly *adverb* **1.** in a kind way • *He spoke kindly to the little boy.* **2.** please • *Kindly close the door.*
kindly *adjective* kindlier, kindliest kind • *She gave a kindly smile.* kindliness *noun* kindliness is being kindly

king *noun* **1.** a man who has been crowned as the ruler of a country **2.** a piece in chess that has to be captured to win the game **3.** a playing card with a picture of a king on it

kingdom *noun* a country that is ruled by a king or queen

kingfisher *noun* a brightly-coloured bird that lives near water and catches fish

king-size or **king-sized** *adjective* larger than the usual size

kink *noun* a short twist in a rope or wire

kiosk *noun* (**kee**-osk) **1.** a telephone box **2.** a small hut or stall where you can buy newspapers, sweets and drinks

kiss *noun* touching someone with your lips as a sign of affection or greeting
kiss *verb* to kiss someone is to give them a kiss

kit *noun* **1.** equipment or clothes that you need to do a sport, a job or some other activity **2.** a set of parts sold to be fitted together to make something • *a model aircraft kit*

kitchen *noun* a room where food is prepared and cooked

kite *noun* a light frame covered with cloth or paper that you fly in the wind at the end of a long piece of string

kitten *noun* a very young cat

kitty *noun* kitties **1.** an amount of money that you can win in a card game **2.** an amount of money that you put aside for a special purpose

kiwi *noun* (**kee**-wee) a New Zealand bird that cannot fly

kiwi fruit *noun* a fruit with thin hairy skin, soft green flesh and black seeds

km short for **kilometre** or **kilometres**

knack *noun* a special skill or talent

knapsack *noun* a bag carried on the back

knead *verb* to knead dough is to press and stretch it with your hands, to make it ready for baking

knee *noun* the joint in the middle of your leg

kneecap *noun* the bony part at the front of your knee

kneel *verb* kneeling, knelt to kneel is to bend your legs so you are resting on your knees

knickers *plural noun* underpants worn by women or girls

knife *noun* knives a cutting instrument made of a short blade set in a handle

knife *verb* to knife someone is to stab them with a knife

knight *noun* **1.** a man who has been given the honour that lets him put 'Sir' before his name **2.** a warrior who had been given the rank of a nobleman, in the Middle Ages **3.** a piece in chess, with a horse's head **knighthood** *noun* a man receives a knighthood when he is made a knight

knight *verb* to knight someone is to make them a knight

knit *verb* knitting, knitted to knit something is to make it by looping together threads of wool or other material, using long needles or a machine

knitting *noun* knitting is the activity of making things by knitting

knitting needle *noun* a long large needle used in knitting

knob *noun* **1.** the round handle of a door or drawer **2.** a control to adjust a radio or television set **knobbly** *adjective* having a lumpy or bumpy surface

knock *verb* **1.** to knock something is to hit it hard or bump into it • *Oops, I knocked the vase over.* **2.** to knock is to hit something with your hand or fist • *Who's knocking at the door?* to knock someone out is to hit them so that they become unconscious

knock *noun* the act or sound of hitting something

knocker *noun* a device for knocking on a door

knockout *noun* **1.** knocking someone out **2.** a game or contest in which the loser in each round has to drop out

knot *noun* **1.** a fastening made by tying or looping two ends of string, rope or ribbon together **2.** a round spot on a piece of wood where a branch once joined it **3.** a unit for measuring the speed of ships and aircraft, 1,852 metres (or 2,025 yards) per hour **4.** a knot of people is a small group of them standing close together

knot *verb* knotting, knotted to knot something is to tie or fasten it with a knot

knotty *adjective* knottier, knottiest full of knots

know *verb* knowing, knew, known **1.** to have something in your mind that you have learned or discovered • *Do you know the answer?* **2.** to know a person or place is to recognize it or be familiar with it • *I've known him for years.*

knowledge *noun* (**nol**-ij) knowledge is the facts or information that someone knows

knowledgeable *adjective* (**nol**-ij-a-bul) knowing a lot about something **knowledgeably** *adverb*

knuckle *noun* a joint in your finger

koala *noun* (koh-**ah**-la) a furry Australian animal that looks like a small bear

Koran *noun* (kor-**ahn**) the holy book of Islam, believed by Muslims to contain the words of Allah

kosher *adjective* (**koh**-sher) kosher food is food prepared according to Jewish religious law

label *noun* a piece of paper or cloth fixed to something and providing information about it
label *verb* **labelling**, **labelled** to label something is to put a label on it

laboratory *noun* **laboratories** (la-**bo**-ra-ter-i) a room or building equipped for scientific work

laborious *adjective* needing a lot of effort; very hard

labour *noun* **1.** labour is hard work **2.** labour is also the movements of a woman's womb when a baby is born **Labour** the Labour Party, one of the main British political parties

labourer *noun* someone who does hard work with their hands

labyrinth *noun* a complicated set of passages or paths

lace *noun* **1.** lace is thin material with decorative patterns of holes in it **2.** a lace is a piece of thin cord used to tie up a shoe or boot **lacy** *adjective* like lace or made of lace
lace *verb* to lace up a shoe or boot is to fasten it with a lace

lack *noun* there is a lack of something when there isn't any of it or there isn't enough of it
lack *verb* to lack something is to be without it • *He lacks courage.*

lacquer *noun* lacquer is a kind of varnish

lad *noun* a boy or young man

ladder *noun* **1.** a device to help you climb up or down something, made of upright pieces of wood, metal or rope with crosspieces called rungs **2.** a tear in tights or a stocking

laden *adjective* carrying a heavy load

ladle *noun* a large deep spoon with a long handle, which you use for serving soup or other liquids

lady *noun* **ladies 1.** a polite name for a woman **2.** a well-mannered woman or a woman who is high up in society **Lady** the title of a noblewoman or the wife of a knight

ladybird *noun* a small flying beetle, usually red with black spots

ladylike *adjective* polite and quiet

lag[1] *verb* **lagging**, **lagged** to lag is to go too slowly and not keep up with others

lag[2] *verb* **lagging**, **lagged** to lag pipes or boilers is to wrap them with insulating material to keep in the heat

lager *noun* (**lah**-ger) a light beer

lagoon *noun* a lake separated from the sea by sandbanks or reefs

lair *noun* the place where a wild animal lives

lake *noun* a large area of water completely surrounded by land

lama *noun* a Buddhist priest or monk in Tibet and Mongolia

lamb *noun* **1.** a lamb is a young sheep **2.** lamb is the meat from young sheep

lame *adjective* **1.** not able to walk normally **2.** weak and not very convincing • *What a lame excuse.* **lamely** *adverb* **lameness** *noun*

lamp *noun* a device for producing light from electricity, gas or oil

lamp post *noun* a tall post in a street or public place, with a lamp at the top

lampshade *noun* a cover for the bulb of an electric lamp

lance *noun* a long spear once used by soldiers on horseback

land *noun* **1.** land or the land is all the dry parts of the world's surface **2.** land is an area of ground **3.** a land is a country or nation

land *verb* **1.** to land is to come down to the ground from the air • *Where did the arrow land?* **2.** to land is also to arrive in a ship or aircraft **3.** to land something or someone is to bring them to a place by means of a ship or aircraft

landing *noun* the floor at the top of a flight of stairs

landlady *noun* landladies **1.** a woman who owns a house or rooms that people can rent **2.** a woman who looks after a pub

landlord *noun* **1.** a person who owns a house or rooms that people can rent **2.** a person who looks after a pub

landmark *noun* an object on land that you can easily see from a distance

landowner *noun* a person who owns a large amount of land

landscape *noun* **1.** a view of a particular area of town or countryside **2.** a picture of the countryside

landslide *noun* a landslide is when earth or rocks slide down the side of a hill

lane *noun* **1.** a narrow road, especially in the country **2.** a strip of road for a single line of traffic **3.** a strip of track or water for one runner or swimmer in a race

language *noun* **1.** language is the use of words in speech and writing **2.** a language is the words used in a particular country or by a particular group of people **3.** a language is also a system of signs or symbols giving information, especially in computing

lanky *adjective* lankier, lankiest very tall and thin lankiness *noun*

lantern *noun* a transparent case for holding a light and shielding it from the wind

lap[1] *noun* **1.** the flat area from the waist to the knees, formed when a person is sitting down **2.** going once round a racecourse

lap[1] *verb* lapping, lapped to lap someone in a race round a track is to be so far ahead of them that you pass them from behind

lap[2] *verb* lapping, lapped **1.** to lap liquid is to drink it with the tongue, as a cat or dog does **2.** waves lap when they make a gentle splash on rocks or the shore

lapel *noun* (la-**pel**) the flap folded back at each front edge of a coat or jacket

lapse *noun* **1.** a slight mistake or fault **2.** the passing of time

lapse *verb* a contract or document lapses when it is no longer valid • *My passport has lapsed.*

laptop *noun* a small portable computer

lard *noun* lard is white greasy fat from pigs, used in cooking

larder *noun* a cupboard or small room for storing food

large *adjective* more than the ordinary or average size; big to be at large is to be free and dangerous • *The escaped prisoners were still at large.* largeness *noun*

largely *adverb* mainly; mostly • *His success is largely a matter of hard work.*

lark *noun* a small sandy-brown bird; a skylark

larva *noun* larvae an insect in the first stage of its life, after it comes out of the egg

lasagne *noun* (la-**zan**-ya) lasagne is pasta in the form of flat sheets, cooked with minced meat or vegetables and a white sauce

laser *noun* (**lay**-zer) a device that makes a very strong narrow beam of light

lash *noun* **1.** an eyelash **2.** a stroke with a whip

lash *verb* **1.** to lash someone or something is to hit them with a whip or like a whip • *Rain lashed the window.* **2.** to lash something is to tie it tightly

lass *noun* a girl or young woman

lasso *noun* lassos (la-**soo**) a rope with a loop at the end which tightens when you pull the rope, used for catching cattle

last[1] *adjective* **1.** coming after all the others; final • *Try not to miss the last bus.* **2.** most recent or latest • *Where were you last night?*
last[1] *adverb* at the end; after everything or everyone else • *He came last in the race.*
last[1] *noun* a person or thing that is last • *I think I was the last to arrive.* at last finally; at the end

last[2] *verb* **1.** to continue • *The journey lasts for two hours.* **2.** to go on without being used up • *Our supplies won't last much longer.*

lastly *adverb* in the last place; finally

latch *noun* a small bar fastening a gate or door

late *adjective, adverb* **1.** after the proper or expected time • *a late arrival* **2.** near the end of a period of time • *They came late in the afternoon.* **3.** recent • *Have you heard the latest news?* **4.** no longer alive • *They saw the tomb of the late king.* **lateness** *noun*

lately *adverb* recently • *She has been very tired lately.*

lathe *noun* (layth) a machine for holding and turning pieces of wood or metal while you shape them

lather *noun* **lathers** the thick foam you get when you mix soap with water

Latin *noun* Latin is the language of the ancient Romans

latitude *noun* the distance of a place north or south of the equator, measured in degrees

latter *adjective* later • *We'd like a holiday in the latter part of the year.*

laugh *verb* to laugh is to make sounds that show you are happy or that you think something is funny

laugh *noun* the sound you make when you laugh

laughter *noun* laughter is laughing or the sound of laughing

launch[1] *verb* **1.** to launch a ship is to send it into the water for the first time **2.** to launch a rocket is to send it into space **3.** to launch a new idea or product is to make it available for the first time

launch[1] *noun* the launching of a ship or spacecraft

launch[2] *noun* a large motor boat

launderette *noun* a shop with washing machines that people pay to use

laundry *noun* **laundries** **1.** laundry is clothes to be washed **2.** a laundry is a place where clothes are sent or taken to be washed

laurel *noun* an evergreen bush with smooth shiny leaves

lava *noun* lava is molten rock that flows from a volcano

lavatory *noun* **lavatories** a toilet

lavender *noun* **1.** lavender is a shrub with pale purple flowers that smell very sweet **2.** a pale purple colour

lavish *adjective* **1.** generous • *They are lavish with their gifts.* **2.** plentiful • *What a lavish meal!*

law *noun* **1.** a rule or set of rules that everyone must keep **2.** a scientific rule about something that always happens, for example the law of gravity

lawcourt *noun* a room or building where a judge and jury or a magistrate decide whether someone has broken the law

lawful *adjective* allowed or accepted by the law **lawfully** *adverb*

lawn *noun* an area of mown grass in a garden

lawnmower *noun* a machine you use for cutting grass

lawyer *noun* a person whose job is to help people with the law

lax *adjective* not strict; tolerant • *Discipline was very lax.*

lay *verb* **laying**, **laid** **1.** to lay something somewhere is to put it down in a particular place or in a particular way **2.** to lay a table is to arrange things on it for a meal **3.** to lay an egg is to produce it **to lay something on** is to supply or provide it

layer *noun* something flat that lies on or under something else

layout *noun* the arrangement or design of something

laze *verb* to laze is to spend time in a lazy way

lazy *adjective* **lazier**, **laziest** not wanting to work; doing as little as possible **lazily** *adverb* **laziness** *noun*

lb. short for **pound** or **pounds** in weight

lead[1] *verb* **leading, led** (leed) **1.** to lead a person or animal is to guide them, especially by going in front **2.** to lead an activity is to be in charge of it **3.** to lead in a race or contest is to be winning it **4.** a road or path leads somewhere when it goes in that direction • *This road leads to the beach.* **to lead to something** is to cause it • *Their carelessness led to the accident.*

lead[1] *noun* (leed) **1.** the first or front place or position • *Who's in the lead now?* **2.** help or guidance • *Just follow my lead.* **3.** a strap or cord for leading a dog **4.** an electric wire • *Don't trip over that lead.*

lead[2] *noun* (led) **1.** lead is a soft heavy grey metal **2.** a lead is the writing substance (graphite) in the middle of a pencil

leader *noun* someone who leads or is in charge **leadership** *noun* the ability to be a good leader

leaf *noun* **leaves 1.** a flat and usually green growth on a tree or plant, growing from its stem **2.** a page of a book **3.** a very thin sheet of metal, such as gold leaf **leafy** *adjective* having a lot of leaves or trees

leaflet *noun* a piece of paper printed with information

league *noun* (leeg) a group of teams that play matches against each other

leak *noun* a hole or crack through which liquid or gas escapes **leaky** *adjective* a leaky pipe or tap has a leak

leak *verb* **1.** something leaks when it lets something out through a hole or crack **2.** liquid or gas leaks out when it escapes from a container **leakage** *noun* an escape of liquid or gas from a container

lean[1] *verb* **leaning, leaned** or **leant 1.** to lean is to bend your body towards something or over it **2.** to lean something is to put it into a sloping position • *Do not lean bicycles against the window.* **3.** to lean against something is to rest against it

lean[2] *adjective* **1.** lean meat has little fat **2.** a lean person is thin

leap *noun* a high or long jump
leap *verb* **leaping, leapt** or **leaped 1.** to leap is to jump high or a long way **2.** to leap is also to increase or advance suddenly

leap year *noun* a year with an extra day in it, on 29 February

learn *verb* to learn something is to find out about it and gain knowledge or skill in it

learned *adjective* (**ler**-nid) clever and knowledgeable

learner *noun* someone who is learning something, for example how to drive a car

lease *noun* an agreement to let someone use a building or land for a fixed period in return for a payment

leash *noun* a strap or cord for leading a dog

least *determiner, adverb* smallest; less than all the others • *I'll get the least expensive bike.* • *I like this one least.* **at least** not less than what is mentioned • *It will cost at least £50.*
least *noun* the smallest amount

leather *noun* a strong material made from animals' skins **leathery** *adjective* tough, like leather

leave *verb* **leaving, left 1.** to leave a person, place or group is to go away from them **2.** to leave something is to let it stay where it is or remain as it is • *You can leave your bags by the door.* **3.** to leave something to someone is to give it to them in a will **to be left over** is to remain when other things have been used
leave *noun* permission to be away from work

lecture *noun* a talk about a subject to an audience or a class
lecture *verb* to lecture is to give a lecture
lecturer *noun* someone who gives a lecture

ledge *noun* a narrow shelf

leek *noun* a long green and white vegetable with broad leaves

leer *verb* to leer at someone is to look at them in an unpleasant way

left *adjective, adverb* on or towards the west if you think of yourself as facing north

left *noun* the left side

left-hand *adjective* on the left side of something

left-handed *adjective* using the left hand more than the right hand

leftovers *plural noun* food that has not been eaten by the end of a meal

leg *noun* **1.** one of the parts of a human's or animal's body on which they stand or move **2.** one of the parts of a pair of trousers that cover your leg **3.** each of the supports of a chair or other piece of furniture **4.** one part of a journey **5.** each of a pair of matches between the same teams in a competition

legacy *noun* legacies something given to someone in a will

legal *adjective* **1.** allowed by the law **2.** to do with the law or lawyers legality *noun* the legality of something is whether it is legal or not legally *adverb*

legalize *verb* to legalize something is to make it legal This word can also be spelled **legalise**.

legend *noun* (**lej**-end) an old story handed down from the past legendary *adjective* to do with legends; very famous • *the legendary knight Sir Galahad*

legible *adjective* clear enough to read • *Make sure your writing is legible.* legibility *noun* how easily you can read something legibly *adverb*

legion *noun* a division of the ancient Roman army

legitimate *adjective* (li-**jit**-i-mat) **1.** allowed by a law or rule **2.** (*old use*) born of parents who were married to each other legitimacy *noun* whether or not something is allowed by a law or rule legitimately *adverb*

leisure *noun* leisure is free time, when you can do what you like

leisurely *adjective* done in a relaxed way, without hurrying • *They took a leisurely stroll down to the river.*

lemon *noun* **1.** a yellow citrus fruit with a sour taste **2.** a pale yellow colour

lemonade *noun* a drink with a lemon flavour

lend *verb* lending, lent **1.** to lend something to someone is to let them have it for a short time **2.** to lend someone money is to give them money which they must pay back plus an extra amount called interest

length *noun* **1.** how long something is **2.** a piece of something cut from a longer piece, for example rope, wire or cloth **3.** the distance of a swimming pool from one end to the other

lengthen *verb* **1.** to lengthen something is to make it longer **2.** to lengthen is to become longer

lengthy *adjective* lengthier, lengthiest going on for a long time • *a lengthy speech*

lenient *adjective* (**lee**-ni-ent) not strict in the way you punish someone leniency *noun* when someone is not as strict as expected leniently *adverb*

lens *noun* **1.** a curved piece of glass or plastic used to focus the light in a camera or a pair of glasses **2.** the transparent part of the eye, behind the pupil

Lent *noun* Lent is a period of about six weeks before Easter when some Christians give up something they enjoy

lentil *noun* a kind of small bean

leopard *noun* (**lep**-erd) a large spotted wild animal of the cat family

leotard *noun* **leotards** (**lee**-o-tard) a close-fitting piece of clothing worn by acrobats and dancers

less *determiner, adverb* smaller; not so much • *Make less noise.* • *It is less important.*

less *noun* a smaller amount • *I have less than you.*

lessen *verb* **1.** to lessen something is to make it smaller or not so much **2.** to lessen is to become smaller or not so much

lesson *noun* **1.** the time when someone is teaching you **2.** something that you have to learn **3.** a passage from the Bible read aloud as part of a church service

let *verb* **letting, let 1.** to let someone do something is to allow them to do it **2.** to let something happen is to cause it or not prevent it • *Don't let your bike slide into the ditch.* **3.** to let a house or room or building is to allow someone to use it in return for payment **4.** to let someone in or out is to allow them to go in or out **to let someone down** is to disappoint them **to let someone off** is to excuse them from a punishment

lethal *adjective* something that is lethal can kill you

let's *verb* (*informal*) shall we? • *Let's go to the park.*

letter *noun* **1.** one of the symbols used for writing words, such as a, b or c **2.** a written message sent to another person

letter box *noun* a box or slot into which letters are delivered or posted

lettering *noun* lettering is letters drawn or painted

lettuce *noun* a green vegetable with crisp leaves used in salads

leukaemia *noun* (lew-**kee**-mi-a) a serious disease in which there are too many white cells in the blood

level *adjective* **1.** flat or horizontal • *The ground is level near the house.* **2.** at the same height or position • *Are these pictures level?* **3.** equal or even • *After half an hour the scores were still level.*

level *verb* **levelling, levelled 1.** to level something is to make it flat or horizontal **2.** to level or to level out, is to become horizontal

level *noun* **1.** height or position • *Fix the shelf at eye level.* **2.** a standard or grade of achievement **3.** a device that shows if something is horizontal

level crossing *noun* a place where a road crosses a railway at the same level

lever *noun* a bar that is pushed or pulled to lift something heavy, force something open or make a machine work

liable *adjective* **1.** likely to do or get something • *They are liable to forget things.* **2.** responsible for something • *If there is any damage you will be liable.*

liar *noun* someone who tells lies

Liberal *noun* a member of the Liberal Democrat party, a British political party

liberal *adjective* **1.** tolerant of other people's point of view **2.** generous • *She is liberal with her money.* **liberally** *adverb* in large amounts or generously • *Pour the cream on liberally.*

liberate *verb* to liberate someone is to set them free **liberation** *noun* setting someone free

liberty *noun* **liberties** liberty is freedom

librarian *noun* someone who works in a library

library *noun* **libraries** a place where books are kept for people to use or borrow

lice plural of **louse**

licence *noun* an official document allowing someone to do or use or own something

license *verb* to license someone to do something is to give them a licence to do it • *We are not licensed to sell alcoholic drinks.*

lichen *noun* (**ly**-ken) a dry-looking plant that grows on the surface of rocks, walls or trees

lick *verb* to lick something is to move your tongue over it

lick *noun* the act of moving your tongue over something

lid *noun* **1.** a cover for a box or jar **2.** an eyelid

lie[1] *verb* lying, lay, lain **1.** to lie is to be in or get into a flat position, especially to rest with your body flat as it is in bed • *He lay on the grass.* **2.** to lie is also to be or remain a certain way • *The castle was lying in ruins.*

lie[2] *verb* lying, lied to lie is to say something that you know is not true

lie[2] *noun* something you say that you know is not true

lieutenant *noun* (lef-**ten**-ant) an officer in the army or navy

life *noun* lives **1.** a person's or animal's life is the time between their birth and death **2.** life is being alive and able to grow **3.** life is also all living things • *Is there life on Mars?* **4.** life is also liveliness • *She is full of life.*

lifebelt *noun* a large ring that will float, used to support someone's body in water

lifeboat *noun* a boat for rescuing people at sea

life cycle *noun* the series of changes in the life of a living thing

lifeguard *noun* someone whose job is to rescue swimmers who are in difficulty

life jacket *noun* a special safety jacket that will help a person to float in water

lifeless *adjective* dead or appearing to be dead

lifelike *adjective* looking exactly like a real person or thing

lifespan *noun* how long a person or animal or plant lives

lifetime *noun* the period of time during which someone is alive

lift *verb* **1.** to lift something is to pick it up or move it to a higher position **2.** to lift is to rise or go upwards • *The fog was beginning to lift.*

lift *noun* **1.** a movement upwards **2.** a device for taking people or goods from one floor to another in a building **3.** a ride in someone else's car or other vehicle

lift-off *noun* the moment when a rocket leaves the ground

light[1] *noun* **1.** light is the form of energy that makes things visible, the opposite of darkness • *There was not enough light to see the garden.* **2.** a light is something that provides light or a flame • *Switch on the light.*

light[1] *adjective* **1.** full of light; not dark **2.** pale • *a light blue dress*

light[1] *verb* lighting, lit or lighted **1.** to light something is to start it burning **2.** to light is to begin to burn • *The fire won't light.* **3.** to light a place is to give it light • *The streets were lit by gaslamps.*

light[2] *adjective* **1.** not heavy; weighing little **2.** not large or strong • *a light wind* **3.** not needing much effort • *They were doing some light work in the garden.* **4.** pleasant and entertaining rather than serious • *We prefer light music.* lightly *adverb* gently or only a little • *He kissed her lightly on the cheek.* • *It began to snow lightly.*

lighten *verb* **1.** to lighten something is to make it lighter or brighter **2.** to lighten is to become lighter

lighter *noun* a device for lighting a cigarette or a fire

light-hearted *adjective* **1.** cheerful; free from worry **2.** not serious

lighthouse *noun* a tower with a bright light at the top to guide ships and warn them of danger

lightning *noun* lightning is a flash of bright light in the sky during a thunderstorm

light year *noun* the distance that light travels in one year (about 9.5 million million kilometres or 6 million million miles)

like[1] *verb* to like someone or something is to think they are pleasant or satisfactory should like or would like to want • *I should like to see him.*

like[1] *noun* **1.** a simliar person or thing • *We shall not see his like again* **2.** a symbol on a social media website that shows that someone agrees with or likes something

like² *preposition* **1.** resembling; similar to; in the manner of • *She looks like her mother.* • *He cried like a baby.* **2.** such as • *We need things like knives and forks.* **3.** typical of • *It's not like her to be late.*

likeable *adjective* pleasant and easy to like

likely *adjective* likelier, likeliest probable; expected to happen or to be true or suitable • *It's likely that it will rain this afternoon.*

likeness *noun* a resemblance

likewise *adverb* similarly; in the same way

liking *noun* a feeling that you like something or someone • *She has a great liking for chocolate.*

lily *noun* lilies a trumpet-shaped flower grown from a bulb

limb *noun* a leg or an arm

lime¹ *noun* a green fruit like a small round lemon

lime² *noun* a tree with yellow blossom

lime³ *noun* a white chalky powder used in making cement or as a fertilizer

limelight *noun* to be in the limelight is to get a lot of publicity and attention

limerick *noun* (**lim**-er-ik) an amusing poem with five lines and a strong rhythm

limestone *noun* limestone is rock from which lime (the chalky powder) is made, used in building and in making cement

limit *noun* a line or point that you cannot or should not pass • *What is the speed limit on this road?*
limit *verb* to limit something or someone is to keep them within a limit limitation *noun* something that limits what you can do

limited *adjective* kept within limits; not great • *The choice was limited.*

limp¹ *verb* to limp is to walk with difficulty because something is wrong with your leg or foot
limp¹ *noun* a limping movement

limp² *adjective* not stiff or firm; without much strength • *He gave me a limp handshake.*
limply *adverb* something hangs limply when it does so in a limp way • *Her hair hung limply over her forehead.*

limpet *noun* a small shellfish that clings firmly to rocks

line¹ *noun* **1.** a long thin mark made on a surface **2.** a row or series of people or things **3.** a length of something long and thin like rope, string or wire **4.** a number of words together in a play, film, poem or song **5.** a railway or a length of railway track in line **1.** forming a straight line **2.** obeying or behaving well

line¹ *verb* **1.** to line something is to mark it with lines **2.** to line a place is to form an edge or border along it • *People lined the streets to watch the race.* to line up is to form lines or rows

line² *verb* to line material or a piece of clothing is to put a lining in it

linen *noun* **1.** linen is cloth made from flax, used to make things such as shirts or sheets **2.** linen is also things made of this cloth

liner *noun* a large passenger ship or aircraft

linesman *noun* linesmen an official in football, tennis and other games who decides whether the ball has crossed a line

linger *verb* to linger is to stay for a long time or be slow to leave

linguist *noun* an expert in languages or someone who can speak several languages well linguistic *adjective* to do with languages

lining *noun* a layer of material covering the inside of something

link *noun* **1.** one of the rings in a chain **2.** a connection between two things

link *verb* to link things is to join them together to link up is to become connected

lino *noun* lino is linoleum

linoleum *noun* (lin-**oh**-li-um) linoleum is a stiff shiny floor covering

lint *noun* lint is a soft material for covering wounds

lion *noun* a large strong flesh-eating animal of the cat family, found in Africa and India

lioness *noun* a female lion

lip *noun* **1.** each of the two fleshy edges of the mouth **2.** the edge of something

lip-read *verb* to lip-read is to understand what someone is saying by watching the movements of their lips, not by hearing their voice

lipstick *noun* a stick of a waxy substance for colouring the lips

liquid *noun* a substance (such as water or oil) that can flow but is not a gas
liquid *adjective* in the form of a liquid; flowing freely

liquor *noun* (**lik**-er) liquor is strong alcoholic drink

liquorice *noun* (**lik**-er-iss) liquorice is a soft black sweet with a strong taste, which comes from the root of a plant

lisp *noun* a way of speaking, in which *s* and *z* are pronounced like *th*
lisp *verb* to lisp is to speak with a lisp

list[1] *noun* a number of names or figures or items written or printed one after another
list[1] *verb* to list things is to write or say them one after another

list[2] *verb* a ship lists when it leans over to one side in the water

listen *verb* to listen to someone or something is to pay attention so that you can hear them **listener** *noun* someone who is listening

literacy *noun* (**lit**-er-a-si) the ability to read and write

literal *adjective* **1.** meaning exactly what it says **2.** word for word • *Write out a literal translation.*

literally *adverb* really; exactly as the words say • *The noise made me literally jump out of my seat.*

literary *adjective* (**lit**-er-er-i) to do with literature; interested in literature

literate *adjective* (**lit**-er-at) able to read and write

literature *noun* literature is books, plays or poems that people think are good or important

litmus *noun* litmus is a blue substance used to show whether something is an acid or an alkali

litre *noun* (**lee**-ter) a measure of liquid, 1,000 cubic centimetres or about 1¾ pints

litter *noun* **1.** litter is rubbish or untidy things left lying about **2.** a litter is a number of young animals born to one mother at one time
litter *verb* to litter a place is to make it untidy with litter

little *adjective, determiner* less or littler, least or littlest **1.** small; not great or not much • *the baby's little toes* • *We have very little time.* **2.** a small amount of something • *We just need a little bit of luck.*
little *adverb* not much • *They go swimming very little now.*

live[1] *verb* (rhymes with give) **1.** to live is to be alive **2.** to live in a particular place is to have your home there • *She is living in Glasgow.* **to live on something** is to have it as food or income • *The islanders lived mainly on fish.* • *No one can live on £50 a week.*

live[2] *adjective* (rhymes with hive) **1.** alive **2.** carrying electricity **3.** broadcast while it is actually happening, not from a recording

livelihood *noun* (**lyv**-li-huud) a person's livelihood is the way in which they earn a living

lively *adjective* livelier, liveliest full of life and energy; cheerful **liveliness** *noun*

liver *noun* **1.** a large organ in the body that helps keep the blood clean **2.** an animal's liver used as food

livestock *noun* farm animals

livid *adjective* very angry

living *noun* **1.** the way that a person lives • *They have a good standard of living.* **2.** a means of earning money • *She makes a living selling jewellery.*

living room *noun* a room for sitting and relaxing in

lizard *noun* a reptile with a scaly skin, four legs and a long tail

llama *noun* (**lah**-ma) a South American animal that has woolly fur and looks like a small camel without a hump

load *noun* something large or heavy that has to be carried

load *verb* **1.** to load something is to put things into it so they can be carried • *I loaded the case into the boot of the car.* **2.** to load a gun is to put a bullet or shell into it **3.** to load a machine is to put something into it so that it can be operated **4.** to load a computer is to enter programs or data on it

loaf[1] *noun* loaves a shaped mass of bread baked in one piece

loaf[2] *verb* to loaf or loaf about is to loiter or waste time

loan *noun* something that has been lent to someone, especially money on loan being lent • *The books are on loan from the library.*
loan *verb* to loan something is to lend it

loathe *verb* (rhymes with clothe) to loathe something or someone is to dislike them very much

loathsome *adjective* making you feel disgusted; horrible

lob *verb* lobbing, lobbed to lob something is to throw or hit it high into the air

lobby *noun* lobbies an entrance hall

lobe *noun* the rounded part at the bottom of your ear

lobster *noun* a large shellfish with eight legs and two claws

local *adjective* belonging to a particular place or area • *Where is your local library?*
locally *adverb* nearby, in the area where you are • *Do you live locally?*
local *noun* (informal) someone who lives in a particular district

locate *verb* **1.** to locate something is to discover where it is • *I have located the fault.* **2.** to be located in a place is to be situated there • *The cinema is located in the High Street.*

location *noun* the place where something is; when a film is filmed on location it is filmed in natural surroundings, not in a studio

loch *noun* a lake in Scotland

lock[1] *noun* locks **1.** a device for fastening a door or window or container, needing a key to open it **2.** a section of a canal or river with gates at each end, so that the level of water can be raised or lowered to allow boats to pass from one level to another
lock[1] *verb* **1.** to lock a door or window or lid is to fasten it with a lock **2.** to lock something somewhere is to put it in a safe place that can be fastened with a lock

lock[2] *noun* a few strands of hair formed into a loop

locker *noun* a small cupboard for keeping things safe, often in a changing room

locket *noun* a small case holding a photograph or lock of hair, worn on a chain round the neck

locomotive *noun* a railway engine

locust *noun* an insect like a large grasshopper, that flies in swarms which eat all the plants in an area

lodge *noun* a small house, often at the entrance to a large house
lodge *verb* **1.** to lodge is to become fixed or get stuck somewhere • *The ball lodged in the branches.* **2.** to lodge somewhere is to stay there as a lodger

lodger *noun* someone who pays to live in someone else's house

lodgings *plural noun* a room that you rent in someone else's house

loft *noun* the room or space under the roof of a house

lofty *adjective* **loftier**, **loftiest** high or tall

log *noun* **1.** a large piece of a tree that has fallen or been cut down **2.** a daily record of what happens on a journey or voyage

log *verb* **logging**, **logged** to log information is to put it in a log **to log in** or **to log on** is to gain access to a computer **to log out** or **to log off** is to finish using a computer

logic *noun* a way of thinking and working out ideas that makes sense

logical *adjective* using logic or worked out by logic **logically** *adverb*

logo *noun* **logos** an image that is used as the official symbol of a company or organization

loiter *verb* to loiter is to stand about not doing anything

lollipop *noun* a hard sticky sweet on the end of a stick

lolly *noun* **lollies** *(informal)* a lolly is a lollipop or an ice lolly

lone *adjective* on its own; solitary • *a lone rider*

lonely *adjective* **lonelier**, **loneliest** **1.** unhappy because you are on your own **2.** far from other inhabited places • *a lonely stretch of road* **loneliness** *noun*

long[1] *adjective* **1.** measuring a lot from one end to the other • *They walked up a long path.* **2.** taking a lot of time • *I'd like a long holiday.* **3.** measuring from one end to the other • *The river is 10 miles long.*

long[1] *adverb* **1.** for a long time • *Have you been waiting long?* **2.** a long time before or after • *They left long ago.* **as long as** or **so long as** provided that; on condition that • *I'll come as long as I can bring my dog.*

long[2] *verb* **to long for something** is to want it very much

longitude *noun* (**long**-i-tewd or **lon**-ji-tewd) longitude is the distance of a place east or west, measured in degrees from an imaginary line that passes through Greenwich in London

long-sighted *adjective* able to see things clearly when they are at a distance but not when they are close

look *verb* **1.** to look is to use your eyes to see something or to turn your eyes towards

something **2.** to look in a particular direction is to face it • *Look right and left before you cross.* **3.** to look (for example) happy or sad is to appear that way **to look after something** or **someone** is to protect them or take care of them **to look down on someone** is to despise them **to look for something** or **someone** is to try to find them **to look forward to something** is to be waiting eagerly for it to happen **to look out** is to be careful **to look up to someone** is to admire or respect them

look *noun* **1.** a look is the act of looking • *Take a look at this.* **2.** the expression on someone's face • *She gave me a surprised look.* **3.** the look of someone or something is their appearance • *I don't like the look of that dog.*

looking-glass *noun* *(old use)* a glass mirror

lookout *noun* **1.** a place from which you watch for something **2.** someone whose job is to keep watch

loom[1] *noun* a machine for weaving cloth

loom[2] *verb* to loom or loom up is to appear large and threatening • *An iceberg loomed out of the fog.*

loop *noun* the shape made by a curve crossing itself; a piece of string, ribbon or wire made into this shape

loop *verb* to loop something is to make it into a loop

loophole *noun* a way of getting round a law or rule without quite breaking it

loose *adjective* **1.** not tight or firmly fixed • *a loose tooth* **2.** not tied up or shut in • *The dog got loose.* **loosely** *adverb* not firmly or tightly • *She tied the scarf loosely round her waist.*

loosen *verb* **1.** to loosen something is to make it loose **2.** to loosen is to become loose

loot *noun* loot is stolen things

loot *verb* to loot a place is to rob it violently, especially during a war or riot **looter** *noun* someone who loots a place

lopsided *adjective* uneven, with one side lower than the other • *She had a lopsided smile.*

lord *noun* a nobleman, especially one who is allowed to use the title 'Lord' in front of his name **Lord** a name used by Christians for God or Jesus Christ

lorry *noun* lorries a large motor vehicle for carrying goods

lose *verb* losing, lost **1.** to lose something is to no longer have it, especially because you can't find it • *I've lost my hat.* **2.** to lose a contest or game is to be beaten in it • *We lost last Friday's match.* **3.** a clock or watch loses time when it gives a time that is earlier than the correct time to lose your way is not to know where you are loser *noun* someone who loses a game or who often loses or fails at things

loss *noun* **1.** losing something **2.** something you have lost to be at a loss is to be puzzled or unable to do something

lost *adjective* **1.** not knowing where you are or not able to find your way • *I think we're lost.* **2.** missing or strayed • *a lost dog*

lot *noun* **1.** a lot is a large number of people or things **2.** a lot can also mean very much • *Thanks a lot.* to draw lots is to choose one person or thing from a group by a method that depends on chance the lot or the whole lot everything

lotion *noun* a liquid that you put on your skin to clean or soothe it

lottery *noun* lotteries a game in which prizes are given to people who have winning tickets that are chosen by a draw

loud *adjective* **1.** noisy; easily heard **2.** bright or gaudy • *The room was painted in loud colours.* loudly *adverb* loudness *noun*

loudspeaker *noun* the part of a radio or music system that produces the sound

lounge *noun* a room in a house, hotel or airport for sitting in and relaxing
lounge *verb* to lounge is to sit or stand in a relaxed or lazy way

louse *noun* lice a small insect that sucks the blood of humans or animals

love *noun* **1.** love is a feeling of liking someone or something very much; great affection or kindness **2.** someone's love is a person that they love **3.** in games, love is a score of nothing to be in love is to love another person very deeply
love *verb* to love someone or something is to like them very much lovable *adjective* easy to love lovingly *adverb* in a way that shows love

lovely *adjective* lovelier, loveliest **1.** beautiful **2.** (*informal*) very pleasant or enjoyable loveliness *noun*

low[1] *adjective* **1.** only reaching a short way up; not high **2.** below average in amount or importance • *Prices are low.* **3.** unhappy • *I'm feeling low.* **4.** a low note is one at the bottom end of a musical scale

low[2] *verb* to low is to make a sound like a cow

lower *verb* **1.** to lower something is to move it down **2.** to lower a sound is to make it less loud • *Please lower your voices.*

lowly *adjective* lowlier, lowliest humble

loyal *adjective* always true to your friends; faithful loyally *adverb* in a faithful way loyalty *noun* being true to your friends

lozenge *noun* a small sweet tablet that contains medicine

lubricant *noun* oil or grease for lubricating machinery

lubricate *verb* to lubricate machinery is to put oil or grease on it so that it moves smoothly lubrication *noun* putting oil or grease on something so that it moves smoothly

luck *noun* **1.** luck is the way things happen by chance, without being planned **2.** luck is also good fortune

luckily *adverb* by a lucky chance; fortunately

lucky *adjective* luckier, luckiest having or bringing good luck

ludicrous *adjective* (**loo**-di-krus) extremely silly or absurd

lug *verb* lugging, lugged to lug something heavy is to carry it or drag it with difficulty

luggage *noun* luggage is the suitcases and bags you take on a journey

lukewarm *adjective* slightly warm

lull *verb* to lull someone is to soothe or calm them
lull *noun* a short period of quiet or rest • *There was a lull in the fighting.*

lullaby *noun* lullabies a song that you sing to send a baby to sleep

lumber *verb* to lumber is to move along clumsily and heavily

lumberjack *noun* someone whose job is to cut down trees and transport them

luminous *adjective* (**loo**-mi-nus) shining or glowing in the dark luminosity *noun* luminosity is being luminous

lump *noun* **1.** a solid piece of something **2.** a swelling lumpy *adjective* having lots of lumps

lump *verb* to lump different things together is to put them together in the same group

lunacy *noun* lunacy is madness

lunar *adjective* to do with the moon

lunatic *noun* an insane person

lunch *noun* a meal eaten in the middle of the day

lung *noun* each of the two organs in your chest that you use for breathing

lunge *verb* to lunge is to make a sudden movement forwards

lurch *verb* to lurch is to stagger or lean suddenly

lurch *noun* a sudden staggering or leaning movement

lure *verb* to lure a person or animal is to tempt them into a trap or difficulty

lurk *verb* to lurk is to wait threateningly where you can't be seen

luscious *adjective* (**lush**-us) tasting or smelling delicious • *luscious fruit*

lush *adjective* growing thickly and healthily • *lush grass*

lustre *noun* (**lus**-ter) a thing's lustre is its brightness or brilliance lustrous *adjective* shining brightly

lute *noun* A lute is a musical instrument rather like a guitar but with a deeper and rounder body. It was used a lot in the Middle Ages.

luxury *noun* luxuries **1.** a luxury is something expensive that you enjoy but don't really need **2.** luxury is having a very comfortable and expensive way of life • *They led a life of luxury.* luxurious *adjective* very comfortable and expensive

lynch *verb* to lynch someone is to execute them without a proper trial

lyre *noun* lyres an ancient musical instrument like a small harp

lyrical *adjective* sounding like a song or a poem

lyrics *plural noun* the words of a popular song

There are no English words that rhyme with *month*.

m short for **metre, metres, miles** or **millions**

mac *noun (informal)* a mackintosh

macaroni *noun* macaroni is pasta in the form of short tubes

> The word **macaroni** comes from an Italian word *maccaroni*, which in turn comes from a Greek word *makaria* meaning 'food made from barley'.

machine *noun* a piece of equipment made of moving parts that work together to do a job

machine-gun *noun* a gun that can keep firing bullets quickly one after another

machinery *noun* machinery is machines or the moving parts of a machine

mackerel *noun* mackerel a sea fish used as food

mackintosh *noun* a raincoat

mad *adjective* madder, maddest **1.** mentally ill **2.** very foolish **3.** very keen • *She's mad about rock music.* **4.** *(informal)* angry **madness** *noun*

madam *noun* a word sometimes used when speaking or writing politely to a woman, instead of her name • *Can I help you, madam?*

madden *verb* to madden someone is to make them mad or angry

madly *adverb* extremely; very much • *They are madly in love.*

magazine *noun* **1.** a kind of newspaper with articles or stories, which comes out every week or every month **2.** the part of a gun that holds the cartridges **3.** a store for weapons and ammunition or for explosives

maggot *noun* the larva of some kinds of fly

magic *noun* **1.** magic is the power to make impossible things happen **2.** magic is also performing clever tricks

magical *adjective* **1.** done by magic or as if by magic **2.** wonderful; marvellous

magician *noun* **1.** someone who does magic tricks **2.** a man with magic powers; a wizard

magistrate *noun* a judge in a local court who deals with some less serious cases

magnesium *noun* magnesium is a silvery-white metal that burns with a very bright flame

magnet *noun* a piece of metal that can attract iron or steel and that points north and south when it is hung in the air **magnetism** *noun* the attraction of a magnet

magnetic *adjective* having or using the powers of a magnet

magnetize *verb* to magnetize something is to make it into a magnet This word can also be spelled **magnetise**.

magnificent *adjective* **1.** looking splendid or impressive **2.** excellent • *We had a magnificent meal.* **magnificence** *noun* being magnificent **magnificently** *adverb*

magnify *verb* magnifies, magnifying, magnified to magnify something is to make it look bigger than it really is **magnification** *noun* magnification is making something look bigger than it really is

magnifying glass *noun* a lens that magnifies things

magnitude *noun* magnitude is how large or important something is

magpie *noun* magpies a black and white bird with a long tail, which likes to collect bright objects

mahogany *noun* (ma-**hog**-a-ni) mahogany is a hard brown wood used for making furniture

maid *noun* **1.** a female servant in a hotel or private house **2.** *(old use)* a girl

maiden *noun (old use)* a girl

maiden name *noun* a woman's family name before she gets married

maiden voyage or **maiden flight** *noun* a ship's first voyage or an aircraft's first flight

mail[1] *noun* **1.** mail is letters and parcels sent by post **2.** mail is also email

mail[1] *verb* to mail something is to send it by post or by email

mail[2] *noun* armour made of metal rings joined together

maim *verb* to maim someone is to injure them so badly that part of their body is damaged for life

main *adjective* largest or most important

main *noun* the main pipe or cable in a system carrying water, gas or electricity to a building

mainland *noun* the mainland is the main part of a country or continent, not the islands around it

mainly *adverb* chiefly or usually; almost completely

maintain *verb* **1.** to maintain something is to keep it in good condition **2.** to maintain a belief is to have it or state it • *I maintain that animals should not be hunted.* **3.** to maintain someone is to provide money for them

maintenance *noun* maintenance is keeping something in good condition

maize *noun* maize is a tall kind of corn with large seeds

majestic *adjective* stately and dignified **majestically** *adverb*

majesty *noun* majesties **1.** the title of a king or queen **2.** majesty is the quality of being stately and dignified

major *adjective* more important; main • *The major roads are shown in red on the map.*

major *noun* an army officer above captain in rank

majority *noun* majorities (ma-**jo**-ri-ti) **1.** the greatest part of a group of people or things; more than half • *The majority of the class wanted a quiz.* **2.** the amount by which the winner in an election beats the loser • *She had a majority of 25 over her opponent.*

make *verb* making, made **1.** to make something is to build or produce it • *They are making a raft out of logs.* **2.** to make someone or something do something is to cause it to happen • *The bang made him jump.* **3.** to make money is to get it or earn it • *She makes £30,000 a year.* **4.** in a game, to make a score is to achieve it • *He has made 20 runs so far.* **5.** to make a certain point is to reach it • *The swimmer just made the shore.* • *Do you think we can make the 7 o'clock train?* **6.** to make something is to estimate it or reckon it • *What do you make the time?* **7.** several numbers make a total when they add up to it • *4 and 6 make 10.* **8.** to make (for example) a suggestion or promise is to give it to someone **9.** to make a bed is to tidy it or arrange it for use **to make do** is to manage with something that is not what you really want **to make off** is to leave quickly **to make something** or **someone out** is to manage to see or hear or understand them **to make something up** is to invent a story or excuse **to make up** is to be friendly again after a disagreement **to make up for something** is to give or do something in return for a loss or difficulty **to make up your mind** is to decide

make *noun* a brand of goods; something made by a particular firm • *What make of car is that?*

make-believe *noun* make-believe is pretending or imagining things

makeshift *adjective* used because you have nothing better • *We'll use the desk as a makeshift table.*

make-up *noun* make-up is creams and powders for making your skin look beautiful or different

malaria *noun* (ma-**lair**-i-a) a tropical disease spread by mosquito bites, that causes fever

male *adjective* of the sex that produces young by fertilizing the female's egg cells

male *noun* a male person or animal

malevolent *adjective* wanting to harm other people **malevolence** *noun* malevolence is wanting to harm people

malice *noun* malice is a desire to harm other people

malicious *adjective* intending to do harm **maliciously** *adverb*

mall *noun* a large covered shopping centre

mallet *noun* a large wooden hammer

malnutrition *noun* malnutritian is bad health caused by not having enough food **malnourished** *adjective* suffering from malnutrition

malt *noun* malt is dried barley used in brewing and making vinegar

mammal *noun* any animal of which the female gives birth to live young and can feed them with her own milk

mammoth *noun* an extinct kind of hairy elephant with long curved tusks

man *noun* men **1.** a man is a grown-up male human being **2.** a man is also any individual person • *No man is perfect.* **3.** man is all the people in the world • *Look what harm man is doing to the environment.* **4.** a man is one of the pieces used in a board game

man *verb* manning, manned to man something is to supply people to work it • *Man the pumps!*

manage *verb* **1.** to manage something is to be able to do it although it is difficult **2.** to manage a shop or factory or other business is to be in charge of it

manageable *adjective* able to be managed or done

management *noun* **1.** management is being in charge of something **2.** the management of a business is the people in charge of it

manager *noun* a person who manages a business or part of it

manageress *noun* a woman manager of a shop or restaurant

mane *noun* the long hair along the back of the neck of a horse or lion

manger *noun* (**mayn**-jer) a trough in a stable for animals to feed from

mangle *verb* to mangle something is to crush or twist it so it is badly damaged

mango *noun* mangoes a juicy tropical fruit with yellow flesh

manhole *noun* a hole with a cover, through which a person can get into a sewer or boiler to inspect or repair it

mania *noun* mania is violent madness

maniac *noun* a person who acts in a violent and wild way

manic *adjective* manic behaviour is busy and excited

manipulate *verb* **1.** to manipulate something is to handle it skilfully **2.** to manipulate someone is to get them to do what you want by skilfully influencing them **manipulation** *noun* manipulating something or someone **manipulator** *noun* a person who manipulates something or someone

mankind *noun* mankind is all the people in the world • *This is a discovery for the good of all mankind.*

manly *adjective* manlier, manliest **1.** strong or brave **2.** suitable for a man or like a man **manliness** *noun*

manner *noun* the way that something happens or is done

manners *plural noun* a person's manners are how they behave with other people; behaving politely

manoeuvre *noun* (ma-**noo**-ver) a skilful or clever action

manoeuvre *verb* **1.** to manoeuvre something is to move it skilfully into position **2.** to manoeuvre is to move skilfully or cleverly **manoeuvrable** *adjective* easy to move into position

manor *noun* a large important house in the country

mansion *noun* a grand house

manslaughter *noun* (**man**-slaw-ter) manslaughter is the crime of killing someone without intending to

mantelpiece *noun* a shelf above a fireplace

manual *adjective* manual work is work you do with your hands **manually** *adverb* using your hands

manual *noun* a handbook or book of instructions

manufacture *verb* to manufacture things is to make them with machines in a factory **manufacturer** *noun* a business that manufactures things

manure *noun* animal dung added to the soil to make it more fertile

manuscript *noun* something written or typed before it has been printed

many *determiner* more, most large in number • *There were many people at the party.* • *How many potatoes do you want?*

many *noun* a large number of people or things • *Many of them wanted to stay.*

Maori *noun* (**mow**-ri) **1.** a member of the aboriginal people of New Zealand **2.** their language

map *noun* a diagram of part or all of the earth's surface, showing features such as towns, mountains and rivers

map *verb* mapping, mapped to map an area is to make a map of it

maple *noun* a tree with broad leaves

mar *verb* marring, marred to mar something is to spoil it

marathon *noun* a long-distance running race on roads, usually 26 miles (42 kilometres) long

marble *noun* **1.** a marble is a small glass ball used in games **2.** marble is a hard kind of limestone that is polished and used for building or sculpture

March *noun* the third month of the year

march *verb* **1.** to march is to walk with regular steps **2.** to march someone is to make them walk somewhere • *He marched them up to the top of the hill.*

march *noun* **1.** a march is a large group of people marching **2.** a march is also a piece of music suitable for marching to

mare *noun* a female horse or donkey

margarine *noun* (mar-ja-**reen**) margarine is a soft creamy food used like butter, made from animal or vegetable fats

margin *noun* **1.** the empty space between the edge of a page and the writing or pictures **2.** the small difference between two scores or prices • *She won by a narrow margin.*

marine *adjective* (ma-**reen**) to do with the sea

marine *noun* a soldier trained to serve on land and sea

mark *noun* **1.** a spot, dot, line or stain on something **2.** a number or letter put on a piece of work to show how good it is **3.** a special feature or sign of something • *They kept a minute's silence as a mark of respect.*

mark *verb* **1.** to mark something is to put a mark on it **2.** to mark a piece of work is to give it a number or letter to show how good it is **3.** in football, netball or hockey, to mark a player on the other team is to keep close to them to stop them getting the ball

market *noun* **1.** a place where things are bought and sold, usually from stalls in the open air **2.** a demand for goods

marksman *noun* marksmen an expert in shooting at a target marksmanship *noun* the skill of shooting at a target

marmalade *noun* jam made from oranges or lemons

maroon *verb* to maroon someone is to abandon them in a place far away from other people • *He was shipwrecked and marooned on a desert island.*

marquee *noun* (mar-**kee**) a large tent used for a party or exhibition

marriage *noun* **1.** marriage is the state of being married **2.** a marriage is a wedding

marrow *noun* **1.** a marrow is a large green or yellow vegetable with a hard skin **2.** marrow is the soft substance inside your bones

marry *verb* marries, marrying, married **1.** to marry someone is to become their husband or wife **2.** to marry two people is to perform a marriage ceremony

marsh *noun* a low-lying area of very wet ground marshy *adjective* marshy ground is low-lying and very wet

marshal *noun* **1.** an official who supervises a contest or ceremony **2.** a law officer in the USA

marshmallow *noun* marshmallow is a soft spongy sweet

marsupial *noun* (mar-**soo**-pi-al) A marsupial is an animal such as a kangaroo, wallaby or koala. The female has a pouch for carrying her young.

martial arts *plural noun* martial arts are fighting sports such as karate and judo

martyr *noun* (**mar**-ter) someone who is killed or suffers because of their beliefs
martyrdom *noun* becoming a martyr

marvel *noun* a wonderful thing
marvel *verb* marvelling, marvelled to marvel at something is to be filled with wonder or astonishment by it

marvellous *adjective* wonderful
marvellously *adverb*

marzipan *noun* marzipan is a soft sweet food made from almonds and sugar

mascot *noun* a person, animal or object that people think will bring them good luck

masculine *adjective* **1.** to do with men or like men; suitable for men **2.** in some languages, belonging to the class of words that refer to men **masculinity** *noun* being masculine

mash *verb* to mash something is to crush it into a soft mass
mash *noun* (informal) mashed potatoes

mask *noun* a covering that you wear over your face to disguise or protect it
mask *verb* **1.** to mask your face is to cover it with a mask **2.** to mask something is to hide it

mason *noun* someone who builds or works with stone

masonry *noun* masonry is the stone parts of a building

Mass *noun* the Communion service in a Roman Catholic church

mass *noun* **1.** a large amount of something **2.** a lump or heap **3.** (in science) the amount of matter in an object, measured in grams
mass *verb* to mass is to collect into a mass • *Protesters began massing in the main square.*

massacre *verb* (**mas**-a-ker) to massacre people is to kill a large number of them
massacre *noun* the killing of a large number of people

massage *verb* (**mas**-ahzh) to massage the body is to rub and press it to make it less stiff or less painful
massage *noun* massaging someone's body

massive *adjective* very big; large and heavy
massively *adverb* hugely

mast *noun* a tall pole that holds up a ship's sails or a flag or aerial

master *noun* **1.** a man who is in charge of something **2.** a male teacher **3.** someone who is very good at what they do, such as a great artist or composer **4.** something from which copies are made **Master** (old use) a title put before a boy's name
master *verb* **1.** to master a subject or skill is to learn it completely **2.** to master a fear is to control it • *She succeeded in mastering her fear of heights.*

mastermind *noun* **1.** a very clever person **2.** someone who organizes a scheme or crime

masterpiece *noun* a very fine piece of art, literature or music or the best that someone has produced

mastery *noun* mastery is complete control or knowledge of something

mat *noun* **1.** a small piece of material that partly covers a floor **2.** a small piece of material put on a table to protect the surface

match[1] *noun* a small thin stick with a chemical substance at one end that gives a flame when rubbed on something rough

match[2] *noun* **1.** a game or contest between two teams or players **2.** one person or thing that is equal or similar to another • *Can you find a match for this sock?*
match[2] *verb* **1.** to match another person or thing is to be equal to them **2.** one thing

matches another when it goes well with it
• *Your jacket matches your shoes.*

mate[1] *noun* **1.** a friend or companion **2.** one of a pair of animals that produce young together **3.** one of the officers on a ship
mate[1] *verb* animals mate when they come together in order to have offspring

mate[2] *noun* checkmate in chess

material *noun* **1.** anything used for making something else **2.** cloth or fabric

maternal *adjective* to do with a mother

maternity *noun* maternity is having a baby

mathematician *noun* (math-em-a-**tish**-an) an expert in mathematics

mathematics *noun* mathematics is the study of numbers, measurements and shapes **mathematical** *adjective* to do with mathematics

maths *noun* maths is mathematics

matinee *noun* (**mat**-i-nay) an afternoon performance at a theatre or cinema

matrimony *noun* (**mat**-ri-mo-ni) matrimony is marriage **matrimonial** *adjective* to do with marriage

matt *adjective* not shiny • *matt paint*

matted *adjective* tangled

matter *noun* **1.** something you need to think about or do • *It is a serious matter.* **2.** a substance • *vegetable matter* what's the matter? what is wrong?
matter *verb* to matter is to be important

mattress *noun* a thick layer of soft or springy material covered in cloth and used on a bed

mature *adjective* **1.** fully grown or developed **2.** behaving in a sensible adult manner **maturity** *noun* maturity is being fully grown or behaving in a sensible adult manner
mature to become fully grown or developed

maximum *noun* maxima the greatest number or amount possible • *Each team can use a maximum of three substitutes.*
maximum *adjective* the greatest possible • *The maximum speed is 60 miles per hour.*

May *noun* the fifth month of the year

may *verb* past tense might **1.** may means to be allowed to • *May I have a sweet?* **2.** may also means that something will possibly happen or has possibly happened • *He may come tomorrow.* • *He might have missed the train.*

maybe *adverb* perhaps

mayonnaise *noun* (may-on-**ayz**) mayonnaise is a creamy sauce made from eggs, oil and vinegar and used on salads

mayor *noun* the person in charge of the council in a town or city

mayoress *noun* a woman who is a mayor

maze *noun* a complicated arrangement of paths or lines to follow your way through as a game or puzzle

me *pronoun* a word used for *I*, usually when it is the object of a sentence or when it comes after a preposition • *She likes me.* • *She gave it to me.*

meadow *noun* a field of grass

meagre *adjective* (**meeg**-er) very little; barely enough

meal *noun* a meal is the food eaten at one time, such as breakfast, lunch or dinner

mean[1] *verb* meaning, meant **1.** to mean something is to have that as its explanation or equivalent or to convey that as its sense • *What does this word mean?* **2.** to mean to do something is to intend to do it • *I meant to tell him, but I forgot.*

mean[2] *adjective* **1.** not generous; selfish • *What a mean man.* **2.** unkind or spiteful • *That was a mean trick.* meanly *adverb* meanness *noun*

mean[3] *adjective* (in mathematics) average • *Work out the mean temperature.*

meaning *noun* what something means meaningless *adjective* having no meaning or purpose

means *noun* a means of doing something is a way or method of doing it • *email and other means of communication*
means *plural noun* money or other resources for doing things

meantime *noun*
in the meantime meanwhile

meanwhile *adverb* while something else is happening • *I'll cut the cake up. Meanwhile, you get the plates out.*

measles *plural noun* measles is an infectious disease that causes small red spots on the skin

measure *verb* 1. to measure something is to find out how big it is 2. to measure (for example) two metres is to be two metres long
measure *noun* 1. a unit used for measuring something 2. a device used for measuring 3. the size of something 4. something done for a particular purpose; a law or rule • *We are bringing in new measures to deal with bullies.*

measurement *noun* 1. a measurement is the size or length of something 2. measurement is when you measure something

meat *noun* meat is animal flesh that is cooked as food **meaty** *adjective* full of meat or like meat

mechanic *noun* someone who maintains and repairs machinery

mechanical *adjective* to do with machines

mechanism *noun* 1. the moving parts of a machine 2. the way a machine works

medal *noun* a piece of metal shaped like a coin, star or cross, given to someone for bravery or for achieving something

medallist *noun* a winner of a medal

meddle *verb* to meddle in something is to interfere in it **meddlesome** *adjective* always interfering

media *plural noun* (**mee**-di-a) the media newspapers, radio, television and the Internet, which provide information about current events to the public

medical *adjective* to do with the treatment of disease **medically** *adverb* by medical means

medicine *noun* 1. a medicine is a substance, usually swallowed, used to try to cure an illness 2. medicine is the treatment of disease and injuries **medicinal** *adjective* something is medicinal when it helps to cure an illness

medieval *adjective* (med-i-**ee**-val) to do with the Middle Ages

mediocre *adjective* (meed-i-**oh**-ker) not very good **mediocrity** *noun* being mediocre

meditate *verb* to meditate is to think deeply and seriously, usually in silence **meditation** *noun* when someone meditates

medium[1] *adjective* average; of middle size

medium[2] *noun* 1. media a thing in which something exists, moves or is expressed • *Air is the medium in which sound travels.* 2. mediums someone who claims to communicate with the dead

meek *adjective* quiet and obedient **meekly** *adverb* quietly and obediently **meekness** *noun*

meet *verb* meeting, met 1. to meet is to come together from different places • *We all met in London.* • *There is a statue where the two roads meet.* 2. to meet someone is to come face to face with them, especially for the first time or by an arrangement • *I met her at a party.* • *I'll meet you at the station.*

meeting *noun* a time when people come together to discuss something

megabyte *noun* (in computing) a unit that measures data or memory, roughly equal to one million bytes

megaphone *noun* a funnel-shaped device for making someone's voice sound louder

melancholy *adjective* sad and gloomy

mellow *adjective* having a soft rich sound or colour

melody *noun* melodies a pleasant tune **melodic** *adjective* having a pleasant tune

melon *noun* a large juicy fruit with yellow or green skin

melt *verb* **1.** to melt something solid is to make it liquid by heating it **2.** to melt is to become liquid by heating

member *noun* someone who belongs to a society or group **membership** *noun* being a member of a society or group

Member of Parliament *noun* someone who has been elected by the people of an area to speak for them in Parliament

memorable *adjective* **1.** worth remembering • *It was a memorable holiday.* **2.** easy to remember • *He has a memorable name.* memorably *adverb*

memorial *noun* something set up to remind people of a person or an event • *a war memorial*

memorize *verb* to memorize something is to learn it and remember it exactly This word can also be spelled **memorise**.

memory *noun* memories **1.** memory is the ability to remember things **2.** a memory is something that you remember, usually something interesting or special **3.** a computer's memory is the part where information is stored

menace *verb* to menace someone is to threaten them with harm or danger

menace *noun* something that threatens people with harm or danger

mend *verb* to mend something that is broken or damaged is to make it as good as it was before

menstruation *noun* menstruation is the natural flow of blood from a woman's womb, normally happening every 28 days menstrual *adjective* to do with menstruation

mental *adjective* to do with the mind • *mental arithmetic* mentally *adverb* in your head or mind

mention *verb* to mention someone or something is to speak about them briefly

mention *noun* when someone or something is mentioned • *Our school got a mention in the local paper.*

menu *noun* (**men**-yoo) **1.** a list of the food that is available in a restaurant or served at a meal **2.** *(in computing)* a list of possible actions, displayed on a screen, from which you choose what you want a computer to do

mercenary *noun* mercenaries a soldier hired to fight for a foreign country

merchandise *noun* merchandise is goods for buying or selling

merchant *noun* someone involved in trade

merciful *adjective* showing mercy mercifully *adverb*

merciless *adjective* showing no mercy; cruel mercilessly *adverb*

mercury *noun* mercury is a heavy silvery metal that is usually liquid, used in thermometers

mercy *noun* mercies **1.** mercy is kindness or pity shown towards someone instead of harming them or punishing them **2.** a mercy is something to be thankful for

mere *adjective* not more than • *He's a mere child.*

merely *adverb* only; simply • *I was merely repeating what he told me.*

merge *verb* **1.** to merge things is to combine or blend them **2.** to merge is to be combined

meringue *noun* (mer-**rang**) a crisp cake made from the whites of eggs mixed with sugar and baked

merit *noun* something that deserves praise

mermaid *noun* in stories, a sea creature with a woman's body and a fish's tail

merry *adjective* merrier, merriest happy and cheerful merrily *adverb*

merry-go-round *noun* a large roundabout with horses and other things to ride on

mesh *noun* mesh is material made like a net, with open spaces between the wire or threads

mess *noun* **1.** something untidy or dirty **2.** a difficult or confused situation **3.** a place where soldiers or sailors eat their meals to make a mess of something is to do it very badly

mess *verb* to mess about is to waste time behaving stupidly or doing things slowly • *Stop messing about and give me a hand.* to mess something up is to do it very badly

message *noun* a piece of information that one person sends to another

messenger *noun* someone who carries a message

messy *adjective* messier, messiest **1**. untidy or dirty **2**. difficult or complicated • *I'm afraid it's a messy situation.*

metal *noun* a hard substance that melts when it is heated, such as gold, silver, copper and iron **metallic** *adjective* like metal, especially sounding like it or shining like it

meteor *noun* (**meet**-i-er) a piece of rock or metal that moves through space and burns up as it enters the earth's atmosphere

meteorite *noun* (**meet**-i-er-ryt) the remains of a meteor that has landed on the earth

meteorology *noun* (meet-i-er-**ol**-o-ji) meteorology is the study of the weather **meteorological** *adjective* to do with meteorology **meteorologist** *noun* an expert on the weather

meter *noun* a device for measuring something, especially for measuring how much of something has been used

method *noun* a method is a way of doing something

methodical *adjective* (mi-**thod**-i-kal) done carefully and in a logical way **methodically** *adverb*

meticulous *adjective* very careful and precise **meticulously** *adverb*

metre *noun* (**meet**-er) **1**. the main unit of length in the metric system, equal to 100 centimetres or about 39½ inches **2**. a particular type of rhythm in poetry

metric system *noun* a measuring system based on decimal units (the metre, litre and gram)

miaow *verb* (mee-**ow**) to make a sound like a cat

microbe *noun* (**my**-krohb) a tiny organism that you need a microscope to see

microchip *noun* a very small piece of silicon working as an electric circuit, used in computers

microphone *noun* an electrical device that picks up sound waves for recording them or making them louder

microscope *noun* (**my**-kro-skohp) a device with lenses that make tiny objects appear larger so you can study them

microscopic *adjective* (my-kro-**skop**-ik) too small to be seen without a microscope; tiny

microwave *noun* a kind of oven which heats things quickly by using energy in very short waves

microwave *verb* to microwave food is to cook it in a microwave

mid *adjective* in the middle of • *The holiday is from mid-July to mid-August.*

midday *noun* the middle of the day; noon

middle *noun* the middle of something is the place or part that is at the same distance from all its sides or edges or from both its ends

middle *adjective* placed in the middle

middle-aged *adjective* aged between about 45 and 65

Middle Ages *noun* the period in history from about AD 1100 to 1500

Middle East *noun* the countries to the east of the Mediterranean Sea, from Egypt to Iran

middle school *noun* a school for children aged from about 9 to 13

midge *noun* a small insect like a gnat

midnight *noun* twelve o'clock at night

midst *noun* to be in the midst of something is to be in the middle of it

midsummer *noun* the middle of summer, when the days are longest

midway *adverb* halfway

midwife *noun* midwives a person trained to look after a woman who is giving birth to a baby

might[1] past tense of **may**

might[2] *noun* great power or strength

mighty *adjective* mightier, mightiest very strong or powerful **mightily** *adverb* very much indeed • *I was mightily relieved to see her.*

migraine *noun* (**mee**-grayn) a severe kind of headache

migrant *noun* (**my**-grant) **1.** a person who moves from one place to another **2.** a bird or animal that moves from one region to another

migrate *verb* (my-**grayt**) **1.** to migrate is to move from one place to another **2.** birds migrate when they fly to a warmer region for the winter **migration** *noun* migrating to another country

mild *adjective* gentle; not harsh or severe **mildly** *adverb* slightly • *She looked mildly surprised.* **mildness** *noun*

mile *noun* a measure of distance, equal to 1,760 yards or about 1.6 kilometres

mileage *noun* the number of miles you have travelled

milestone *noun* **1.** an important event in history or in a person's life **2.** a stone placed beside a road to mark the distance between towns

military *adjective* to do with soldiers or the armed forces

milk *noun* milk is a white liquid that female mammals produce in their bodies to feed to their young

milk *verb* to milk a cow or other animal is to get milk from it

milk shake *noun* a frothy drink of milk mixed with a sweet fruit flavouring

milky *adjective* **milkier, milkiest 1.** like milk; white **2.** made with a lot of milk

mill *noun* **1.** a building with machinery for grinding corn to make flour **2.** a factory for making materials, such as a paper mill or a steel mill **3.** a machine for grinding something such as coffee or pepper

mill *verb* **1.** to mill something is to grind or crush it in a mill **2.** people mill or mill about when they move in a confused crowd

millennium *noun* a period of 1,000 years

miller *noun* someone who runs a flour mill

milligram *noun* one thousandth of a gram

millilitre *noun* one thousandth of a litre

millimetre *noun* one thousandth of a metre

million *noun* a thousand thousands (1,000,000) **millionth** *adjective, noun* 1,000,000th

millionaire *noun* a rich person who has at least a million pounds or dollars

mime *verb* to mime is to tell a story by using movements of the body without speaking

mime *noun* mime is the art of telling a story by using movements of the body without speaking

mimic *verb* **mimicking, mimicked** to mimic someone is to imitate them, especially to make people laugh

mimic *noun* a person who is good at imitating other people

minaret *noun* a tall tower on a mosque

The word **minaret** comes from an Arabic word *manara* meaning 'lighthouse'.

mince *noun* mince is meat that has been cut up into very small pieces

mince *verb* to mince food is to cut it up into very small pieces

mincemeat *noun* mincemeat is a sweet mixture of currants, raisins and chopped fruit, used in pies

mince pie *noun* a pie containing mincemeat

mind *noun* **minds** the ability of your brain to think, feel, understand and remember; your thoughts and feelings **to change your mind** is to have a new opinion or make a different decision about something

mind *verb* **1.** to mind something is to be bothered or upset about it • *I don't mind missing the party.* **2.** to mind someone or something is to look after them for a time • *He was minding the baby.* **3.** to mind or to mind out, is to be careful or watch out for something • *Mind you don't trip on the step.*

mindless *adjective* done without thinking; stupid or pointless

mine[1] *adjective, pronoun* belonging to me • *That book is mine.*

mine[2] *noun* **1.** a place where coal, metal or precious stones are dug out of the ground **2.** a type of bomb hidden under the ground or in the sea that explodes when anything touches it

mine[2] *verb* **1.** to mine something is to dig it from a mine **2.** to mine a place is to lay explosives in it

minefield *noun* an area where explosive mines have been laid

miner *noun* someone who works in a mine

mineral *noun* a hard substance that can be dug out of the ground, such as coal and iron ore

mineral water *noun* Mineral water is water that comes from a natural spring. It can be fizzy or still.

mingle *verb* 1. things mingle when they become mixed together 2. to mingle things is to mix or blend them

miniature *adjective* (**min**-i-cher) very small; made in a much smaller size than usual

minibus *noun* a small bus

minim *noun* a musical note equal to two crotchets or half a semibreve, written ♩

minimum *noun* minima the smallest number or amount possible • *We want the minimum of fuss.*
minimum *adjective* least or smallest • *The minimum charge is £5.*

minister *noun* 1. a member of the government who is in charge of a department 2. a member of the clergy

ministry *noun* ministries 1. a government department 2. the work of a minister in the church

mink *noun* 1. a mink is a small animal rather like a stoat 2. mink is this animal's valuable brown fur

minnow *noun* a tiny freshwater fish

minor *adjective* not very important, especially when compared to something else

minority *noun* minorities (myn-**o**-ri-ti) 1. the smaller part of a group of people or things • *There was a minority who wanted to leave.* 2. a small group that is different from others

minstrel *noun* a travelling singer and musician in the Middle Ages

mint¹ *noun* 1. mint is a green plant with strong-smelling leaves used for flavouring 2. a mint is a sweet flavoured with peppermint

mint² *noun* a place where a country's coins are made

mint² *verb* to mint coins is to make them

minus *preposition* 1. less; with the next number taken away • *Eight minus two equals six (8-2 = 6).* 2. less than zero • *The temperature is minus 5 degrees.*

minute¹ *noun* (**min**-it) one-sixtieth of an hour

minute² *adjective* (my-**newt**) 1. tiny • *The insect was minute.* 2. very detailed • *He gave it a minute examination.* minutely *adverb* in a very detailed way

miracle *noun* a wonderful or magical happening that cannot be explained miraculous *adjective* wonderful or magical miraculously *adverb*

mirage *noun* (**mi**-rahzh) something that seems to be visible but is not really there, like a lake in a desert

mirror *noun* a sheet of glass painted with silver on the back so that it reflects things clearly

The word **mirror** comes from a Latin word *mirare* meaning 'to look at'.

mirth *noun* mirth is laughter or cheerfulness

misbehave *verb* to misbehave is to behave badly misbehaviour *noun* when someone behaves badly

miscarriage *noun* a woman has a miscarriage when she gives birth to a baby before it is old enough to survive

miscellaneous *adjective* (mis-el-**ay**-ni-us) a miscellaneous group is one that is made up of different kinds of things

mischief *noun* mischief is naughty or troublesome behaviour

mischievous *adjective* full of mischief

miser *noun* someone who stores money away and spends as little as they can miserly *adjective* hating to spend money

miserable *adjective* 1. very unhappy • *He felt miserable.* 2. unpleasant • *What miserable weather!* miserably *adverb*

misery *noun* misery is great unhappiness or suffering

misfire verb **1.** a gun misfires when it fails to fire **2.** a plan or idea or joke misfires when it goes wrong

misfit noun someone who does not fit in well with other people

misfortune noun **1.** a misfortune is an unlucky event or an accident **2.** misfortune is bad luck

mishap noun (**mis**-hap) an unfortunate accident

misjudge verb to misjudge someone or something is to form a wrong idea or opinion about them

mislay verb mislaying, mislaid to mislay something is to lose it for a short time

mislead verb to mislead someone is to give them a wrong idea or impression deliberately

misprint noun a mistake in printing, such as a spelling mistake

Miss noun a title you put before the name of a girl or unmarried woman

miss verb **1.** to miss something is to fail to hit, reach, catch, see, hear or find it • The bullet missed him by inches. • I missed the last episode. **2.** to miss someone or something is to be sad because they are not with you • I missed my sister when she was in hospital. **3.** to miss a train, bus or plane is to arrive too late to catch it **4.** to miss a lesson or other activity is to fail to attend it • How many classes have you missed? **5.** to miss something is also to notice that it isn't where it should be • When did you first miss your wallet?

miss noun not hitting, reaching or catching something

missile noun **1.** a weapon that is fired a long distance and explodes when it lands **2.** an object thrown at someone

missing adjective something is missing when it is lost or not in the proper place

mission noun **1.** an important job that someone is sent to do or that someone feels they must do **2.** a place or building where missionaries work

missionary noun missionaries someone who goes to another country to spread a religious faith

misspell verb misspelling, misspelt or misspelled to misspell a word is to spell it wrongly

mist noun **1.** damp cloudy air like a thin fog **2.** condensed water vapour on a window or mirror

mistake noun something done or said wrongly
mistake verb mistaking, mistook, mistaken to mistake one person or thing for another is to confuse them

mistaken adjective to be mistaken is to be incorrect or wrong

mistletoe noun mistletoe is a plant with green leaves and white berries in winter

mistreat verb to mistreat someone is to treat them badly or unfairly
mistreatment noun treating someone badly or unfairly

mistress noun **1.** a woman who is in charge of something **2.** a woman who teaches in a school **3.** the woman owner of a dog or other animal

mistrust verb to mistrust someone or something is not to trust them

misty adjective mistier, mistiest if it is misty outside there is a lot of mist

misunderstand verb misunderstanding, misunderstood to misunderstand something is to get a wrong idea or impression about it **misunderstanding** noun a wrong idea or impression

misuse verb (mis-**yooz**) to misuse something is to use it in the wrong way or treat it badly
misuse noun (mis-**yooss**) misuse is using something in the wrong way

mite noun a tiny insect found in food

mitten noun a kind of glove without separate parts for the fingers

mix verb **1.** to mix different things is to stir or shake them together to make one thing **2.** to mix is to get on well with other people • She mixes well. to mix up people or things is to confuse them **mixer** noun a machine for mixing food

mixed adjective containing two or more kinds of things or people • a bag of mixed nuts

mixture *noun* something made of different things mixed together

mm short for **millimetre** or **millimetres**

moan *noun* **1.** a long low sound, usually of suffering **2.** a complaint or grumble
moan *verb* **1.** to moan is to make a long low sound **2.** to moan is also to complain or grumble

moat *noun* a deep ditch round a castle, usually filled with water

mob *noun* a large crowd of people who are hard to control
mob *verb* **mobbing**, **mobbed** people mob someone when they crowd round them

mobile *adjective* able to be moved or carried about easily **mobility** *noun* the ability to move easily from place to place
mobile *noun* **1.** a decoration made to be hung up from threads so that it moves about in the air **2.** *(informal)* a mobile phone

mobile phone *noun* a telephone you can carry around with you

mock *verb* to mock someone or something is to make fun of them **mockery** *noun* making fun of someone or something
mock *adjective* not real or genuine • *They fought a mock battle.*

mode *noun* the way that something is done • *Flying is the fastest mode of transport.*

model *noun* **1.** a small copy of an object • *He makes models of aircraft.* **2.** a particular version or design of something • *We saw the latest models at the motor show.* **3.** someone who displays clothes by wearing them or who poses for an artist or photographer
model *adjective* **1.** being a small copy of something • *a model railway* **2.** being a good example for people to follow • *a model pupil*
model *verb* **modelling**, **modelled** **1.** to model something is to make it out of a material such as clay **2.** to model one thing on another is to use the second thing as a pattern for the first • *The building is modelled on an Egyptian temple.* **3.** to model or to model clothes, is to work as an artist's model or a fashion model

modem *noun* *(in computing)* a piece of equipment that links a computer to a telephone line

moderate *adjective* (**mod**-er-at) a moderate amount or level is not too little and not too

much **moderately** *adverb* fairly but not very **moderation** *noun* being moderate

modern *adjective* belonging to the present day or recent times

modest *adjective* **1.** not thinking or talking too much about how good you are **2.** quite small in amount • *Their needs were modest.* **modestly** *adverb* **modesty** *noun* being modest

modify *verb* **modifies**, **modifying**, **modified** to modify something is to change it slightly **modification** *noun* a slight change in something

module *noun* (**mod**-yool) a separate section or part of something larger, such as a spacecraft or building

moist *adjective* slightly wet

moisten *verb* (**moi**-sen) to moisten something is to make it slightly wet

moisture *noun* moisture is tiny drops of water in the air or on a surface

mole *noun* **1.** a small furry animal that digs holes under the ground **2.** a small dark spot on the skin

molecule *noun* (**mol**-i-kewl) *(in science)* the smallest part into which a substance can be divided without changing its chemical nature; a group of atoms

mollusc *noun* an animal with a soft body and usually a hard shell, such as a snail or an oyster

molten *adjective* molten rock or metal has been made into liquid by great heat • *Molten lava flowed down the side of the volcano.*

moment *noun* **1.** a very short period of time • *Wait a moment.* **2.** a particular time • *At that moment, all the lights went out.* **at the moment** now

momentous *adjective* (moh-**ment**-us) very important

momentum *noun* (moh-**ment**-um) momentum is the force developed by something moving • *The rock gained momentum as it rolled down the hill.*

monarch *noun* a king, queen, emperor or empress ruling a country

monarchy *noun* monarchies **1**. monarchy is rule by a monarch **2**. a monarchy is a country ruled by a monarch

monastery *noun* monasteries (**mon**-a-ster-i) a building where monks live and work monastic *adjective* to do with monks or monasteries

Monday *noun* the second day of the week

money *noun* money is coins and notes used by people to buy things

mongrel *noun* (**mung**-rel) a dog of mixed breeds

monitor *noun* **1**. a device used for checking how something is working **2**. a computer or television screen
monitor *verb* to monitor something or someone is to watch or test them to see how they are working

monk *noun* a member of a religious community of men

monkey *noun* monkeys an animal with long arms, hands with thumbs and a tail

monopolize *verb* to monopolize something is to keep it to yourself without letting other people use it This word can also be spelled **monopolise**.

monopoly *noun* monopolies a situation where one person or company is the only one to sell something that people need

monotonous *adjective* (mon-**ot**-on-us) boring because it does not change • *This is monotonous work.* monotonously *adverb* monotony *noun* when something is boring because it does not change; dullness

monsoon *noun* a strong wind in and around the Indian Ocean, bringing heavy rain in summer

monster *noun* a huge frightening creature

monstrous *adjective* **1**. like a monster; huge **2**. very shocking or cruel • *It was a monstrous crime.* monstrosity *noun* a monstrous thing

month *noun* one of the twelve parts into which a year is divided

monthly *adjective, adverb* something happens monthly when it happens every month

monument *noun* a statue, building or column put up to remind people of some person or event

moo *verb* to make the sound of a cow

mood *noun* the way someone feels at a particular time

moody *adjective* moodier, moodiest **1**. gloomy or bad-tempered **2**. likely to have sudden changes of mood moodily *adverb* moodiness *noun*

moon *noun* **1**. the natural satellite which orbits the earth and shines in the sky at night **2**. a similar object which orbits another planet

moonlight *noun* moonlight is the light reflected from the moon moonlit *adjective* a moonlit night is one that is lit by the moon

moor[1] *noun* an area of rough land covered with bracken and bushes

moor[2] *verb* to moor a boat is to tie it up to the land

moose *noun* moose a North American elk

mop *noun* a piece of soft material on the end of a stick, used for cleaning floors
mop *verb* mopping, mopped to mop something is to clean it with a mop

mope *verb* to mope is to be miserable and not interested in doing anything

moped *noun* (**moh**-ped) a kind of small motorcycle with pedals

moral *adjective* **1**. to do with people's behaviour and what is right and wrong **2**. being or doing good and what is right • *We are expected to lead moral lives.* morality *noun* how moral someone or something is morally *adverb*
moral *noun* a lesson taught by a story or event

morale *noun* (mo-**rahl**) morale is confidence or courage

morals *plural noun* standards of behaviour

morbid *adjective* thinking too much about gloomy things such as death

more *adjective* greater in number or amount • *We need more money.* • *She is more beautiful.*
more *noun* a larger number or amount • *I want more.*

more adverb 1. to a greater extent • *You must work more.* 2. again • *I'll tell you once more.* more or less almost; approximately • *I've more or less finished the work.*

morning noun the early part of the day before noon or before lunchtime

morphine noun (**mor**-feen) morphine is a drug made from opium, used to relieve pain

morris dance noun a traditional English dance performed by people in costume with ribbons and bells

Morse code noun a code for sending messages by radio, using dots and dashes to represent letters and numbers

morsel noun a small piece of food

mortal adjective 1. certain to die • *All men are mortal.* 2. causing death • *He received a mortal wound.* mortality noun being certain to die mortally adverb someone who is mortally wounded or ill is certain to die from their wounds or illness

mortar noun 1. mortar is a mixture of sand, cement and water used in building to stick bricks together 2. a mortar is a small cannon

mortgage noun (**mor**-gij) an arrangement to borrow money to buy a house, repaid over many years

mortuary noun mortuaries a place where dead bodies are kept before they are buried or cremated

mosaic noun (moh-**zay**-ik) a picture or design made from small coloured pieces of glass or stone

mosque noun (mosk) a building where Muslims worship

mosquito noun mosquitoes (mos-**kee**-toh) an insect that sucks blood and carries disease

moss noun a plant that grows in damp places and has no flowers mossy adjective covered in moss

most adjective greatest in number or amount • *Most people came by bus.*
most noun the greatest number or amount • *They've eaten most of the food.*
most adverb more than any other • *I liked this book most.*

mostly adverb mainly

motel noun (moh-**tel**) a hotel for people travelling by road, with parking near the rooms

moth noun an insect rather like a butterfly, that usually flies around at night

mother noun your female parent

mother-in-law noun mothers-in-law the mother of your husband or wife

motion noun a way of moving; movement

motionless adjective not moving

motive noun a person's motive is what makes them do something

motor noun a machine that provides power to drive machinery

motorbike noun (informal) a motorcycle

motorcycle noun a two-wheeled vehicle with an engine motorcyclist noun someone who rides a motorcycle

motorist noun someone who drives a car

motorway noun a wide road with two or more lanes for fast traffic

mottled adjective marked with spots or patches of colour

motto noun mottoes a short saying used as a guide for behaviour

mould[1] noun a mould is a container for making liquid things like jelly or plaster form a special shape when they harden
mould[1] verb to mould something is to make it have a particular shape

mould[2] noun mould is a furry growth that appears on some damp surfaces or stale food

mouldy adjective mouldier, mouldiest something is mouldy when it has mould on it

moult verb (mohlt) animals or birds moult when they lose hair or feathers

mound noun a pile of earth or stones; a small hill

mount verb 1. to mount a horse or bicycle is to get on it 2. to mount is to increase in amount • *The excitement was mounting.*
mount noun a mountain, especially in names such as *Mount Everest*

a
b
c
d
e
f
g
h
i
j
k
l
m
n
o
p
q
r
s
t
u
v
w
x
y
z

mountain *noun* **1.** a very high hill **2.** a large amount • *We've got a mountain of work to do.* **mountainous** *adjective* a mountainous place has a lot of mountains

mountaineer *noun* someone who climbs mountains **mountaineering** *noun* the sport of climbing mountains

mourn *verb* to mourn is to be sad because someone has died **mourner** *noun* mourners are the people who go to a funeral

mournful *adjective* sad and sorrowful

mouse *noun* mice **1.** a small animal with a long tail and a pointed nose **2.** a small device that you move around with your hand to control the movements of a cursor on a computer screen

mousse *noun* (mooss) **1.** a creamy pudding flavoured with chocolate or fruit **2.** a frothy substance that you use to style your hair

moustache *noun* (mus-**tahsh**) a strip of hair that a man grows above his upper lip

mouth *noun* **1.** the part of the face that opens for eating and speaking **2.** the place where a river flows into the sea

mouthful *noun* an amount of food you put in your mouth

mouth organ *noun* a small musical instrument you play by blowing and sucking while passing it along your lips

mouthpiece *noun* the part of a musical instrument or other device that you put to your mouth

movable *adjective* able to be moved

move *verb* **1.** to move something is to take it from one place to another **2.** to move is to go from one place to another **3.** to move someone is to affect their feelings • *Their story moved us deeply.*
move *noun* **1.** a movement **2.** a player's turn in a game

movement *noun* **1.** movement is moving or being moved **2.** a movement is a group of people working together to achieve something **3.** a movement is also one of the main parts of a long piece of classical music

movie *noun* a cinema film

moving *adjective* making you feel strong emotion, especially sadness or pity

mow *verb* mowing, mowed, mown to mow grass is to cut it with a machine **mower** *noun* a machine for mowing grass

MP short for **Member of Parliament**

m.p.h. short for *miles per hour*

Mr *noun* (**mis**-ter) a title you put before a man's name

Mrs *noun* (**mis**-iz) a title you put before a married woman's name

Ms *noun* (miz) a title you put before a woman's name, whether or not she is married

much *adjective* existing in a large amount • *There is much work to do.*
much *noun* a large amount of something • *£5 is not very much.*
much *adverb* greatly; considerably • *They came, much to my surprise.*

muck *noun* **1.** muck is farmyard manure **2.** *(informal)* muck is dirt or filth

mucky *adjective* muckier, muckiest dirty or messy

mud *noun* mud is wet soft earth **muddy** *adjective* covered with mud

muddle *verb* **1.** to muddle things is to mix them up **2.** to muddle someone is to confuse them
muddle *noun* a confusion or mess • *I've got these papers in a bit of a muddle.*

mudguard *noun* a curved cover fixed over a bicycle wheel to stop mud and water being thrown up on to the rider

muesli *noun* (**mooz**-li) muesli is a breakfast food made of cereals, nuts and dried fruit

muffle *verb* to muffle a sound is to make it quieter by covering the place that it is coming from

mug *noun* a large cup, usually used without a saucer
mug *verb* mugging, mugged to mug someone is to attack and rob them in the street **mugger** *noun* a person who attacks and robs someone in the street

muggy *adjective* muggier, muggiest a muggy day is unpleasantly warm and damp

mule *noun* an animal that is the offspring of a male donkey and a female horse

multiple *adjective* having many parts

multiple *noun* a number that can be divided exactly by another number • *30 and 50 are multiples of 10.*

multiply *verb* multiplies, multiplying, multiplied to multiply a number is to add it to itself a certain number of times • *Five multiplied by four equals twenty (5 x 4 = 20).* multiplication *noun* multiplication is when you multiply numbers

multiracial *adjective* (mul-ti-**ray**-shal) a multiracial area has people living there of many different races

multitude *noun* a very large number of people or things

mum *noun (informal)* mother

mumble *verb* to mumble is to speak softly and unclearly

mummy *noun* mummies in ancient Egypt, a dead body wrapped in cloth and treated with oils for burial

mumps *noun* mumps is an infectious disease that makes your neck swell painfully

munch *verb* to munch food is to chew it noisily

mural *noun* a picture painted on a wall

murder *verb* to murder someone is to kill them deliberately murderer *noun* someone who commits murder

murder *noun* 1. murder is the crime of deliberately killing someone 2. a murder is a deliberate killing of someone

murky *adjective* murkier, murkiest dark and gloomy

murmur *noun* a low or soft continuous sound of people speaking

murmur *verb* to murmur is to speak softly with a low continuous sound

muscle *noun* a bundle of fibres that can stretch or tighten to make a part of your body move

muscular *adjective* having strong muscles

museum *noun* a place where interesting old or valuable objects are displayed for people to see

mushroom *noun* a fungus with a dome-shaped top, some of which can be eaten

music *noun* 1. music is pleasant or interesting sounds made by instruments or by the voice 2. music is also a set of written symbols for making this kind of sound

musical *adjective* 1. to do with music 2. good at music or interested in it musically *adverb*

musical *noun* a play or film with music and songs

musician *noun* someone who plays a musical instrument

musket *noun* an old type of rifle

Muslim *noun* (**muuz**-lim) someone who follows the religious teachings of Muhammad, as set out in the Koran

muslin *noun* fine cotton cloth

mussel *noun* a black shellfish, often found sticking to rocks

must *verb* a word used with another verb to show 1. that someone has to do something • *I must go home soon.* 2. that something is certain • *You must be joking!*

mustard *noun* mustard is a yellow paste or powder used to give food a hot taste

muster *verb* to muster something is to assemble or gather it together • *He put all the enthusiasm he could muster into his voice.*

musty *adjective* mustier, mustiest smelling or tasting mouldy or stale mustiness *noun*

mute *adjective* not speaking or able to speak

mutilate *verb* to mutilate something is to damage it by breaking or cutting off part of it mutilation *noun* when someone mutilates something

mutiny *noun* mutinies (**mew**-tin-i) a rebellion by sailors or soldiers against their officers **mutinous** *adjective* rebellious; taking part in a mutiny

mutiny *verb* mutinies, mutinying, mutinied (**mew**-tin-i) to mutiny is to take part in a mutiny

mutter *verb* to mutter is to speak in a low quiet voice that is difficult to understand

mutton *noun* mutton is meat from an adult sheep

mutual *adjective* (**mew**-tew-al) given or done to each other • *They have mutual respect.* **mutually** *adverb* equally to two or more people • *Let's arrange a mutually convenient time to meet.*

muzzle *noun* **1.** an animal's nose and mouth **2.** a cover put over an animal's nose and mouth so that it cannot bite **3.** the open end of a gun

muzzle *verb* to muzzle an animal is to put a muzzle on it

my *determiner* belonging to me • *This is my book.*

myself *pronoun* me and nobody else, used to refer back to the person who is speaking • *I have hurt myself.* **by myself** on my own; alone • *I did the work all by myself.*

mysterious *adjective* strange and puzzling **mysteriously** *adverb*

mystery *noun* mysteries something strange or puzzling • *Exactly why the ship sank is a mystery.*

mystify *verb* mystifies, mystifying, mystified to mystify someone is to puzzle them very much

myth *noun* **1.** an old story about gods and heroes in ancient times **2.** an untrue story or belief • *It is a myth that carrots make you see better.*

mythical *adjective* only found in myths

mythology *noun* mythology is a collection of myths or the study of myths **mythological** *adjective* mythological creatures or characters are found in myths

No is one of the most frequently used words in English.

nag *verb* nagging, nagged to nag someone is to keep criticizing them or complaining to them

nail *noun* **1.** the hard covering on the end of one of your fingers or toes **2.** a small piece of metal with a sharp point, used to fix pieces of wood together
nail *verb* to nail something is to fasten it with nails

naked *adjective* (**nay**-kid) without any clothes or coverings on **to look at something with the naked eye** is to look at it with your eyes without the help of a telescope or microscope **nakedness** *noun*

name *noun* what you call a person or thing
name *verb* **1.** to name someone or something is to give them a name **2.** to name someone or something is to say what they are called • *Can you name these plants?*

nameless *adjective* not having a name

namely *adverb* that is to say • *I will invite two friends, namely Vicky and Tom.*

nanny *noun* nannies a person, usually a woman, whose job is to look after small children

nap *noun* a short sleep

napkin *noun* a piece of cloth or paper for wiping your lips or hands at meals

nappy *noun* nappies a piece of cloth or an absorbent pad put round a baby's bottom

narrate *verb* to narrate a story or experiences is to tell them to someone **narration** *noun* telling a story

narrative *noun* a story or account that someone tells

narrator *noun* the person who is telling a story

narrow *adjective* **1.** not wide **2.** with only a small margin of error or safety • *We all had a narrow escape.* **narrowly** *adverb* only just • *She narrowly escaped injury.*

narrow-minded *adjective* not liking or understanding other people's ideas or beliefs

nasal *adjective* to do with the nose

nasty *adjective* **nastier, nastiest** not pleasant; unkind **nastily** *adverb* **nastiness** *noun*

nation *noun* **1.** a large group of people of the same race who speak the same language • *The Czechs are a very musical nation.* **2.** a country and the people who live there • *Athletes from 16 nations took part in the tournament.*

national *adjective* belonging to a nation or country **nationally** *adverb* over the whole of a country

nationality *noun* **nationalities** the nation someone belongs to

nationwide *adjective, adverb* over the whole of a country

native *noun* a person born in a particular place • *He is a native of Sweden.*

native *adjective* of the country where you were born • *English is my native language.*

Native American *noun* one of the original inhabitants of North or South America

Nativity *noun* (na-**tiv**-i-ti) the Nativity is the birth of Jesus Christ

natural *adjective* **1.** made or done by nature, not by people or machines **2.** normal; not surprising • *It was only natural that she was nervous.* **3.** a natural ability is something you are born with **4.** in music, not sharp or flat

natural *noun* **1.** a natural note in music; a sign (♮) that shows a note is natural **2.** someone who is naturally good at something • *She's a natural at juggling.*

natural history *noun* natural history is the study of plants and animals

naturalist *noun* someone who studies natural history

naturally *adverb* **1.** in a natural way • *The gas is produced naturally.* **2.** as you would expect • *Naturally I will pay your train fare.*

nature *noun* **1.** nature is everything in the world that was not made by people, such as plants, animals, mountains and rivers **2.** a person's or thing's nature is the qualities or characteristics they have • *She has a loving nature.*

nature reserve *noun* an area of land set aside to keep wild life

naughty *adjective* **naughtier, naughtiest** not behaving as you should; disobedient or rude **naughtily** *adverb* **naughtiness** *noun*

nausea *noun* nausea is a feeling of sickness or disgust **nauseous** *adjective* feeling sick

nautical *adjective* to do with ships or sailors

naval *adjective* to do with a navy

nave *noun* the main central part of a church

navel *noun* the small hollow at the front of your stomach, where the umbilical cord was attached

navigate *verb* to navigate is to make sure that an aircraft, ship or vehicle is going in the right direction **navigation** *noun* making sure that an aircraft, ship or vehicle is going in the right direction **navigator** *noun* a person who navigates

navy *noun* **navies** **1.** a fleet of ships and the people trained to use them **2.** dark blue

near *adverb, adjective* not far away
near *preposition* not far away from something • *She lives near the town.*
near *verb* to near a place is to come close to it • *The ships were nearing the harbour.*

nearby *adjective, adverb* near; not far away • *We live in a nearby town.* • *My sister lives nearby.*

nearly *adverb* almost • *It was nearly midnight.* **not nearly** not at all • *There is not nearly enough food.*

neat *adjective* **1.** tidy and carefully arranged **2.** without water added • *They were drinking neat orange juice.* **neatly** *adverb* **neatness** *noun*

necessarily *adverb* for certain; definitely • *It won't necessarily cost you a lot.*

a b c d e f g h i j k l m n o p q r s t u v w x y z

necessary *adjective* needed very much; essential

necessity *noun* **necessities 1.** necessity is need • *There is no necessity for you to come too.* **2.** a necessity is something needed • *Water is one of the basic necessities of life.*

neck *noun* **1.** the part of the body that joins the head to the shoulders **2.** a narrow part of something, especially of a bottle

neckerchief *noun* a square of cloth worn round the neck, for example by Scouts

necklace *noun* a piece of jewellery you wear round your neck

nectar *noun* nectar is a sweet liquid collected by bees from flowers

nectarine *noun* a kind of peach with a smooth skin

need *verb* **1.** to need something is to be without it when you should have it **2.** to need to do something is to have to do it • *I needed to get a haircut.*

need *noun* **1.** a need is something that you need **2.** need is a situation in which something is necessary • *There's no need to shout.* **to be in need** is to need money or help **needless** *adjective* unnecessary

needle *noun* **1.** a very thin pointed piece of metal used for sewing **2.** something long, thin and sharp, such as a knitting needle or a pine needle **3.** the pointer of a meter or compass

needlework *noun* needlework is sewing or embroidery

needy *adjective* **needier, neediest** needy people are very poor and don't have what they need to live properly

negative *adjective* **1.** a negative statement or answer is one that says 'no' **2.** not definite or helpful **3.** a negative number is one that is less than nought **4.** a negative electric charge is one that carries electrons **negatively** *adverb*

negative *noun* **1.** something that means 'no' **2.** a photograph or film with the dark parts light and the light parts dark, from which prints are made

neglect *verb* **1.** to neglect something or someone is to fail to look after them or deal with them **2.** to neglect to do something is to fail to do it

neglect *noun* neglect is failing to look after someone or do something

negotiate *verb* (nig-**oh**-shi-ayt) to negotiate is to try to reach an agreement about something by discussing it **negotiation** *noun* negotiations are discussions where people have to try to reach an agreement about something **negotiator** *noun* one of the people involved in negotiations

neigh *verb* to make the sound of a horse

neighbour *noun* someone who lives next door or near to you **neighbouring** *adjective* the neighbouring house or town is the one next to where you live

neighbourhood *noun* the area you live in

neighbourly *adjective* someone is neighbourly when they are friendly and helpful to people who live near them

neither *determiner, pronoun* (**ny**-ther or **nee**-ther) not either • *Neither light was working.* • *Neither of them likes cabbage.*

neither *conjunction* **neither … nor …** not one thing and not the other • *I neither know nor care.*

neon *noun* (**nee**-on) neon is a gas that glows when electricity passes through it, used in street lighting and signs

nephew *noun* the son of a person's brother or sister

nerve *noun* **1.** a nerve is one of the fibres inside your body that carry messages to and from your brain, so that parts of your body can feel and move **2.** nerve is courage and calmness in a dangerous situation • *Don't lose your nerve.* **3.** (*informal*) nerve is cheek or rudeness • *He had the nerve to ask for more.* **to get on someone's nerves** is to irritate them **nerves** nervousness • *I always suffer from nerves before an exam.*

nervous *adjective* **1.** easily upset or agitated; timid **2.** to do with the nerves **nervously** *adverb* in a way that shows you are nervous **nervousness** *noun*

nest *noun* **1.** the place where a bird lays its eggs and feeds its young **2.** a warm place where some small animals live

nest *verb* birds or animals nest when they make or have a nest

nestle *verb* to nestle is to curl up comfortably

net *noun* **1.** net is material made of pieces of thread, cord or wire joined together in a criss-cross pattern with holes between **2.** a net is a piece of this material • *a fishing net* **3.** the net is the Internet

netball *noun* netball is a game in which two teams try to throw a ball through a high net hanging from a ring

nettle *noun* a wild plant with leaves that sting when you touch them

network *noun* **1.** a criss-cross arrangement of lines **2.** a system with many connections or parts, such as a railway or computer system

neuter *adjective* (**new**-ter) **1.** neither male nor female **2.** in some languages, belonging to the class of words that are neither masculine nor feminine
neuter *verb* (**new**-ter) to neuter an animal is to remove its sexual organs so that it cannot breed

neutral *adjective* (**new**-tral) **1.** not supporting either side in a war or quarrel **2.** not distinct or distinctive • *The room was painted in neutral colours.* **3.** a neutral gear is one that is not connected to the driving parts of an engine neutrality *noun* neutrality is not supporting either side in a war or quarrel

neutralize *verb* to neutralize something is to take away its use or effect This word can also be spelled **neutralise**.

neutron *noun* a particle of matter with no electric charge

never *adverb* at no time; not ever; not at all

nevertheless *conjunction, adverb* in spite of this; although that is a fact

new *adjective* **1.** not existing before; just bought, made or received • *Do you like my new shoes?* **2.** different or unfamiliar • *They've moved to a new area.* newly *adverb* recently newness *noun*

newcomer *noun* someone who has recently arrived in a place

new moon *noun* the moon at the beginning of its cycle, when it appears as a thin crescent

news *noun* **1.** news is new information about people or recent events • *I've got some good* news. **2.** news is also a broadcast report about important events

newsagent *noun* a shopkeeper who sells newspapers and magazines

newspaper *noun* **1.** a newspaper is set of large sheets of printed paper containing news reports and articles which is published daily or weekly **2.** newspaper is the paper these are printed on • *Wrap it in newspaper.*

newt *noun* a small animal rather like a lizard, that lives near or in water

next *adjective* the nearest; following immediately after
next *adverb* **1.** in the nearest place **2.** at the nearest time • *What comes next?*

nib *noun* the pointed metal part at the end of a pen

nibble *verb* to nibble something is to take small or gentle bites at it

nice *adjective* pleasant or kind nicely *adverb* in a nice way • *Ask me nicely and I might say yes.* niceness *noun*

nick *noun* a small cut or notch
nick *verb* to nick something is to make a small cut in it

nickel *noun* a silvery-white metal

nickname *noun* an informal name given to someone instead of their real name

nicotine *noun* (**nik**-o-teen) nicotine is a poisonous substance found in tobacco

niece *noun* the daughter of a person's brother or sister

night *noun* the time when it is dark, between sunset and sunrise

nightfall *noun* nightfall is the time when it becomes dark just after sunset

nightingale *noun* a small brown bird that sings sweetly

nightly *adjective* happening every night

nightmare *noun* a frightening or unpleasant dream nightmarish *adjective* terrifying

nil *noun* nothing • *We lost three-nil.*

nimble *adjective* moving quickly or easily nimbly *adverb*

a
b
c
d
e
f
g
h
i
j
k
l
m
n
o
p
q
r
s
t
u
v
w
x
y
z

nine *noun* the number 9

nineteen *noun* the number 19
nineteenth *adjective, noun* 19th

ninety *noun* nineties the number 90
ninetieth *adjective, noun* 90th

ninth *adjective, noun* the next after the eighth

nip *verb* nipping, nipped to nip someone is to pinch or bite them sharply
nip *noun* **1.** a quick pinch or bite **2.** a cold feeling • *There's a nip in the air.*

nipple *noun* one of the two small parts that stick out at the front of a person's chest

nit *noun* a louse or its egg

nitrogen *noun* (**ny**-tro-jen) nitrogen is a gas that makes up about four-fifths of the air

no *interjection* a word you use to refuse something or say that you don't agree
no *determiner, adverb* not any • *We have no money.* • *She is no better.*

nobility *noun* **1.** the nobility is the nobles or the aristocracy **2.** nobility is being noble

noble *adjective* nobler, noblest **1.** coming from the highest class in society **2.** having a good and generous nature • *He is a noble king.* **nobly** *adverb*
noble *noun* a person who comes from a noble family, for example a duke or an earl

nobleman or **noblewoman** *noun* noblemen or noblewomen a man or woman from the highest class in society

nobody *pronoun* no person; not anyone • *Nobody knows.*

nocturnal *adjective* (nok-**ter**-nal) happening or active at night • *Badgers are nocturnal animals.*

nod *verb* nodding, nodded to nod or nod your head, is to move your head up and down as a way of agreeing with someone

noise *noun* a loud sound, especially one that is unpleasant or unwanted

noisy *adjective* noisier, noisiest making a lot of noise **noisily** *adverb*

nomad *noun* (**noh**-mad) a member of a tribe that moves from place to place

nomadic *adjective* nomadic people move around from place to place

no man's land *noun* the land between two armies in a war

nominate *verb* to nominate someone is to suggest that they should be a candidate in an election or should be given a job or award **nomination** *noun* when someone is nominated for a job or award

none *pronoun* not any; not one • *None of us went.*

none *adverb* not at all • *He's none too pleased.*

nonetheless *conjunction, adverb* in spite of this; nevertheless

non-existent *adjective* not existing

non-fiction *noun* writing that is not fiction; books about real things and true events

nonsense *noun* **1.** nonsense is words that do not mean anything or make any sense **2.** nonsense is also absurd or silly ideas or behaviour **nonsensical** *adjective* not making any sense

non-stop *adverb, adjective* **1.** not stopping • *They talked non-stop all morning.* **2.** not stopping until the end of a journey • *a non-stop flight to Los Angeles*

noodles *plural noun* pasta made in thin strips, used in soups and stir-fries

noon *noun* twelve o'clock midday

no one *pronoun* no person; not anyone

noose *noun* a loop in a rope that gets smaller when the rope is pulled

nor *conjunction* and not • *She cannot do it; nor can I.*

normal *adjective* usual or ordinary • *It's normal to want a holiday.* normality *noun* a situation where things are normal

normally *adverb* **1**. usually • *The journey normally takes an hour.* **2**. in the usual way • *Just breathe normally.*

north *noun* **1**. north is the direction to the left of a person facing east **2**. north is also the part of a country or city that is in this direction
north *adjective, adverb* **1**. towards the north or in the north **2**. coming from the north • *a north wind*

north-east *noun, adjective, adverb* midway between north and east

northern *adjective* from or to do with the north

northerner *noun* someone who lives in the north of a country

northward or **northwards** *adjective, adverb* towards the north

north-west *noun, adjective, adverb* midway between north and west

nose *noun* **1**. the part of your face that you use for breathing and smelling **2**. the front part of something, especially a vehicle or aircraft
nose *verb* to nose forward or through is to move slowly forward • *The ship nosed through the ice.*

nostalgia *noun* (nos-**tal**-ja) you feel nostalgia when you fondly remember something that made you happy in the past
nostalgic *adjective* making you long for something in the past

nostril *noun* each of the two openings in your nose

nosy *adjective* nosier, nosiest *(informal)* always wanting to know other people's business nosiness *noun*

not *adverb* a word you use to change the meaning of something to its opposite

notable *adjective* remarkable or famous
notably *adverb* especially or remarkably

notch *noun* a small V-shaped cut or mark

note *noun* **1**. something you write down as a reminder or help **2**. a short letter **3**. a single sound in music **4**. a sound or tone that indicates something • *There was a note of anger in his voice.* **5**. a piece of paper money • *a five-pound note* to take note of something is to listen to it and understand it
note *verb* to note something is to pay attention to it or to write it down as a reminder or help

notebook *noun* a book in which you write things down

notepaper *noun* notepaper is paper for writing letters

nothing *noun* nothing is not anything

notice *noun* **1**. a notice is something written or printed and displayed for people to see **2**. to take notice of something is to pay attention to it • *It escaped my notice.* **3**. a warning that something is going to happen
notice *verb* to notice something is to see it or become aware of it

noticeable *adjective* easy to see or notice
noticeably *adverb*

noticeboard *noun* a board on which notices can be displayed

notion *noun* an idea, especially one that is vague or uncertain • *The notion that the earth is flat was disproved long ago.*

notorious *adjective* (noh-**tor**-i-us) well-known for doing something bad • *He was a notorious criminal.* notoriety *noun* being well-known for doing something bad
notoriously *adverb*

nougat *noun* (**noo**-gah) nougat is a chewy sweet made from nuts and sugar or honey

nought *noun* (nawt) the figure 0

noun *noun* a word that names a person or thing

nourish *verb* to nourish someone is to give them enough good food to keep them alive and well

nourishment *noun* nourishment is the food someone needs to keep them alive and well

novel *noun* a book containing one long story
novel *adjective* unusual • *What a novel idea.*

novelist *noun* (**nov**-el-ist) someone who writes novels

novelty *noun* novelties **1.** novelty is being new or unusual • *The novelty of living in a cave soon wore off.* **2.** a novelty is something new and unusual

November *noun* the eleventh month of the year

novice *noun* a beginner

now *adverb* **1.** at this time • *I am now living in Glasgow.* **2.** without any delay • *Do it now!*
now and again or now and then occasionally
now *conjunction* since or as • *I do remember, now you mention it.*
now *noun* this moment • *They should be home by now.*

nowadays *adverb* at the present time

nowhere *adverb* not anywhere; in no place or to no place

nozzle *noun* the part at the end of a hose or pipe from which liquid flows

nuclear *adjective* (**new**-kli-er) **1.** to do with a nucleus, especially of an atom **2.** using the energy that is created by the splitting of atoms • *nuclear weapons*

nucleus *noun* nuclei (**new**-kli-us) the central part of an atom or cell

nude *adjective* not wearing any clothes
nude *noun* a nude person, especially in a work of art **nudity** *noun* nudity is not wearing any clothes

nudge *verb* to nudge someone is to touch or push them with your elbow

nugget *noun* a rough lump of gold from the ground

nuisance *noun* an annoying person or thing

numb *adjective* part of your body is numb when you can't feel anything in it
numbness *noun*

number *noun* **1.** a symbol or word that tells you how many of something there are **2.** a quantity of people or things • *Do you know the number of bones in your body?* **3.** a person's number is their telephone number **4.** a song or piece of music
number *verb* **1.** to number things is to count them or mark them with numbers • *Please*

number the pages of your essay. **2.** to number a certain amount is to reach it • *The crowd numbered 10,000.*

numeracy *noun* numeracy is the ability to understand and work with numbers

numeral *noun* a symbol or figure that stands for a number

numerical *adjective* to do with numbers

numerous *adjective* many • *There are numerous kinds of cat.*

nun *noun* a member of a religious community of women

nurse *noun* a person trained to look after people who are ill or injured
nurse *verb* to nurse someone is to look after them when they are ill or injured

nursery *noun* nurseries a place where young children are looked after or play

nursery rhyme *noun* a simple poem or song that young children like

nursery school *noun* a school for very young children

nurture *verb* to nurture children is to look after them and educate them

nut *noun* **1.** a fruit with a hard shell **2.** the eatable part of this kind of fruit **3.** a hollow piece of metal for screwing on to a bolt
nutty *adjective* tasting of nuts or full of nuts

nutcrackers *plural noun* pincers for cracking the shells of nuts

nutmeg *noun* a hard seed that is made into a powder and used as a spice

nutrition *noun* (new-**trish**-on) nutrition is the food someone needs to keep them alive and well

nutritious *adjective* (new-**trish**-us) nutritious food helps you to grow and keep well

nuzzle *verb* to nuzzle someone is to rub gently against them with the nose, in the way that some animals do • *The kitten nuzzled her arm.*

nylon *noun* nylon is a lightweight synthetic cloth or fibre

nymph *noun* in myths, a young goddess who lives in trees or rivers or the sea

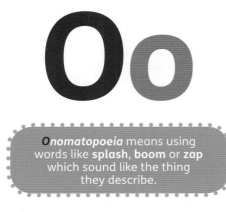

Oo

Onomatopoeia means using words like **splash**, **boom** or **zap** which sound like the thing they describe.

oak *noun* a large tree that produces seeds called acorns

oar *noun* a pole with a flat blade at one end, used for rowing a boat

oasis *noun* **oases** (oh-**ay**-sis) a fertile place with water and trees in a desert

oath *noun* **1.** a solemn promise **2.** a swear word

oats *plural noun* a cereal used to make food for humans and animals

obedient *adjective* doing what someone tells you to do; willing to obey **obedience** *noun* obedience is doing what you are told **obediently** *adverb*

obey *verb* **1.** to obey someone is to do what they tell you **2.** to obey a rule or law is to do what it says

object *noun* (**ob**-jikt) **1.** something that can be seen or touched **2.** the purpose of something **3.** *(in grammar)* the word naming the person or thing that the action of the verb affects, for example *him* in the sentence *I chased him*

object *verb* (ob-**jekt**) to object to something or someone is to say that you do not like them or do not agree with them

objection *noun* **1.** objection is objecting to something **2.** an objection is a reason for objecting

objective *noun* what you are trying to reach or do; an aim

obligation *noun* a duty

obligatory *adjective* something is obligatory when you must do it because of a rule or law • *Games are obligatory.*

oblige *verb* **1.** to oblige someone to do something is to force them to do it **2.** to oblige someone is to help and please them • *Will you oblige me by closing the window?*

oblong *noun* a four-sided shape with right angles that is longer than it is wide

oblong *adjective* having the shape of an oblong

obnoxious *adjective* really horrible

oboe *noun* (**oh**-boh) a high-pitched woodwind instrument **oboist** *noun* a person who plays the oboe

obscure *adjective* **1.** difficult to see or understand; very unclear **2.** not well-known **obscurity** *noun* obscurity is being not well-known

observant *adjective* quick at noticing things

observation *noun* **1.** observation is noticing or watching something carefully **2.** an observation is a comment or remark

observatory *noun* **observatories** (ob-**zerv**-a-ter-i) a building equipped with telescopes for looking at the stars or weather

observe *verb* **1.** to observe someone or something is to watch them carefully **2.** to observe something is to notice it **3.** to observe a law or custom is to obey it or keep it **observer** *noun* someone who watches something

obsessed *adjective* always thinking about something • *He is obsessed with his work.* **obsession** *noun* something that you think about too much

obsolete *adjective* not used any more; out of date

obstacle *noun* something that gets in your way or makes it difficult for you to do something

obstinate *adjective* not willing to change your ideas or ways, even though they may be wrong **obstinacy** *noun* obstinacy is being obstinate **obstinately** *adverb*

obstruct *verb* to obstruct someone or something is to stop them from getting

a
b
c
d
e
f
g
h
i
j
k
l
m
n
o
p
q
r
s
t
u
v
w
x
y
z

past or to hinder them **obstruction** *noun* something causing a blockage

obtain *verb* to obtain something is to get it or be given it **obtainable** *adjective* able to be bought or got

obtuse angle *noun* an angle of between 90 and 180 degrees

obvious *adjective* easy to see or understand

obviously *adverb* it's obvious that; clearly

occasion *noun* 1. the time when something happens • *On this occasion, we will not take any action.* 2. a special event • *The wedding was a marvellous occasion.*

occasional *adjective* happening from time to time, but not often and not regularly **occasionally** *adverb*

occupation *noun* 1. a person's occupation is their job or profession 2. the occupation of a country or territory is when an army captures it and stays there

occupy *verb* **occupies, occupying, occupied** 1. to occupy a place or building is to live in it 2. to occupy a space or position is to fill it 3. in a war, to occupy territory is to capture it and keep an army in it 4. to occupy someone is to keep them busy or interested

occur *verb* **occurring, occurred** 1. an event occurs when it happens or takes place • *An earthquake occurred on the island in 1953.* 2. something occurs to you when it suddenly comes into your mind

occurrence *noun* something that happens or exists

ocean *noun* 1. the ocean is the area of salt water surrounding the land of the earth 2. an ocean is a large part of this water, such as the Pacific Ocean

o'clock *adverb* used with numbers to show an exact hour • *Lunch is at one o'clock.*

octagon *noun* a flat shape with eight sides **octagonal** *adjective* having eight sides

octave *noun* 1. the interval between one musical note and the next note of the same name above or below it 2. these two notes played together

October *noun* the tenth month of the year

octopus *noun* **octopuses** a sea creature with eight arms (called *tentacles*)

The word **octopus** comes from a Greek word *oktopous*, which in turn comes from the words *okto* meaning 'eight' and *pous* meaning 'foot'.

odd *adjective* 1. strange or unusual 2. an odd number is one that cannot be divided by 2, such as 5 or 31 3. left over or spare • *I've got an odd sock.* 4. of various kinds; occasional • *He's doing odd jobs.* **oddity** *noun* something that is odd or strange

odds *plural noun* the chances that something will happen

odour *noun* a smell, usually an unpleasant one

of *preposition* 1. belonging to • *She is the mother of the child.* 2. coming from • *He is a native of Italy.* 3. about; concerning • *Is there any news of your father?* 4. from; out of • *The house is built of stone.*

off *adverb* 1. not on; away • *His hat blew off.* 2. not working or happening • *The heating is off.* • *The match is off because of snow.* 3. beginning to go bad • *I think the milk is off.*

off *preposition* 1. not on; away or down from • *He fell off his chair.* 2. not taking or wanting • *She is off her food.* 3. taken away from • *There is £5 off the normal price.*

offence *noun* 1. an offence is a crime or something illegal 2. offence is a feeling of annoyance or hurt **to cause offence** is to hurt someone's feelings **to take offence** is to be upset by what someone has said or done

offend *verb* 1. to offend someone is to hurt their feelings or be unpleasant to them 2. to offend is to break a law or do something wrong **offender** *noun* someone who breaks a law or does something wrong

offensive *adjective* 1. insulting or causing offence 2. used for attacking • *He was arrested for carrying an offensive weapon.* **offensively** *adverb*

offer *verb* 1. to offer something is to hold it out so that someone can take it if they want it 2. to offer to do something is to say that you are willing to do it 3. to offer a sum of money is to say how much you are willing to pay for something

offer *noun* **1.** the action of offering something • *Thank you for your offer of help.* **2.** an amount of money that you are willing to pay for something

offhand *adjective* **1.** said without much thought **2.** rude or abrupt

office *noun* **1.** a room or building where people work, often at desks **2.** a place where you can go for tickets, information or some other purpose • *a lost property office* **3.** an important job or position • *He was honoured to hold the office of President.*

officer *noun* **1.** someone who is in charge of other people, especially in the armed forces **2.** a policeman or policewoman

official *adjective* **1.** done or said by someone with authority **2.** connected with the job of someone in a position of authority • *The prime minister will make an official visit to Australia next month.* **officially** *adverb*

official *noun* someone who has power or makes decisions as part of their job

off-licence *noun* a shop with a licence to sell alcoholic drinks for people to take away

offside *adjective (in sport)* in a position which is not allowed by the rules

offspring *noun* offspring a child or young animal

often *adverb* many times; in many cases

ogre *noun* a cruel giant in stories

oil *noun* **1.** an oil is a thick slippery liquid that does not mix with water **2.** oil is a thick sticky liquid that is found underground and used to make fuel and to keep machinery working smoothly

oil *verb* to oil something is to put oil on it to make it work smoothly

oil painting *noun* a painting done using paints made with oil

oil rig *noun* a structure set up to support the equipment for drilling for oil

oil well *noun* a hole drilled in the ground or under the sea to get oil

oily *adjective* oilier, oiliest like oil or covered in oil

ointment *noun* a cream that you put on sore skin and cuts

OK *adverb, adjective (informal)* all right

old *adjective* **1.** not new; born or made a long time ago **2.** of a particular age • *I'm ten years old.* **3.** former or original • *I liked my old school better than the one I go to now.*

old age *noun* old age is the time when a person is old

old-fashioned *adjective* of a kind that was usual a long time ago; out of date

olive *noun* **1.** an evergreen tree with a small bitter fruit **2.** the black or green fruit of this tree, used for eating and to make olive oil

omelette *noun* (**om**-lit) a food consisting of eggs beaten together and fried

omen *noun* an event that some people see as a sign that something is going to happen

ominous *adjective* suggesting that trouble is coming • *There was an ominous rumble from inside the tunnel.* **ominously** *adverb*

omission *noun* something left out or not done

omit *verb* omitting, omitted to omit something is to leave it out • *Several names have been omitted from the list.*

omnivorous *adjective* an omnivorous animal is one that eats plants as well as meat

on *preposition* **1.** at or over the top or surface of something • *Sit on the floor.* **2.** at the time of • *Come on Monday.* **3.** about; concerning • *We went to a talk on snakes.* **4.** towards or near • *They advanced on the town.*

on *adverb* **1.** so as to be on something • *Put your hat on.* **2.** forwards • *Move on.* **3.** working; in action • *Is the heater on?*

once *adverb* **1.** at one time • *I once lived in Leeds.* **2.** one time only • *I've only met him once.*

once *conjunction* as soon as • *We can get out once I open this door.* **at once** immediately

one noun the smallest whole number, 1

one pronoun a person or thing on their own • *One of my friends is ill.* **one another** each other

one adjective single • *I have one packet left.*

oneself pronoun one's own self; yourself • *One should not always think of oneself.*

one-way adjective a one-way street is one where traffic is only allowed to go in one direction

onion noun a round vegetable with a strong flavour

online adjective, adverb connected to a computer

only adjective being the one person or thing of a kind • *He's the only person we can trust.*

only adverb no more than • *There are only three cakes.*

only conjunction but then; however • *I want to come, only I'm very busy.*

onomatopoeia (on-om-at-o-**pee**-a) noun forming or using words that sound like the thing they stand for, e.g. *cuckoo, plop, sizzle*

onto preposition to a position on • *They fell onto the floor.*

onward or **onwards** adverb forward or forwards

ooze verb oozes, oozing, oozed a thick liquid oozes when it flows out slowly • *Blood oozed from his wound.*

opaque adjective (oh-**payk**) something that is opaque doesn't allow light through and so can't be seen through

open adjective 1. allowing people or things to pass through; not shut • *The door is open.* • *The bottles need to be open.* 2. not enclosed • *There were miles of open land.* 3. not folded; spread out • *She greeted us with open arms.* 4. honest; not secret or secretive • *They were quite open about what they had done.* **in the open air** outdoors; not inside a building

open verb 1. to open something is to make it open 2. to open is to become open 3. a shop opens when it starts business for the day • *What time do you open?*

opener noun a device for opening a bottle or can

opening noun 1. a space or gap in something 2. the beginning of something

openly adverb to do something openly is to do it for all to see, not secretly

open-minded adjective ready to listen to other people's ideas and opinions; not having fixed ideas

opera noun a form of drama in which the characters sing all or most of the words, with an orchestra operatic adjective to do with opera

operate verb 1. to operate something is to make it work 2. to operate is to work or be in action 3. to operate on someone is to perform a surgical operation on them

operation noun 1. something done to a patient's body by a surgeon to remove or repair a part of it 2. a carefully planned activity to be in operation is to be working

operator noun someone who works something, especially a telephone switchboard or exchange

opinion noun what you think of something; a belief or judgement

opponent noun someone who is against you in a contest, war or argument

opportunity noun opportunities a good time or chance to do something

oppose verb to oppose someone or something is to be against them or disagree with them to be opposed to something is to disagree strongly with it • *We are opposed to the war.*

opposite adjective, adverb 1. on the other side; facing • *She lives on the opposite side of the road to me.* • *I'll sit opposite.* 2. completely different • *They went in opposite directions.*
opposite noun something that is completely different from something else • *'Happy' is the opposite of 'sad'.*

opposition noun opposition is opposing something the Opposition the chief political party opposing the one that has formed the government

oppress verb to oppress people is to govern them or treat them cruelly or unjustly oppression noun treating people cruelly or unjustly oppressor noun someone who treats people cruelly or unjustly

oppressive *adjective* **1**. harsh and cruel • *He was an oppressive ruler.* **2**. hot and tiring • *The weather can be very oppressive in July.*

opt *verb* to opt for something or to do something is to choose it **to opt out of something** is to decide not to join in with it

optical *adjective* to do with sight or the eyes **optically** *adverb* as far as sight or the eyes are concerned

optician *noun* (op-**tish**-an) someone who tests your eyesight and makes and sells glasses

optimist *noun* someone who usually expects things to turn out well **optimism** *noun* the feeling that things will turn out well

optimistic *adjective* expecting things to turn out well **optimistically** *adverb*

option *noun* **1**. one of the things that you can choose • *Your options are to travel by bus or by train.* **2**. the right to choose; choice • *You have the option of staying.*

optional *adjective* something is optional when you can choose whether to do it or not • *You have to study French, but German is optional.*

or *conjunction* used to show that there is a choice or alternative • *Do you want a cake or a biscuit?*

oral *adjective* **1**. spoken, not written **2**. to do with the mouth or using your mouth **orally** *adverb* by speaking or using your mouth • *Most medicine is taken orally.*

orange *noun* **1**. a round juicy fruit with thick reddish-yellow peel **2**. a reddish-yellow colour **orange** *adjective* reddish-yellow

orang-utan *noun* (o-rang-u-**tan**) a large kind of ape found in Borneo and Sumatra

orbit *noun* the curved path taken by something moving round a planet or other body in space **orbit** *verb* to orbit a planet or other body in space is to move round it

orchard *noun* a piece of ground with fruit trees

orchestra *noun* a group of musicians playing various instruments together **orchestral** *adjective* orchestral music is written to be played by an orchestra

orchid *noun* (**or**-kid) a type of brightly coloured flower

ordeal *noun* a difficult or unpleasant experience

order *noun* **1**. a command **2**. a request for something to be supplied • *The waiter took our order.* **3**. the way things are arranged • *The words are in alphabetical order.* **4**. obedience or good behaviour • *Can we have some order please?* **5**. tidiness or neatness **6**. a group of religious monks, priests or nuns **in order that** or **in order to** for the purpose of **to be out of order** is to be broken or not working **order** *verb* **1**. to order someone to do something is to tell them to do it **2**. to order something is to ask for it to be supplied to you

orderly *adjective* **1**. arranged tidily or well; methodical **2**. well-behaved; obedient

ordinary *adjective* normal or usual; not special **ordinarily** *adverb* normally or usually

ore *noun* rock with metal in it, such as iron ore

organ *noun* **1**. a musical instrument from which sounds are produced by air forced through pipes, played by keys and pedals **2**. a part of your body which does a particular job, for example the liver which cleans the blood

organic *adjective* **1**. organic food is grown or produced without using artificial chemicals **2**. made by or found in living things

organism *noun* a living animal or plant

organist *noun* someone who plays the organ

organization *noun* **1**. an organization is a group of people who work together to do something **2**. organization is planning or arranging things This word can also be spelled **organisation**.

organize *verb* **1**. to organize people is to get them together to do something **2**. to organize something is to plan or arrange it • *We organized a picnic.* **3**. to organize things is to put them in order **organizer** *noun* someone who organizes something This word can also be spelled **organise**.

oriental *adjective* to do with the countries east of the Mediterranean Sea, especially China and Japan

origin *noun* the start of something; the point where something began • *a book about the origins of life on earth*

original *adjective* **1**. existing from the start; earliest • *They were the original inhabitants.* **2**. new; not a copy or an imitation • *It is an original design.* **3**. producing new ideas; inventive • *She was an original thinker.* **originality** *noun* originality is being original or inventive **originally** *adverb* in the beginning

originate *verb* **1**. to originate something is to create it or develop it **2**. to originate is to start in a certain way • *Supermarkets originated in America.*

ornament *noun* an object you wear or display as a decoration **ornamental** *adjective* used to decorate something

ornithology *noun* (or-ni-**thol**-o-ji) ornithology is the study of birds **ornithological** *adjective* to do with birds **ornithologist** *noun* a person who studies birds

orphan *noun* a child whose parents are dead

orphanage *noun* a home for orphans

orthodox *adjective* having beliefs that are correct or generally accepted

ostrich *noun* a large long-legged bird that can run fast but cannot fly

other *determiner* not the same as this; different • *Play some other tune.* • *Try the other shoe.* **every other day** every second day, for example Monday, Wednesday and Friday **the other day** or **the other week** a few days or weeks ago

other *noun* **others** the other person or thing • *Where are the others?*

otherwise *adverb* **1**. if you do not; if things happen differently • *Write it down, otherwise you'll forget it.* **2**. in other ways • *It rained a lot but otherwise the holiday was good.*

otter *noun* an animal with thick fur, webbed feet and a flat tail, that lives near water

ought *verb* used with other words to show **1**. what you should or must do • *You ought to do your music practice.* **2**. what is likely to happen • *With all these dark clouds it ought to rain.*

ounce *noun* a unit of weight equal to ¹⁄₁₆ of a pound or about 28 grams

our *determiner* belonging to us • *This is our house.*

ours *pronoun* belonging to us • *This house is ours.*

ourselves *pronoun* us and nobody else, used to refer back to the subject of a verb • *We have hurt ourselves.* **by ourselves** on our own; alone • *We did the work all by ourselves.*

out *adverb* **1**. away from a place or not in it; not at home **2**. into the open or outdoors • *Are you going out today?* **3**. not burning or working • *The fire has gone out.* **4**. loudly • *She cried out.* **5**. dismissed from a game • *Another batsman is out.* **to be out of something** is to have no more of it left **out of date** old-fashioned; not used any more **out of doors** in the open air **out of the way** remote or distant

outback *noun* the remote inland areas of Australia

outbreak *noun* the sudden start of a disease, war or show of anger

outburst *noun* the sudden occurrence of anger or laughter

outcast *noun* someone who has been rejected by family, friends or society

outcome *noun* the result of what happens or has happened

outcry *noun* **outcries** a strong protest from many people • *There was an outcry over the rise in bus fares.*

outdated *adjective* out of date

outdoor *adjective* done or used outside • *You'll need your outdoor clothes.*

outdoors *adverb* in the open air • *It is cold outdoors.*

outer *adjective* nearer the outside; external

outer space *noun* outer space is the universe beyond the earth's atmosphere

outfit *noun* a set of clothes you wear together

outgrow *verb* outgrowing, outgrew, outgrown to outgrow something such as clothes or a habit is to grow too big or too old for them

outing *noun* a trip or short journey you make for pleasure

outlaw *noun* a robber or bandit who is hiding to avoid being caught and is not protected by the law
outlaw *verb* to outlaw something is to make it illegal

outlet *noun* 1. a way for something to get out • *The tank has an outlet at the bottom.* 2. a place to sell goods • *We need to find fresh outlets for our products.*

outline *noun* a line round the outside of something; a line showing the shape of a thing
outline *verb* to outline something is to draw a line round it to show its shape

outlook *noun* 1. a person's outlook is the way that they look at and think about things • *She has a positive outlook on life.* 2. what seems likely to happen in the future • *The outlook is bright.*

outnumber *verb* to outnumber something else is to be greater in number than it

outpatient *noun* a patient who visits a hospital for treatment but does not stay there overnight

output *noun* 1. the amount produced, especially by a factory or business 2. information produced by a computer
output *verb* outputting, output to output information is to get it from a computer

outrage *noun* 1. outrage is the anger you feel when something shocking happens 2. an outrage is something very shocking or cruel
outrage *verb* to outrage someone is to make them very shocked and angry

outrageous *adjective* shocking or dreadful

outright *adverb* 1. completely • *We won outright.* 2. all at once; in one go • *They were able to buy their house outright.*

outside *noun* the outer side or surface of a thing
outside *adjective* 1. on or coming from the outside 2. slight or remote • *There is an outside chance of snow.*
outside *adverb, preposition* on or to the outside of something • *Go outside.* • *It's outside the house.*

outsider *noun* 1. someone who is not a member of a particular group of people 2. a horse or person that people think has no chance of winning a race or contest

outskirts *plural noun* the areas on the edge of of a town or city

outspoken *adjective* speaking frankly even though it might offend people

outstanding *adjective* 1. extremely good or distinguished • *She is an outstanding athlete.* 2. not yet dealt with • *What are your outstanding debts?*

outward *adjective* 1. going outwards 2. on the outside

outwardly *adverb* on the outside; for people to see • *They were outwardly calm.*

outwards *adverb* towards the outside

outwit *verb* outwitting, outwitted to outwit someone is to deceive or defeat them by being more clever

oval *adjective* shaped like an egg
oval *noun* an oval shape

oven *noun* a closed space, often part of a cooker, in which things are cooked or heated

over *adverb* 1. down or sideways; out and down from the top or edge • *He fell over.* 2. across to a place • *We walked over to the house.* 3. so that a different side shows • *Turn the sheet over.* 4. finished • *The lesson is over.* 5. left or remaining • *There are a few apples over.* 6. through or thoroughly • *Think it over.*
over and over repeatedly; many times
over *preposition* 1. above or covering • *There's a light over the door.* 2. across • *They ran over the road.* 3. more than • *The house is over a mile away.* 4. concerning; about • *They quarrelled over money.* 5. during • *We can talk over dinner.*

over *noun* in cricket, a series of six balls bowled by one person

overall *adjective, adverb* including everything; total • *What is the overall cost?*

overalls *plural noun* clothes that you wear over your other clothes to protect them when you are working

overboard *adverb* to fall or jump overboard is to go over the side of a boat into the water

overcast *adjective* covered with cloud

overcoat *noun* a warm outdoor coat

overcome *verb* overcoming, overcame, overcome **1.** to overcome a problem or difficulty is to succeed in dealing with it or controlling it **2.** to be overcome by something is to become helpless from it • *She was overcome by the fumes.*

overdose *noun* too large a dose of a drug or medicine

overdue *adjective* something is overdue when it is later than it should be

overflow *verb* to overflow is to flow over the edges or limits of something

overgrown *adjective* a place is overgrown when it is thickly covered with weeds

overhaul *verb* to overhaul a machine or vehicle is to check it thoroughly and repair it if necessary

overhead *adjective, adverb* above your head; in the sky

overhear *verb* to overhear something is to hear it accidentally or without the speaker knowing

overlap *verb* overlapping, overlapped one thing overlaps another when it lies across part of it

overlook *verb* **1.** to overlook something is not to notice it **2.** to overlook a mistake or offence is not to punish it **3.** to overlook a place is to have a view over it • *The hotel overlooks the sea.*

overnight *adverb, adjective* for or during a night • *We stayed overnight in a hotel.* • *There will be an overnight stop in Paris.*

overpower *verb* to overpower someone is to defeat them because you are stronger
overpowering *adjective* very strong

overrun *verb* overrunning, overran, overrun **1.** to overrun an area is to spread harmfully over it • *The place is overrun with mice.* **2.** something overruns when it goes on longer than it should

overseas *adverb* abroad • *They travelled overseas.*

overseas *adjective* from abroad; foreign • *overseas students*

oversight *noun* a mistake you make by not noticing something

oversleep *verb* oversleeping, overslept to sleep longer than you meant to

overtake *verb* overtaking, overtook, overtaken to overtake a moving vehicle or person is to move past them in the same direction

overthrow *verb* overthrowing, overthrew, overthrown to overthrow a government is to remove it from power by force

overthrow *noun* the overthrow of a government is when it is forced out of power

overtime *noun* time someone spends working outside their normal hours

overture *noun* a piece of music played at the start of a concert, opera or ballet

overturn *verb* **1.** to overturn something is to make it turn over or fall over **2.** to overturn is to turn over

overweight *adjective* too heavy

overwhelm *verb* **1.** to overwhelm someone is to have a very strong effect on them • *I was overwhelmed by everyone's kindness.* **2.** to overwhelm someone is to defeat them completely

owe *verb* **1.** to owe something, especially money, is to have a duty to pay or give it to someone • *I owe you a pound.* **2.** to owe something to someone is to have it thanks to them • *They owed their lives to the pilot's skill.*
owing to something because of it • *The train was late owing to leaves on the line.*

owl *noun* a bird of prey with large eyes and a short beak, which hunts at night

own *adjective* belonging to yourself or itself **on your own** by yourself; alone • *I did it all on my own.* • *I had to sit on my own.*
own *verb* to own something is to have it as your property **to own up to something** *(informal)* is to admit that you did it

owner *noun* the person who owns something **ownership** *noun* ownership is owning something

ox *noun* **oxen** a male animal of the cow family, used for pulling loads

oxygen *noun* oxygen is one of the gases in the air that people need to stay alive

oyster *noun* a kind of shellfish whose shell sometimes contains a pearl

ozone *noun* ozone is a strong-smelling gas that is a form of oxygen

ozone layer *noun* a layer of ozone high in the atmosphere, which protects the earth from the sun's radiation

Pp

Plurals do not have apostrophes in them.

p short for **penny** or **pence**

pace *noun* **1.** one step in walking, marching or running **2.** speed • *He set a fast pace.*
pace *verb* to pace is to walk up and down with slow or regular steps

pacifist *noun* (**pas**-i-fist) someone who believes that war is always wrong **pacifism** *noun* the belief that war is always wrong

pacify *verb* **pacifies, pacifying, pacified** (**pas**-i-fy) to pacify someone is to calm them down

pack *noun* **1.** a collection of things wrapped or tied together **2.** a set of playing cards **3.** a strong bag carried on your back **4.** a group of hounds, wolves or other animals **5.** a group of people, especially a group of Brownies or Cub Scouts
pack *verb* **1.** to pack a suitcase or bag is to put things in it so that you can take them somewhere **2.** to pack a room or building is to fill it • *The hall was packed.*

package *noun* a parcel or packet

package holiday *noun* a holiday in which all the travel and accommodation is arranged and included in the price

packet *noun* a small parcel

pad[1] *noun* **1.** a number of sheets of blank or lined paper joined together along one edge **2.** a thick piece of soft material used to protect something or to make it more comfortable **3.** a flat surface from which helicopters take off or rockets are launched

pad[1] *verb* **padding**, **padded** to pad something is to put a piece of soft material on it or into it in order to protect it or to make it more comfortable

pad[2] *verb* **padding**, **padded** to pad is to walk softly

padding *noun* padding is soft material used to protect something or make it more comfortable

paddle *verb* **1.** to paddle is to walk about with bare feet in shallow water **2.** to paddle a boat is to move it along with a short oar

paddle *noun* **1.** a time spent paddling in water **2.** a short oar with a broad blade

paddock *noun* a small field for keeping horses

paddy *noun* **paddies** a field where rice is grown

padlock *noun* a lock with a metal loop that you can use to fasten a gate or lock a bicycle

page[1] *noun* a piece of paper that is part of a book or newspaper; one side of this piece of paper

page[2] *noun* a boy who acts as an attendant or runs errands

pageant *noun* (**paj**-ent) **1.** a play or entertainment about historical events and people **2.** a procession of people in costume **pageantry** *noun* pageantry is elaborate display that is part of a ceremony or procession

pagoda *noun* (pa-**goh**-da) a Buddhist tower or Hindu temple in the Far East

pail *noun* a bucket

pain *noun* **1.** pain or a pain is an unpleasant feeling caused by injury or disease • *Are you in pain?* **2.** pain is also mental suffering **to take pains** is to make a careful effort or take trouble over something

painful *adjective* causing you pain • *My ankle is too painful to walk on.* **painfully** *adverb* to be (for example) painfully thin or painfully slow is to be extremely thin or slow

painstaking *adjective* making a careful effort

paint *noun* a liquid substance put on something to colour or cover it

paint *verb* **1.** to paint something is to put paint on it **2.** to paint a picture is to make it with paints **3.** to paint someone or something is to make a picture of them using paint

paintbrush *noun* a brush used in painting

painter *noun* **1.** an artist who paints pictures **2.** a person whose job is painting walls and houses

painting *noun* **1.** painting is using paints to make a picture • *She likes painting.* **2.** a painting is a painted picture

pair *noun* **1.** two things or people that go together or are the same kind • *a pair of shoes* **2.** something made of two parts joined together • *a pair of scissors*

palace *noun* a large and splendid house where a king or queen or other important person lives

palate *noun* (**pal**-at) the roof of your mouth

pale *adjective* **1.** almost white • *a pale face* **2.** not bright in colour; faint • *pale blue* **paleness** *noun*

palette *noun* (**pal**-it) a board on which an artist mixes colours

pallid *adjective* pale, especially because of illness

palm *noun* **1.** the inner part of your hand, between your fingers and wrist **2.** a tropical tree with large leaves and no branches

paltry *adjective* not very much or not very valuable

pamper *verb* to pamper someone is to make them feel comfortable and let them have whatever they want

pamphlet *noun* a thin book with a paper cover

> The word **pamphlet** comes from *Pamphilet*, the name of a 12th-century Latin love poem about someone called Pamphilus.

pan *noun* a pot or dish with a flat base, used for cooking

pancake *noun* a flat round cake of batter fried on both sides

panda *noun* a large black and white bear-like animal found in China

pandemonium *noun* you say there is pandemonium when there is a loud noise or disturbance

pane *noun* a sheet of glass in a window

panel *noun* **1.** a long flat piece of wood, metal or other material that is part of a door, wall or piece of furniture **2.** a group of people chosen to judge a competition or take part in a television quiz

pang *noun* a sudden feeling of pain or strong emotion

panic *noun* panic is sudden fear that makes you behave wildly **panicky** *adjective* feeling panic
panic *verb* **panicking**, **panicked** to panic is to be overcome with fear or anxiety and behave wildly

panorama *noun* a view or picture of a wide area

pansy *noun* **pansies** a small brightly-coloured garden flower

pant *verb* you pant when you take short quick breaths after running or working hard

panther *noun* a leopard

pantomime *noun* a Christmas show with dancing and songs, based on a fairy tale

pantry *noun* **pantries** a cupboard or small room for storing food

pants *plural noun* **1.** (*informal*) underpants or knickers **2.** (*in America*) trousers

paper *noun* **1.** paper is a thin substance made in sheets and used for writing or printing or drawing on or for wrapping things **2.** a paper is a newspaper
paper *verb* to paper a wall or room is to cover it with wallpaper

paperback *noun* a book with a paper cover

papier mâché *noun* (pap-yay **mash**-ay) papier mâché is a mixture of paper pulp and glue you use to make models or ornaments

papyrus *noun* **papyri** (pa-**py**-rus) papyrus is a kind of paper made from the stems of reeds, used in ancient Egypt

parable *noun* a story told to teach people something, especially one of the stories told by Jesus Christ

parachute *noun* an umbrella-shaped device on which people or things can float slowly down to the ground from an aircraft **parachutist** *noun* someone who uses a parachute

parade *noun* **1.** a line of people or vehicles moving forward through a place as a celebration **2.** soldiers are on parade when they assemble for an inspection or drill
parade *verb* **1.** to parade is to move forward through a place as a celebration **2.** soldiers parade when they assemble for an inspection or drill

paradise *noun* **1.** paradise is heaven or, in the Bible, the Garden of Eden **2.** you can describe a wonderful or perfect place as a paradise

paraffin *noun* paraffin is a kind of oil used as fuel

paragraph *noun* one of the group of sentences that a piece of writing is divided into, beginning on a new line

parallel *adjective* parallel lines are lines that are the same distance apart for their whole length, like railway lines

parallelogram *noun* a four-sided figure with its opposite sides parallel to each other and equal in length

paralyse *verb* to paralyse someone is to make them unable to feel anything or to move

paralysis *noun* (pa-**ral**-i-sis) paralysis is being unable to move or feel anything

parapet *noun* a low wall along the edge of a balcony, bridge or roof

parasite *noun* an animal or plant that lives in or on another and gets its food from it **parasitic** *adjective* a parasitic animal or plant lives as a parasite on another

parasol *noun* a lightweight umbrella you use to shade yourself from the sun

paratroops *plural noun* troops trained to be dropped from aircraft by parachute **paratrooper** *noun* a soldier in the paratroops

parcel *noun* something wrapped up in paper for sending in the post

parched *adjective* very dry or thirsty

parchment *noun* parchment is a kind of heavy paper originally made from animal skins

pardon *verb* to pardon someone is to forgive or excuse them

pardon *noun* 1. forgiveness; when someone is pardoned 2. used as an exclamation to mean 'I didn't hear or understand what you said' or 'I apologize'

parent *noun* your parents are your father and mother **parental** *adjective* to do with parents

parish *noun* a district that has its own church **parishoner** *noun* a person who regularly goes to a particular church

park *noun* a large area with grass and trees, for public use

park *verb* to park a vehicle is to leave it somewhere for a time

parliament *noun* the group of people that make a country's laws **parliamentary** *adjective* to do with a parliament

parole *noun* (pa-**rohl**) parole is letting someone out of prison before they have finished their sentence, on condition that they behave well • *He was on parole.*

parrot *noun* a brightly-coloured bird with a curved beak, that can learn to repeat words or sounds

parsley *noun* parsley is a plant with crinkled green leaves used to flavour and decorate food

parsnip *noun* a pale yellow vegetable

parson *noun* a member of the Christian clergy, especially a vicar

part *noun* 1. some but not all of a thing or a number of things; anything that belongs to something bigger 2. the character played by an actor or actress; the words spoken by a character in a play

part *verb* 1. to part people or things is to separate them or divide them 2. to part is to separate 3. to part hair is to divide it so that it goes in two different directions **to part with something** is to give it away or get rid of it

partial *adjective* 1. not complete or total • *a partial eclipse of the sun* 2. unfairly showing more support for one person or side than another **partially** *adverb* partly or not completely

participate *verb* to participate in something is to take part in it **participant** *noun* someone who takes part in something **participation** *noun* taking part in something

participle *noun* a word formed from a verb and used as part of the verb or as an adjective, for example *going, gone* or *sailed, sailing*

particle *noun* a very small piece or amount

particular *adjective* 1. only this one and no other • *Are you looking for a particular book?* 2. fussy; hard to please • *He is very particular about his clothes.* **in particular** especially;

chiefly **particularly** *adverb* you can say something is (for example) particularly good or useful when it is especially good or useful

parting *noun* **1**. leaving or separation **2**. the line where hair is combed in different directions

partition *noun* a thin wall that divides a space into separate areas

partly *adverb* not completely; in some ways

partner *noun* **1**. one of a pair of people who do something together, especially dancing, running a business or playing a game **2**. someone's partner is the person they are married to or live with **partnership** *noun* partnership is being partners

part of speech *noun* each of the groups (also called **word classes**) into which words can be divided in grammar: noun, adjective, verb, pronoun, adverb, preposition, conjunction, determiner

partridge *noun* a bird with brown feathers that some people shoot as a sport

part-time *adjective, adverb* working for only some of the normal hours

party *noun* **parties** **1**. a time when people get together to enjoy themselves **2**. a group of people working or travelling together • *a search party* **3**. an organized group of people with similar political beliefs • *the Labour Party*

pass *verb* **1**. to pass something or someone is to go past them **2**. to pass in a certain direction is to move or go that way • *They passed over the bridge.* **3**. to pass something to someone is to give it or hand it to them • *Can you pass the butter, please?* **4**. to pass an examination is to be successful in it **5**. to pass time is to use time doing something **6**. to pass is to finish or no longer be there • *His opportunity passed.* **7**. to pass a law or rule is to approve or accept it

pass *noun* **1**. when a ball is kicked, hit or thrown from one player to another in a game **2**. a success in an examination **3**. a card or ticket that allows you to go in or out of a place

passage *noun* **1**. a corridor or narrow space between two walls **2**. a section of a piece of writing or music **3**. a journey by sea or air **4**. passing • *the passage of time*

passageway *noun* a passage or way through, especially between buildings

passenger *noun* someone who is driven in a car or travels by public transport

passer-by *noun* **passers-by** someone who happens to be going past when something happens

passion *noun* passion is strong feeling or emotion

passionate *adjective* full of passion or strong feeling **passionately** *adverb*

passive *adjective* not active; not resisting or fighting against something **passively** *adverb*

Passover *noun* Passover is a Jewish religious festival, celebrating the escape of the ancient Jews from slavery in Egypt

passport *noun* an official document that allows you to travel abroad

password *noun* a secret word or phrase that you need to know to be allowed to go somewhere or to use a computer, interface or system

past *noun* **1**. the time that has gone by • *Try to forget the past.* **2**. the form of a verb used to describe an action that happened at a time before now, for example *came* in the sentence *My uncle came to visit us*
past *adjective* of the time gone by • *He was thinking about his past achievements.*
past *preposition* **1**. beyond • *Go past the school and turn right.* **2**. later than • *It is past midnight.*

pasta *noun* pasta is a food made as a dried paste of flour, water and often eggs, formed into various shapes

paste *noun* a soft and moist or gluey substance
paste *verb* to paste something is to stick it to a surface with paste

pastel *noun* **1**. a crayon that is like a slightly greasy chalk **2**. a light delicate colour

pasteurize *verb* (**pahs**-cher-ryz) to pasteurize milk is to purify it by heating and then cooling it **pasteurization** *noun* the process of pasteurizing milk This word can also be spelled **pasteurise**.

pastime *noun* something you do to pass time pleasantly; a hobby

past participle *noun* a form of a verb used after *has, have, had, was, were,* to describe an action that happened at a time before now, for example *done, overtaken* and *written*

pastry *noun* pastries **1.** pastry is dough made from flour, fat and water rolled flat and baked **2.** a pastry is a cake made from this dough

pasture *noun* land covered with grass where cattle, sheep or horses can feed

pasty[1] *noun* pasties (**pas**-ti) a small meat or vegetable pie

pasty[2] *adjective* pastier, pastiest (**pay**-sti) looking pale and unhealthy

pat *verb* patting, patted to pat something or someone is to tap them gently with your open hand
pat *noun* a patting movement or sound

patch *noun* **1.** a piece of material put over a hole or damaged place **2.** an area that is different from its surroundings • *We have a black cat with a white patch on its chest.* **3.** a small area of land **4.** a small piece of something • *There are patches of ice on the road.*
patch *verb* to patch something is to put a piece of material on it to repair it to patch something up is to repair it roughly

patchwork *noun* patchwork is small pieces of different cloth sewn together

patchy *adjective* patchier, patchiest occurring in some areas but not others; uneven • *There may be some patchy rain.*

paternal *adjective* to do with a father or like a father

path *noun* **1.** a narrow way to walk or ride along **2.** the line along which something moves • *the path of the meteor*

pathetic *adjective* **1.** sad and pitiful **2.** sadly or comically weak or useless • *He made a pathetic attempt to climb the tree.* pathetically *adverb*

patience *noun* (**pay**-shens) patience is the ability to stay calm, especially when you have to wait for a long time

patient *adjective* (**pay**-shent) **1.** able to wait for a long time without getting anxious or angry **2.** able to bear pain or trouble patiently *adverb*

patient *noun* (**pay**-shent) a person who is getting treatment from a doctor or dentist

patio *noun* patios (**pat**-i-oh) a paved area beside a house

> The word **patio** is a Spanish word and in Spanish it means 'a courtyard'.

patriot *noun* (**pay**-tri-ot or **pat**-ri-ot) someone who loves and supports their country patriotic *adjective* loyal to your country patriotism *noun* patriotism is loving and supporting your country

patrol *verb* patrolling, patrolled to walk or travel regularly round a place or a thing to guard it and make sure it is secure
patrol *noun* **1.** a group of people or vehicles patrolling a place **2.** a group of Scouts or Guides to be on patrol is to be patrolling a place

patron *noun* (**pay**-tron) **1.** someone who supports a person or cause with money or encouragement **2.** a regular customer of a shop or business

patter *noun* a series of light tapping sounds
patter *verb* to patter is to make light tapping sounds • *The rain was pattering on the glass roof.*

pattern *noun* **1.** a decorative arrangement of lines or shapes **2.** a thing that you copy so that you can make something, such as a piece of clothing

pause *noun* a short stop before continuing with something
pause *verb* **1.** to pause to stop for a short time before continuing with something **2.** to pause (for example) a television programme is to make it stop for a short time

pave *verb* to pave a road or path is to put a hard surface on it

pavement *noun* a path with a hard surface, along the side of a street

pavilion *noun* a building at a sports ground for players and spectators to use

paw *noun* an animal's foot
paw *verb* an animal paws something when it touches it with its paw

pawn *noun* one of the sixteen pieces in chess that are at the front on each side and are the least valuable

pawn *verb* to pawn something is to leave it with a pawnbroker in exchange for money

pawnbroker *noun* someone who lends money in return for objects which are later sold if the money is not paid back

pay *verb* paying, paid **1.** to pay for something is to give money in return for it • *Have you paid for your lunch?* **2.** to pay someone is to give them money for something they have done • *Wash my car and I'll pay you £5.* **3.** to pay is to be profitable or worthwhile • *It pays to be honest.* **4.** to pay (for example) attention or a compliment is to give someone your attention or a compliment **5.** to pay for something you have done wrong is to suffer for it • *I'll make you pay for this!* to pay someone back is to pay money that you owe them

pay *noun* pay is the money you earn when you work

payment *noun* **1.** payment is when you pay someone or are paid for something **2.** a payment is money you pay

PC short for **personal computer, police constable**

PE short for **physical education**

pea *noun* a small round green seed of a climbing plant, growing inside a pod and used as a vegetable

peace *noun* **1.** peace is a time when there is no war or violence • *At last the country was at peace.* **2.** peace is also quietness and calm

peaceful *adjective* **1.** quiet and calm **2.** not involving violence peacefully *adverb*

peach *noun* a soft round juicy fruit with a slightly furry skin and a large stone

peacock *noun* A peacock is a large male bird with a long brightly coloured tail that it can spread out like a fan. The female is called a *peahen.*

peak *noun* **1.** the top of a mountain **2.** the highest or best point of something • *Traffic reaches its peak at 5 o'clock.* **3.** the part of a cap that sticks out in front peaked *adjective* a peaked hat or cap is one with a peak

peal *verb* bells peal when they make a loud ringing sound

peal *noun* a loud ringing sound made by bells

peanut *noun* a small round nut that grows in a pod in the ground

pear *noun* a juicy fruit that gets narrower near the stalk

pearl *noun* a small shiny white ball found in some oysters and used as a jewel

peasant *noun* a person who works on the land, especially in poor areas of the world or in the Middle Ages peasantry *noun* the peasants of a region or country

peat *noun* peat is rotted plant material that can be dug out of the ground and used as fuel or fertilizer

pebble *noun* a small round stone found on the beach pebbly *adjective* a pebbly beach is one with lots of pebbles

peck *verb* when a bird pecks something, it bites it or eats it with its beak

peck *noun* a short sharp bite with a bird's beak

peckish *adjective* (informal) slightly hungry

peculiar *adjective* strange or unusual to be peculiar to someone or something is to belong to a particular people or place • *This species of bird is peculiar to Asia.*

pedal *noun* a lever that you press with your foot to operate a bicycle, car or machine or to play some musical instruments

pedal *verb* pedalling, pedalled to pedal is to push or turn the pedals of a bicycle

pedestal *noun* the base that supports a statue or pillar

pedestrian *noun* someone who is walking in the street

pedigree *noun* a list of a person's or animal's ancestors, especially to show how well an animal has been bred

peel *noun* the skin of some fruit and vegetables

peel *verb* **1.** to peel a piece of fruit or a vegetable is to remove the peel or covering from it **2.** to peel is to lose a covering or skin • *The paint on the walls was peeling.*

peep *verb* to peep is to look quickly or secretly or through a narrow opening

peep *noun* a quick look

peer[1] *verb* to peer at something or someone is to look at them closely or with difficulty

peer[2] *noun* **1.** a nobleman or noblewoman **2.** your peers are the people who are the same age as you

peg *noun* a clip for fixing things in place or for hanging things on

peg *verb* **pegging**, **pegged** to peg something is to fix it with pegs

pelican *noun* a large bird with a pouch in its long beak for storing fish

pellet *noun* a tiny ball of metal, food, wet paper or other substance

pelt[1] *verb* **1.** to pelt someone with things is to throw a lot of things at them **2.** it pelts down when it is raining very hard

pelt[2] *noun* an animal skin, especially with the fur or hair still on it

pen[1] *noun* a device with a metal point for writing with ink

pen[2] *noun* an enclosure for cattle or other animals

penalize *verb* **1.** to penalize someone is to punish them **2.** in a game, to penalize someone is to award a penalty against them This word can also be spelled **penalise**.

penalty *noun* **penalties** **1.** a punishment **2.** a point or advantage given to one side in a game when a member of the other side breaks a rule

pence *plural noun* pennies

pencil *noun* a device for drawing or writing, made of a thin stick of graphite or coloured chalk inside a cylinder of wood

pendulum *noun* a weight hung at the end of a rod so that it swings to and fro, especially to keep a clock working

penetrate *verb* to penetrate something is to find a way through it or into it
penetration *noun* penetrating something

penfriend *noun* someone in another country you write to, usually without meeting them

penguin *noun* an Antarctic sea bird that cannot fly but uses its wings as flippers for swimming

penicillin *noun* penicillin is a drug that kills bacteria, used to cure infections

peninsula *noun* a long piece of land that is almost surrounded by water

penis *noun* the part of the body with which a male person or animal urinates and has sexual intercourse

penknife *noun* **penknives** a small folding knife

penniless *adjective* having no money; very poor

penny *noun* **pennies** or **pence** a British coin worth a hundredth of a pound

pension *noun* an income of regular payments made to someone who has retired
pensioner *noun* someone who is receiving a pension

pentagon *noun* a flat shape with five sides

pentathlon *noun* (pent-**ath**-lon) a sports competition that has five different events

people *plural noun* **1.** people are human beings **2.** the people of a particular country or area are the men, women and children who live there

people *noun* a people is a community or nation • *They are a peaceful people.*

pepper *noun* **1.** pepper is a hot-tasting powder used to flavour food **2.** a pepper is a bright green, red or yellow vegetable

peppermint *noun* **1.** peppermint is a kind of mint used for flavouring **2.** a peppermint is a sweet flavoured with this mint

per *preposition* for each • *The charge is £2 per person.*

perceive *verb* to perceive something is to see or notice it or understand it

per cent *adverb* for every hundred • *We pay interest at 5 per cent (5%).* • *Fifty per cent of the pupils walk to school.*

percentage *noun* an amount or rate expressed as a proportion of 100

perceptible *adjective* able to be seen or noticed

perception *noun* perception is the ability to see, notice or understand something

perceptive *adjective* quick to notice or understand things

perch[1] *noun* a place where a bird sits or rests
perch[1] *verb* to perch is to sit or stand on the edge of something or on something small

perch[2] *noun* perch a freshwater fish used for food

percussion *noun* percussion is musical instruments that you play by hitting them or shaking them, such as drums and cymbals
percussionist *noun* someone who plays percussion instruments

perennial *adjective* lasting or occurring for many years
perennial *noun* a plant that lives for many years

perfect *adjective* (**per**-fikt) **1.** so good that it cannot be made any better **2.** complete • *The man is a perfect stranger.* **perfection** *noun* when something is perfect

perfect *verb* (per-**fekt**) to perfect something is to make it perfect

perfectly *adverb* **1.** completely • *She stood perfectly still.* **2.** without any faults • *The toaster works perfectly now.*

perforate *verb* to perforate something is to make a hole or holes in it

perform *verb* **1.** to perform something is to present it in front of an audience **2.** to perform something is also to carry it out or complete it • *The surgeon performed the operation on Tuesday.* **performer** *noun* someone who performs an entertainment

performance *noun* the showing of something in front of an audience

perfume *noun* **1.** a sweet-smelling liquid that people put on their skin **2.** a sweet or pleasant smell

perhaps *adverb* it may be; possibly

peril *noun* peril is danger • *She was in great peril.* **perilous** *adjective* dangerous • *It was a perilous climb.* **perilously** *adverb* dangerously • *We came perilously close to disaster.*

perimeter *noun* (per-**im**-it-er) **1.** a boundary • *A fence marks the perimeter of the airfield.* **2.** the distance round the edge of something

period *noun* **1.** a length of time **2.** the time every month when a woman or girl bleeds from her womb in menstruation

periodical *noun* a magazine published regularly, usually once a month

periscope *noun* a device with a tube and mirrors that lets you see things at a higher level, used for example in submarines

perish *verb* **1.** to perish is to die or be destroyed **2.** to perish is also to rot • *The tyres have perished.* **perishable** *adjective* perishable food is likely to go off quickly

permanent *adjective* lasting for ever or for a long time **permanently** *adverb* for ever or for a long time

permission *noun* you have permission to do something when you are allowed to do it

permissive *adjective* letting people do what they wish

permit *verb* **permitting, permitted** (per-**mit**) **1.** to permit someone to do something is to allow them to do it **2.** to permit something is to allow it to be done

permit *noun* (**per**-mit) a written or printed statement that says you are allowed to do something

perpendicular *adjective* standing upright or at a right angle to a line or surface

perpetual *adjective* lasting for ever or for a long time **perpetually** *adverb* continually

perplex *verb* to perplex someone is to puzzle them very much

persecute *verb* to persecute someone is to be continually cruel to them, especially because you disagree with their beliefs **persecution** *noun* when someone is being persecuted **persecutor** *noun* the person who is persecuting someone

persevere *verb* to persevere is to continue trying to do something even though it is difficult **perseverance** *noun* you show perseverance when you persevere

persist *verb* **1.** to persist is to keep on firmly or obstinately doing something • *She persists in breaking the rules.* **2.** to persist is also to last for a long time

persistent *adjective* **1.** refusing to give up **2.** lasting for a long time • *The rain was persistent.* **persistence** *noun* you show persistence when you keep on doing something without giving up **persistently** *adverb*

person *noun* **people** or **persons** a human being

personal *adjective* **1.** belonging to, done by or concerning a particular person • *Keep your personal belongings with you.* **2.** private • *I can't tell you about that because it's personal.*

personal computer *noun* a small computer designed to be used by one person

personality *noun* **personalities** your personality is your nature and character • *a cheerful personality*

personally *adverb* **1.** in person; being actually there • *The head thanked me personally.* **2.** as far as I am concerned • *Personally, I'd rather stay here.*

personnel *noun* (per-so-**nel**) the personnel in a business or organization are the people who work there

perspective *noun* **1.** perspective is the impression of depth and space in a picture or scene **2.** your perspective on a situation is your point of view **in perspective** giving a balanced view of things • *Try to see the problem in perspective.*

perspire *verb* to perspire is to sweat **perspiration** *noun* sweat

persuade *verb* to persuade someone is to get them to agree about something or do something, by giving them reasons **persuasion** *noun* when you persuade someone to do or believe something **persuasive** *adjective* good at persuading people

pessimist *noun* someone who expects things to turn out badly **pessimism** *noun* the feeling that things will turn out badly

pessimistic *adjective* expecting things to turn out badly

pest *noun* **1.** a destructive insect or animal, such as a locust or a mouse **2.** an annoying person; a nuisance

pester *verb* to pester someone is to annoy them with frequent questions or interruptions

pet *noun* a tame animal that you keep at home

petal *noun* each of the separate coloured outer parts of a flower

petition *noun* a written request for someone in authority to do something, usually signed by a large number of people

petrify *verb* **petrifies, petrifying, petrified** to petrify someone is to make them so terrified that they cannot move

petrol *noun* petrol is a liquid made from oil, used as a fuel for engines

petticoat *noun* a piece of women's clothing worn under a skirt or dress

petty *adjective* **pettier, pettiest** **1.** minor and unimportant • *petty rules and regulations* **2.** mean and selfish about small things **pettiness** *noun*

pew *noun* one of the long wooden seats in a church

pewter *noun* pewter is a grey alloy of tin and lead

pH *noun* PH is a measure of how much acid or alkali a solution contains. Acids have a pH between 0 and 7 and alkalis have a pH between 7 and 14.

phantom *noun* a ghost

pharmacy *noun* **pharmacies** a shop that sells medicines

phase *noun* a stage in the progress or development of something

pheasant *noun* (**fez**-ant) a bird with a long tail that some people shoot as a sport

phenomenal *adjective* amazing or remarkable

phenomenon *noun* **phenomena** an event or fact, especially one that is remarkable or unusual

philosophical *adjective* **1.** to do with philosophy **2.** calmly accepting disappointment or suffering • *He was philosophical about losing.* **philosophically** *adverb*

philosophy *noun* **philosophies** (fil-**os**-o-fi) **1.** philosophy is the study of what life and human behaviour are all about **2.** a philosophy is a way of thinking or a system of beliefs **philosopher** *noun* someone who studies philosophy

phobia *noun* (**foh**-bi-a) a great fear of something

phone *noun* a telephone
phone *verb* to phone someone is to telephone them

phone-in *noun* a radio or TV programme in which people telephone the studio and take part in a discussion

phosphorescent *adjective* shining or glowing in the dark **phosphorescence** *noun* being phosphorescent

phosphorus *noun* phosphorus is a yellowish substance that glows in the dark

photo *noun* **photos** (*informal*) a photograph

photocopier *noun* a machine that makes photocopies

photocopy *noun* **photocopies** a copy of a document or page made by a photocopier
photocopy *verb* **photocopies, photocopying, photocopied** to photocopy a document is to make a copy of it with a photocopier

photograph *noun* a picture made using a camera
photograph *verb* to photograph someone or something is to take a photograph of them

photographer *noun* someone who takes photographs

photography *noun* photography is taking photographs with a camera **photographic** *adjective* to do with photography

phrase *noun* **1.** a group of words that do not make a complete sentence, for example *in the garden* in the sentence *The Queen was in the garden* **2.** a short section of a tune

physical *adjective* **1.** to do with the body rather than the mind or feelings **2.** to do with things you can touch or see **physically** *adverb* in a way that is connected with the body rather than the mind or feelings

physical education *noun* physical education is exercise that children do at school

physics *noun* physics is the study of matter and energy, including movement, heat, light and sound **physicist** *noun* an expert in physics

pianist *noun* someone who plays the piano

piano *noun* **pianos** a large musical instrument with a row of black and white keys on a keyboard

piccolo *noun* **piccolos** a small high-pitched flute

pick *verb* **1.** to pick something or someone is to choose them • *Pick a card from this pack.* **2.** to pick flowers or fruit is to cut or pull them off the plant or tree **3.** to pick someone's pocket is to steal from it **4.** to pick a lock is to open it without using a key **5.** to pick bits off or out of something is to pull them away from it **to pick on someone** is to keep criticizing or bothering them **to pick someone up** is to give them a lift in a vehicle **to pick something up** is to take it from the ground or a surface
pick *noun* a choice • *Take your pick.*

pickaxe *noun* a heavy pointed tool with a long handle, used for breaking up concrete or hard ground

picket *noun* a group of workers on strike who try to persuade other people not to go into the place where they work

pickle *noun* a strong-tasting food made of vegetables preserved in vinegar

pickle *verb* to pickle food is to preserve it in vinegar or salt water

pickpocket *noun* a thief who steals from people's pockets or bags

picnic *noun* a meal eaten in the open air away from home
picnic *verb* picnicking, picnicked to picnic is to have a picnic picnicker *noun* someone having a picnic

pictorial *adjective* with or using pictures pictorially *adverb*

picture *noun* 1. a painting, drawing or photograph 2. a film at the cinema
picture *verb* 1. to picture someone or something is to show them in a picture 2. to picture someone or something in your mind is to imagine them

picturesque *adjective* (pik-cher-**esk**) a picturesque place is attractive or charming • *a picturesque village*

pie *noun* a baked dish of meat or fruit covered with pastry

piece *noun* 1. a part of something 2. a work of art or writing or music • *a nice piece of music* 3. one of the objects you use on a board to play a game • *a chess piece* 4. a coin • *a 20p piece*
piece *verb* to piece things together is to join them to make something

pier *noun* a long structure built out into the sea for people to walk on

pierce *verb* to pierce something is to make a hole through it

piercing *adjective* 1. a piercing sound is loud and high-pitched • *a piercing shriek* 2. a piercing wind is very cold

pig *noun* 1. a fat animal with short legs and a blunt snout, kept for its meat 2. *(informal)* you can describe someone as a pig when they are greedy, dirty or unpleasant

pigeon *noun* a common grey bird with a small head and large chest

piggyback *noun* a ride on someone's back

piglet *noun* a young pig

pigment *noun* a substance that colours something

pigmy *noun* pigmies another spelling of pygmy

pigsty *noun* pigsties 1. a place for keeping pigs 2. *(informal)* you can describe a very untidy or dirty place as a pigsty

pigtail *noun* a single plait of hair worn hanging at the back of the head

pike *noun* 1. a large fish that lives in rivers and lakes 2. a heavy spear

pile *noun* a number of things on top of one another; a large amount of something
pile *verb* to pile things is to put them into a pile

pilgrim *noun* someone who goes on a journey to a holy place

pilgrimage *noun* a journey to a holy place

pill *noun* a small piece of medicine that you swallow the pill a pill taken regularly by a woman to prevent becoming pregnant

pillar *noun* a tall stone post supporting part of a building

pillion *noun* a seat for a passenger behind the driver's seat on a motorcycle

The word **pillion** comes from a Scottish Gaelic word meaning 'cushion'.

pillow *noun* a cushion to rest your head on in bed

pillowcase *noun* a cloth cover for a pillow

pilot *noun* 1. someone who flies an aircraft 2. someone who helps to steer a ship in and out of a port
pilot *verb* to pilot an aircraft is to be the pilot of it

pimple *noun* a small round swelling on your skin pimply *adjective* having pimples

pin *noun* a short piece of metal with a sharp point and a rounded head, used to fasten pieces of cloth together pins and needles a tingling feeling in the skin
pin *verb* pinning, pinned to pin something is to fasten it with a pin

pincer *noun* the claw of a shellfish such as a lobster

pincers *plural noun* a tool for gripping and pulling things out

pinch *verb* **1.** to pinch something is to squeeze it tightly between your finger and thumb **2.** *(informal)* to pinch something is to steal it

pinch *noun* **1.** a firm squeezing movement **2.** the amount of a substance that you can pick up between the tips of your finger and thumb • *a pinch of salt*

pine¹ *noun* an evergreen tree with leaves shaped like needles

pine² *verb* to pine for someone or something is to feel a strong longing for them

pineapple *noun* a large tropical fruit with yellow flesh and prickly leaves and skin

ping-pong *noun* ping-pong is table tennis

pink *adjective* pale red
pink *noun* a pink colour

pint *noun* a measure of liquid, an eighth of a gallon or about 568 millilitres

pioneer *noun* one of the first people to go to a place or do something new

pious *adjective* very religious or devout **piously** *adverb*

pip *noun* a small hard seed of a fruit such as an apple, orange or pear

pipe *noun* **1.** a tube for carrying water, gas or oil from one place to another **2.** a short tube with a small bowl at one end, used to smoke tobacco **3.** a musical instrument in the shape of a small tube

pipe *verb* **1.** to pipe something is to send it along pipes or wires **2.** to pipe is to play music on a pipe or the bagpipes

pipeline *noun* a pipe for carrying oil, water or gas over a long distance

piper *noun* someone who plays a pipe or the bagpipes

piping *adjective* **piping hot** very hot, ready to eat

pirate *noun* a sailor who attacks and robs other ships **piracy** *noun* piracy is robbing ships

pistol *noun* a small gun held in the hand

piston *noun* a disc that moves up and down inside a cylinder in an engine

pit *noun* **1.** a deep hole or hollow **2.** a coal mine **3.** the part of a race circuit where cars get fuel and new tyres during a race

pitch¹ *noun* **1.** a pitch is a piece of ground marked out for cricket, football or another game **2.** pitch is how high or low a voice or musical note is

pitch¹ *verb* **1.** to pitch something is to throw it **2.** to pitch a tent is to put it up **3.** to pitch is to fall heavily • *He tripped and pitched forward.* **4.** a ship pitches when it moves up and down on a rough sea

pitch² *noun* pitch is a black sticky substance like tar

pitch-black *adjective* completely black or dark, with no light at all

pitcher *noun* a large jug, usually with two handles

pitchfork *noun* a large fork with two prongs for lifting hay

pitfall *noun* a hidden danger or difficulty

pitiful *adjective* making you feel pity • *It was a pitiful sight.* **pitifully** *adverb*

pitiless *adjective* having or showing no pity

pitta bread *noun* pitta bread is a flat, round piece of bread that you can open and fill with food

pity *noun* **1.** pity is the feeling of being sorry because someone is suffering or in trouble • *I feel pity for the homeless people.* **2.** a pity is something that you regret • *It's a pity they can't come.* **to take pity on someone** is to help someone who is in trouble

pity *verb* **pities, pitying, pitied** to pity someone is to feel sorry for them

pivot *noun* a point on which something turns or balances

pixie *noun* a small fairy or elf

pizza *noun* (**peet**-sa) a food made as a layer of dough covered with tomatoes, cheese and meat or vegetables and baked

placard *noun* a large poster or notice carried at a demonstration

place *noun* **1.** a particular part of space, especially where something belongs; an area or position **2.** a position in a race or competition **3.** a seat • *Save me a place.* in place in the proper position in place of something or someone instead of them out of place **1.** in the wrong position **2.** unsuitable • *Jeans and sandals are out of place in a smart restaurant.* to take place is to happen

place *verb* to place something somewhere is to put it in a particular place

placid *adjective* calm and gentle

plague *noun* **1.** a dangerous illness that spreads very quickly **2.** a large number of pests • *The crops were devastated by a plague of insects.*

plague *verb* to plague someone is to pester or annoy them continuously • *They have been plagued with complaints.*

plaice *noun* plaice a flat sea fish used for food

plain *adjective* **1.** simple; not decorated **2.** not pretty **3.** easy to understand or see • *It was plain that he was lying.* plainness *noun*

plain *noun* a large area of flat country without trees

plainly *adverb* **1.** clearly or obviously • *The clock tower was plainly visible in the distance.* **2.** simply • *She was plainly dressed.*

plait *noun* (plat) a length of hair or rope made by twisting several strands together

plait *verb* (plat) to plait hair or rope is to make it into a plait

plan *noun* **1.** a way of doing something that you think out in advance **2.** a drawing showing how the parts of something are arranged **3.** a map of a town or district

plan *verb* planning, planned **1.** to plan something is to think out in advance how you are going to do it **2.** to plan to do something is to intend to do it

plane *noun* **1.** an aeroplane **2.** a tool for making wood smooth **3.** a flat or level surface

plane *verb* to plane wood is to smooth it with a plane

planet *noun* A planet is one of the bodies that move in an orbit round the sun. The planets of the solar system are Mercury, Venus, Earth, Mars, Jupiter, Saturn, Uranus and Neptune.

plank *noun* a long flat piece of wood

plankton *noun* plankton is made up of tiny creatures that float in the sea and lakes

plant *noun* **1.** a living thing that grows out of the ground, including flowers, bushes, trees and vegetables **2.** a factory or its equipment

plant *verb* **1.** to plant something such as a tree or flower is to put it in the ground to grow **2.** to plant something is also to put it firmly in place • *He planted his feet on the ground and took hold of the rope.* **3.** to plant something is to secretly put it somewhere • *Someone planted a bomb on the train.*

plantation *noun* an area of land where a crop such as tobacco, tea or rubber is planted

plaque *noun* (plak or plahk) **1.** a plaque is a metal or porcelain plate fixed on a wall as a memorial or an ornament **2.** plaque is a substance that forms on your teeth, allowing bacteria to develop

plaster *noun* **1.** a plaster is a small covering you put over a cut or wound to protect it **2.** plaster is a mixture of lime, sand and water, used to cover walls and ceilings

plaster *verb* **1.** to plaster a wall or ceiling is to cover it with plaster **2.** to plaster a surface with something is to cover it thickly • *His clothes were plastered with mud.* plasterer *noun* someone who plasters walls and ceilings

plastic *noun* a strong light synthetic substance that can be moulded into different shapes

plastic *adjective* made of plastic • *a plastic bag*

Plasticine *noun* (trademark) Plasticine is a soft and easily shaped substance used for making models

plastic surgery *noun* plastic surgery is work done by a surgeon to change or improve the look of someone's body

plate *noun* **1.** a flat dish, used for eating **2.** a thin flat sheet of metal, glass or other hard material **3.** an illustration on a separate page in a book

plate *verb* to plate metal is to cover it with a thin layer of gold, silver, tin or other soft metal

plateau *noun* plateaux (**plat**-oh) a flat area of high land

platform *noun* **1.** a flat raised area along the side of the line at a railway station **2.** a raised area for speakers or performers in a hall

platinum *noun* platinum is a valuable silver-coloured metal used in jewellery

platoon *noun* a small unit of soldiers

platypus *noun* an Australian animal with a beak and webbed feet

play *verb* **1.** to play or play a game, is to take part in a game or other amusement **2.** to play music or a musical instrument, is to make music or sound with it **3.** to play a part in a film or play is to perform it **4.** to play a CD or DVD is to put it in a machine and listen to it or watch it to play about or around is to have fun or be mischievous to play someone up is to tease them or annoy them **player** *noun* someone who plays a game or a musical instrument

play *noun* **1.** a play is a story acted on a stage or broadcast on radio or television **2.** play is playing or having fun

playful *adjective* **1.** wanting to play; full of fun **2.** not serious **playfully** *adverb* **playfulness** *noun*

playground *noun* a place out of doors where children can play

playgroup *noun* a place where very young children can play together and are looked after by parents and other helpers

playing card *noun* one of a set of cards (usually 52) used for playing games

playing field *noun* a grassy field for outdoor games

playtime *noun* the time when young schoolchildren go out to play

playwright *noun* someone who writes plays

plea *noun* **1.** a request or appeal **2.** a statement of 'guilty' or 'not guilty' made in a lawcourt by someone accused of a crime

plead *verb* to plead with someone is to beg them to do something to plead guilty or not guilty is to state in a lawcourt that you are guilty or not guilty of a crime

pleasant *adjective* pleasing or enjoyable or friendly **pleasantly** *adverb* in a pleasant way • *I was pleasantly surprised.*

please *verb* **1.** to please someone is to make them happy or satisfied **2.** used when you want to ask something politely • *Please shut the door.*

pleasure *noun* **1.** pleasure is a feeling of being pleased **2.** a pleasure is something that pleases you with pleasure gladly; willingly

pleat *noun* a fold made in cloth by pressing or sewing it **pleated** *adjective*

pledge *noun* a solemn promise
pledge *verb* to pledge something is to promise it

plentiful *adjective* large in amount

plenty *noun* to have plenty of something is to have a lot of it or more than enough

pliers *plural noun* pincers with flattened jaws for gripping something or for breaking wire

plight *noun* a difficult and sad situation • *They were stranded for several days before anyone knew of their plight.*

plod *verb* plodding, plodded to plod is to walk slowly and with heavy steps

plop *noun* the sound of something dropping into a liquid
plop *verb* plopping, plopped to plop is to fall into a liquid with a plop

plot *noun* **1.** a secret plan, especially to do something illegal or bad **2.** what happens in a story, film or play **3.** a piece of land for a house or garden
plot *verb* plotting, plotted **1.** to plot is to make a secret plan to do something **2.** to plot a chart or graph is to make it, marking all the points on it **plotter** *noun* plotters are people who take part in a plot

plough *noun* (plow) a large farm tool pulled by a tractor or animal, used for turning over the soil

plough *verb* to plough the soil is to turn it over with a plough

pluck *verb* **1**. to pluck a bird is to pull the feathers off it to prepare it for cooking **2**. to pluck a flower or fruit is to pick it **3**. in music, to pluck a string is to pull it and let it go again to pluck up courage is to be brave and overcome fear

pluck *noun* pluck is courage or bravery

plucky *adjective* pluckier, pluckiest brave or courageous

plug *noun* **1**. a plastic or metal object used to fill the hole in a sink or bath **2**. a device that is used to connect a piece of electric equipment to a socket

plug *verb* plugging, plugged **1**. to plug a hole is to fill it up **2**. *(informal)* to plug an event or product is to publicize it to plug something in is to connect it to an electric socket with a plug

plum *noun* a soft juicy red or purple fruit with a stone in the middle

plumage *noun* (**ploo**-mij) a bird's plumage is its feathers

plumber *noun* someone who fits and mends water pipes in a building

plumbing *noun* **1**. plumbing is the work of a plumber **2**. the plumbing in a building is all the water pipes and water tanks

plume *noun* **1**. a large feather **2**. something shaped like a feather • *We saw a plume of smoke in the distance.*

plump *adjective* rounded or slightly fat

plunder *verb* to plunder a place is to rob it violently during a war plunderer *noun* someone who plunders a place

plunder *noun* **1**. plunder is plundering a place **2**. plunder is also goods taken by plundering

plunge *verb* **1**. to plunge into water is to jump or dive into it with force **2**. to plunge something into a liquid or something soft is to put it in with force

plunge *noun* a sudden fall or dive

plural *noun* the form of a word meaning more than one person or thing, such as *cakes* and *children*

plural *adjective* in the plural; meaning more than one • *'Mice' is a plural noun.*

plus *preposition* with the next number or thing added • *2 plus 2 equals 4 (2 + 2 = 4).*

p.m. short for Latin *post meridiem* which means 'after midday'

pneumatic *adjective* (new-**mat**-ik) filled with air or worked by compressed air • *a pneumatic tyre* • *a pneumatic drill*

pneumonia *noun* (new-**moh**-ni-a) pneumonia is a serious disease of the lungs

poach *verb* **1**. to poach food is to cook it in or over boiling water **2**. to poach animals is to hunt them illegally on someone else's land poacher *noun* someone who hunts animals illegally on someone else's land

pocket *noun* part of a piece of clothing shaped like a small bag, for keeping things in

pocket *adjective* small enough to carry in your pocket • *Use a pocket calculator.*

pocket *verb* to pocket something is to put it in your pocket

pocket money *noun* pocket money is money given to a child to spend

pod *noun* a long seed-container on a pea or bean plant

podgy *adjective* podgier, podgiest short and fat

poem *noun* a piece of writing arranged in short lines, often with a particular rhythm and sometimes rhyming

poet *noun* someone who writes poetry

poetry *noun* poetry is poems as a form of literature

point *noun* **1**. the narrow or sharp end of something • *Don't hold the knife by its point.* **2**. a written dot • *Put in a decimal point.* **3**. a single mark in a game or quiz • *How many points did I get?* **4**. a particular place or time • *They gave up at this point.* **5**. something that someone says during a discussion • *That's a very good point.* **6.** a detail or special feature • *He has some good points.* **7.** purpose or advantage • *There's no point in hurrying.* **8.** the points on a railway line are the movable parts that allow trains to change from one track to another

point *verb* **1.** to point to something is to show where it is, especially by holding out your finger towards it **2.** to point something is to aim it or direct it • *The fireman pointed the hose at the fire.* to point something out is to show it or explain it

point-blank *adjective, adverb* **1.** close to the target **2.** directly and completely • *He refused point-blank.*

pointed *adjective* having a point at the end

pointless *adjective* something is pointless when it has no purpose or meaning pointlessly *adverb*

point of view *noun* a way of looking or thinking of something

poise *noun* poise is a dignified and self-confident manner

poise *verb* **1.** to poise something is to balance it or keep it steady **2.** to be poised to do something is to be ready to do it

poison *noun* a substance that can kill or harm living things if they eat or absorb it

poison *verb* **1.** to poison someone is to kill or harm them with poison **2.** to poison something is to put poison in it poisoner *noun* a person who kills someone using poison

poisonous *adjective* **1.** a poisonous chemical, gas or plant can kill or harm you if you swallow it or breathe it in **2.** poisonous animals or insects can kill or harm you with poison if they bite you

poke *verb* to poke something or someone is to push or jab them hard with your finger or a pointed object

poke *noun* a prod or jab

poker *noun* **1.** a poker is a metal rod for stirring a fire **2.** poker is a card game in which the players bet on who has the best cards

polar *adjective* to do with the North or South Pole or near one of them

polar bear *noun* a powerful white bear living near the North Pole

pole[1] *noun* a long thin piece of wood or metal

pole[2] *noun* **1.** each of the two points on the earth that are furthest from the equator, the **North Pole** and the **South Pole 2.** each end of a magnet

pole vault *noun* the pole vault is an athletic event in which you jump over a high bar with the help of a long springy pole

police *noun* the police are the people whose job is to catch criminals and make sure that people obey the law

policeman or **policewoman** *noun* policemen or policewomen a man or woman member of the police

police officer *noun* a member of the police

policy *noun* policies the aims or plans of a person or group of people

polio *noun* (**poh**-li-oh) a disease that paralyses the body

polish *verb* to polish something is to make its surface shiny or smooth

polish *noun* **1.** polish is a substance used in polishing **2.** a polish is a shine got by polishing • *He gave his shoes a good polish.*

polite *adjective* having good manners; respectful and thoughtful towards other people politely *adverb* politeness *noun*

political *adjective* to do with the governing of a country politically *adverb* in a way that is to do with politics

politician *noun* someone who is involved in politics

politics *noun* politics is political matters; the business of governing a country

poll *noun* **1.** a round of voting at an election **2.** a survey of what people think about something

pollen *noun* pollen is yellow powder found inside flowers, containing male seeds for fertilizing other flowers

pollinate *verb* to pollinate a flower or plant is to put pollen into it so that it becomes fertilized pollination *noun* the process of pollinating a flower or plant

pollute *verb* to pollute a place or thing is to make it dirty or impure

pollution *noun* pollution is substances that make the air, water and soil dirty or impure

poltergeist *noun* (**pol**-ter-gyst) a ghost that makes things move around

polygon *noun* a figure or shape with many sides, such as a hexagon or octagon

polythene *noun* (**pol**-i-theen) polythene is a lightweight plastic used to make bags and wrappings

pomp *noun* pomp is the dignified and solemn way in which an important ceremony is carried out

pompous *adjective* someone is being pompous when they are thinking too much of their own importance **pomposity** *noun* behaviour that shows that someone thinks they are more important than other people **pompously** *adverb*

pond *noun* a small lake

ponder *verb* to ponder something is to think carefully and seriously about it

pony *noun* ponies a small horse

ponytail *noun* a bunch of long hair tied at the back of the head

poodle *noun* a dog with long curly hair

pool[1] *noun* **1.** a small area of liquid in a hollow place **2.** a swimming pool

pool[2] *noun* **1.** a group of things shared by several people **2.** the fund of money that can be won in a gambling game **3.** pool is a game similar to snooker but played on a smaller table **the pools** a system of gambling on the results of football matches

poor *adjective* **1.** having very little money • *a poor family* **2.** not good or adequate • *This is poor work.* **3.** unfortunate • *Poor fellow!*

poorly *adverb* quite badly • *She did poorly in the test.*

poorly *adjective* unwell • *I'm feeling poorly today.*

pop[1] *noun* **1.** a pop is a small sharp bang **2.** pop is a fizzy drink
pop[1] *verb* popping, popped **1.** to pop is to make a small sharp bang **2.** *(informal)* to pop somewhere is to go there quickly • *I'm just popping out to the shops.*

pop[2] *noun* pop is modern popular music

popcorn *noun* a snack made from grains of maize heated till they burst and form light fluffy balls

Pope *noun* the Pope is the leader of the Roman Catholic Church

poppy *noun* poppies a plant with large red flowers

popular *adjective* liked or enjoyed by a lot of people **popularity** *noun* being liked or enjoyed by a lot of people

populated *adjective* a place is populated when it has people living there • *The land is thinly populated.*

population *noun* the population of a particular place is all the people who live there; the total number of people who live there

porcelain *noun* (**por**-se-lin) porcelain is a fine kind of china

porch *noun* a covered area in front of the door of a building

porcupine *noun* a small animal covered with long prickles

> The word **porcupine** comes from old French words meaning 'prickly pig'.

pore *noun* one of the tiny openings in your skin which sweat can pass through

pork *noun* pork is meat from a pig

porous *adjective* something is porous when it allows liquid or air to pass through

porpoise *noun* (**por**-pus) a sea animal rather like a dolphin or a small whale

porridge *noun* porridge is a food made by boiling oatmeal to make a thick paste

port[1] *noun* **1.** a port is a harbour **2.** a port is also a city or town with a harbour **3.** port is the left-hand side of a ship or aircraft when you are facing forward

port[2] *noun* port is a strong red Portuguese wine

portable *adjective* able to be carried easily

portcullis *noun* a heavy grating that can be lowered to block the gateway to a castle

porter *noun* **1.** someone whose job is to carry things around at a railway station, hotel or hospital **2.** someone whose job is to look after the entrance to a large building

porthole *noun* a small round window in the side of a ship or aircraft

portion *noun* **1.** a part or share given to someone **2.** an amount of food for one person

portrait *noun* a picture of a person

portray *verb* to portray something or someone is to describe or show them in a certain way • *The play portrays the king as a kind man.* **portrayal** *noun* how a person or thing is described or shown

pose *noun* a way of standing or sitting for a portrait or photograph to be made of you
pose *verb* **1.** to pose is to sit or stand in a special position **2.** to pose as someone is to pretend to be them • *The man posed as a police officer.* **3.** to pose a question or problem is to present it • *Ice always poses a problem to motorists.*

posh *adjective* (*informal*) very smart or high-class • *a posh hotel* • *a posh accent*

position *noun* **1.** the place where something is or should be **2.** the way in which someone or something is placed or arranged • *He was sleeping in an uncomfortable position.* **3.** a person's place in a race or competition **4.** a regular job

positive *adjective* **1.** sure or definite • *I am positive I saw him.* **2.** agreeing or saying 'yes' • *We received a positive answer.* **3.** a positive number is one that is greater than nought **4.** a positive electric charge is one that does not carry electrons **positively** *adverb*
positive *noun* a photographic print made from a negative

posse *noun* (**poss**-i) a group of people who help a sheriff in the USA

possess *verb* to possess something is to own or have it **possessor** *noun* a person who owns or has something

possessed *adjective* someone is possessed when they are behaving as if they are controlled by an outside force

possession *noun* something that you own

possessive *adjective* you are being possessive when you want to get and keep things for yourself

possibility *noun* **possibilities** **1.** possibility is being possible • *Is there any possibility of changing your mind?* **2.** a possibility is something that is possible • *There are many possibilities.*

possible *adjective* able to exist, happen, be done or be used

possibly *adverb* **1.** in any way • *That cannot possibly be right.* **2.** perhaps • *I will arrive at six o'clock or possibly earlier.*

post[1] *noun* an upright piece of wood, concrete or metal fixed in the ground

post[2] *noun* **1.** the post is the collecting and delivering of letters and parcels **2.** post is letters and parcels carried by post; mail **3.** a message sent to an Internet site; a piece of writing on a blog
post[2] *verb* **1.** to post a letter or parcel is to send it to someone by post **2.** to send a message to an Internet site; to display information online

post[3] *noun* **1.** a regular job **2.** the place where a sentry stands
post[3] *verb* to be posted somewhere is to be sent there for a time as part of your job

postage *noun* postage is the cost of sending a letter or parcel by post

postal *adjective* to do with the post; by post

postbox *noun* a box into which you put letters to be sent by post

postcard *noun* a card that you can write a message on and post without an envelope

postcode *noun* a group of letters and numbers put at the end of an address to help in sorting the post

poster *noun* a large picture or public notice giving information or advertising something

postman *noun* postmen someone who collects and delivers letters and parcels

postmark *noun* an official mark stamped on something sent by post, showing when and where it was posted

post office *noun* a place where you can post letters and parcels and buy stamps

postpone *verb* to postpone a meeting or event is to arrange for it to take place later than was originally planned • *The match had to be postponed.* postponement *noun* when something is postponed

posture *noun* the way that a person stands, sits or walks

posy *noun* posies a small bunch of flowers

pot *noun* **1.** a deep round container **2.** a flowerpot
pot *verb* potting, potted **1.** to pot a plant is to put it into a flowerpot **2.** to pot a ball in a game such as snooker or pool is to hit it into a pocket

potassium *noun* potassium is a soft silvery-white metallic substance that living things need

potato *noun* potatoes a vegetable that grows underground

potent *adjective* powerful potency *noun* the potency of something is how powerful it is

potential *adjective* possible or capable of happening in the future • *She is a potential star.* potentially *adverb* as a possibility in the future • *He is potentially one of our best players.*
potential *noun* to have potential is to be capable of becoming important or useful in the future

pothole *noun* **1.** a deep natural hole in the ground **2.** a hole in a road

potion *noun* (**poh**-shon) a drink containing medicine or poison

potter *noun* someone who makes pottery

pottery *noun* potteries **1.** pottery is pots, cups, plates and other things made of baked clay **2.** pottery is also the craft of making pottery

potty *noun* potties *(informal)* a small bowl used by young children as a toilet

pouch *noun* **1.** a small bag or pocket **2.** a fold of skin in which a kangaroo keeps its young

poultry *noun* poultry are birds such as chickens, geese and turkeys, kept for their eggs and meat

pounce *verb* to pounce on someone or something is to jump on them or attack them suddenly

pound[1] *noun* **1.** a unit of money, in Britain equal to 100 pence **2.** a unit of weight equal to 16 ounces or about 454 grams

pound[2] *verb* **1.** to pound something is to hit it repeatedly to crush it **2.** your heart is pounding when it beats heavily, making a dull thumping sound

pour *verb* **1.** to pour a liquid is to make it flow out of a container **2.** to pour is to flow in a large amount • *Blood was pouring from the wound.* **3.** it is pouring when it is raining heavily **4.** to pour in or out is to come or go in large numbers or amounts • *Fans began pouring out of the stadium.*

pout *verb* you pout when you stick out your lips because you are annoyed or sulking

poverty *noun* poverty is being poor

powder *noun* **1.** a mass of tiny pieces of something dry, like flour or dust **2.** make-up in the form of powder powdery *adjective* like powder
powder *verb* to powder something is to put powder on it • *She powdered her face.* powdered *adjective* made into a powder • *powdered milk*

power *noun* **1.** power is strength or great energy **2.** power is also control over other people **3.** the power to do something is the ability to do it • *Humans have the power of speech.* **4.** a power is a powerful country **5.** power is also electricity or another form of energy **6.** *(in mathematics)* the power of a number is the result obtained by multiplying the number by itself one or more times • *27 is the third power of 3 (3 x 3 x 3 = 27).* powered *adjective* a device is (for example) electric-powered or solar-powered when it is worked by electricity or by the sun's energy

powerful *adjective* having a lot of power or influence powerfully *adverb*

powerless *adjective* someone is powerless if they are unable to act or control things

power station *noun* a building where electricity is produced

practical *adjective* 1. someone is practical when they are able to do or make useful things 2. something is practical when it is likely to be useful • *That is a practical idea.* 3. concerned with doing or making things • *He has had practical experience.*

practical *noun* a lesson or examination in which you actually do or make something rather than reading or writing about it

practical joke *noun* a trick played on someone

practically *adverb* almost • *It's practically ready now.*

practice *noun* 1. practice is doing something often and regularly so that you get better at it • *I must do my piano practice.* 2. practice is also actually doing something rather than thinking or talking about it • *It's time to put this theory of yours into practice.* 3. a practice is the business of a doctor or lawyer

practise *verb* 1. to practise something is to do it often so that you get better at it 2. to practise an activity or custom is to do it regularly • *She practises yoga.* 3. to practise (for example) medicine or law is to work as a doctor or lawyer

prairie *noun* a large area of flat grass-covered land in North America

praise *verb* to praise someone or something is to say that they are good or have done well

praise *noun* praise is words that praise someone or something

pram *noun* a small open carriage for a baby, pushed by a person walking

prance *verb* to prance or prance about, is to jump about in a lively way

prank *noun* a trick played on someone for mischief

prawn *noun* a shellfish like a large shrimp, used for food

pray *verb* 1. to pray is to talk to God 2. to pray is also to wish or hope strongly for something • *We are praying for good weather.*

prayer *noun* 1. prayer is praying 2. a prayer is what you say when you pray

preach *verb* to preach is to give a talk about religion or about right and wrong
preacher *noun* someone who preaches

precarious *adjective* (pri-**kair**-i-us) not at all safe or secure • *That vase is in a precarious position.* **precariously** *adverb*

precaution *noun* something you do to prevent trouble or danger in the future

precede *verb* one thing precedes another when it comes or goes in front of the other thing

precinct *noun* (**pree**-sinkt) a part of a town where traffic is not allowed • *The town has a large shopping precinct.*

precious *adjective* very valuable or loved

precipice *noun* the steep face of a mountain or cliff

precise *adjective* 1. clear and accurate • *I gave them precise instructions.* 2. exact • *At that precise moment, the doorbell rang.* **precisely** *adverb* accurately and carefully **precision** *noun* being exact or accurate

predator *noun* (**pred**-a-ter) an animal that hunts other animals **predatory** *adjective* hunting other animals

predict *verb* to predict something is to say that it will happen in the future **predictable** *adjective* likely or expected **prediction** *noun* something that you predict

preen *verb* a bird preens when it smoothes and cleans its feathers using its beak

preface *noun* (**pref**-ass) an introduction at the beginning of a book

prefect *noun* an older pupil in some schools who is given authority to help to keep order

prefer *verb* preferring, preferred to prefer one thing to another is to like it better than the other thing **preference** *noun* what you prefer

prefix *noun* a group of letters joined to the front of a word to change or add to its meaning, as in *disorder*, *overflow* and *unhappy*

pregnant *adjective* a pregnant woman has an unborn baby growing inside her womb **pregnancy** *noun* a time of being pregnant

prehistoric *adjective* belonging to a very long time ago, before written records were kept **prehistory** *noun* prehistoric times

prejudice *noun* a prejudice is an unfair opinion you have about someone that is not based on facts or reason **prejudiced** *adjective* having a prejudice

preliminary *adjective* coming before something or preparing for it

prelude *noun* (**prel**-yood) an introduction to a play, poem or event

premature *adjective* happening or coming before the proper time • *a premature baby*

première *noun* (**prem**-yair) the first public performance of a play or showing of a film

premises *plural noun* an organization's premises are the building and land it uses

premium *noun* (**pree**-mi-um) an amount paid regularly to an insurance company

preparation *noun* **1.** preparation is getting something ready **2.** preparations are things you do in order to get ready for something

prepare *verb* to prepare something is to get it ready **to be prepared to do something** is to be ready or willing to do it

preposition *noun* a word which usually comes before a noun or pronoun, showing place, direction or time or cause

prescribe *verb* to prescribe something is to say what medicine or treatment a patient should have

prescription *noun* a doctor's written order for a chemist to prepare a medicine for a patient

presence *noun* your presence somewhere is the fact that you are there • *Your presence is expected.*

present[1] *adjective* (**prez**-ent) **1.** in a particular place; here • *Nobody else was present.* **2.** existing or happening now • *Who is the present Queen?*

present[1] *noun* (**prez**-ent) **1.** the present is the time now • *Our teacher is away at present.* **2.** the form of a verb that describes something that is happening now, for example *likes* in *he likes swimming*

present[2] *noun* (**prez**-ent) something that you give to someone or receive from them
present[2] *verb* (pri-**zent**) **1.** to present something to someone is to give it to them at a ceremony • *Who will present the prizes this year?* **2.** to present a play or other entertainment is to perform it **3.** to present a radio or television programme is to introduce it to the audience **4.** to present something is to show or describe it to people

presentation *noun* **1.** a formal talk showing or demonstrating something **2.** a ceremony in which someone is given a gift or prize

presenter *noun* someone who presents something, especially a radio or television programme

presently *adverb* soon; in a while • *They will be here presently.*

present participle *noun* a form of a verb that ends in *-ing* and describes something that is or was happening, for example the sentences *I am watching television* and *they were watching television*

preservative *noun* a substance added to food to preserve it

preserve *verb* to preserve something is to keep it safe or in good condition **preservation** *noun* preserving something

president *noun* **1.** the head of a country that is a republic **2.** the person in charge of a society, business or club **presidency** *noun* the job of being a president **presidential** *adjective* to do with a president

press *verb* **1.** to press something is to push it firmly or squeeze it • *Press the red button.* **2.** to press clothes is to make them flat and smooth with an iron

press noun **1.** the action of squeezing or pushing on something **2.** the press are newspapers and journalists **3.** a machine for printing things

pressure noun **1.** pressure is continuous pushing or squeezing • *Apply pressure to stop the cut bleeding.* **2.** pressure is also the force with which a liquid or gas pushes against something **3.** there is pressure on you when someone is trying to persuade or force you to do something

prestige noun (pres-**tee**zh) prestige is the respect something has because it is important or of a high quality

presumably adverb probably; I suppose

presume verb to presume something is to think it is probably true • *I had presumed he was dead.*

pretence noun a pretence is an attempt to pretend something

pretend verb **1.** to pretend is to behave as if something untrue or imaginary is true **2.** to pretend something is to claim it dishonestly • *They pretended they were policemen.*

pretty adjective prettier, prettiest pleasant to look at or hear; attractive prettily adverb prettiness noun

pretty adverb (informal) quite; moderately • *It's pretty cold outside.*

prevent verb **1.** to prevent something is to stop it from happening or make it impossible **2.** to prevent someone is to stop them from doing something prevention noun stopping something bad from happening preventive adjective meant to help prevent something • *preventive medicine*

preview noun a showing of a film or play before it is shown to most people

previous adjective coming before this; preceding • *I was in London the previous week.* previously adverb before or earlier

prey noun (pray) an animal that is hunted or killed by another animal for food

prey verb (pray) to prey on something is to hunt and kill an animal for food

price noun **1.** the amount of money for which something is sold **2.** what you have to give or do to get something • *Giving up this land was*

a small price to pay for peace. **pricey** adjective expensive

priceless adjective very valuable

prick verb to prick something is to make a tiny hole in it

pride noun **1.** pride is a feeling of being very pleased with yourself or with someone else who has done well • *My heart swelled with pride.* **2.** pride is also being too satisfied because of who you are or what you have done **3.** a pride is a group of lions

priest noun **1.** a member of the clergy **2.** someone who performs religious ceremonies; a religious leader priesthood noun the position of being a priest

priestess noun a female priest in a non-Christian religion

prim adjective primmer, primmest liking things to be correct and easily shocked by anything rude primly adverb

primary adjective first; most important primarily adverb mainly; most importantly

primary colour noun one of the colours from which all other colours can be made by mixing: red, yellow and blue for paint and red, green and blue for light

primary school noun a first school for children from the age of 5 onwards

prime adjective **1.** most important • *The weather was the prime cause of the accident.* **2.** of the best quality

prime minister noun the leader of a government

prime number noun a number that can only be divided exactly by itself and the number one, for example 2, 3, 5, 7 and 11

primitive adjective **1.** at an early stage of development or civilization • *Primitive humans were hunters rather than farmers.* **2.** basic or simple • *Our accommodation was fairly primitive.*

prince noun **1.** the son of a king or queen **2.** a man or boy in a royal family

princess noun **1.** the daughter of a king or queen **2.** a woman or girl in a royal family **3.** the wife of a prince

principal *adjective* chief or most important
principally *adverb* chiefly or mainly
principal *noun* the head of a college or school

principle *noun* **1.** a general rule or truth • *the principles of geometry* **2.** someone's principles are the basic rules and beliefs they have about how they should behave **in principle** in general, not in detail • *I agree with your plan in principle.*

print *verb* **1.** to print words, pictures or photographs is to put them on paper with a machine **2.** to print letters is to write them separately and not joined together
print *noun* **1.** print is printed words or pictures **2.** a print is a mark made by something pressing on a surface • *a thumb print* **3.** a print is also a photograph made from a negative

printer *noun* **1.** a machine that prints on paper from data in a computer **2.** someone who prints books or newspapers

printout *noun* the information printed on paper from data in a computer

priority *noun* **priorities** (pry-**o**-ri-ti) **1.** a priority is something that is more urgent or important than other things and needs to be dealt with first • *Repairing the roof is a priority.* **2.** priority is the right to go first or be considered before other things • *People in need of urgent medical help will have priority.*

prise *verb* to prise something open is to force or lever it open

prism *noun* a piece of glass that breaks up light into the colours of the rainbow

prison *noun* a place where people are locked up as a punishment for crimes

prisoner *noun* someone who is kept in a prison or who is a captive

privacy *noun* privacy is being private or away from other people

private *adjective* **1.** belonging to a particular person or group of people • *a private road* **2.** meant to be kept secret • *These letters are private.* **3.** away from other people • *Is there a private place to swim?* **in private** where only particular people can see or hear; not in public **privately** *adverb* separately; not with other people • *Can we speak privately?*
private *noun* a soldier of the lowest rank

privilege *noun* a special right or advantage given to one person or group of people
privileged *adjective* having special advantages that other people don't have

prize *noun* something you get for winning a game or competition or for doing well in an examination
prize *verb* to prize something is to value it highly

probable *adjective* likely to be true or to happen **probability** *noun* the probability of something is how likely it is to happen
probably *adverb*

probation *noun* probation is a time when someone is tried out in a new job to make sure they are suitable for the work

probe *noun* **1.** a long thin instrument used to look closely at something **2.** an investigation
probe *verb* to probe is to investigate or look at something closely

problem *noun* something that is difficult to answer or deal with

procedure *noun* a fixed or special way of doing something

proceed *verb* (pro-**seed**) to proceed is to go on or continue

proceedings *plural noun* things that happen; activities

proceeds *plural noun* (**proh**-seedz) the proceeds of a sale or event are the money made from it

process *noun* a series of actions for making or doing something
process *verb* to process something is to treat it or deal with it by a process so that it can be used • *He took the film to the chemist to be processed.*

procession *noun* a number of people or vehicles moving steadily forwards

proclaim *verb* to proclaim something is to announce it officially or publicly
proclamation *noun* a public announcement

prod *verb* **prodding, prodded** to prod something or someone is to poke or jab them

produce *verb* (pro-**dewss**) **1.** to produce something is to make or create it **2.** to produce something that is hidden or put away is to bring it out so that people can see it **3**. to produce a play or film or other entertainment is to organize the performance of it **producer** *noun* someone who produces a play or film

produce *noun* (**prod**-yewss) produce is food grown by farmers

product *noun* **1**. something someone makes or produces for sale **2**. the result of multiplying two numbers • *12 is the product of 4 and 3.*

production *noun* **1**. production is the process of making or creating something • *car production* **2**. a production is a version of a play or film

productive *adjective* producing a lot of good or useful things **productivity** *noun* the rate at which someone works or produces things

profession *noun* a type of work for which you need special knowledge and training, for example medicine, law or teaching

professional *adjective* **1**. doing a certain type of work to earn money • *a professional footballer* **2**. to do with a profession **3**. done with great skill and to a high standard **professionally** *adverb*

professional *noun* someone doing a certain type of work to earn money

professor *noun* a teacher of the highest rank in a university

proficient *adjective* (pro-**fish**-ent) to be proficient at something is to be able to do it well **proficiency** *noun* the ability to do something well **proficiently** *adverb*

profile *noun* **1**. a person's profile is a side view of their face **2**. a short description of someone or something

profit *noun* **1**. the extra money you get by selling something for more than it cost to buy or make **2**. an advantage or benefit

profit *verb* to profit from something is to get an advantage from it

profitable *adjective* making a profit; bringing in money

profound *adjective* **1**. very deep or intense • *His death had a profound effect on us all.* **2**. showing or needing great knowledge or thought • *The poem she wrote was quite profound.* **profoundly** *adverb*

program *noun* a series of instructions for a computer to carry out

program *verb* **programming**, **programmed** to program a computer is to prepare or control it by means of a program

programme *noun* **1**. a show, play or talk on radio or television **2**. a list of a planned series of events **3**. a leaflet or pamphlet that gives details of a play, concert or other event

progress *noun* (**proh**-gress) **1**. progress is forward movement • *The procession made slow progress.* **2**. progress is also development or improvement • *You have made a lot of progress this term.*

progress *verb* (pro-**gress**) **1**. to progress is to move forward **2**. to progress is also to develop or improve **progression** *noun* when something develops or moves forward

prohibit *verb* to prohibit something is to forbid it, especially by law **prohibition** *noun* forbidding something

project *noun* (**proj**-ekt) **1**. a task in which you find out as much as you can about something and write about it **2**. a plan or scheme

project *verb* (pro-**jekt**) **1**. to project is to stick out **2**. to project a picture or film is to show it with a projector on a screen **projection** *noun* **1**. something that sticks out **2**. showing a picture or film on a screen

projector *noun* a machine for showing films or photographs on a screen

prologue *noun* (**proh**-log) an introduction to a play or a long poem or story

prolong *verb* to prolong something is to make it last longer

promenade *noun* (prom-en-**ahd**) a wide path for walking beside the sea

prominent *adjective* **1**. easily seen; standing out **2**. important **prominence** *noun* being prominent

promise *noun* **1**. a promise is a statement that you will definitely do or not do something **2**. something shows promise when it shows signs that it will be successful in the future

promise *verb* to promise to do something is to say that you will definitely do it

promising *adjective* likely to be good or successful • *a promising athlete*

promote *verb* **1.** to be promoted is to be given a more senior or more important job or rank **2.** a sports team is promoted when it moves to a higher division or league **3.** to promote a product or cause is to make people more aware of it

promotion *noun* **1.** promotion is when someone is given a more senior or more important job or rank **2.** promotion is also when a sports team moves to a higher division or league **3.** a promotion is a piece of publicity or advertising

prompt *adjective* happening soon or without delay • *We need a prompt reply.* **promptly** *adverb* without delay

prompt *verb* **1.** to prompt someone to do something is to cause or encourage them to do it **2.** to prompt an actor is to remind them of their words if they forget them during a play

prone *adjective* to be prone to something is to be likely to do it or suffer from it

prong *noun* one of the pointed spikes at the end of a fork

pronoun *noun* a word used instead of a noun, such as *he, her, it, them, those*

pronounce *verb* **1.** to pronounce a word is to say it in a particular way • *'Too' and 'two' are pronounced the same.* **2.** to pronounce something is to declare it formally • *I now pronounce you husband and wife.*

pronunciation *noun* (pro-nun-si-**ay**-shon) the way a word is pronounced

proof *noun* proof is a fact which shows that something is true or exists

proof *adjective* giving protection against something • *a bullet-proof jacket*

prop[1] *noun* a wooden or metal support
prop[1] *verb* **propping, propped** to prop something somewhere is to lean it there so that it doesn't fall over

prop[2] *noun* an object used on stage in a theatre

propaganda *noun* propaganda is false information that political organizations use to make people believe something

propel *verb* **propelling, propelled** to propel something is to send it rapidly forward

propeller *noun* a set of blades on a hub that spin round to drive an aircraft or ship

proper *adjective* **1.** suitable or right • *This is the proper way to hold a bat.* **2.** respectable • *You must behave in a proper fashion.* **3.** *(informal)* complete; real • *I haven't had a proper meal for days.* **properly** *adverb* in a way that is correct or suitable

proper noun *noun* the name given to one person or thing, such as *Mary* and *Tokyo* and usually written with a capital first letter

property *noun* **properties 1.** a person's property is a thing or all the things, that belong to them **2.** a property is buildings or land belonging to someone **3.** a property is also a quality or characteristic that something has • *the plant's healing properties*

prophecy *noun* **prophecies** (**prof**-i-si) something that someone has said will happen in the future

prophesy *verb* **prophesies, prophesying, prophesied** (**prof**-i-sy) to prophesy something is to say that it will happen in the future

prophet *noun* **1.** someone who makes prophecies **2.** a religious teacher who is inspired by God **the Prophet** a name for Muhammad, the founder of the Muslim faith

prophetic *adjective* saying or showing what will happen in the future

proportion *noun* **1.** a fraction or share of something • *Water covers a large proportion of the earth's surface.* **2.** the proportion of one thing to another is how much there is of one compared to the other • *What is the proportion of girls to boys at the school?* **3.** the correct relationship between the size, amount or importance of two things • *You've drawn the head out of proportion with the body.* **proportions** size or scale

proportional or **proportionate** *adjective* in proportion; according to a ratio **proportionately** *adverb* in proportion

proposal *noun* **1.** a suggestion or plan **2.** when someone asks another person to marry them

propose *verb* **1.** to propose a plan is to suggest it **2.** to propose to someone is to ask them to marry you

proprietor *noun* (pro-**pry**-et-er) the owner of a shop or business

propulsion *noun* propulsion is propelling something or driving it forward

prose *noun* prose is writing that is like ordinary speech, not poetry

prosecute *verb* to prosecute someone is to make them go to a lawcourt to be tried for a crime **prosecution** *noun* the process of prosecuting someone **prosecutor** *noun* an official who prosecutes people

prospect *noun* (**pros**-pekt) a possibility or hope; what may happen in the future • *There's no prospect of the weather improving.*

prosper *verb* to prosper is to be successful or do well

prosperous *adjective* successful or rich **prosperity** *noun* being successful or rich

protect *verb* to protect someone or something is to keep them safe **protection** *noun* keeping someone or something safe **protector** *noun* a person who protects someone or something

protective *adjective* 1. a person is protective when they want to protect someone or something 2. a thing is protective when it is meant to protect something

protein *noun* (**proh**-teen) protein is a substance found in some types of food which your body needs to help you grow and be healthy

protest *noun* (**proh**-test) something you say or do because you disapprove of someone or something

protest *verb* (pro-**test**) to protest about something is to say publicly that you think it is wrong **protester** *noun* someone who protests about something

Protestant *noun* (**prot**-is-tant) a member of a western Christian Church other than the Roman Catholic Church

proton *noun* a particle of matter with a positive electric charge

protractor *noun* a device in the shape of a semicircle, used for measuring and drawing angles

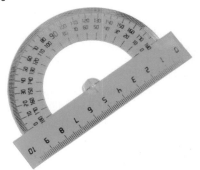

proud *adjective* 1. very pleased with yourself or with someone else who has done well • *I am proud of my sister.* 2. too satisfied because of who you are or what you have done • *They were too proud to ask for help.* **proudly** *adverb*

prove *verb* 1. to prove something is to show that it is true 2. to prove to be something is to turn out to be that way

proverb *noun* a short well-known saying that gives advice or says something about life, for example *many hands make light work*

provide *verb* 1. to provide something is to supply it 2. to provide for something is to prepare for it • *They have provided for all possible disasters.* **provided** or **providing** on condition; on condition that • *You can come providing you bring some food.*

province *noun* a region or division of a country

provision *noun* provision is providing something • *the provision of free meals for old people*

provisional *adjective* arranged or agreed on for the time being, but not yet definite • *21 July is the provisional date for the summer fair.*

provisions *plural noun* supplies of food and drink

provocative *adjective* likely to make someone angry

provoke *verb* 1. to provoke someone is to deliberately make them angry 2. to provoke a feeling is to arouse or cause it • *His* remarks provoked a great deal of criticism. **provocation** *noun* saying or doing something to deliberately make someone angry

prow *noun* the front end of a ship

prowl *verb* to prowl is to move about quietly and secretly, as some animals do when they are hunting **prowler** *noun* someone who prowls threateningly

proximity *noun* to be in the proximity of something is to be near it

prudent *adjective* (**proo**-dent) sensible and careful

prune[1] *noun* a dried plum

prune[2] *verb* to prune a tree or bush is to cut unwanted parts from it

pry *verb* pries, prying, pried to pry is to be nosy or inquisitive about someone else's business

PS something you write at the end of a letter when you want to add something else to it

psalm *noun* (sahm) a religious song from the Bible

pseudonym *noun* (s'**yoo**-do-nim) a name used by an author instead of their real name

psychiatrist *noun* (sy-**ky**-a-trist) a doctor who treats mental illness

psychiatry *noun* (sy-**ky**-a-tree) psychiatry is the treatment of mental illness **psychiatric** *adjective* to do with psychiatry

psychic *adjective* (**sy**-kik) someone is psychic when they can tell the future or read other people's minds

psychologist *noun* (sy-**kol**-o-jist) someone who studies how the mind works

psychology *noun* psychology is the study of the mind and the way people behave **psychological** *adjective* to do with psychology

pub *noun* (informal) a building where people can buy and drink alcoholic drinks

puberty *noun* (**pew**-ber-ti) puberty is the time when a young person starts to become an adult and their body starts to change

public *adjective* belonging to everyone or known or used by everyone • *public transport*

public *noun* the public is people in general in public openly; where anyone can see or take part **publicly** *adverb* in public

publication *noun* **1.** a publication is a book or magazine that is printed and sold **2.** publication is printing and selling books or magazines

publicity *noun* publicity is information or advertising that makes people know about someone or something

public school *noun* a secondary school that charges fees

publish *verb* **1.** to publish books or magazines is to print and sell them **2.** to publish information is to make it known publicly **publisher** *noun* a person or company that publishes books or magazines

pudding *noun* **1.** a hot sweet cooked food • *rice pudding* **2.** a savoury food made with flour or suet • *Yorkshire pudding* **3.** the sweet course of a meal • *What's for pudding?*

puddle *noun* a small pool of rainwater

puff *verb* **1.** to puff smoke or steam is to blow it out **2.** you puff when you breathe with difficulty **3.** to puff something or to puff it out, is to inflate or swell it

puff *noun* a small amount of breath, wind, smoke or steam

puffin *noun* a seabird with a large striped beak

pull *verb* **1.** to pull something is to get hold of it and make it come towards you or follow behind you **2.** to pull is to move with an effort • *She tried to grab the boy but he pulled away.* to pull out is to decide to stop taking part in something to pull someone's leg is to tease them to pull something off is to achieve it to pull through is to recover from an illness to pull up is to stop • *A car pulled up and two men got out.* to pull yourself together is to become calm or sensible

pull *noun* a pull is an action of pulling • *Give the handle a good pull.*

pulley *noun* pulleys a wheel with a groove round it to take a rope, used for lifting heavy things

pullover *noun* a knitted piece of clothing for the top half of your body, that you put on over your head

pulp *noun* a soft wet mass of something

pulpit *noun* a raised platform in a church, from which the priest or minister speaks to the congregation

pulse *noun* your pulse is the regular beat as your heart pumps your blood through your arteries. You can feel your pulse in your wrist or neck.

puma *noun* a large wild cat of North America

pumice *noun* (**pum**-iss) pumice is a kind of soft stone used to clean or polish surfaces

pump *noun* **1.** a device that forces air or liquid into or out of something or along pipes **2.** a lightweight shoe

pump *verb* to pump air or liquid is to force it into or out of something with a pump to pump something up is to fill a balloon or tyre with air or gas

pumpkin *noun* a large round fruit with a hard yellow skin

pun *noun* A pun is a joke made by using a word with two different meanings or two words that sound the same, as in *Choosing where to bury him was a grave decision.*

punch¹ *verb* **1.** to punch someone is to hit them with your fist **2.** to punch something is to make a hole in it • *The guard checked and punched our tickets.*

punch¹ *noun* **1.** a punch is a blow or hit with the fist **2.** a punch is also a device for making holes in paper or metal

punch² *noun* punch is a hot alcoholic drink

punchline *noun* the last part of a joke or story, that makes it funny

punctual *adjective* you are punctual when you arrive exactly on time, not late **punctuality** *noun* how punctual someone is **punctually** *adverb* in good time

punctuate *verb* to punctuate a piece of writing is to put the commas, full stops and other punctuation in it

punctuation *noun* punctuation is the set of marks such as commas, full stops and brackets put into a piece of writing to make it easier to understand

puncture *noun* a small hole made in a tyre by a sharp object

punish *verb* to punish someone is to make them suffer in some way because they have done something wrong **punishment** *noun* a way of punishing someone

puny *adjective* **punier**, **puniest** (**pew**-ni) small and weak

pup *noun* a puppy

pupa *noun* **pupae** (**pew**-pa) an insect at the stage of development between a larva and an adult insect; a chrysalis

pupil *noun* **1.** someone who is being taught by a teacher **2.** the opening in the centre of your eye

puppet *noun* a kind of doll that can be made to move by fitting it over your fingers or hand or by pulling strings or wires attached to it

puppy *noun* **puppies** a young dog

purchase *verb* to purchase something is to buy it **purchaser** *noun* someone who buys something

purchase *noun* **1.** a purchase is something you have bought **2.** purchase is the fact of buying something • *Keep the receipt as proof of purchase.*

pure *adjective* **1.** not mixed with anything else • *Use pure olive oil.* **2.** clean or clear • *They washed in a pure cold mountain stream.*

purely *adverb* only, simply • *They did it purely for the money.*

purify *verb* **purifies**, **purifying**, **purified** to purify something is to make it pure **purification** *noun* purification is purifying something

purity *noun* purity is the state of being pure

purple *noun* and *adjective* a deep reddish-blue

purpose *noun* the reason why you do something; what something is for to do something on purpose is to do it deliberately

purposely *adverb* on purpose

purr *verb* a cat purrs when it makes a gentle murmuring sound because it is pleased

purse *noun* a small bag for holding money

pursue *verb* **1.** to pursue someone or something is to chase them **2.** to pursue an activity is to continue to do it or work

at it • *She pursued her studies at college.*
pursuer *noun* a person who chases someone

pursuit *noun* **1.** pursuit is the action of chasing someone **2.** a pursuit is something you spend a lot of time doing

pus *noun* pus is a thick yellowish substance produced in boils and other sore places on your body

push *verb* **1.** to push something is to move it away from you by pressing against it **2.** to push something is also to press it in • *Try pushing the button.*

push *noun* a pushing movement

pushchair *noun* a small folding chair with wheels, in which a child can be pushed along

puss or **pussy** *noun* pusses or pussies (*informal*) a cat

put *verb* putting, put **1.** to put something in a place is to move it there • *Put the shopping down here.* **2.** to put also means to affect someone or something in a particular way • *They've put me in a bad mood.* **3.** to put an idea in a certain way is to express it using particular words • *She put it very tactfully.* to put someone off is to make them less keen on something • *Seeing you eat so much has put me off my food.* to put something off is to decide to do it later instead of now • *We'll have to put off the party if you're ill.* to put something on **1.** is to switch on an electrical device, for example a light or a television **2.** is to start wearing a piece of clothing • *I'll just put on my coat.* to put something out is to stop a fire or light from burning or shining to put someone up is to give them a place to sleep • *Can we put them up for the night?* to put something up is to raise it or make it upright • *Let's put up the tent.* to put up with something is to be willing to accept it without complaining

putty *noun* putty is a soft paste that sets hard, used to fit windows in their frames

puzzle *noun* **1.** a tricky game that you have to solve **2.** a difficult question; a problem

puzzle *verb* **1.** to puzzle someone is to give them a problem that is hard to understand **2.** to puzzle over something is to think hard about it

pygmy *noun* pygmies (**pig**-mi) an unusually small person or animal

pyjamas *plural noun* a loose lightweight set of jacket and trousers that you wear in bed

pylon *noun* a metal tower for supporting electric cables

pyramid *noun* **1.** an object with a square base and four sloping sides coming to a point **2.** a massive ancient Egyptian monument shaped like this

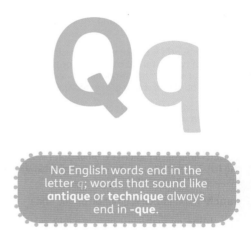

python *noun* a large snake that crushes its prey

No English words end in the letter *q*; words that sound like **antique** or **technique** always end in **-que**.

quack *verb* a duck quacks when it makes a short loud sound

quack *noun* the sound made by a duck

quad *noun* (*informal*) **1.** a quadrangle **2.** a quadruplet

quadrangle *noun* a rectangular courtyard with large buildings round it

quadrant *noun* a quarter of a circle

quadrilateral *noun* a flat shape with four straight sides

quadruple *adjective* **1.** four times as much or as many **2.** having four parts

quadruplet *noun* each of four children born to the same mother at one time

quail *noun* a bird that looks like a small partridge

quaint *adjective* attractive in an unusual or old-fashioned way

quake *verb* to quake is to tremble or shake

qualification *noun* **1.** a skill or ability to do a job **2.** an examination or course you have passed that shows you have a level of knowledge or skill in a subject

qualify *verb* qualifies, qualifying, qualified **1.** to qualify for a job is to be suitable for it or show you have the ability or qualifications to do it **2.** to qualify for a competition is to reach a high enough standard to take part in it

quality *noun* qualities **1.** the quality of something is how good or bad it is **2.** what something is like • *The paper had a shiny quality.*

quantity *noun* quantities how much there is of something or how many things there are of one sort

quarantine *noun* (**kwo**-ran-teen) quarantine is a period when a person or animal is kept apart from others to prevent a disease from spreading

quarrel *noun* a strong or angry argument
quarrel *verb* quarrelling, quarrelled to quarrel with someone is to argue fiercely with them

quarry *noun* quarries **1.** a place where stone or slate is dug out of the ground **2.** an animal that is being hunted

quart *noun* (kwort) a measure of liquid, a quarter of a gallon or about 1.14 litres

quarter *noun* **1.** each of four equal parts into which something is divided or can be divided **2.** three months, one-fourth of a year • *We get a phone bill every quarter.* at close quarters close together • *They fought at close quarters.*

quarters *plural noun* where someone lives for a time; lodgings

quartet *noun* (kwor-**tet**) a group of four musicians or singers

quartz *noun* (kworts) quartz is a hard mineral, used in making accurate electronic watches and clocks

quay *noun* (kee) a harbour wall or pier where ships can load and unload

queasy *adjective* queasier, queasiest you feel queasy when you feel slightly sick

queen *noun* **1.** a woman who has been crowned as the ruler of a country **2.** a king's wife **3.** a female bee or ant that produces eggs **4.** a piece in chess, the most powerful on the board **5.** a playing card with a picture of a queen on it

queer *adjective* strange or odd

quench *verb* **1.** to quench your thirst is to drink until you are no longer thirsty **2.** to quench a fire is to put it out

query *noun* queries (**kweer**-i) a question
query *verb* queries, querying, queried to query something is to question whether it is true or correct

quest *noun* a long search for something important

question *noun* **1.** something you ask **2.** a problem or subject for discussion to be out of the question is to be impossible

question *verb* **1.** to question someone is to ask them questions **2.** to question something is to be doubtful about it questioner *noun* someone who asks a question

question mark *noun* the punctuation mark (?) put at the end of a question

questionnaire *noun* (kwes-chon-**air**) a set of questions asked to get information for a survey

queue *noun* (kew) a line of people or vehicles waiting for something

queue *verb* (kew) people queue or queue up, when they wait in a queue

quick *adjective* **1**. taking only a short time • *You were quick.* **2**. done in a short time • *She gave a quick answer.* **3**. able to learn or think fast **quickly** *adverb* in a short time; fast

quicken *verb* **1**. to quicken something is to make it quicker • *She quickened her pace.* **2**. to quicken is to become quicker

quicksand *noun* quicksand is an area of loose wet sand that sucks in anything that falls into it

quiet *adjective* **1**. silent **2**. not loud • *He spoke in a quiet voice.* **3**. calm and peaceful • *They lead a quiet life.* **quietly** *adverb*

quiet *noun* quiet is a time when it is calm and peaceful • *Let's have a bit of quiet now.*

quieten *verb* **1**. to quieten something or someone is to make them quiet **2**. to quieten is to become quiet

quill *noun* a pen made from a large feather

quilt *noun* a thick soft cover for a bed

quintet *noun* a group of five musicians or singers

quit *verb* **quitting, quitted** or **quit** to quit something is to leave or abandon it

quite *adverb* **1**. rather or fairly • *He's quite a good swimmer.* **2**. completely or entirely • *I haven't quite finished.*

quiver[1] *verb* to quiver is to tremble

quiver[2] *noun* a long container for arrows

quiz *noun* **quizzes** a competition or game in which you have to answer questions

quota *noun* (**kwoh**-ta) a fixed share or amount

quotation *noun* an interesting sentence or set of words taken from a book or speech

quotation marks *plural noun* inverted commas, used to mark a quotation

quote *verb* to quote words is to use them in a quotation

quotient *noun* (**kwoh**-shent) the result of dividing one number by another • *The quotient of 12 divided by 3 is 4.*

The mnemonic '**r***hythm* **helps **y**our **t**wo **h**ips **m**ove' can help you to spell the word **rhythm**.

rabbi *noun* (**rab**-I) a Jewish religious leader

rabbit *noun* a furry animal with long ears that digs burrows

rabies *noun* (**ray**-beez) rabies is a fatal disease which causes madness in dogs and cats and can be passed to humans

raccoon *noun* a small North American animal with a bushy, striped tail

race[1] *noun* a competition to be the first to reach a particular place or to do something

race[1] *verb* **1**. to race someone is to have a race against them **2**. to race is to move very fast • *The train raced along the track.* **racer** *noun* a competitor in a race

race[2] *noun* a large group of people who have the same ancestors and share certain physical features such as the colour of their skin and hair

racecourse *noun* a place where horse races are run

racial *adjective* to do with a person's race **racially** *adverb*

racism *noun* (**ray**-sizm) racism is believing that one race of people is better than all the others and treating people unfairly because they belong to a different race **racist** *noun* someone who practises racism **racist** *adjective* showing racism

rack *noun* **1**. a framework used as a shelf or container • *a plate rack* **2**. an ancient device for torturing people by stretching them

rack *verb* **to rack your brains** is to think hard to remember something or solve a problem

racket[1] *noun* a bat with strings stretched across a frame, used in tennis and similar games

racket[2] *noun* to make a racket is to make a loud noise

radar *noun* (**ray**-dar) radar is a system that uses radio waves to show the position of ships or aircraft which cannot be seen because of distance or poor visibility

radiant *adjective* 1. radiating light or heat 2. you can say someone is radiant when they look happy and beautiful **radiance** *noun* brightness **radiantly** *adverb*

radiate *verb* to radiate heat, light or other energy is to send it out in rays

radiation *noun* 1. radiation is heat, light or other energy given out by something 2. radiation is also energy or particles sent out by something radioactive

radiator *noun* 1. a device that gives out heat, especially a metal container through which steam or hot water flows 2. a device that cools a car's engine

radical *adjective* 1. thorough and complete • *The new government made radical changes.* 2. wanting to make changes or reforms • *He is a radical politician.* **radically** *adverb* to be radically different is to be completely different

radio *noun* **radios** 1. radio is sending or receiving sound by means of electrical waves 2. a radio is an apparatus for receiving broadcast sound programmes or for receiving and sending messages

radioactive *adjective* radioactive substances have atoms that break up and give out dangerous radiation **radioactivity** *noun* the state of being radioactive

radish *noun* a small hard red vegetable with a hot taste, eaten raw in salads

radius *noun* **radii** 1. a straight line from the centre of a circle to the circumference 2. the length of this line

raffle *noun* a way of raising money by selling numbered tickets, some of which win prizes

raffle *verb* to raffle something is to give it as a prize in a raffle

raft *noun* a floating platform of logs or barrels tied together

rafter *noun* each of the long sloping pieces of wood that hold up a roof

rag *noun* an old or torn piece of cloth

rage *noun* great or violent anger
rage *verb* 1. to rage is to be very angry 2. to rage is also to be violent or noisy • *The storm was raging outside.*

ragged *adjective* (**rag**-id) torn or frayed

raid *noun* 1. a sudden attack 2. an unexpected visit from police to search a place or arrest people
raid *verb* to raid a place is to make a raid on it **raider** *noun* raiders are people who attack a place in a raid

rail *noun* 1. a bar or rod that you can hang things on or that forms part of a fence or banisters 2. a long metal strip that is part of a railway track **by rail** on a train

railings *plural noun* a fence made of metal bars

railway *noun* 1. a system of transport with trains running on rails 2. the parallel metal strips that trains travel on

rain *noun* rain is drops of water that fall from the sky
rain *verb* 1. to fall as rain • *It is still raining.* 2. to rain is to come down like rain • *Fragments of glass rained on them from above.*

rainbow *noun* a curved band of colours that you can sometimes see in the sky when the sun shines through rain

raincoat *noun* a waterproof coat

raindrop *noun* a single drop of rain

rainfall *noun* rainfall is the amount of rain that falls in a particular place or time

rainforest *noun* a dense tropical forest in an area of very heavy rainfall

raise *verb* 1. to raise something is to move it to a higher place or to an upright position 2. to raise money is to succeed in collecting it 3. to raise your voice is to speak loudly 4. to raise a subject or idea is to mention it for people to think about 5. to raise children is to bring them up and educate them **6**. to raise animals is to breed them

raisin *noun* a dried grape

rake *noun* a gardening tool with a row of short spikes fixed to a long handle
rake *verb* to rake something is to move it with a rake

rally *noun* rallies **1**. a large public meeting **2**. a competition to test skill in driving **3**. a series of strokes and return strokes of the ball in tennis or squash
rally *verb* rallies, rallying, rallied **1**. to rally people is to bring them together for a special effort **2**. to rally or rally round, is to come together to support someone **3**. to rally is to recover after an illness or setback • *The team rallied when they realized they could win.*

ram *noun* a male sheep
ram *verb* ramming, rammed to ram something is to push one thing hard against another

Ramadan *noun* (ram-a-**dan**) Ramadan is the ninth month of the Muslim year, when Muslims do not eat or drink during the daytime.

ramble *noun* a long walk in the country
ramble *verb* **1**. to ramble is to go for a long walk in the country **2**. to ramble is also to say a lot without keeping to a subject
rambler *noun* someone who goes rambling in the country

ramp *noun* a slope joining two different levels

rampage *verb* (ram-**payj**) to rampage is to rush about wildly or violently

ranch *noun* a large cattle-farm in America

random *noun* at random by chance; without any purpose or plan
random *adjective* done or taken at random • *They took a random sample.*

range *noun* **1**. a collection of different things of the same type • *The shop sells a wide range of games and puzzles.* **2**. the limits of something, from the highest to the lowest • *Most of the children here are in the 8-11 age range.* **3**. a line of hills or mountains **4**. the distance that a gun can shoot or an aircraft can fly or a sound can be heard **5**. a place with targets for shooting practice **6**. a kitchen fireplace with ovens

range *verb* **1**. to range between two limits is to extend from one to the other • *Prices ranged from £1 to £50.* **2**. to range is to wander over a wide area • *Hens ranged all over the farm.*

Ranger *noun* a senior member of the Guides

ranger *noun* someone who looks after a park or forest

rank *noun* **1**. a position in a series of people or things • *He was promoted to the rank of captain.* **2**. a line of people or things
rank *verb* to rank is to have a certain rank or place • *She ranks among the world's greatest writers.*

ransack *verb* to ransack a place is to search it thoroughly, looking for something to steal and leave it in a mess

ransom *noun* money paid so that someone who has been kidnapped can be set free to hold someone to ransom is to keep them prisoner and demand a ransom

rap *verb* rapping, rapped to rap is to knock quickly and loudly
rap *noun* **1**. a rap is a rapping movement or sound **2**. rap is a kind of pop music in which you speak words rapidly in rhythm

rapid *adjective* moving or working at speed
rapidity *noun* speed **rapidly** *adverb* very quickly

rapids *plural noun* part of a river where the water flows very fast over rocks

rare *adjective* unusual; not often found or experienced • *She died of a rare disease.*
rarely *adverb* not very often **rarity** *noun* something that is rare

rascal *noun* a dishonest or mischievous person

rash[1] *adjective* you are rash when you do something too quickly without thinking properly about it **rashly** *adverb*

rash[2] *noun* an outbreak of red spots or patches on the skin

rasher *noun* a slice of bacon

raspberry *noun* raspberries a small soft red fruit

Rastafarian *noun* (ras-ta-**fair**-i-an) a member of a religious group that started in Jamaica

rat *noun* an animal like a large mouse

rate *noun* **1**. how fast or how often something happens • *The train moved at a great rate.* **2**. a charge or payment • *What is the rate for a letter to Italy?* at any rate anyway at this rate if this is typical or true
rate *verb* to rate something or someone is to regard them in a certain way or as having a certain value • *Drivers rate the new car very highly.*

rather *adverb* **1**. slightly; somewhat • *It was rather dark.* **2**. you would rather do one thing than another thing if you would prefer to do it • *I think I'd rather do this later.* **3**. more truly or correctly • *He lay down or rather fell, on the bed.*

ratio *noun* ratios (**ray**-shi-oh) the relationship between two numbers; how many times one number goes into another • *In a group of 2 girls and 10 boys, the ratio of girls to boys is 1 to 5.*

ration *noun* (**rash**-on) the amount of something one person is allowed to have
ration *verb* (**rash**-on) to ration something is to give it out in fixed amounts because there is not a lot of it to share

rational *adjective* (**rash**-o-nal) reasonable or sensible • *No rational person would do such a thing.* rationally *adverb*

rattle *verb* **1**. to rattle is to make a series of short sharp hard sounds **2**. to rattle something is to make it rattle
rattle *noun* **1**. a rattling sound **2**. a baby's toy that rattles when you shake it

rattlesnake *noun* a poisonous American snake that makes rattling sounds with its tail

rave *verb* **1**. to be raving is to be talking wildly **2**. to rave about something is to talk very enthusiastically about it

rave *noun* a big party held in a large building with loud electronic music to dance to

raven *noun* a large black bird

ravenous *adjective* (**rav**-e-nus) very hungry
ravenously *adverb*

ravine *noun* (ra-**veen**) a very deep narrow gorge

ravioli *noun* ravioli is small squares of pasta filled with meat or cheese

raw *adjective* **1**. raw food is not cooked **2**. raw (for example) cotton or sugar is in its natural state before being processed **3**. sore because the skin has been removed **4**. cold and damp • *There was a raw wind.*

ray[1] *noun* a thin line of light, heat or other energy

ray[2] *noun* a large sea fish with a flat body and a long tail

razor *noun* a device with a very sharp blade, used for shaving

reach *verb* **1**. to reach a place is to go as far as it and arrive there **2**. to reach or reach out, is to stretch out your hand to get or touch something **3**. to reach something is to be long enough to touch it • *The carpet doesn't reach the wall.*
reach *noun* **1**. the distance you can reach with your hand **2**. a distance that you can easily travel • *I'd like to live within reach of the sea.*

react *verb* to react is to act in response to another person or thing

reaction *noun* what you feel or say or do when something happens or when someone does something

reactor *noun* an apparatus for producing nuclear power

read *verb* reading, read **1**. to read something written is to look at it and understand it or say it aloud **2**. a gauge or instrument reads a certain amount when that is what it shows • *The thermometer reads 20°.*

reader *noun* **1**. someone who reads **2**. a book that helps you learn to read

readily *adverb* **1**. willingly or eagerly • *She readily agreed to help.* **2**. quickly and without any difficulty • *All the ingredients you need are readily available.*

reading noun **1**. reading is the action of reading something written or printed **2**. a reading is an amount shown on a gauge or instrument

ready adjective readier, readiest **1**. prepared so that you can do something straight away; able or willing to do something • *Are you ready to leave?* **2**. prepared for use • *Is dinner ready?* readiness noun readiness is being ready for something

real adjective **1**. true or existing; not imaginary **2**. genuine; not a copy • *Are those pearls real?*

realistic adjective **1**. true to life • *It is a very realistic painting.* **2**. seeing things as they really are • *She is realistic about her chances of winning.* realistically adverb

reality noun realities reality is what is real

realize verb to realize something is to understand it or accept that it is true realization noun when you realize something This word can also be spelled **realise**.

really adverb truly; certainly; in fact

realm noun (relm) **1**. a kingdom **2**. an area of knowledge or activity

reap verb **1**. to reap corn is to cut it down and gather it in when it is ripe **2**. to reap a benefit is to gain it

reappear verb to reappear is to appear again reappearance noun a time when someone or something appears again

rear[1] adjective placed or found at the back • *I was looking out of the rear window.*

rear[1] noun the back part of something

rear[2] verb **1**. to rear young children or animals is to bring them up or help them grow **2**. a horse rears or rears up, when it rises up on its hind legs so that its front legs are in the air

reason noun **1**. the reason for something is why it happens **2**. reason is thinking in a clear and logical way • *He wouldn't listen to reason.*

reason verb **1**. to reason is to think in a logical way **2**. to reason with someone is to try to persuade them of something

reasonable adjective **1**. sensible or logical **2**. fair or moderate • *These are reasonable prices for what you get.*

reasonably adverb **1**. in a reasonable way; sensibly • *They were behaving quite reasonably.* **2**. fairly; somewhat • *She can swim reasonably well.*

reassure verb to reassure someone is to take away their doubts or fears reassurance noun something you say that reassures someone

rebel verb rebelling, rebelled (ri-**bel**) to rebel is to refuse to obey someone in authority

rebel noun (**reb**-el) someone who refuses to obey or fights against people who are in charge

rebellion noun **1**. rebellion is when people refuse to obey or fight against people in charge **2**. a rebellion is a fight against someone in authority, especially the government

rebellious adjective someone is rebellious when they refuse to obey people in charge or are likely to rebel

rebound verb to rebound is to bounce back after hitting something

rebuild verb rebuilding, rebuilt to rebuild something is to build it again after it has been destroyed

recall verb **1**. to recall something is to remember it **2**. to recall someone is to tell them to come back

recap verb recapping, recapped (informal) to recap is to summarize what has been said

recapture verb to recapture something or someone is to capture them again after they have escaped

recede verb **1**. to recede is to go back • *The floods have receded.* **2**. a man's hair is receding when he starts to go bald at the front

receipt noun (ri-**seet**) a written statement saying that a payment has been received or goods have been delivered

receive verb **1**. to receive something is to get it when it is given or sent to you **2**. to receive visitors is to greet them formally

receiver noun **1**. the part of a telephone that you hold to your ear **2**. a radio or television set

recent *adjective* made or happening a short time ago **recently** *adverb* only a short time ago

receptacle *noun* a container used for holding something

reception *noun* 1. the sort of welcome that someone gets • *We were given a friendly reception.* 2. a formal party to receive guests • *a wedding reception* 3. a place in a hotel or office where visitors report or check in 4. the quality of the signals your radio or television set receives • *We don't get good reception here.*

receptionist *noun* someone in an office or hotel who deals with visitors and answers the telephone

recession *noun* a time when a country is not trading well and a lot of people can't find jobs

recipe *noun* (**ress**-i-pi) a list of ingredients and instructions for preparing or cooking food

recital *noun* (ri-**sy**-tal) a performance of music or poetry by one person

recite *verb* to recite a poem is to say it aloud

reckless *adjective* someone is reckless when they do things without thinking or caring about what might happen **recklessly** *adverb* **recklessness** *noun*

reckon *verb* 1. to reckon something is to calculate or count it 2. to reckon something is to think it or have an opinion about it • *I reckon it's about to rain.*

recline *verb* to recline is to lean or lie back

recognize *verb* 1. to recognize someone or something is to know who they are because you have seen them before 2. to recognize a fault or mistake is to admit to it • *We recognize that we may have acted unfairly.* This word can also be spelled **recognise**. **recognition** *noun* recognizing someone or something **recognizable** *adjective* able to be recognized

recoil *verb* to recoil is to move backwards suddenly

recollect *verb* to recollect something is to remember it **recollection** *noun* a memory of something; being able to remember something

recommend *verb* 1. to recommend something is to suggest it because you think it is good or suitable • *I recommend the strawberry ice cream.* 2. to recommend an action is to advise someone to do it • *We recommend that you wear strong shoes on the walk.* **recommendation** *noun* something that you recommend

reconcile *verb* 1. to be reconciled with someone is to become friendly with them again after a quarrel 2. you are reconciled to something when you are persuaded to put up with it • *He soon became reconciled to wearing glasses.* **reconciliation** *noun* becoming friendly with someone again after a quarrel

reconstruction *noun* 1. reconstruction is building something up again 2. a reconstruction is acting out an event that took place in the past • *The police did a reconstruction of the bank robbery.*

record *noun* (**rek**-ord) 1. a disc with recorded sound on it 2. the best performance in a sport or the most remarkable event of its kind 3. a set of facts or information about something that you write down and keep
record *verb* (ri-**kord**) 1. to record music or sound or a television programme is to store it using electronic equipment 2. to record things that have happened is to put them down in writing

recorder *noun* 1. a wooden musical instrument that you play by blowing into one end and covering holes with your fingers 2. a person or thing that records something

recount *verb* to tell someone about something true that has happened

recover *verb* 1. to recover is to get better after being ill 2. to recover something is to get it back after losing it **recovery** *noun* getting better after being ill; getting something back after it was lost

recreation *noun* something you do for fun or enjoyment **recreational** *adjective* to do with recreation

recruit *noun* someone who has just joined the armed forces or a business or club
recruit *verb* to recruit someone is to get them to join the organization or club you belong to

rectangle *noun* a shape with four straight sides and four right angles **rectangular** *adjective* in the form of a rectangle

recuperate *verb* to recuperate is to get better after you have been ill

recur *verb* **recurring, recurred** something recurs when it happens again **recurrence** *noun* a recurrence of something is when it happens again

recycle *verb* to recycle waste material is to treat it so that it can be used again

red *adjective* **redder, reddest** 1. of the colour of blood 2. red hair is orangey-brown in colour
red *noun* a red colour **to see red** is to become suddenly angry

redden *verb* to redden is to become red

red-handed *adjective* to catch someone red-handed is to catch them while they are actually committing a crime or doing something wrong

redhead *noun* a person with reddish-brown hair

reduce *verb* to reduce something is to make it smaller or less

reduction *noun* 1. there is a reduction in something when it becomes smaller or less 2. the amount by which something is reduced • *They gave us a reduction of £5.*

redundant *adjective* 1. to be redundant is to be no longer needed 2. someone is made redundant when they lose their job because it is no longer needed **redundancy** *noun* when someone loses their job because it is no longer needed

reed *noun* 1. a plant that grows in or near water 2. a thin strip that vibrates to make the

sound in some wind instruments, such as a clarinet, saxophone or oboe

reef *noun* a line of rocks or sand just below the surface of the sea

reek *verb* to reek is to have a strong unpleasant smell

reel *noun* 1. a round device on which cotton or thread is wound 2. a lively Scottish dance

refer *verb* **referring, referred** 1. to refer to someone or something is to mention them or speak about them 2. to refer to (for example) a dictionary or encyclopedia is to look at it so that you can find something out 3. to refer a question or problem to someone else is to give it to them to deal with

referee *noun* someone who makes sure that people keep to the rules of a game
referee *verb* to referee a game is to act as referee in it

reference *noun* 1. a mention of something 2. a place in a book or file where information can be found 3. a letter or note about how well someone has done their work, used when applying for a job

reference book *noun* a book that gives information, such as a dictionary or encyclopedia

referendum *noun* (ref-er-**en**-dum) a vote on an important matter by all the people in a country

refill *verb* to refill something is to fill it again
refill *noun* a container used to replace something that has been used up • *My pen needs a refill.*

refine *verb* to refine something is to purify or improve it

refined *adjective* 1. refined (for example) sugar or oil has been made pure by taking other substances out of it 2. someone is refined when they have good manners and are well educated

refinement *noun* **1.** refinement is the process of refining something **2.** a refinement is something special that improves a thing

refinery *noun* refineries a factory for refining a product, such as oil

reflect *verb* **1.** something reflects light or heat or sound when it sends them back from a surface **2.** a mirror or other shiny surface reflects something when it forms an image of it **3.** you reflect on something when you think seriously about it

reflection *noun* the image you can see in a mirror or other shiny surface

reflex *noun* (**ree**-fleks) a movement or action that you do without any conscious thought

reform *verb* **1.** to reform a person or thing is to improve them by getting rid of their faults **2.** someone reforms when they improve their behaviour
reform *noun* **1.** reform is changing something to improve it **2.** a reform is a change in a system or law reformer *noun* someone who tries to change a system

refrain¹ *verb* to refrain from something is to keep yourself from doing it

refrain² *noun* the chorus of a song

refresh *verb* to refresh someone who is tired is to make them feel fresh and strong again

refreshments *plural noun* food and drink

refrigerator *noun* a cabinet in which you can store food at a low temperature to keep it fresh

refuel *verb* refuelling, refuelled to refuel a ship or aircraft is to supply it with more fuel

refuge *noun* a place where someone can go to be safe from danger

refugee *noun* (ref-yoo-**jee**) someone who has had to leave their home or country because of war or persecution or disaster

refund *verb* (ri-**fund**) to refund money is to pay it back
refund *noun* (**ree**-fund) money that is paid back to you

refuse *verb* (ri-**fewz**) to refuse something or to do something, is to say that you will not

accept it or do it refusal *noun* when someone refuses something
refuse *noun* (**ref**-yooss) rubbish or waste material

regain *verb* to regain something is to get it back

regard *verb* to regard someone or something as something is to think of them in a certain way • *I regard her as a friend.*
regard *noun* with regard to something about it; in connection with it

regarding *preposition* to do with; about • *There are rules regarding use of the library.*

regardless *adjective, adverb* paying no attention to something • *Buy it, regardless of the cost.* • *We asked her to stop, but she carried on regardless.*

regards *plural noun* kind wishes you send in a message

regatta *noun* (ri-**gat**-a) a meeting for boat or yacht races

reggae *noun* (**reg**-ay) reggae is a West Indian style of music with a strong beat

regiment *noun* a large army unit regimental *noun* to do with or belonging to a regiment

region *noun* a part of a country or the world regional *adjective* belonging to a particular region

register *noun* an official list of names or information
register *verb* **1.** to register something or someone is to put their name on an official list **2.** a gauge or instrument registers a certain amount when that is what it shows • *The thermometer registered 25°.* registration *noun* making an official record of something

regret *noun* you feel regret when you feel sorry or sad about something
regret *verb* regretting, regretted to regret something is to feel sorry or sad about it

regrettable *adjective* you say something is regrettable when you wish it hadn't happened

regular *adjective* **1.** always happening at certain times • *You need regular meals.* **2.** even or symmetrical • *She has beautiful regular teeth.* **3.** normal or correct • *Do you want a regular or large milkshake?* regularity *noun* being regular regularly *adverb*

regulate *verb* to regulate something is to adjust or control it

regulation *noun* a regulation is a rule or law

rehearse *verb* to rehearse (for example) a play or piece of music is to practise it before you perform it rehearsal *noun* when you practise something before performing it

reign *verb* to reign is to rule as a king or queen

reign *noun* the time when someone is king or queen

rein *noun* a strap used by a rider to guide a horse

reindeer *noun* reindeer a kind of deer that lives in Arctic regions

reinforce *verb* to reinforce something is to strengthen it

reinforcement *noun* a thing that strengthens something reinforcements extra troops sent to strengthen a military force

reject *verb* (ri-**jekt**) **1.** to reject something or someone is to refuse to accept them • *They have rejected my offer of help.* **2.** to reject something is to get rid of it • *Faulty parts are rejected at the factory.* rejection *noun* being rejected

reject *noun* (**ree**-jekt) a thing that is rejected because it is faulty or poorly made

rejoice *verb* to rejoice is to be very happy or pleased

relate *verb* **1.** things relate to each other when there is a connection between them **2.** to relate a story is to tell it

related *adjective* **1.** two people are related when they belong to the same family **2.** two things are related when they are connected or linked in some way

relation *noun* a relation is someone who is related to you

relationship *noun* **1.** the way people or things are connected with each other **2.** the way people get on with one another • *There is a good relationship between the teachers and the children.* **3.** a close friendship or connection between two people

relative *noun* your relatives are the people who are related to you

relative *adjective* **1.** connected or compared with something **2.** compared with the average • *They live in relative comfort.*

relatively *adverb* compared with other people or things • *Books are relatively cheap.*

relax *verb* **1.** to relax is to become less anxious or worried **2.** to relax is also to rest or stop working **3.** to relax a part of you is to make it less stiff or tense • *Try to relax your arm.* relaxation *noun* relaxing

relay *noun* a race between two teams in which each member of the team runs part of the distance

release *verb* **1.** to release something or someone is to set them free or unfasten them **2.** to release a film or recording is to make it available to the public

release *noun* **1.** release is being released **2.** a release is a new film or recording

relegate *verb* (**rel**-i-gayt) a sports team is relegated when it goes down into a lower division of a league relegation *noun* when a sports team is relegated

relent *verb* to relent is to be less angry or severe than you were going to be

relentless *adjective* never stopping or letting up • *Their criticism was relentless.* relentlessly *adverb*

relevant *adjective* connected with what you are discussing or dealing with relevance *noun* how relevant something is

reliable *adjective* able to be trusted or depended on reliability *noun* how reliable something is reliably *adverb*

relic *noun* something that has survived from an ancient time

relief *noun* **1.** a good feeling you get because something unpleasant has stopped or is not going to happen • *It was such a relief when we reached dry land.* **2.** relief is the ending or lessening of pain or suffering **3.** aid or help given to people in need • *famine relief*

relieve *verb* to relieve pain or suffering is to end or lessen it

relieved *adjective* feeling good because something unpleasant has stopped or is not going to happen

religion *noun* what people believe about God or gods and how they worship

religious *adjective* **1.** to do with religion **2.** believing in a religion

reluctant *adjective* you are reluctant to do something when you don't want to do it **reluctance** *noun* not wanting to do something **reluctantly** *adverb*

rely *verb* **relies, relying, relied** to rely on someone or something is to trust them or need them to help or support you

remain *verb* **1.** to remain is to continue in the same place or condition • *It will remain cloudy all day.* **2.** to remain is also to be left over • *A lot of food remained after the party.*

remainder *noun* **1.** something left over **2.** *(in mathematics)* the amount that is left over when you divide one number into another

remains *plural noun* **1.** something left over **2.** ruins or relics **3.** a dead body

remark *verb* to remark on something is to say something that you have thought or noticed

remark *noun* something you say

remarkable *adjective* so unusual or impressive that you notice or remember it **remarkably** *adverb* unusually or noticeably

remedy *noun* **remedies** a cure for an illness or problem

remember *verb* **1.** to remember something is to keep it in your mind or bring it into your mind when you need to **2.** to remember someone is to be thinking about them **remembrance** *noun* you do something in remembrance of someone or something when you do it as a way of remembering them

remind *verb* to remind someone is to help or make them remember something • *The girl in that painting reminds me of you.* **reminder** *noun* something that makes you think about or remember a person or thing

remnant *noun* a small piece of something left over

remorse *noun* remorse is deep regret for something wrong you have done **remorseful** *adjective* feeling remorse

remote *adjective* **1.** far away • *a remote island* **2.** unlikely or slight • *Their chances of winning were remote.* **remoteness** *noun*

remote control *noun* **1.** remote control is controlling something from a distance, using radio or electronic signals **2.** a remote control is a device for doing this

removal *noun* removing or moving something

remove *verb* to remove something is to take it away or take it off

rendezvous *noun* **rendezvous** (**ron**-day-voo) an arrangement to meet someone

renew *verb* to renew something is to make it as it was before or replace it with something new **renewal** *noun* when something begins again or is replaced with something new

renewable *adjective* able to be renewed or replaced; never completely used up • *Wind is a renewable source of energy.*

renowned *adjective* famous • *She is renowned for her generosity.*

rent *noun* a regular payment for using a house or flat

rent *verb* to rent something is to pay money to use it

repair *verb* to repair something is to mend it

repair *noun* **1.** repair is mending something • *The car is in for repair.* **2.** a repair is a mended place

repay *verb* **repaying, repaid 1.** to repay money is to pay it back **2.** to repay someone's kindness is to do something for them in return **repayment** *noun* paying money back

repeat *verb* to repeat something is to say it or do it again

repeat *noun* something that is repeated, especially a television programme

repeatedly *adverb* again and again

repel *verb* **repelling, repelled** to repel someone or something is to drive or force them away or apart

repent *verb* to repent is to be sorry for what you have done **repentance** *noun* repentance is being sorry for what you have done **repentant** *adjective* sorry for what you have done

repetition *noun* **1.** repeating or doing something again **2.** something repeated

repetitive *adjective* something is repetitive when it is repeated too much and so becomes boring

replace *verb* **1.** to replace something is to put it back in its place **2.** to replace someone or something is to take their place **3.** to replace something is to put a new thing in the place of it • *I promise I'll replace the book I lost.*

replacement *noun* **1.** replacement is when something or someone is replaced for another **2.** a replacement is something used or given in place of another

replay *noun* **1.** a football match played for a second time after the first match has ended in a draw **2.** the playing or showing again of a recording

replica *noun* (**rep**-li-ka) an exact copy

reply *noun* replies what you say or write when someone asks or says something

reply *verb* replies, replying, replied to reply is to give a reply

report *verb* **1.** to report something is to describe something that has happened or something you have studied **2.** to report someone is to complain about them to a person in authority **3.** to report to someone is to tell them you have arrived

report *noun* **1.** a description or account of something **2.** a regular statement of how a student has worked or behaved

reporter *noun* someone whose job is to collect news for a newspaper or for radio or television

represent *verb* **1.** to represent something or someone is to be a picture or model or symbol of them • *The dotted lines represent county boundaries.* **2.** to represent someone else is to speak or act on their behalf **representation** *noun* a representation of a thing is something that shows or describes it

representative *noun* a person who acts or speaks for other people
representative *adjective* typical of a group

reprieve *noun* (ri-**preev**) someone is given a reprieve when their punishment is postponed or cancelled

reprieve *verb* to reprieve someone is to cancel or postpone their punishment

reprimand *verb* to reprimand someone is to tell them off
reprimand *noun* a telling-off

reprisal *noun* (ri-**pry**-zal) an act of revenge

reproach *verb* to reproach someone is to blame them for something and show you are disappointed with them
reproach *noun* reproach is blame or criticism • *His behaviour was beyond reproach.*

reproduce *verb* **1.** to reproduce something is to make it be heard or seen again • *CDs can reproduce sound.* **2.** to reproduce something is also to copy it **3.** animals and people reproduce when they produce offspring
reproductive *adjective* to do with producing offspring

reproduction *noun* **1.** reproduction is the process of producing offspring **2.** a reproduction is a copy of something

reptile *noun* a cold-blooded animal that creeps or crawls, such as snakes and lizards

> The word **reptile** comes from a Latin word **repere** meaning 'to crawl'.

republic *noun* a country ruled by a president and government that are chosen by the people

repulsive *adjective* disgusting

reputation *noun* what most people think about a person or thing • *He has a reputation for being honest.*

request *verb* to request something is to ask politely or formally for it
request *noun* what someone asks for

require *verb* **1.** to require something is to need or want it **2.** you are required to do something when you have to do it • *Pedestrians are required to walk on the pavements.* **requirement** *noun* something that is needed

rescue *verb* to rescue someone is to save them from danger or capture
rescue *noun* when someone is rescued
rescuer *noun* a person who rescues someone

research *noun* research is careful study to learn more about a subject **researcher** *noun* someone who does research

resemblance *noun* there is a resemblance between two or more things when they are similar

resemble *verb* to resemble someone or something is to look or sound like them

resent *verb* to resent something is to feel angry about it because you think it is unfair **resentful** *adjective* angry about something that you think is unfair **resentment** *noun* a feeling of resenting something

reservation *noun* 1. arranging for (for example) a restaurant table or seat on a train to be kept for you 2. an area of land kept for a special purpose 3. you have reservations about something when you feel doubtful or uneasy about it

reserve *verb* to reserve something is to keep it or order it for a particular person or for a special use

reserve *noun* 1. a person kept ready to be used if necessary, especially an extra player in a sports team 2. an area of land kept for a special purpose • *a nature reserve*

reserved *adjective* 1. kept for someone • *These seats are reserved.* 2. someone is reserved when they are shy or unwilling to show their feelings

reservoir *noun* (**rez**-er-vwar) an artificial lake where water is stored

residence *noun* a place where someone lives

resident *noun* someone who lives in a particular place

resign *verb* to resign is to give up your job or position **to resign yourself to something** is to accept a difficulty without complaining or arguing

resignation *noun* 1. resignation is accepting a difficulty without complaining 2. a resignation is a letter saying you are resigning from your job

resin *noun* (**rez**-in) resin is a sticky substance that comes from plants or is made artificially

resist *verb* 1. to resist someone or something is to oppose them or try to stop them 2. you cannot resist something when you cannot

stop yourself doing it **resistance** *noun* fighting back or taking action against someone or something **resistant** *adjective* to be resistant to something is not to be affected or damaged by it

resolute *adjective* (**rez**-o-loot) determined or firm **resolutely** *adverb*

resolution *noun* 1. resolution is being determined or firm 2. a resolution is something you have decided to do

resolve *verb* 1. to resolve to do something is to decide to do it 2. to resolve a problem is to deal with it successfully

resort *noun* a place where people go for a holiday, especially by the sea **the last resort** the only thing you can do when everything else has failed

resort *verb* to resort to something is to make use of it, especially when everything else has failed • *In the end they resorted to violence.*

resource *noun* resources are things that you have and are able to use • *The land is rich in natural resources.*

respect *noun* 1. respect is admiration for someone's good qualities or achievements 2. respect is also consideration or concern • *Have respect for people's feelings.* 3. a respect is a detail or aspect • *In some respects, he is like his sister.*

respect *verb* to respect someone is to have respect for them

respectable *adjective* 1. a respectable person has good manners and character 2. something respectable is of a good size or standard **respectability** *noun* respectability is being respectable **respectably** *adverb*

respectful *adjective* showing respect; polite **respectfully** *adverb*

respective *adjective* belonging to each one of several • *We went to our respective rooms.*

respectively *adverb* in the same order as the people or things already mentioned • *Emma and I went to London and Paris respectively.*

respiration *noun* respiration is breathing **respiratory** *adjective* to do with breathing

respond *verb* to respond to someone or something is to reply or react to them

a b c d e f g h i j k l m n o p q r s t u v w x y z

response *noun* how you reply or react to something

responsibility *noun* responsibilities **1.** responsibility is being responsible for something **2.** a responsibility is something for which you are responsible

responsible *adjective* **1.** looking after something and likely to take the blame if anything goes wrong **2.** able to be trusted **3.** important and needing trust • *She has a responsible job.* **4.** to be responsible for something is to be the cause of it • *Faulty wiring was responsible for the fire.* responsibly *adverb* in a way that shows you can be trusted

rest¹ *noun* **1.** a time when you can sleep or relax **2.** a support for something

rest¹ *verb* **1.** to rest is to sleep or relax **2.** to rest on or against something is to lean on it • *The ladder is resting against the wall.* **3.** to rest something is to lean or support it somewhere • *Rest the ladder on the roof.*

rest² *noun* the rest the part that is left; the others

restaurant *noun* a place where you can buy a meal and eat it

restless *adjective* you are restless when you can't relax or keep still restlessly *adverb* restlessness *noun*

restore *verb* to restore something is to repair it so that it looks new again restoration *noun* when something is restored

restrain *verb* to restrain someone or something is to hold them or keep them tightly controlled restraint *noun* self-control

restrict *verb* to restrict someone or something is to keep them within certain limits or stop them from acting freely restriction *noun* something that restricts you

result *noun* **1.** a thing that happens because something else has happened **2.** the score or situation at the end of a game or competition or race **3.** the answer to a sum or problem

result *verb* to result is to happen as a result to result in something is to have it as a result

retain *verb* to retain something is to keep it

retina *noun* (**ret**-i-na) a layer at the back of your eyeball that is sensitive to light

retire *verb* **1.** someone retires when they give up regular work at a certain age **2.** to retire is also to retreat or withdraw or to go to bed • *He was so exhausted he had to retire from the race.* retirement *noun* the time when someone gives up regular work

retrace *verb* to retrace your steps is to go back the way you came

retreat *verb* to retreat is to go back when you are attacked or defeated

retrieve *verb* to retrieve something is to get it back or find it again retrieval *noun* retrieval is retrieving something

return *verb* **1.** to return is to come or go back to a place **2.** to return something is to give it or send it back

return *noun* **1.** when you come back to a place **2.** something that is given or sent back **3.** a ticket for a journey to a place and back again • *Do you want a single or return?*

reunion *noun* a meeting of people who have not met for some time

rev *verb* revving, revved to rev an engine is to make it run quickly

reveal *verb* to reveal something is to show it or make it known revelation *noun* a surprising fact that is made known

revenge *noun* revenge is harming someone because they have done harm to you

revenue *noun* (**rev**-e-nyoo) revenue is money that a business or organization receives

revere *verb* (ri-**veer**) to revere someone or something is to respect them deeply or religiously

reverence *noun* reverence is great respect or awe, especially towards God or holy things reverent *adjective* feeling or showing awe or respect

Reverend *noun* the title of a member of the Christian clergy

reverse *noun* **1.** the opposite way or side **2.** the gear used to drive a vehicle backwards in reverse going in the opposite direction

reverse *verb* **1.** to reverse something is to turn it round **2.** to reverse is to go backwards in a vehicle **3.** to reverse a decision is to change or cancel it reversal *noun* when something is reversed reversible *adjective* reversible clothing can be worn with either side on the outside

review *noun* **1.** a published description and opinion of a book or film or play or a piece of music **2.** an inspection or survey of something

review *verb* **1.** to review a book or play or film or a piece of music, is to write a review of it **2.** to review something is to inspect or survey it **reviewer** *noun* someone who writes a review

revise *verb* **1.** before you do an examination, you revise when you go over work that you have already done **2.** to revise something is to correct or change it **revision** *noun* a change or correction; learning work before you do an examination

revive *verb* **1.** to revive something is to start using it again **2.** to revive someone is to make them conscious again after fainting **revival** *noun* when something improves or becomes popular again

revolt *verb* **1.** to revolt is to rebel **2.** something revolts you when it disgusts or horrifies you **revolting** *adjective* very unpleasant or disgusting

revolt *noun* a rebellion

revolution *noun* **1.** a rebellion that overthrows the government **2.** a complete change **3.** one turn of a wheel or engine

revolutionary *adjective* **1.** to do with a revolution **2.** completely new or original

revolve *verb* something revolves when it goes round in a circle

revolver *noun* a small gun with a revolving cylinder that holds the bullets

reward *noun* something you are given in return for doing something good

reward *verb* to reward someone is to give them a reward

rewarding *adjective* satisfying and worth doing

rewrite *verb* **rewriting, rewrote, rewritten** to rewrite something is to write it again or differently

rheumatism *noun* (**roo**-ma-tizm) rheumatism is a disease that causes pain and stiffness in the joints and muscles

rhinoceros *noun* **rhinoceroses** or **rhinoceros** (ry-**noss**-er-os) a large heavy animal with a horn or two horns on its nose

rhombus *noun* a shape with four equal sides and no right angles, like a diamond on a playing card

rhubarb *noun* rhubarb is a plant with pink or green stalks that you can cook and eat

rhyme *noun* **1.** similar sounds in the endings of words, as in *bat* and *mat*, *batter* and *matter* **2.** a short rhyming poem

rhyme *verb* **1.** a poem rhymes when it has rhymes at the ends of its lines **2.** one word rhymes with another word when it forms a rhyme with it • *Bat rhymes with hat.*

rhythm *noun* a regular pattern of beats, sounds or movements in music and poetry **rhythmic** or **rhythmical** *adjective* having a rhythm **rhythmically** *adverb*

rib *noun* your ribs are the curved bones above your waist

ribbon *noun* a strip of nylon, silk or other material

rice *noun* rice is white seeds from a cereal plant, used as food

rich *adjective* **1.** someone is rich when they have a lot of money or property **2.** something is rich when it is full of goodness, quality or strength • *Fruit is rich in vitamins.* **richness** *noun*

riches *plural noun* wealth

richly *adverb* thoroughly, completely • *They richly deserved their punishment.*

rickety *adjective* unsteady and likely to break or fall down • *a rickety chair*

rickshaw *noun* a two-wheeled carriage pulled by one or more people, used in the Far East

The word **rickshaw** is from Japanese and is a shorter form of *jinriksha* which means 'people-power vehicle'.

ricochet *verb* (**rik**-o-shay) to ricochet is to bounce off something

rid *verb* ridding, rid to rid a person or place of something unwanted is to free them from it to get rid of something or someone is to cause them to go away • *I wish I could get rid of these spots.*

riddance *noun* good riddance used to show that you are glad that something or someone has gone

riddle *noun* a puzzling question with a clever answer

ride *verb* riding, rode, ridden **1.** to ride a horse or bicycle is to sit on it and be carried along on it **2.** to ride is to travel in a vehicle rider *noun* someone who rides a horse

ride *noun* a journey on a horse or bicycle or in a vehicle

ridge *noun* a long narrow part higher than the rest of something • *a mountain ridge*

ridicule *verb* to ridicule someone or something is to make fun of them

ridiculous *adjective* extremely silly or absurd ridiculously *adverb*

rifle *noun* a long gun that you hold against your shoulder when you fire it

rift *noun* **1.** a crack or split **2.** a disagreement or a break in a friendship

rig *verb* rigging, rigged **1.** to rig a ship is to fit it with rigging, sails and other equipment **2.** to rig an election or competition is to control the result dishonestly to rig something up is to make it quickly

rigging *noun* rigging is the ropes that support a ship's masts and sails

right *adjective* **1.** on or towards the east if you think of yourself as facing north **2.** correct • *Is this sum right?* **3.** fair or honest • *It's not right to cheat.*

right *adverb* **1.** on or towards the right • *Turn right.* **2.** completely • *Turn right round.* **3.** exactly • *She stood right in the middle.* **4.** straight; directly • *Go right ahead.* right away immediately

right *noun* **1.** the right side **2.** what is fair or just; something that people ought to be allowed • *They fought for their rights.* • *He had no right to talk to you like that.*

right *verb* to right something is to put it right • *The fault might right itself.*

right angle *noun* an angle of 90 degrees, like angles in a rectangle

rightful *adjective* deserved or proper

right-hand *adjective* on the right side of something

right-handed *adjective* using the right hand more than the left hand

rightly *adverb* correctly or fairly

rigid *adjective* (**rij**-id) **1.** firm or stiff **2.** strict or harsh • *The rules are rigid.* rigidity *noun* how rigid something is rigidly *adverb*

rim *noun* the outer edge of a cup or wheel or other round object

rind *noun* the tough skin on bacon, cheese or fruit

ring[1] *noun* **1.** something in the shape of a circle **2.** a thin circular piece of metal you wear on a finger **3.** the place where a boxing match or other contest is held **4.** the space where a circus performs

ring[2] *verb* ringing, rang, rung **1.** to ring a bell is to make it sound **2.** a bell rings when it makes a clear musical sound **3.** to ring someone is to telephone them

ring[2] *noun* a ringing sound to give someone a ring (informal) is to telephone them

ringleader *noun* someone who leads other people in doing wrong

ringlet *noun* a long curled piece of hair

ringmaster *noun* the person who is in charge of a performance in the circus ring

ring road *noun* a road that takes traffic round a town rather than through it

rink *noun* a place made for skating

rinse *verb* to rinse something is to wash it in clean water without soap
rinse *noun* a wash in clean water without soap

riot *noun* violent behaviour by a crowd of people in a public place
riot *verb* people riot when they behave violently in a public place

rip *verb* ripping, ripped to rip something is to tear it roughly
rip *noun* a torn place

ripe *adjective* ready to be harvested or eaten ripeness *noun*

ripen *verb* 1. to ripen something is to make it ripe 2. to ripen is to become ripe

ripple *noun* a small wave on the surface of water
ripple *verb* water ripples when it forms small waves on the surface

rise *verb* rising, rose, risen 1. to rise is to go upwards • *Smoke was rising from the fire.* 2. to rise is also to get larger or more • *Prices rose this year.* 3. a person rises when they get up from sleeping or sitting • *They all rose as she came in.*
rise *noun* 1. an increase 2. an upward slope

risk *verb* to risk something is to take a chance of damaging or losing it • *They risked their lives during the rescue.*
risk *noun* a chance that something bad will happen risky *adjective* dangerous; involving risk

rite *noun* a ceremony or ritual

ritual *noun* a regular ceremony or series of actions

rival *noun* a person or thing that competes with another or tries to do the same thing rivalry *noun* when two people compete against each other

rival *verb* rivalling, rivalled to rival someone or something is to be as good as they are

river *noun* a large natural stream of water that flows into the sea or into a lake

rivet *noun* a strong metal pin for holding pieces of metal together
rivet *verb* 1. to rivet something is to fasten it with rivets 2. to rivet someone is to hold them still • *She stood riveted to the spot.* 3. to be riveted by something is to be fascinated by it • *The children were riveted by his story.* riveting *adjective* fascinating; holding your attention

road *noun* a level way with a hard surface made for traffic to go along

roam *verb* to roam is to wander

roar *noun* a loud deep sound of the kind that a lion makes
roar *verb* to roar is to make a loud deep sound

roast *verb* to roast food is to cook it in an oven

rob *verb* robbing, robbed to rob someone or a place is to steal something from them • *The bank's been robbed.* robber *noun* someone who steals something robbery *noun* when something is stolen

robe *noun* a long loose piece of clothing

robin *noun* a small brown bird with a red breast

robot *noun* a machine that can move and do work

robust *adjective* tough and strong

rock[1] *noun* **1.** a rock is a large stone **2.** rock is a large mass of stone **3.** rock is also a hard sweet shaped like a stick

rock[2] *verb* **1.** to rock is to move gently backwards and forwards or from side to side **2.** to rock something is to make it do this

rock[2] *noun* rock music

rocket *noun* **1.** a firework that shoots high into the air **2.** a pointed tube-shaped vehicle propelled into the air by hot gases, especially as a spacecraft or weapon

rocking chair *noun* a chair which can be rocked by the person sitting in it

rocky *adjective* rockier, rockiest **1.** a rocky place is full of rocks **2.** unsteady or shaky

rod *noun* **1.** a long thin stick or bar **2.** a rod with a line attached for fishing

rode past tense of **ride** verb

rodent *noun* an animal that has large front teeth for gnawing things, such as a rat, mouse or squirrel

rodeo *noun* rodeos (roh-**day**-oh or **roh**-di-oh) a display or contest in which cowboys show their skills in riding and in controlling cattle

rogue *noun* a dishonest or mischievous person roguish *adjective* a roguish smile is a mischievous one

role *noun* **1.** the part that an actor plays in a play, film or story **2.** the purpose something has • *Computers have a role in language learning.*

roll *verb* **1.** to roll is to move along by turning over and over, like a ball **2.** to roll something is to make it do this **3.** to roll something or roll something up, is to form it into the shape of

a cylinder or ball **4.** to roll something soft is to flatten it by moving a round heavy object over it **5.** a ship rolls when it sways from side to side

roll *noun* **1.** a cylinder made by rolling something up **2.** a small round loaf of bread **3.** a list of names **4.** the rumbling sound of drums or thunder

roller *noun* a cylinder-shaped object, especially one used for flattening things

roller skate *noun* roller skates are boots with two pairs of wheels fitted underneath, so that you can move smoothly over the ground

rolling pin *noun* a heavy cylinder you roll over pastry to flatten it

Roman Catholic *noun* a member of the Church with the Pope in Rome at its head

romance *noun* **1.** romance is experiences and feelings connected with love **2.** a romance is a love affair or a love story

Roman numerals *plural noun* letters that represent numbers, as used by the ancient Romans (compare *Arabic figures*): I = 1, V = 5, X = 10, L = 50, C = 100 and M = 1000

romantic *adjective* to do with love or romance romantically *adverb*

romp *verb* to romp is to play in a lively way

roof *noun* **1.** the part that covers the top of a building, shelter or vehicle **2.** the upper part of your mouth

rook *noun* **1.** a black bird that looks like a crow **2.** a piece in chess, also called a *castle*

room *noun* **1.** a room is a part of a building with its own walls and ceiling **2.** room is space for someone or something • *Is there room for me?*

roomy *adjective* roomier, roomiest somewhere is roomy when there is plenty of room or space inside

roost *noun* the place where a bird rests

root *noun* **1.** the part of a plant that grows under the ground **2.** a source or basis of something • *People say that money is the root of all evil.* **3.** a number that gives another number when multiplied by itself • *9 is the square root of 81.* to take root is to grow roots or to become established

root *verb* to root is to take root in the ground **to root something out** is to find it and get rid of it

rope *noun* a strong thick cord made of strands twisted together **to show someone the ropes** is to show them how to do a job

rose *noun* a scented flower with a long thorny stem

rosy *adjective* rosier, rosiest **1**. pink **2**. hopeful or cheerful • *The future looks rosy.*

rot *verb* rotting, rotted to rot is to go soft or bad so that it is useless • *This wood has rotted.*
rot *noun* rot is decay

rota *noun* a list of tasks to be done and the people who have to do them

rotate *verb* **1**. to rotate is to go round like a wheel **2**. to rotate is to take turns at something • *The job of treasurer rotates.*

rotation *noun* **1**. rotation or a rotation, is when something goes round like a wheel **2**. rotation is also taking turns to do something

rotor *noun* the part of a machine that goes round, especially the large rotating blade on top of a helicopter

rotten *adjective* **1**. rotted or decayed • *rotten fruit* **2**. *(informal)* nasty or very bad • *rotten weather*

rough *adjective* **1**. not smooth; uneven **2**. violent; not gentle • *He is a rough boy.* **3**. not exact; done quickly • *It's only a rough guess.* **roughness** *noun*

roughly *adverb* **1**. approximately; not exactly • *There were roughly a hundred people there.*

2. in a rough way; not gently • *She pushed him roughly out of the way.*

round *adjective* **1**. shaped like a circle or ball or cylinder **2**. a round trip is one that returns to the start

round *adverb* **1**. in a circle or curve • *Go round to the back of the house.* **2**. in every direction or to every person • *Hand the cakes round.* **3**. in a new direction • *Turn your chair round.* **4**. to someone's house or place of work • *Come round at lunchtime.*

round *preposition* **1**. on all sides of • *We'll put a fence round the field.* **2**. in a curve or circle about • *The earth moves round the sun.* **3**. to every part of • *Show them round the house.*

round *noun* **1**. each stage in a competition • *The winners go on to the next round.* **2**. a series of visits or calls made by a doctor, postman or other person **3**. a whole slice of bread or a sandwich made from two whole slices of bread **4**. a shot or series of shots from a gun; a piece of ammunition **5**. a song in which people sing the same words but start at different times

round *verb* to round a place is to travel round it • *A car rounded the corner.* **to round a number down** is to decrease it to the nearest lower number • *123.4 may be rounded down to 123.* **to round a number up** is to increase it to the nearest higher number • *123.7 may be rounded up to 124.* **to round up people or things** is to gather them together

roundabout *noun* **1**. a road junction at which traffic has to pass round a circular island **2**. a merry-go-round

rounders *noun* rounders is a game in which players try to hit a ball and run round a circuit

roundly *adverb* thoroughly or severely • *We were roundly told off for being late.*

rouse *verb* to rouse someone is to wake them up or make them excited

rout *verb* (rowt) to rout an enemy is to defeat them and chase them away

route *noun* (root) the way you have to go to get to a place

routine *noun* (roo-**teen**) a regular or fixed way of doing things

rove *verb* to rove is to roam or wander • *Her eyes roved arond the classroom.* **rover** *noun* someone who roves

row[1] *noun* (rhymes with go) a line of people or things

row[2] *verb* (rhymes with go) to row a boat is to use oars to make it move **rower** *noun* someone who rows a boat

row[3] *noun* (rhymes with cow) **1.** a great noise or disturbance **2.** a noisy quarrel or argument
row[3] *verb* people row when they have a noisy argument

rowdy *adjective* **rowdier**, **rowdiest** noisy and disorderly **rowdiness** *noun*

rowing boat *noun* a small boat that you move forward by using oars

royal *adjective* to do with a king or queen **royalty** *noun* the members of a royal family

rub *verb* **rubbing**, **rubbed** to rub something is to move it backwards and forwards while pressing it on something else **to rub something off** or **out** is to make it disappear by rubbing it
rub *noun* when you rub something

rubber *noun* **1.** rubber is a strong elastic substance used for making tyres, balls, hoses and other things **2.** a rubber is a piece of rubber for rubbing out pencil marks **rubbery** *adjective* soft and easy to stretch

rubbish *noun* **1.** things that are not wanted or needed **2.** nonsense

rubble *noun* rubble is broken pieces of brick or stone

ruby *noun* **rubies** a red jewel

rucksack *noun* a bag with shoulder straps that you carry on your back

rudder *noun* a flat hinged device at the back of a ship or aircraft, used for steering it

ruddy *adjective* **ruddier**, **ruddiest** red and healthy-looking • *a ruddy face*

rude *adjective* **1.** not polite; not showing respect for other people **2.** indecent or improper • *a rude joke* **rudely** *adverb* **rudeness** *noun*

ruffian *noun* a rough violent person

ruffle *verb* to ruffle something is to make it untidy or less smooth • *The bird ruffled its feathers.*

rug *noun* **1.** a thick piece of material that partly covers a floor **2.** a thick blanket

rugby or **rugby football** *noun* rugby is a kind of football game using an oval ball that players may kick or carry

rugged *adjective* (**rug**-id) something rugged has a rough or uneven surface or outline • *a rugged coastline*

ruin *verb* to ruin something is to spoil it or destroy it completely
ruin *noun* **ruins** **1.** a ruin is a building that has been so badly damaged that it has almost all fallen down **2.** ruin is when something is ruined or destroyed **ruinous** *adjective* leading to ruin

rule *noun* **1.** a rule is something that people have to obey **2.** rule is ruling or governing • *The country used to be under French rule.* **as a rule** usually; normally
rule *verb* **1.** to rule people is to govern them; to rule is to be a ruler **2.** to rule something is to make a decision • *The referee ruled that it was a foul.*

ruler *noun* **1.** someone who governs a country **2.** a strip of wood, plastic or metal with straight edges, used for measuring and drawing straight lines

ruling *noun* a judgement or decision

rum *noun* rum is a strong alcoholic drink made from sugar cane

rumble *verb* to rumble is to make a deep heavy sound like thunder
rumble *noun* a long deep heavy sound

rummage *verb* to rummage is to turn things over or move them about while looking for something

rumour *noun* something that a lot of people are saying, although it may not be true

rump *noun* the back part of an animal, above its hind legs

run *verb* **running**, **ran**, **run** **1.** to run is to move with quick steps and with both feet off the ground for a time **2.** to run is also to move or go or travel • *Tears ran down his cheeks.* **3.** a tap or your nose runs when liquid flows from it **4.** an engine or machine runs when it is working • *The engine was running smoothly.* **5.** to run something is to manage it or organize it • *She runs a corner shop.* **to**

run a risk is to take a chance **to run away** is to leave a place quickly or secretly **to run into someone** is to meet them unexpectedly **to run out of something** is to have used up a supply of it **to run someone over** is to knock them down with a car

run *noun* **1.** a spell of running • *Let's go for a run.* **2.** a point scored in cricket or baseball **3.** a series of damaged stitches in a pair of tights or other piece of clothing **4.** a continuous series of events • *They've had a run of good luck.* **to be on the run** is to be running away from the police

runaway *noun* someone who has run away from home

rung *noun* each of the steps on a ladder

runner *noun* **1.** a person or animal that runs in a race **2.** the part of a sledge that slides along the ground

runner-up *noun* **runners-up** someone who comes second in a race or competition

runny *adjective* **runnier, runniest** flowing or moving like liquid

runway *noun* a long strip with a hard surface for aircraft to take off and land

rural *adjective* to do with the countryside; in the country

rush[1] *verb* **1.** to rush is to move or go very quickly • *When the doorbell rang I rushed to see who it was.* **2.** to rush someone is to make them hurry • *I'm trying not to rush you.*
rush[1] *noun* a rush is a hurry • *I can't stop – I'm in a rush.*

rush[2] *noun* rushes are plants with thin stems that grow in wet or marshy places

rusk *noun* a kind of hard dry biscuit for babies to chew

rust *noun* rust is a red or brown substance formed on metal when it gets wet
rust *verb* metal rusts when it becomes covered with rust

rustle *verb* **1.** to rustle is to make a gentle sound like dry leaves being blown by the wind **2.** to rustle horses or cattle is to steal them

rusty *adjective* **rustier, rustiest** **1.** coated with rust **2.** not as good as it used to be because you have not had enough practice • *My French is a bit rusty.*

rut *noun* a deep groove made by wheels in soft ground **to be in a rut** is to have a dull life with no changes

ruthless *adjective* someone is ruthless when they are determined to get what they want and don't care if they hurt other people **ruthlessly** *adverb* **ruthlessness** *noun*

rye *noun* rye is a cereal used to make bread and biscuits

There is **a rat** in s**eparate**. If you can see it, it will help you spell it.

sabbath *noun* the sabbath is the weekly day for rest and prayer, Saturday for Jews, Sunday for Christians

sabotage *noun* (**sab**-o-tahzh) sabotage is deliberately damaging machinery or equipment
sabotage *verb* to sabotage machinery or equipment is to deliberately damage it **saboteur** *noun* someone who commits sabotage

sac *noun* any bag-like part of an animal or plant

sachet *noun* (**sash**-ay) a small sealed packet of something such as shampoo

sack *noun* a large bag made of strong material **to get the sack** (*informal*) is to be dismissed from your job
sack *verb* (*informal*) to sack someone is to dismiss them from their job

sacred *adjective* to do with God or a god; holy

a
b
c
d
e
f
g
h
i
j
k
l
m
n
o
p
q
r
s
t
u
v
w
x
y
z

sacrifice *noun* **1.** giving up a thing that you value so that something good may happen **2.** an animal or person that is killed as an offering to a god **sacrificial** *adjective* offered as a sacrifice

sacrifice *verb* **1.** to sacrifice something is to give it up so that something good may happen **2.** to sacrifice an animal or person is to kill them as an offering to a god

sad *adjective* **sadder**, **saddest** unhappy; showing sorrow **sadly** *adverb* in a sad way **sadness** *noun*

sadden *verb* something saddens you when it makes you sad

saddle *noun* **1.** a seat that you put on the back of a horse so that you can ride it **2.** the seat of a bicycle

saddle *verb* to saddle an animal is to put a saddle on its back

safari *noun* (sa-**far**-i) an expedition to see wild animals or hunt them

The word **safari** comes from an Arabic word *safara* meaning 'to travel'.

safari park *noun* a large park where wild animals can roam around freely and visitors can watch them from their cars

safe *adjective* **1.** free from danger; protected **2.** not causing danger • *Drive at a safe speed.* **safely** *adverb* without risk or danger • *The plane landed safely.*

safe *noun* a strong cupboard or box in which valuable things can be locked away to keep them safe

safeguard *noun* something that protects you against danger

safeguard *verb* to safeguard something is to protect it from danger

safety *noun* safety is being safe; protection

safety belt *noun* a belt to hold someone securely in a seat

safety pin *noun* a curved pin made with a clip that closes to cover the point

sag *verb* **sagging**, **sagged** something sags when it sinks slightly in the middle because something heavy is pressing on it

saga *noun* a long story with many adventures

sail *noun* **1.** a large piece of strong cloth attached to a mast to make a boat move **2.** an arm of a windmill **to set sail** is to start on a voyage in a ship

sail *verb* **1.** to sail somewhere is to travel there in a ship **2.** a ship or boat sails when it starts out on a voyage **3.** to sail a ship or boat is to control it

sailor *noun* **1.** a member of a ship's crew **2.** someone who sails

saint *noun* a holy or very good person **saintly** *adjective* very good or holy

sake *noun* **for the sake of something** in order to do it or get it • *He'll do anything for the sake of money.* **for someone's sake** in order to help them or please them • *She went to a lot of trouble for his sake.*

salad *noun* a mixture of vegetables eaten cold and often raw

salary *noun* **salaries** a regular wage, usually paid every month

sale *noun* **1.** the selling of something **2.** a time when a shop sells things at reduced prices **for sale** or **on sale** able to be bought

salesperson *noun* someone whose job is to sell things **salesman** *noun* **saleswoman** *noun*

saliva *noun* (sa-**ly**-va) saliva is the natural liquid in your mouth

salmon *noun* **salmon** a large fish with pink flesh, used for food

salon *noun* a room or shop where a hairdresser or a beauty specialist works

salt *noun* salt is the white substance that gives sea water its taste and is used for flavouring food **salty** *adjective* tasting of salt

salt *verb* to salt food is to use salt to flavour or preserve it

salute *verb* to salute is to raise your hand to your forehead as a sign of respect or greeting
salute *noun* the act of saluting

salvage *verb* to salvage something such as a damaged ship is to save or rescue it or parts of it

salvation *noun* salvation is saving someone or something

same *adjective* not different; exactly equal or alike • *We are the same age.*

samosa *noun* a small case of crisp pastry filled with a mixture of spicy meat or vegetables

sample *noun* a small amount that shows what something is like
sample *verb* **1.** to sample something is to take a sample of it • *Scientists sampled the lake water.* **2.** to sample something is also to try part of it • *She sampled the cake.*

sanctuary *noun* **sanctuaries** **1.** a safe place, especially for someone who is being chased or attacked **2.** a place where wildlife is protected

sand *noun* sand is the tiny grains of rock that form beaches and deserts

sandal *noun* a light shoe with straps that go round your foot

sandpaper *noun* sandpaper is strong paper coated with hard grains, rubbed on rough surfaces to make them smooth

sandwich *noun* slices of bread with meat, cheese or some other filling between them

sandy *adjective* **sandier, sandiest** made of sand; covered with sand

sane *adjective* having a healthy mind; not mad

sanitary *adjective* free from germs and dirt; hygienic

sanitation *noun* sanitation is arrangements for drainage and getting rid of sewage

sanity *noun* sanity is being sane

sap *noun* sap is the juice inside a tree or plant
sap *verb* **sapping, sapped** to sap someone's strength or energy is to use it up or weaken it gradually

sapling *noun* a young tree

sapphire *noun* a bright blue jewel

sarcastic *noun* you are being sarcastic when you mock someone or something by saying the opposite of what you mean **sarcastically** *adverb* **sarcasm** *noun* when someone is being sarcastic

sardine *noun* a small sea fish, usually sold packed tightly in tins

sari *noun* (**sar**-i) a long length of cloth worn as a dress, especially by Indian women and girls

sash *noun* a strip of cloth worn round the waist or over one shoulder

satchel *noun* a bag you wear over your shoulder or on your back, especially for carrying school books

satellite *noun* **1.** a spacecraft sent into space to move in an orbit round a planet **2.** a moon that moves in orbit round a planet

satellite dish *noun* a dish-shaped aerial for receiving television signals sent by satellite

satin *noun* satin is a silky material that is shiny on one side

satire *noun* **1.** satire is using humour or exaggeration to show the faults of a person or thing, especially the government **2.** a satire is a play or piece of writing that does this **satirical** *adjective* using satire to criticize someone **satirist** *noun* someone who writes satire

satisfaction *noun* satisfaction is the feeling of being satisfied

satisfactory *adjective* good enough; acceptable **satisfactorily** *adverb* in a satisfactory way

satisfy *verb* **satisfies, satisfying, satisfied** **1.** to satisfy someone is to give them what they need or want **2.** to be satisfied is to be sure of something • *I am satisfied that you have done your best.*

saturate *verb* to be saturated is to be soaking wet • *My shirt was saturated with sweat.* **saturation** *noun* saturation is being saturated

Saturday *noun* the seventh day of the week

sauce *noun* a sauce is a thick liquid served with food to add flavour

saucepan *noun* a metal cooking pan with a long handle

saucer *noun* a small curved plate for a cup to stand on

sauna *noun* (**saw**-na or **sow**-na) a room filled with steam where people sit and sweat a lot

saunter *verb* to saunter is to walk about in a leisurely way

sausage *noun* a tube of edible skin or plastic stuffed with meat and other ingredients

savage *adjective* wild and fierce; cruel **savagely** *noun* in a violent or cruel way **savagery** *noun* cruel and violent behaviour **savage** *verb* an animal savages someone when it attacks them and bites or scratches them fiercely

savannah *noun* (sa-**van**-a) a grassy plain in a hot country, with few trees

save *verb* **1.** to save someone or something is to free them from danger or harm **2.** to save money is to keep it so that it can be used later **3.** to save a document is to store it a computer's hard disk **4.** in football, to save a shot is to stop the ball going into your goal

savings *plural noun* your savings are the money that you have saved

saviour *noun* a person who saves someone

savoury *adjective* savoury food is tasty but not sweet

saw *noun* a tool with sharp teeth for cutting wood
saw *verb* **sawing, sawed, sawn or sawed** to saw wood is to cut it with a saw

sawdust *noun* sawdust is powder that comes from wood when it is cut with a saw

saxophone *noun* a wind instrument with a tube that curves upward with a wider opening

> The word **saxophone** comes from the name of Adolphe Sax, a Belgian instrument-maker.

say *verb* **saying, said** **1.** to say something is to speak words **2.** to say something is also to give information or instructions • *The notice said 'Keep Out'.*

saying *noun* a well-known phrase or proverb

scab *noun* a hard covering that forms over a cut or graze while it is healing

scabbard *noun* a cover for a sword or dagger

scaffold *noun* a platform on which criminals were executed in the past

scaffolding *noun* scaffolding is a structure of poles and planks for workers to stand on when they are building or repairing a house

scald *verb* to scald your skin is to burn it with very hot liquid or steam

scale[1] *noun* **1.** a series of units or marks for measuring something • *This ruler has one scale in centimetres and another in inches.* **2.** the relationship between the size of something on a map or model and its actual size • *The scale of this map is one inch to the mile.* **3.** a series of musical notes going up or down in a fixed pattern **4.** the relative size or importance of something • *The scale of the task is massive.*

scale[1] *verb* to scale something is to climb up it

scale[2] *noun* one of the thin overlapping parts on the outside of fish, snakes and other animals scaly *adjective* covered in scales

scales *plural noun* a device for weighing things

scalp *noun* the skin on the top of your head

scamper *verb* to scamper is to run quickly with short steps

scan *verb* scanning, scanned **1.** to scan something is to look at every part of it **2.** to scan a piece of writing is to read it quickly **3.** to scan an area or a part of the body, is to send an electronic beam over it in order to find something **4.** poetry scans when it has a regular rhythm

scan *noun* a search or examination using a scanner

scandal *noun* a scandal is a shameful or disgraceful action scandalous *adjective* shocking or disgraceful

scanner *noun* **1.** a machine used to examine part of the body, using an electronic beam **2.** a machine that copies documents and pictures onto a computer

scanty *adjective* scantier, scantiest hardly big enough; small scantily *adverb* barely; just sufficiently

scapegoat *noun* someone who is blamed for something that other people have done

scar *noun* a mark left on your skin by a cut or burn after it has healed

scar *verb* scarring, scarred an injury scars you when it leaves a permanent mark on your skin

scarce *adjective* not enough to supply people • *Wheat was scarce because of the bad harvest.* scarcity *noun* a shortage of something

scarcely *adverb* hardly; only just • *She could scarcely walk.*

scare *verb* to scare someone is to frighten them

scare *noun* a scare is a fright

scarecrow *noun* a figure of a person dressed in old clothes, put in a field of crops to frighten away birds

scarf *noun* scarves a strip of material that you wear round your neck or head

scarlet *adjective* bright red

scary *adjective* scarier, scariest *(informal)* frightening

scatter *verb* **1.** to scatter things is to throw them in all directions **2.** to scatter is to move quickly in all directions

scavenge *verb* an animal or bird scavenges when it eats dead animals that have been killed by another animal scavenger *noun* an animal or bird that scavenges

scene *noun* **1.** the place where something happens • *the scene of the crime* **2.** a part of a play or film **3.** a view you can see **4.** an angry or noisy outburst

scenery *noun* **1.** scenery is the natural features of an area **2.** scenery is also the painted panels and other things put on a stage to make it look like a place

scent *noun* (sent) **1.** a pleasant smell or perfume **2.** an animal's smell, that other animals can follow scented *adjective* having a strong pleasant smell

scent *verb* to scent something is to discover it by its scent

sceptic *noun* (**skep**-tik) someone who doesn't believe things easily or readily

sceptical *adjective* (**skep**-tik-al) you are sceptical when you don't believe things easily or readily **scepticism** *noun* scepticism is not believing things easily or readily

schedule *noun* (**shed**-yool) a timetable of things that have to be done **to be on schedule** is to be on time; not late

scheme *noun* a plan of what to do

scheme *verb* to scheme is to make secret plans

scholar *noun* 1. someone who studies a subject thoroughly 2. someone who has been given a scholarship

scholarly *adjective* showing knowledge and learning

scholarship *noun* 1. a scholarship is a grant of money given to someone for their education 2. scholarship is knowledge and learning

school¹ *noun* 1. a place where children go to be taught 2. the children who go there • *The whole school had a holiday.* 3. a place where you can learn a skill • *a driving school*

school² *noun* a group of whales or fish swimming together

schoolchild *noun* schoolchildren a child who goes to school

schoolteacher *noun* a teacher at a school

schooner *noun* (**skoo**-ner) a fast sailing ship with two or more masts

science *noun* science is the study of objects and happenings in the world that can be observed and tested

> The word **science** comes from a Latin word *scientia* meaning 'knowledge'.

science fiction *noun* science fiction is stories about imaginary worlds, especially in space and in the future

scientific *adjective* 1. to do with science 2. studying things carefully and logically

scientist *noun* someone who studies science or is an expert in science

scissors *plural noun* a cutting device made of two movable blades joined together

scoff *verb* to scoff at someone or something is to make fun of them

scold *verb* to scold someone is to tell them off harshly

scone *noun* (skon or skohn) a small plain cake, usually eaten with butter and jam

scoop *noun* 1. a deep spoon for serving soft food such as ice cream or mashed potato 2. an important piece of news that one newspaper prints before all the others

scoop *verb* to scoop something or to scoop it out, is to take it out with a scoop or the palm of your hand

scooter *noun* 1. a simple type of bicycle for a child, with two wheels and a narrow platform for riding on 2. a kind of motorcycle with small wheels

scope *noun* 1. an opportunity or possibility for something • *There is scope for improvement.* 2. what something deals with or includes • *That question doesn't come within the scope of this book.*

scorch *verb* to scorch something is to make it go brown by slightly burning it

score *noun* 1. the number of points or goals you get in a game • *What's the score?* 2. (old use) a score is twenty • *He reached the age of four-score (= 80) years.*

score *verb* 1. to score a goal or point in a game is to get it 2. to score is to keep a count of the score in a game • *I thought you were scoring.* 3. to score a surface is to scratch it **scorer** *noun* someone who scores a goal or point

scorn *noun* scorn is treating a person or thing with contempt

scorn *verb* to scorn someone or something is to have contempt for them **scornful** *adjective* full of contempt and showing no respect **scornfully** *adverb*

scorpion *noun* an animal related to the spider, with pincers and a poisonous sting in its curved tail

Scot *noun* a person from Scotland

Scottish *adjective* to do with Scotland

scoundrel *noun* a wicked or dishonest person

scour *verb* **1**. to scour (for example) a pan or bath is to rub it hard with something rough until it is clean and bright **2**. to scour an area is to search it thoroughly

Scout *noun* a member of the Scout Association

scout *noun* someone sent out ahead of a group in order to collect information

scowl *verb* to scowl is to look bad-tempered
scowl *noun* an angry look

scramble *verb* **1**. to scramble is to move quickly and awkwardly • *We scrambled up the steep slope.* **2**. to scramble eggs is to cook them by mixing them and heating them in a pan
scramble *noun* **1**. a difficult climb or walk **2**. a struggle to get something • *There was a scramble for the best seats.* **3**. a motorcycle race across rough country

scrap[1] *noun* **1**. a scrap is a small piece of something **2**. scrap is unwanted metal that has been thrown away
scrap[1] *verb* scrapping, scrapped to scrap something is to get rid of it when you do not want it

scrap[2] *noun* (*informal*) a fight
scrap[2] *verb* scrapping, scrapped to scrap is to fight or quarrel

scrape *verb* **1**. to scrape something is to rub it with something rough, hard or sharp **2**. to scrape past or through is to only just get past or succeed • *She scraped through her exams.* **3**. to scrape something together is to collect it with difficulty • *They scraped together enough money for a holiday.* **scraper** *noun* a device for scraping something clean
scrape *noun* **1**. a scraping movement or sound **2**. a mark made by scraping something

scrappy *adjective* scrappier, scrappiest done carelessly or untidily

scratch *verb* **1**. to scratch a surface is to damage it by rubbing something sharp over it **2**. you scratch your skin when you rub it with your fingers because it itches
scratch *noun* **1**. a mark or cut made by scratching **2**. the action of scratching • *I need to have a scratch.* to start from scratch is to begin at the very beginning to be up to scratch is to be up to the proper standard

scrawl *noun* untidy writing
scrawl *verb* to scrawl something is to write it in a hurried or careless way

scream *noun* a loud high-pitched cry of pain or fear or anger
scream *verb* to scream is to make a loud high-pitched cry

screech *noun* a harsh high-pitched sound • *There was a screech of tyres as the car sped off.*
screech *verb* to screech is to make a harsh high-pitched sound

screen *noun* **1**. a surface on which films or television programmes or computer data are shown **2**. a movable panel used to hide or protect something **3**. a windscreen
screen *verb* **1**. to screen a film or television programme is to show it **2**. to screen something is to hide it or protect it with a screen **3**. to screen people is to test them to find out if they have a disease

screw *noun* a metal pin with a spiral ridge round it, which holds things by being twisted into them
screw *verb* **1**. to screw something is to fix it with screws **2**. to screw something in or on is to fit it by turning it • *Screw the lid on to the jar.* to screw something up is to twist or squeeze it into a tight ball

screwdriver *noun* a tool for putting in or taking out screws

a b c d e f g h i j k l m n o p q r s t u v w x y z

scribble *verb* to scribble is to write untidily or carelessly or to make meaningless marks

script *noun* **1.** the words of a play, film or broadcast **2.** handwriting **3.** something you write, especially the answers you write to exam questions

scripture *noun* a sacred writings of a religion, especially the Bible

scroll *noun* a roll of paper or parchment with writing on it

scroll *verb* you scroll up or down on a computer screen when you move the text up or down on the screen to read it

scrounge *verb* (*informal*) to scrounge something is to get it without paying for it **scrounger** *noun* someone who tries to get things without paying for them

scrub[1] *verb* scrubbing, scrubbed to scrub something is to rub it with a hard brush
scrub[1] *noun* the action of scrubbing

scrub[2] *noun* scrub is low trees and bushes or land covered with them

scruffy *adjective* scruffier, scruffiest shabby and untidy

scrum or **scrummage** *noun* (in rugby football) a group of players from each side who push against each other and try to win the ball with their feet

scuba diving *noun* scuba diving is swimming underwater, breathing air from a supply carried on your back

scuffle *noun* a confused struggle or fight
scuffle *verb* people scuffle when they fight in a confused way

sculptor *noun* someone who makes sculptures

sculpture *noun* **1.** a sculpture is something carved or shaped out of a hard material such as stone, clay or metal **2.** sculpture is the art or work of a sculptor

scum *noun* scum is froth or dirt on the top of a liquid

scurvy *noun* scurvy is a disease caused by lack of fresh fruit and vegetables

scuttle[1] *noun* a container for coal, kept by a fireplace

scuttle[2] *verb* to scuttle a ship is to sink it deliberately by making holes in the side or bottom

scythe *noun* a tool with a long curved blade for cutting grass or corn

sea *noun* **1.** the salt water that covers most of the earth's surface **2.** a large lake or area of water, such as the Mediterranean Sea or the Sea of Galilee **3.** a large area of something • *I looked down at the sea of faces in the audience.* **at sea** on the sea

seabed *noun* the seabed is the bottom of the sea

seafaring *adjective, noun* travelling or working on the sea **seafarer** *noun* someone who travels or works at sea

seafood *noun* seafood is fish or shellfish from the sea eaten as food

seagull *noun* a sea bird with long wings

sea horse *noun* a small fish that swims upright, with a head like a horse's head

seal[1] *noun* a furry sea animal that breeds on land

seal[2] *noun* **1.** something designed to close an opening and stop air or liquid getting in or out **2.** a design pressed into a soft substance such as wax or lead

seal[2] *verb* to seal something is to close it by sticking two parts together

sea level *noun* sea level is the level of the sea halfway between high and low tide

sea lion *noun* a large kind of sea

seam *noun* **1.** the line where two edges of cloth join together **2.** a layer of coal in the ground

seaman *noun* seamen a sailor

search *verb* **1.** to search for something or someone is to look very carefully for them **2.** to search a person or place is to look very carefully for something they may have searcher *noun* someone who is trying to find something or someone

search *noun* **1.** a very careful look for someone or something **2.** when you look for information in a computer database or on the Internet

search engine *noun* a computer program that helps you find information on the Internet

searchlight *noun* a light with a strong beam that can be turned in any direction

seashore *noun* the seashore is the land close to the sea

seasick *adjective* someone is seasick when they are sick because of the movement of a ship seasickness *noun* feeling sick

seaside *noun* the seaside is a place by the sea where people go on holiday

season *noun* **1.** one of the four main parts of the year: spring, summer, autumn and winter **2.** the time of year when a sport or other activity happens • *When does the football season start?*

season *verb* to season food is to put salt, pepper or other strong-tasting things on it to flavour it

seasonal *adjective* happening only at certain times of the year • *Fruit-picking is seasonal work.*

seasoning *noun* seasoning is something strong-tasting like salt and pepper, used to season food

season ticket *noun* a ticket that you can use as often as you like for a certain period

seat *noun* **1.** something used for sitting on **2.** a place in parliament or on a council or a board of directors

seat *verb* a place seats a certain number of people when it has that many seats for them

seat belt *noun* a strap to hold a person securely in the seat of a vehicle or aircraft

seaweed *noun* seaweed is plants that grow in the sea

secateurs *plural noun* (**sek**-a-terz) a garden tool used for pruning plants

secluded *adjective* a secluded place is away from large numbers of people; quiet and hidden • *a secluded beach* seclusion *noun* seclusion is being private or hidden

second *adjective, noun* the next after the first to have second thoughts is to wonder whether your decision was really right

second *noun* **1.** a very short period of time, one-sixtieth of a minute **2.** a person or thing that is second **3.** someone who helps a fighter in a boxing match or duel

second *verb* to second a proposal or motion is to support it formally

secondary *adjective* coming second; not original or essential • *This is of secondary importance.*

secondary school *noun* a school for children more than about 11 years old

second-hand *adjective, adverb* bought or used after someone else has used it • *a second-hand car*

secondly *adverb* as the second thing • *Secondly, I'd like to thank my parents.*

secrecy *noun* secrecy is being secret

secret *adjective* **1.** that must not be told or shown to other people **2.** that is not known by many people; hidden • *The house had a secret passage.* secretly *adverb* without telling other people

secret *noun* something that is secret to do something in secret is to do it secretly

secretary *noun* secretaries (**sek**-re-tri) someone whose job is to type letters, keep files, answer the telephone and make business arrangements for a person or organization

secrete *verb* (si-**kreet**) to secrete a substance in the body is to release it • *Saliva is secreted in the mouth.* secretion *noun* a substance that is secreted

secretive *adjective* (**seek**-rit-iv) liking or trying to keep things secret secretively *adverb*

sect *noun* a group of people who have special or unusual religious opinions or beliefs

section *noun* a part of something

sector *noun* a part of an area or activity

secure *adjective* 1. firmly fixed • *Is that ladder secure?* 2. made safe or protected from attack • *Check that all the doors and windows are secure.* securely *adverb*

secure *verb* to secure something is to make it safe or firmly fixed

security *noun* 1. security is being secure or safe 2. security is also measures taken to prevent theft, spying or terrorism

sedate *adjective* (si-**dayt**) calm and dignified sedately *adverb*

sedative *noun* (**sed**-a-tiv) a medicine that makes a person calm or helps them sleep

sediment *noun* sediment is solid matter that settles at the bottom of a liquid

see *verb* seeing, saw, seen 1. to see something or someone is to use your eyes to notice them or be aware of them 2. to see someone is to meet or visit them • *See me after class.* 3. to see something is to understand it • *I see what you mean.* 4. to see someone as something is to imagine them being it • *Can you see yourself as a teacher?* 5. to see that something happens is to make sure of it • *See that the windows are shut.* 6. to see someone somewhere is to escort or lead them • *I'll see you to the door.* to see through something or someone is not to be deceived by them to see to something is to deal with it

seed *noun* a tiny part of a plant that can grow in the ground to make a new plant

seedling *noun* a very young plant

seek *verb* seeking, sought to seek a person or thing is to try to find them

seem *verb* to seem to be something or to have some quality is to appear that way or give that impression • *They seem happy in their new house.*

seep *verb* a liquid or gas seeps when it flows slowly through or into or out of something • *Water was seeping into the cellar.* seepage *noun* when something is seeping

see-saw *noun* a plank balanced in the middle so that people can sit at each end and make it go up and down

seethe *verb* 1. a liquid seethes when it boils or bubbles 2. you are seething when you are very angry

segment *noun* a part that is cut off or can be separated from the rest of something • *the segments of an orange* •

segregate *verb* (**seg**-ri-gayt) to segregate people of different races or religions is to keep them apart and make them live separately segregation *noun* when people of different races or religions are kept apart and made to live separately

seize *verb* (seez) 1. to seize someone or something is to take hold of them suddenly or firmly 2. to seize a place is to capture it using force

seizure *noun* a seizure is a sudden attack of an illness

seldom *adverb* not often • *I seldom cry.*

select *verb* to select a person or thing is to choose them carefully

select *adjective* small and carefully chosen • *a select group of athletes*

self *noun* selves the type of person you are; your individual nature • *You'll soon be feeling your old self again.*

self-centred *adjective* selfish; thinking about yourself too much

self-confident *adjective* confident in what you can do self-confidence *noun* being self-confident

self-conscious *adjective* embarrassed or shy because you know people are watching you

self-control *noun* self-control is the ability to control your own behaviour or feelings
self-controlled *adjective* able to control your own behaviour or feelings

self-defence *noun* **1.** you act in self-defence when you do something defending yourself against attack **2.** self-defence is also skill in defending yourself if someone attacks you

self-employed *adjective* someone who is self-employed works independently and not for an employer

selfish *adjective* having or doing what you want without thinking of other people
selfishly *adverb* **selfishness** *noun*

selfless *adjective* thinking of other people rather than yourself; not selfish

self-service *adjective* a self-service restaurant is one where customers serve themselves

sell *verb* **selling, sold** to sell goods or services is to offer them in exchange for money **to sell out** is to sell all your stock of something

semaphore *noun* semaphore is a system of signalling by holding flags in positions to indicate letters of the alphabet

semibreve *noun* (**sem**-i-breev) the longest musical note normally used, written ᵒ

semicircle *noun* half a circle
semicircular *adjective* in the form of a semicircle

semicolon *noun* a punctuation mark (;) marking a more definite break in a sentence than a comma

semi-detached *adjective* a semi-detached house is one that is joined to another house on one side

semi-final *noun* a match played to decide who will take part in the final
semi-finalist *noun* a contestant in a semi-final

semitone *noun* half a tone in music

senate *noun* (**sen**-at) **1.** the higher-ranking section of the parliament in France, the USA and some other countries **2.** the governing council in ancient Rome **senator** *noun* a member of a senate

send *verb* **sending, sent 1.** to send something somewhere is to make something go or be taken somewhere **2.** to send someone somewhere is to tell them to go there **to send for someone** is to ask for them to come to you

senior *adjective* **1.** older than someone else **2.** higher in rank • *He is a senior officer in the navy.* **seniority** *noun* a person's seniority is how old or high in rank they are
senior *noun* someone is your senior when they are older or higher in rank than you are

senior citizen *noun* an elderly person, especially a pensioner

sensation *noun* **1.** a feeling • *There's an itchy sensation in my leg.* **2.** a very exciting event or the excitement caused by it • *The news caused a great sensation.*

sensational *adjective* causing great excitement or shock

sense *noun* **1.** the ability to see, hear, smell, touch or taste things **2.** the ability to feel or appreciate something • *She has a good sense of humour.* **3.** the power to think or make good judgements • *He had enough sense to switch off the electricity first.* **4.** meaning • *The word 'set' has many senses.* **to make sense** is to have a meaning you can understand

sense *verb* **1.** to sense something is to feel it or be aware of it • *I sensed that she did* not like me. **2.** to sense something is also to detect it • *This device senses radioactivity.*

senseless *adjective* **1.** stupid; not sensible • *I am sick of all this senseless fighting.* **2.** unconscious • *He fell senseless to the ground.*

sensible *adjective* wise; having or showing good sense **sensibly** *adverb*

sensitive *adjective* **1.** affected by the sun or chemicals or something else physical • *sensitive skin* **2.** easily offended or upset • *He's quite sensitive about being criticized.* **3.** aware of other people's feelings **sensitively** *adverb* in a way that shows you are aware of other people's feelings **sensitivity** *noun* being sensitive

sensor *noun* a device or instrument for detecting something physical such as heat or light

sentence *noun* **1.** a group of words that express a complete thought and form a statement or question or command **2.** the punishment given to a convicted person in a lawcourt
sentence *verb* to sentence someone is to give them a sentence in a lawcourt

sentiment *noun* **1.** a sentiment is a feeling or opinion **2.** sentiment is a show of feeling or emotion

sentimental *adjective* showing or making you feel emotion, especially too much sad emotion **sentimentality** *noun* sentimentality is being too sentimental **sentimentally** *adverb*

sentry *noun* **sentries** a soldier guarding something

separate *adjective* (**sep**-er-at) **1.** not joined to anything; on its own **2.** not together; not with other people • *They lead separate lives.* **separately** *adverb* not together • *They arrived together but left separately.*
separate *verb* (**sep**-er-ayt) **1.** to separate things or people is to take them away from others **2.** to separate is to become separate or move away from each other **3.** two people separate when they stop living together as a couple **separation** *noun* when people are apart from each other

September *noun* the ninth month of the year

septic *adjective* a wound goes septic when it becomes infected with harmful bacteria

sequel *noun* (**see**-kwel) a book or film that continues the story of an earlier one

sequence *noun* (**see**-kwenss) a series of things coming in a particular order

sequin *noun* (**see**-kwin) sequins are tiny bright discs sewn on clothes to decorate them

serene *adjective* calm and peaceful **serenely** *adverb* **serenity** *noun* serenity is being calm and peaceful

sergeant *noun* (**sar**-jent) a soldier or police officer who is in charge of others

serial *noun* a story that is shown or printed in several separate parts

series *noun* **series** **1.** a number of things following each other or connected with each other **2.** a set of television or radio programmes with the same title

serious *adjective* **1.** not funny; important • *We need a serious talk.* **2.** thoughtful or solemn • *His face was serious.* **3.** very bad • *a serious accident* **seriously** *adverb* **seriousness** *noun*

sermon *noun* a talk given by a preacher during a religious service

serpent *noun* a snake

servant *noun* a person whose job is to work in someone else's house

serve *verb* **1.** to serve people in a shop is to help them find the things they want to buy **2.** to serve food or drink is to give it to people at a meal **3.** to serve a person or organization is to work for them **4.** to serve is to be suitable for a purpose • *This tree stump will serve as a table.* **5.** *(in tennis)* to serve is to start play by hitting the ball to your opponent **server** *noun* the player who starts play by serving in tennis
serve *noun* the action of serving in tennis

service *noun* **1.** service is working for someone or something • *He retired after forty years' service.* **2.** a service is something that helps people or supplies what they want • *There is a good bus service into town.* **3.** a service is also a religious ceremony in a church **4.** a vehicle or machine has a service when someone examines and maintains it

5. *(in tennis)* a service is a serve **the services** the armed forces of a country

service *verb* to service a vehicle or machine is to check it and repair it if necessary

service station *noun* a place beside the road where you can buy petrol

serviette *noun* a cloth or paper napkin that you can wipe your hands and mouth on

session *noun* **1.** a time spent doing a particular thing • *They were in the middle of a recording session.* **2.** a meeting or series of meetings • *The Queen will open the next session of Parliament.*

set *verb* **setting, set** This word has many meanings, depending on the words that go with it: **1.** to set something somewhere is to put or place it there • *Set the vase on the table.* **2.** to set a device is to make it ready to work • *Have you set the alarm?* **3.** to set is to become solid or hard • *The jelly has set now.* **4.** the sun sets when it goes down towards the horizon at the end of the day **5.** to set someone doing something is to start them doing it • *The news set me thinking.* **6.** to set someone a task or problem is to give it to them to do or solve • *I'd better set you some more work.* **to set off** or **set out** is to begin a journey **to set something up** is to place it in position or get it started • *We want to set up a playgroup.*

set *noun* **1.** a group of people or things that belong together **2.** a radio or television receiver **3.** a series of games in a tennis match **4.** the scenery or furniture on a stage or in a film

setback *noun* something that causes a difficulty for a while

set square *noun* a device in the shape of a right-angled triangle, used for drawing parallel lines and to draw angles

settee *noun* a sofa

setting *noun* **1.** the setting of a story is the place and time in which it happens **2.** the land and buildings around something

settle *verb* **1.** to settle a problem, difficulty or argument is to solve it or decide about it **2.** to settle or settle down, is to become relaxed or make yourself comfortable • *He settled down in the armchair.* **3.** to settle somewhere is to go and live there **4.** something light such as dust or snow settles when it comes to rest on something **5.** to settle a bill or debt is to pay it

settlement *noun* **1.** a settlement is a group of people or houses in a new area **2.** a settlement is also an agreement to end an argument

settler *noun* one of the first people to settle in a new area

set-up *noun* *(informal)* the way that something is organized or arranged

seven *noun* the number 7

seventeen *noun* the number 17 **seventeenth** *adjective, noun* 17th

seventh *adjective, noun* the next after the sixth

seventy *noun* **seventies** the number 70 **seventieth** *adjective, noun* 70th

sever *verb* to sever something is to cut or break it off

several *determiner* more than two but not many

severe *adjective* **1.** strict or harsh; not gentle or kind **2.** very bad or serious • *a severe cold* • *severe weather* **severely** *adverb* harshly or seriously **severity** *noun* being severe or how severe something is

sew *verb* **sewing, sewed, sewn** or **sewed** (so) **1.** to sew material is to use a needle and cotton to join it or form it into clothing **2.** to sew is to work with a needle and thread or with a sewing machine

sewage *noun* (**soo**-ij) sewage is waste matter carried away in drains

sewer *noun* (**soo**-er) an underground drain that carries away sewage

sex *noun* **1.** a sex is each of the two groups, male or female, that people and animals belong to **2.** sex is the physical act by which people and animals produce offspring **sexual** *adjective* to do with sex or the sexes

sexism *noun* sexism is the unfair or offensive treatment of people of a particular sex, especially women **sexist** *adjective* offensive to people of a particular sex, especially women **sexist** *noun* someone who treats people of a particular sex, especially women, in an unfair or offensive way

shabby *adjective* **shabbier, shabbiest** very old and worn • *She was wearing a shabby grey coat.*

shack *noun* a roughly-built hut

shade *noun* **1**. shade is an area sheltered from bright sunlight **2**. a shade is a colour or how light or dark a colour is **3**. a shade is also a device that reduces or shuts out bright light

shade *verb* **1**. to shade something or someone is to shelter them from bright light **2**. to shade a drawing is to make parts of it darker than the rest **shading** *noun* the parts of a drawing that you make darker than the rest

shadow *noun* **1**. a shadow is a dark shape that falls on a surface when something is between it and the light **2**. shadow is an area that is dark because the light is blocked • *His face was in shadow.* **shadowy** *adjective* dark or hard to see

shady *adjective* **shadier**, **shadiest** **1**. giving shade • *We sat under a shady tree.* **2**. situated in the shade • *Find a shady spot.* **3**. dishonest or suspect • *He's always making shady deals.*

shaft *noun* **1**. a long thin rod or straight part of something **2**. a deep narrow hole in a mine or building • *a lift shaft* **3**. a beam of light

shaggy *adjective* **shaggier**, **shaggiest** having long untidy hair

shake *verb* **shaking**, **shook**, **shaken** **1**. to shake something is to move it quickly up and down or from side to side • *Have you shaken the bottle?* **2**. to shake is to move in this way **3**. to shake someone is to shock or upset them • *The news shook her.* **4**. to shake is to tremble • *His voice was shaking.* **to shake hands** is to clasp someone's right hand as a greeting or as a sign that you agree

shake *noun* a quick movement up and down or from side to side • *Give the bottle a shake.*

shaky *adjective* **shakier**, **shakiest** shaking or likely to fall down **shakily** *adverb*

shall *verb* past tense **should** used with *I* and *we* to refer to the future • *We shall arrive tomorrow.* • *We told them we should arrive the next day.*

shallow *adjective* not deep

sham *noun* a person or thing that is not genuine or what they claim to be

shambles *noun* a scene of confusion and chaos; a mess • *The rehearsal was a complete shambles.*

shame *noun* **1**. shame is a feeling of great sorrow or guilt because you have done something wrong **2**. you say something is a shame when it is something that you regret or are sorry about • *What a shame you won't be able to come.*

shame *verb* to shame someone is to make them feel ashamed

shameful *adjective* causing shame; disgraceful **shamefully** *adverb*

shameless *adjective* feeling or showing no shame **shamelessly** *adverb*

shampoo *noun* shampoo is liquid soap for washing things, especially your hair or a carpet

shampoo *verb* to shampoo your hair is to wash it with shampoo

> The word **shampoo** comes from a Hindi word *campo* meaning 'press!' (as an instruction).

shamrock *noun* shamrock is a small plant like clover, with leaves divided in three

shandy *noun* **shandies** shandy is a mixture of beer with lemonade

shanty[1] *noun* **shanties** a sailor's traditional song

shanty[2] *noun* **shanties** a roughly-built hut

shape *noun* **1**. the outline of something or the way it looks **2**. something that has a definite or regular form, such as a square, circle or triangle **3**. the condition that something is in • *The garden isn't in very good shape.* **to take shape** is to start to develop properly

shape *verb* to shape something is to give it a shape

share *noun* **1**. one of the parts into which something is divided between several people or things **2**. part of a company's money, lent by someone who is then given part of the profits in return

share *verb* **1**. to share something or share it out, is to divide it between several people or things **2**. to share something is to use it when someone else is also using it • *She shared a room with me.*

shark *noun* a large sea fish with sharp teeth

sharp *adjective* **1.** a sharp object has an edge or point that can cut or make holes • *a sharp knife* **2.** quick to learn or notice things • *It was sharp of you to spot that mistake.* **3.** sudden or severe • *We came to a sharp bend in the road.* • *a sharp pain* **4.** slightly sour • *The apples taste sharp.* **5.** above the proper musical pitch **sharply** *adverb* **sharpness** *noun*

sharp *adverb* **1.** with a sudden change of direction • *Now turn sharp right.* **2.** punctually; exactly • *Be there at six o'clock sharp.*

sharp *noun* the note that is a semitone above a particular musical note; the sign that indicates this (♯)

sharpen *verb* to sharpen something is to make it sharp or pointed **sharpener** *noun* a device for sharpening a pencil

shatter *verb* **1.** to shatter is to break suddenly into lots of tiny pieces **2.** to shatter something is to break it in this way **3.** someone is shattered when they are very upset by something or very tired • *We were shattered by the news.*

shave *verb* **1.** someone shaves when they scrape hair from their skin with a razor **2.** to shave something is to cut or scrape a thin slice off it **shaver** *noun* an electric razor

shave *noun* the act of shaving the face *a close shave* (*informal*) a narrow escape

shavings *plural noun* thin strips that have been shaved off a piece of wood or metal

shawl *noun* a large piece of material for covering the shoulders or wrapping a baby

she *pronoun* a female person or animal

sheaf *noun* **sheaves** **1.** a bundle of papers **2.** a bundle of corn stalks tied together after reaping

shear *verb* **shearing**, **sheared**, **shorn** or **sheared** to shear a sheep is to cut the wool from it **shearer** *noun* someone who shears sheep

shears *plural noun* a tool like a very large pair of scissors for trimming grass and bushes or for shearing sheep

sheath *noun* a cover for the blade of a sword or dagger

shed[1] *noun* a simple building used for storing things or sheltering animals, or as a workshop

shed[2] *verb* **shedding**, **shed** to shed something is to let it fall off • *The trees are shedding their leaves.* • *He was so badly hurt he was shedding blood.*

sheen *noun* a soft shine on a surface

sheep *noun* **sheep** a grass-eating animal kept by farmers for its wool and meat

sheepdog *noun* a dog trained to guard and control sheep

sheepish *adjective* someone looks sheepish when they look shy or embarrassed **sheepishly** *adverb*

sheer *adjective* **1.** complete or total • *There was a look of sheer misery on his face.* **2.** extremely steep; vertical • *To the right of the road there was a sheer drop.* **3.** sheer material is so thin that you can see through it

sheet *noun* **1.** a large piece of light material put on a bed **2.** a whole flat piece of paper, glass or metal **3.** a wide area of water, snow, ice or flame

sheikh *noun* (shayk) the leader of an Arab tribe or village

shelf *noun* **shelves** **1.** a flat piece of hard material fitted to a wall or in a piece of furniture so that you can put things on it **2.** a flat level surface that sticks out from a cliff or under the sea

shell *noun* **1.** the hard outer covering round a nut or egg or round an animal such as a snail or tortoise **2.** a metal case filled with explosive, fired from a large gun

shell *verb* **1.** to shell something is to take it out of its shell **2.** to shell a building, ship, town, etc., is to fire explosive shells at it

shellfish *noun* shellfish a sea animal that has a shell

shelter *noun* **1.** a shelter is a place that protects people from danger or from the weather **2.** shelter is being protected from danger or from the weather • *We found shelter from the rain.*

shelter *verb* **1.** to shelter somewhere is to stay there because you are protected from danger or from the weather **2.** to shelter something or someone is to protect or cover them • *The hill shelters the house from the wind.*

shelve *verb* to shelve an idea or piece of work is to reject or postpone it

shepherd *noun* someone whose job is to look after sheep

sherbet *noun* a fizzy sweet powder or drink

sheriff *noun* in the USA, the chief law officer in a county

sherry *noun* sherries a kind of strong wine

shield *noun* **1.** a large piece of metal or wood a person carries to protect their body in fighting **2.** a design or trophy in the shape of a shield **3.** a protection from harm • *The spacecraft's heat shield protects it as it enters the planet's atmosphere.*

shield *verb* to shield someone or something is to protect them

shift *noun* **1.** a change of position or condition **2.** a group of workers who start work as another group finishes; the time when they work • *He's on the night shift this month.*

shift *verb* **1.** to shift something is to move it **2.** to shift is to change position

shilling *noun* an old British coin that was worth a twentieth of a pound (now 5 pence)

shimmer *verb* to shimmer is to shine with a quivering light

shin *noun* the front of your leg between your knee and your ankle

shine *verb* shining, shone or, in 'polish' sense, shined **1.** to shine is to give out or reflect bright light **2.** to shine a torch or light somewhere is to point the light in that direction **3.** to shine something is to polish it

shine *noun* **1.** shine is brightness **2.** a shine is an act of polishing • *Give your shoes a good shine.*

shingle *noun* shingle is pebbles on a beach

shiny *adjective* shinier, shiniest bright or glossy

ship *noun* a large boat, especially one that goes to sea

ship *verb* shipping, shipped to ship something is to send it on a ship

shipwreck *noun* **1.** when a ship is wrecked in a storm or accident at sea **2.** the remains of a wrecked ship shipwrecked *adjective* left somewhere after your ship has been wrecked at sea

shipyard *noun* a place where ships are built and repaired

shirk *verb* you shirk a task or duty when you avoid doing it

shirt *noun* a piece of clothing you wear on the top half of the body, with a collar and sleeves

shiver *verb* you shiver when you tremble with cold or fear shivery *adjective* unable to stop yourself shivering

shiver *noun* an act of shivering

shoal *noun* a large number of fish swimming together

shock *noun* **1.** a shock is a sudden unpleasant surprise **2.** a shock is also a violent knock or jolt **3.** shock is weakness caused by severe pain or injury **4.** a shock or electric shock, is a painful feeling caused by electricity passing through your body

shock verb **1.** to shock someone is to give them a shock **2.** to shock someone is also to make them feel disgusted or upset

shocking adjective horrifying or disgusting

shoddy adjective shoddier, shoddiest of poor quality; badly made • This is shoddy work.

shoe noun **1.** a strong covering you wear on your foot **2.** a horseshoe

shoelace noun a cord for fastening a shoe

shoot verb shooting, shot **1.** to shoot a gun or other weapon is to fire it **2.** to shoot a person or animal is to fire a gun at them **3.** to shoot somewhere is to move very fast • The car shot past. **4.** (in football) to shoot is to kick or hit a ball at a goal **5.** to shoot a film or scene is to film or photograph it

shoot noun a young branch or new growth of a plant

shooting star noun a meteor

shop noun a building where people buy things

shop verb shopping, shopped to shop is to go and buy things at shops shopper noun someone who goes shopping

shopkeeper noun someone who owns or looks after a shop

shoplifter noun someone who steals from shops shoplifting noun stealing things from shops

shopping noun **1.** shopping is buying things at shops • I like shopping. **2.** shopping is also things that you have bought in shops • Let me help you carry your shopping.

shore noun **1.** the seashore **2.** the land along the edge of a lake

short adjective **1.** not long; not lasting long • I went for a short walk. **2.** not tall • He is a short man. **3.** not sufficient; scarce • Water is short. **4.** bad-tempered • He was rather short with me. short for something a shorter form of something • Jo is short for Joanna. to be short of something is to not have enough of it • We seem to be short of chairs. shortness noun

short adverb **1.** before reaching the point aimed at • My ball landed just short of the hole. **2.** suddenly • The horse stopped short.

shortage noun there is a shortage when there is not enough of something

shortbread noun shortbread is a rich sweet biscuit made with butter

shortcoming noun a fault or weakness • He has many shortcomings.

short cut noun a route or method that is quicker than the usual one

shorten verb **1.** to shorten something is to make it shorter **2.** to shorten is to become shorter

shorthand noun shorthand is a set of special signs for writing words down as quickly as people say them

shortly adverb soon • I'll be there shortly.

shorts plural noun trousers with legs that stop at or above the knee

short-sighted adjective **1.** unable to see things clearly when they are further away **2.** not thinking enough about what may happen in the future

shot[1] noun **1.** a shot is the firing of a gun or other weapon **2.** shot is lead pellets fired from small guns **3.** a good or bad shot is a person judged by their skill in shooting **4.** a shot is a stroke in a game with a ball, such as tennis or snooker **5.** in photography, a shot is a photograph or filmed sequence **6.** a shot at something is an attempt to do it

shot[2] past tense and past participle of **shoot** verb

shotgun noun a gun that fires small lead pellets

should verb used to express **1.** what someone ought to do • You should have told me. **2.** what someone expects • They should be here soon.

shoulder noun the part of your body between your neck and your arm

shoulder blade noun each of the two large flat bones at the top of your back

shout verb to shout is to speak or call very loudly

shout noun a loud cry or call

shove *verb* (shuv) to shove something is to push it hard

shovel *noun* (**shuv**-el) a tool like a spade with the sides turned up, for lifting and moving things like earth or snow

shovel *verb* shovelling, shovelled to shovel (for example) earth or snow is to move it or clear it with a shovel

show *verb* showing, showed, shown **1.** to show something is to let people see it • *She showed me her new bike.* **2.** to show something to someone is to explain it to them • *Can you show me how to do it?* **3.** to show someone somewhere is to guide or lead them there • *I'll show you to your seat.* **4.** to show is to be visible • *That stain won't show.* to show off is to try to impress people to show something off is to be proud of letting people see it

show *noun* **1.** an entertainment • *She loves TV game shows.* **2.** a display or exhibition • *Have you been to the flower show?*

show business *noun* show business is the entertainment business; the theatre, films, radio and television

shower *noun* **1.** a brief fall of light rain **2.** a lot of small things coming or falling like rain • *They were met by a shower of stones.* **3.** a device for spraying water to wash your body; a wash in this

shower *verb* **1.** to shower is to fall like rain **2.** to shower someone with things is to give a lot of them • *He showered her with presents.* **3.** to shower is to wash under a shower

showery *adjective* raining occasionally

showjumping *noun* showjumping is a competition in which riders make their horses jump over fences and other obstacles **showjumper** *noun* someone who takes part in showjumping

show-off *noun* someone who is trying to impress other people

showy *adjective* showier, showiest likely to attract attention; bright or highly decorated **showily** *adverb* **showiness** *noun*

shrapnel *noun* shrapnel is pieces of metal scattered from an exploding shell

shred *noun* a tiny strip or piece torn or cut off something • *His jeans had been ripped to shreds.* **2.** a very small amount of something • *There's not a shred of evidence for what you say.*

shred *verb* shredding, shredded to shred something is to tear or cut it into tiny strips or pieces

shrew *noun* a small animal rather like a mouse

shrewd *adjective* having common sense and showing good judgement **shrewdly** *adverb* **shrewdness** *noun*

shriek *noun* a shrill cry or scream

shriek *verb* to shriek is to give a shrill cry or scream

shrill *adjective* a shrill sound is very high and loud • *There was a shrill blast of the whistle.* **shrilly** *adverb* **shrillness** *noun*

shrimp *noun* a small shellfish

shrine *noun* an altar or chapel or other sacred place

shrink *verb* shrinking, shrank, shrunk **1.** to shrink is to become smaller • *My dress has shrunk.* **2.** to shrink something is to make it smaller, usually by washing it • *Their jeans have been shrunk.*

shrivel *verb* shrivelling, shrivelled to shrivel is to become wrinkled and dry

shroud *noun* a sheet in which a dead body is wrapped

shroud *verb* to shroud something is to cover or conceal it • *The mountain was shrouded in mist.*

shrub *noun* a bush or small tree

shrubbery *noun* shrubberies an area where shrubs are grown

shrug *verb* shrugging, shrugged you shrug when you raise your shoulders slightly as a sign that you don't care or don't know **shrug** *noun* the act of shrugging

shrunken *adjective* smaller than it used to be because it has shrunk

shudder *verb* you shudder when you shake because you are cold or afraid **shudder** *noun* the act of shuddering

shuffle *verb* **1.** to shuffle is to drag your feet along the ground as you walk **2.** to shuffle playing cards is to mix them by sliding them over each other several times
shuffle *noun* the act of shuffling • *Give the cards a quick shuffle.*

shunt *verb* to shunt a railway train or wagons is to move them from one track to another

shut *verb* **shutting, shut 1.** to shut a door or window or a lid or cover, is to move it so that it blocks up an opening **2.** to shut is to become closed • *The door shut suddenly.* **to shut down** is to stop work or business **to shut up** *(informal)* is to stop talking
shut *adjective* closed • *Keep your eyes shut.*

shutter *noun* **1.** a panel or screen that can be closed over a window **2.** the device in a camera that opens and closes to let light fall on the film

shuttle *noun* **1.** a train or bus or aircraft that makes frequent short journeys between two places **2.** a space shuttle **3.** the part of a loom that carries the thread from side to side

shuttlecock *noun* a small rounded piece of cork or plastic with a ring of feathers fixed to it, that you use in the game of badminton

shy *adjective* timid and afraid to meet or talk to other people **shyly** *adverb* **shyness** *noun*

sibling *noun* your siblings are your brothers and sisters

sick *adjective* **1.** ill or unwell • *He looks after sick animals.* **2.** you feel sick when you feel that you are going to vomit; you are sick when you vomit **to be sick of something** or **someone** is to be tired of them or fed up with them

sicken *verb* **1.** to sicken someone is to disgust them **2.** to sicken is to start feeling ill

sickly *adjective* **sicklier, sickliest 1.** often ill; unhealthy • *a sickly child* **2.** making people feel sick • *The drink had a sickly taste.*

sickness *noun* an illness or disease

side *noun* **1.** a flat surface, especially one that joins the top and bottom of something **2.** a line that forms the edge of a shape • *A triangle has three sides.* **3.** the outer part of something that is not the front or the back • *The instructions are on the side of the box.* **4.** a position or space to the left or right of something • *There's a window on either side of the door.* **5.** your sides are the parts of your body from your armpits to your hips • *I've got a pain down my right side.* **6.** a group of people playing, arguing or fighting against another group • *They are on our side.*
side *verb* to side with someone is to support them in a quarrel or argument

sideboard *noun* a long heavy piece of furniture with drawers and cupboards and a flat top

sideshow *noun* a small entertainment forming part of a fair

sideways *adverb, adjective* **1.** to or from the side • *Crabs walk sideways.* **2.** with one side facing forward • *We sat sideways in the bus.*

siding *noun* a short railway line leading off the main line

siege *noun* (seej) when an army surrounds a place until the people inside surrender

sieve *noun* (siv) a device made of mesh or perforated metal or plastic, used to separate harder or larger parts from liquid or powder

sift *verb* **1.** to sift a fine or powdery substance is to pass it through a sieve **2.** to sift facts or information is to examine or select them

sigh *noun* a sound you make by breathing out heavily when you are sad, tired or relieved
sigh *verb* to sigh is to make a sigh

sight *noun* **1.** sight is the ability to see • *She has very good sight.* **2.** a sight is something that you see • *That sunset is a sight I'll never forget.* **3.** the sights of a place are the interesting places worth seeing there • *Visit the sights of Paris.* **4.** a sight on a gun is a device that helps you to aim it **to be in sight** is to be able to be seen **to be out of sight** is to be no longer able to be seen
sight *verb* to sight something is to see it or observe it

sightseeing *noun* sightseeing is going round looking at interesting places **sightseer** *noun* someone who goes sightseeing

sign *noun* **1.** a mark or symbol that stands for something • *a minus sign* **2.** a board or notice that tells or shows people something **3.** something that shows that a thing exists • *There are signs of rust.*

sign *verb* **1.** you sign your name when you write your signature on something **2.** to sign someone is to give them a contract for a job, especially in a professional sport • *They have signed three new players.*

signal *noun* **1.** a device or gesture or sound or light that gives information or a message **2.** a series of radio waves sent out or received

signal *verb* **signalling, signalled** to signal to someone is to give them a signal

signature *noun* your name written by yourself

significant *adjective* something is significant when it has a meaning or importance **significance** *noun* the significance of something is its meaning or importance **significantly** *adverb* in a way that is important or has a meaning

signify *verb* **signifies, signifying, signified** to signify something is to mean it or indicate it

signing or **sign language** *noun* signing is a way of communicating by using movements of your hands instead of sounds, used by deaf people

signpost *noun* a sign at a road junction showing the names and distances of the places that each road leads to

Sikh *noun* (seek) someone who believes in **Sikhism**, a religion of India having one God and some Hindu and Islamic beliefs

silence *noun* silence is when no sound can be heard

silence *verb* to silence someone or something is to make them silent

silencer *noun* a device designed to reduce the sound made by an engine or a gun

silent *adjective* without any sound; not speaking **silently** *adverb*

silhouette *noun* (sil-oo-**et**) a dark outline of something seen against a light background

silicon *noun* silicon is a substance found in many rocks and used in making microchips

silk *noun* **1.** silk is a fine soft thread produced by silkworms for making their cocoons **2.** silk is also smooth shiny cloth made from this thread **silken** *adjective* made of silk **silky** *adjective* soft, smooth and shiny like silk

silkworm *noun* a kind of caterpillar that covers itself with a cocoon of fine threads when it is ready to turn into a moth

sill *noun* a strip of stone or wood or metal underneath a window or door

silly *adjective* **sillier, silliest** foolish or unwise **silliness** *noun*

silver *noun* **1.** silver is a shiny white precious metal **2.** silver is also coins made of this metal or a metal that looks like it **3.** silver is also a greyish-white colour **silvery** *adjective* like silver • *the moon's silvery light*

similar *adjective* one thing is similar to another when it is like it in some ways but not exactly the same **similarity** *noun* the similarity between two things is the fact that they are similar **similarly** *adverb* in a similar way

simile *noun* (**sim**-i-li) a kind of expression in which you describe something by comparing it with something else, such as *bold as brass* or *as brave as a lion*

simmer *verb* food simmers when it boils very gently over a low heat **to simmer down** is to become calm after being anxious or angry

simple *adjective* **1.** easy • *That's a simple question to answer.* **2.** not complicated • *It was a simple plan, but it worked.* **3.** plain • *She was wearing a simple dress.* **simplicity** *noun* how simple something is

simplify *verb* **simplifies, simplifying, simplified** to simplify something is to make it easier to do or understand **simplification** *noun* something that has been made simpler

simply *adverb* **1.** in a simple way • *Explain it simply.* **2.** completely • *It's simply delicious.*

3. only or merely • *It's simply a question of time.*

simulate *verb* to simulate something is to reproduce its conditions or appearance • *The machine simulates a space flight.* **simulation** *noun* when something is simulated **simulator** *noun* a machine for reproducing the conditions for something, such as flying an aeroplane

simultaneous *adjective* (sim-ul-**tay**-ni-us) two things are simultaneous when they happen at the same time **simultaneously** *adverb* two things happen simultaneously when they happen at the same time

sin *noun* an action that breaks a religious or moral law
sin *verb* **sinning, sinned** to sin is to commit a sin **sinful** *adjective* guilty of sin **sinner** *noun* someone who sins

since *conjunction* **1**. from the time when • *Where have you been since I last saw you?* **2**. because • *Since we have missed the bus, we must walk home.*
since *preposition* from a certain time • *I have been here since Christmas.*
since *adverb* between then and now • *He has not been seen since.*

sincere *adjective* you are being sincere when you mean what you say and express your true feelings **sincerely** *adverb* **sincerity** *noun* sincerity is being sincere

sinew *noun* strong tissue that joins a muscle to a bone

sing *verb* **singing, sang, sung 1**. to sing is to make musical sounds with your voice **2**. birds and insects sing when they make musical sounds **singer** *noun* someone who sings

singe *verb* (sinj) to singe something is to burn it slightly

single *adjective* **1**. only one; not double **2**. designed for one person • *a single bed* **3**. not married
single *noun* **1**. a ticket for a journey you make to a place but not back again **2**. one song or short piece of music **3**. you play singles in tennis when you play against only one other person
single *verb* to single someone out is to pick them from other people

single file *noun* **in single file** in a line, one behind the other

single-handed *adjective* by your own efforts; without any help

single parent *noun* a person who is bringing up a child or children without a partner

singular *noun* the form of a word meaning only one person or thing, such as *cake* and *child*
singular *adjective* in the singular; meaning only one • *'Mouse' is a singular noun.*

sinister *adjective* looking or seeming evil or harmful

sink *verb* **sinking, sank** or **sunk, sunk 1**. to sink is to go under water • *The ship sank in a storm.* **2**. to sink something is to make it go under water • *They fired on the ship and sank it.* **3**. to sink or to sink down, is to go or fall down to the ground • *He sank to his knees.*
sink *noun* a fixed basin with taps to supply water

sinus *noun* (**sy**-nus) your sinuses are the hollows in the bones of your skull, connected with your nose

sip *verb* **sipping, sipped** to sip a drink is to drink it slowly in small mouthfuls

siphon *noun* a bent tube used for taking liquid from one container to another at a lower level
siphon *verb* to siphon liquid is to transfer it with a siphon

sir *noun* a word sometimes used when speaking politely to a man, instead of his name • *Can I help you, sir?* **Sir** the title given to a knight • *Sir Francis Drake.*

siren *noun* a device that makes a loud hooting or screaming sound, usually as a warning signal

sister *noun* **1**. your sister is a woman or girl who has the same parents as you **2**. a senior nurse in a hospital

sister-in-law *noun* **sisters-in-law** a person's sister-in-law is the sister of their husband or wife or the wife of their brother

sit *verb* sitting, sat **1.** to sit is to rest on your bottom, as you do when you are on a chair **2.** to sit an exam or test is to take it **3.** to sit somewhere is to be situated or positioned there • *The house sits on top of a hill.*
sitter *noun* a babysitter

site *noun* **1.** the place where something has been built or will be built • *a building site* **2.** a place used for something or where something happened • *a camping site* • *the site of a famous battle*

sitting room *noun* a room with comfortable chairs for sitting in

situated *adjective* to be situated in a particular place or position is to be placed there • *They lived in a town situated in a valley.*

situation *noun* **1.** a place or position; where something is **2.** all the things that are happening to someone at a particular time; the way things are • *We're now in a difficult situation because we've run out of money.* **3.** a job or employment

six *noun* the number 6

sixteen *noun* the number 16
sixteenth *adjective, noun* 16th

sixth *adjective, noun* the next after the fifth

sixty *noun* sixties the number 60
sixtieth *adjective, noun* 60th

size *noun* **1.** how big a person or thing is **2.** the measurement something is made in • *I wear a size eight shoe.*

sizzle *verb* to sizzle is to make a crackling and hissing sound

skate *noun* **1.** a boot with a steel blade attached to the sole, used for sliding smoothly over ice **2.** a roller skate

skate *verb* to skate is to move around on skates **skater** *noun* someone who skates

skateboard *noun* a small board with wheels, used for standing and riding

skeleton *noun* the framework of bones in a person's or animal's body

sketch *noun* **1.** a quick or rough drawing **2.** a short amusing play
sketch *verb* to sketch something or someone is to make a sketch of them

sketchy *adjective* sketchier, sketchiest roughly drawn or described, without any detail

skewer *noun* a long wooden or metal or plastic pin that you push through meat to hold it together while it is being cooked

ski *noun* (skee) a long flat strip of wood or metal or plastic, fastened to each foot for moving quickly over snow
ski *verb* skiing, skied to ski is to travel on snow wearing skis **skier** *noun* someone who skis

skid *verb* skidding, skidded to skid is to slide accidentally, especially in a vehicle
skid *noun* a skidding movement • *The car went into a skid on the icy road.*

skilful *adjective* having or showing a lot of skill **skilfully** *adverb*

skill *noun* **1.** to do something with skill is to do it well **2.** an ability that you learn through training and practice • *He's been learning some new football skills.* **skilled** *adjective* having a skill or skills

skim *verb* skimming, skimmed to skim is to move quickly over a surface
skimmed *adjective* skimmed milk has had the cream removed

skin *noun* **1.** the outer covering of a person's or animal's body **2.** the outer covering of a fruit or vegetable

skin *verb* skinning, skinned to skin something is to take the skin off it

skinny *adjective* skinnier, skinniest very thin

skip[1] *verb* skipping, skipped **1.** to skip is to jump or move along by hopping from one foot to the other **2.** to skip is also to jump with a skipping rope **3.** to skip something is to miss it out or ignore it • *You can skip the last chapter.*

skip[1] *noun* a skipping movement

skip[2] *noun* a large metal container for taking away builders' rubbish

skipper *noun* the captain of a ship or team

skirt *noun* a piece of clothing for a woman or girl that hangs down from her waist

skirt *verb* to skirt something is to go round the edge of it

skittle *noun* a piece of wood or plastic shaped like a bottle, that people try to knock down with a ball in a game of **skittles**

skull *noun* the framework of bones in your head which contains your brain

skunk *noun* a black and white furry animal from North America that can make an unpleasant smell

sky *noun* skies the space above the earth, where you can see the sun, moon and stars

skylark *noun* a small brown bird that sings as it hovers high in the air

skylight *noun* a window in a roof

skyscraper *noun* a very tall building

slab *noun* a thick flat piece of something hard

slack *adjective* **1.** loose; not pulled tight • *The rope was slack.* **2.** not busy

slacken *verb* to slacken something is to loosen it

slam *verb* slamming, slammed **1.** to slam (for example) a door is to shut it hard or loudly **2.** to slam something is to hit it with great force • *He slammed the ball into the net.*

slang *noun* slang is a kind of colourful language that you use when speaking to your friends but not in writing or when you want to be polite

slant *verb* to slant is to slope or lean

slant *noun* a sloping or leaning position

slap *verb* slapping, slapped **1.** to slap someone is to hit them with the palm of your hand **2.** to slap something somewhere is to put it there forcefully or carelessly • *We slapped paint on the walls.*

slap *noun* to give someone a slap is to slap them

slapstick *noun* slapstick is noisy lively comedy, with people hitting each other, throwing things and falling over

slash *verb* **1.** to slash something is to make large cuts in it **2.** to slash prices or costs is to reduce them a lot

slash *noun* **1.** a large cut **2.** a sloping line (/) used to separate words or letters

slat *noun* a thin strip of wood or plastic, usually arranged to overlap with others, for example in a blind or screen

slate *noun* **1.** slate is a kind of grey rock that is easily split into flat plates **2.** slates are flat pieces of this rock used to cover a roof

slaughter *verb* (**slor**-ter) **1.** to slaughter an animal is to kill it for food **2.** to slaughter people or animals is to kill a lot of them

slaughter *noun* slaughter is the killing of a lot of people or animals

slave *noun* a person who is owned by someone else and has to work for them without being paid

slave *verb* to slave over something is to work very hard

slavery *noun* slavery is being a slave or the system of having slaves

slay *verb* slaying, slew, slain (*old use*) to slay someone is to kill them

sledge or **sled** *noun* a vehicle for travelling over snow, with strips of metal or wood instead of wheels

sledgehammer *noun* a very large heavy hammer

sleek *adjective* smooth and shiny • *the cat's sleek fur*

sleep *noun* **1.** sleep is the condition in which your eyes are closed, your body is relaxed and your mind is unconscious • *You need some sleep.* **2.** a sleep is a time when you are sleeping • *Did you have a good sleep?*

sleep *verb* sleeping, slept to sleep is to have a sleep

sleeper *noun* **1.** someone who is asleep • *I am a heavy sleeper.* **2.** each of the wooden or concrete beams on which a railway line rests **3.** a railway carriage equipped for sleeping in

sleeping bag *noun* a warm padded bag for sleeping in, especially when you are camping

sleepless *adjective* unable to sleep; without sleep • *We've had a sleepless night.*

sleepwalker *noun* someone who walks around while they are asleep sleepwalking *noun* what a sleepwalker does

sleepy *adjective* sleepier, sleepiest feeling tired and wanting to go to sleep sleepily *adverb* sleepiness *noun*

sleet *noun* sleet is a mixture of rain with snow or hail

sleeve *noun* the part of a piece of clothing that covers your arm sleeveless *adjective* not having sleeves

sleigh *noun* (slay) a large sledge pulled by horses

slender *adjective* slim or thin

slice *noun* a thin flat piece cut off something
slice *verb* to slice something is to cut it into slices

slick *noun* a large patch of oil floating on water

slide *verb* sliding, slid to slide is to move smoothly over a flat or polished or slippery surface
slide *noun* **1.** a sliding movement **2.** a structure for children to play on, with a smooth slope for sliding down **3.** a type of photograph that lets light through and that can be shown on a screen **4.** a small glass plate on which you can examine things under a microscope **5.** a decorative clip for keeping your hair tidy

slight *adjective* very small; not serious or important

slightly *adverb* in a slight way; not seriously • *They were slightly hurt.*

slim *adjective* slimmer, slimmest **1.** thin and graceful **2.** small; hardly enough • *We have a slim chance of winning.*

slim *verb* slimming, slimmed to slim is to try to make yourself thinner, especially by dieting slimmer *noun* someone who is slimming

slime *noun* slime is unpleasant wet slippery stuff • *The pond was covered in slime.*
slimy *adjective* covered in slime

sling *verb* slinging, slung **1.** to sling something somewhere is to throw it there roughly or carelessly • *Sling your wet clothes into the washing machine.* **2.** to sling something is also to hang it up or support it so that it hangs loosely • *He had slung the bag round his neck.*

sling *noun* **1.** a piece of cloth tied round your neck to support an injured arm **2.** a device for throwing stones

slink *verb* slinking, slunk to slink somewhere is to move there slowly and quietly because you feel guilty or don't want to be noticed

slip *verb* slipping, slipped **1.** to slip is to slide without meaning to or to fall over **2.** to slip somewhere is to move there quickly and quietly • *He slipped out of the house before anyone was awake.* **3.** to slip something somewhere is to put it there quickly without being seen • *She slipped the letter into her pocket.* to slip up is to make a mistake

slip *noun* **1.** an accidental slide or fall • *One slip and you could fall into the river.* **2.** a small mistake **3.** a small piece of paper **4.** a piece of women's underwear like a thin dress or skirt to give someone the slip is to escape from them or avoid them

slipper *noun* a soft comfortable shoe for wearing indoors

slippery *adjective* smooth or wet so that it is difficult to stand on or hold

slit *noun* a long narrow cut or opening
slit *verb* slitting, slit to slit something is to make a slit in it

slither *verb* to slither is to slip or slide along, often unsteadily • *We were slithering around on the ice.*

sliver *noun* (**sli**-ver) a thin strip of wood, glass or other material

slog *verb* slogging, slogged **1**. to slog something is to hit it hard or wildly **2**. to slog is to work hard • *I'm slogging away at my essay.* **3**. to slog is also to walk with effort • *We slogged through the snow.*

slog *noun* a piece of hard work or effort • *Climbing the hill was a real slog.*

slogan *noun* a short catchy phrase used to advertise something or to sum up an idea

slop *verb* slopping, slopped **1**. to slop liquid is to spill it over the edge of its container **2**. liquid slops when it spills in this way

slope *verb* to slope is to go gradually downwards or upwards or to have one end higher than the other

slope *noun* **1**. a sloping surface **2**. the amount by which a surface slopes • *The hill has a slope of 30°.*

sloppy *adjective* sloppier, sloppiest **1**. liquid and spilling easily **2**. careless or badly done • *Their work is sloppy.* **3**. (informal) too sentimental sloppily *adverb* sloppiness *noun*

slot *noun* a narrow opening to put things through

sloth *noun* (rhymes with both) **1**. sloth is laziness **2**. a sloth is a long-haired South American animal that lives in trees and moves very slowly

slouch *verb* to slouch is to move or stand or sit in a lazy way, especially with your head and shoulders bent forwards

slovenly *adjective* (**sluv**-en-li) careless or untidy

slow *adjective* **1**. not quick; taking more time than usual **2**. a clock or watch is slow when it shows a time earlier than the correct time

slow *adverb* at a slow rate; slowly • *Go slow.* slowly *adverb* at a slow rate or speed slowness *noun* slowness is being slow

slow *verb* **1**. to slow or to slow down, is to go slower **2**. to slow something or to slow it down, is to make it go slower

sludge *noun* sludge is thick sticky mud

slug *noun* a small slimy animal like a snail without its shell

slum *noun* an area of dirty and crowded houses in a city

slumber *noun* slumber is peaceful sleep

slumber *verb* to slumber is to sleep peacefully

slump *verb* to slump is to fall heavily or suddenly

slush *noun* slush is snow that is melting on the ground slushy *adjective* slushy snow is melting and wet

sly *adjective* cunning or mischievous slyly *adverb* slyness *noun*

smack *verb* to smack someone is to slap them with your hand

smack *noun* a slap with your hand

small *adjective* not large; less than the normal size

smart *adjective* **1**. neat and well dressed **2**. clever smartly *adverb*

smart *verb* to smart is to feel a stinging pain

smarten *verb* to smarten yourself or something up is to make them neater • *You need to smarten yourself up a bit.*

smash *verb* **1**. to smash is to break into pieces noisily and violently **2**. to smash something is to break it in this way **3**. to smash into something is to hit it with great force

smash *noun* **1**. the act or sound of smashing **2**. a collision between vehicles

smear *verb* to smear something dirty or greasy is to rub it thickly over a surface

smear *noun* a dirty or greasy mark made by smearing

smell *verb* smelling, smelt or smelled **1**. you smell something when you use your nose to sense it **2**. to smell is to give out a smell • *The cheese smells funny.*

smell *noun* **1**. a smell is something you can smell, especially something unpleasant **2**. smell is the ability to smell things • *Dogs have a good sense of smell.*

smelly *adjective* smellier, smelliest having an unpleasant smell

smelt *verb* to smelt ore is to melt it in order to get metal from it

smile *noun* an expression on your face that shows you are pleased or amused, with your lips stretched and curving upwards

smile *verb* to smile is to give a smile

smith *noun* someone who makes things out of metal

smock *noun* a loose piece of clothing like a very long shirt

smog *noun* smog is a mixture of smoke and fog

smoke *noun* smoke is the grey or blue mixture of gas and particles that rises from a fire **smoky** *adjective* full of smoke

smoke *verb* **1.** something smokes when it gives out smoke • *The fire is smoking.* **2.** someone is smoking when they have a lit cigarette in their mouth and are breathing in the smoke from it **smoker** *noun* someone who smokes cigarettes

smooth *adjective* **1.** having an even surface without any marks or roughness **2.** a smooth liquid or substance has no lumps in it **3.** moving without bumps or jolts • *We had a smooth ride.* **4.** not harsh • *It has a rich, smooth taste.* **smoothly** *adverb* in a smooth way; evenly **smoothness** *noun*

smooth *verb* to smooth something is to make it smooth and flat

smother *verb* **1.** to smother someone is to cover their face so that they can't breathe **2.** to smother something is to cover it thickly • *He brought in a cake smothered in icing.* **3.** to smother a fire is to put it out by covering it

smoulder *verb* to smoulder is to burn slowly without a flame

smudge *noun* a dirty or messy mark made by rubbing something

smudge *verb* to smudge paint or ink is to touch it while it is still wet and make it messy

smug *adjective* **smugger, smuggest** too pleased with yourself **smugly** *adverb* **smugness** *noun*

smuggle *verb* to smuggle something is to bring it into a country secretly and illegally **smuggler** *noun* someone who smuggles goods

snack *noun* a quick light meal

snag *noun* an unexpected problem

snail *noun* a small animal with a soft body in a hard shell

snake *noun* a reptile with a long narrow body and no legs

snap *verb* **snapping, snapped** **1.** something snaps when it breaks suddenly with a sharp noise **2.** an animal snaps when it bites suddenly or quickly • *The dog snapped at me.* **3.** to snap something is to say it quickly and angrily • *There's no need to snap.* **4.** to snap your fingers is to make a sharp snapping sound with them

snap *noun* **1.** a snap is the act or sound of snapping **2.** a snap is also an informal photograph taken quickly **3.** snap is a card game in which players shout 'Snap!' when they spot two similar cards

snappy *adjective* **snappier, snappiest** quick and lively

snapshot *noun* an informal photograph taken quickly

snare *noun* a trap for catching animals

snare *verb* to snare an animal is to catch it in a snare

snarl *verb* an animal snarls when it growls angrily

snarl *noun* a snarling sound

snatch *verb* to snatch something is to grab it quickly

sneak *verb* to sneak somewhere is to move there quietly and secretly

sneak *noun (informal)* a person who tells tales

sneaky *adjective* sneakier, sneakiest dishonest or deceitful

sneer *verb* to sneer is to speak or behave in a scornful way

sneeze *verb* you sneeze when you push air through your nose suddenly and uncontrollably

sneeze *noun* the action or sound of sneezing

sniff *verb* **1.** to sniff is to make a noise by drawing air in through your nose **2.** to sniff something is to smell it with a sniff

sniff *noun* the action or sound of sniffing or smelling something

sniffle *verb* to keep sniffing because you have a cold or are crying

snigger *verb* to snigger is to give a quiet sly laugh

snigger *noun* a quiet sly laugh

snip *verb* snipping, snipped to snip something is to cut a small piece or pieces off it

snip *noun* an act of snipping something

sniper *noun* someone who shoots at people from a hiding place

snippet *noun* a short piece of news or information

snivel *verb* snivelling, snivelled to snivel is to cry or complain in a whining way

snob *noun* someone who looks down on people who have not got wealth or power or particular tastes or interests **snobbery** *noun* snobbery is being a snob **snobbish** *adjective* thinking or behaving like a snob

snooker *noun* snooker is a game played with long sticks (called *cues*) and 22 coloured balls on a cloth-covered table

snoop *verb* to snoop is to pry or try to find out about someone else's business **snooper** or **snoop** *noun* someone who snoops

snore *verb* to snore is to breathe noisily while you are sleeping

snorkel *noun* a tube with one end above the water, worn by an underwater swimmer to get air

snort *verb* to snort is to make a loud noise by forcing air out through your nose

snort *noun* a snorting noise

snout *noun* an animal's snout is the front part sticking out from its head, with its nose and mouth

snow *noun* snow is frozen drops of water falling from the sky as small white flakes

snow *verb* to fall as snow

snowball *noun* snow pressed into the shape of a ball for throwing

snowdrop *noun* a small white flower that blooms in early spring

snowflake *noun* a flake of snow

snowman *noun* snowmen a figure of a person made of snow

snowplough *noun* a vehicle with a large blade at the front for clearing snow from a road or railway track

snowstorm *noun* a storm with snow falling

snowy *adjective* snowier, snowiest **1.** with snow falling • *We're expecting snowy weather.* **2.** covered with snow • *The roofs looked snowy.* **3.** brightly white

snub *verb* snubbing, snubbed to snub someone is to treat them in a scornful or unfriendly way

snug *adjective* snugger, snuggest warm and cosy • *We found a snug corner by the fire.* **snugly** *adverb* in a snug way • *The little ones are tucked up snugly in bed.*

snuggle *verb* to snuggle is to curl up in a warm comfortable place

so *adverb* **1.** in this way; to such an extent • *Why are you so cross?* **2.** very • *Cricket is so boring.* **3.** also • *I was wrong but so were you.* and so on and other similar things • *They took food, water, spare clothing and so on.* or so or about that number • *We need about fifty or so.* so as to in order to so far up to now so what? *(informal)* what does that matter?

so *conjunction* for that reason • *It was dark, so we took a torch.*

soak *verb* to soak someone or something is to make them very wet or leave them in water to soak something up is to take in a liquid in the way that a sponge does

soap *noun* **1.** soap is a substance you use with water for washing and cleaning things **2.** *(informal)* a soap is a soap opera soapy *adjective* full of soap or covered in soap

soap opera *noun* a television serial about the ordinary life of a group of imaginary people

soar *verb* **1.** to soar is to rise or fly high in the air **2.** to soar is also to increase a lot • *Prices were soaring.*

sob *verb* sobbing, sobbed to sob is to cry with gasping noises
sob *noun* a sound of sobbing

sober *adjective* **1.** not drunk **2.** calm and serious • *She had a sober expression.* **3.** not bright or showy • *The room was painted in sober colours.*

so-called *adjective* having the name but perhaps not deserving it • *Even the so-called experts couldn't solve the problem.*

soccer *noun* soccer is a game played by two teams which try to kick a ball into their opponents' goal

sociable *adjective* (**soh**-sha-bul) sociable people are friendly and like to be with other people

social *adjective* (**soh**-shal) **1.** to do with people meeting one another in their spare time • *a social club* **2.** living in groups, not alone • *Bees are social insects.* **3.** to do with society or a community • *They were writing a social history of the area.* socially *adverb* in your spare time, not at work

social media *noun* websites and computer programs that people use to communicate on the Internet, using mobile phones, computers, etc.

social work *noun* social work is work helping people in a community who have problems social worker *noun* someone who has a job in social work

society *noun* societies **1.** a society is a community of people; society is people living together in a group or nation **2.** a society is also a group of people organized for a particular purpose • *He's joined a dramatic society.*

sock *noun* a soft piece of clothing that covers your foot and the lower half of your leg

socket *noun* a hole that an electric plug or bulb fits into

soda *noun* **1.** soda is a substance made from sodium **2.** soda is also soda water

soda water *noun* soda water is fizzy water used in drinks

sodium *noun* (**soh**-di-um) sodium is a soft silvery-white metal

sofa *noun* a long soft seat with sides and a back

soft *adjective* **1.** not hard or firm • *a soft pillow* **2.** smooth • *soft fur* **3.** gentle; not loud • *He spoke in a soft voice.* softly *adverb* in a gentle way; quietly • *She closed the door softly behind her.* softness *noun*

soft drink *noun* a drink that does not contain alcohol

soften *verb* **1.** to soften something is to make it softer **2.** to soften is to become softer

software *noun* (in computing) software is the programs that tell a computer what to do, which are not part of the machinery (the *hardware*) of a computer

soggy *adjective* soggier, soggiest very wet and soft

soil¹ *noun* soil is the loose earth that plants grow in

soil² *verb* to soil something is to make it dirty

solar *adjective* to do with the sun or powered by the sun's energy

solar system *noun* the solar system is the sun and the planets that revolve round it

solder *noun* solder is a soft alloy that is melted to join pieces of metal together

solder *verb* to solder two pieces of metal is to join them together with solder

soldier *noun* a member of an army

sole[1] *noun* **1.** the bottom part of a shoe or foot **2.** a flat sea fish used for food

sole[2] *adjective* single or only • *She was the sole survivor.* **solely** *adverb*

solemn *adjective* serious and dignified **solemnity** *noun* solemnity is being solemn **solemnly** *adverb* in a serious and dignified way

solicitor *noun* a lawyer who advises clients and prepares legal documents

solid *adjective* **1.** keeping its shape; not a liquid or gas **2.** not hollow; with no space inside • *These bars are made of solid steel.* **3.** firm or strongly made • *The house is built on solid foundations.* **4.** strong and reliable • *They gave solid support.* **solidly** *adverb* something is solidly built when it is firmly and strongly built; to rain solidly is to rain continuously **solidity** *noun* how solid something is

solid *noun* **1.** a solid thing **2.** a three-dimensional shape, such as a cube, sphere or cone

solitary *adjective* **1.** alone; on your own • *He lived a solitary life.* **2.** single • *There was a solitary van in the car park.*

solitude *noun* solitude is being on your own

solo *noun* **solos** something sung or performed by one person alone

soloist *noun* someone who plays or sings a solo

soluble *adjective* a soluble substance is able to be dissolved

solution *noun* **1.** the answer to a problem or puzzle **2.** a liquid with something dissolved in it

solve *verb* to solve a problem or puzzle is to find an answer to it

sombre *adjective* gloomy or dark

some *determiner* **1.** a few or a little • *I'd like some biscuits and some sugar.* **2.** a certain amount of • *Would you like some cake?* **3.** an unknown person or thing • *Some fool left the window open.*

some *pronoun* a certain or unknown number or amount • *Some of them were late.*

somebody *pronoun* someone; some person

somehow *adverb* in some way • *We must finish the work somehow.*

someone *pronoun* some person

somersault *noun* (**sum-er-solt**) a movement in which you turn head over heels and land on your feet

something *pronoun* a certain or unknown thing

sometime *adverb* at some time • *I saw her sometime last year.*

sometimes *adverb* at some times but not always • *We sometimes walk to school.*

somewhat *adverb* to some extent; rather • *He was somewhat annoyed.*

somewhere *adverb* in or to some place

son *noun* a boy or man who is someone's child

sonar *noun* sonar is a system using the echo from sound waves to locate objects underwater

song *noun* **1.** a song is a tune with words for singing **2.** a bird's song is the musical sounds it makes **3.** song is singing • *He burst into song.*

songbird *noun* a bird that sings sweetly

sonic *adjective* to do with sound or sound waves

sonnet *noun* a kind of poem with 14 lines

soon *adverb* **1.** in a short time from now **2.** not long after something • *She became ill, but was soon better.* **3.** early or quickly • *You spoke too soon.* sooner or later at some time in the future

soot *noun* soot is the black powder left by smoke in a chimney or on a building sooty *adjective* covered in soot

soothe *verb* **1.** to soothe someone is to make them calm **2.** to soothe a pain or ache is to make it hurt less

sophisticated *adjective* (sof-**iss**-ti-kay-tid) **1.** someone is sophisticated when they live a fashionable or cultured life and know a lot about things such as art or food **2.** something is sophisticated when it is complicated and highly developed • *a sophisticated machine* sophistication *noun* sophistication is being sophisticated

sopping *adjective* very wet; soaked

soppy *adjective* soppier, soppiest *(informal)* sentimental or silly

soprano *noun* sopranos (so-**prah**-noh) a woman or young boy with a high singing voice

sorcerer *noun* someone who can do magic sorcery *noun* magic or witchcraft

sorceress *noun* a woman who can do magic

sore *adjective* painful or smarting • *I've got a sore throat.* soreness *noun*

sore *noun* a red and painful place on your skin

sorely *adverb* seriously; very • *I was sorely tempted to run away.*

sorrow *noun* sorrow is sadness or regret sorrowful *adjective* feeling sorrow sorrowfully *adverb*

sorry *adjective* sorrier, sorriest **1.** you are sorry that you did something when you regret doing it or want to apologize • *I'm sorry I forgot to send you a birthday card.* **2.** you feel sorry for someone when you feel pity for them or are sad that something bad has happened to them • *I'm sorry you've been ill.*

sort *noun* a group of things or people that are similar; a kind • *What sort of fruit do you like?*

sort *verb* to sort things is to arrange them in groups or kinds to sort something out is to organize it or arrange it

SOS *noun* an SOS is an urgent appeal for help from someone whose life is in danger

soul *noun* a person's invisible spirit that some people believe goes on living after the body has died

sound[1] *noun* **1.** sound is vibrations in the air that you can detect with your ear **2.** a sound is something that you can hear

sound[1] *verb* **1.** to sound is to make a sound • *The trumpets sounded.* **2.** to sound something is to make a sound with it • *Don't forget to sound your horn.* **3.** to sound a certain way is to give that impression when heard • *You sound in a good mood.* • *The car sounds as if it needs a service.*

sound[2] *verb* to sound someone out is to try to find out what they think or feel about something

sound[3] *adjective* **1.** not damaged; in good condition **2.** healthy **3.** reasonable or correct • *His ideas are sound.* **4.** reliable or secure • *They made a sound investment.* **5.** thorough or deep • *She has a sound knowledge of the subject.* • *I am a sound sleeper.* soundly *adverb* thoroughly or completely soundness *noun* being reliable or sensible

sound effects *plural noun* special sounds produced to make a play or film more realistic

soundtrack *noun* the sound or music that goes with a film or television programme

soup *noun* a liquid food made from vegetables or meat

sour *adjective* having a sharp taste like vinegar or lemons sourness *noun*

source *noun* **1.** the place where something comes from **2.** the place where a river starts

south *noun* **1.** the direction to the right of a person facing east **2.** the part of a country or city that is in this direction
south *adjective, adverb* **1.** towards the south or in the south **2.** coming from the south • *A south wind was blowing.*

south-east *noun, adjective, adverb* midway between south and east

southern *adjective* (**suth**-ern) from or to do with the south

southerner noun (**suth**-er-ner) someone who lives in the south of a country

southward or **southwards** adjective, adverb towards the south

south-west noun, adjective, adverb midway between south and west

souvenir noun (soo-ven-**eer**) something that you buy or keep to remind you of a person, place or event

sovereign noun (**sov**-rin) 1. a king or a queen 2. an old British gold coin that was worth £1

sow[1] verb sowing, sowed, sown or sowed (rhymes with go) to sow seeds is to put them into the ground so that they will grow into plants

sow[2] noun (rhymes with cow) a female pig

soya bean noun a bean that is rich in protein, used to make kinds of oil and flour

space noun 1. space is the whole area outside the earth, where the stars and planets are 2. space is also an area or volume • There isn't enough space for a car. 3. a space is an empty area or gap • There is a space at the back of the cupboard.
space verb to space things or space things out, is to arrange them with gaps or periods of time between them

spacecraft noun spacecraft a vehicle for travelling in outer space

spaceship noun a spacecraft

space shuttle noun a spacecraft that can travel into space and return to earth

space station noun a satellite which orbits the earth and is used as a base by scientists and astronauts

spade noun 1. a tool with a long handle and a wide blade for digging 2. a playing card with black shapes like upside-down hearts on it

spaghetti noun (spa-**get**-i) spaghetti is pasta made in long strings

span noun 1. the length from one end of something to the other 2. a part of a bridge between two supports 3. a period of time
span verb to span something is to reach from one side or end of it to the other • A wooden bridge spanned the river.

spank verb to spank someone is to smack them several times on the bottom as a punishment

spanner noun a tool for tightening or loosening a nut

spar verb sparring, sparred to spar is to practise boxing

spare verb 1. to spare something is to afford it or be able to give it to someone • Can you spare a moment? 2. to spare someone is to avoid harming them or making them suffer something unpleasant
spare adjective not used but kept ready in case it is needed; extra • Where's the spare wheel?
spare noun a spare thing or part • The local garage sells spares.

spark noun 1. a tiny flash of electricity 2. a tiny glowing piece of something hot
spark verb to spark is to give off sparks

sparkle verb to sparkle is to shine with a lot of tiny flashes of bright light

sparkler noun a firework that sparkles

sparrow noun a small brown bird

sparse adjective small in number or amount; thinly scattered • Vegetation on the island is sparse. sparsely adverb a sparsely populated area is one with only a few people

spatter verb to spatter something is to splash it or scatter it in small drops or pieces

spawn noun spawn is the eggs of frogs, fish and other water animals

speak verb speaking, spoke, spoken 1. to speak is to say something • I spoke to them this morning. 2. to speak a language is to be able to talk in it to speak up is to say something more clearly or loudly

speaker noun 1. a person who is speaking or making a speech 2. the part of a radio, CD player or computer etc. that the sound comes out of

spear noun a long pole with a sharp point, used as a weapon
spear verb to spear something is to pierce it with a spear or something pointed

special adjective 1. different from other people or things; unusual 2. meant for a particular person or purpose • *You'll need special training.*

specialist *noun* an expert in a particular subject

speciality *noun* specialities something that you are especially good at doing

specially *adverb* for a special purpose • *I came specially to see you.*

species *noun* species (**spee**-shiz) a group of animals or plants that have similar features and can breed with each other

specific *adjective* 1. definite or precise 2. to do with a particular thing • *The money was given for a specific purpose.*

specifically *adverb* 1. in a special way or for a special purpose • *These scissors are designed specifically for left-handed people.* 2. clearly and precisely • *I specifically said we had to go.*

specify *verb* specifies, specifying, specified to specify a person or thing is to name or mention them precisely • *The recipe specified brown sugar, not white.*

specimen *noun* a small amount or sample of something

speck *noun* a tiny mark or piece of something

speckled *adjective* covered with small spots

spectacle *noun* an exciting sight or display

spectacles *plural noun* a pair of lenses in a frame, which you wear over your eyes to help improve your eyesight

spectacular *adjective* exciting to see

spectator *noun* a person who watches a game or show

spectrum *noun* spectra the band of colours like those in a rainbow

speech *noun* 1. speech is the ability to speak or a person's way of speaking 2. a speech is a talk given to a group of people

speechless *adjective* unable to speak, especially because you are surprised or angry

speech marks *plural noun* inverted commas (" ") used to show that someone is speaking

speed *noun* 1. the speed of something is the rate at which it moves or happens 2. speed is being quick or fast at speed fast; quickly
speed *verb* speeding, sped or speeded to speed is to go very fast or too fast to speed up is to become quicker to speed something up is to make it go or happen faster

speedboat *noun* a fast motor boat

speedometer *noun* (spee-**dom**-it-er) a gauge in a vehicle that shows its speed

speedy *adjective* speedier, speediest quick or fast • *We need a speedy reply.*
speedily *adverb* fast or quickly

spell[1] *verb* spelling, spelt or spelled to spell a word is to give its letters in the right order

spell[2] *noun* a short time when there is a particular type of weather • *a cold spell*

spell[3] *noun* a set of words that is supposed to have magic power

spelling *noun* 1. the way in which letters are put together to form words 2. how well someone can spell • *Her spelling is poor.*

spend *verb* 1. to spend money is to use it to pay for things 2. to spend time is to pass it doing something 3. to spend energy or effort is to use it up

sphere *noun* a perfectly round solid shape; a globe or ball spherical *adjective* shaped like a ball

spice *noun* a strong-tasting substance used to flavour food, often made from the dried parts of plants spicy *adjective* having a strong flavour; full of spices

spider *noun* a small animal with eight legs that spins webs to catch insects

spike *noun* a pointed piece of metal; a sharp point spiky *adjective* full of spikes or sharp points • *She has short spiky hair.*

spill *verb* spilling, spilt or spilled 1. to spill something is to let it fall out of a container by accident 2. to spill is to fall out of a container • *The coins came spilling out.*
spill *noun* when something gets spilt • *an oil spill*

spin *verb* spinning, spun 1. to spin is to turn round and round quickly 2. to spin something is to make it spin 3. to spin is also to make pieces of wool or cotton into thread by twisting them **4.** to spin a web or cocoon is to make it out of threads

spinach *noun* spinach is a vegetable with dark green leaves

spindle *noun* **1.** a thin rod on which you wind thread **2.** a pin or bar that turns round or on which something turns round

spine *noun* **1.** the line of bones down the middle of your back **2.** a sharp point on an animal or plant • *This cactus has sharp spines.* **3.** the back part of a book where the pages are joined together **spinal** *adjective* to do with your spine **spiny** *adjective* covered in spines

spine-chilling *adjective* frightening and exciting

spinning wheel *noun* a machine for spinning thread out of wool or cotton

spinster *noun* a woman who has not married

spiral *adjective* going round and round a central point, getting further from it with each turn
spiral *noun* something with a spiral shape

spire *noun* a tall pointed part on top of a church tower

spirit *noun* **1.** a person's spirit is their soul or their deepest thoughts and feelings **2.** a spirit is a ghost or other supernatural being **3.** spirit is courage or liveliness **4.** a person's spirits are their mood or the way they feel • *She was in good spirits after the exam.* **5.** a spirit is also a strong alcoholic drink

spiritual *adjective* **1.** to do with the human soul and with a person's deepest thoughts and feelings **2.** to do with religious beliefs **spiritually** *adverb*
spiritual *noun* a religious song originally sung by Black Americans

spit[1] *verb* **spitting, spat** to spit is to shoot drops of liquid out of your mouth
spit[1] *noun* saliva that has been spat out

spit[2] *noun* a long thin metal spike put through meat to hold it while it is roasted

spite *noun* spite is a desire to hurt or annoy someone **in spite of something** although something has happened or is happening • *They went out in spite of the rain.*

spiteful *adjective* wanting to hurt or annoy someone **spitefully** *adverb*

splash *verb* **1.** to splash liquid is to make it fly about, as you do when you jump into water **2.** to splash is to fly about in drops • *The water splashed all over me.* **3.** to splash someone or something is to make them wet by sending drops of liquid towards them • *The bus splashed us as it went past.*
splash *noun* the action or sound of splashing

splashdown *noun* the landing of a spacecraft in the sea

splendid *adjective* magnificent **splendidly** *adverb*

splendour *noun* splendour is a brilliant display or appearance

splint *noun* a straight piece of wood or metal that is tied to a broken arm or leg to hold it firm

splinter *noun* a small sharp piece of wood or glass broken off a larger piece
splinter *verb* to splinter is to break into splinters

split *verb* **splitting, split** **1.** to split is to break into parts **2.** to split something is to divide it into parts **to split up** **1.** is to divide into parts **2.** is to separate after being together for some time
split *noun* a crack or tear in something, where it has split

splutter *verb* to splutter is to make a quick series of spitting or coughing sounds • *The smoke made him splutter.*

spoil *verb* **spoiling, spoilt** or **spoiled** **1.** to spoil something is to make it less enjoyable or useful • *The rain spoilt our holiday.* **2.** to spoil someone is to make them selfish by always letting them have what they want

spoilsport *noun* someone who spoils other people's fun

spoke *noun* one of the rods that go from the centre of a wheel to the rim

sponge *noun* **1.** a lump of soft material containing lots of tiny holes, used for washing **2.** a sea creature from which this kind of material is made **3.** a soft lightweight cake or pudding
sponge *verb* to sponge something is to wash it with a sponge

spongy *adjective* spongier, spongiest soft and absorbent like sponge

sponsor *verb* **1.** to sponsor someone is to promise to give them money for a charity if they do something difficult **2.** to sponsor something or someone is to provide money to support them
sponsor *noun* someone who provides money to support a person or thing or who supports someone who sets out to do something for charity **sponsorship** *noun* the money someone provides to support a person or thing

spontaneous *adjective* (spon-**tay**-ni-us) happening or done without being planned; not forced or suggested by someone else • *Everyone burst into spontaneous applause.* spontaneously *adverb* spontaneity *noun* behaving in a spontaneous way

spooky *adjective* spookier, spookiest (informal) frighteningly strange; haunted by ghosts

spool *noun* a rod or reel for winding on something such as thread or film or tape

spoon *noun* a tool used for lifting food to your mouth or for stirring or measuring, consisting of a small bowl with a handle
spoon *verb* to spoon something is to lift it or take it with a spoon

sport *noun* **1.** a sport is a game that exercises your body, especially one played outside **2.** sport is games of this sort • *Are you keen on sport?*

sporting *adjective* **1.** connected with sport **2.** behaving fairly and unselfishly

sportsman or **sportswoman** *noun* sportsmen or sportswomen a man or woman who takes part in sport

sportsmanship *noun* sportsmanship is behaving fairly and generously in sport

spot *noun* **1.** a small round mark **2.** a pimple on your skin **3.** a small amount of something • *We've had a spot of bother.* **4.** a place • *This is a nice spot.* on the spot immediately; there and then • *We can repair your bike on the spot.*
spot *verb* spotting, spotted to spot someone or something is to notice them or see them

spotless *adjective* perfectly clean
spotlessly *adverb* to be spotlessly clean is to be perfectly clean

spotlight *noun* a strong light with a beam that shines on a small area

spotty *adjective* spottier, spottiest marked with spots

spout *noun* **1.** a pipe or opening from which liquid can pour **2.** a jet of liquid
spout *verb* to spout is to come out in a jet of liquid

sprain *verb* you sprain your ankle or wrist when you injure it by twisting it
sprain *noun* an injury by spraining

sprawl *verb* **1.** you sprawl when you sit or lie with your arms and legs spread out **2.** to be sprawled is to be spread out loosely or untidily • *There were books and papers sprawled all over the floor.*

spray *verb* to spray liquid is to scatter it in tiny drops over something; to spray something is to cover it with liquid in this way
spray *noun* **1.** tiny drops of liquid sprayed on something **2.** a device for spraying liquid

spread *verb* spreading, spread **1.** to spread something is to lay or stretch it out to its full size • *The bird spread its wings and flew away.* **2.** to spread something over a surface is to make it cover the surface • *He spread a thick layer of jam on his toast.* **3.** to spread news or information is to make it widely known **4.** news or information spreads when it becomes widely known • *The story spread quickly round the village.*
spread *noun* **1.** something you can spread on bread **2.** (informal) a large meal

sprightly *adjective* sprightlier, sprightliest lively and energetic

spring *noun* **1.** spring is the season of the year when most plants start to grow, between winter and summer **2.** a spring is a coil of wire that goes back to its original shape after being squeezed **3.** a spring is also a sudden upward movement **4.** a spring is also a place where water rises out of the ground and becomes a stream
spring *verb* springing, sprang, sprung **1.** to spring is to move quickly or suddenly **2.** to spring or spring up, is to develop or come from something • *This argument has sprung from a misunderstanding.* **3.** to spring something on someone is to surprise them with it

springboard *noun* a springy board from which people jump or dive

springtime *noun* springtime is the season of spring

springy *adjective* springier, springiest able to spring back to its original position after being squeezed

sprinkle *verb* to sprinkle liquid or powder is to make tiny drops or pieces of it fall on something **sprinkler** *noun* a device for sprinkling liquid

sprint *verb* to sprint is to run very fast for a short distance **sprinter** *noun* someone who sprints

sprint *noun* a short fast race

sprout *verb* a plant sprouts when it starts to produce leaves or shoots

sprout *noun* a green vegetable like a tiny cabbage

spruce *noun* a kind of fir tree

spud *noun* (informal) a potato

spur *noun* a sharp spike that a rider wears on the heel of their boot to urge a horse to go faster **on the spur of the moment** on an impulse; without planning

spur *verb* spurring, spurred to spur someone or to spur someone on, is to encourage them

spurt *verb* a liquid spurts when it gushes out or up

spurt *noun* a jet of liquid

spy *noun* spies someone who works secretly to find out things about another country or person

spy *verb* spies, spying, spied **1.** to spy is to be a spy or to watch secretly • *He was spying on us.* **2.** to spy someone or something is to see them or notice them • *We spied a house in the distance.*

squabble *verb* people squabble when they quarrel about something unimportant

squabble *noun* a minor quarrel or argument

squad *noun* a small group of people working or being trained together

squadron *noun* part of an army, navy or air force

squalid *adjective* dirty and unpleasant • *He lived in a squalid little flat.* **squalor** *noun* squalor is being squalid

squander *verb* to squander money or time is to waste it

square *noun* **1.** a shape with four equal sides and four right angles **2.** in a town, an area surrounded by buildings **3.** the result of multiplying a number by itself • *9 is the square of 3.*

square *adjective* **1.** shaped like a square **2.** used for units of measurement that give an area. For example, a square metre is the size of a square with each side one metre long. **3.** equal or even • *The teams are all square with six points each.*

square *verb* to square a number is to multiply it by itself • *3 squared is 9.*

squarely *adverb* directly or exactly • *The ball hit him squarely in the mouth.*

square root *noun* the number that gives a particular number if it is multiplied by itself • *3 is the square root of 9.*

squash *verb* **1.** to squash something is to squeeze it so that it loses its shape **2.** to squash a person or thing into something is to force them into a space that is too small

squash *noun* **1.** a squash is when people or things are pressed together because there is not enough space • *There was a tremendous squash outside the football ground.* **2.** squash is a fruit-flavoured drink **3.** squash is also a game played with rackets and a small ball in a special indoor court

squat *verb* squatting, squatted **1.** to squat is to sit back on your heels **2.** to squat in an unoccupied house is to live there without permission **squatter** *noun* someone who squats in a house

squat *adjective* short and fat

squaw *noun* a Native American woman

squawk *verb* to squawk is to make a loud harsh cry

squawk *noun* a loud harsh cry

squeak *verb* to make a short high-pitched sound or cry

squeak *noun* a short high-pitched sound or cry **squeaky** *adjective* making squeaks • *a squeaky floorboard*

squeal *verb* to squeal is to make a long shrill sound

squeal *noun* a long shrill sound

squeeze *verb* **1**. to squeeze something is to press it from opposite sides, especially so that you get liquid out of it **2**. to squeeze somewhere is to force a way into or through a place or gap
squeeze *noun* **1**. the action of squeezing **2**. a tight fit • *We all got on the bus but it was a bit of a squeeze.*

squelch *verb* to squelch is to make a sound like someone treading in thick mud
squelch *noun* a squelching sound

squid *noun* squid or squids a sea animal with eight short arms and two long ones

squiggle *noun* a short curly or wavy line

squint *verb* **1**. to squint at something is to look at it with half-shut eyes **2**. to squint is to have eyes that look in different directions
squint *noun* a fault in someone's eyesight that makes them squint

squire *noun* **1**. the man who owns most of the land in a country district **2**. in the Middle Ages, a young nobleman who served a knight

squirm *verb* to squirm is to wriggle about when you feel embarrassed

squirrel *noun* a small animal with grey or red fur and a bushy tail, that lives in trees and eats nuts

squirt *verb* to squirt something is to send it out in a strong jet of liquid; to squirt is to come out like this

St. or **St** short for **Saint** or **Street**

stab *verb* stabbing, stabbed to stab someone is to pierce or wound them with something sharp
stab *noun* **1**. the action of stabbing **2**. a sudden sharp pain

stability *noun* stability is being stable or firm

stabilizer *noun* a small extra wheel on a bicycle to make it stable This word can also be spelled **stabiliser**.

stable[1] *adjective* steady or firmly fixed
stably *adverb*

stable[2] *noun* a building where horses are kept

stack *noun* **1**. a neat pile of things **2**. a large amount of something • *I've got a stack of work to do.* **3**. a single small chimney

stack *verb* to stack things is to pile them up neatly

stadium *noun* stadiums or stadia a large sports ground surrounded by seats for spectators

The word **stadium** comes from a Greek word *stadion*, which originally meant a measure of length of about 185 metres. This was the usual length of a race in an ancient stadium.

staff *noun* **1**. the people who work in an office or shop **2**. the teachers in a school or college **3**. a thick stick for walking with

stag *noun* a male deer

stage *noun* **1**. a platform for performances in a theatre or hall **2**. the point that you have reached in a process or journey • *The final stage is to paint the model.*
stage *verb* **1**. to stage a performance is to present it on a stage **2**. to stage an event is to organize it

stagecoach *noun* a kind of horse-drawn coach that used to travel regularly along the same route

stagger *verb* **1**. to stagger is to walk unsteadily **2**. to stagger someone is to amaze or shock them • *I was staggered at the price.* **3**. to stagger events is to arrange them so that they do not all happen at the same time staggering *adjective* very surprising or shocking

stagnant *adjective* stagnant water is not flowing or fresh

stain *noun* a dirty mark that is difficult to remove
stain *verb* **1**. to stain something is to make a stain on it **2**. to stain material or wood is to colour it

stainless steel *noun* stainless steel is steel that does not rust easily

stair *noun* each of a series of steps that take you from one floor to another in a building

staircase *noun* a set of stairs

stake *noun* stakes **1**. a thick pointed stick to be driven into the ground **2**. the thick post to which people used to be tied for execution by being burnt alive **3**. an amount of money you bet on something **to be at stake** is to be at risk of being lost

stake *verb* **stakes, staking, staked** to stake money is to use it on a bet **to stake a claim** is to claim something or get a right to it

stalactite *noun* a stony spike hanging like an icicle from the roof of a cave

stalagmite *noun* a stony spike standing like a pillar on the floor of a cave

stale *adjective* no longer fresh • *stale bread*

stalk[1] *noun* the main part of a plant, from which the leaves and flowers grow

stalk[2] *verb* to stalk a person or animal is to follow or hunt them stealthily

stall[1] *noun* **1.** a table or small open-fronted shop where things are sold, usually outdoors **2.** a place for one animal in a stable or shed

stall[1] *verb* a vehicle stalls when the engine stops suddenly

stall[2] *verb* to stall is to delay or hold things up to give yourself more time

stallion *noun* a male horse

stalls *plural noun* the seats on the ground floor of a theatre or cinema

stamen *noun* (**stay**-men) the part of a flower that produces pollen

stamina *noun* (**stam**-in-a) stamina is the strength and energy you need to keep doing something for a long time

stammer *verb* to stammer is to keep repeating the sounds at the beginning of words

stammer *noun* when someone stammers a lot

stamp *noun* **1.** a small piece of gummed paper with a special design on it, which you stick on a letter or parcel to show you have paid the postage **2.** when you bang your foot on the ground **3.** a small block with raised letters for printing words or marks on something; the words or marks made with this

stamp *verb* **1.** to stamp is to bang your foot heavily on the ground **2.** to stamp an envelope or parcel is to put a postage stamp on it **3.** to stamp something is also to put

marks on it with a stamp • *The librarian stamped my books.*

stampede *noun* a sudden rush of animals or people

stampede *verb* animals or people stampede when they rush in a stampede

stand *verb* **standing, stood** **1.** to stand is to be on your feet without moving • *She stood at the back of the hall.* **2.** to stand something somewhere is to put it upright there • *Stand the vase on the table.* **3.** something stands somewhere when that is where it is • *The castle stood on the top of a hill.* **4.** something stands when it stays unchanged • *My offer still stands.* **5.** to stand a difficulty or hardship is to be able to bear it • *I can't stand the heat.* **to stand by** is to be ready for action **to stand for something** **1.** is to tolerate it • *She won't stand for any arguments.* **2.** is to mean something • *'Dr' stands for 'Doctor'.* **to stand out** is to be clear or obvious **to stand up** is to rise to your feet **to stand up for someone** is to support them or defend them

stand *noun* **1.** something made for putting things on • *The statue had fallen off its stand.* **2.** a stall where things are sold or displayed **3.** a structure at a sports ground with rows of seats for spectators **4.** when someone resists an attack or defends their opinion • *She was determined to make a stand for her rights.*

standard *noun* **1.** how good something is • *They reached a high standard of work.* **2.** a thing used to measure or judge something else • *The metre is the standard for length.* **3.** a flag used by an army

standard *adjective* of the usual or ordinary kind

standard of living *noun* **standards of living** the level of comfort and wealth that a person or country has

standstill *noun* a complete stop • *The blizzard brought traffic to a standstill.*

stanza *noun* a group of lines in a poem

staple[1] *noun* **1.** a tiny piece of metal used to fasten pieces of paper together **2.** a U-shaped nail **stapler** *noun* a machine for putting staples in paper

staple[1] *verb* to fasten pieces of paper together with a staple

staple[2] *adjective* main or normal • *Rice is the staple food in many countries.*

star *noun* **1.** a large mass of burning gas that you see as a bright speck of light in the sky at night **2.** a shape with five or six points **3.** one of the main performers in a film or show; a famous entertainer **starry** *adjective* a starry sky or night is full of stars

star *verb* **starring, starred 1.** to star in a film or show is to be one of the main performers **2.** a film or show stars someone when it has them as a main performer

starboard *noun* starboard is the right-hand side of a ship or aircraft when you are facing forward

starch *noun* **1.** starch is a white substance found in bread, potatoes and other food, which is an important part of the human diet **2.** starch is also a form of this substance used to stiffen clothes **starchy** *adjective* like starch or containing starch

stare *verb* to look hard at someone or something without moving your eyes

stare *noun* a long fixed look

starfish *noun* **starfish** or **starfishes** a sea animal shaped like a star with five points

starling *noun* a common bird with dark shiny feathers

start *verb* **1.** to start something is to take the first steps in doing it **2.** to start or start out, is to begin a journey **3.** to start is also to make a sudden movement of surprise • *They all started at the noise outside.*

start *noun* **1.** the act of starting • *We need to make an early start tomorrow.* **2.** the point or place where something starts • *Saturday is the start of the new season.* **3.** an advantage that someone starts with • *We gave the young ones 10 minutes' start.* **4.** a sudden movement of surprise • *It gave me quite a start when the hooter sounded.*

startle *verb* to startle a person or animal is to surprise or alarm them

starve *verb* **1.** someone starves when they suffer or die because they do not have enough food **2.** to starve someone is to make them suffer or die in this way • *The prisoners had been starved to death.* **3.** *(informal)* to be starving is to be very hungry **starvation** *noun* when someone does not have enough food and so dies

state *noun* **1.** the condition that someone or something is in • *The room was in an untidy state.* **2.** a nation or country **3.** a division of a country **4.** you can refer to a government and its officials as the state

state *verb* to state something is to say it clearly or formally

statement *noun* **1.** words that state something **2.** a formal account of something that happened • *a witness statement* **3.** a report made by a bank about the money in a person's account

statesman or **stateswoman** *noun* **statesmen** or **stateswomen** someone who is important or skilled in governing a state

static *adjective* not moving or changing

static electricity *noun* electricity which is present in something but does not flow as a current

station *noun* **1.** a place where people get on or off trains or buses **2.** a building for police or firemen **3.** a place from which radio or television broadcasts are made

station *verb* to station a person somewhere is to place them there for a particular purpose

> The word **station** comes from a Latin word *stare* meaning 'to stand', because a station was originally a place where someone stood.

stationary *adjective* not moving

stationery *noun* stationery is paper, envelopes and other things used for writing

statistic *noun* a piece of information expressed as a number • *These statistics show that the population has doubled.* **statistical** *adjective* statistical information is expressed as numbers **statistically** *adverb*

statue *noun* a model made of stone or metal to look like a person or animal

status *noun* a person's status is their position or rank in relation to other people • *What is her status in the company?*

staunch *adjective* firm and loyal • *They are the team's most staunch supporters.*

stave *noun* a set of five lines on which music is written
stave *verb* **to stave something off** is to delay something unwelcome • *I ate a banana to stave off my hunger.*

stay *verb* 1. to stay somewhere is to continue to be there or to remain there 2. to stay somewhere or with someone is to spend time as a visitor • *We stayed in a little hotel near the sea.*
stay *noun* a period of time spent somewhere • *I enjoyed my stay in France.*

steady *adjective* **steadier, steadiest** 1. not shaking or moving; firm 2. regular or constant; not changing much • *They kept up a steady pace.* **steadily** *adverb* in a steady way; gradually
steady *verb* **steadies, steadying, steadied** to steady something is to make it steady

steak *noun* a thick slice of meat or fish

steal *verb* **stealing, stole, stolen** 1. to steal something is to take and keep it when it does not belong to you 2. to steal somewhere is to move there quietly without being noticed

stealthy *adjective* **stealthier, stealthiest** moving or doing something secretly and quietly so that you are not noticed

stealth *noun* stealth is being stealthy **stealthily** *adverb*

steam *noun* steam is the gas or vapour that comes from boiling water **steamy** *adjective* full of steam
steam *verb* 1. to steam is to give out steam 2. to steam somewhere is to move using the power of steam • *The boat steamed down the river.* 3. to steam food is to cook it in steam **to steam up** is to be covered with mist or condensation

steam engine *noun* a railway engine driven by steam

steamer *noun* a steamship

steamroller *noun* a heavy vehicle with wide metal wheels, used to flatten surfaces when making roads

steamship *noun* a ship driven by steam

steed *noun* (old or poetical use) a horse

steel *noun* steel is a strong metal made from iron and carbon **steely** *adjective* hard, cold or grey like steel
steel *verb* **to steel yourself** is to find the courage to do something difficult

steel band *noun* a band of musicians who play instruments made from oil drums

steep *adjective* rising or sloping sharply **steeply** *adverb* **steepness** *noun*

steeple *noun* a church tower with a spire

steeplechase *noun* a race across country or over hedges and fences

steer[1] *verb* to steer a vehicle is to make it go in the direction you want

steer[2] *noun* a young bull kept for its beef

steering wheel *noun* a wheel for steering a vehicle

stem *noun* 1. the main long thin part of a plant above the ground, that the leaves and flowers grow from; a stalk 2. the thin part of a wine glass
stem *verb* **stemming, stemmed** to stem from something is to start there or come from it

stench *noun* a very unpleasant smell

stencil *noun* a piece of card or metal or plastic with pieces cut out of it, used to produce a picture or design

step *noun* **1.** a movement you make with your foot when you are walking, running or dancing **2.** the sound you make when you put your foot down to walk **3.** each of the level surfaces on a stair or ladder **4.** each of a series of actions • *The first step is to make a plan.*

step *verb* stepping, stepped to step is to tread or walk to step something up is to increase it

stepchild *noun* stepchildren A stepchild is a child that someone's husband or wife has from an earlier marriage. A boy is a **stepson** and a girl is a **stepdaughter**.

stepfather *noun* a man who is married to your mother but is not your own father

stepladder *noun* a folding ladder with flat treads

stepmother *noun* a woman who is married to your father but is not your own mother

stepping stone *noun* stepping stones are a line of stones put in a river or stream to help people walk across

steps *plural noun* a stepladder

stereo *noun* stereos a system for playing recorded music using two speakers to spread the sound

sterile *adjective* **1.** clean and free from germs **2.** not able to have children or young **sterility** *noun* sterility is being sterile

sterilize *verb* **1.** to sterilize something is to make it free from germs **2.** to sterilize a person or animal is to make them unable to bear young **sterilization** *noun* sterilization is sterilizing something or someone This word can also be spelled **sterilise**.

sterling *noun* sterling is British money

stern[1] *adjective* strict and severe **sternly** *adverb* **sternness** *noun*

stern[2] *noun* the back part of a ship

stethoscope *noun* (**steth**-o-skohp) a device used by doctors for listening to a patient's heartbeat or breathing

stew *verb* to stew food is to cook it slowly in liquid

stew *noun* a dish of meat and vegetables cooked slowly in liquid

steward *noun* **1.** a man whose job is to look after the passengers on a ship or aircraft **2.** an official who looks after the arrangements at a public event

stewardess *noun* a woman whose job is to look after the passengers on a ship or aircraft

stick[1] *noun* **1.** a long thin piece of wood **2.** a walking stick **3.** a long piece of wood used to hit the ball in some ball games **4.** a long thin piece of something • *a stick of rock*

stick[2] *verb* sticking, stuck **1.** to stick something sharp into a thing is to push it in roughly or carelessly • *He stuck a pin in her finger.* **2.** to stick things is to fasten or join them **3.** something sticks when it becomes fixed or jammed • *The door keeps sticking.* to stick out is to come out from a surface or be noticeable to stick together is to stay loyal to one another to stick up for someone *(informal)* is to support them or defend them

sticker *noun* a label or sign for sticking on something

stick insect *noun* an insect with a long thin body that looks like a twig

stickleback *noun* a small fish with sharp spines on its back

sticky *adjective* stickier, stickiest able or likely to stick to things **stickiness** *noun*

stiff *adjective* **1.** not able to bend or change its shape easily **2.** difficult • *a stiff test* **3.** formal; not friendly **4.** strong or severe • *a stiff breeze* **stiffness** *noun*

stiffen *verb* **1.** to stiffen something is to make it stiff **2.** to stiffen is to become stiff

stifle *verb* **1.** to be stifled is to find it difficult or impossible to breathe **2.** to stifle something is to stop it happening • *She stifled a yawn.*

stile *noun* a set of steps or bars in a wall, for people to climb over

Sidebar letters: A B C D E F G H I J K L M N O P Q R S T U V W X Y Z

still *adjective* **1.** not moving **2.** quiet and peaceful • *The streets were still.* **3.** not fizzy
stillness *noun* stillness is being quiet and not moving

still *adverb* **1.** up to this or that time • *He was still there.* **2.** even more • *They wanted still more food.* **3.** however • *They lost. Still, they have another game.*

still *verb* to still something is to make it stop moving

stilts *plural noun* **1.** a pair of poles on which you can walk high above the ground **2.** supports for a house built over water

stimulate *verb* to stimulate someone is to make them excited or interested
stimulation *noun* being stimulated or excited

stimulus *noun* **stimuli** something that encourages a thing to develop or produces a reaction

sting *noun* **1.** the part of an insect or plant that can cause pain or a wound **2.** a painful area or wound caused by an insect or plant
sting *verb* **stinging, stung 1.** an insect or plant stings you when it wounds or hurts you with a sting **2.** part of your body stings when you feel a sharp or throbbing pain there

stingy *adjective* **stingier, stingiest** (**stin**-ji) mean; not generous

stink *noun* an unpleasant smell
stink *verb* **stinking, stank** or **stunk, stunk** to stink is to have an unpleasant smell

stir *verb* **stirring, stirred 1.** to stir something liquid or soft is to move it round and round with a spoon **2.** to stir is to move slightly or start to move after sleeping or being still • *She didn't stir all afternoon.* **to stir something up** is to excite or arouse it • *They are always stirring up trouble.*
stir *noun* **1.** an act of stirring • *Give it a stir.* **2.** a fuss or disturbance • *The news caused a stir.*

stirrup *noun* a metal loop that hangs down on each side of a horse's saddle to support the rider's foot

stitch *noun* **1.** a loop of thread made in sewing or knitting **2.** a sudden pain in your side caused by running
stitch *verb* to stitch something is to sew it with stitches

stoat *noun* an animal rather like a weasel

stock *noun* **1.** a stock of things is an amount of them kept ready to be sold or used **2.** stock is a collection of farm animals, also called livestock **3.** stock is a liquid used in cooking, made from the juices you get by stewing meat, fish or vegetables **4.** stock is also a number of a company's shares

stock *verb* **1.** a shop stocks goods when it keeps a supply of them to sell **2.** to stock a place is to provide it with a stock of things • *The explorers stocked their base camp with tinned food.*

stocking *noun* a piece of clothing that covers the whole of someone's leg and foot

stocks *plural noun* a wooden framework with holes for people's legs and arms, in which criminals were locked as a punishment in the past

stocky *adjective* **stockier, stockiest** short and solidly built

stodgy *adjective* **stodgier, stodgiest** thick and heavy; not easy to digest • *The pudding's very stodgy.*

stoke *verb* to stoke a furnace or fire is to add fuel to it

stomach *noun* **1.** the part of your body where food starts to be digested **2.** the front part of your body that contains your stomach; your abdomen
stomach *verb* to stomach something is to put up with it

stone *noun* **stones** or, for the unit of weight, **stone 1.** stone is the hard solid mineral of which rocks are made **2.** a stone is a piece of this mineral **3.** a stone is also a jewel **4.** a stone is also the hard seed in the middle of some fruits, such as a cherry, plum or peach **5.** a stone is also a unit of weight equal to 14 pounds or about 6.35 kilograms
stone *verb* to stone someone is to throw stones at them

stone-deaf *adjective* completely deaf

stony *adjective* **stonier, stoniest 1.** stony ground is full of stones **2.** unfriendly or hostile • *Our question was met by a stony silence.*

stool *noun* a small seat without a back

stoop *verb* to stoop is to bend your body forwards and downwards

stop *verb* stopping, stopped **1.** to stop something is to finish doing it or make it finish **2.** to stop is to be no longer moving or working or to come to an end **3.** to stop something is to prevent it happening or continuing • *I must go out and stop that noise.* **4.** to stop at a place is to stay there briefly

stop *noun* **1.** when something stops or ends • *She brought the car to a stop.* **2.** a place where a bus or train stops regularly

stopper *noun* something that fits into the top of a bottle or jar to close it

stopwatch *noun* a watch that you can start or stop, used for timing races

storage *noun* storage is the storing of things

store *verb* to store things is to keep them until they are needed

store *noun* **1.** a place where things are stored **2.** a supply of things kept for future use **3.** a shop, especially a large one to be in store is to be waiting to happen soon • *There is a treat in store for you.*

storey *noun* storeys one whole floor of a building

stork *noun* a large bird with long legs and a long beak

storm *noun* **1.** a period of bad weather with strong winds, rain or snow and often thunder and lightning **2.** a violent attack or outburst • *There was a storm of protest.*

storm *verb* **1.** to storm is to move or shout angrily • *He stormed out of the room.* **2.** soldiers or police storm a place when they attack it suddenly

stormy *adjective* stormier, stormiest **1.** likely to end in a storm • *The weather is stormy*

today. **2.** loud and angry • *We had a stormy meeting.*

story *noun* stories **1.** an account of real or imaginary events **2.** *(informal)* a lie • *Don't tell stories!*

stout *adjective* **1.** rather fat **2.** thick and strong • *She carried a stout stick.* **3.** brave • *The defenders put up a stout resistance.* stoutly *adverb* stoutness *noun*

stove *noun* a device that produces heat for warming a room or cooking

stow *verb* to stow something is to pack it or store it away to stow away is to hide on a ship or aircraft so that you can travel without paying

stowaway *noun* someone who stows away on a ship or aircraft

straddle *verb* **1.** to straddle something is to sit or stand with your legs either side of it **2.** to straddle something is also to be built across it • *A long bridge straddles the river.*

straggle *verb* **1.** to straggle is to walk too slowly and not keep up with the rest of a group **2.** to straggle is also to grow or move in an untidy way • *Brambles straggled across the path.* straggler *noun* someone who does not keep up with the rest of a group straggly *adjective* growing or hanging untidily

straight *adjective* **1.** going continuously in one direction; not curving or bending **2.** level • *Is this picture straight?* **3.** tidy; in proper order **4.** honest or frank • *Give me a straight answer.*

straight *adverb* **1.** in a straight line • *Go straight on, then turn left.* **2.** at once; directly • *I came straight here.*

straightaway *adverb* immediately; at once

straighten *verb* **1.** to straighten something is to make it straight **2.** to straighten is to become straight

straightforward *adjective* **1.** easy to understand or do; not complicated **2.** honest or frank

strain *verb* **1.** to strain something is to stretch it or push it or pull it hard or too hard **2.** to strain is to make a great effort to do something **3.** to strain liquid is to put it through a sieve to take out any lumps or other things in it

strain *noun* **1.** the strain on something is when it is stretched or pulled too hard • *The rope broke under the strain.* **2.** a strain is an injury caused by straining **3.** strain is the effect on someone of too much work or worry

strait *noun* a narrow stretch of water connecting two seas

strand *noun* **1.** each of the threads or wires twisted together to make a rope or cable **2.** a lock of hair

stranded *adjective* **1.** left on sand or rocks in shallow water • *We could see a stranded ship.* **2.** left in a difficult or lonely position • *They were stranded in the desert.*

strange *adjective* **1.** unusual or surprising **2.** not known or experienced before **strangely** *adverb* in a strange way • *The house was strangely quiet.* **strangeness** *noun*

stranger *noun* **1.** a person you do not know **2.** a person who is in a place they do not know

strangle *verb* to strangle someone is to kill them by pressing their throat so they can't breathe

strap *noun* a flat strip of leather or cloth or plastic for fastening things together or holding them in place
strap *verb* **strapping, strapped** to strap something is to fasten it with a strap or straps

strategy *noun* **strategies** **1.** a strategy is a plan to achieve something **2.** strategy is planning a war **strategic** *adjective* done as part of a plan to achieve or win something

stratum *noun* **strata** (**strah**-tum) a layer or level • *You can see several strata of rock in the cliffs.*

straw *noun* **1.** straw is dry cut stalks of corn **2.** a straw is a narrow tube that you can drink through

strawberry *noun* **strawberries** a small red juicy fruit, with its seeds on the outside

stray *verb* to stray is to wander or become lost
stray *adjective* **1.** wandering around lost • *a stray cat* **2.** out of place; separated from all the others • *a stray hair*
stray *noun* a stray dog or cat

streak *noun* **1.** a long thin line or mark **2.** a streak of something is a trace or sign of it • *He has a cruel streak.* **streaky** *adjective* marked with streaks

streak *verb* **1.** to streak something is to mark it with streaks **2.** to streak somewhere is to move there very quickly

stream *noun* **1.** a narrow river or brook **2.** a flow of liquid **3.** a number of things moving in the same direction, such as traffic **4.** a group in a school containing children of similar ability

stream *verb* **1.** to stream is to move in a strong or fast flow • *Traffic streamed across the junction.* **2.** to stream is also to produce a flow of liquid • *Blood was streaming from her cut hand.*

streamer *noun* a long strip of paper or ribbon

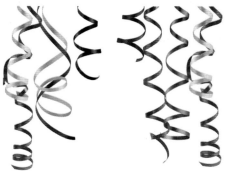

streamlined *adjective* a streamlined vehicle or object has a smooth shape that helps it to move easily through air or water

street *noun* a road with houses beside it in a city or town

strength *noun* **1.** strength is how strong a person or thing is **2.** a person's strengths are their good points or the things they are good at

strengthen *verb* **1.** to strengthen something or someone is to make them stronger **2.** to strengthen is to become stronger

strenuous *adjective* needing great physical effort **strenuously** *adverb*

stress *noun* **1.** a stress is a force or pressure that pulls or pushes or twists something **2.** stress is the effect on someone of too much work or worry **3.** stress is also the extra emphasis you give to a word or part of a word when you say it

stress *verb* **1.** to stress a word or part of a word is to pronounce it with extra emphasis **2.** to stress a point or idea is to emphasize it

stretch *verb* **1.** to stretch something is to pull it so that it becomes longer or wider **2.** something stretches when it becomes longer or wider when it is pulled **3.** you stretch when you extend your arms or arms as far as possible **4.** to stretch somewhere is to extend or continue there • *The wall stretches all the way round the park.*

stretch *noun* **1.** the action of stretching something **2.** a continuous period of time or area of land or water

stretcher *noun* a framework like a light folding bed with handles at each end, for carrying a sick or injured person

strew *verb* *strewing, strewed, strewn* or *strewed* to strew things is to scatter them over a surface

strict *adjective* **1.** demanding that people obey rules and behave well • *The teachers are all fairly strict.* **2.** complete or exact • *He's not really a hero in the strict sense of the word.* **strictly** *adverb* completely or exactly • *Taking photographs here is strictly forbidden.*

stride *verb* to stride is to walk with long steps

stride *noun* a long step you take when walking or running

strike *verb* *striking, struck* **1.** to strike something or someone is to hit them **2.** to strike people or a place is to attack them suddenly • *A hurricane struck the village.* **3.** to strike a match is to light it by rubbing it against something rough **4.** a clock strikes (for example) seven when it rings seven chimes at seven o'clock **5.** workers strike when they stop working as a protest **6.** to strike oil or gold is to find it by drilling or mining **7.** to strike someone in some way is to make them think that way • *The film struck me as rather violent.*

strike *noun* **1.** a hit **2.** when workers refuse to work, as a way of making a protest *to go on strike* is to stop working as a protest

striker *noun* **1.** a worker who is on strike **2.** in football, an attacking player who tries to score goals

striking *adjective* so impressive, interesting or attractive that you can't help noticing it

string *noun* **1.** string is thin rope or cord for tying things; a string is a piece of thin rope **2.** a string is a piece of stretched wire or nylon used in a musical instrument to make sounds **3.** a string of things is a line or series of them • *There was a string of buses along the High Street.*

string *verb* *stringing, strung* **1.** to string something is to hang it on a string **2.** to string pearls or beads is to thread them on a string **3.** to string a racket or musical instrument is to put strings on it

stringed *adjective* stringed instruments are ones that have strings

strings *plural noun* the stringed instruments in an orchestra

stringy *adjective* *stringier, stringiest* **1.** long and thin like string **2.** stringy meat contains tough fibres

strip¹ *verb* *stripping, stripped* **1.** to strip something is to take a covering off it **2.** to strip is to take all your clothes off **3.** to strip someone of something is to take it away from them
strip¹ *noun* the special outfit worn by a sports team

strip² *noun* a long narrow piece of something

stripe *noun* a long narrow band of colour
striped or **stripy** *adjective* having stripes

strive *verb* *striving, strove, striven* to strive to do something is to try hard to do it

strobe *noun* a light that flickers on and off continuously

stroke¹ *noun* **1.** a hit or movement made by swinging your arm **2.** a swimming style **3.** a line drawn by a pen or brush **4.** a sudden illness that often causes someone to be paralysed

stroke² *verb* to stroke something is to move your hand gently along it

stroll *verb* to stroll is to walk slowly
stroll *noun* a short leisurely walk

strong *adjective* **1.** having great power, energy or effect **2.** not easily broken or damaged • *The gate was held by a strong chain.* **3.** having a lot of flavour or smell • *Do you like your tea strong?*

stronghold *noun* a fortress or other place that is well defended

strongly adverb **1.** in a strong way; with strength • *They fought back strongly.* **2.** very much • *The room smelt strongly of perfume.*

structure noun **1.** a structure is something that has been built or put together **2.** a thing's structure is the way that it is built or made **structural** adjective to do with the way that something is built or made

struggle verb **1.** to struggle is to move your body about violently while you are fighting or trying to get free **2.** to struggle to do something is to make strong efforts to do it **struggle** noun **1.** fighting or trying to get free **2.** a great effort

strum verb strumming, strummed to strum a guitar is to play it by running your finger across its strings

strut verb strutting, strutted to strut is to walk proudly or stiffly **strut** noun a bar of wood or metal that strengthens a framework

stub verb stubbing, stubbed you stub your toe when you knock it against something hard **stub** noun a short piece of something left after the rest has been used up or worn down

stubble noun **1.** stubble is the short stalks of corn left in the ground after a harvest **2.** stubble is also the short stiff hairs growing on a man's chin when he has not shaved

stubborn adjective not willing to change your ideas or ways; obstinate **stubbornly** adverb **stubbornness** noun

stuck adjective unable to move or make progress • *Is anyone stuck?*

stuck-up adjective (informal) unpleasantly proud or snobbish

stud noun a small metal button or knob fixed into something

student noun someone who studies, especially at a college or university

studio noun studios **1.** a place where radio or television broadcasts are made **2.** a place where cinema or television films are made **3.** the room where an artist or photographer works

studious adjective fond of studying; studying hard **studiously** adverb

study verb studies, studying, studied **1.** to study is to spend time learning about something **2.** to study something is to look at it carefully **study** noun studies **1.** study is the process of studying **2.** a study is a room used for studying or writing

stuff noun **1.** stuff is a substance or material • *What's this stuff at the bottom of the glass?* **2.** stuff is also a group of things or a person's possessions • *Will you move your stuff off the table?* **stuff** verb **1.** to stuff something is to fill it tightly, especially with stuffing **2.** to stuff one thing inside another is to push it in carelessly

stuffing noun **1.** stuffing is material used to fill the inside of something **2.** stuffing is also a savoury mixture you put into meat or poultry before cooking it

stuffy adjective stuffier, stuffiest **1.** a stuffy room does not have enough fresh air **2.** formal and boring **stuffiness** noun

stumble verb **1.** to stumble is to lose your balance or fall over something **2.** to stumble when you are speaking is to make mistakes or hesitate to stumble across something or stumble on something is to find it by chance

stump noun **1.** the bottom of a tree trunk left in the ground when the tree has fallen or been cut down **2.** (in cricket) each of the three upright sticks of a wicket **stump** verb **1.** (in cricket) to stump the person batting is to get them out by touching the stumps with the ball when they are not standing in the correct place **2.** something stumps you when it is too difficult for you • *The last question stumped everyone.*

stun verb stunning, stunned **1.** to stun someone is to knock them unconscious **2.** something stuns you when it shocks or confuses you

stunt noun **1.** something dangerous done in a film or as part of a performance **2.** something unusual done to attract publicity or attention

stupendous adjective amazing; tremendous

stupid adjective not sensible; not clever or thoughtful **stupidity** noun stupidity is being stupid **stupidly** adverb

sturdy adjective sturdier, sturdiest strong and solid **sturdily** adverb **sturdiness** noun

stutter *verb* to stutter is to keep repeating the sounds at the beginning of words
stutter *noun* a habit of stuttering

sty¹ *noun* **sties** a pigsty

sty² or **stye** *noun* **sties** or **styes** a sore swelling on your eyelid

style *noun* **1.** a style is the way that something is done, made, said or written **2.** style is being smart and elegant

stylish *adjective* fashionable and smart
stylishly *adverb*

subcontinent *noun* a large area of land that forms part of a continent • *the Indian subcontinent*

subdue *verb* to subdue someone is to overcome them or bring them under control

subject *noun* (**sub**-jikt) **1.** the person or thing that is being talked or written about **2.** something that you can study **3.** (*in grammar*) the person or thing that is doing the action of the verb in a sentence, for example *dog* in the sentence *the dog chewed a bone* **4.** someone who must obey the laws of a particular ruler or government
subject *verb* (sub-**jekt**) to subject someone to something is to make them experience or suffer it

submarine *noun* a type of ship that can travel under water

submerge *verb* **1.** to submerge is to go under water **2.** to submerge something or someone is to put them under water

submit *verb* **submitting, submitted 1.** to submit to someone is to give in to them or agree to obey them **2.** to submit something to someone is to give it to be judged or considered **submission** *noun* submission is submitting to someone **submissive** *adjective* willing to obey

subscribe *verb* to subscribe to something is to pay money to receive it regularly or to be a member of a club or society **subscriber** *noun* someone who subscribes to something

subscription *noun* money you pay to receive something regularly or to be a member of a club or society

subsequent *adjective* coming later or after something else • *Subsequent events proved that she was right.* **subsequently** *adverb* later

subside *verb* **1.** to subside is to sink • *After a few days the flood water began to subside.* **2.** to subside is also to become quiet or normal • *The noise subsided after midnight.* **subsidence** *noun* when a building or piece of land sinks into the ground

subsidy *noun* **subsidies** money paid to keep prices low or to support an industry or activity **subsidize** *verb* to subsidize someone or something is to help pay the cost of something

substance *noun* something that you can touch or see; what something is made of

substantial *adjective* **1.** large or important **2.** strong and solid **substantially** *adverb* mostly

substitute *verb* to substitute one thing or person for another is to use the first one instead of the second **substitution** *noun* when one thing or person is used instead of another
substitute *noun* a person or thing that is used instead of another

subtle *adjective* (**sut**-el) **1.** slight and delicate • *This soup has a subtle flavour.* **2.** clever but not obvious • *Your jokes are too subtle for me.* **subtly** *adverb* in a subtle way **subtlety** *noun* subtlety is being subtle or delicate

subtract *verb* to subtract one amount from another is to take it away • *If you subtract 2 from 7, you get 5.* **subtraction** *noun* the taking of one amount from another

suburb *noun* an area of houses on the edge of a city or large town **suburban** *adjective* in or relating to a suburb

subway *noun* an underground passage for pedestrians

succeed *verb* **1.** to succeed is to do or get what you wanted or intended **2.** to succeed someone is to be the next person to do their job

success *noun* **1.** success is doing or getting what you wanted or intended **2.** a success is a person or thing that does well • *The plan was a great success.*

successful *adjective* having success; doing well **successfully** *adverb*

succession *noun* **1.** a number of people or things coming one after another • *The cooks* *brought in a succession of dishes.* **2**. the right to be the next king or queen

successor *noun* someone who has a position or does a job after someone else

such *adjective* **1**. of that kind; of the same kind • *Try not to think about such things.* **2**. so great or so much • *That was such fun!*

suck *verb* **1**. to suck liquid or air is to take it in through your mouth • *I sucked milk through a straw.* **2**. to suck something is to move it around inside your mouth so that you can taste it • *She was sucking a sweet.* **3**. to suck something is also to draw it in or absorb it • *The boat was sucked into the whirlpool.* • *He sucked in his cheeks.*
suck *noun* the action of sucking

suction *noun* suction is the process of drawing in liquid or air by creating a vacuum

sudden *adjective* happening or done quickly and unexpectedly **suddenness** *noun*

suddenly *adverb* quickly and unexpectedly

suds *plural noun* froth on soapy water

sue *verb* to sue someone is to start a claim in a lawcourt to get money from them

suede *noun* (swayd) suede is leather with one side soft and velvety

suffer *verb* **1**. to suffer is to feel pain or misery **2**. to suffer something unpleasant is to have to put up with it

suffering *noun* suffering is pain or misery

sufficient *adjective* enough
sufficiently *adverb* to a sufficient degree

suffix *noun* a word or syllable joined to the end of a word to change or add to its meaning, as in forget*ful*, lion*ess* and rust*y*

suffocate *verb* **1**. to suffocate is to die because you cannot breathe **2**. to suffocate someone is to kill them by stopping them breathing **suffocation** *noun* suffocation is when someone dies because they cannot breathe

sugar *noun* sugar is a sweet food obtained from the juices of various plants, such as sugar beet or sugar cane **sugary** *adjective* full of sugar; sweet

suggest *verb* **1**. to suggest something is to mention it as an idea or possibility **2**. to

suggest something is also to give an idea or impression of something • *Your smile suggests that you agree with me.*

suggestion *noun* something that you mention to someone as an idea or possibility

suicide *noun* suicide is killing yourself deliberately • *He committed suicide.*
suicidal *adjective* wanting to commit suicide

suit *noun* **1**. a matching set of jacket and trousers or jacket and skirt **2**. a set of clothing for a particular activity • *a diving suit* **3**. each of the four sets in a pack of playing cards: spades, hearts, diamonds and clubs

suit *verb* **1**. to suit someone or something is to be suitable or convenient for them • *What time would suit you?* **2**. a piece of clothing or hairstyle suits you when it looks good on you

suitable *adjective* satisfactory or right for a particular person, purpose or occasion **suitability** *noun* how suitable something is **suitably** *adverb*

suitcase *noun* a container with a lid and a handle, for carrying your clothes when travelling

suite *noun* (sweet) **1**. a set of rooms in a hotel **2**. a set of matching furniture

suitor *noun* a man who wants to marry a particular woman

sulk *verb* to sulk is to be silent and bad-tempered because you are not pleased

sulky *adjective* sulkier, sulkiest sulking or moody **sulkily** *adverb* **sulkiness** *noun*

sullen *adjective* silent and moody **sullenly** *adverb* **sullenness** *noun*

sulphur *noun* sulphur is a yellow chemical used in industry and medicine

sultan *noun* the ruler of certain Muslim countries

sultana *noun* a raisin without seeds

sum *noun* **1**. a total or the amount you get when you add numbers together **2**. a problem in arithmetic **3**. an amount of money

sum *verb* summing, summed to sum up is to give a summary at the end of a discussion or talk

summarize *verb* to summarize something is to give a short statement of its main points This word can also be spelled **summarise**.

summary *noun* **summaries** a short statement of the main points of something that someone has said or written

summer *noun* the warm season between spring and autumn **summery** *adjective* like summer or suitable for summer

summertime *noun* summertime is the season of summer

summit *noun* **1.** the top of a mountain or hill **2.** a meeting between the leaders of powerful countries

summon *verb* to summon someone is to order them to come or appear

sun *noun* **1.** the star round which the earth travels and from which it gets warmth and light **2.** warmth and light from the sun • *Shall we sit in the sun?*
sun *verb* **sunning, sunned** to sun yourself is to warm yourself in the sun

sunbathe *verb* to sunbathe is to sit or lie in the sun to get a suntan

sunburn *noun* sunburn is the redness of the skin someone gets if they are in the sun for too long **sunburned** or **sunburnt** *adjective* affected by sunburn

sundae *noun* (**sun**-day) a mixture of ice cream with fruit, nuts and cream

Sunday *noun* the first day of the week

sundial *noun* a device that shows the time by a shadow made by the sun

sunflower *noun* a tall flower with a large round yellow head

sunglasses *plural noun* dark glasses you wear to protect your eyes from strong sunlight

sunlight *noun* sunlight is light from the sun **sunlit** *adjective* lit by sunlight

sunny *adjective* **sunnier, sunniest** **1.** having a lot of sunshine • *It's a sunny day.* **2.** full of sunshine • *What a sunny room.*

sunrise *noun* sunrise is the time when the sun first appears; dawn

sunset *noun* sunset is the time when the sun sets

sunshine *noun* sunshine is warmth and light that come from the sun

sunstroke *noun* sunstroke is an illness caused by being in the sun for too long

suntan *noun* a brown colour of the skin caused by the sun **suntanned** *adjective* having a suntan

super *adjective* (*informal*) excellent or very good

superb *adjective* magnificent or excellent **superbly** *adverb*

superficial *adjective* **1.** on the surface • *It's only a superficial cut.* **2.** not deep or thorough • *His knowledge of French is fairly superficial.* **superficially** *adverb*

superintendent *noun* **1.** someone who is in charge **2.** a police officer above the rank of inspector

superior *adjective* **1.** higher in rank than someone else **2.** better than another person or thing **3.** showing that you think you are better than other people **superiority** *noun* being better than something else; behaviour that shows you think you are better than other people
superior *noun* someone of higher rank than another person

supermarket *noun* a large self-service shop that sells food and other goods

supernatural *adjective* not belonging to the natural world or having a natural explanation

supersonic *adjective* faster than the speed of sound

superstition *noun* a belief or action that is not based on reason or evidence

superstitious *adjective* believing in superstitions

supervise *verb* to supervise someone or something is to be in charge of them **supervision** *noun* being in charge of someone or something **supervisor** *noun* someone who supervises you

supper *noun* a meal or snack that you eat in the evening

supple *adjective* able to bend easily; flexible, not stiff **suppleness** *noun* suppleness is being supple

supplement *noun* something added as an extra **supplementary** *adjective* added as an extra

supply *verb* supplies, supplying, supplied to supply something is to give or sell it to people who need it **supplier** *noun* someone who supplies something

supply *noun* supplies **1.** a supply of something is an amount of it kept ready to be used when needed • *We keep a supply of paper in the cupboard.* **2.** supplies are food, medicines or equipment needed by an army or an expedition

support *verb* **1.** to support something is to hold it so that it does not fall down **2.** to support someone or something is to give them help or encouragement **3.** to support a sports team is to like them and want them to do well

support *noun* **1.** support is help or encouragement **2.** a support is something that holds another thing up

supporter *noun* someone who supports a sports team or political party

suppose *verb* to suppose something is to think that it is likely or true **to be supposed to do something** is to have to do it as an order or duty

suppress *verb* to suppress something is to keep it hidden or stop it happening • *He managed to suppress a smile.* **suppression** *noun* suppression is suppressing something

supreme *adjective* highest or greatest; most important **supremacy** *noun* having more power or a higher position than anyone else **supremely** *adverb* extremely

sure *adjective* **1.** confident about something; having no doubts • *Are you sure you locked the door?* **2.** certain to happen • *Don't worry, we're sure to win.* **3.** completely true or known • *One thing is sure: she is not here at the moment.* **4.** reliable • *Visiting places is a sure way of getting to know them.* **to make sure of something** is to find out that it is true or right

sure *adverb* (*informal*) certainly; of course • *Sure I'll come with you.*

surely *adverb* **1.** certainly or definitely **2.** it must be true; I feel sure • *Surely I met you last year.*

surf *noun* surf is the white foam of waves breaking on rocks or the seashore

surf *verb* **1.** to surf is to go surfing **2.** to surf the Internet is to browse through it

surface *noun* **1.** the outside of something **2.** each of the sides of something, especially the top part

surface *verb* **1.** to surface is to come up to the surface from under water • *The submarine slowly surfaced.* **2.** to surface a road or path is to give it a hard covering layer

surfboard *noun* a board used in surfing

surfing *noun* surfing is the sport of riding waves while standing on a flat board **surfer** *noun* someone who goes surfing

surge *verb* to surge is to move powerfully forwards or upwards

surge *noun* a sudden rush forward or upward

surgeon *noun* a doctor who deals with disease or injury by cutting or repairing the affected parts of the body

surgery *noun* surgeries **1.** a surgery is a building or room where a doctor or dentist sees patients **2.** surgery is the time when patients can see a doctor or dentist • *Surgery will close at 6 o'clock today.* **3.** surgery is also the work of a surgeon

surgical *adjective* to do with a surgeon or surgery **surgically** *adverb* by means of surgery

surname *noun* your last name, which you share with other members of your family

surpass *verb* to surpass someone is to do better or be better than them

surplus *noun* an amount left over after you have spent or used what you need

surprise *noun* **1.** a surprise is something that you did not expect **2.** surprise is the feeling you have when something unexpected happens
surprise *verb* **1.** to surprise someone is to be a surprise to them **2.** to surprise someone is also to catch or attack them unexpectedly

surrender *verb* **1.** to surrender to someone is to stop fighting them and admit that you have been beaten **2.** to surrender something to someone is to hand it over to them
surrender *noun* when someone surrenders

surround *verb* to surround someone or something is to be or come all round them

surroundings *plural noun* the things or conditions around a person or place

survey *noun* (**ser**-vay) **1.** a general look at a topic or activity **2.** a detailed inspection or examination of a building or area
survey *verb* (ser-**vay**) to survey something is to inspect it or make a survey of it

surveyor *noun* someone whose job is to survey buildings and land

survive *verb* **1.** to survive is to stay alive **2.** to survive an accident or disaster is to remain alive in spite of it **3.** to survive someone is to continue living after they have died **survival** *noun* survival is staying alive **survivor** *noun* someone who survives after an accident or disaster

suspect *verb* (su-**spekt**) **1.** to suspect something unwelcome is to think that it is likely or possible **2.** to suspect someone is to think that they have done something wrong or are not to be trusted
suspect *noun* (**sus**-pekt) someone who is thought to have done something wrong

suspend *verb* **1.** to suspend something that is happening is to stop it for a time **2.** to suspend someone is to take away their job or position for a time **3.** to suspend something is to hang it up

suspense *noun* suspense is an anxious or uncertain feeling you have while you are waiting for something to happen or for news about something • *Don't keep us in suspense – who won?*

suspension *noun* **1.** suspension is suspending something or someone **2.** a vehicle's suspension is the parts that make the ride more comfortable

suspension bridge *noun* a bridge supported by cables

suspicion *noun* **1.** suspicion is feeling that someone has done something wrong or cannot be trusted **2.** a suspicion is an uncertain feeling about something or someone

suspicious *adjective* **1.** making you suspect someone or something • *There are suspicious footprints along the path.* **2.** suspecting someone or something • *I'm suspicious about what happened.* **suspiciously** *adverb*

sustain *verb* to sustain something is to keep it going

swagger *verb* to walk or behave in a conceited way

swallow[1] *verb* to swallow something is to make it go down your throat

swallow[2] *noun* a small bird with a forked tail and pointed wings

swamp *verb* **1.** to swamp something is to flood it **2.** to be swamped is to be overwhelmed with a large number of things • *They have been swamped with complaints.*
swamp *noun* a marsh **swampy** *adjective* full of swamps

swan *noun* a large white water bird with a long neck and powerful wings

swap *verb* **swapping, swapped** *(informal)* to swap something is to exchange one thing for another
swap *noun* a swap is an act of swapping

swarm *noun* a large number of bees or other insects flying or moving about together

swarm *verb* **1.** bees or other insects swarm when they move in a swarm **2.** to be swarming is to be crowded with people • *The town is swarming with tourists in summer.*

swat *verb* swatting, swatted (swot) to swat a fly or other insect is to hit or crush it swatter *noun* a device for swatting flies

sway *verb* to sway is to move gently from side to side

swear *verb* swearing, swore, sworn **1.** to swear is to make a solemn promise • *She swore to tell the truth.* **2.** to swear is also to use very rude or offensive words

swear word *noun* a word that is very rude or offensive, used especially by someone who is very angry

sweat *verb* (swet) you sweat when you give off moisture through the pores of your skin when you are hot
sweat *noun* (swet) sweat is moisture that comes out of your skin when you are hot sweaty *adjective* covered with sweat

sweater *noun* (**swet**-er) a jumper or pullover

sweatshirt *noun* a thick cotton jersey

swede *noun* a large kind of turnip with purple skin and yellow flesh

sweep *verb* sweeping, swept **1.** to sweep an area is to clean it with a broom or brush • *He swept the floor.* **2.** to sweep something away is to move or change it quickly • *The flood has swept away the bridge.* **3.** to sweep somewhere is to go there swiftly or grandly • *She swept out of the room.* sweeper *noun* a machine for sweeping floors
sweep *noun* **1.** a sweeping action or movement • *Give this room a sweep.* **2.** someone who cleans out a chimney

sweet *adjective* **1.** tasting of sugar or honey **2.** very pleasant • *There was a sweet smell in the room.* **3.** charming or delightful • *What a sweet little cottage.* sweetly *adverb* in a very pleasant way • *She smiled sweetly at him.* sweetness *noun* sweetness is tasting sweet
sweet *noun* **1.** a small piece of sweet food made from sugar or chocolate **2.** a pudding; the sweet course in a meal

sweetcorn *noun* sweetcorn is the juicy yellow seeds of maize

sweeten *verb* to sweeten something is to make it sweet sweetener *noun* something used instead of sugar to make food or drink taste sweeter

sweetheart *noun* a person you love very much

swell *verb* swelling, swelled, swollen or swelled to swell is to get bigger or louder swollen *adjective* having swelled a lot • *My wrist is still very swollen where I bumped it.*
swell *noun* the rise and fall of the sea's surface

swelling *noun* a swollen place on your body

swelter *verb* to swelter is to be uncomfortably hot

swerve *verb* to swerve is to move suddenly to one side
swerve *noun* a swerving movement

swift *adjective* quick; moving quickly and easily swiftly *adverb* quickly swiftness *noun*
swift *noun* a small bird rather like a swallow

swill *verb* to swill something is to rinse or flush it
swill *noun* swill is a sloppy mixture of waste food given to pigs

swim *verb* swimming, swam, swum **1.** to swim is to move yourself through the water or to be in the water for pleasure **2.** to swim a stretch of water is to cross it by swimming • *She has swum the Channel.* **3.** to be swimming in liquid or with liquid is to be covered in it or full of it • *Their eyes were swimming with tears.* **4.** your head swims when you feel dizzy
swim *noun* a spell of swimming

swimmer *noun* someone who swims

swimming bath or **swimming pool** *noun* a specially built pool with water for people to swim in

swimming costume *noun* a piece of clothing for swimming in

swimsuit *noun* a one-piece swimming costume

swindle *verb* to swindle someone is to get money or goods from them dishonestly swindler *noun* someone who swindles people
swindle *noun* a trick to swindle someone

swine *noun* swine a pig

swing *verb* *swinging, swung* **1.** to swing is to move to and fro or in a curve **2.** to swing something is to turn it quickly or suddenly • *He swung the car round to avoid the bus.*

swing *noun* **1.** a swinging movement • *He took a swing at the ball.* **2.** a seat hung on chains or ropes so that it can move backwards and forwards **to be in full swing** is to be full of activity

swipe *verb* **1.** to swipe someone or something is to give them a hard hit **2.** to swipe a credit card is to pass it through a special reading device when you make a payment
swipe *noun* a hard hit

swirl *verb* to swirl is to move around quickly in circles; to swirl something is to make it do this • *The water swirled down the plug hole.*
swirl *noun* a swirling movement

swish *verb* to swish is to move quickly in the air with a hissing sound
swish *noun* a swishing movement

switch *noun* **1.** a device that you press or turn to start or stop an electrical device **2.** a sudden change of opinion or methods
switch *verb* **1.** to switch a device on or off is to use a switch to make it work or stop working • *Shall I switch the light on?* **2.** to switch something is to change it suddenly

switchboard *noun* a place in a large building or organization where telephone calls are connected

swivel *verb* *swivelling, swivelled* to swivel is to turn round

swoop *verb* to swoop is to dive down suddenly • *The eagle swooped down on its prey.*
swoop *noun* a sudden dive

swop *verb* *swopping, swopped* (*informal*) to swap

sword *noun* (sord) a weapon with a long pointed blade fixed in a handle

swot *verb* *swotting, swotted* (*informal*) to swot is to study hard
swot *noun* (*informal*) someone who swots

sycamore *noun* a tall tree with winged seeds

syllable *noun* a word or part of a word that has one separate sound when you say it

• *'Cat' has one syllable, 'el-e-phant' has three syllables.*

syllabus *noun* (**sil**-a-bus) a list of things to be studied by a class or for an examination

symbol *noun* **1.** a mark or sign with a special meaning **2.** a thing that stands for something • *The crescent is a symbol of Islam.*

symbolic *adjective* acting as a symbol of something **symbolically** *adverb*

symmetrical *adjective* (sim-**et**-rik-al) having two halves which are exactly the same shape and size **symmetrically** *adverb* in a symmetrical way **symmetry** *noun* symmetry is the quality of being symmetrical

sympathetic *adjective* feeling sympathy or understanding for someone **sympathetically** *adverb* in a way that shows you feel sympathy for someone

sympathize *verb* to sympathize with someone is to feel sympathy for them This word can also be spelled **sympathise**.

sympathy *noun* *sympathies* **1.** sympathy is the sharing or understanding of other people's feelings or opinions **2.** sympathy is also the feeling of being sorry for someone's unhappiness or suffering

symphony *noun* *symphonies* a long piece of music for an orchestra **symphonic** *adjective* to do with a symphony

symptom *noun* something wrong with you that is a sign that you have an illness • *Red spots are a symptom of measles.*

synagogue *noun* (**sin**-a-gog) a building where Jews meet to worship

> The word **synagogue** comes from a Greek word *synagoge* meaning 'assembly'.

synonym *noun* (**sin**-o-nim) a word that means the same or nearly the same as another word, such as *big* and *large* **synonymous** *adjective* two words are synonymous when they have the same or nearly the same, meaning

synthesizer *noun* an electronic musical instrument that can make many different sounds This word can also be spelled **synthesiser**.

synthetic *adjective* artificially made; not natural **synthetically** *adverb*

syringe *noun* a device with a tube and a long needle, used for sucking in liquid and giving injections

syrup *noun* a thick sweet liquid

system *noun* **1.** a set of parts or things or ideas that work together • *the digestive system* • *the Solar System* **2.** a well-organized way of doing something • *We have a new system for taking books out of the library.*

systematic *adjective* using a system; careful and well planned **systematically** *adverb*

Therefore has five words in it without rearranging the letters: **the, there, for, fore** and **ore.**

tab *noun* a small strip or flap that sticks out

tabby *noun* tabbies a grey or brown cat with dark streaks in its fur

table *noun* **1.** a piece of furniture with a flat top supported on legs **2.** a list of facts or numbers arranged in rows and columns

tablecloth *noun* a cloth for covering a table

tablespoon *noun* a large spoon used for serving food

tablet *noun* **1.** a pill **2.** a flat piece of stone or wood with words cut into it **3.** a small flat computer that you use by touching the screen

table tennis *noun* table tennis is a game played on a table divided in the middle by a net, over which you hit a small ball with bats

tack *noun* a short nail with a flat top **to change tack** or **try a different tack** is to find a different way of doing something

tack *verb* **1.** to tack something is to nail it with tacks **2.** to tack material is to sew it together quickly with long stitches **3.** to tack is to sail a zigzag course to get full benefit from the wind

tackle *verb* **1.** to tackle a task is to start doing it **2.** in football or hockey, to tackle a player is to try to get the ball from them or (in rugby) to bring them to the ground

tackle *noun* **1.** tackle is equipment, especially for fishing **2.** a tackle is when you tackle someone in football or rugby or hockey

tacky *adjective* tackier, tackiest sticky or not quite dry • *Be careful! The paint is still tacky on that bench.*

tact *noun* tact is skill in not offending or upsetting people

tactful *adjective* careful not to offend or upset people by saying something unkind **tactfully** *adverb*

tactics *plural noun* someone's tactics are the methods they use to achieve or win something **tactical** *adjective* done to help you achieve or win something **tactically** *adverb*

tactless *adjective* likely to offend or upset people by saying the wrong thing **tactlessly** *adverb*

tadpole *noun* a young frog or toad at a stage when it has an oval head and a long tail and lives in water

tag[1] *noun* a label tied or stuck to something

tag[1] *verb* tagging, tagged to tag something is to fix a tag or label on it **to tag along** is to go along with other people

tag[2] *noun* tag is a children's game in which one child chases the others

tail *noun* **1.** the part that sticks out from the rear end of the body of an animal or bird **2.** the back part of an aircraft **3.** the side of a coin opposite the head **tailless** *adjective* not having a tail

tail *verb* to tail someone is to follow them without them seeing you **to tail off** is to become less and less or smaller and smaller

tailback *noun* a long line of traffic stretching back from an obstruction

tailor *noun* someone whose job is to make clothes

take *verb* taking, took, taken This word has many meanings, depending on the words that go with it: **1.** to take something or someone is to get hold of them or bring them into your possession • *He took a cake from the plate.* • *Did you take the money?* • *They took many prisoners.* **2.** to take someone or something somewhere is to carry or drive them there • *Shall I take you to the station?* • *Take this parcel to the post.* **3.** to take something useful or pleasant is to make use of it • *Do you take sugar?* • *You must take a holiday this year.* • *Do take a seat.* **4.** to take someone or something is to need them for a purpose • *It will take two people to lift the table.* **5.** to take a piece of information is to make a note of it • *Take their names and addresses.* **6.** to take a class for a subject is to teach it to them • *Who takes you for English?* **7.** to take one number from another is to subtract it • *Take two from ten and you get eight.* **8.** to take an exam or test is to do it **9.** to take a joke is to accept it well. **10.** to take a photograph **to take off** is to leave the ground at the beginning of a flight **to take part in something** is to share in doing it **to take place** is to happen **to take someone in** is to fool or deceive them **to take something off** is to remove it **to take something over** is to take control of it **to take something up** is to start doing it • *I've taken up yoga.*

takeaway *noun* **1.** a place that sells cooked food for customers to take away **2.** a meal from a takeaway

takings *plural noun* money that has been received by a shop

talcum powder or **talc** *noun* talcum powder is a perfumed powder you put on your skin to dry it or make it smell pleasant

tale *noun* a story

talent *noun* a natural ability or skill to do something well • *She has a talent for singing.* **talented** *adjective* good at doing something

talk *verb* to talk is to speak or have a conversation **talker** *noun* someone who talks a lot or talks in a particular way

talk *noun* **1.** a conversation or discussion **2.** a lecture

talkative *adjective* someone is talkative when they talk a lot

tall *adjective* **1.** higher than the average • *They sat under a tall tree.* **2.** measured from the bottom to the top • *The bookcase is two metres tall.* **a tall story** is a story that is hard to believe

Talmud *noun* a collection of writings on Jewish religious law

talon *noun* a strong claw, especially on a bird of prey

tambourine *noun* a round musical instrument like a small drum with metal discs fixed around the edge so that it jingles when you shake it or hit it

tame *adjective* **1.** a tame animal is one that is gentle and not afraid of people **2.** something is tame when it is dull or uninteresting **tamely** *adverb* **tameness** *noun*

tame *verb* to tame a wild animal is to make it used to being with people **tamer** *noun* someone who tames wild animals • *a lion-tamer*

tamper *verb* **to tamper with something** is to interfere with it or change it so that it will not work properly

tan *noun* **1.** a tan is a suntan **2.** tan is a yellowish-brown colour

tan *verb* tanning, tanned **1.** to tan your skin is to make it brown with a suntan **2.** to tan the skin of a dead animal is to make it into leather

tandem *noun* a bicycle for two riders, one behind the other

tang *noun* a strong flavour or smell

tangent *noun* (**tan**-jent) a straight line that touches the outside of a curve or circle

tangerine *noun* (tan-jer-**een**) a kind of small orange

> The word **tangerine** is named after Tangier in Morocco, where the fruit originally came from.

tangle *verb* you tangle something or it tangles up, when it becomes twisted or muddled • *My fishing line has tangled.*

tangle *noun* a twisted or muddled mass of (for example) hair or wire

tank *noun* **1.** a large container for a liquid or gas **2.** a large heavy vehicle with guns, used in war

tankard *noun* a large heavy mug for drinking from

tanker *noun* **1.** a large ship for carrying oil **2.** a large lorry for carrying a liquid

tantalize *verb* to tantalize someone is to torment them by showing them something good that they cannot have This word can also be spelled **tantalise**.

tantrum *noun* an outburst of bad temper

tap[1] *noun* a device for letting out liquid or gas in a controlled flow

tap[1] *verb* tapping, tapped to tap a telephone is to fix a device to it so that you can hear someone else's conversation

tap[2] *noun* a tap is a quick light hit or the sound it makes • *I gave him a tap on the shoulder.*

tap[2] *verb* tapping, tapped to tap someone or something is to give them a tap or gentle hit

tap-dancing *noun* tap-dancing is dancing in hard shoes that make sharp tapping sounds on the floor tap-dance *noun* a dance of this kind tap-dancer *noun* someone who does tap-dancing

tape *noun* **1.** tape is soft material such as cloth or paper or plastic in a thin strip; a tape is a piece of this **2.** tape is also a narrow plastic strip coated with a magnetic substance and used for making recordings

tape *verb* **1.** to tape something is to fasten it by sticking it or tying it with tape **2.** to tape music or sound or a television programme is to record it on magnetic tape

tape measure *noun* a long strip marked in centimetres or inches for measuring things

taper *verb* something tapers when it gets narrower towards one end

tape recorder *noun* a machine for recording or playing music or sound on magnetic tape tape recording *noun* a recording made with magnetic tape

tapestry *noun* tapestries (**tap**-i-stree) a piece of strong cloth with pictures or patterns woven or embroidered on it

tar *noun* tar is a thick black sticky liquid made from coal or wood and used in making roads

tar *verb* tarring, tarred to tar something is to cover it with tar

tarantula *noun* (ta-**ran**-tew-la) a large hairy poisonous spider found in warm countries

target *noun* something that you aim at and try to hit or reach

tarmac *noun* tarmac is a mixture of tar and small stones, used for making the surface of roads

tarnish *verb* **1.** metal tarnishes when it becomes stained and less shiny **2.** to tarnish something is to spoil it • *The scandal tarnished his reputation.*

tarpaulin *noun* a large sheet of waterproof canvas

tart[1] *noun* a pie containing fruit or jam

tart[2] *adjective* sour-tasting • *The apples are tart.*

tartan *noun* a Scottish woollen cloth with a pattern of squares and stripes in different colours

task *noun* a piece of work that needs to be done

tassel *noun* a bundle of threads tied together at the top and used to decorate something

taste *verb* **1.** to taste food or drink is to eat or drink a small amount to see what it is like **2.** food or drink tastes a certain way when it has a particular flavour • *The milk tastes sour.*

taste *noun* **1.** the taste of something is the flavour it has when you taste it • *The milk has a strange taste.* **2.** taste is the ability to taste things **3.** your tastes are the things you like or prefer • *What are your tastes in music?* **4.** you show taste when you are able to choose things that are of good quality or go together well • *The way she dresses shows good taste.*

tasteful *adjective* showing good taste
tastefully *adverb*

tasteless *adjective* showing poor taste
tastelessly *adverb*

tasty *adjective* tastier, tastiest tasty food has a strong pleasant taste

tattered *adjective* tattered clothing is badly torn and ragged

tatters *plural noun* in tatters badly torn

tattoo[1] *noun* a picture or pattern made on someone's skin with a needle and dye
tattoo[1] *verb* tattooing, tattooed someone is tattooed when they have a tattoo on their skin

tattoo[2] *noun* an outdoor entertainment including military music and marching

tatty *adjective* tattier, tattiest shabby and worn

taunt *verb* to taunt someone is to jeer at them or insult them
taunt *noun* an insulting or mocking remark

taut *adjective* stretched tightly **tautly** *adverb*
tautness *noun*

tavern *noun* (old use) an inn or pub

tax *noun* an amount of money that people and businesses have to pay to the government to pay for things like hospitals and schools
tax *verb* **1.** to tax someone is to charge them a tax **2.** to tax goods or someone's income is to put a tax on them **taxation** *noun* money that has to be paid as taxes

taxi *noun* a car with a driver which you can hire for journeys
taxi *verb* an aircraft taxis when it moves slowly along the ground before taking off or after landing

tea *noun* **1.** tea is a drink made by pouring hot water on the dried leaves of a shrub grown in Asia **2.** tea is also the dried leaves of this shrub **3.** tea is also a meal eaten in the late afternoon or early evening

The word **tea** comes from a Chinese word *te.*

teabag *noun* a small bag of tea for making tea in a cup

teach *verb* teaching, taught **1.** to teach someone is to show them how to do something or give them knowledge about something **2.** to teach a subject is to give lessons in it • *She taught us history last year.*

teacher *noun* someone who teaches people at a school or college

teak *noun* teak is a hard strong wood from Asia

team *noun* **1.** a set of players who form one side in a game or sport **2.** a group of people who work together

teapot *noun* a pot with a handle and spout, for making and pouring out tea

tear¹ *verb* tearing, tore, torn (tair) **1.** to tear something is to make a split in it or to pull it apart **2.** to tear something is also to pull or remove it with force • *He tore the picture off the wall.* **3.** to tear is to become torn • *Paper tears easily.* **4.** to tear somewhere is to move very quickly there • *He tore down the street.*
tear¹ *noun* (tair) a hole or split made by tearing something

tear² *noun* (teer) a drop of water that comes from your eye when you cry

tearful *adjective* in tears; crying easily tearfully *adverb*

tease *verb* to tease someone is to make fun of them and say things to make them annoyed

teaspoon *noun* a small spoon for stirring drinks

teat *noun* **1.** a nipple through which a baby drinks milk **2.** the cap of a baby's feeding bottle

technical *adjective* to do with technology or the way things work technically *adverb*

technician *noun* someone whose job is to look after scientific equipment and do practical work in a laboratory

technique *noun* (tek-**neek**) a particular method of doing something skilfully

technology *noun* technologies technology is using science and machines to help you make things and do things technological *adjective* to do with technology

teddy bear *noun* teddy bears a soft furry toy bear

tedious *adjective* (**tee**-di-us) annoyingly slow or long; boring tediously *adverb* tediousness *noun*

tedium *noun* tedium is a dull or boring time or experience • *He hated the tedium of visiting his grandparents.*

teem *verb* **1.** to teem with something is to be full of it • *The river was teeming with fish.* **2.** to teem or teem down, is to rain very hard

teenage or **teenaged** *adjective* in your teens; to do with teenagers

teenager *noun* a person in their teens

teens *plural noun* the time of your life between the ages of 13 and 19

teetotal *adjective* never drinking alcoholic drink teetotaller *noun* someone who is teetotal

telecommunications *plural noun* telecommunications is sending news and information over long distances by telephone, television, radio or on the Internet

telegram *noun* a message sent by telegraph

telegraph *noun* telegraph is a way of sending messages by using electric current along wires or by radio

telepathy *noun* (til-**ep**-a-thee) telepathy is understanding another person's thoughts without them speaking, writing or making gestures telepathic *adjective* able to know what someone else is thinking

telephone *noun* a device that enables you to speak to someone who is some distance away
telephone *verb* to telephone someone is to speak to them by telephone

telescope *noun* a tube with lenses at each end, through which you can see distant objects more clearly

telescopic *adjective* to do with telescopes

teletext *noun* teletext is a system for displaying news and information on a television screen

televise *verb* to televise an event is to film it and put it on television

television *noun* **1.** television is a way of sending and receiving information by radio waves (wireless), through cables, or through the Internet **2.** A television or television receives and uses this information as an electrical signal. It changes the signal into pictures on a screen and sound in loudspeakers.

tell *verb* telling, told **1.** to tell something to someone is to give them information by speaking to them **2.** to tell someone to do something is to give them instructions to do it **3.** to tell is to reveal a secret • *Promise you won't tell.* **4.** to tell something is to recognize it • *Can you tell the difference between butter and margarine?* **to tell someone off** is to tell them severely that they have done wrong

temper *noun* **1.** a person's mood • *He is in a good temper.* **2.** an angry mood • *She was in a temper.* **to lose your temper** is to become very angry

temperature *noun* **1.** the temperature of something is how hot or cold it is **2.** an unusually high body temperature • *She's feverish and has a temperature.*

tempest *noun* (old use) a violent storm

temple[1] *noun* a building where a god is worshipped

temple[2] *noun* the part of your head between your forehead and your ear

tempo *noun* tempos the tempo of a piece of music is its speed

temporary *adjective* only lasting or used for a short time temporarily *adverb* for a short time only

tempt *verb* to tempt someone is to try to make them do something, especially something they ought not to do temptation *noun* when someone is being tempted tempting *adjective* hard to resist

ten *noun* the number 10

tenant *noun* someone who rents a house or building or a piece of land from a landlord tenancy *noun* the time when someone is a tenant

tend[1] *verb* something tends to happen when it is likely to happen or is what usually happens

tend[2] *verb* to tend something or someone is to look after them • *She tends her garden with care.*

tendency *noun* tendencies the way a person or thing is likely to behave • *She has a tendency to be lazy.*

tender *adjective* **1.** not tough or hard; easy to chew **2.** delicate or sensitive • *These are more tender plants.* **3.** gentle or loving • *She gave a tender smile.* tenderly *adverb* gently or lovingly tenderness *noun*

tendon *noun* a piece of strong tissue in the body that joins a muscle to a bone

tennis *noun* tennis is a game played with rackets and a ball on a court with a net across the middle

tenor *noun* a male singer with a high voice

tenpin bowling *noun* tenpin bowling is a game in which you knock down sets of ten skittles with a ball

tense[1] *adjective* **1.** tightly stretched • *tense muscles* **2.** to be tense is to be nervous and not able to relax **3.** a tense situation makes people feel nervous and unable to relax tensely *adverb*

tense[2] *noun* The tense of a verb is the form that shows when something happens. The past tense of come is *came* and the present tense is *come*.

tension *noun* **1.** tension is a feeling of anxiety or nervousness about something about to happen **2.** tension is also how tightly stretched a rope or wire is

tent *noun* a shelter made of canvas or cloth supported by upright poles

tentacle *noun* a long bending part of the body of an octopus and some other animals

tenth *adjective, noun* the next after the ninth

tepid *adjective* tepid liquid is only slightly warm; lukewarm

term *noun* **1.** a part of the year when a school or college does its teaching **2.** a definite period • *He was sentenced to a term of imprisonment.* **3.** a word or expression with a special meaning • *I don't understand these technical terms.* **4.** the terms of an agreement are the conditions offered or agreed • *They won't agree to our terms.* **to be on good** or **bad terms** is to be friendly or unfriendly with someone

terminal *noun* **1.** a building where passengers arrive or depart • *an airport terminal* **2.** a place where a wire is connected to a battery or electric circuit **3.** a computer keyboard and screen used for sending data to or from the main computer

terminal *adjective* a terminal illness is one that cannot be cured and that the person will die from

terminate *verb* you terminate something or it terminates, when it ends or stops • *This train terminates here.* **termination** *noun* ending or stopping something

terminus *noun* **termini** the station at the end of a railway or bus route

termite *noun* a small insect that eats wood and lives in large groups

terrace *noun* **1.** a row of houses joined together **2.** a level area on a slope or hillside **3.** a paved area beside a house

terrapin *noun* a kind of small turtle that lives in water

terrible *adjective* awful; very bad

terribly *adverb* awfully; badly • *I'm terribly sorry I kept you waiting.* • *He was missing his parents terribly.*

terrific *adjective* (*informal*) **1.** very good or excellent • *That's a terrific idea.* **2.** very great • *They went at a terrific speed.* **terrifically** *adverb* very; greatly

terrify *verb* **terrifies, terrifying, terrified** to terrify a person or animal is to make them very frightened

territory *noun* **territories** an area of land, especially an area that belongs to a country or person **territorial** *adjective* to do with territory

terror *noun* terror is great fear

terrorism *noun* terrorism is the use of violence, such as setting off bombs, for political purposes **terrorist** *noun* someone who takes part in terrorism

terrorize *verb* to terrorize someone is to terrify them with threats This word can also be spelled **terrorise**.

test *noun* **1.** a short set of questions to check someone's knowledge, especially in school **2.** a medical examination • *Amy went to have*

an eye test.. **3.** a trial or experiment to find out what something is like • *Tests have shown there is a high level of pollution in the water.* **4.** (*informal*) a test match

test *verb* **1.** to test someone is to give them a test **2.** to test something is to use it so that you can find out whether it works properly or find out more about it

testament *noun* **1.** a written statement **2.** each of the two main parts of the Bible, the **Old Testament** and the **New Testament**

testify *verb* **testifies, testifying, testified** to testify is to give evidence in a lawcourt

testimony *noun* **testimonies** evidence; what someone testifies

test match *noun* a cricket or rugby match between teams from different countries

test tube *noun* a tube of thin glass closed at one end, used for experiments in chemistry

tether *verb* to tether an animal is to tie it up so that it cannot move far

tether *noun* a rope for tying an animal to be at the end of your tether is to be unable to stand something any more

text *noun* **1.** the words of something printed or written **2.** a text message

text *verb* you text someone when you send them a text message

textbook *noun* a book that teaches you about a subject

textiles *plural noun* kinds of cloth; fabrics

text message *noun* a written message sent using a mobile phone

texture *noun* the way that the surface of something feels when you touch it • *Silk has a smooth texture.*

than *conjunction* compared with another person or thing • *Claire is taller than David.*

thank *verb* to thank someone is to tell them you are grateful for something they have given you or done for you **thank you** words that you say when you thank someone

thankful *adjective* feeling glad that someone has done something for you **thankfully** *adverb* used to show that you are pleased and relieved about something • *Thankfully no one was hurt.*

thanks *plural noun* **1.** words that thank someone **2.** *(informal)* a short way of saying 'Thank you' thanks to someone or something because of them • *Thanks to you, we succeeded.*

that *determiner* the one there • *Whose is that book?*

that *conjunction* used to introduce a fact or statement or result • *I hope that you are well.* • *Do you know that it is one o'clock?* • *The puzzle was so hard that no one could solve it.*

that *pronoun* **1.** the one there • *Whose book is that?* **2.** which or who • *This is the book that I wanted.* • *Are you the person that I saw the other day?*

thatch *noun* thatch is straw or reeds used to make a roof
thatch *verb* to thatch a roof is to make it with straw or reeds

thaw *verb* something thaws when it melts and is no longer frozen

the *determiner* (called the definite article) a particular one; that or those

theatre *noun* **1.** a building where people go to see plays or shows **2.** a special room where you go to have an operation

theatrical *adjective* to do with plays or acting

theft *noun* theft is stealing

their *determiner* belonging to them • *This is their house.*

theirs *pronoun* belonging to them • *This house is theirs.*

them *pronoun* a word used for *they* when it is the object of a verb or when it comes after a preposition • *I like them.* • *I gave it to them.*

theme *noun* **1.** a main idea or subject of something such as a book or speech **2.** a short tune or melody

theme park *noun* an amusement park with rides and activities connected with a special subject or theme

themselves *plural noun* them and nobody else, used to refer back to the subject of a verb • *They have hurt themselves.* by themselves on their own; alone

then *adverb* **1.** at that time • *I lived in London then.* **2.** after that; next • *Then they came*

home. **3.** in that case; therefore • *If you are going, then I can stay.*

theology *noun* theology is the study of God and religion theological *adjective* to do with theology

theoretical *adjective* based on theory and not on practice or experience theoretically *adverb* in theory

theory *noun* theories **1.** a theory is an idea or set of ideas suggested to explain something **2.** the theory of a subject is the ideas and principles behind it, rather than the practice in theory according to what should happen

therapy *noun* therapies a way of treating an illness of the mind or the body, usually without using surgery or artificial medicines therapist *noun* an expert in therapy • *a speech therapist*

there *adverb* **1.** in or to that place **2.** a word that you say to call attention to someone or something or to refer to them • *There's a spider in the bath.*

therefore *adverb* for that reason; and so

thermal *adjective* to do with heat; using heat

thermometer *noun* a device for measuring temperature

thermostat *noun* a device that automatically controls the temperature of a room or piece of equipment

thesaurus *noun* thesauruses or thesauri a kind of dictionary in which words with similar meanings are listed in groups together, instead of one long list in alphabetical order

these *determiner, pronoun* the people or things here

they *pronoun* **1.** the people or things that someone is talking about **2.** people in general • *They say it's a very good film.*

thick *adjective* **1.** measuring a lot from one side to the other • *a thick slice of cake* **2.** measured from one side to the other • *The wall is ten centimetres thick.* **3.** dense or closely packed together • *thick fog* **4.** not very runny • *I love thick gravy.* thickly *adverb* in thick pieces or in a deep layer thickness *noun* how thick something is

thicken *verb* you thicken something or it thickens, when it becomes thicker

thicket *noun* a group of trees and shrubs growing close together

thief *noun* thieves someone who steals things

thigh *noun* the part of your leg above your knee

thimble *noun* a metal or plastic cover that you put on the end of your finger to protect it when you are sewing

thin *adjective* thinner, thinnest 1. measuring a small amount from one side to the other 2. not fat 3. not dense or closely packed together 4. runny or watery thinly *adverb* in thin pieces or in a thin layer thinness *noun* thinness is being thin

thin *verb* thins, thinning, thinned 1. to thin something is to make it less thick 2. to thin or thin out, is to become less crowded • *The crowds had thinned by late afternoon.*

thing *noun* an object; anything that can be touched or seen or thought about

think *verb* thinking, thought 1. to think is to use your mind 2. to think something is to have it as an idea or opinion • *I think that's a good idea.* 3. to be thinking of doing something is to be planning to do it thinker *noun* someone who thinks about things

third *adjective, noun* the next after the second thirdly *adverb* as the third thing

third *noun* each of three equal parts into which something can be divided

Third World *noun* the poor or developing countries of Asia, Africa and South and Central America

thirst *noun* thirst is the feeling that you need to drink

thirsty *adjective* thirstier, thirstiest feeling that you need to drink

thirteen *noun* the number 13 thirteenth *adjective, noun* 13th

thirty *noun* thirties the number 30 thirtieth *adjective, noun* 30th

this *determiner, pronoun* the one here • *Take this pen.* • *This is the one.*

thistle *noun* a wild plant with prickly leaves and purple or white or yellow flowers

thorn *noun* a sharp point growing on the stem of roses and other plants

thorny *adjective* thornier, thorniest full of thorns

thorough *adjective* done properly and carefully • *This is a thorough piece of work.* thoroughly *adverb* properly and carefully; completely thoroughness *noun* doing things properly and carefully

those *determiner, pronoun* the ones there • *Where are those cards?* • *Those are the ones I want.*

though *conjunction* in spite of the fact that; even if • *It is not true, though he says it is.* **though** *adverb* however; all the same • *She's right, though.*

thought *noun* 1. a thought is something that you think; an idea or opinion 2. thought is thinking • *I'll give the matter some thought.*

thoughtful *adjective* 1. looking or sounding as if you are thinking a lot about something 2. thinking of other people and what they would like thoughtfully *adverb* thoughtfulness *noun*

thoughtless *adjective* not thinking of other people and what they would like; inconsiderate thoughtlessly *adverb* thoughtlessness *noun*

thousand *noun* the number 1,000 thousandth *adjective, noun* 1,000th

thrash *verb* 1. to thrash someone is to keep hitting them hard with a stick or whip 2. to thrash a person or team is to defeat them completely in a game or sport 3. to thrash or thrash about, is to fling your arms and legs about wildly

thread *noun* **1.** a long piece of cotton used for sewing **2.** a long thin piece of something **3.** the spiral ridge round a screw or bolt
thread *verb* **1.** to thread a needle is to put a thread through its eye **2.** to thread a long and thin material is to put it through or round something **3.** to put beads on a thread

threadbare *adjective* clothes are threadbare when they are worn thin with threads showing

threat *noun* **1.** a warning that you will punish or harm someone if they do not do what you want **2.** a danger

threaten *verb* **1.** to threaten someone is to warn them that you will punish or harm them if they do not do what you want **2.** to threaten is to be a danger to someone or something • *The quarrel threatened to turn violent.*

three *noun* the number 3

three-dimensional *adjective* having three dimensions: length, width and height or depth

thresh *verb* to thresh corn is to beat it so that you separate the grain from the husks

threshold *noun* **1.** the entrance to a room or building or the area in front of a door **2.** the beginning of something important • *We are on the threshold of a great discovery.*

thrift *noun* thrift is being careful with money and not wasting it

thrifty *adjective* thriftier, thriftiest careful with money and not wasting it

thrill *noun* **1.** a sudden feeling of excitement **2.** something that gives you this feeling
thrill *verb* something thrills you when it gives you a sudden feeling of excitement
thrilling *adjective* very exciting

thriller *noun* an exciting story or film, usually about crime

thrive *verb* thriving, thrived or throve, thrived or thriven to thrive is to grow strongly or do well

throat *noun* **1.** the front of your neck **2.** the tube in your neck that takes food and air into your body

throb *verb* throbbing, throbbed to throb is to beat or vibrate with a strong rhythm
throb *noun* a throbbing sound or feeling

throne *noun* **1.** a special chair for a king or queen **2.** the position of being king or queen • *The Prince of Wales is heir to the throne.*

throng *noun* a large crowd of people

throttle *verb* to throttle someone is to strangle them
throttle *noun* a device to control the flow of fuel to an engine

through *adverb* and *preposition* **1.** from one end or side to the other • *I can't get through.* • *Climb through the window.* **2.** because of; by means of • *We'll do it through hard work.*

throughout *preposition, adverb* all the way through

throw *verb* throwing, threw, thrown **1.** to throw something or someone is to send them through the air **2.** to throw something somewhere is to put it there carelessly • *He threw his coat on the chair.* **3.** to throw a part of your body is to move it quickly • *She threw her head back and laughed.* **4.** to throw someone into a certain state is to put them in that state • *We were thrown into confusion.* to throw something away is to get rid of it
throw *noun* a throwing action or movement

thrush *noun* a bird that has a white front with brown spots

thrust *verb* to thrust something somewhere is to push it there with a lot of force • *He thrust his hands into his pockets.*

thud *noun* the dull sound of something heavy falling
thud *verb* thudding, thudded to fall with a thud

thumb *noun* the short thick finger at the side of each hand

thump *verb* 1. to thump someone or something is to hit them heavily 2. to thump is to make a dull heavy sound
thump *noun* an act or sound of thumping

thunder *noun* thunder is the loud rumbling noise that you hear with lightning during a storm
thunder *verb* to thunder is to make the noise of thunder

thunderous *adjective* extremely loud • *The curtain came down to thunderous applause.*

thunderstorm *noun* a storm with thunder and lightning

Thursday *noun* the fifth day of the week

thus *adverb* 1. in this way • *We did it thus.* 2. therefore • *Thus, we must try again.*

tick *noun* 1. a small mark (✓) made next to something when checking it as a sign that it is correct or has been done 2. each of the regular clicking sounds that a clock or watch makes
tick *verb* 1. to tick something is to mark it with a tick • *She ticked the correct answers.* 2. a clock or watch ticks when it makes regular clicking sounds to tick someone off (informal) is to tell them off

ticket *noun* a piece of paper or card that allows you to do something such as see a show or travel on a bus or train

tickle *verb* 1. to tickle someone is to keep touching their skin lightly so that they get a tingling feeling that can make them laugh and wriggle 2. to tickle is to have a tickling or itching feeling 3. to tickle someone is also to please or amuse them

ticklish *adjective* someone is ticklish when they are likely to laugh or wriggle if they are tickled

tidal *adjective* to do with tides or affected by tides

tidal wave *noun* a huge sea wave moving with the tide

tiddler *noun* (informal) a very small fish

tide *noun* the regular rising or falling of the sea, which usually happens twice a day

tide *verb* to tide someone over is to give them what they need, especially money, for the time being

tidy *adjective* tidier, tidiest 1. a tidy place is neat and orderly, with things in the right place 2. a tidy person keeps things neat and in the right place 3. (informal) fairly large • *That's a tidy sum of money.* tidily *adverb* tidiness *noun*

tidy *verb* tidies, tidying, tidied to tidy a place is to make it neat by putting things away in the right place

tie *verb* ties, tying, tied 1. to tie something is to fasten it with string, rope or ribbon 2. to tie a knot or bow is to make one in a strip of material 3. two players or teams tie when they finish a game or competition with an equal score or position

tie *noun* 1. a thin strip of material tied round the collar of a shirt with a knot at the front 2. the result of a game or competition in which two players or teams have the same position or score 3. one of the matches in a competition

tiger *noun* a large wild animal of the cat family, with yellow and black stripes

tight *adjective* **1.** fitting very closely or firmly fastened • *These shoes are a bit tight.* **2.** fully stretched • *Is this string tight enough?* **tightly** *adverb* **tightness** *noun*

tight *adverb* **1.** firmly • *Hold on tight.* **2.** fully stretched • *Now pull the string tight.*

tighten *verb* **1.** to tighten something is to make it tighter • *These screws need to be tightened.* **2.** to tighten is to become tighter

tightrope *noun* a tightly stretched rope above the ground, for acrobats to perform on

tights *plural noun* a piece of clothing that fits tightly over the lower parts of the body including the legs and feet

tigress *noun* a female tiger

tile *noun* a thin piece of baked clay or other hard material used in rows to cover roofs, walls or floors **tiled** *adjective* covered with tiles

till[1] *preposition, conjunction* until

till[2] *noun* a drawer or box for money in a shop; a cash register

till[3] *verb* to till soil or land is to plough it ready to grow crops

tiller *noun* a handle used to turn a boat's rudder

tilt *verb* **1.** to tilt is to slope or lean **2.** to tilt something is to tip it or make it slope

tilt *noun* a sloping position

timber *noun* **1.** timber is wood used for building or making things **2.** a timber is a beam of wood

time *noun* **1.** time is a measure of the passing of years, months, days and other units **2.** you ask the time when you want to know what point in the day it is, as shown on a watch or clock • *What's the time?* **3.** a time is a particular moment or period of things existing or happening • *There was a time when I would have agreed with you.* • *Come back another time.* • *There were fields here in past times.* **4.** a time is also an occasion • *This is the first time I've been here.* **5.** a time is also a period for which something lasts • *She spent a long time in the library.* **6.** time is the rhythm and speed of a piece of music **at times** or **from time to time** sometimes or occasionally **in time** or **on time** soon or early enough; not late

time *verb* **1.** to time something is to measure how long it takes **2.** to time an event or activity is to arrange the time when it will happen • *You timed your arrival perfectly.*

timer *noun* a device for timing things

times *plural noun* multiplied by • *5 times 3 is 15 (5 x 3 = 15).*

timetable *noun* a list of the times when things happen, such as buses and trains leaving and arriving and when school lessons take place

timid *adjective* nervous and easily frightened **timidly** *adverb* **timidity** *noun* timidity is being timid

timing *noun* timing is choosing the right time to do something • *Arriving at lunchtime was good timing.*

tin *noun* **1.** tin is a soft white metal **2.** a tin is a metal container for preserving food **tinned** *adjective* tinned food is preserved in a tin

tingle *verb* part of your body tingles when you have a slight stinging or tickling feeling there

tingle *noun* a tingling feeling

tinker *verb* to tinker with something is to try to mend or improve it, often without really knowing how to

tinker *noun* (old use) someone who travelled around mending pots and pans

tinkle *verb* something tinkles when it makes a gentle ringing sound

tinkle *noun* a tinkling sound

tinny *adjective* tinnier, tinniest a tinny sound is unpleasant and high-pitched

tinsel *noun* tinsel is strips of glittering material used for decoration

tint *noun* a shade of a colour

tint *verb* to tint something is to colour it slightly

tiny *adjective* tinier, tiniest very small

tip¹ *noun* the part at the very end of something

tip² *noun* 1. a small amount of money given to thank someone who has helped you 2. a useful piece of advice or information

tip² *verb* tipping, tipped to tip someone is to give them a small amount of money to thank them for helping you

tip³ *verb* tipping, tipped to tip something is to turn it upside down or tilt it • *She tipped the water out of the bucket.* • *He tipped his head back and laughed.*

tip³ *noun* 1. a place where rubbish is left 2. a very untidy place

tiptoe *verb* to tiptoe is to walk on your toes very quietly or carefully

tiptoe *noun* on tiptoe walking or standing on your toes

tire *verb* 1. to tire someone is to make them tired 2. to tire is to become tired

tired *adjective* feeling that you need to sleep or rest to be tired of something is to have had enough of it

tiresome *adjective* annoying or tedious

tissue *noun* 1. tissue or tissue paper, is thin soft paper 2. a tissue is a piece of this, used for blowing your nose 3. tissue is also the substance of which an animal or plant is made

title *noun* 1. the name of something such as a book, film, painting or piece of music 2. a word that shows a person's position or profession, such as • *Sir, Lady, Dr, Mrs.*

titter *verb* to titter is to giggle or laugh in a silly way

to *preposition* 1. towards • *They set off to London.* 2. as far as; so as to reach • *I am soaked to the skin.* 3. compared with; rather than • *She prefers cats to dogs.* 4. used with a verb to make an infinitive • *I want to see him.*

to *adverb* to the usual or closed position • *Push the door to.* to and fro backwards and forwards

toad *noun* an animal like a large frog, that lives on land

toadstool *noun* a fungus that looks like a mushroom and is often poisonous

toast *verb* 1. to toast food is to cook it by heating it under a grill or in front of a fire 2. to toast someone or something is to have a drink in their honour

toast *noun* 1. toast is toasted bread 2. a toast is when people are asked to toast someone or something with a drink

toaster *noun* an electrical device that makes toast

tobacco *noun* tobacco is the dried leaves of certain plants used for smoking in cigarettes, cigars or pipes

toboggan *noun* a small sledge for sliding downhill

today *noun* this day • *Today is Monday.*
today *adverb* 1. on this day • *I saw him today.* 2. nowadays • *Today we don't have slaves.*

toddler *noun* a young child who is just learning to walk

toe *noun* each of the five separate parts at the end of each foot

toffee *noun* 1. toffee is a sticky sweet made from butter and sugar 2. a toffee is a piece of this

together *adverb* with another person or thing; with each other • *They went to school together.* • *Now glue the two parts together.*

toil *verb* to toil is to work hard

toilet *noun* **1.** a large bowl with a seat that you use for getting rid of waste from your body **2.** a room with a toilet in it

token *noun* **1** a card or voucher that you can exchange for goods in a shop **2.** a piece of metal or plastic that you use instead of money to pay for something **3.** a sign or signal of something • *Please accept these flowers as a small token of my gratitude.*

tolerable *adjective* able to be tolerated; bearable

tolerant *adjective* accepting or putting up with other people's behaviour and opinions when you don't agree with them
tolerance *noun* being willing to accept other people's behaviour and opinions
tolerantly *adverb*

tolerate *verb* to tolerate something is to allow it or put up with it although you do not approve of it

toll[1] *noun* **1.** a payment charged for using a bridge or road **2.** an amount of loss or damage • *The death toll in the earthquake is rising.*

toll[2] *verb* to toll a bell is to ring it slowly

tom or **tomcat** *noun* a male cat

tomahawk *noun* an axe used by Native Americans

tomato *noun* **tomatoes** a soft round red fruit with seeds inside it, eaten as a vegetable

tomb *noun* (toom) a place where a dead body is buried; a grave

tomboy *noun* a girl who enjoys rough noisy games and activities

tombstone *noun* a memorial stone put on a grave

tomorrow *noun* and *adverb* the day after today

ton *noun* **1.** a unit of weight equal to 2,240 pounds or about 1,016 kilograms **2.** *(informal)* a large amount • *There's tons of room.*

tone *noun* **1.** the nature or quality of a sound • *I don't like the tone of your voice.* **2.** a sound in music **3.** a shade of a colour
tone *verb* to tone something down is to make it softer or quieter

tongs *plural noun* a tool with two arms joined at one end, used to pick things up or hold them

tongue *noun* **1.** the long soft part that moves about inside your mouth **2.** a language **3.** the flap of material under the laces of a shoe

tongue-tied *adjective* to be tongue-tied is to feel too shy or embarrassed to speak

tongue-twister *noun* a sentence or phrase that is very difficult to say

tonic *noun* something that makes a person healthier or stronger

tonight *adverb, noun* this evening or night

tonne *noun* a unit of weight equal to 1,000 kilograms

tonsillitis *noun* tonsillitis is a disease that makes your tonsils extremely sore

tonsils *plural noun* your tonsils are the two small masses of soft flesh inside your throat

too *adverb* **1.** also • *I'd like to come too.* **2.** more than is wanted or allowed or wise • *You're driving too fast.*

tool *noun* a device that you use to help you do a particular job, such as a hammer or saw

tooth *noun* **teeth 1.** each of the hard white bony parts that grow in your gums, used for biting and chewing **2.** each in a row of sharp points on a saw or comb

toothache *noun* toothache is a pain in one of your teeth

toothbrush *noun* a small brush on a long handle, for brushing your teeth

toothpaste *noun* toothpaste is a creamy paste for cleaning your teeth

top[1] *noun* **1.** the highest part of something **2.** the upper surface of something **3.** the covering or stopper of a jar or bottle **4.** a piece of clothing you wear on the upper part of your body

top[1] *adjective* highest, fastest or most successful • *We live on the top floor.* • *They were travelling at top speed.* • *one of our top tennis players*

top[1] *verb* topping, topped **1.** to top something is to put a top on it • *The cake was topped with icing.* **2.** to top something is also to be at the top of it • *She tops the class in maths.* **to top something up** is to fill it to the top when it is already partly full

top[2] *noun* a toy that can be made to spin on its point

top hat *noun* a man's tall stiff black or grey hat worn with formal clothes

topic *noun* a subject that you are writing or talking or learning about

topical *adjective* to do with things that are happening or in the news now

topping *noun* food that is put on the top of a cake, pudding or pizza

topple *verb* **1.** to topple or topple over, is to fall over **2.** to topple something is to make it fall over **3.** to topple someone in power is to overthrow them

top secret *adjective* extremely secret

topsy-turvy *adverb, adjective* in a muddle

torch *noun* **1.** a small electric lamp that you hold in your hand **2.** a stick with burning material on the end, used as a light

torment *verb* **1.** to torment someone is to make them suffer or feel pain **2.** to torment someone is also to keep annoying them deliberately **tormentor** *noun* the person who is tormenting someone

torment *noun* torment is great suffering

tornado *noun* tornadoes (tor-**nay**-doh) a violent storm or whirlwind

torpedo *noun* torpedoes a long tube-shaped missile sent under water to destroy ships and submarines

torpedo *verb* torpedoes, torpedoing, torpedoed to torpedo a ship is to attack it with a torpedo

torrent *noun* a very strong stream or fall of water **torrential** *adjective* torrential rain pours down very heavily

torso *noun* torsos the main part of the human body, not including the head, arms or legs

tortoise *noun* (**tor**-tus) a slow-moving animal with a shell over its body

torture *verb* to torture someone is to make them feel great pain, especially so that they will give information

torture *noun* torture is something done to torture a person

toss *verb* **1.** to toss something is to throw it into the air **2.** to toss a coin is to throw it in the air and see which side is showing when it lands, as a way of deciding something **3.** to toss is to move about restlessly in bed

total *noun* the amount you get by adding everything together

total *adjective* **1.** including everything • *What is the total amount?* **2.** complete; utter • *There was total darkness outside.* **totally** *adverb* completely • *Now I'm totally confused.*

total *verb* totalling, totalled **1.** to total something is to add it up **2.** to total an amount is to reach it as a total • *Sales totalled over £50,000 this month.*

totem pole *noun* a large pole carved or painted by Native Americans

totter *verb* to totter is to walk unsteadily or wobble

toucan *noun* a tropical bird with a large brightly-coloured beak

touch *verb* **1.** you touch something when you feel it lightly with your hand or fingers **2.** to touch something is to come into contact with it or hit it gently **3.** to be touching something is to be next to it so that there is no space in between **4.** to touch an amount is to just reach it • *His temperature touched 104 degrees.* **5.** to touch someone is to affect their emotions • *We were deeply touched by his sad story.* to touch down is to land in an aircraft or spacecraft to touch something up is to improve it by making small changes or additions

touch *noun* **1.** a touch is an act of touching **2.** touch is the ability to feel things by touching them **3.** a touch is also a small thing that greatly improves something • *We're just putting the finishing touches to it.* **4.** touch is also communication with someone • *We have lost touch with them.*

touch and go *adjective* uncertain or risky

touchy *adjective* touchier, touchiest easily or quickly offended

tough *adjective* **1.** strong; hard to break or damage • *You'll need tough shoes for the climb.* **2.** tough food is hard to chew **3.** rough or violent • *The police were dealing with tough criminals.* **4.** firm or severe • *It's time to get tough with football hooligans.* **5.** difficult • *It was a tough decision.* toughness *noun*

toughen *verb* toughens, toughening, toughened to toughen someone or something or toughen them up, is to make them tougher

tour *noun* a journey in which you visit several places

tourist *noun* someone who is travelling or on holiday abroad tourism *noun* travelling or being on holiday abroad

tournament *noun* a competition in which there is a series of games or contests

tow *verb* (rhymes with go) to tow a vehicle is to pull it along behind another vehicle

tow *noun* an act of towing

towards or **toward** *preposition* **1.** in the direction of • *She walked towards the sea.*

2. in relation to • *He behaved kindly towards his children.* **3.** as a contribution to • *Put the money towards a new bicycle.*

towel *noun* a piece of soft cloth used for drying yourself

tower *noun* a tall narrow building or part of a building

tower *verb* to tower above or over things is to be much taller than them • *Skyscrapers tower above the city.*

tower block *noun* a tall building containing offices or flats

town *noun* a place with many houses, shops, schools, offices and other buildings

town hall *noun* a building with offices for the local council and usually a hall for public events

towpath *noun* a path beside a canal or river

toxic *adjective* poisonous

toy *noun* something to play with

toy *verb* to toy with an idea is to think about it casually or idly

trace *noun* **1.** a mark or sign left by a person or thing • *He vanished without a trace.* **2.** a very small amount of something • *They found traces of blood on the carpet.*

trace *verb* **1.** to trace someone or something is to find them after a search **2.** to trace a picture or map is to copy it by drawing over it on thin paper you can see through

track *noun* **1.** a path made by people or animals **2.** tracks are marks left by a person or thing **3.** a set of rails for trains or trams to run on **4.** a road or area of ground prepared for racing **5.** a metal belt used instead of wheels on a heavy vehicle such as a tank or tractor **6.** one song or item on a album to keep track of something or someone is to know where they are or what they are doing

track *verb* to track a person or animal is to follow them by following the signs they leave to track something down is to find it after it has been lost tracker *noun* someone who tracks people or animals

tracksuit *noun* a warm loose suit of a kind worn for sport

tractor *noun* a motor vehicle with large rear wheels, used for pulling farm machinery or heavy loads

trade *noun* **1.** trade is the business of buying or selling or exchanging things **2.** a trade is a job or occupation, especially a skilled craft

trade *verb* to trade is to buy or sell or exchange things **to trade something in** is to give it towards the cost of something new • *He traded in his motorcycle for a car.* **trader** *noun* someone who buys and sells things in trade

trademark *noun* a symbol or name that only one manufacturer is allowed to use

tradesman *noun* **tradesmen** someone who sells or delivers goods

trade union *noun* an organization of workers in a particular industry, set up to help improve pay and work conditions

tradition *noun* **1.** tradition is the passing down of customs and beliefs from one generation to the next **2.** a tradition is a custom or belief passed on in this way

traditional *adjective* **1.** passed down from one generation to the next • *a traditional recipe* **2.** of a kind that has existed for a long time • *I went o a very traditional school.* **traditionally** *adverb*

traffic *noun* **1.** traffic is vehicles, ships or aircraft moving along a route **2.** traffic is also trade in something illegal or wrong

traffic *verb* **trafficking**, **trafficked** to traffic in something is to trade in it illegally

traffic lights *plural noun* a set of coloured lights used to control road traffic

traffic warden *noun* an official whose job is to make sure that vehicles are parked legally

tragedy *noun* **tragedies** **1.** a story or play with unhappy events or a sad ending **2.** a very sad event

tragic *adjective* **1.** very sad or distressing **2.** to do with tragedy **tragically** *adverb*

trail *noun* **1.** a path or track through the countryside or a forest **2.** the marks left behind by an animal as it moves **3.** marks left behind by something that has passed

trail *verb* **1.** to trail an animal is to follow the scent or marks it has left behind **2.** you trail something or it trails, when it drags along the ground behind you **3.** to trail behind someone is to follow them more slowly or at a distance • *A few walkers trailed behind the others.*

trailer *noun* **1.** a truck or other container that is pulled along by a car or lorry **2.** a short film advertising a film or television programme

train *noun* **1.** a group of railway coaches or trucks joined together and pulled by an engine **2.** a number of people or animals moving along together, especially in a desert • *a camel train* **3.** a series of things • *The train of events began in London.* **4.** a long part of a dress that trails behind on the ground

train *verb* **1.** to train someone is to give them skill or practice in something **2.** to train is to learn how to do a job • *He's training to be a doctor.* **3.** to train is also to practise for a sporting event • *She was training for the race.* **4.** to train a gun is to aim it at a target

trainer *noun* **1.** a person who trains people or animals **2.** a soft shoe with a rubber sole, worn for sport

traitor *noun* someone who betrays their country or friends

tram *noun* a passenger vehicle that runs along rails set in the road

tramp *noun* **1.** a person without a home or job who walks from place to place **2.** a long walk **3.** the sound of heavy footsteps

tramp *verb* to tramp is to walk with heavy footsteps

trample *verb* to trample something or to trample on it, is to crush it by treading heavily on it

trampoline *noun* (**tramp**-o-leen) a large piece of canvas joined to a frame by springs, used by gymnasts for jumping on

trance *noun* a dreamy or unconscious state like sleep

tranquil *adjective* quiet and peaceful
tranquillity or **tranquility** *noun* being quiet and peaceful

tranquillizer *noun* a drug used to make a person feel calm and relaxed

transaction *noun* a piece of business that involves buying and selling something

transfer *verb* **transferring**, **transferred** (trans-**fer**) to transfer someone or something is to move them from one place to another
transfer *noun* (**trans**-fer) **1.** the process of moving a person or thing from one place to another **2.** a piece of paper with a picture or design that can be transferred to another surface by soaking or heating the paper

transform *verb* to transform a person or thing is to change their form or appearance to something quite different • *The caterpillar is transformed into a butterfly.*
transformation *noun* a complete change in the form or appearance of something

transfusion *noun* putting blood taken from one person into another person's body

transistor *noun* **1.** a tiny electronic device that controls a flow of electricity **2.** a portable radio that uses transistors

transition *noun* a change from one thing to another

translate *verb* to translate speech or writing in one language is to change it into another language **translation** *noun* something translated from another language **translator** *noun* someone who translates language

transmission *noun* **1.** transmission is transmitting something **2.** a transmission is a radio or television broadcast

transmit *verb* **transmitting**, **transmitted** **1.** to transmit a broadcast or signal is to send it out **2.** to transmit something is to send it or pass it from one person or place to another • *We don't know how the disease is transmitted.*

transmitter *noun* a piece of equipment for transmitting radio or television signals

transparent *adjective* something is transparent when you can see through it **transparency** *noun* how transparent something is

transplant *verb* **1.** to transplant a body organ is to remove it from one person and put it in the body of a person who is ill **2.** to transplant a plant is to move it from one place to another **transplantation** *noun* transplantation is transplanting something
transplant *noun* an operation to transplant a body organ

transport *verb* (trans-**port**) to transport people or things is to take them from one place to another
transport *noun* (**trans**-port) **1.** transport is the process of transporting people or things **2.** transport is also vehicles used to do this

trap *noun* **1.** a device for catching and holding animals **2.** a plan or trick to capture or cheat someone **3.** a two-wheeled carriage pulled by a horse
trap *verb* **trapping**, **trapped** **1.** to trap a person or animal is to catch them in a trap **2.** to trap someone is to capture or cheat them **3.** to be trapped is to be stuck in a dangerous situation you can't escape from • *They were trapped in the burning building.*

trapdoor *noun* a door in a floor, ceiling or roof

trapeze *noun* a bar hanging from two ropes high above the ground, used as a swing by acrobats

trapezium *noun* a four-sided figure that has only two parallel sides, which are of different length

trash *noun* trash is rubbish or nonsense
trashy *adjective* worthless or rubbish

travel *verb* **travelling**, **travelled** to travel is to go from one place to another
travel *noun* travel is going on journeys

travel agent *noun* a person or business whose job is to arrange travel and holidays for people

traveller *noun* **1.** someone who is travelling or who often travels **2.** a gypsy

trawler *noun* a fishing boat that pulls a large net behind it

tray *noun* a flat piece of wood or metal or plastic, used for carrying food and drink

treacherous *adjective* **1.** betraying someone; not loyal **2.** dangerous or unreliable • *Snow had made the roads treacherous* . **treacherously** *adverb* **treachery** *noun* doing something that betrays someone

treacle *noun* treacle is a thick sweet sticky liquid made from sugar

tread *verb* **treading, trod, trodden** to tread on something is to walk on it or put your foot on it

tread *noun* **1.** the sound someone makes when they walk **2.** the part of a staircase or ladder that you put your foot on **3.** the part of a tyre that touches the ground

treason *noun* treason is betraying your country

treasure *noun* treasure is a collection of valuable things like jewels or money
treasure *verb* to treasure something is to think that it is very precious

treasurer *noun* an official who is in charge of the money of an organization or club

treasury *noun* **treasuries** a place where treasure or money is stored **the Treasury** the government department in charge of a country's income

treat *verb* **1.** to treat someone or something in a certain way is to behave towards them in that way • *She treats her friends very kindly.* **2.** to treat a person or animal is to give them medical care • *He was treated for sunstroke.* **3.** to treat something is to put it through a process to improve it • *The woodwork needs treating so that it doesn't rot.* **4.** to treat someone is to pay for their food or drink or entertainment • *I'll treat you to an ice cream.*
treat *noun* **1.** something special that gives someone pleasure **2.** the act of treating someone by paying for them • *This is my treat.*

treatment *noun* **1.** your treatment of someone is the way you treat them **2.** treatment is medical care

treaty *noun* **treaties** a formal agreement between two or more countries, for example to end a war

treble *adjective* three times as much or three times as many
treble *noun* **1.** treble the amount of something is three times as much or as many **2.** a treble is a boy with a high singing voice
treble *verb* **1.** to treble something is to make it three times as big **2.** to treble is to become three times as big

tree *noun* a tall plant with leaves, branches and a thick wooden trunk

trek *verb* **trekking, trekked** to trek is to make a long walk or journey
trek *noun* a long walk or journey

trellis *noun* a framework of crossing wooden or metal bars, used to support climbing plants

tremble *verb* to tremble is to shake gently, especially because you are afraid
tremble *noun* a trembling movement or sound

tremendous *adjective* **1.** very large or very great • *There was a tremendous explosion.* **2.** excellent **tremendously** *adverb* very much

tremor *noun* **1.** a shaking or trembling **2.** a small earthquake

trench *noun* a long hole or ditch dug in the ground

trend *noun* the general direction in which something is going or developing

trendy *adjective* **trendier, trendiest** (*informal*) fashionable **trendily** *adverb* **trendiness** *noun*

trespass *verb* to trespass is to go on someone's land or property without their permission **trespasser** *noun* someone who is trespassing

trestle *noun* each of a set of supports on which you place a board to make a table

trial *noun* **1.** trying or testing something to see how well it works **2.** the process of hearing all the evidence about a crime in a lawcourt to find out whether someone is guilty of it **by trial and error** by trying out different methods until you find one that works **on trial** being tried out or being tried in a lawcourt

triangle *noun* **1.** a flat shape with three straight sides and three angles **2.** a musical instrument made from a metal rod bent

A
B
C
D
E
F
G
H
I
J
K
L
M
N
O
P
Q
R
S
T
U
V
W
X
Y
Z

into a triangle and played by striking it
triangular *adjective* in the shape of a triangle

tribe *noun* a group of families living together, ruled by a chief **tribal** *adjective* to do with tribes or a tribe • *a tribal leader*

tributary *noun* **tributaries** a river or stream that flows into a larger river or a lake

tribute *noun* something you say or do as a mark of respect or admiration for someone

trick *noun* **1.** something done to deceive or fool someone **2.** a clever or skilful action • *a card trick*

trick *verb* to trick someone is to deceive or fool them **trickery** *noun* doing something to deceive or fool someone

trickle *verb* liquid trickles when it flows slowly in small quantities

trickle *noun* a slow gradual flow

tricky *adjective* **trickier**, **trickiest** difficult or awkward • *There were a couple of tricky questions in the quiz.*

tricolour (tick-ol-er) *noun* **tricolours** a flag with three coloured stripes, e.g. the national flag of France or Ireland

tricycle *noun* a child's bicycle with three wheels

trifle *noun* **trifles 1.** a pudding made of sponge cake covered with custard, fruit and cream **2.** something that has little importance or is very small

trifling *adjective* very small or unimportant

trigger *noun* a lever that is pulled to fire a gun

trillion *noun* a million million (1,000,000,000,000) or sometimes a million million million (1,000,000,000,000,000,000)

trilogy *noun* **trilogies** a group of three books or films about the same characters

trim *adjective* **trimmer**, **trimmest** neat and tidy

trim *verb* **trimming**, **trimmed 1.** you trim something when you cut the edges or unwanted parts from it **2.** to trim clothing is to decorate its edges • *The gown was trimmed with fur.*

trim *noun* an act of trimming • *My hair needs a quick trim.*

Trinity *noun* **the Trinity** in Christianity, the union of Father, Son and Holy Spirit in one God

trio *noun* **trios 1.** three people or things **2.** a group of three musicians

trip *verb* **tripping**, **tripped 1.** to trip or trip over, is to catch your foot on something and fall or stumble **2.** to trip someone or trip them up, is to make them fall or stumble

trip *noun* **1.** a short journey or outing **2.** the action of tripping or stumbling

triple *adjective* **1.** three times as much or three times as many **2.** consisting of three parts or involving three people or groups

triple *verb* to triple something is to make it three times as big

triple jump *noun* an athletics event in which athletes try to jump as far as possible with a hop, step and jump

triplet *noun* each of three children or animals born at the same time to the same mother

tripod *noun* (**try**-pod) a stand with three legs, for supporting a camera or other instrument

triumph *noun* **1.** a triumph is a great success or victory **2.** triumph is a feeling of victory or success • *They returned home in triumph.*

triumph *verb* to triumph is to win or succeed

triumphant *adjective* enjoying a victory or celebrating one **triumphantly** *adverb*

trivial *adjective* not important or valuable **trivially** *adverb* **triviality** *noun* triviality is being unimportant

troll *noun* a creature in Scandinavian mythology, either a dwarf or a giant

trolley *noun* **trolleys 1.** a basket on wheels, used in supermarkets • *a shopping trolley* **2.** a small table on wheels, used for serving food and drink

trombone *noun* a large brass musical instrument with a sliding tube

troop *noun* a group of soldiers or Scouts

troop *verb* people troop when they move along in large numbers

troops *plural noun* soldiers

trophy *noun* trophies a cup or other prize you get for winning a competition

tropic *noun* a line of latitude about 23½° north of the equator (**Tropic of Cancer**) or about 23½° south of the equator (**Tropic of Capricorn**) the tropics the hot regions between these two latitudes
tropical *adjective* to do with the tropics or from the tropics

trot *verb* trotting, trotted **1.** a horse trots when it runs gently without cantering or galloping **2.** a person trots when they run gently with short steps
trot *noun* a slow or gentle run

trouble *noun* trouble is something that causes worry or difficulty to be in trouble is to be likely to get punished because of something you have done to take trouble is to take great care in doing something
trouble *verb* **1.** to trouble someone is to cause them worry or difficulty **2.** to trouble someone is also to bother or disturb them • *Sorry to trouble you, but can you spare a minute?* **3.** to trouble to do something is to make an effort to do it • *Nobody troubled to ask us what we wanted.*

troublesome *adjective* causing trouble or worry

trough *noun* (trof) a long narrow box for animals to eat or drink from

trousers *plural noun* a piece of clothing worn over the lower half of your body, with two parts to cover your legs

trout *noun* trout a freshwater fish

trowel *noun* **1.** a tool for digging small holes or lifting plants **2.** a tool with a flat blade for spreading mortar

truant *noun* a child who stays away from school without permission to play truant is to stay away from school without permission
truancy *noun* being absent from school without permission

truce *noun* an agreement to stop fighting for a while

truck *noun* **1.** a lorry **2.** an open railway wagon for carrying goods

trudge *verb* to trudge is to walk slowly and heavily

true *adjective* truer, truest **1.** real or correct; telling what actually exists or happened • *a true story* **2.** genuine or proper • *He was the true heir.* **3.** loyal and faithful • *You are a true friend.* to come true is to actually happen

truly *adverb* **1.** truthfully **2.** sincerely or genuinely • *We are truly grateful.*

trump *noun* a playing card of a suit that ranks above the others for one game or round of play
trump *verb* to trump a card is to beat it by playing a trump

trumpet *noun* a brass musical instrument with a narrow tube that widens at the end
trumpeter *noun* someone who plays the trumpet
trumpet *verb* an elephant trumpets when it makes a loud sound

truncheon *noun* a short thick stick carried as a weapon by a police officer

trundle *verb* to trundle is to move along heavily, especially on wheels

trunk *noun* **1.** the main stem of a tree **2.** an elephant's long flexible nose **3.** a large box with a hinged lid, for carrying or storing things **4.** the human body except for the head, legs and arms

trunks *plural noun* shorts worn by men and boys for swimming, boxing and other activities

trust *verb* to trust someone or something is to believe that they are good or truthful or reliable to trust someone with something is to let them use it or look after it
trust *noun* **1.** trust is the feeling that a person or thing can be trusted **2.** trust is also responsibility or being trusted

trustworthy *adjective* able to be trusted; reliable

trusty *adjective* trustworthy or reliable

truth noun truth is the quality of being true; the facts about something

truthful adjective **1.** telling the truth • Be truthful with me. **2.** true • a truthful account of what happened **truthfully** adverb **truthfulness** noun

try verb tries, trying, tried **1.** to try to do something is to make an effort to do it or to see if you can do it • Try to keep still. **2.** to try something is to use it to see if it works or taste it to see if you like it • Try this can opener. **3.** to try someone in a lawcourt is to find out whether they are guilty of a crime, by hearing all the evidence about it **4.** to try someone is also to annoy them over a long time • You really do try me with your constant complaining. **to try something on** is to put on clothes to see if they fit or look good **to try something out** is to use it to see if it works

try noun tries **1.** a go at trying something; an attempt **2.** (in rugby football) putting the ball down on the ground behind your opponents' goal to score points

T-shirt noun T-shirts a shirt or vest with short sleeves

tub noun a round container for liquids or soft stuff such as ice cream

tuba noun (**tew**-ba) a large brass musical instrument that makes a deep sound

tube noun **1.** a tube is a long thin hollow piece of material such as metal, plastic, rubber or glass **2.** a tube is also a long hollow container for something soft such as toothpaste **3.** the Tube is the underground railway in London

tuber noun a thick rounded plant root or stem that produces buds

tubular adjective shaped like a tube

tuck verb to tuck something somewhere is to push a loose edge of it there so that it is tidy or hidden **to tuck in** (informal) is to eat heartily **to tuck someone up** or or **in** is to put the bedclothes snugly round them

Tuesday noun the third day of the week

tuft noun a bunch of soft or fluffy things such as grass, hair or feathers

tug verb tugging, tugged to tug something is to pull it hard

tug noun **1.** a hard or sudden pull **2.** a small powerful boat used for towing ships

tug-of-war noun a contest between two teams pulling a rope from opposite ends

tulip noun a large bright cup-shaped flower that grows on a tall stem from a bulb

tumble verb to tumble is to fall over or fall down clumsily

tumbler noun a drinking glass with no stem or handle

tummy noun tummies (informal) your stomach

tumour noun (**tew**-mer) an abnormal growth on or in your body

tumultuous adjective noisy and excited • The teams came out to tumultuous applause.

tuna noun tuna or tunas (**tew**-na) a large sea fish used for food

tundra noun tundra is a large area of flat land in cold regions (especially northern Canada and Siberia) with no trees and with soil that is frozen for most of the year

tune noun a short piece of music; a pleasant series of musical notes **to be in tune** is to be at the correct musical pitch

tune verb **1.** to tune a musical instrument is to adjust it to be in tune **2.** to tune a radio or television is to adjust it to receive a particular broadcasting station **3.** to tune an engine is to adjust it so that it works smoothly

tuneful adjective having a pleasant tune

tunic noun (**tew**-nik) **1.** a jacket that is part of some uniforms **2.** a loose piece of clothing with no sleeves

tunnel noun a passage made underground or through a hill

tunnel verb tunnelling, tunnelled to tunnel is to make a tunnel

turban noun a covering for the head made by wrapping a long strip of cloth round it, worn especially by Sikh, Hindu or Muslim men

turbine noun a machine or motor that is driven by a flow of water or gas

turbulent adjective moving violently; heaving • The seas in March can be turbulent. **turbulence** noun violent and uneven movement of air or water, causing aircraft and ships to be tossed about

turf *noun* **turfs** or **turves** **1**. turf is short grass with the soil it is growing in **2**. a turf is a piece of grass and soil cut out of the ground

turkey *noun* **turkeys** a large bird kept for its meat

turmoil *noun* turmoil is a great disturbance or confusion

turn *verb* **1**. to turn is to move round or move to a new direction; to turn something is to make it move in this way **2**. to turn (for example) pale is to change appearance and become pale **3**. to turn into something is to change into it **4**. to turn something into something else is to change it • *You can turn milk into cheese.* **5**. to turn a device on or off is to use a switch to make it work or stop working; to turn (for example) a radio or television up or down is to make it louder or softer **to turn out** is to happen a certain way • *The weather's turned out fine.* **to turn something down** is to refuse it **to turn something out** is to empty it **to turn up** is to appear or arrive unexpectedly

turn *noun* **1**. the action of turning; a turning movement **2**. a place where a road bends; a junction **3**. a task or duty that people do one after the other • *It's your turn to wash up.* **a good turn** is a favour you do for someone **in turn** first one and then the other; following one after another

turnip *noun* a plant with a large round white root used as a vegetable

turnstile *noun* a revolving gate that lets one person through at a time

turntable *noun* the part of a record player that you put the record on

turpentine *noun* (**ter**-pen-tyn) turpentine is a kind of oil used to make paint thinner and to clean paintbrushes

turquoise *noun* (**ter**-kwoiz) **1**. a sky-blue or greenish-blue colour **2**. a blue jewel

turret *noun* **1**. a small tower in a castle **2**. a revolving structure containing a gun

turtle *noun* a sea animal that looks like a tortoise

tusk *noun* one of a pair of long pointed teeth that stick out of the mouth of an elephant or walrus or boar

tussle *noun* a hard struggle or fight
tussle *verb* to tussle is to struggle or fight over something

tutor *noun* a teacher who teaches one person or a small group at a time

TV short for **television**

tweak *verb* to tweak something is to twist it or pull it sharply

tweed *noun* tweed is a thick rough woollen cloth

tweet *noun* **1**. the chirping sound made by a small bird **2**. a short message sent on the social network Twitter
tweet *verb* **1**. a small bird tweets when it makes a chirping sound **2**. to send a message on the social network Twitter

tweezers *plural noun* a small tool for gripping or picking up small things like stamps and hairs

twelve *noun* the number 12
twelfth *adjective, noun* 12th

twenty *noun* **twenties** the number 20
twentieth *adjective, noun* 20th

twice *adverb* **1**. two times; on two occasions **2**. double the amount

twiddle *verb* to twiddle something is to turn it round or over and over in an idle way

twig *noun* a short thin piece from a branch of a tree

twilight *noun* twilight is the time of dim light just after sunset

twin *noun* each of two children or animals born at the same time from one mother

twine *noun* twine is strong thin string

twinge *noun* a sudden sharp pain

twinkle *verb* to twinkle is to sparkle or shine with flashes of bright light
twinkle *noun* a twinkling light

twirl *verb* to twirl is to turn round and round quickly; to twirl something is to make it do this
twirl *noun* a twirling movement

twist *verb* **1**. to twist something is to turn its ends in opposite directions **2**. to twist is to turn round or from side to side • *The* road twisted through the hills. **3.** to twist something is to bend it out of its proper shape • *I think I've twisted my ankle.*

twist *noun* a twisting movement or action

twitch *verb* to twitch is to jerk or move suddenly and quickly; to twitch something is to make it do this

twitch *noun* a twitching movement

twitter *verb* birds twitter when they make quick chirping sounds

two *noun* the number 2

type *noun* **1.** a type is a group or class of similar people or things; a kind or sort **2.** type is letters and figures designed for use in printing

type *verb* to type something is to write it with a typewriter or computer

typewriter *noun* a machine with keys that you press to print letters or figures on a sheet of paper **typewritten** *adjective* written with a typewriter

typhoon *noun* a violent tropical storm with strong winds and rain

typical *adjective* **1.** usual or normal • *It was just a typical day, like any other.* **2.** as you would expect from a particular person or thing • *She worked with typical thoroughness.* **typically** *adverb* usually

typist *noun* a person who types, especially as their job

tyranny *noun* tyrannies (**ti**-ra-nee) tyranny is a cruel or unjust way of ruling people **tyrannical** *adjective* a tyrannical ruler uses their power in a cruel or unjust way

tyrant *noun* (**ty**-rant) someone who rules people cruelly or unjustly

tyre *noun* a covering of rubber fitted round the rim of a wheel to make it grip the road and run smoothly

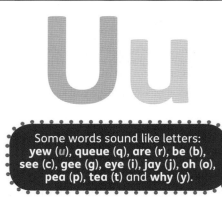

Some words sound like letters: **yew** (*u*), **queue** (**q**), **are** (**r**), **be** (**b**), **see** (**c**), **gee** (**g**), **eye** (**i**), **jay** (**j**), **oh** (**o**), **pea** (**p**), **tea** (**t**) and **why** (**y**).

udder *noun* the bag-like part of a cow, goat or ewe, from which milk is taken

UFO *noun* short for *unidentified flying object*, a flying object that no one can explain

ugly *adjective* uglier, ugliest **1.** not beautiful; unpleasant to look at **2.** threatening or dangerous • *The crowd was in an ugly mood.* **ugliness** *noun*

ulcer *noun* a sore on your skin or the inside of your body

ultimate *adjective* furthest in a series of things; final **ultimately** *adverb* finally or eventually

ultraviolet *adjective* ultraviolet light is light beyond the violet end of the spectrum, that causes your skin to tan

umbilical cord *noun* the tube through which a baby receives nourishment in the mother's womb, connected to the baby's navel

umbrella *noun* an object that you hold above your head to protect yourself from rain

The word **umbrella** comes from an Italian word *ombrella* meaning 'a little shade'.

umpire *noun* someone who makes sure that people keep to the rules in cricket, tennis and some other games

unable *adjective* not able • *She was unable to hear.*

unanimous *adjective* (yoo-**nan**-i-mus) a unanimous decision or vote is one where everyone agrees **unanimously** *adverb* with everyone agreeing • *She was elected unanimously.*

unavoidable *adjective* not able to be avoided; bound to happen

unaware *adjective* not knowing about something

unawares *adjective* unexpectedly • *His question caught me unawares.*

unbearable *adjective* very painful or unpleasant **unbearably** *adverb* in an unbearable way • *It was unbearably hot.*

unbelievable *adjective* **1.** difficult to believe **2.** amazing **unbelievably** *adverb*

uncalled for *adjective* not justified or necessary • *Your rudeness is uncalled for.*

uncanny *adjective* **uncannier, uncanniest** strange and mysterious • *There was an uncanny silence.*

uncertain *adjective* **1.** not certain • *He is uncertain about what to do.* **2.** not reliable • *The weather is uncertain at the moment.* **uncertainty** *noun* uncertainty is being uncertain about something

uncle *noun* **1.** the brother of your father or mother **2.** your aunt's husband

uncomfortable *adjective* not comfortable

unconscious *adjective* not awake or knowing what is happening around you because you have fainted or been knocked out **unconsciousness** *noun* being unconscious

uncouth *adjective* (un-**koo**th) rude and rough in manner

uncover *verb* **1.** to uncover something is to take the cover or top off it **2.** to uncover a secret or something unknown is to discover it • *The police have uncovered a huge fraud.*

undecided *adjective* you are undecided about something when you have not made up your mind about it

undeniable *adjective* impossible to deny; certainly true

under *preposition* **1.** lower than; below • *Hide it under the desk.* **2.** less than • *They are under 5 years old.* **3.** ruled or controlled by • *The army is under his command.* **4.** in the process of; undergoing • *The road is under repair.*

5. using; moving by means of • *The machine moves under its own power.*

under *adverb* in or to a lower place • *Slowly the diver went under.*

underarm *adjective, adverb* with the arm kept below shoulder level and moving forward and upwards

undercarriage *noun* an aircraft's undercarriage is its landing wheels and the parts that support them

underclothes *plural noun* or **underclothing** *noun* underwear

underdog *noun* the person or team in a contest that is expected to lose

underdone *adjective* not properly done or cooked

underfoot *adverb* on the ground where you are walking • *It was slippery underfoot.*

undergo *verb* **undergoes, undergoing, underwent, undergone** to undergo something is to experience something or have to do it

undergraduate *noun* a student at a university who has not yet taken a degree

underground *adjective, adverb* **1.** under the ground **2.** done or working in secret **underground** *noun* a railway that runs through tunnels under the ground

undergrowth *noun* undergrowth is bushes and other plants growing close together under tall trees

underhand *adjective* secret and deceitful

underline *verb* **1.** to underline something you have written is to draw a line under it **2.** to underline a fact is to emphasize it or show it clearly • *This accident underlines the need to be careful all the time.*

undermine *verb* to undermine someone's efforts or plans is to weaken them gradually

underneath *preposition, adverb* below or beneath

underpants *plural noun* a piece of men's underwear worn under trousers

underpass *noun* a place where one road or path goes under another

A
B
C
D
E
F
G
H
I
J
K
L
M
N
O
P
Q
R
S
T
U
V
W
X
Y
Z

underprivileged *adjective* people who are underprivileged don't have the same opportunities or standard of living as most people

understand *verb* **1**. to understand something is to know what it means or how it works **2**. to understand something is also to have heard about it • *I understand you've not been well.* **3**. to understand someone is to know what they are like and why they behave the way they do **understandable** *adjective* able to be understood; easy to understand

understanding *noun* **1**. understanding is the power to understand or think; intelligence **2**. an understanding is when people have an agreement • *In the end the two brothers came to an understanding.* **3**. understanding is also sympathy or tolerance

understanding *adjective* sympathetic and helpful • *He was very understanding when I was ill.*

understudy *noun* **understudies** an actor who learns a part in a play so that they can play the part if the usual actor isn't able to perform

undertake *verb* **undertaking**, **undertook**, **undertaken** to undertake something is to agree or promise to do it

undertaker *noun* someone whose job is to arrange funerals

undertaking *noun* something that someone agrees to do

underwater *adjective* placed or used or done below the surface of water

underwear *noun* underwear is clothes you wear next to your skin, under your main clothes

underworld *noun* **1**. in legends, the underworld is the place for the spirits of the dead; hell **2**. the underworld is also people who are regularly involved in crime

undeveloped *adjective* not yet developed

undo *verb* **undoes**, **undoing**, **undid**, **undone** **1**. to undo something is to unfasten or unwrap it • *Can you undo this knot?* **2**. to undo something already done is to cancel the effect of it • *He has undone all our careful work.*

undoubted *adjective* definite or certain **undoubtedly** *adverb* certainly

undress *verb* **1**. to undress is to take your clothes off **2**. to undress someone is to take their clothes off

unearth *verb* **1**. to unearth something is to dig it up **2**. to unearth something is also to find it after searching for it

unearthly *adjective* supernatural; strange and frightening

uneasy *adjective* **uneasier**, **uneasiest** anxious or worried **uneasily** *adverb* in a way that shows you are anxious or worried

unemployed *adjective* to be unemployed is to be without a job **unemployment** *noun* being without a job; the number of people without a job

uneven *adjective* not level, flat or regular **unevenly** *adverb* **unevenness** *noun*

unexpected *adjective* not expected; surprising **unexpectedly** *adverb* when you are not expecting it

unfair *adjective* not fair; unjust **unfairly** *adverb* **unfairness** *noun*

unfaithful *adjective* not faithful or loyal

unfamiliar *adjective* not familiar

unfasten *verb* to unfasten something is to open it when it has been fastened

unfinished *adjective* not finished

unfit *adjective* **1**. someone is unfit when they are not fit or fully healthy **2**. to be unfit for something is to be not suitable • *He is unfit for the job.*

unfold *verb* **1**. to unfold something is to open it or spread it out • *She unfolded the map.*

2. a story unfolds when it becomes known gradually

unforgettable *adjective* impossible to forget

unforgivable *adjective* not able to be forgiven

unfortunate *adjective* **1.** unlucky **2.** you say something is unfortunate when you wish it hadn't happened; regrettable • *It was an unfortunate remark.* unfortunately *adverb* used to say you are sad about something • *Unfortunately he wasn't able to come to the party.*

unfriendly *adjective* unfriendlier, unfriendliest not friendly

ungrateful *adjective* not grateful

unhappy *adjective* unhappier, unhappiest **1.** not happy or pleased **2.** you say something is unhappy when you wish it hadn't happened; regrettable • *It was an unhappy choice of words.* unhappily *adverb* unhappiness *noun*

unhealthy *adjective* unhealthier, unhealthiest **1.** not in good health **2.** not good for you • *an unhealthy diet*

unheard-of *adjective* never known or done before; extraordinary

unicorn *noun* (**yoo**-ni-korn) an imaginary animal in stories, like a horse with a long straight horn growing out of the front of its head

uniform *noun* the special clothes worn by members of an army or school or organization

uniform *adjective* always the same; not changing uniformly *adverb*

uniformity *noun* uniformity is being uniform or the same

unify *verb* unifies, unifying, unified to unify several things, especially countries, is to join them into one thing; to unify is to join together unification *noun* when several things are joined together into one thing

unimportant *adjective* not important

uninhabited *adjective* a place is uninhabited when there is nobody living there

unintentional *adjective* not done deliberately unintentionally *adverb* not on purpose

uninterested *adjective* not interested

uninteresting *adjective* not interesting

union *noun* **1.** the joining of things together; a united thing **2.** a trade union

Union Jack *noun* Union Jacks the flag of the United Kingdom

unique *adjective* (yoo-**neek**) something is unique when it is the only one of its kind • *Everyone's fingerprints are unique.* uniquely *adverb* uniqueness *noun*

unisex *adjective* designed to be suitable for either men or women

unison *noun* (**yoo**-ni-son) in unison said or done by people together at the same time

unit *noun* **1.** an amount used in measuring or counting, such as a centimetre or a pound **2.** a single person or thing **3.** a group of people or things that belong together

unite *verb* **1.** to unite several people or things is to form them into one thing or group **2.** people or things unite when they join together

unity *noun* unities unity is being united or having agreement

universal *adjective* including everyone and everything universally *adverb* by everyone • *This theory is now universally accepted.*

universe *noun* the universe is everything that exists, including the earth and living things and all the stars and planets

university *noun* universities a place where people go to study for a degree after they have left school

unjust *adjective* not fair or just unjustly *adverb*

unkind *adjective* cruel and not kind unkindly *adverb* unkindness *noun*

unless *conjunction* except when; if not • *We cannot go unless we are invited.*

unlike *preposition* not like • *Unlike me, she enjoys sport.*

unlikely *adjective* unlikelier, unlikeliest not likely to happen or be true

unload *verb* to unload a container or vehicle is to remove the things it carried

unlock *verb* to unlock a door or container is to open it with a key

unlucky *adjective* unluckier, unluckiest not lucky unluckily *adverb*

unmistakable *adjective* not likely to be mistaken for something or someone else; clear and definite

unnatural *adjective* not natural or normal unnaturally *adverb*

unnecessary *adjective* not needed unnecessarily *adverb* when it is not needed

unoccupied *adjective* a house is unoccupied when it is empty, with no one living there

unpack *verb* to unpack a suitcase or bag is to take out the things in it

unpleasant *adjective* not pleasant unpleasantly *adverb* unpleasantness *noun*

unplug *verb* unplugging, unplugged to unplug an electrical device is to disconnect it by taking its plug out of the socket

unpopular *adjective* not liked or enjoyed by people unpopularity *noun* the fact that a person or thing is unpopular

unravel *verb* unravelling, unravelled to unravel something is to unwind it or disentangle it

unreal *adjective* not real; existing only in the imagination

unreasonable *adjective* not reasonable or fair

unrest *noun* unrest is trouble caused by people feeling unhappy

unroll *verb* to unroll something is to open it when it has been rolled up

unruly *adjective* unrulier, unruliest (un-**roo**-lee) badly behaved and difficult to control unruliness *noun*

unsafe *adjective* not safe; dangerous

unscrew *verb* to unscrew something is to undo it by turning it or by removing screws

unseen *adjective* not seen or noticed • *He managed to slip out of the room unseen.*

unselfish *adjective* not selfish; not thinking only about yourself unselfishly *adverb* unselfishness *noun*

unsightly *adjective* not pleasant to look at; ugly

unsteady *adjective* unsteadier, unsteadiest shaking or wobbling or likely to fall unsteadily *adverb* unsteadiness *noun*

unsuccessful *adjective* not successful unsuccessfully *adverb*

unsuitable *adjective* not suitable unsuitably *adverb*

unthinkable *adjective* too bad or unlikely to be worth thinking about

untidy *adjective* untidier, untidiest messy and not tidy untidily *adverb* untidiness *noun*

untie *verb* unties, untying, untied to untie something is to undo it when it has been tied

until *preposition, conjunction* up to a particular time or event • *The shop is open until 8 o'clock.* • *We will stay with you until the train comes.*

untold *adjective* too great to be counted or measured • *The hurricane caused untold damage.*

untrue *adjective* not true

unused *adjective* (un-**yoozd**) not yet used

unusual *adjective* different from what is usual or normal; strange or rare unusually *adverb*

unwell *adjective* not well; ill

unwilling *adjective* you are unwilling to do something when you don't want to do it unwillingly *adverb* unwillingness *noun*

unwind *verb* unwinding, unwound (rhymes with find) **1.** to unwind something is to unroll it **2.** to unwind is to become unrolled **3.** (informal) to unwind is also to relax after you have been working hard

unwrap *verb* to unwrap something is to take it out of its wrapping

unzip *verb* unzipping, unzipped to unzip something is to undo it when it is zipped up

up *adverb* **1.** in or to a standing or upright position • *Stand up.* **2.** in or to a high or higher place or level • *Put it up on the shelf.*

• *Prices are going up.* **3**. completely • *Eat up your carrots.* **4**. out of bed • *It's time to get up.* **5**. finished • *Your time is up.* **6**. *(informal)* happening • *Something is up.* ups and downs changes of luck, sometimes good and sometimes bad to be up to something is to be doing something mysterious or suspicious • *What are they up to?*

up *preposition* in or to a higher position on something • *Let's climb up that tree.*

upbringing *noun* your upbringing is the way you have been brought up

update *verb* to update something is to bring it up to date

upgrade *verb* to upgrade a machine is to improve it by installing new parts in it

upheaval *noun* a sudden violent change or disturbance

uphill *adjective, adverb* **1**. sloping upwards; going up a slope **2**. difficult • *It was an uphill struggle.*

uphold *verb* upholding, upheld to uphold a decision or belief is to support it or agree with it

upholstery *noun* upholstery is covers and padding for furniture

upkeep *noun* the upkeep of something is the cost of looking after it and keeping it in good condition

uplands *plural noun* the highest part of a country or region

upon *preposition* on

upper *adjective* higher in position or rank

upright *adjective* **1**. standing straight up; vertical **2**. honest

upright *noun* an upright post or support

uprising *noun* a rebellion or revolt against the government

uproar *noun* uproar is a loud or angry noise or disturbance • *The room was in uproar.*

upset *adjective* (up-**set**) unhappy or anxious about something

upset *verb* upsetting, upset (up-**set**) to upset someone is to make them unhappy or anxious

upset *noun* (**up**-set) a slight illness • *a stomach upset*

upside down *adjective, adverb* **1**. with the upper part underneath instead of on top; the wrong way up **2**. in disorder or confusion • *The thieves turned the place upside down.*

upstairs *adverb, adjective* to or on a higher floor in a house or other building

upstream *adjective, adverb* in the direction opposite to the flow of a river or stream

uptight *adjective (informal)* upset or nervous about something

up-to-date *adjective* **1**. modern or fashionable **2**. having the latest information

upward *adjective, adverb* going towards what is higher

upwards *adverb* towards what is higher

uranium *noun* (yoor-**ay**-ni-um) uranium is a radioactive metal used as a source of atomic energy

urban *adjective* to do with a town or city

Urdu *noun* Urdu is a language related to Hindi, spoken in northern India and Pakistan

urge *verb* **1**. to urge someone to do something is to try to persuade them to do it **2**. to urge people or animals is to drive them forward

urge *noun* a sudden strong desire or wish

urgent *adjective* needing to be done or dealt with immediately urgency *noun* urgency is when something needs to be done or dealt with immediately urgently *adverb*

urinate *verb* (**yoor**-i-nayt) to urinate is to pass urine out of your body urination *noun* urination is passing urine

urine *noun* (**yoor**-in) urine is the waste liquid that collects in your bladder and is passed out of your body

urn *noun* **1**. a large metal container with a tap, in which water is heated **2**. a container shaped like a vase with a base, especially one for holding the ashes of a cremated person

us *pronoun* a word used for *we*, usually when it is the object of a sentence or when it comes after a preposition • *She likes us.* • *She gave it to us.*

usage *noun* (**yoo**-sij) the way that something is used, especially the way that words and language are used

use *verb* (yooz) to use something is to perform an action or job with it • *Are you using my pen?* **used to** did in the past • *I used to live in Glasgow.* **to be used to something** or **someone** is to know them well or be familiar with them • *We're used to hard work.* **to use something up** is to use all of it, so that none is left

use *noun* (yooss) **1.** the action of using something or being used **2.** the purpose or value of something • *Can you find a use for this box?*

used *adjective* (yoozd) not new; second-hand • *used cars*

useful *adjective* able to be used a lot or do something that needs doing **usefully** *adverb* **usefulness** *noun*

useless *adjective* **1.** not having any use **2.** *(informal)* not very good at something • *I'm useless at drawing.* **uselessly** *adverb* **uselessness** *noun*

user *noun* someone who uses something

user-friendly *adjective* **user-friendlier,** **user-friendliest** designed to be easy to use

usher *noun* someone who shows people to their seats in a church or cinema or theatre

usherette *noun* a woman who shows people to their seats in a cinema or theatre

usual *adjective* as happens often or all the time; expected • *He sat in his usual chair by the fire.* • *She was late as usual.* **usually** *adverb* on most occasions; normally

utensil *noun* (yoo-**ten**-sil) a tool or device, especially one you use in the house

utmost *adjective* greatest • *Look after it with the utmost care.*

utter[1] *verb* to utter something is to say it clearly or to make a sound with your mouth **utterance** *noun* something that someone says

utter[2] *adjective* complete or absolute **utterly** *adverb* • *You look utterly ridiculous.*

Vv

No English word ends in just the letter *v*.

vacancy *noun* **vacancies** a job or a room in a guest house, that is available and not taken

vacant *adjective* **1.** empty; not filled or occupied • *There were no vacant seats.* **2.** not showing any expression • *He gave a vacant stare.*

vacate *verb* to vacate a place is to leave it empty

vacation *noun* (vay-**kay**-shon) a holiday, especially between the terms at a university

vaccinate *verb* (**vak**-si-nayt) to vaccinate someone is to protect them from a disease by injecting them with a vaccine **vaccination** *noun* when you are vaccinated against a disease

vaccine *noun* (**vak**-seen) a type of medicine injected into people to protect them from disease

> It is called **vaccine** from the Latin word *vacca* meaning 'cow', because the first vaccine was taken from cows.

vacuum *noun* a completely empty space; a space without any air in it

vacuum *verb* to clean something using a vacuum cleaner

vacuum cleaner *noun* an electrical device that sucks up dust and dirt from the floor

vacuum flask *noun* a container with double walls that have a vacuum between them, for keeping liquids hot or cold

vagina *noun* (va-**jy**-na) the passage in a woman's body that leads from the outside of her body to her womb

vague *adjective* not definite or clear • *I only have a vague memory of his face.* **vaguely** *adverb* not clearly **vagueness** *noun*

vain *adjective* 1. too proud of yourself, especially of how you look 2. unsuccessful or useless • *They made vain attempts to save him.* **in vain** with no result; without success • *I tried in vain to call for help.* **vainly** *adverb* without success

valentine *noun* 1. a card sent on St Valentine's Day (14 February) to someone you love 2. the person you send a valentine to

valiant *adjective* brave or courageous **valiantly** *adverb*

valid *adjective* able to be used or accepted; legal • *My passport is no longer valid.* **validity** *noun* the fact that something is acceptable or legal

valley *noun* **valleys** an area of low land between hills

valour *noun* valour is bravery, especially in a battle

valuable *adjective* 1. worth a lot of money 2. very useful or important • *She gave me valuable advice.*

valuables *plural noun* things that are worth a lot of money

value *noun* 1. the amount of money that something could be sold for 2. how useful or important something is

value *verb* 1. to value something is to think that it is important or worth having • *I value her friendship.* 2. to value something is also to work out how much it could be sold for • *The estate agent is coming to value the house.* **valuation** *noun* an estimate of what something is worth **valuer** *noun* someone who values something

valve *noun* a device used to control the flow of gas or liquid

vampire *noun* in stories, a creature that sucks people's blood

van *noun* a small lorry with a covered area for goods at the back

vandal *noun* someone who deliberately breaks or damages things **vandalism** *noun* doing deliberate damage to something

vanilla *noun* vanilla is a flavouring made from the pods of a tropical plant

vanish *verb* to vanish is to disappear completely

vanity *noun* vanity is being too proud of your appearance or abilities

vanquish *verb* to vanquish someone is to win a victory over them

vapour *noun* a visible gas, such as mist or steam, which some liquids and solids can be turned into by heat

variable *adjective* able or likely to change

variation *noun* 1. a change in something • *There have been slight variations in temperature.* 2. a different form of something

varied *adjective* of various kinds; full of variety • *She has varied interests.*

variety *noun* **varieties** 1. a variety is a number of different kinds of the same thing • *There was a variety of cakes to choose from.* 2. a variety is a particular kind of something • *rare varieties of butterfly* 3. variety is a situation where things are not always the same • *My work is full of variety.*

various *determiner* of different kinds • *They came for various reasons.* **variously** *adverb* in several different ways

varnish *noun* a liquid that dries to form a hard shiny surface on wood
varnish *verb* to varnish wood is to put varnish on it

vary *verb* varies, varying, varied **1.** to vary is to keep changing • *The weather varies a lot here.* **2.** things vary when they are different from each other • *The cars are the same, although the colours vary.* **3.** to vary something is to make changes to it

vase *noun* (vahz) a jar used for holding flowers or as an ornament

vast *adjective* very large or wide
vastly *adverb* greatly; very • *They are from vastly different backgrounds.* **vastness** *noun* being very large or wide

VAT short for *value-added tax*, a tax on goods and services

vat *noun* a very large container for holding liquid

vault *verb* you vault something or vault over it, when you jump over it, using your hands to support you or with the help of a pole
vault *noun* **1.** a jump done by vaulting **2.** an underground room for storing money and valuables

VDU short for visual display unit

veal *noun* veal is the meat from a calf

vector *noun* (in mathematics) a quantity that has size and direction, such as velocity (which is speed in a certain direction)

Veda *plural noun* the ancient writings of the Hindu religion

veer *verb* to veer is to swerve or change direction suddenly

vegan *noun* (**vee**-gan) someone who does not use or eat any products made from animals

vegetable *noun* a plant that can be used as food

vegetarian *noun* (vej-i-**tair**-i-an) someone who does not eat meat

vegetation *noun* vegetation is plants that are growing

vehicle *noun* a means of carrying people or things, especially on land. Cars, buses, trains and lorries are vehicles.

veil *noun* a piece of thin material to cover a woman's face or head **veiled** *adjective* covered with a veil; partially hidden

vein *noun* **1.** your veins are the tubes in your body that carry blood towards your heart **2.** a line or streak on a leaf or rock or insect's wing **3.** a long deposit of a mineral in the middle of rock

velocity *noun* velocities (vil-**os**-i-tee) velocity is speed in a particular direction

velvet *noun* velvet is a soft material with short furry fibres on one side
velvety *adjective* soft, like velvet

vendetta *noun* a long-lasting quarrel or feud

Vendetta is an Italian word, which comes from a Latin word *vindicta* meaning 'vengeance'.

vending machine *noun* a machine that you can buy food, drinks or other things from

venerable *adjective* worthy of respect or honour because of being so old

venetian blind *noun* a blind for a window, made of thin horizontal slats which you can move to control the amount of light that comes through

vengeance *noun* vengeance is harming or punishing someone because they have done harm to you **vengeful** *adjective* a vengeful person wants to punish someone who has harmed them

venison *noun* venison is the meat from a deer

Venn diagram *noun* (in mathematics) a diagram using circles to show how sets of things relate to one another

venom *noun* venom is the poison of snakes **venomous** *adjective* poisonous

vent *noun* an opening in something, especially to let out smoke or gas

ventilate *verb* to ventilate a place is to let fresh air come into it and move around it **ventilation** *noun* letting fresh air move freely around a place **ventilator** *noun* a machine that breathes for someone in hospital

ventriloquist *noun* (ven-**tril**-o-kwist) an entertainer who speaks without moving their lips, so that it looks as though a dummy is speaking **ventriloquism** *noun* what a ventriloquist does

venture *noun* something new that you decide to do that is risky or daring
venture *verb* to venture somewhere is to go there even though you know it might be difficult or dangerous

veranda *noun* (ver-**an**-da) an open terrace with a roof along the outside of a house

verb *noun* a word that shows what someone or something is doing, such as *be, go, sing, take*

verbal *adjective* spoken rather than written • *We had a verbal agreement.* **verbally** *adverb* in spoken words, not in writing

verdict *noun* the decision reached by a judge or jury about whether someone is guilty of a crime

verge *noun* a strip of grass beside a road or path **on the verge of** about to do something • *She was on the verge of leaving.*

verify *verb* verifies, verifying, verified to verify something is to find or show whether it is true or correct **verification** *noun* verification is verifying something

vermin *noun* vermin are animals or insects that damage crops or food or carry disease, such as rats and fleas

verruca *noun* (ver-**oo**-ka) a kind of wart on the sole of your foot

versatile *adjective* (**ver**-sa-tyl) able to do or be used for many different things **versatility** *noun* versatility is being able to do or be used for many different things

verse *noun* 1. verse is writing in the form of poetry 2. a verse is a group of lines in a poem or song 3. a verse is also each of the short numbered sections of a chapter in the Bible

version *noun* 1. someone's account of something that has happened • *His version of the accident is different from mine.* 2. a different form of a thing • *I don't like their version of the song.*

versus *preposition* against or competing with, especially in sport • *The final will be Brazil versus Germany.*

vertebra *noun* vertebrae (**ver**-ti-bra) each of the bones that form your backbone

vertebrate *noun* (**ver**-ti-brit) an animal with a backbone

vertical *adjective* going directly upwards, at right angles to something level or horizontal **vertically** *adverb* in a vertical direction

vertigo *noun* vertigo is feeling dizzy because you are high up

very *adverb* to a great amount; extremely • *It is very cold.*
very *adjective* 1. exact or actual • *That's the very thing we need!* 2. extreme • *We've reached the very end.*

Vesak *noun* (**ves**-ak) Vesak is an important festival of Buddhism, held in April to May

vessel *noun* 1. a boat or ship 2. a container for liquids 3. a tube inside an animal or plant, carrying blood or some other liquid

vest *noun* a piece of underwear you wear on the top half of your body

vet *noun* a person trained to treat sick animals

veteran *noun* 1. a person with long experience of something 2. a soldier who has returned from a war

veterinary *adjective* (**vet**-rin-ree) to do with the medical treatment of animals

veto *noun* vetoes (**vee**-toh) 1. a refusal to let something happen 2. the right to stop something from happening
veto *verb* vetoes, vetoing, vetoed to veto something is to refuse to let it happen

vex *verb* to vex someone is to annoy or worry them **vexation** *noun* vexation is vexing someone

via *preposition* (**vy**-a) going through; stopping at • *This train goes from Edinburgh to London via York.*

viaduct *noun* (**vy**-a-dukt) a long bridge with many arches, carrying a road or railway over low ground

vibrate *verb* to vibrate is to move quickly from side to side and with small movements **vibration** *noun* when something vibrates

vicar *noun* a minister of the Church of England who is in charge of a parish

vicarage *noun* the house of a vicar

vice[1] *noun* **1.** a vice is a bad or evil habit **2.** vice is evil or wickedness

vice[2] *noun* a device with jaws for holding something tightly in place while you work on it

vice-president *noun* a deputy to a president

vice versa *adverb* (vys-**ver**-sa) the other way round • *'We need them and vice versa' means 'We need them and they need us'.*

vicinity *noun* vicinities the area near or surrounding a particular place • *Are there any parks in the vicinity?*

vicious *adjective* (**vish**-us) **1.** cruel and aggressive **2.** severe or violent viciously *adverb* viciousness *noun*

victim *noun* **1.** a person who suffers from something • *He is a polio victim.* **2.** someone who is killed, injured or robbed • *The murderer lay in wait for his victim.*

victor *noun* the winner of a battle or contest

victory *noun* victories winning a battle or contest or game victorious *adjective* someone is victorious when they win a battle or contest or game

video *noun* videos **1.** a system of recording moving pictures and sound, especially as a digital file • *The accident was captured on video.* **2.** a short film or recording that you can watch on a computer or mobile phone, especially over the Internet **3.** a copy of a film or television programme that has been recorded
video *verb* videoes, videoing, videoed to record something on video

> The word **video** comes from a Latin word *videre* meaning 'to see'. The -o ending is based on *audio* in *audiovisual*.

view *noun* **1.** what you can see from one place • *There's a fine view from the top of the hill.* **2.** someone's opinion • *She has strong views about smoking.* on view shown for people to see
view *verb* **1.** to view something is to look at it carefully **2.** to view something or someone in a certain way is to think about them in that way • *They seemed to view us with suspicion.*

viewer *noun* someone who watches something, especially a television programme

vigilant *adjective* (**vij**-i-lant) someone is vigilant when they are watching carefully for something vigilantly *adverb* vigilance *noun* vigilance is watching carefully for something

vigorous *adjective* full of strength and energy vigorously *adverb*

vigour *noun* vigour is strength and energy

Viking *noun* a Scandinavian pirate or trader in the 8th to 10th centuries

vile *adjective* disgusting or bad • *What a vile smell.*

villa *noun* a house, especially a large one in its own grounds or one used for holidays abroad

village *noun* a group of houses and other buildings in the country, smaller than a town villager *noun* someone who lives in a village

villain *noun* a wicked person or criminal villainous *adjective* wicked villainy *noun* wicked behaviour

vine *noun* a plant on which grapes grow

vinegar *noun* vinegar is a sour liquid used to flavour food

vineyard *noun* (**vin**-yard) an area of land where vines are grown to produce grapes for making wine

vintage *noun* the wine made in a particular year

vinyl *noun* (**vy**-nil) vinyl is a kind of plastic

viola *noun* (vee-**oh**-la) a stringed instrument rather like a violin but slightly larger and with a lower pitch

violence *noun* **1.** violence is when someone uses force to hurt or kill people **2.** violence is also force that damages things • *We weren't prepared for the violence of the storm.* violent *adjective* using violence; strong and forceful violently *adverb* with violence or great force

violet *noun* **1.** a bluish-purple colour **2.** a small plant that usually has purple flowers

violin *noun* a musical instrument with four strings, played with a bow **violinist** *noun* someone who plays a violin

VIP short for *very important person*

viper *noun* a small poisonous snake

virtual *adjective* **1.** almost the same as the real thing • *His silence was a virtual admission of guilt.* **2.** using virtual reality • *Click here to go on a virtual tour of the gallery.*

virtually *adverb* in effect; nearly • *She comes here so often she's virtually a member of the family.*

virtual reality *noun* virtual reality is an image or environment created by a computer that make you feel as if you are in a place

virtue *noun* **1.** a virtue is a good quality in a person's character • *Honesty is a virtue.* **2.** virtue is moral goodness **virtuous** *adjective* behaving in a very good way

virus *noun* (**vy**-rus) **1.** a microscopic creature that can cause disease **2.** a disease caused by a virus **3.** a hidden set of instructions in a computer program that is designed to destroy data

visa *noun* an official mark put on someone's passport to show that the person has permission to enter a country

visibility *noun* visibility is how far you can see clearly • *Visibility is down to 20 metres.*

visible *adjective* able to be seen • *The ship was visible on the horizon.*

vision *noun* **1.** vision is the ability to see **2.** a vision is something that you see or imagine, especially in a dream **3.** vision is also imagination and understanding • *They need a leader with vision.*

visit *verb* to visit a place or person is to go to see them or stay there

visit *noun* a short stay at a place or with a person

visitor *noun* someone who is visiting or staying at a place

visor *noun* (**vy**-zer) the clear part of a helmet that closes over the face

visual *adjective* to do with seeing; used for seeing **visually** *adverb* in a way that is connected with your ability to see

visual display unit *noun* a screen on which a computer displays information; a monitor

vital *adjective* **1.** extremely important; essential • *It is vital that we get there on time.* **2.** connected with life; needed in order to live **vitally** *adverb*

vitality *noun* vitality is liveliness or energy

vitamin *noun* each of several substances which are present in some foods and which you need to stay healthy

vivid *adjective* bright and clear • *The colours are very vivid.* • *She gave a vivid description of the storm.* **vividly** *adverb* **vividness** *noun*

vixen *noun* a female fox

vocabulary *noun* **vocabularies** **1.** the vocabulary of a language is all the words used in it **2.** a person's vocabulary is the words that they know and use

vocal *adjective* to do with the voice; using your voice

vocation *noun* a job or activity that you feel strongly you want to do

voice *noun* **1.** the sound you make when you speak or sing **2.** the ability to speak or sing • *She has lost her voice.*

volcano *noun* **volcanoes** a mountain with a hole at the top formed by molten lava which has burst through the earth's crust **volcanic** *adjective* caused or produced by a volcano

The word **volcano** is Italian and comes from Vulcan, the name of the Roman god of fire.

vole *noun* a small animal rather like a rat

volley *noun* volleys **1.** a number of bullets or shells fired at the same time **2.** in ball games, hitting or kicking the ball back before it touches the ground

volleyball *noun* volleyball is a game in which two teams hit a large ball to and fro over a net with their hands

volt *noun* a unit for measuring the force of an electric current

voltage *noun* voltage is electric force measured in volts

volume *noun* **1.** the amount of space filled by something **2.** the strength or power of sound • *Turn down the volume!* **3.** an amount • *The volume of traffic has increased.* **4.** a book, especially one of a set

voluntary *adjective* done or doing something because you want to, not for pay **voluntarily** *adverb* because you want to

volunteer *verb* **1.** to volunteer is to offer to do something that you do not have to do **2.** to volunteer information or time is to provide it willingly without being asked for it
volunteer *noun* someone who volunteers to do something

vomit *verb* to vomit is to bring food back from the stomach through your mouth

vote *verb* **1.** to vote for someone or something is to show which you prefer by putting up your hand or making a mark on a piece of paper **2.** to vote to do something is to say that you want to do it • *I vote we go away this weekend.*
vote *noun* **1.** a way of choosing someone or something by getting people to put up their hand or make a mark on a piece of paper **2.** a choice you make by voting **3.** the right to vote

voter *noun* someone who votes, especially in an election

voucher *noun* a piece of paper showing that you are allowed to pay less for something or that you can get something in exchange

vow *verb* to vow is to make a solemn promise to do something
vow *noun* a solemn promise

vowel *noun* any of the letters a, e, i, o, u and sometimes y

voyage *noun* a long journey by ship or in a spacecraft

vulgar *adjective* without good manners or good taste

vulgar fraction *noun* a fraction shown by numbers above and below a line (such as ½ and ⅞), not a decimal fraction

vulnerable *adjective* able to be harmed or attacked easily

vulture *noun* a large bird that eats the flesh of dead animals

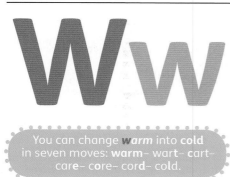

You can change **warm** into **cold** in seven moves: **warm**– war**t**– **c**art– car**e**– co**r**e– cor**d**– col**d**.

wad noun a pad or bundle of soft material or pieces of paper

waddle verb to waddle is to walk with short steps, rocking from side to side, like a duck

wade verb to wade through water or mud is to walk through it

wafer noun a thin kind of biscuit

waffle noun 1. a waffle is a crisp square pancake with a pattern of squares on it 2. waffle is talking for a long time without saying anything important or interesting
waffle verb to talk or write for a long time without saying anything important or interesting

wag verb wagging, wagged 1. a dog wags its tail when it moves it quickly from side to side because it is happy or excited 2. you wag your finger when you move it up and down or from side to side
wag noun a wagging movement

wage noun or **wages** plural noun the money paid to someone for the job they do
wage verb to wage a war or campaign is to fight it

wager noun (**way**-jer) a bet
wager verb to wager someone is to make a bet with them

wagon noun 1. a cart with four wheels, pulled by a horse or ox 2. an open railway truck

wail verb to wail is to make a long sad cry
wail noun a sound of wailing

waist noun the narrow part in the middle of your body

waistcoat noun a close-fitting jacket without sleeves, worn over a shirt and under a jacket

wait verb 1. to wait or to wait for someone or something, is to stay in a place or situation until something happens 2. to wait is also to be a waiter
wait noun a time spent waiting

waiter noun a man who serves people with food in a restaurant

waitress noun a woman who serves people with food in a restaurant

wake[1] verb waking, woke, woken 1. you wake or wake up, when you stop sleeping 2. to wake someone or wake them up, is to make them stop sleeping • You have woken the baby.

wake[2] noun the trail left on the water by a ship or boat

walk verb to walk is to move along on your feet at an ordinary speed
walk noun 1. a journey on foot 2. the way that someone walks • He has a funny walk. 3. a path or route for walking • There are some lovely walks near here.

walker noun someone who goes for a walk, especially a long one

walkie-talkie noun a small portable radio transmitter and receiver

walking stick noun a stick a person carries or uses as a support while walking

wall noun 1. a structure built of brick or stone and forming one of the sides of a building or room or going round a space 2. the outer surface of something, such as the stomach
wall verb to wall something or wall it in, is to surround or enclose it with a wall

wallaby noun wallabies (**wol**-a-bee) a kind of small kangaroo

wallet noun a small flat folding case for holding paper money, credit cards and small documents

wallow verb 1. to wallow is to roll about in water or mud 2. to wallow in, for example, sadness is seem to enjoy being sad

wallpaper noun wallpaper is paper used to cover the walls of rooms

walnut *noun* a kind of nut with a wrinkled surface

walrus *noun* a large Arctic sea animal that looks like a large seal and has two long tusks

waltz *noun* a dance with three beats to a bar

waltz *verb* to waltz is to dance a waltz

wand *noun* a short thin rod used by a magician, wizard or fairy

wander *verb* 1. to wander is to go about without trying to reach a particular place 2. to wander or wander off, is to stray or get lost • *Don't let the sheep wander.*
wanderer *noun* someone who keeps travelling from place to place

wane *verb* 1. the moon wanes when its bright area gets gradually smaller 2. to wane is to become less • *His popularity was waning.*

want *verb* 1. to want something is to feel that you would like to have it or do it 2. to want something is also to need it • *Your hair wants cutting.*

want *noun* 1. a want is a wish to have something 2. want of something is a lack of it • *Children are dying for want of clean water.*

wanted *adjective* someone is wanted when they are being looked for by the police as a suspected criminal

war *noun* 1. war is fighting between nations or armies; a war is a period of fighting 2. a war is also a serious struggle or effort against an evil such as crime or disease

warble *verb* to warble is to sing gently, the way some birds do

ward *noun* 1. a long room with beds for patients in a hospital 2. a child looked after by a guardian 3. an area of a town or city represented by a councillor

ward *verb* to ward something off is to keep it away

warden *noun* an official in charge of a hostel, college or other building

warder *noun* an official who guards prisoners in a prison

wardrobe *noun* 1. a cupboard to hang your clothes in 2. a stock of clothes or costumes

warehouse *noun* a large building where goods are stored

wares *plural noun* goods offered for sale

warfare *noun* warfare is fighting or waging war

warhead *noun* the part of a missile that explodes

warlike *adjective* warlike people are fond of fighting or are likely to start a war

warm *adjective* 1. fairly hot; not cold or cool 2. warm clothes are thick and keep you warm 3. a warm person is enthusiastic or friendly • *They gave us a warm welcome.*
warmly *adverb*

warm *verb* 1. to warm something or someone is to make them warm 2. to warm or warm up, is to become warm to warm up is to do gentle exercises before playing sport

warm-blooded *adjective* having blood that does not change temperature according to the surroundings

warmth *noun* 1. warmth is being warm or keeping warm • *The cattle huddled together for warmth.* 2. warmth is also being friendly and enthusiastic • *She was touched by the warmth of their welcome.*

warn *verb* to warn someone is to tell them about a danger or difficulty that might affect them

warning *noun* something that tells someone about a danger

warp *verb* (worp) to warp or be warped, is to become bent or twisted out of shape because of dampness or heat

warrant *noun* a document that gives the police the right to arrest someone or search a place

warren *noun* a piece of ground where there are many rabbit burrows

warrior *noun* someone who fights in battles

warship *noun* a ship designed for use in war

wart *noun* a small hard lump on your skin

wary *adjective* warier, wariest cautious and careful warily *adverb* cautiously wariness *noun*

wash *verb* 1. to wash something is to clean it with water 2. you wash when you clean yourself with water 3. to wash is to flow over or against something • *Waves washed over* the beach. **4.** to be washed somewhere is to be carried along by the force of moving water • *The boxes were washed overboard.* to wash up is to wash the dishes and cutlery after a meal

wash *noun* **1.** the action of washing **2.** the disturbed water behind a moving ship **3.** a thin coating of colour or paint

washer *noun* a small ring of metal or rubber placed between two surfaces so that they fit tightly together

washing *noun* washing is clothes that need to be washed or have been washed

washing-up *noun* washing the dishes and cutlery after a meal; the things that need to be washed

wasp *noun* a stinging insect with black and yellow stripes across its body

wastage *noun* wastage is losing something by waste

waste *verb* **1.** to waste something is to use more of it than you need to or to use it without getting much value from it **2.** to waste something is also to fail to use it • *You are wasting a good opportunity.* to waste away is to become thinner and weaker

waste *adjective* **1.** left over or thrown away because it is not wanted • *waste paper* **2.** not used or usable • *waste land*

waste *noun* **1.** a waste is wasting something or not using it well • *It's a waste of time.* **2.** waste is things that are not wanted or used **3.** a waste is also an area of desert or frozen land

wasteful *adjective* wasting things or not using them well **wastefully** *adverb*

watch *verb* **1.** to watch someone or something is to look at them for some time **2.** to watch or watch out, is to be on guard or ready for something to happen **3.** to watch something is also to take care of it to watch out is to be careful about something **watcher** *noun* someone who watches something

watch *noun* **1.** a device like a small clock, usually worn on a person's wrist **2.** a period of being on guard or on duty

watchdog *noun* a dog kept to guard buildings

watchful *adjective* alert and watching carefully **watchfulness** *noun*

water *noun* **1.** water is a transparent colourless liquid that falls as rain and is found in seas, rivers and lakes **2.** a water is a sea or lake

water *verb* **1.** to water a plant is to sprinkle water over it **2.** to water an animal is to give it water to drink **3.** your eyes or mouth water when they produce tears or saliva to water something down is to dilute it or make it weaker

watercolour *noun* **1.** a paint that can be mixed with water **2.** a painting done with this kind of paint

waterfall *noun* a place where a river or stream flows over a cliff or large rock

watering can *noun* a container with a long spout, for watering plants

waterlogged *adjective* waterlogged ground is so wet it cannot soak up any more water

watermark *noun* a faint design in some types of paper, which you can see if you hold it up to the light

waterproof *adjective* able to keep water out

water-skiing *noun* the sport of moving over the surface of water on flat boards (**water-skis**) while being pulled along by a boat

watertight *adjective* made so that water cannot get into it

waterway *noun* a river or canal that ships or boats can travel on

waterworks *noun* a place with pumping machinery for supplying water to a district

watery *adjective* **1.** like water • *The paint is too watery.* **2.** full of water • *You have watery eyes.*

watt *noun* a unit of electric power

wave *verb* **1.** to wave is to move your hand from side to side, usually to say hello or goodbye **2.** you wave something or it waves, when it moves from side to side or up and down • *Flags were waving in the wind.*

wave *noun* **1.** a moving ridge on the surface of water, especially on the sea **2.** a curling piece of hair **3.** *(in science)* one of the vibrating movements in which sound and light and electricity travel **4.** the action of waving your hand **5.** a sudden increase in an emotion or activity • *She felt a wave of anger.*

wavelength *noun* the size of a sound wave or electric wave

waver *verb* to waver is to hesitate or be uncertain • *They wavered between two choices.*

wavy *adjective* **wavier, waviest** full of waves or curves

wax[1] *noun* wax is a soft substance that melts easily, used for making candles, crayons and polish **waxy** *adjective* looking or feeling like wax

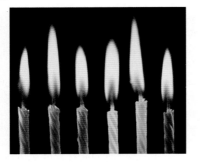

wax[1] *verb* to wax something is to cover it with wax

wax[2] *verb* the moon waxes when its bright area gets gradually larger

waxwork *noun* a full-sized wax model of a person

way *noun* **1.** how something is done; a method or manner **2.** the way to a place is how you get there **3.** a distance • *Is it a long way?* **4.** a respect • *It's a good idea in some ways.* **5.** a condition or state • *Things are in a bad way.* **to get your own way** is to make people let you have what you want **in the way** blocking your path so that you can't move or see properly

we *pronoun* a word used by someone to mean 'I and someone else' or 'I and others'

weak *adjective* **1.** without much strength or energy **2.** easy to break, bend or defeat **3.** poor at doing something **weakly** *adverb* **weakness** *noun* weakness is being weak; a weakness is a fault you have or something you don't do well

weaken *verb* **1.** to weaken something is to make it weaker **2.** to weaken is to become weaker

weakling *noun* a weak person

wealth *noun* **1.** wealth is a lot of money or property **2.** a wealth of something is a lot of it

wealthy *adjective* **wealthier, wealthiest** someone is wealthy when they have a lot of money or property

weapon *noun* something used to harm or kill people in a battle or fight

wear *verb* **wearing, wore, worn** **1.** to wear something is to be dressed in it **2.** to wear something is to damage it by rubbing or using it; to wear is to become damaged like this • *The carpet has worn thin.* **3.** to last • *This cloth wears well.* **to wear off** is to become less strong or intense **to wear out** is to become weak or useless **to wear someone out** is to make them very tired

wear *noun* **1.** wear is clothes • *Where can I find children's wear?* **2.** wear is gradual damage done by rubbing or using something

weary *adjective* **wearier, weariest** very tired **wearily** *adverb* **weariness** *noun*

weasel *noun* a small fierce animal with a slender body

weather *noun* weather is the rain, snow, wind, sunshine and temperature at a particular time or place **to be under the weather** is to feel ill

weather *verb* **1.** to weather is to become worn because of being exposed to the weather **2.** to weather something is to make it suffer the effects of the weather • *The wind and rain have weathered the cliffs.* **3.** you weather a difficulty when you come through it successfully

weathercock *noun* or **weathervane** a pointer that turns in the wind and shows which way the wind is blowing

weave *verb* **weaving, wove, woven** **1.** to weave material or baskets is to make them by crossing threads or strips over and under each other **2.** to weave is to twist and turn • *The bike was weaving in and out of traffic.* **weaver** *noun* someone who weaves material

web *noun* **1.** a net of thin sticky threads that spiders spin to catch insects **2.** a computer network, especially the Internet

webbed or **web-footed** *adjective* webbed feet have toes joined by pieces of skin, as ducks' feet do

website *noun* a place on the Internet where you can get information

wed *verb* wedding, wedded or wed to wed someone is to marry them

wedding *noun* the ceremony when two people get married

wedge *noun* a piece of something that is thick at one end and thin at the other

wedge *verb* to wedge something is to hold it in place with a wedge

Wednesday *noun* the fourth day of the week

weed *noun* a wild plant that grows where it is not wanted

weed *verb* to weed the ground is to remove weeds from it

weedy *adjective* weedier, weediest 1. full of weeds 2. thin and weak

week *noun* 1. a period of seven days, especially from Sunday to the following Saturday 2. the part of the week that doesn't include the weekend

weekday *noun* any day except Saturday and Sunday

weekend *noun* Saturday and Sunday

weekly *adjective, adverb* every week

weep *verb* weeping, wept to weep is to cry

weigh *verb* 1. to weigh something is to find out how heavy it is 2. to weigh a certain amount is to have that as its weight • *How much do you weigh?* to weigh anchor is to raise the anchor and start a voyage to weigh something down is to hold it down with something heavy to weigh something up is to think about it carefully before deciding what to do

weight *noun* 1. weight is the measure of how heavy someone or something is 2. a weight is a heavy piece of metal that people lift to make their muscles bigger and stronger weightless *adjective* astronauts are weightless when they float around because there is no gravity

weightlifting *noun* weightlifting is the sport or exercise of lifting heavy weights

weighty *adjective* weightier, weightiest 1. important or serious • *These are weighty matters.* 2. heavy

weir *noun* (weer) a small dam across a river or canal to control the flow of water

weird *adjective* (weerd) very strange or unnatural weirdly *adverb* weirdness *noun*

welcome *adjective* 1. that you are glad to get or see • *This is a welcome surprise.* 2. allowed or free to do or take something • *You are welcome to use my bicycle.*
welcome *verb* to welcome someone or something is to show that you are pleased when they arrive
welcome *noun* a kind or friendly greeting or reception

weld *verb* to weld pieces of metal or plastic together is to join them by using heat or pressure welder *noun* someone who welds things together

welfare *noun* welfare is people's health, happiness and comfort

well¹ *noun* a deep hole dug or drilled to get water or oil out of the ground

well² *adverb* better, best 1. in a good or successful way • *He can play the piano quite well now.* 2. thoroughly • *Wash your hands well.* 3. actually; probably • *It may well be our last chance.* as well also to be well off is to be fairly rich or fortunate
well² *adjective* 1. in good health • *She is not well.* 2. good or satisfactory • *All is well.*

well-being *noun* well-being is health or happiness

wellington boots or **wellingtons** *plural noun* rubber or plastic waterproof boots

> The word **wellingtons** comes from the name of the Duke of Wellington, the British statesman and soldier who defeated Napoleon at the Battle of Waterloo in 1815.

well-known *adjective* known to many people; famous

werewolf *noun* in stories, a person who changes into a wolf

west *noun* **1.** the direction where the sun sets **2.** the part of a country or city that is in this direction

west *adjective, adverb* **1.** towards the west or in the west **2.** coming from the west • *a west wind blowing*

western *adjective* from or to do with the west

western *noun* a film or story about American cowboys

westward or **westwards** *adjective, adverb* towards the west

wet *adjective* wetter, wettest **1.** covered or soaked in water or other liquid **2.** not yet set or dry • *Watch out for wet paint.* **3.** rainy • *It's been wet here all day.* **wetness** *noun*

wet *verb* wetting, wetted to wet something is to make it wet

wet suit *noun* a tight-fitting piece of rubber clothing worn by divers and surfers to keep them warm and dry

whack *verb* to whack someone or something is to hit them hard

whack *noun* a hard hit or blow

whale *noun* a very large sea animal

whaling *noun* whaling is hunting whales

wharf *noun* wharves or wharfs (worf) a quay where ships are loaded or unloaded

what *determiner* **1.** used to ask questions about something • *What kind of bike have you got?* **2.** used to say how strange or great a person or thing is • *What a fool you are!*

what *pronoun* the thing or things that have been said or described • *What did you say?* • *This is what you must do.*

whatever *pronoun* **1.** anything or everything • *Do whatever you like.* **2.** no matter what • *I'll be there whatever happens.*

whatever *determiner* of any kind or amount • *Get whatever help you can.*

wheat *noun* wheat is a cereal plant from which flour is made

wheel *noun* a round device that turns on an axle passing through its centre

wheel *verb* **1.** to wheel a bicycle or cart is to push it along on its wheels **2.** to wheel is to move in a curve or circle • *The column of soldiers wheeled to the right.*

wheelbarrow *noun* a small cart with one wheel at the front and two handles at the back

wheelchair *noun* a chair on wheels for a person who cannot walk

wheeze *verb* to wheeze is to make a whistling or gasping noise as you breathe

whelk *noun* a shellfish that looks like a snail

when *adverb* at what time • *When can you come to tea?*

when *conjunction* **1.** at the time that • *The bird flew away when I moved.* **2.** because; considering that • *Why are you wearing a coat when it's so hot?*

whenever *conjunction* at any time; every time • *Whenever I see him, he's smiling.*

where *adverb, conjunction* **1.** in or to what place • *Where have you put the glue?* **2.** in or to that place • *Leave it where it is.*

whereabouts *adverb* roughly where; in what area • *Whereabouts is Timbuktu?*

whereabouts *noun* the place where something is • *Have you any idea of her whereabouts?*

whereas *conjunction* but on the other hand • *Some people like sailing, whereas others hate it.*

whereupon *adverb* after that; and then

wherever *adverb, conjunction* in or to whatever place; no matter where

whether *conjunction* used to introduce more than one possibility • *I don't know whether they are here or not.*

whey *noun* (way) whey is the watery liquid left when milk forms curds

which *determiner* what particular • *Which way did he go?*

which *pronoun* **1.** what person or thing • *Which is your desk?* **2.** the person or thing just mentioned • *Here's my book, which you asked me to bring.*

whichever *determiner, pronoun* that or those which; any which • *Choose whichever brand you like.* • *Lemonade or coke? You can have whichever you prefer.*

whiff *noun* a slight smell of something

while *conjunction* **1.** during the time that; as long as • *She was singing while she worked.* **2.** but; although • *She is fair, while her sister is dark.*

while *noun* a period of time • *We have waited all this while.*

while *verb* to while away time is to pass it doing something leisurely

whilst *conjunction* while

whim *noun* a sudden desire to do or have something

whimper *verb* to whimper is to cry with a low trembling voice

whimper *noun* a sound of whimpering

whine *verb* **1.** to whine is to make a long high piercing sound **2.** to whine is also to complain in an annoying way

whine *noun* a whining sound

whip *noun* a cord or strip of leather fixed to a handle and used for hitting people or animals

whip *verb* whipping, whipped **1.** to whip a person or animal is to beat them with a whip **2.** to whip cream is to beat it until it becomes thick and frothy

whirl *verb* you whirl something round or it whirls, when it turns or spins very quickly

whirl *noun* when something turns or spins very quickly

whirlpool *noun* a strong current of water going round in a circle and pulling things towards it

whirlwind *noun* a very strong wind that whirls around or blows in a spiral

whirr *verb* to whirr is to make a continuous buzzing sound

whirr *noun* a continuous buzzing sound

whisk *verb* **1.** to whisk cream or eggs is to beat them until they are thick or frothy **2.** to whisk something somewhere is to move it there very quickly • *A waiter whisked away my plate.*

whisk *noun* **1.** a device for whisking eggs or cream **2.** a whisking movement

whisker *noun* **1.** whiskers are the long stiff hairs on the face of a cat or other animal **2.** whiskers are also the hair growing on a man's face

whisky *noun* whiskies a strong alcoholic drink

whisper *verb* to whisper is to speak very softly or secretly

whisper *noun* a very soft voice or sound

whistle *verb* **1.** you whistle when you make a shrill or musical sound by blowing through your lips **2.** something whistles when it makes a shrill sound • *The kettle was whistling away.*

whistle *noun* **1.** a whistling sound **2.** a device that makes a shrill sound when you blow into it

white *adjective* **1.** of the very lightest colour, like snow or milk **2.** having light-coloured skin **whiteness** *noun*

white *noun* **1.** a white colour **2.** the substance round the yolk of an egg, which turns white when it is cooked

whitewash *noun* whitewash is a white liquid made from lime and chalk and painted on walls and ceilings

whitewash *verb* to whitewash a wall or ceiling is to coat it with whitewash

whizz *verb* whizzes, whizzing, whizzed **1**. to whizz is to move very quickly **2**. to whizz is also to sound like something rushing through the air

who *pronoun* **1**. which person or people • *Who threw that?* **2**. the person or people spoken about • *These are the boys who did it.*

whoever *pronoun* any person who • *Whoever comes is welcome.*

whole *adjective* all of something; without anything missing • *Could you eat a whole pizza?*

whole *noun* a complete thing; all the parts of something on the whole considering everything; mainly

wholefood *noun* wholefood is food that has been produced without using artificial fertilizers

wholemeal *adjective* wholemeal flour or bread is made from the whole grain of wheat

whole number *noun* a number without a fraction

wholesale *adjective, adverb* **1**. sold in large quantities to be sold again by others **2**. on a large scale; including everybody or everything • *There has been wholesale destruction.*

wholesome *adjective* healthy and good for you

wholly *adverb* completely or entirely • *He's not wholly to blame.*

whom *pronoun* a word used for **who** when it is the object of a verb or comes after a preposition, as in *the boy whom I saw* or *the boy to whom I spoke*

whooping cough *noun* (**hoop**-ing-kof) whooping cough is an illness that makes you cough and gasp

who's short for *who has* or *who is*

whose *adjective, pronoun* **1**. belonging to what person • *Whose bike is that?* **2**. of which; of whom • *The girl whose party we went to.*

why *adverb* for what reason or purpose • *Why have you come?*

wick *noun* the string that goes through the middle of a candle, which you light to give a flame

wicked *adjective* **1**. very bad or cruel; doing things that are wrong **2**. mischievous • *He gave a wicked smile.* wickedly *adverb* wickedness *noun* doing bad things

wicker or **wickerwork** *noun* wicker or wickerwork is reeds or canes woven together to make baskets and furniture

wicket *noun* in cricket, each set of three stumps with two bails on top of them

wicketkeeper *noun* the fielder in cricket who stands behind the batsman's wicket

wide *adjective* **1**. measuring a lot from one side to the other • *The river was wide.* **2**. from one side to the other • *The room is 4 metres wide.* **3**. covering a large range • *She has a wide knowledge of birds.*

wide *adverb* **1**. you are wide awake when you are fully awake **2**. to open or spread something wide is to open or spread it as far as possible **3**. far from the target • *The shot went wide.*

widely *adverb* commonly; among many people • *They are widely admired.*

widen *verb* to widen something is to make it wider; to widen is to become wider

widespread *adjective* existing or found in many places; common

widow *noun* a woman whose husband has died

widower *noun* a man whose wife has died

width *noun* the width of something is how much it measures from one side to the other

wield *verb* (weeld) to wield a weapon or tool is to hold it and use it

wife *noun* wives the woman that a man is married to

> The word **wife** comes from an Anglo-Saxon word *wif* meaning 'woman'.

wig *noun* a covering of false hair worn on the head

wiggle *verb* to wiggle something is to move it from side to side

wiggle *noun* a wiggling movement

wigwam *noun* the tent of a Native American

wild *adjective* **1.** wild animals and plants live or grow in their natural state and are not looked after by people **2.** not controlled; violent or angry • *His behaviour became more and more wild.* • *She went wild when she saw the mess.* **3.** very foolish or unreasonable • *They do have wild ideas.* **wildly** *adverb* in a way that is not controlled • *My heart was beating wildly.*

wild *noun* animals live in the wild when they live in their natural environment

wilderness *noun* an area of natural country with no buildings or people

wildlife *noun* wildlife is wild animals in their natural setting

wilful *adjective* **1.** someone is wilful when they are determined to do exactly what they want **2.** something is wilful when it is done deliberately • *This is wilful disobedience.* **wilfully** *adverb* **wilfulness** *noun*

will¹ *verb* past tense **would** used to refer to the future • *I will be there at 12 o'clock.* • *He said he would come later.*

will² *noun* **1.** will is the power to use your mind to decide and control what you do **2.** someone's will is what they choose or want • *He was forced to write the letter against his will.* **3.** a will is a legal document saying what is to be done with someone's possessions after they die

willing *adjective* ready and happy to do what is wanted **willingly** *adverb* **willingness** *noun*

willow *noun* a tree with long thin branches, often growing near water

wilt *verb* a plant wilts when it loses freshness and droops

wily *adjective* **wilier, wiliest** crafty or cunning **wiliness** *noun*

win *verb* **winning, won 1.** to win a contest or game or battle is to do better than your opponents **2.** to win something is to get it by using effort or in a competition • *She won second prize.*

win *noun* a success or victory

wince *verb* to wince is to make a slight movement because you are in pain or embarrassed

winch *noun* a device for lifting or pulling things, using a rope or cable that goes round a wheel

winch *verb* to winch something is to lift it or pull it with a winch

wind¹ *noun* (rhymes with tinned) **1.** wind or a wind, is a current of air **2.** wind is gas in the stomach or intestines that makes you uncomfortable **3.** wind is also breath used for a purpose, such as running

wind² *verb* (rhymes with find) **1.** something like a road or river winds when it twists and turns • *The river winds down the valley.* **2.** to wind something is to wrap or twist it round something else • *She wound her scarf round her neck.* **3.** to wind or wind up, a watch or clock is to tighten its spring so that it works

windfall *noun* **1.** a fruit blown down from a tree **2.** a piece of unexpected good luck, especially a sum of money

wind instrument *noun* a musical instrument played by blowing, such as a flute or clarinet

windmill *noun* a mill with four long arms called *sails* which are turned by the wind

window *noun* **1.** an opening in a wall or roof with glass in it **2.** *(in computing)* an area on a computer screen used for a particular purpose

windpipe *noun* the tube through which air reaches your lungs

windscreen *noun* the window at the front of a motor vehicle

a
b
c
d
e
f
g
h
i
j
k
l
m
n
o
p
q
r
s
t
u
v
w
x
y
z

windsurfing *noun* windsurfing is surfing on a board with a sail fixed to it **windsurfer** *noun* someone who goes windsurfing

windy *adjective* **windier, windiest** with a lot of wind • *It's a windy day today.*

wine *noun* an alcoholic drink made from grapes or other plants

wing *noun* **1.** a bird's or insect's wings are the parts it uses for flying **2.** an aircraft's wings are the long flat parts that stick out from its sides **3.** a part of a building that is built at the side and is joined to the main part **4.** each side of a theatre stage, out of sight of the audience **5.** the part of a car's body above a wheel **6.** the wings of a sports field are the far left or right parts of it **on the wing** flying **to take wing** is to fly away **winged** *adjective* having wings • *winged insects*

wingspan *noun* the distance across the wings of a bird or aeroplane

wink *verb* you wink when you close and open one of your eyes quickly

wink *noun* **1.** when you close and open one of your eyes quickly **2.** a short period of sleep • *I didn't sleep a wink.*

winkle *noun* a shellfish that is used for food

winner *noun* a person who wins something

winnings *plural noun* the money someone wins in a game or by betting

winter *noun* the coldest season of the year, between autumn and spring **wintry** *adjective* cold, like winter

wintertime *noun* wintertime is the season of winter

wipe *verb* to wipe something is to rub it gently to dry it or clean it **to wipe something out** is to destroy it or cancel it • *He's wiped out his debt.*

wipe *noun* when you wipe something

wire *noun* a thin length of metal used to carry electric current or for making fences

wire *verb* to wire something or wire it up, is to connect it with wires to carry electricity

wireless *adjective* something that is wireless can send and receive signals without using wires

wireless *noun* (old use) a radio set

wiring *noun* wiring is the system of wires carrying electricity in a building or in a device

wiry *adjective* **wirier, wiriest 1.** a wiry person is lean and strong **2.** wiry hair is tough and stiff

wisdom *noun* wisdom is being wise

wisdom tooth *noun* **wisdom teeth** a tooth that may grow at the back of your jaw much later than the other teeth

wise *adjective* knowing or understanding many things and so able to make sensible decisions **wisely** *adverb* when it is the sensible thing to do • *He wisely decided to tell the truth.*

wish *verb* **1.** to wish something or wish to do something, is to think or say that you would like it **2.** to wish someone something is to say that you hope they will get it • *They wished us luck.*

wish *noun* **1.** something you want **2.** when you wish for something • *Make a wish.*

wishbone *noun* a forked bone from the breast of a chicken or other bird

wisp *noun* a thin piece or line of something light or fluffy, such as hair or smoke **wispy** *adjective* thin and fluffy

wistful *adjective* thinking sadly about something you can no longer have **wistfully** *adverb* **wistfulness** *noun*

wit *noun* **1.** wit is intelligence or cleverness **2.** wit is also a clever kind of humour **3.** a wit is a witty person **to keep your wits about you** is to stay alert

witch *noun* a woman who is believed to use magic

witchcraft *noun* witchcraft is using magic, especially to make bad things happen

with *preposition* there are many meanings, of which the most important are: **1.** having • *I saw a man with a wooden leg.* **2.** in the company of or accompanied by • *I came with a friend.* **3.** using • *Hit it with a hammer.* **4.** against • *They fought with each other.* **5.** because of • *He shook with laughter.*

withdraw *verb* **withdrawing, withdrew, withdrawn 1.** to withdraw something is to take it away or take it back • *She withdrew her offer.* **2.** to withdraw is to retreat or drop out of something • *The troops have withdrawn* *from the frontier. • His injury meant he had to withdraw from the race.* withdrawal *noun* when someone withdraws something or withdraws from a place

wither *verb* a plant withers when it shrivels and starts to die

withhold *verb* withholding, withheld to withhold something is to refuse to give it to someone • *He has withheld his permission.*

within *preposition, adverb* inside; not beyond something • *Is the top shelf within your reach?*

without *preposition* not having; free from • *It is difficult to live without money.*

withstand *verb* to withstand something is to resist it or put up with it successfully • *The bridge is designed to withstand high winds.*

witness *noun* 1. a person who sees something happen and can describe it 2. a person who gives evidence in a lawcourt

witty *adjective* wittier, wittiest clever and amusing wittily *adverb*

wizard *noun* a man who has magic powers wizardry *noun* the impressive things that a computer or other machine can do

wobble *verb* to wobble is to move unsteadily from side to side

wobble *noun* a wobbling movement wobbly *adjective* moving unsteadily from side to side

woe *noun* 1. someone's woes are their troubles and misfortunes 2. woe is great sorrow woeful *adjective* very sad; very bad or serious woefully *adverb*

wok *noun* a deep round-bottomed frying-pan used in Chinese cookery

wolf *noun* wolves a wild animal like a large dog

woman *noun* women a grown-up female human being

womb *noun* (woom) the part of a female's body where her baby develops before it is born

wonder *verb* to wonder about something is to be trying to decide about it or to be curious about it • *I wonder what we should do next.* • *I wonder what's for dinner.*

wonder *noun* 1. wonder is a feeling of surprise and admiration 2. a wonder is something that makes you feel surprised and admiring no wonder it is not surprising

wonderful *adjective* marvellous or excellent wonderfully *adverb* extremely; very well

won't short for *will not*

wood *noun* 1. wood is the substance that trees are made of 2. a wood is a lot of trees growing together

wooded *adjective* a wooded area is covered with growing trees

wooden *adjective* made of wood

woodland *noun* land covered with trees

woodlouse *noun* woodlice a small crawling creature with seven pairs of legs, living in rotten wood or damp soil

woodpecker *noun* a bird that taps tree trunks with its beak to find insects

woodwind *noun* in an orchestra, the woodwind is the wind instruments that are usually made of wood, such as the clarinet and oboe

woodwork *noun* 1. woodwork is making things with wood 2. woodwork is also things made out of wood

woodworm *noun* woodworm or woodworms the larva of a beetle that bores into wood

woody *adjective* woodier, woodiest 1. like wood or made of wood 2. full of trees

wool *noun* 1. wool is the thick soft hair of sheep or goats 2. wool is also thread or cloth made from this hair

woollen *adjective* made of wool

woolly *adjective* woollier, woolliest 1. made of wool or looking like wool 2. vague and not clear • *a woolly idea* woolliness *noun*

word *noun* 1. a set of sounds or letters that has a meaning and is written with a space before and after it 2. a brief talk with someone • *Can I have a word with you?* 3. your word is when you promise to do something • *He gave me his word.* 4. a command or signal to do something • *Run when I give the word.* 5. a message or piece of news • *We sent word that we had arrived safely.*

word *verb* to word something is to express it in words • *I'm not sure how to word this question.*

word class *noun* each of the groups (also called **parts of speech**) into which words can be divided in grammar: noun, adjective, pronoun, adverb, preposition, conjunction, verb, determiner

wording *noun* the wording of something is the words used to say it

word processing *noun* word processing is using a computer for producing and printing out documents **word processor** *noun* a computer used for word processing

work *verb* **1.** to work is to spend time doing something that needs effort or energy **2.** to work is also to have a job or be employed • *She works in a bank.* **3.** something works when it operates correctly or successfully • *Is the lift working?* **4.** to work something is to make it act or operate • *Can you work the lift?* **to work out** is to happen in a certain way • *Things have worked out well for her.* **to work something out** is to find the answer to it

work *noun* **1.** work is something that you have to do that needs effort or energy • *Digging is hard work.* **2.** a person's work is their job • *What work do you do?* **3.** at school, your work is something you write or produce • *Please get on with your work quietly.* **4.** a work is a piece of writing or music or painting • *The book has all the works of Shakespeare.* **to be at work** is to be working

worker *noun* **1.** someone who does work **2.** a bee or ant that does the work in a hive or colony but does not produce eggs

workman *noun* **workmen** a man who does manual work

workmanship *noun* workmanship is skill in making something

works *plural noun* **1.** the moving parts of a machine **2.** a factory or industrial site

worksheet *noun* a sheet of paper with a set of questions about a subject for students

workshop *noun* a place where things are made or mended

world *noun* **1.** the world is the earth with all its countries and peoples **2.** a world is a planet • *The film is about creatures from another world.* **3.** everything to do with a particular subject or activity • *He knows a lot about the world of sport.*

worldly *adjective* **worldlier, worldliest** to do with life on earth

worldwide *adjective, adverb* over the whole world

World Wide Web *noun* the system connecting computers all over the world, allowing people to find information on the Internet

worm *noun* a small thin wriggling animal without legs

worn *adjective* damaged because it has been rubbed or used so much **to be worn out** is to be very tired

worry *verb* **worries, worrying, worried 1.** to worry is to feel anxious or troubled about something **2.** to worry someone is to make them feel anxious or troubled about something **worried** *adjective* anxious or troubled about something **worrier** *noun* someone who worries a lot

worry *noun* **worries 1.** worry is worrying or being anxious **2.** a worry is something that makes you anxious

worse *adjective, adverb,* more bad or more badly; less good or less well

worsen *verb* **1.** to worsen is to become worse **2.** to worsen something is to make it worse

worship *verb* **worshipping, worshipped 1.** to worship God or a god is to give them praise or respect **2.** to worship someone is to adore them or have great respect for them **worshipper** *noun* someone who worships

worship *noun* worship is worshipping; religious ceremonies or services

worst *adjective, adverb* most bad or most badly; least good or least well

worth *adjective* **1.** having a certain value • *This stamp is worth £100.* **2.** deserving something; good or important enough for something • *That book is worth reading.*

worth *noun* a thing's worth is its value or usefulness

worthless *adjective* having no value; useless

worthwhile *adjective* important or good enough to be worth doing

worthy *adjective* worthier, worthiest deserving respect or support • *The sale is for a worthy cause.* to be worthy of something is to deserve or be good enough for something • *This charity is worthy of your support.* worthiness *noun* worthiness is being deserving or good enough for something

would *verb* **1.** past tense of the verb will[1] • *We said we would do it.* **2.** used in polite questions or requests • *Would you like some tea?*

wound *noun* (woond) a deep cut in a part of a person's or animal's body, caused by a weapon such as a knife or spear or by a bullet
wound *verb* to wound a person or animal is to give them a wound

wrap *verb* wrapping, wrapped to wrap something is to put paper or some other covering round it

wrapper *noun* a piece of paper or plastic that something is wrapped in

wrapping *noun* wrapping is material used to wrap something

wrath *noun* (rhymes with cloth) *(old-fashioned use)* anger

wreath *noun* (reeth) flowers and leaves and branches bound together to make a circle

wreck *verb* to wreck something is to damage or ruin it so badly that it cannot be used again
wreck *noun* a badly damaged ship or car

wreckage *noun* wreckage is the pieces of something that has been wrecked

wren *noun* a very small brown bird

wrench *verb* to wrench something is to pull or twist it suddenly or violently • *He wrenched the door open.*
wrench *noun* **1.** a wrenching movement **2.** a tool for gripping and turning bolts or nuts

wrestle *verb* **1.** to wrestle with someone is to fight them by grasping them and trying to throw them to the ground **2.** to wrestle with a problem or difficulty is to struggle to solve it wrestler *noun* someone who wrestles for sport wrestling *noun*

wretch *noun* someone who is unhappy, poor or disliked

wretched *adjective* (**rech**-id) **1.** poor and unhappy • *a wretched beggar* **2.** not satisfactory or pleasant • *This wretched car won't start.*

wriggle *verb* to wriggle is to twist and turn your body
wriggle *noun* a wriggling movement wriggly *adjective* wriggling a lot

wring *verb* wringing, wrung **1.** to wring something wet or to wring it out, is to squeeze or twist it to get the water out of it **2.** to wring something is to squeeze it violently • *I'll wring your neck!* wringing wet very wet; soaked

wrinkle *noun* **1.** wrinkles are the small lines and creases that appear in your skin as you get older **2.** a small crease or line on the surface of something
wrinkle *verb* something wrinkles when wrinkles appear in or on it wrinkled *adjective* wrinkled skin or clothing has wrinkles

wrist *noun* the joint that connects your hand to your arm

write *verb* writing, wrote, written **1.** to write words or signs is to put them on paper or some other surface so that people can read them **2.** to write a story or play or a piece of music is to be the author or composer of it **3.** to write to someone is to send them a letter to write something off is to think it is lost or useless

writer *noun* a person who writes; an author

writhe *verb* (ryth) to writhe is to twist your body about because you are in pain or discomfort

writing *noun* **1.** writing is something you write **2.** your writing is the way you write

wrong *adjective* **1.** not fair or morally right • *It is wrong to cheat.* **2.** incorrect • *That's the wrong answer.* **3.** not working properly • *There's something wrong with the engine.* wrongly *adverb* in a way that is unfair or incorrect
wrong *adverb* wrongly • *You guessed wrong.*
wrong *noun* something that is wrong to be in the wrong is to have done or said something wrong
wrong *verb* to wrong someone is to do wrong to them

wry *adjective* slightly mocking or sarcastic
• *He gave a wry smile.*

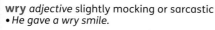

Xmas *noun (informal)* Christmas

X-ray *noun* a photograph of the inside of something, especially a part of the body, made by a kind of radiation that can pass through something solid

X-ray *verb* to X-ray something is to make an X-ray of it

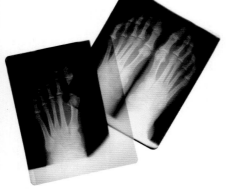

xylophone *noun* (zy-lo-fohn) a musical instrument made of wooden bars of different lengths, that you hit with small hammers

The word **xylophone** comes from Greek words *xylon* meaning 'wood' and *phone* meaning 'sound' (the same word as in *telephone*).

yacht *noun* (yot) a boat used for sailing or racing

yam *noun* a tropical vegetable that grows underground

yank *verb* to yank something is to pull it strongly and suddenly

yard[1] *noun* a measure of length, 36 inches or about 91 centimetres

yard[2] *noun* a piece of ground beside a building

yarn *noun* **1.** yarn is thread spun by twisting fibres together **2.** a yarn is a tale or story

yashmak *noun* a veil covering most of the face, worn by some Muslim women

yawn *verb* you yawn when you open your mouth wide and breathe in deeply because you are tired or bored
yawn *noun* an act of yawning

year *noun* the time that the earth takes to go right round the sun, about 365¼ days or twelve months

yearly *adjective, adverb* every year

yearn *verb* to yearn for something is to long for it

yeast *noun* yeast is a substance used in baking bread and in making beer and wine

yell *noun* a loud cry or shout
yell *verb* to yell is to cry or shout loudly

yellow *noun* the colour of ripe lemons and buttercups

yellow *adjective* yellow in colour

yelp *verb* to yelp is to make a shrill bark or cry, as a dog does when it is hurt

yelp *noun* a yelping sound

yes *interjection* a word used for agreeing to something

yesterday *noun, adverb* the day before today

yet *adverb* 1. up to now; by this time • *Has the postman called yet?* 2. eventually; still • *I'll get even with him yet.* 3. in addition; even • *She became yet more excited.*

yet *conjunction* nevertheless • *It is strange, yet it is true.*

yew *noun* an evergreen tree with red berries and dark leaves like needles

yield *verb* 1. to yield is to surrender or give in • *He yielded to persuasion.* 2. to yield a crop or profit is to produce it • *These trees yield good apples.*

yield *noun* an amount produced by something

yodel *verb* **yodelling, yodelled** to yodel is to sing or shout with your voice going rapidly from low to high notes

yoga *noun* yoga is a Hindu system of exercise and meditation

yoghurt *noun* (**yog**-ert) yoghurt is milk made thick by the addition of bacteria, giving it a sharp taste

yoke *noun* a curved piece of wood put across the necks of animals pulling a cart

yoke *verb* to yoke animals is to harness them or link them with a yoke

yolk *noun* (rhymes with coke) the yellow part of an egg

Yom Kippur *noun* the Day of Atonement, an important Jewish religious festival

you *pronoun* 1. the person or people someone is speaking to • *Who are you?* 2. people; anyone • *You can never be too sure.*

young *adjective* having lived or existed only a short time; not old

young *plural noun* an animal's or bird's young are its babies

youngster *noun* a young person or child

your *determiner* belonging to you

yours *pronoun* belonging to you • *Is this house yours?*

yourself *pronoun* **yourselves** you (referring to one person) and nobody else, used to refer back to the subject of a verb • *Have you hurt yourself?* **by yourself** or **yourselves** on your own • *Did you do the work all by yourself?*

youth *noun* 1. youth is being young or the time when you are young 2. a youth is a young man 3. youth also means young people • *The youth of today are much more serious.* **youthful** *adjective* looking young or behaving like a young person

youth club *noun* a club providing leisure activities for young people

youth hostel *noun* a hostel where young people can stay cheaply when they are on holiday

Zzzzz is for snoring!

zany *adjective* **zanier, zaniest** funny in a crazy kind of way

> The word **zany** comes from the Italian name *Gianni*, a shortening of Giovanni, which is the name often used for 'clown' in an old form of Italian comedy.

zap *verb* **zapping, zapped** (*slang*) to zap something or someone is to attack or destroy them, especially in a computer game

zeal *noun* zeal is enthusiasm or eagerness, especially in doing what you believe to be right

zealous *adjective* (**zel**-us) very enthusiastic or keen **zealously** *adverb*

a b c d e f g h i j k l m n o p q r s t u v w x **y** z

zebra *noun* an African animal like a horse with black and white stripes

zebra crossing *noun* part of a road marked with broad white stripes for pedestrians to cross

zero *noun* zeros nought; the figure 0

> The word **zero** comes from French, Italian and Spanish words that in turn come from an Arabic word *sifr*.

zest *noun* zest is great enjoyment or enthusiasm

zigzag *noun* a line or route full of sharp turns from one side to the other
zigzag *verb* zigzagging, zigzagged to zigzag is to move in a series of sharp turns from one side to the other

zinc *noun* zinc is a white metal

zip *noun* a device with two rows of small teeth that fit together, used to join two pieces of material
zip *verb* zipping, zipped to zip something or zip it up, is to fasten it with a zip

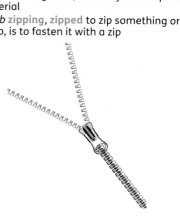

zodiac *noun* (**zoh**-di-ak) an area of the sky divided into twelve equal parts, called **signs of the zodiac**, each named after a constellation

zone *noun* a district or area set aside for a particular use • *a pedestrian zone*

zoo *noun* a place where wild animals are kept so that people can look at them or study them

zoology *noun* (zoh-**ol**-o-jee) zoology is the study of animals zoological *adjective* to do with zoology zoologist *noun* an expert in zoology

zoom *verb* to zoom is to move very quickly

zoom lens *noun* a camera lens that you can use to make distant objects appear closer

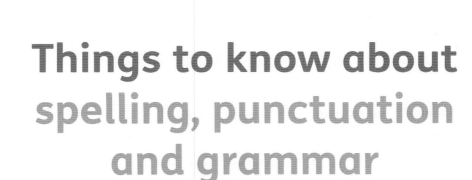

Things to know about
spelling, punctuation and grammar

Things to know about
spelling . . .

Spelling can be tricky but it is important. Here are some things to know that will help you remember how to spell tricky words.

Sometimes words have silent letters in them

silent k	knot know knight knife knock
silent g	gnaw gnome sign design
silent w	sword two who answer write
silent l	should calf half talk yolk
silent h	ghost what hour honest heir
silent u	guess guilt tongue guard guitar
silent b	thumb crumb doubt comb climb
silent n	solemn condemn autumn

Some letters combine to make a sound

ch sometimes makes a **k** sound	school choir chemist
ph usually makes an **f** sound	photograph phrase
ch sometimes makes a **sh** sound	chateau chef brochure
sc sometimes makes an **s** sound	science scene fascinate

Sometimes there are words hidden in other words

See if you can find words inside tricky words. It will help you to break the word down into smaller memorable sections.

ball in ba**ll**oon   **gate** in navi**gate**   **scribe** in de**scribe**

a rat in sep**arat**e   **to get her** in al**together**   **ear** in **ear**ly

rite in favou**rite**   **pie** in **pie**ce   **air** in st**air**

Look out: there is no **mini** in minute!

You can make up your own mnemonic

A **mnemonic** is a pattern of words to help you remember a tricky spelling. Try to make up some mnemonics of your own for words you often misspell.

Here are some good mnemonics:

because   Big elephants can always understand small elephants.

people   People eat omelettes. People like eggs.

rhythm   Rhythm helps your two hips move.

ocean   Only cats' eyes are narrow.

Some words have prefixes or suffixes

A **prefix** is a group of letters that can be added to the beginning of a root word to make a new word.

impossible = **im** + possible   uncomfortable = **un** + comfortable

Different **prefixes** have different meanings, so when you add a prefix you change the meaning of a word. Here are some common prefixes and their meanings:

prefix	meaning	example
re-	again	**re**cycle, **re**use
pre-	before	**pre**historic
bi-	two, twice	**bi**cycle
trans-	across	**trans**port
super-	above, over, beyond	**super**man, **super**size
over-	excessively	**over**used, **over**excited
ex-	out, outside of	**ex**port, **ex**claim

Look out: the prefix **in-** can mean **not**, **in** or **into**!

A **suffix** is a group of letters that can be added to the end of a root word to make a new word. Sometimes you can add the suffix straight on to the root word, without changing anything else.

hope + ful = hopeful   kind + ness = kindness

Different **suffixes** have different meanings, so when you add a suffix you change the meaning of a word. Here are some common suffixes and their meanings:

suffix	meaning	example
-er	more	faster
-est	most	fastest
-ible/-able	able to be	possible, washable
-hood	nouns of state or condition	childhood, boyhood
-ness	nouns of state or condition	kindness, tiredness
-tion/ -ation	nouns of action or condition	direction, information
-ment	nouns of action or purpose	enjoyment, advertisement

The letters **-al** can be a **prefix** or a **suffix** – you can add them to the beginning of some words, and to the end of other words.

altogether, although   (prefix)

personal, national, historical, arrival   (suffix)

Things to know about
punctuation

Punctuation marks make meaning clear. It is important to use the correct punctuation marks in your writing, so that your sentences are easy to read and understand. Here are the punctuation marks that you can use:

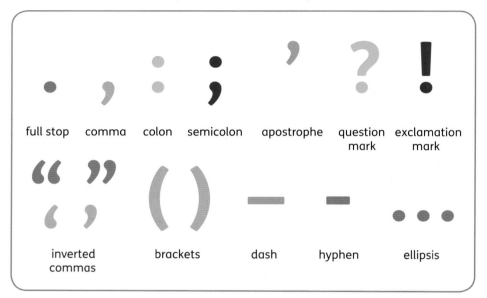

| full stop | comma | colon | semicolon | apostrophe | question mark | exclamation mark |

| inverted commas | brackets | dash | hyphen | ellipsis |

full stops

A **full stop** comes at the **end** of a sentence. It shows that the sentence is complete.

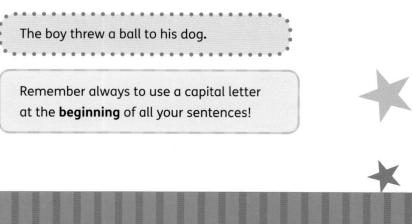

The boy threw a ball to his dog.

Remember always to use a capital letter at the **beginning** of all your sentences!

commas

A **comma** separates things in a list.

> Mum bought apples, bread, milk, juice and cheese.

Commas can make meaning clear.

> I'd like a milkshake, and some water for the dog.

Commas can separate clauses in sentences.

> Jamal, who was my best friend, came to the party with me.
>
> We're finishing dinner, and then we're playing football.
>
> If we're really quiet, we won't wake up Granddad.

A **comma** can follow an adverbial at the start of a sentence.

> Luckily, I managed to dodge the headteacher.

colons

Colons introduce lists, examples or explanations.

> They come in four colours: red, blue, yellow and green.
>
> Rabbits are very furry: they need to keep warm in winter.

apostrophes

Apostrophes show that something belongs to someone or something.

Lucy's cake was the best. (The cake belonged to Lucy.)

Apostrophes also show that letters are missing out of a word.
This is called a contraction.

it is → it's	has not → hasn't
you are → you're	did not → didn't

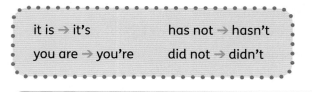

Remember you do not need to add an apostrophe to make a plural!

question marks

Question marks go at the end of a sentence which is asking a question.

Would you like a piece of cake?   Who are you?

exclamation marks

Exclamation marks go at the end of sentence, to show surprise, anger or that
something is urgent. They are used in place of a full stop.

It's a goal!   Everyone sit down!

inverted commas

Inverted commas, or speech marks, show when people are actually speaking.

> "Would you like to come to the park?" asked Dad.

Inverted commas can be written as single ' ' or double " " speech marks. You'll need to decide which you want to use before you start writing and be consistent.

> Remember, the punctuation (full stop, comma, question mark or exclamation mark) at the end of the spoken words always comes **inside** the final inverted commas!

brackets

Brackets separate a word or a phrase that has been added to a sentence to give more information or explanation. Your sentence should still make sense without the words in the brackets.

> Joe put on a red shirt **(which was his favourite)** and a hoody and jeans.

dashes

A **dash** can introduce further information, especially in informal text.

> Gemma went to the cinema – she had the best time ever!

semicolons

Semicolons can be used between two main clauses instead of 'and' or 'but' to join two sentences together.

> The netball team wear yellow bibs for their tournaments; they wear blue tops for practice.

Semicolons can separate longer phrases in a list.

> We all wore different things to the fancy dress party: a clown costume; an animal suit; a pirate hat; and a prince's crown.

hyphens

A **hyphen** joins two or more words that should be read as a single unit. It is shorter than a dash.

> Out hopped a pink-headed, green-clawed bird with a loud squawk.

Using a **hyphen** can make meaning clear sometimes.

> a man-eating fish   a man eating fish

ellipses

An **ellipsis** shows that a word has been missed out or a sentence is not finished.

> Don't tell me . . .

Things to know about
grammar

The words we use all do different jobs in sentences. They have different **word classes**. The word classes work together to make sure that the meaning of a sentence is clear.

> The little boy kicked a football.

- The words **the** and **a** are determiners.
- The word **little** is an adjective.
- The word **kicked** is a verb.
- The words **boy** and **football** are nouns.

nouns

A **noun** names a person or a thing. Nouns can be common nouns or proper nouns.

A **common noun** names something in general.

> table   boy   flower   bird

A **proper noun** names a specific person, place or thing. Proper nouns always start with a capital letter.

> France   Jenny   Thursday

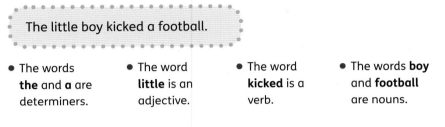

Collective nouns refer to groups of people or things.

> family   class   shoal   team

Decide if you mean the whole group or each individual member of the group to work out whether you need a singular or plural verb.

> **The team is** determined to win.   **The team are** determined to win.

adjectives

An **adjective** gives you more information about a noun. Adjectives normally go before nouns, or after **is**, **am**, **are**, **was** or **were**.

> The scary spider was **hairy** and **black**.

You can use more than one **adjective** to describe a noun. Adjectives make your writing more interesting for the reader.

> The **little white shaggy** dog ate his **huge juicy** bone.

verbs

A **verb** often (but not always) names an action. It can also be a 'being' word.

> The dog **chases** the ball. The dog **is** happy.

Verbs can be made into a past tense. The tense tells you **when** the action takes place, for example, the present or the past.

> The dog **chases** the ball. The dog **is** happy. (**present tense**)
>
> The dog **chased** the ball. The dog **was** happy. (**past tense**)

adverbs

Adverbs tell you how, where, when or how often something happens. They can also link ideas, make comments or say how likely something is.

eagerly   noisily   later   twice   however   fortunately   perhaps

Sometimes **adverbs** are also used for emphasis.

very polite   **quite** silly   **super** strong

Adverbs often end in the suffix **-ly**. Keep an eye on your spelling though – sometimes you can just add **-ly**, but sometimes you will need to lose or change a letter!

nice → nicely

bad → badly

happy → happily

easy → easily

simple → simply

comfortable → comfortably

pronouns

Pronouns can be used instead of a noun or a noun phrase. Using a pronoun means that you do not need to repeat the same noun over and over again.

> The girl bought an apple and ate **it** as **she** walked home.

- The pronoun **it** replaces the words 'an apple'.
- The pronoun **she** replaces the words 'The girl'.

Possessive pronouns tell you who or what owns a noun.

> James said the black coat and hat were **his**.

- The pronoun **his** shows that the coat and hat belonged to James.

determiners

A **determiner** goes in front of a noun and the adjectives describing it. It tells you which person or thing the sentence is about.

> **The** circus came to town and put **a** tent up in **the** field.

> Remember to change **a** to **an** if the word after it starts with a vowel!

> an apple   an angry lion   an igloo   an octopus   an umbrella

A **determiner** can also tell you how much or how many.

> Granny bought **one** loaf of bread.
>
> There were **many** apples on the tree.

prepositions

Prepositions usually come before a noun or pronoun. They describe **place**, **direction** or **when** something happens.

> My teacher was **behind** us in the queue at the supermarket! (place)
>
> My mum walked **through** the food aisle. (direction)
>
> **After** the shopping, I went to the adventure playground. (when)

Prepositions show how things are related to one another. They can link nouns and pronouns to other words in a sentence.

conjunctions

A **conjunction** links words or groups of words.

The **conjunction** 'and' is a **coordinating conjunction** – it links words in the sentence which are of the same importance.

> The goalkeeper dived for the ball **and** he saved a goal.

Here are some more:

> and   but   or   nor   yet

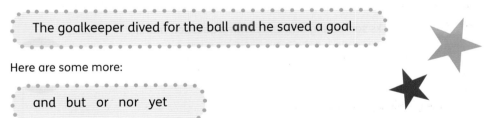

The **conjunction** 'because' is a **subordinating conjunction** – it joins words or groups of words which add extra meaning, but which are not as important as the rest of the sentence.

> The team scored five goals **because** they had done lots of training.

Here are some more:

> after   although   as   before   if   since   unless   when   though